The Encyclopedia of
HOUSE PLANTS

The Encyclopedia of
HOUSE
PLANTS

IN THE HOME • ON THE PATIO
IN THE WINDOW BOX

Grange
BOOKS

The Encyclopedia of
HOUSE PLANTS

Published in 1993 by Grange Books
An imprint of Grange Books PLC
The Grange
Grange Yard
LONDON SE1 3AG

This material has previously appeared in
partwork form as Greenleaf.

Printed in Hungary

ISBN: 1-85627-347-4

PICTURE ACKNOWLEDGEMENTS

The Publishers gratefully acknowledge the following agencies
and individuals who have supplied pictures:

A-Z Collection; Bernard Alfieri; Heather Angel; Autogrow Products Ltd; Gillian Beckett; Ken Beckett;
BEF Products (Essex) Ltd, Billericay; Biofotos; David Birch; Pat Brindley; Richard Bryant; Bob Challiner;
Clive Corless; Eric Crichton; George Crowner; EWA; Vaughan Fleming; John Glover; Jerry Harpur;
Neil Holmes; Ian Howes; Hozelock ASL; Impact; Alan Lawson; Edward Lock; Ward Lock; Marrex;
Maison de Marie Claire; Peter McHoy; Bill McLoughlin; Michael Boys Syndication; Tania Midgley;
Ken Muir; Jo Reid and John Peck; David Ridge; John Russell; Harry Smith; Daam Smit; David Squire;
Jesslen Strang; Peter Stiles; Thorn EMI Lighting; Michael Warren; Don Wildridge; J. O. Willow.

CONTENTS

CHAPTER I

Display and Design

How to display your houseplants

There can't be many homes without a few houseplants dotted about, and you will probably already have a fairly wide selection. But are you doing them justice and displaying them to their greatest effect? It's true that even a solitary African Violet on a coffee table will make a room look better, but why not go further and use plants to change the whole image of your home?

Use foliage plants and flowers as an important part of your interior design, and transform a bare bathroom into a lush jungle or a drab kitchen into a leafy bower. Anything's possible, and you don't need a magic wand or lots of money.

Taking stock of your rooms

Once you realise just how versatile your houseplants can be, you'll be itching to use them in many different ways. There are absolutely no strict rules to follow, though there are a few guidelines that will help to guarantee success.

It makes good sense to choose plants that will be happy in the normal conditions of your home. Find out which plants will flourish in your particular surroundings — there's no point in trying to nurture a sub-tropical

Plants against a pattern
The shape and effect of this Ivy and Dieffenbachia are lost against such a heavily patterned background. Instead, use a plant like an Aspidistra or Rubber Plant with well-defined leaves.

Plants against a plain ground
The plain background makes all the difference to the colours and impact of the arrangement. Any plant stands out well and looks good against a pale, plain, unfussy background.

This striking spiky yucca emphasises the height of the elegant French windows and makes a dramatic focal point. A number of smaller plants would fail to give as much impact to the design of the room.

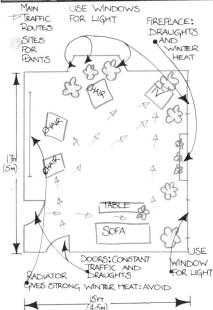

Draw a sketch of your room to tell you where there's scope for houseplants. Put in doors, windows, furniture, heating and traffic ways to show possibilities.

The clever use of mirrors gives a room the illusion of more space and makes the plants look bigger and better. On the table sit a couple of Gloxinias and a Nicotiana. A Beaucarnea enjoys the window and a Dracaena lives on the right.

orchid which needs hot-house temperatures if you've got a cold flat.

It's worth doing a quick sketch of each room, just to map out where the light comes from — windows, skylights, doors which are left permanently open — and don't forget that there's furniture to fit in too!

Measure the distances as well, so there's no guesswork when it comes to investing in large plants, as you'll be sure that there's enough room for them. A good tip is to draw arrows to show the well-worn traffic routes and avoid such mistakes as putting the most delicately arranged group of plants slap in the middle of the children's bee-line from the front door to the kitchen.

Now think about your four walls and the height of the ceiling — their scale and proportion are important, for practical as well as design reasons. A gorgeous collection of small houseplants would get lost in a large open-plan room, while a splendid weeping fig in the cloakroom would mean there's no room for you or anything else!

If you are lucky enough to have high-ceilinged rooms you have twice the canvas to work with — you can use plants to fill the otherwise empty upper part of the room, by cascading down to meet those growing upward from floor level. As a general rule of thumb, the bigger the room, the larger the plants it can accommodate and vice versa, and the better the effect if the plants and room are all in proportion.

Design for effect

Next look at your colour scheme — too often it's something many of us forget to

3

consider. Houseplants can look good against plain white or soft pastel colour walls — the colours that reflect light. But if you do have a dark, heavily patterned wallpaper, avoid putting plants with brilliantly coloured leaves against it — they'll just cancel each other out. Try instead the calmer effect of simple plain green foliage plants which will stand out against a detailed background without competing with it.

Still at the planning stage, try to think of plants being used in conjunction with other features, particularly your furniture. There's a whole world of possibilities — why not twine ivy or Kangaroo Vine (*Cissus*) around bannisters, or create a living green frame for a favourite picture you can't afford to have framed professionally.

Best of all, try to use mirrors in at least one display. Using reflected light and images is one of the magical ways to add an entirely new visual dimension to a room, and like an illusionist you can produce something from nothing — a double size sitting room, a seemingly flower-filled alcove, twice the sunlight — try it and see.

A point to remember although not exactly a guideline: do experiment, as the unexpected effect can often be the most dramatic. The final choice of plants and their arrangement is up to your personal taste, and the joy of houseplants, unlike garden flowers, is that you can change your mind and move them around until you arrive at something you love. Once you start thinking, you'll get ideas at every turn, and soon everywhere you look will inspire you — magazine features, shop displays, other people's windows . . .

Good companions

Grouping plants together is the most effective and immediately dramatic way of displaying your houseplants. Plants love each other's company and really do thrive in a group — they create their own mini environment with the higher group humidity, and watering is made easier too!

Of course some plants merit solitary confinement to show off the beauty of their form. Large specimens such as Howea palms and mature castor oil plants *(Ricinus communis)* are sufficiently imposing standing alone.

If you decide to plan a group, the possibilities are endless, and the only

Grouping houseplants

Informal plant group
Provide unity by growing your plants in the same type of container. Baskets are effective as you can get them in a good range of sizes and interesting shapes and their natural colours blend well with the green leaves of the plants.

Group in a large container
Fill the main pot with peat and plunge the plants still in their individual pots into the peat; then you can change them around whenever you want. Set a stately Mother-in-Law's Tongue against a small leaved ficus and a tall arching palm to get a geometric contrast of leaf shapes; and use just one flowering plant such as a Busy Lizzie to provide a vivid splash of colour in the centre.

A formal group
Grow a row of the same plant in the same type of container to create a formal grouping. You can do this with lots of different plants - palms, crotons, ivies, geraniums or, as here, Sword Ferns.

A permanent room divider can be emphasised by a plant trough: fill it with plants which like artificial light, such as ferns, ivies and peperomias.

To fix glass shelves securely, run a double row of metal struts either side of your window, and fix the shelves with special glass shelving clips. The best ones have smooth jaws into which the glass slides. The height of the different shelves can be adjusted to fit the size of your plants.

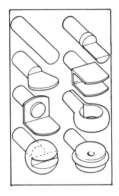

thing to ensure is that all the plants have the same likes and dislikes — don't put a thirsty, humidity-loving Philodendron next to a cactus that loves to be parched.

A group can be just that — any number of plants standing together; there's no limitation. They can be free-standing, shoulder to shoulder, or sharing the same container. This last method is probably one of the best ways and all you need is a container large enough to take all the plants. Fill the container with peat and plunge your chosen plants (still in their individual pots) into the peat. Keep standing back to check the balance of your display as you go, then when you've finished, water the whole lot well. For best results, the plant pots should be clay rather than plastic, as clay is porous and allows the moisture from the damp peat to get through to the plant.

How to balance a display

This is the chance to use all those design talents you know you have. Look at florists' displays and other people's successful groupings and notice how it seems instinctive and natural to balance shapes — tall and narrow with low and bushy; to contrast textures with something like a feathery fern against the arching leaves of a Spider Plant and

to use colour and variegated leaves together, such as a delicately speckled Dumb Cane with a dark green Sweetheart Vine.

When designing a display don't forget those houseplants with bright coloured foliage, as they add a touch of real flamboyance. Only include one variety in any group and don't let it overpower the others: the plants should complement each other, like jewels in a lovely setting.

Containers

What you display your plants in can be as important as the plants themselves, though this doesn't mean the container need be an expensive one. Almost anything will do — but try for one which enhances the effect you're aiming at, rather than detracting from it. A large specimen plant or tree that you want to use as a focal point for a room will do a handsome Victorian jardinière proud, while a waterfall of trailing plants will hide the prettiest pot in no time.

If you like the unusual, and haven't much money, rummage in junk shops and rubbish skips — it's amazing what you can find; and instead of ripping out that old iron fire grate, why not give it a lick of paint and fill it with a froth of ferns? But one word of caution — many

glazed china pots will let water seep through and leave nasty white water rings on your furniture or stains on your carpet. So either paint the inside of the pot with polyurethane varnish or put an old plate underneath to catch all the drips and you won't have any accidents!

Some more display ideas

Learning to display your houseplants to better effect can have a practical as well as a visually pleasing result, and you'll find too that designing with plants is about the cheapest way of decorating. Here are some unusual ideas:

● Create a curtain effect using plants; hang pots at different levels from secure hooks in the ceiling and choose plants that climb, arch or trail. They act as a privacy screen as well so you can manage without net curtains.

● Have you ever thought of dividing a large room with a screen or trellis of plants? You can group several large varieties together, or build a proper plant trough.

● Do you want to disguise an ugly view? One of the prettiest ways of hiding the fact that you're just 3 feet away from the house next door, or overlooking a row of dustbins, is to use plants instead of a roller blind. Put glass shelves up at a window — make sure they're secure — and fill every inch with plants. The glass shelves don't blot out any light and the plants let the sun through in a lovely dappled way.

Once your enthusiasm has been fired, the sky (or the ceiling) is the limit. The pleasure in having achieved the effect you want is amazing, so sit back and enjoy it — you deserve to.

Overleaf: use plants to add a real touch of tropical lushness to bathtime, and they enjoy the steamy warmth too!

Plants for hallways

Your hall provides the first impression a visitor receives as he comes through your front door, and it is often one that will endure. An eyecatching and decorative arrangement of your favourite houseplants — or even one single, but well chosen plant — can do much to create a welcoming atmosphere in those first few seconds.

Even the smallest hall can benefit from the homely, brightening touch that houseplants can bring. Warm colour-schemes, tasteful furnishings and a well-planned interior are all helpful and, on the practical side, plenty of cupboard space for coats and shoes will cut down the clutter. But, for the finishing touches, there's nothing like living greenery for making people feel instantly 'at home'. Good quality plants, thoughtfully displayed, can transform even the smallest and dullest space into something worthy of a second look.

Unfortunately, from the plant's point of view, a hall is just about the most inhospitable room in the house. Often dark, chilly and draughty, halls aren't the place for the same sort of plants that you would grow in your living-room. But the plants don't have to be boring because they are tough; there are very many interesting plants you can grow.

An Aspidistra, *above*, catches the light in front of an unused door.

Making a hallway display

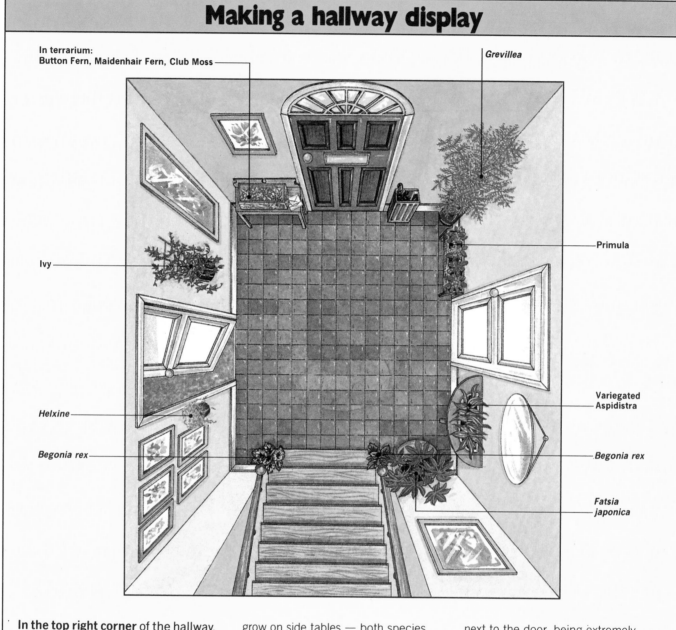

In terrarium:
Button Fern, Maidenhair Fern, Club Moss

Grevillea

Ivy

Helxine

Begonia rex

Primula

Variegated
Aspidistra

Begonia rex

*Fatsia
japonica*

In the top right corner of the hallway, *above*, a *Grevillea* makes the most of the sheltered space, set off by the pretty colours of the Primulas on a low trestle next to it. Variegated Aspidistras and a Figleaf Palm grow on side tables — both species are able to endure a wide range of conditions. *Begonia rex* is a good choice to adorn the bottom of the stairs, since it doesn't grow too tall. The pale green *Helxine* will be happy next to the door, being extremely adaptable, while the Ivy is an excellent choice for an unheated room. In the terrarium are more delicate plants, protected by the glass from draughts and knocks.

And, if you are prepared to hunt them out, there are some very special new plants around that are perfect for halls. What's more, you'll have something that very few people will ever have come across before!

Assessing the setting

The first step is to take stock of the conditions you can offer houseplants in your hall. You may, for instance, have an open stairwell, where you can make a feature of climbing plants, or plants of various heights. A beautiful cascading effect can be created, if you have an open landing gallery, by growing trailing plants along its edge and letting them hang down into the hallway.

However, it's the amount of light available that is probably the most important factor, though usually it's a case of little, or none at all. Even the best of halls are generally quite a bit darker than living-rooms. What natural light there is probably comes from glass panels in the front door. But, unpromising though it sounds, this will generally be enough to grow plants that are dedicated shade lovers. To qualify as a good candidate for hallways, plants will need to be tough enough to tolerate draughts, and won't mind the occasional knock.

Among the suitable kinds of plant, you can choose from traditional species and exciting newcomers, so there's bound to be something you fancy.

Success with shade

Some halls have no natural light at all, yet even here it is possible to grow successful plants, as long as you think of them as temporary visitors and not permanent decorations. Just select any of the plants from those mentioned, but move them back to a lighter position every few days. Alternatively, you could stick to annual flowering plants that like it cool, such as *Cineraria (right)* or *Primula.*

Some outdoor plants, such as the Christmas Rose (*Helleborus niger*) and *Polyanthus*, are often grown in pots and sold in flower by garden centres. These can be brought inside to provide a spot of colour when and where it's needed, and the cool of the hall is the best place for a temporary home. Once you've enjoyed the flowers, just plant them out in the garden as usual for next year. Bulbs are another good bet: Christmas

flowering Hyacinths, Narcissi or even exotic Lilies will last quite well in the cool of a hall, even if there isn't much light. You can still plant the bulbs outside once the flowers are finished.

Starting with old favourites, at the top of the indestructibility ratings and perfect for larger hallways comes the original Cast-Iron Plant, the Aspidistra, now enjoying a new surge in popularity. Aspidistras exist in both plain green and cream-and-green variegated versions. While most people think of the Aspidistra as a non-flowering plant, it does in fact have flowers — if you know where to look for them. Instead of growing on stems, Aspidistra flowers grow pressed close to the compost, for the very good reason that in the wild they are pollinated by slugs. Look out for them in summer: they are dull mauve and about 1in (2.5cm) across.

Then there is the Figleaf Palm *(Fatsia Japonica)*. This has large leaves — 6-12 in (15-30 cm) across, depending on the size of your plant — and grows into a short, shrubby specimen that's almost as robust as the Aspidistra. Both plants look good as large display 'specimens' standing on the floor in ornamental pot holders. Or you can raise them up by supporting the pot in the neck of a large ceramic vase.

Classic foliage plants

Ivy is another rugged individual that's perfect for halls. It is available in a wide range of variegations, in silver, gold and lime green. One of the prettiest is 'Goldheart', a variety with glossy green leaves, each with a splash of gold in the centre. You will also find plain green frilly leaves, arrow-shaped leaves and all sorts of other forms, too. Ivy looks good grown in troughs, where the stems can trail down: but, for a change, why not train it up to make a 'tree'. Simply plant three Ivies in a 10in (25cm) pot, and wire the trailing stems vertically up a moss-covered pole, letting the ends cascade down when they reach the top.

For a nice mossy green creeping plant to fill a hanging basket, choose *Helxine*, otherwise called Mind-Your-Own-Business; a good place to hang this would be at a small window or behind a glass panel alongside the front door. *Grevillea* — the Silk Oak — is a foliage plant very similar to a fern, but it can survive much lower temperatures than the more delicate Maidenhair Fern. To see it at its best, plant three of them in a 5in (13cm) pot — one on its own looks a little sparse. Or you could make up a mixed bowl: plant *Grevillea, Helxine* and a variegated plant such as Japanese Sedge, which has short, pointed, grass-

A sheltered spot with good light is home for an Asparagus Fern, a Tradescantia (*Zebrina pendula*), a *Nephrolepsis exaltata* and a stripy *Dracaena deremensis.*

like leaves in green and gold stripes, or *Euonymus* — a small, evergreen shrubby plant, variegated in green and gold or silver. This makes a perfect 'feature' for a low telephone table.

Alternatively, in a warmer hall where the temperature stays above 50°F (10°C), you could grow Club Moss (*Sellaginella*), or miniature ferns like Button Fern (*Pellaea rotundifolia*) in a terrarium. The glass walls will keep the humidity in and the draughts out, so you'll be able to grow a couple of plants that would otherwise be unhappy there.

Something new

For something that bit different and definitely much more colourful, look out for the newest strain of houseplants — a range of plants that grow naturally out of doors in mild climates, like New Zealand. A few of them are easily mistaken for tropical foliage plants, but need half the heat. Most will be quite happy if you

shut down the heating when you're away — and you won't find many tropical plants surviving that treatment!

For a start, there's *Pseudopanax sabre*, which looks very much like an Aralia with long, narrow, bronze-coloured leaves. This makes a short, elegant, shrubby plant that could be placed on the floor or on a table where it will create an impact as a 'specimen' plant from your collection. Gold Splash, another *Pseudopanax*, looks just like a *Heptapleurum* or *Schleffera*, but has most attractive gold splashes on its foliage, as the name suggests. Very similar in shape and size is *Pseudopanax purpurea*, but instead of being variegated, its leaves are bronze-purple.

Entirely different is *Libertia peregrinans*, with bright red and gold grassy stems 6-8in (15-20cm) high. It looks delightful grown in a planter along with contrasting green foliage plants like *Helxine*. Or how about a small, chunky

The pink of a Cyclamen contrasts with an Ivy and a Parlour Palm.

specimen for a pot of its own — *Astelia* 'Silver Spear,' a little like an Agave with spiky leaves coming from a short, central stem. The *Astelia* can be beautifully highlighted by growing it in a rough, hand-painted pot.

Different levels for a Cast Iron Plant, an *Ananas bracteatus striatus*, a Croton and a *Ficus elastica* 'Black Prince'.

Low-growing plants: an *Asplenium nidus*, a Maidenhair Fern, a *Davallia* and an Ivy contrast with a white-bracted Poinsettia.

Houseplants for the sitting room

Making a focal point of your fireplace

A fireplace is the main feature of most sitting rooms, which makes it an ideal position for displaying houseplants. If your budget can stretch to a really large plant you can create an arrangement such as the display on the *left*. Use a tall plant such as an elegant, arching Palm to emphasise the height and shape of the fireplace. Then, at a lower level, balance the design with an Aspidistra and a Castor Oil Plant. None of these plants need a great deal of light so they should grow well in such a situation, provided they are well looked after.

A more 'cottagey' style of displaying plants around a fireplace is to grow them in a row along the top of the mantelpiece, *right*. You can soften the effect, as we have here, by trailing an Ivy and a Tradescantia over the side edges and sitting a Scindapsus on the hearth stone.

The sitting room is the easiest place in the house to choose plants for as it's light and airy and free of draughts, as well as being comfortably warm in winter. It is a happy coincidence that the same conditions that keep us cosy when we are relaxing are also near-perfect for a wide range of indoor plants.

If you've ever visited the Netherlands the chances are that you have come away thinking what wonderful houseplants they have. Every window is crammed full of plants — so are their living rooms. But, although they look sensational, Dutch houseplants are actually no better than ours. The trick lies in the way they are displayed.

Given a bit of design sense even the most ordinary collection of pot plants can be completely transformed into a stunning arrangement. Don't worry if you aren't particularly artistic; if you have ever decorated a room by teaming wallpaper, soft furnishings and carpet, or chosen an outfit with accessories to match — you're already half way there.

A good focal point

The focal point of a sitting room is usually the fireplace. This is an ideal place to arrange plants, whether in such a way as to hide an ugly fireplace or to emphasise its beauty.

If you block off the shaft to stop draughts whistling down the chimney you can grow all sorts of plants there. Only grow shade-loving houseplants as

Plants give a room a casual atmosphere as well as being a decorative feature in their own right. A sitting room is absolutely perfect for both plants and people as it is designed to be welcoming, warm and comfortable. The plain green leaves of the Ivy, *overleaf*, have been allowed to trail downwards and trained to fill an otherwise blank wall. In the corner a Palm curves in a relaxed fashion over the table.

Points to ponder

● **Dry air.** Central heating makes the air very dry. Most plants other than the real sun lovers such as Bougainvillea and Pony Tail Plant, Cacti and many Succulents, grow best in moist air. Some plants, such as Ferns and African Violets, cannot survive without moisture as this keeps their leaves fresh. These plants must be grown standing in trays of damp gravel to maintain the humidity in a dry heated room.

● **Cold nights.** Tropical houseplants need constant warmth, which they are unlikely to keep when you turn your heating off at night. Unless the temperature stays above 55°F (13°C), you would do better to grow plants which will tolerate lower temperatures. There's a good list to choose from: Aspidistra, Ivy, Hexline, Cyclamen, Azalea, Hydrangea, spring flowering bulbs, Euonymus, Eucalyptus, Cineraria, Aucuba, Grape Ivy, Hoya, Passion Flower, Geranium, Plumbago, Cape Heather, Primula and Schizanthus.

The jungle atmosphere created by the huge Weeping Fig is echoed by the luxuriant Boston Fern on the fireplace and delicate Maidenhair Ferns and flowering Begonias.

Points to watch when placing your houseplant

A shade-loving plant here will be over-exposed to sun in summer. Plants here may get frozen in winter when the curtains are closed at night.

A trailing plant dangling over a fireplace that is used may get scorched.

A plant that sits on top of a television set may get too warm — drying out the leaves and compost.

This plant may be in a draught, and may get knocked over or trodden on.

A plant here may not get enough light. It is far too cramped and the radiator will singe the leaves.

The radiator may overheat the trailing stems, possibly singeing them, and will dry out all the humidity. The draught from the door may brown the plant's leaves.

This plant may be scorched by the radiator, knocked by people coming in and out of the door and subjected to draughts.

the fireplace tends to be well away from the window so there is not much natural light for the plants to use. Don't choose variegated plants as they won't get enough light to keep their patterns. The arrangement can be as permanent as you want, although if you have a working fire in winter make sure that the leaves are not in danger of being scorched, or move your plants away altogether to safety.

Displaying your plants

In a large room large plants look most effective as they echo the scale of the room. Plants used on their own for their design and foliage impact are called 'specimen' plants; choose those with evergreen leaves as they will look good all year round.

The Swiss Cheese Plant and Weeping Fig are popular choices but there are lots of other plants to consider: large-leaved Philodendrons, Cyperus plants including the Papyrus, all sorts of Palm trees, Boston and Ladder Ferns and the unusual Stag's Horn Fern. Try a Norfolk Island Pine, a Castor Oil Plant, a Fiddle Leaf Fig or even a Eucalyptus.

Large specimen plants are expensive, but given time you can grow your own — starting with a good young plant from a garden centre or chain store.

Plants that don't really merit being displayed on their own can be made to look unusually striking if you group them together well. Try growing trailing plants like Ivy or the Sweetheart Vine up a moss-covered pole and then let it trail down from the top. Alternatively, grow a climber like a Black-Eyed Susan with a Kangaroo Vine up a framework of bamboos or branches of contorted willows or even some bare branches collected from the garden.

Experiment with ways of linking plants visually by standing them close together on a polished slice of wood or in a tray of moss or pebbles. Where possible hide the pot if it is not ornamental.

A collection of small plants can be displayed in a group to make the most of the mass effect of the foliage. Such a close arrangement is good for the plants as well, because this way they can create their own mini environment of moist air. For the best results, group together foliage and flowering plants, choosing a selection of tall and spreading kinds with colours which harmonise and shapes that contrast.

Windowsill plants

For a windowsill display to look really good, the plants need to be healthy and for this they must be given an environment that suits them. Depending on whether your windowsill faces north, south, east or west, choose your plants from the information below to make up a healthy and happy display.

North facing windowsill
Grow plants here which actually dislike the sun.

Ivies, Aspidistra, Aucuba, all sorts of Ferns, Streptocarpus, Scindapsus, Grape Ivy, Sweetheart Vine, Peperomia, Maranta, Hibiscus, Palms, Creeping Fig, Cyperus, Kaffir Lily, Cissus, Spider Plant, Bird's Nest Fern, Castor Oil Plant.

South facing windowsill
This position is for sun-loving plants only.

Geraniums (Pelargoniums), lots of Cacti, most succulents such as Sanseveria, Living Stones (Lithops), Aloe, Agave, Crassula. Other plants include Celosia, Oleander, Black-Eyed Susan and Coleus.

East and West facing windowsill

Here you can grow most flowering pot plants and variegated foliage plants without fear of them burning in the strong sun.

Capsicum, Cyclamen, Fuchsia, Calceolaria, Cineraria, Celosia, Busy Lizzies, Pot Chrysanthemum, Aphelandra, Shrimp Plant, Italian Bellflower, Hibiscus, Hoya, Begonia, Azalea, Hippeastrum, Poinsettia, Primula, Winter Cherry, Christmas Cactus, Dracaena, Cordyline, Dieffenbachia, Polka Dot Plant, Pilea, Tradescantia, and also Orchids and carnivorous plants like the Venus Fly Trap and Pitcher Plant.

Windowsills at night

When you draw the curtains at night leaving your plants behind on the windowsill you are trapping them in a pocket of cold air. This is less important in summer than winter when plants run the risk of frost damage. It is much safer to move your plants inside the room at night where they can be protected by curtains.

A Palm and two Cissus vines are ideal companions for a north-facing window.

Plants in a fireplace

An empty fireplace can provide an eye-catching frame for a display of plants. Just as a warming, flickering fire provides a focal point to a room, so too can the twining patterns of leaves and stems, fern fronds and palm stalks, and the subtle contrasts of variegated foliage.

A great advantage of using the fireplace as a display area is the generous amount of space it offers, and the possibility of exploiting different levels to show off different types of plants —

trailing plants on the mantelpiece, small plants bunched together in the grate, tall plants gracefully flanking the chimney-breast — the possibilities are tremendous. Another great plus point about a fireplace display is that it allows the plants themselves to grow in the way they like best — that is, close together, creating their own microclimate.

Planning before planting

There are several things you need to take into account when you get down to

designing your display. These include the shape and size of the room, the height of the ceiling, the amount and type of furniture in the room, and — last but by no means least — the character of the fireplace itself. Classical marble or carved pine, for example, demands a quite different treatment from a cast-iron Victorian grate, or post-war tiles.

The creamy-white flowers of a Hydrangea and a white Gloxinia reflect the colour of a pale marble surround.

15

A range of greens and bright flowers lighten a dark fireplace: Maidenhair and Asparagus Ferns, a scarlet Gloxinia and an orange Begonia.

A word about containers

Much of the effectiveness of your display will come from the containers you choose. The wide mouth of a shiny copper or brass coal-scuttle filled with pink, white, violet and bicoloured African Violets (Saintpaulia) or a variety of different ferns, for example, can be the perfect foil to an old-fashioned fireplace.

Tall coal hods, log boxes and baskets, will all make splendid containers, their glinting metal, gleaming wood or criss-cross wicker contrasting beautifully with the soft tones of plant foliage. China and

pottery are another idea. Those tall, decorated washstand jugs from the Victorian era can still be picked up fairly cheaply in junk shops and street markets, as can pretty chamberpots, vegetable tureens and gravy boats. They can all be planted and used to great advantage, either on the hearth or ranged in a row on the mantel.

Don't neglect the modern fibreglass reproductions of classic garden urns in many garden centres. A pair set on either side of an Adam-style fireplace will look both appropriate and impressive.

A row of flowering plants in small containers, or a fringe of trailing ivies placed along the mantelshelf can look either cluttered or charmingly rustic, depending on the surroundings. And a marble fireplace in a high-ceilinged, rectangular room would be much enhanced by the addition of a Kentia Palm (*Howea forsteriana*) or a Parlour Palm (*Chamaedorea elegans* or *Neanthe bella*), both of which would be too dominating in less spacious surroundings.

Unless you're in favour of a flowering display — in which case you'll need to bear in mind the overall tones of walls and furnishings — colour, fortunately, should not present a problem, since foliage plants have the happy knack of harmonising with everything.

Pleasing your plants

There are very few plants indeed — including the virtually indestructible Cast Iron Plant (Aspidistra) — that can withstand being grown in a draught. Since an open chimney can obviously create quite a severe down-draught, you must make sure that it is adequately blocked.

If you never light an open fire and rely exclusively on central heating, this will probably have been seen to already. But if the fireplace is in use in winter you will have to seal it off temporarily while you are using it as a display area for plants. You should either fit a special throat control (available from builders' merchants) or cut a stout piece of hardboard or plywood which will act as a wedge. Push it into the chimney at an angle of 45°, tilting it *away* from the opening into the room, otherwise the summer's accumulation of soot and grit will fall towards you when you pull the wedge out in the autumn.

Having established that the plants in your fireplace display can be sure of a draught-free environment, the next things to consider are light and warmth. Most shade-loving plants, such as ferns, palms and Aspidistras for instance, will tolerate some indirect light, but never put a plant where there isn't even enough light to read by. And remember that almost all flowering plants, as well as those with variegated leaves, need plenty of light to look their best — so bear this in mind when you are choosing plants for your display.

Room temperature is the other important factor. Most houseplants originated in the tropics, so they'll cope well with central heating, but they also like a humid atmosphere. Give the foliage of your fireplace display plants a spray from time to time, and they'll be all the better for it.

Living together

There are several ways of grouping plants — by standing pots close together on the hearth, taller behind and smaller in front; by standing pots on a tray, chosen to fit the dimensions of the hearth; or by putting several pots into a peat-filled container. Whichever method you decide on will be dictated largely by the shape and size of your fireplace, but a point to remember is that any plants sharing a tray or container should all have the same requirements for water.

Don't, for example, put plants that like to be kept on the dry side — such as Mother-in-Law's Tongue (Sansevieria) and Queen's Tears (*Billbergia nutans*) — with confirmed moisture lovers, such as Plumbago, Fittonia and Umbrella Plant (Cyperus).

Designing the display

The most successful plant displays often have a single theme or idea, which brings a sense of unity and coherence to the design. You might, for example, decide on a colour theme of green and white, and choose a selection of different sizes and leaf shapes — tall and spiky, soft and sprawling — but all variegated, green and white. Thus the wonderfully vigorous Marble Queen (*Scindapsus aureus*), which can either climb or trail, may be used in company with the easy-to-grow, green and white-striped Spider Plant (*Chlorophytum comosum variegatum*), and a trailing, silvery Wandering Jew (*Tradescantia fluminensis variegatum*), which can either droop gracefully from the mantel or be suspended in a hanging basket from a hook below the mantel. Add the beautiful Angel's Wings (Caladium), which has heart-shaped, paper-thin, almost transparent leaves; while a Dumb Cane (Dieffenbachia) and a Parasol Plant (Heptapleurum) will add graceful height to the display, along with a Peace Lily (Spathiphyllum) or a lovely Arum Lily (Zantedeschia); and a variegated Ivy, trained to wind round an overmantel mirror, adds an attractive finishing touch.

Possible alternative themes include a feathery display, featuring numerous

The green and white of Tradescantia and Spider Plant, set off by the darker hues of Begonia and Streptocarpus, enhance the elegance of white paint and shining brass.

types of ferns and palms; or a green and flowery display (best in a light position) of Lilies, the fluffy Jacobinia, Clerodendrum, Abutilon, and a cascade of the spectacular trailing Goldfish Plant (Columnea). Or you could opt for an exotic display, reminiscent of a Rousseau painting, with Bromeliads, a Prayer Plant (Maranta), Rubber Plant (*Ficus elastica*), Umbrella Plant (Cyperus), the large yellow bells of Allamanda and the dramatic, scarlet, lily-like flower spikes of Anthurium. Just let your imagination run wild, and your fireplace could become the frame for the loveliest picture in your home.

Creating a formal display

If you've ever admired the stupendous displays at a flower show and wondered enviously whether you could do the same sort of thing at home, the answer is, quite definitely, yes!

It goes without saying that not everyone has the space to stage a full-sized show exhibit indoors — and certainly not on a permanent basis. But for special occasions there's nothing to beat a large formal display of plants in the entrance hall, sitting or dining room to make your party that bit more special and your guests feel thoroughly welcome.

And on a smaller scale, formal displays translate beautifully into part of your everyday decor. Why settle for a few plants dotted about the place when

you could combine them to make something far more eye-catching?

At major flower shows, of course, the displays are usually created by professional flower designers who, to be really successful, need to be part flower arranger, part interior decorator, and part landscape architect. But there's no reason why a do-it-yourself enthusiast, given a little practice, shouldn't achieve equally stunning results at home.

If you were to commission a professional flower designer to create a display

in your home, there's one thing he or she would need, above all else, before even thinking about plants or containers — a brief. And even when you're doing the job yourself, it's surprising how much it helps to formalise things in your own mind before you actually start to create your display.

This eyecatching permanent display,
above, owes as much to the painted furniture and fine collection of containers as it does to the selection of healthy, well-tended plants.

A careful selection of foliage plants: the tall sword-shaped leaves of Dracaena are set off by the rounded leaves of Croton and Dieffenbachia; in the front are Maranta and rosettes of Pineapple. The background is filled in with Hedera.

draughty areas. Then, if you aren't sure which plants like what, check them out in our A-Z. Temporary displays allow you a bit more leeway when it comes to light, because most plants will tolerate a darker-than-usual spot just for a day or two, provided you return them to a brighter position afterwards. But do avoid keeping plants in too low a temperature in winter or too much sun in summer, even for only a few days — unless it's such an important occasion that you're prepared to risk losing some of your plants.

Once you've arrived at a shortlist of plants that fit the conditions you have to offer them, the other consideration is the decorative one. Are they the right colour, shape and size for the type of display you have in mind, and what will they contribute to your finished design? This is the point where your design really starts to take shape.

Designing your display

Plants come in all shapes, sizes, textures and colours, so how do you decide which will 'go' together? This is no more difficult that choosing clothes that co-ordinate, or curtains, carpets and soft furnishings to complement each other. The easiest way is to spend an afternoon in a plant shop, trying out different combinations of plants together until you end up with something that you like.

But if you want to be sure of getting good results every time — and without spending too long — it pays to know a little about composition. Start by splitting up the problem into its various component parts as listed below.

● **Colour.** This is the first consideration. Most people think of plants as predominantly green, but even foliage plants can be variegated and some, such as Croton (Codiaeum), have very brightly coloured leaves in shades of red, gold or purple.

When it comes to flowers, there is an almost unlimited choice of colours available. Depending on the sort of plants you choose, you'll usually see your flowers set against a background of green leaves but some plants — such as Cineraria (*Senecio cruentus*), Prince of Wales' Feather (*Celosia plumosa*) and Cockscomb (*Celosia cristata*) — are so covered with flowers that you can't see any green at all by the time they have been grouped together in a display. You can choose plants with mixed, bright

So ask yourself the same questions as the professional would ask you. For example, are you after something extravagant for a special occasion, or something rather more down-to-earth that will become part of your permanent room decor? What are the background colours to the display — walls, carpets, curtains and furniture — and are they plain or patterned? What plants, containers and accessories have you already got? And how much are you prepared to spend?

The next thing your professional would do is to look around the house, trying to spot places that lend themselves particularly well to plant decoration — such as fireplaces, alcoves, table tops and deep windowsills. He'd also be on the look-out for places that would

benefit from plants to give them a 'lift' — uninteresting corners, open room dividers, large unfurnished open spaces, or even under the stairs. Don't think that lack of daylight means you can't put plants there: you just need to rig up some special plant lights.

Then, with the basics taken care of, it's time to start getting on with the job.

Choosing plants

There are two quite different considerations to be taken into account when you are choosing your plants. The first is an entirely practical consideration — are the conditions suitable? This is particularly important if you want your display to last. Look especially at the temperature, humidity and amount of light in the room, and take note of any

Cyclamen, Cineraria, Primulas and Bird's Nest Fern make up this fine spring display. The plants have been left in their individual pots to make replacement easy and the Bird's Nest Fern (*centre back*) has been raised to dominate the arrangement.

colours for a really cheerful display, or you may prefer something a little more sophisticated — say, several plants in different shades of one single colour, or perhaps two contrasting colours.

If you want to get technical about this, you might find a flower arranger's colour wheel useful. This will help you to decide which colours tone well together, and which make the most effective contrasts.

Another aspect of choosing colour for displays is the idea of using certain colours to suggest certain seasons or occasions. Use yellow for spring, for example, bronze for autumn, crimson for Christmas, and white for Easter, weddings, christenings and winter.

But while you are thinking of colour, don't think only of the plants — the background they'll be seen against is an equally important factor. And, since you can't usually do much about the colour of the background, it's a case of choosing plants to suit it rather than the other way round. The trick lies in making your display stand out by choosing a contrasting colour to the background — if it's too similar a colour, the plants will simply merge into it and 'disappear'.

Thus if the background is very dark, you'll need to choose flowers with really luminous colours — bright red, white or yellow, for example — which will show up well against it. Most flowers stand out well against a pastel background, but you can go one step further and choose plants that pick out a minor colour from your furnishings to give a well co-ordinated colour scheme.

The best backgrounds are relatively plain and unfussy, because plants don't stand out against violent floral wallpapers, though of course you can always create an artificial background by draping a piece of fabric, such as velvet, say, behind your display, as is often done at flower shows.

● **Shape and texture.** These are two more design elements which are both likely to figure strongly in plant arrangements. Just imagine how uninteresting a display would look if all plants had rounded leaves, or they all grew short and dumpy. But fortunately, plants come in an enormous range of different shapes, so make the most of them. Contrast tall pointed leaves with a mass of small shiny leaves or large round felty ones; upright plants with trailing or climbing ones; and spiky blooms with large flat flower heads.

But quite apart from the shape of plants and their individual flowers and leaves, you also need to think about the overall shape of the display. Formal displays need to have a very definite shape, or they will end up looking somehow not quite right. The basic display shapes, all of which are easily achieved, include flame, round, oval and hedge.

You also need to consider the space round the display, and the relationship between the two. This is particularly important in an enclosed space like an alcove or fireplace, where you have to decide whether to fill the space entirely with your display so that it looks as if it is bursting out of it, or leave a margin around the edge of the display to emphasise its shape.

● **Size.** It's no good putting a tiny little miniature garden into something the size of the Chelsea Flower Show and expecting it to be noticed — you've got to do something big in a big area. So always make your display an appropriate size for the room it's in.

Don't worry if you can't afford large enough plants for the purpose you have in mind. You can create the semblance of a large display by using quite small plants raised up on a table, or banked up in tiers, or simply by including a few standard plants — standard Fuchsias, for example, are easily available.

But basically, any display requires plants of several different sizes to enable you to fill in your shape, from bottom to top, with no empty spaces. The trick here is very simple: put the tallest plants to the back and the shortest to the front; or, if it's a display which you can walk round, then the tallest to the centre and the shortest round the edges.

● **Containers.** These are a much overlooked part of display technique, when in fact they are every bit as much a part of the design as the plants you put in them. A formal display looks best if you use a large, single container to hold all the plants which gives a sense of unity.

All sorts of containers can be used but, as a general rule, the simpler the better. Plain white china, for example, or very shiny good quality plastic, timber, bamboo or wicker are all ideal. They can be any shape you like — urns, troughs, baskets or whatever you fancy.

It is important to choose a container of the right size for the display. As a rough guide, use the 'two-and-a-half

Putting it all together

Planning a display takes a bit of theory and a lot of good ideas, plus the plants and containers to make the arrangement work.

Temporary displays are the easiest to stage manage as plants can be left to fend for themselves for a few days without the need to make too much provision for watering or replacing plants as they outgrow their space.

But permanent displays are a different story. With these, you have to make allowances for upkeep and maintenance as well. One useful tip here is to fill your container with peat and plunge your plants into it, pot and all. This way it's very easy to lift out a flowering plant when it is over, and switch it for another. Anything that grows too big or gets untidy can be

treated in the same way. Plunging your plants, ready-potted, into peat is also a good idea because it keeps the air round them moist and makes it very easy to keep them correctly watered by simply keeping the peat damp. You can even feed the whole display in one go by pushing a few fertiliser spikes into the peat.

And, for the final finishing touch, you could plant Mind Your Own Business, a creeping mossy looking plant, directly into the peat. It does for formal displays what moss does for hanging baskets — dotting the i's and crossing the t's. Or choose some other low growing, spreading plants to cover the soil such as the Fittonia and the trailing Pellionia which have been used in the arrangement above.

times' rule: for a tall, upright display, for example, measure the height of the container and add to this its width across the top; the display should be about two-and-a-half times as tall as this total measurement. And conversely, if your display is a long low one, the container needs to be about two-and-a-half times as long as the display is high.

If the price of really large containers puts you off, you can achieve the same effect much less expensively by simply giving an edging to your display. This can be done using a row of cascading plants round the edge which hides the pots and saucers, or a border of bark, cork, stones, or whatever else you can find which looks attractive.

Plants in the bathroom

The trouble with a bathroom is that it is so changeable — one minute it's nice and warm and steamy and an absolute paradise for tropical, jungle-type plants and the next it can be cold, damp and gloomy and be perfect for almost nothing except mushrooms! But this doesn't mean you can't grow plants; we'll tell you how to adapt to such extremes.

A basic problem in many bathrooms is a lack of natural light. Because the view from a bathroom window is not considered important, an awful lot of bathrooms face north or overlook a brick wall, so that only a tiny trickle of light can find its way in. And this is if you're lucky — some bathrooms don't have any windows at all.

The other thing sadly lacking in most bathrooms is space. Plants have to jostle for elbow-room between bottles of aftershave and perfume and tins of talc — it's enough to give a Sensitive Plant a nervous breakdown or a Weeping Fig a fit of the vapours!

But do not despair. There are lots of plants that can make themselves very much at home in such circumstances. The secret lies in providing extra heat and light and adding that touch of design that lets pot plants work their own miracles.

Heat and light

Start by assessing the amount of light your bathroom receives and how cold it is likely to get. If you aren't sure about the temperature, use an ordinary minimum-maximum thermometer — you can buy one at most garden centres and department stores — and use it to see how much your temperature differs every day.

You can safely assume that humidity will be high, as there is usually a lot of moisture in a bathroom. The light level is more difficult to assess but if there is enough natural light for you to read by, then there is enough to grow low-light tolerant plants. If you have good light then you can happily grow most foliage plants; but to grow flowering plants successfully you need to have a lot of light — though of course you can always move them into your bathroom for a temporary splash of colour.

Even if you have no windows in your bathroom you can still grow some plants under artificial light. Choose plants suited to this way of growing, such as African Violets and all sorts of

Heat

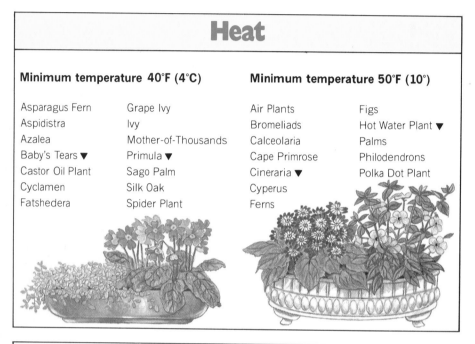

Minimum temperature 40°F (4°C)

Asparagus Fern	Grape Ivy
Aspidistra	Ivy
Azalea	Mother-of-Thousands
Baby's Tears ▼	Primula ▼
Castor Oil Plant	Sago Palm
Cyclamen	Silk Oak
Fatshedera	Spider Plant

Minimum temperature 50°F (10°)

Air Plants	Figs
Bromeliads	Hot Water Plant ▼
Calceolaria	Palms
Cape Primrose	Philodendrons
Cineraria ▼	Polka Dot Plant
Cyperus	
Ferns	

Light

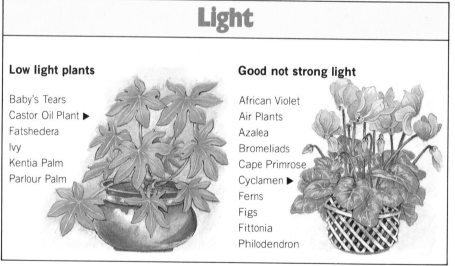

Low light plants

Baby's Tears
Castor Oil Plant ▶
Fatshedera
Ivy
Kentia Palm
Parlour Palm

Good not strong light

African Violet
Air Plants
Azalea
Bromeliads
Cape Primrose
Cyclamen ▶
Ferns
Figs
Fittonia
Philodendron

pretty Ferns. Fix a small wall cabinet with fluorescent tubes, or find a place for a hanging basket lit from above by a special plant light, and you can make an attractive display of plants.

To work out what plants will grow where, check how much light and heat your bathroom gets. You can then make your selection of plants from those listed in the Heat and Light boxes above.

How to find space

Even in the tiniest bathroom there's bound to be a corner of space somewhere. Windowsills are great places for houseplants. Don't worry about frosted glass — it looks as if it cuts out light but it only diffuses the light. This is absolutely perfect for growing a wide range of foliage plants without burning their leaves in the sun.

Narcissus bulbs are specially prepared to flower inside in late winter and early spring.

A variety of heights, leaves and flowers makes for an attractive display.

A dramatic plant — or two — can give a plain bathroom character.

The fresh green foliage of a Maidenhair Fern, a Pteris and an Umbrella Plant have been used to enhance a light, airy bathroom.

Solitary Plants

African Violet
Begonia rex
Cape Primrose ▶
Club Moss
Hot Water Plant
Maidenhair Fern
Maranta tricolor
Primula

Solitary plants

As for other flat surfaces, if you have a cupboard or sink surround, banish all those bottles of potions to under the basin and leave some extra plant standing room. Also have a look at the corners of your bath; they may be just about big enough to stand a plant on. If you do, though, it's essential to pick a plant that will look good on its own, shapewise. Nor must the plant be the least bit top-heavy either, or there's a good chance that it will overbalance and end up joining you in the bath! So choose low, spreading plants or roughly pyramidal kinds. In limited space, choosing the plant with the right shape is half the battle.

Spiky Yucca silhouettes make this room simple yet striking.

Dramatic Plants

Air Plants
Aspidistra
Bromeliads
Coconut Palm
Cyperus ▶
Grape Ivy
Kentia Palm
Parlour Palm
Sago Palm
Silk Oak
Spathiphyllum
Weeping Fig

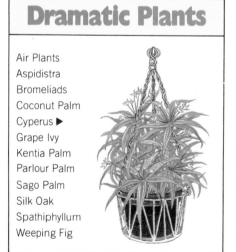

Dramatic plants

If space is a bit more generous, you might also find room for a single dramatic specimen plant.

If there isn't room for an enormous one, create the impression of size by standing a medium size pendulous plant on a pedestal. Or hang it from the ceiling. If the plant is reflected in a mirror, it will look even bigger.

Trailing Plants

Asparagus Fern
Boston Fern
Creeping Fig
Ivy
Mother-of-Thousands ▶
Spider Plant

Trailing plants

There's usually some wall space in the bathroom where you can hang a shelf or two. Instead of cluttering these up with bath salts and empty shells, seize the golden opportunity the shelves offer to grow trailing plants in pretty containers. You can also make an unusual and decorative feature from seashells filled with Air Plants.

Design secrets

The final trick is the designer touch — how to 'make' the room with your plants. In a small space, using a little to achieve a lot is an essential skill; all you need are just two or three really good plants of the right size, colour and shape.

🌱 In a small space lots of different colours give a cluttered and bitty effect, so base your bathroom colour scheme on a single colour, with darker and lighter tones of that colour, and the greens of your plants as a contrast. When choosing flowering plants, you can create a restful effect if you can find flowers that tone in with the rest of your colour scheme.

🌱 You don't have to rely on a single plant to provide an interesting shape; several similar or contrasting plants grouped together can be very effective. Remember that a group of plants should have plenty of room to make them stand out from their surroundings. The space around your plant arrangement is almost as important as the plants themselves.

🌱 A plain, uncluttered background allows plants to stand out well from their surroundings. Unpatterned tiles, whether white or coloured, are one of the best backgrounds for bathroom plants. Cork tiles are great for a touch of luxury, and combine beautifully with

This bathroom would look discouragingly stark without its collection of plants.

Brighten an empty corner with a luxuriant Ladder Fern.

large-leaved plants to create the atmosphere of a jungle.

🌿 Mirrors are another terrific background too. Not only do they create an illusion of space, they also help to make a bathroom lighter and brighter, and you'll get lots of lovely reflections.

🌿 Containers and accessories are the finishing touch for beautiful plants. For a restful effect, choose containers in colours and materials that harmonise well with the rest of your decorative scheme. Baskets and pastel coloured porcelain blend in quietly; or you can make your containers stand out in bright contrast by choosing loud, brilliant colours. If you do this, team them with the colour of your towels or some other highlight in the room.

Creating the display

For best results arrange your larger foliage plants first — then add the smaller plants with coloured leaves and flowers. You can draw attention to particular areas with something really eyecatching.

Air Plants offer plenty of exciting possibilities as they are small and don't have roots — so they can grow without pots. You can mount them on cork tiles in sea shells, or attach them to chunks of semi-precious stone. Grow a collection of them on a piece of driftwood, or make mobiles by dangling Air Plants from lumps of cork or small pieces of wood.

If you're a real plant enthusiast and don't have to share a bathroom with small children, why not allow yourself the luxury of transforming your bathroom into a tropical jungle? For this effect, ignore all the advice about using a little to achieve a lot — go over the top! It's easily done by filling every nook and cranny with vegetation.

Choose good size plants with large leaves like the Swiss Cheese Plant, Philodendrons, Palms, and large Ferns, in as many shades of green as you can find. Use these plants to form the basis of the display, overlapping plants with contrasting leaf shapes; then add highlights in the shape of brightly coloured plants such as Fittonia, *Begonia rex*, African Violet, Maranta or the exotic flowering Spathiphyllum. Gnarled branches draped with Spanish Moss and hung with Air Plants make a very dramatic centrepiece — if you have the room. Then, if you have trouble finding the bath, you can be sure you've got the effect just right!

Plants for kitchens

Because the kitchen is the heart of the home it's only sensible to make it look nice by 'furnishing' it with plants. The idea is to make your kitchen really comfortable, rather than regarding it as just somewhere to work.

The kitchen is the place where all the cooking is done, as well as a hundred and one other things. If you count up all the time you spend in the kitchen you'll probably find that it's more than you spend in any other room except the bedroom — where you're mostly asleep!

A lot of thought goes into planning a kitchen and the permanent equipment, but it takes more than expensive units and the latest equipment to make an ideal kitchen. It's the finishing touches that count, and this is where plants can make all the difference. No matter what style of kitchen you've got, whether it's stripped pine, antique finish, ultra modern or classic, plants will help to make it a welcoming place and the heart of your home.

Practical planning

As the kitchen is essentially a functional place, it is a more challenging environment for your plants than any other room in the house. You have to position your plants quite carefully; you don't want to steam your Philodendron along with the potatoes or blast your African Violets with cold air every time you open the freezer. And as there is always a good deal of coming and going in the kitchen there's the constant risk of plants being knocked over and landing among the breakfast marmalade and toast!

Because of the special nature of the kitchen you'll find that no matter how careful you are there'll inevitably be a few disasters. Even if the plants don't get knocked over and broken, they are likely to show signs of strain by developing dead patches on their leaves or brown crease lines where they've been bent. You'll have to be prepared to replace casualties as necessary.

The biggest problem in kitchens without doubt is lack of space. There's never enough work-top room at the best of times, and plants really don't mix successfully with hot toasters and coffee makers.

Grow plants in hanging baskets if you have a skylight but no spare work top space.

Create an informal kitchen by growing a variety of plants in different kinds of pots.

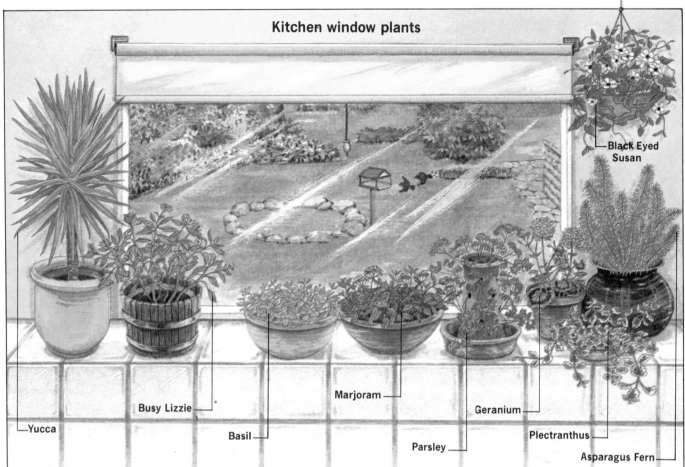

Kitchen window plants

Yucca · Busy Lizzie · Basil · Marjoram · Parsley · Geranium · Plectranthus · Asparagus Fern · Black Eyed Susan

A windowsill is an obvious place to stand pot plants. In many kitchens the sink is in front of a window, and here it's particularly important to have an attractive arrangement simply because you'll be spending quite a bit of time looking at it while you're doing the washing up.

If you have a nice view from your window you won't want to hide it; choose smaller plants so that they don't shut out the scene outside. A row of identical plants, such as African Violets, in a long trough looks perfect here and won't distract from the view. By keeping to one kind of plant, rather than a mixture, you'll get a sophisticated uncluttered look.

There's no need to stick with the same plants all the time — ring the changes. Since your windowsill is the ideal spot for flowering plants, take the opportunity to alternate between winter and summer flowering annuals. Or how about a row of potted herbs? You can snip them for cooking, and replace them with new plants when they are used up.

If you don't have a particularly nice view from your window, you could consider blanking it out entirely with a curtain of trailing plants. By growing plants in hanging containers you can find room for many more. To fill up the window, dangle several plants at different heights.

Kitchen window plants

Summer annuals: Busy Lizzie, Geraniums, Hot Water Plants, Polka Dot Plant, giant double flowered Petunias (these grow far better indoors than they do outside).
Winter annuals: Persian Violets, Cineraria, flowering Azalea (not strictly speaking an annual),Pot Chrysanthemums, Hyacinths (short-lived in the kitchen).
Herbs: any of the small ones — Parsley, Marjoram, Chervil and Basil. Sow new potfuls to replace plants as they are used for cooking.
Trailing plants for windows: Black Eyed Susan, Lipstick Plant, Ceropegia woodii, Creeping Fig.

Lack of light is another common kitchen failing, particularly in older houses and flats. Small windows, blinds and overhanging trees can all cut down the amount of light that enters the room. But this does not have to be a problem: you can choose shade-loving plants for the main part of the room and put flowering plants on the windowsills where the light is strongest.

On the plus side, a kitchen is usually warm enough to keep most plants happy, thanks to the central-heating boiler and the oven. And activities such as washing up and cooking guarantee comfortably high humidity.

Shapes and sizes

When choosing plants for limited spaces it is especially important to take the shape of the plant into account. Avoid rambling, sprawling plants. Choose instead compact, rounded or long narrow plants, or opt for striking sculpted shapes. All of these contrast well with boxy kitchen cupboards, and make the maximum impact in the minimum of space.

Size is another factor to consider. While it is certainly cheaper to buy

Plants for shady shelves

Ivy, all sorts of trailing Asparagus Ferns, Maidenhair Fern, Fittonia, Miniature Bulrush.

Plants for work tops

Boston Fern, Weeping Fig, Mother-in-Law's Tongue, Schefflera, Foxtail Fern and Begonias.

small plants (and lots of fun to watch them grow) it's worth spending rather more to get plants the size you need if you want instant results decor-wise. One or two large plants can look far more striking in a restricted space, and take up less room, than lots of small plants — but it depends entirely on the effect you want to create.

Using colour

The most effective scheme in a room already filled with bits and pieces is to go for plain green foliage plants. These are very restful on the eye and will also blend well with all the various colours of the containers and equipment in your kitchen. If you want your kitchen filled with flowers you'll find it best to stick to a single colour scheme; warm peaches and pinks, for instance, work wonders at brightening up a dark kitchen and highlighting interesting corners.

One of the most difficult kitchen colours to work with — as far as plants

are concerned — is plain white; in theory anything goes with white, but in practice it can make rather a harsh background. Not only does it seem to drain flowers of their colour, but it can also look boring with green. The answer with such a kitchen is to use coloured foliage plants to add warmth and interest to the scheme.

Where to put plants

An effective way of using plants at and above eye level is to stand them on shelves or dressers. Make sure that they are shade tolerant plants, and as long as you don't forget to water them, they'll grow beautifully.

You can make a special feature out of a cork notice board pinned to the wall and covered with Air Plants. These are small plants in a range of strange shapes rather like starfish; because they don't have roots, they can be mounted on bark (which you can get at a garden centre) and pinned to the board. To water them you just give them a light mist spray every day.

If you have the space, work tops are the place for large plants. Here again, you'll probaby need to choose plants that thrive in shade, such as most Ferns and some foliage plants. Alternatively, a small group of plants with colourful or attractively patterned leaves, or in pretty containers, look very attractive. It's wise to avoid flowering plants, or you may end up with unwelcome additions to your cooking!

Ideas for kitchen plant containers

The containers you put your plant pots in are almost as important — in design terms — as the plants themselves, so try and make the most of the opportunity your kitchen offers to get away from the type of container you use around the rest of the house. Containers that look good in 'farmhouse' or natural wood kitchens include brass, copper and rustic pottery. Or, instead of standing the pots in containers, why not just show off plain clay or terracotta pots on matching drip trays. If terracotta doesn't go with your decor, you can use brightly coloured plastics — green, yellow, white or pillar box red.

Another idea is to use old equipment such as saucepans and kettles as containers. Or you can liven up a collection of plates, interesting tins or teapots by placing your plants among them.

Use all the kitchen surfaces — work tops, shelves and windowsills for your plants.

1 Shiny copper kettle with a small and elegant Parlour Palm.

2 Solid stoneware pot looks terrific holding a Croton.

3 A Creeping Fig and a jazzy painted gourd.

4 Heavy kitchen pot with a young Umbrella Plant.

5 A cheerful Oxo tin goes well with a tiny Snakeskin Plant.

6 A large ceramic bowl is useful for a tall Sweetheart Vine.

7 They could be made for each other — a cabbage pot and Azalea.

8 Even a potty comes into its own with a leafy Sword Fern!

9 Put your old teapot to work holding a Maidenhair Fern.

10 This Polka Dot Plant cheers up the sober wine cooler.

Window-box colour

All too often window-boxes are thought of as summer-time spectaculars, but with a little thought and planning they can be filled with colourful plants all the year round. To do this you will have to work out a sequence of plants for the whole year, which can either be bought in flower for instant results, or planted in advance, using bulbs, seeds or cuttings bought from garden centres.

Window-boxes are usually associated with dazzling displays of annuals, but the more subtle shades of the smaller species of herbs, wild flowers or cottage garden plants can make a wonderful display. And even with summer bedding plants it is possible to do something original: try planting just one type of flower or a mixture of different flowers of the same colour for a dazzling effect.

Pastel-coloured flowers look good when set off by grey-leaved plants.

Cultivation

Soil. Use a good brand of potting compost and avoid garden soil.
Watering. Check the moisture of the soil daily in summer and weekly in winter. Vigorous-growing plants like Fuchsias need more water than the slower-growing plants like alpines,

A mixture of upright and trailing plants is the key to a good box.

Plants for spring

There is plenty of scope for window-box planting in spring, but remember to choose plants that flower early and will be finished in time for you to prepare the box for summer planting.
Bulbs. Hyacinths 8×6in (20×15cm); Winter Aconites 3 × 4in (8 × 10cm); Snowdrops 4 × 4in (10 × 10cm); Crocus 5 × 4in (13 × 10cm); Grape Hyacinths 5 × 6in (13 × 15cm); *Anemone blanda* 6 × 4in (15 × 10cm); miniature Narcissi, such as the Hooped Petticoat Daffodil (*Narcissus bulbocodium*) 4 × 3in (10 × 8cm); *Iris reticulata* 6 × 4in (15 × 10cm).
Spring flowering alpines. *Primula farinosa*, *P.denticulata* and *P.auricula* 6 × 6in (15 × 15cm).
Spring bedders. Polyanthus 6 × 6in (15 × 15cm); Primroses 4 × 4in (10 × 10cm); Wallflowers 9 × 5in (23 × 13cm).

Plants for summer

There are many plants that will give a good show of colour in summer. The problem here is choosing plants that will look effective together, so once you have decided on a theme, try and stick to it.
Bedding plants. Lobelia, bushy or trailing, 3 × 2in (8 × 5cm); Salvia, bushy, 6 × 6in (15 × 15cm); Ageratum, bushy, 6 × 4in (15 × 10cm); Impatiens, bushy, 6 × 6in (15 × 15cm); French Marigolds 6 × 8in (15 × 20cm); Petunias, trailing, 8 × 6in (20 × 15cm); Verbena, bushy, 8 × 6in (20 × 15cm); Nasturtiums, bushy, 4 × 4in (10 × 10cm); Sweet Peas, trailing, 12 × 4in (30 × 10cm); Begonias 12 × 6in (30 × 15cm); Fuchsias, trailing, 12 × 8in (30 × 20cm); Geraniums, bushy, 10 × 6in (25 × 15cm). Mimulus 6in (15cm); Mesembryanthemum 4 × 6in (10 × 15cm); *Felicia bergeriana* 8 × 4in (20 × 10cm); White Alyssum 2 × 2in (5 × 5cm); Echeveria 2 × 3in (5 × 8cm).
Other flowering plants. Coleus 10 × 6in (25 × 15cm); Cockscomb 10 × 6in (25 × 15cm); Calceolaria 10 × 6in (25 × 15cm); Cineraria 10 × 6in (25 × 15cm).
Foliage plants. *Helichrysum petiolatum* 6 × 10in (15 × 25cm); Dill 12 × 4in (30 × 10cm); Eau de Cologne Mint 8 × 6in (20 × 15cm); Golden Marjoram 4 × 4in (10 × 10cm); Red Basil 8 × 6in (20 × 15cm).
Rock and alpine plants. Androsace

and even if it is raining check the soil as the wall behind the box tends to deflect the rain away from the plants.
Aspect. Flowering plants and alpines need to be in the sun for at least half the day, so any window-sill facing south-east, south or south-west is an ideal spot for them. Herbs and other non-alpine foliage plants will do well given a north-east or north-west aspect if you don't have a sunnier spot for them. You can also plant summer flowering plants in this position but you may need to replace them once or twice in a season as the poor weather conditions may result in them flowering only once. Ivies are shade-tolerant plants and will thrive even in a north-facing box.
Wind. When you are deciding where to put your window-box it is very important to take wind into consideration. Only the toughest plants, like Ivies, will survive in a windy spot and the larger the flowers of a plant, the less likely they are to thrive, often browning or withering early.

Design

The key to a good window-box is a balanced mixture of upright and trailing plants, creeping plants for ground cover, variegated and plain foliage

plants, and a selection of colourful flowering plants.

With an informal mixed box, keep the taller, upright plants to the back and centre, and use progressively smaller plants as you work towards the edges. Place your creeping or trailing plants at the front. With a more formal box, keep plants of the same height along the full length of the box. Whichever style you choose make sure that you put plenty of plants in – the box should be well-filled, right from the start.

As a rough guide allow half the eventual height between upright plants and half the eventual spread between creeping plants.

When designing a window-box it is important to decide first what you are trying to achieve. For example you might want to create a traditional window-box ablaze with colour, or something along the lines of a miniature landscape, using alpines. You could design a box based on contrasting foliage shapes and colours or on cottage garden plants and flowers. You could even plan an exotic tropical-looking box based on succulent plants and Mesembryanthemum. Here are some suggestions of plants to use and some design ideas.

4 × 4in (10 × 10cm); Aquilegia 10 × 6in (25 × 15cm); Campanula, creeping, 4 × 6in (10 × 15cm); Gentian, bushy, 6 × 6in (15 × 15cm); Edelweiss, creeping, 3 × 6in (8 × 15cm); Lithospermum, bushy, 6 × 6in (15 × 15cm); Aubrieta, creeping, 4 × 6in (10 × 15cm); *Raoulia hookeri* 1/2 × 4in (12mm × 10cm); *Chamaecyparis obtusa* 'Nana Gracilis' 6 × 6in (15 × 15cm). *Saxifraga moschata* 'Cloth of Gold', golden cushions, and *S.* 'Flowers of Sulphur', sulphur green cushions, 2 × 3in (5 × 8cm).

Plants for autumn and winter

Few window-box sized plants are in flower at this time of year so most of your colour will come from evergreen plants. Choose varieties that will give a good contrast of form, shape, colour and texture. Ivies, especially variegated ones, give a good show of colour, but go for trailing rather the climbing types.

Flowers. Miniature cyclamen 6 × 4in (15 × 10cm); *Gentiana macauleyi* and *G.sino-ornata* 6 × 4in (15 × 10cm); Pansy 'Floral Dance' 6 × 4in (15 × 10cm)·

Herbs. Prostrate Rosemary, creeping, 6 × 8in (15 × 20cm); Thyme

Fill your box with only one type of flower such as Pelargonium.

Ivies, Conifers and Winter Cherries make a spectacular display.

'Anderson's Gold', creeping, 4 × 6in (10 × 15cm); Winter Savory, bushy, 6 × 6in (15 × 15cm).

Alpines. *Sedum spathulifolium purpureum* 1 × 4in (2.5 × 10cm); *Sempervivum arachnoideum* (Houseleek) 1in (2.5cm); *Artemisia schmidtiana*, hillocks of silver, 3 × 3in (8 × 8cm).

Ivies. These are all trailing varieties and measure 6 × 10in (15 × 26cm); 'Sagittaefolia', (small, pointed, deep-green leaves); 'Sally Lime' (green and yellow splashed leaves); 'Heise' (silvery grey leaves); 'Fantasia' (yellow leaves covered with green spots and swirls); 'Caecilia' (curly variegated leaves); and 'Fluffy Ruffles' (curly leaves).

Design ideas

Spring

Traditional box. Fill the box with Hyacinths of the same or mixed colours. These look better staggered, so avoid planting in rows and include some Ivy as a contrast.

Connoisseurs' box. *Iris reticulata*; Snowdrops; Winter Aconites; Grape Hyacinths; *Narcissus bulbocodium*; *Hedera helix* 'Sagittaefolia'.

Cottage garden box. Wallflower 'Tom Thumb'; Primroses; *Primula farinosa*; *Hedera congesta*.

Summer

Traditional box. Nasturtium (non-trailing variety); Basil Dark Opal; White Alyssum; Lobelia (trailing variety).

Cottage garden box. *Felicia bergeriana*; Verbena; Golden marjoram; Pelargonium.

Alpine box. *Saxifraga* 'Flowers of Sulphur'; Aquilegia; Campanula; Lithospermum; *Raoulia hookeri*; *Chamaecyparis obtusa nana gracilis* (one small plant).

Exotic tropical box. Mesembryanthemum; Echeveria.

Autumn and winter

Traditional box. Pansy 'Floral Dance'; Ivy *Hedera helix*, any plain-leaved green variety.

Box for foliage contrasts. *Hedera congesta*; *H.helix* 'Fantasia', 'Fluffy Ruffles', 'Sagittaefolia variegata'; *Thymus erectus*; *Thymus* x 'Anderson's Gold'.

Connoisseurs' box. Miniature Cyclamen; *Gentiana sino-ornata*; *Sedum spathulifolium purpureum*; *Sempervivum arachnoideum* (Cobwebbed Houseleek); *Festuca glauca*.

Conservatories and sun rooms

Imagine all the best features of a greenhouse, a living room and a patio rolled into one — a place to relax in comfort and enjoy the sun, to eat summer meals and to entertain. A conservatory isn't just an extra room added on to your house — it's more a way of life! To make the most of it, you should give some thought to the furniture and fittings, but most of all you should choose the right plants.

When it comes to conservatories or sun rooms, don't just settle for more of the same kinds of plants you already have on your windowsills or tables — go for those that are tailor-made for conservatory life. These are the large, flamboyant or fast-growing plants, too big for the greenhouse, and too sun-loving for indoors. They include small trees and shrubs, climbers and wall plants, bulbs — and even water plants! The choice is yours.

Planning for effect

When you're enthusiastic about plants, it can be all too easy to buy anything that takes your fancy, and end up with a miscellaneous collection that has no real coherence or style. This may not matter much with occasional plants in a sitting room, but your conservatory should be the one room where the plants come first, and other things, such as furniture and ornaments, are designed around them.

Be firm from the start: decide what you want and reject anything that

A garden view is framed by Primulas, Cinerarias and Azaleas.

Plants for

CONSERVATORIES HEATED TO 40-45°F (5-7°C)

Abutilon
Trees or shrubs with large orange or red bell-shaped flowers often carried right through the winter.

Acacia (Acacia mimosaceae)
Small evergreen tree or shrub with yellow flowers. Try also A.baileyana purpurea with purple foliage and A.dunnii with silvery blue leaves.

Arum Lily (Zantedeschia aethiopica)
Bulb with white flowers in early spring.

Banana (Musa)
Fast-growing tree and a real conversation piece. Try the dwarf Musa velutina if you want to have fruit, although it will not be edible.

Bougainvillea
Climber available in various colours, including the well-known purple.

Camellia
Flowering shrub. Grow greenhouse C.reticulata varieties for their beautiful blooms.

Castor Oil Plant (Ricinus communis)
Shrub with large, palm-shaped leaves. 'Gibsonii' and 'Impala' have red or bronze foliage and may also produce spiky red fruit.

Citrus
Orange, lemon, kumquat and lime all have glossy leaves, fragrant flowers and should produce ripe, full-sized fruit in a heated conservatory.

Clivia
Bulb with large clusters of orange flowers on thick stems.

Cordyline (Dracaena)
Small shrub that will grow to an imposing height in a conservatory.

Eucalyptus
Try the unusual, lemon-scented Eucalyptus citriodora or, for flowers, the dwarfs E.forrestiana and E.ficifolia.

Floating Water Hyacinth (Eichhornia crassipes)
Aquatic plant with orchid-like flowers.

Ginger Lily (Hedychium)
Tassel-like flowers produced at the ends of tall canes.

Glory Lily (Gloriosa)
Bulb with large red or yellow flowers on long, climbing stems.

House Lime (Sparmannia africana)
An unusual shrub with enormous, heart-shaped, lime green leaves.

Lobster Claw (Clianthus puniceus)
Climber with large flowers, red or turquoise, shaped like claws.

Oleander (Nerium oleander)
Sweet-scented flowering shrub; grow from seed or cuttings.

Passion Flower (Passiflora)
Vigorous climbing plants producing exotic flowers as well as fruit. P.edulis and P.quadrangularis are the most reliable for fruit; P.coccinea has brilliant red flowers.

Plumbago
Unusual climber with striking, blue flowers; easily grown from seed.

Sago Palm (Cycas)
Victorian favourite with unusual fronds growing from a short stump.

Stephanotis
Sweetly scented, slow-growing plant; raise from seeds or cuttings.

Trumpet Flower (Datura)
Exotic, trumpet-shaped flowers in white, purple, yellow or pink.

Water Lily (Nymphaea)
Aquatic plants with large, beautiful flowers. Try the tropical varieties.

A stunning arrangement of flowering plants brightens up a plain wall.

conservatories

UNHEATED CONSERVATORIES

Arum Lily (*Zantedeschia aethiopica*)
The white variety of bulb needs less warmth than the coloured ones.

Black-eyed Susan (*Thunbergia alata*)
Fast-growing annual climber with brilliant orange, black-centred flowers. It is not hardy, so avoid sowing seeds until April or May, when the frosts have finished.

Camellia
Grow outdoor varieties of the shrub in tubs and bring them inside for early spring flowers.

Eucalyptus
Small trees. *Eucalyptus perriniana* and *E.gunnii* both have beautiful, bluish leaves.

Fig (*Ficus*)
Fascinating to grow, with luscious fruit in late summer. Choose indoor varieties for the best flavour, such as 'White Marseilles' or 'Negro Largo'. Can also be grown in a heated conservatory.

Grape Vine (*Vitis*)
Easiest grown in a bed and trained up on roof supports. Mainly ornamental, yet may yield edible fruit. Can also be grown in a heated conservatory.

Guernsey Lily (*Nerine*)
Enormous flower heads in pink or red. Bring indoors during exceptionally cold winter spells.

Hibiscus
Try the large-flowered annuals grown from seed, such as 'Dixie Bell' and 'Southern Belle'.

Kiwi Fruit (*Actinidia chinensis*)
Fast-growing climber; to get it to fruit you will need both a male and a female plant.

Mind Your Own Business (*Helxine*)
Creeping foliage plant, very useful among taller plants to make ground cover or as a fill-in.

Nile Lily (*Agapanthus*)
Bulb with stately stems of blue or white flowers.

Pineapple Flower (*Eucomis*)
Beautiful plant with a flower shaped like a pineapple at the end of a stalk. Bring indoors during exceptionally cold winter spells.

Yucca
Sword-shaped leaves that grow in rosettes; will reach 6ft (1.8m) in a conservatory.

doesn't fit into your scheme. Take into account both the style and the size of your conservatory. If you have an old-fashioned, Victorian-style one, you could arrange it in the authentic fashion, with plants in beds, tiled floors and cast-iron furniture. If the ceiling is high you can go in for tall plants, such as citrus trees or large palms. If you have a much more modern room, with a cleaner, less cluttered look, you could go for a few well-chosen specimen plants to create a sculptural effect.

A flexible approach
You'll probably find that the traditional, Victorian style of laying down permanent beds will be too restricting unless you have a very large conservatory. It's more useful with a smaller conservatory or sun room to stick to plants in individual pots and tubs, so that you can move them around easily. This option also has a practical side to it: if any of your plants become affected by disease, it's much easier to move them out to treat them, reducing the risk of infection being passed to the other plants.

Climbing plants are a boon in a conservatory. You can train them up wire netting or a trellis attached to a wall, and they will eventually hide the brickwork completely.

Making a focal point
Most rooms have a particular feature that draws the eye and provides a starting point for the decor — in living rooms, for example, it's often a fireplace. It's a good idea to aim to create a kind of focal point in your conservatory, too.

You can do this very successfully by designing a particularly attractive group of plants for a corner of the room, or you could be more adventurous and use trailing plants to frame a view into the garden. An even more exciting, and rewarding, feature would be a small water garden (we'll be telling you about indoor water gardens later).

If you don't have enough room for a pool, but like the idea of some water in the conservatory, you can always fill a large glass tank or a half-barrel with water and just float a single tropical Water Lily (*Nymphaea*) or a clump of Floating Water Hyacinth (*Eichhornia crassipes*) in it.

Keeping it warm
When a conservatory takes a certain amount of heat from the house and has

Delicate *Tibouchina urvilleana.*

An Amaryllis stands out among Begonias, Streptocarpus and a scarlet Busy Lizzie.

Colourful Gloxinia and Streptocarpus.

windows that catch the sun, it will be quite warm enough for most of the year without your help. In winter, however, it will get too cold unless you take precautions. You should provide a heater that is capable of keeping the room at a temperature of 40-45°F (5-7°C) at nights. One or two electric heaters controlled by a thermostat will be the most convenient and the most economical, since they operate automatically depending on the air temperature.

Keeping it cool

Even more of a problem than the cold in winter may be the heat in summer! If your conservatory is a real sun trap, it may simply get too hot, causing plants to flag. And too much direct sun can scorch plants, especially if they get too dry. The two things you must provide are ventilation and shade.

As with heating, ventilation that operates automatically is by far the easiest, and doesn't need to be expensive. You can get gadgets that work by using tubes of paraffin wax: when the sun has heated them to a certain temperature,

the wax expands, pushing open the ventilator. When the temperature cools down a little, the wax contracts again and the ventilator closes.

Shading may also be necessary, especially if your conservatory is south-facing. A special liquid is available for greenhouse roofs which you paint on to the glass. It doesn't look very attractive, however, and will remain until you wash it off — not ideal for changeable summer weather. A much better bet is to use blinds. Most domestic blinds will work very well in a conservatory. Venetian blinds stand up well to intense heat and light, and they're easy to clean, but if you prefer roller blinds, choose a plasticised fabric that will not fade in the bright light. You can buy these — and wooden, slatted blinds that you attach to the outside — from greenhouse suppliers, or direct from the manufacturers.

Watering

It's very handy to have a tap in or near the conservatory, since watering can be a long job in summer if you have a lot of plants. You can douse permanent beds

easily with a watering can or hosepipe, but remember that plants in pots dry out more quickly and will therefore need watering more often.

A tiled floor is a must if you want to splash water about to increase the humidity — if possible it should slope a little towards a drain so that water will run off quickly and not remain to make the floor dangerously slippery. You can always brighten up the floor with rugs when you've finished watering.

Where to get your plants

Many of the commoner conservatory plants can easily be obtained from good garden centres. More unusual ones are often available from specialists who advertise in gardening magazines.

Of course, you can always grow your own from seed — indeed, if you want something really out of the way, you'll have to! You may have to wait two or three years before you have a really well established specimen, but the effort will be well worth it when you have a beautiful plant to enjoy and to share with others in the years to come.

A room with a view

However small your garden – whether patio, terrace or balcony outside a window – you can derive tremendous enjoyment from it. One of the most treasured aspects of owning a garden is that it gives you the opportunity to stage-manage the scene you look out on from your window.

Just think how many times a day you glance out of the window. Whether you're having a quiet cup of tea at breakfast, a chat with a friend, or simply taking it easy with a good book, chances are that every so often you'll let your eyes stray to the view that is just outside. So it's really worth while to take some trouble to make the scene outside beautiful and satisfying – even to the extent of deliberately setting out to make for yourself 'a room with a view'.

First things first

If you start by thinking of the view as a picture, with the window as its frame, you'll see that it's not just the view that needs designing but the room that goes with it as well. So first decide which room is going to get the 'treatment' – it will probably be the room you use the most, as long as it is one that does look out on to the garden. Otherwise, you'll probably choose the room that has the best garden view – and you may even decide to alter your living habits accordingly.

Once you have chosen the room and the window, think of the garden outside as a stage. You'll be looking at it throughout the year – and while the different 'sets' (the living plants) may change with the seasons, the underlying construction of the stage will remain the same. For this reason it is vitally important to consider this basic structure first, before deciding on the plantings.

If you have only a very small patio or terrace, it's even more important than it is with a large garden to plan its structure carefully. Three things are fundamental in creating permanent interest in your 'stage'.

● **Different levels.** You should con-

Use different levels and textures to create added interest.

sider giving your stage added interest by creating various levels: terracing, steps, low retaining walls, pergolas, hanging baskets, large plant containers and shelving for pot plants are all possibilities.

● **Textures.** The different textures you can introduce by the use of various paving and walling materials can give your stage an endurable appeal quite apart from the plants you introduce. Cobble-stones, random stone paving, granite setts, weathered brick, concrete paving slabs, tiles, old railway sleepers and timber discs (cut from tree trunks) can all be used to create patterns and textures to marvellous effect.

● **Perspective.** Any stage designer knows that a small stage can be made to appear larger by the subtle use of perspective. Plan your plot so that the eye is drawn to a focal point – maybe a piece of statuary you found in a local junk shop, or a small fountain, or an inviting arrangement of garden furniture. To lead the eye towards this focal point, you can plan a path, or a line of stepping stones or paving, or arrange a narrowing vista of planting.

When it comes to planning the planting for your 'view', remember that this too falls into separate groupings – permanent features that will be there throughout the year, and changing ones that will come into their own at a particular season.

● **Permanent planting.** Your framework of permanent planting is the anchor that will hold all your other plant elements together. If your plot is large enough to take it, you might consider a small tree for the focal point. A basic furnishing of evergreens is a must: it will 'knit together' the tapestry of colours in spring, summer and autumn, and will prevent the garden looking dead in the middle of winter. Evergreens don't have to be gloomy. The splendid *Fatsia japonica*, for instance, puts out handsome bright emerald green leaves in spring to replace its older, darker green ones, and it will bring any patio or terrace to life in November with its spikes of white, waxy flowers. A low bush of the attractive silver leaved *Senecio laxifolius* is a cheerful sight at any time of year, while Bergenias, Yuccas, ferns, Blue Rue and variegated Ivies are all marvellously resilient evergreen plants that will give your view an enduring appeal throughout the year. If you can include at least one grouping of evergreens like these, you will have a point of living interest in the depths of winter when everything else in the garden looks completely dead.

● **Seasonal planting.** It's a good idea to think of each season in turn, and make sure that there will be at least one group of plants that will be at its best at that time. If your plot is small, don't try to cram too much into it – better to aim for one main effect at each season of the year. Once you've got the main planting right, by all means fill remaining spaces with your favourite bulbs and little plants. Look out particularly for very early flowering bulbs – there's nothing that lifts the spirits more than the sight of a mass of the pale-blue *Scilla tubergeniana* covering the ground in early February, or the delightful little *Cyclamen coum* poking their flowers up through the snow in mid-winter.

The picture frame

So much for the picture; now let's look at the frame. From inside the room, the idea is to make as near a perfect setting for your view as possible. This may well involve

Hanging baskets and window-boxes can be used to marvellous effect.

A basic furnishing of evergreens is a 'must' for every balcony.

Make the window a focal point.

re-arranging the furniture: in a room with a huge picture window or double patio doors, the view could well become the focal point of the room, with the furniture arranged facing towards it. But in a room that is dominated by a large fireplace, or that has more than one window, the arrangement of the furniture needs more thought. You can retain the natural focal point of the room, but make sure that nothing obscures the view from the window, and try to organise things so that the natural 'flow' of the room automatically leads the eye towards the window and the view that it frames.

The window itself needs careful treatment too. You want to encourage people to look towards it, and also to carry on looking out through it at the picture beyond. So avoid fussy or overpatterned curtains, distracting ornaments or too-tall pot plants on the window-sill. And make sure the glass is clean! As far as blinds are concerned, stick to plain colours, gentle patterns and muted tones, and avoid anything that contrasts harshly with what is beyond – or the eye will never get that far. And finally, don't forget to open the windows whenever you get the chance. It's the best way of all to bring the outside dimension indoors – wafted on the scent of sun-kissed flowers, grass and herbs.

On the ground

As first impressions are so important ground-level containers should always be attractive to look at and immaculately clean. White or green wooden tubs with black bands (preferably rustproof), oak or teak tubs, white painted wooden troughs, plastic troughs, terracotta clay containers, classical lead troughs and urns are just some of the containers available. Choose them to match the style of your house and make sure that the plants you fill them with are compatible with the style of the container. Remember, also, to lift containers slightly off the ground to encourage good drainage.

Cottage garden look

If you live in the country, aim for containers overflowing with an abundance of colour. Use Pansies, Polyanthus, Mignonette, Sweet William, Marigold, Larkspur, Candytuft, Poppies, Hollyhocks, Foxgloves, Forget-me-Nots, Nepeta, Double Daisies, Wallflowers and Anemones. These are all traditional cottage garden plants, but there is no reason why they shouldn't grow as well in containers as in a border.

Tubs and large containers can also be used to house climbers such as Honeysuckle, Clematis and Roses. Of course if there is soil near the door these climbers can just be planted directly into it.

All these climbers will need support. Square or diamond-shaped trellis, in wood or plastic, and coloured white, green or brown, is ideal. Or you can use galvanised wires attached to masonry nails, or to vine 'eyes' fixed with straining bolts if the weight of the plant growth is likely to be heavy. You could use a rustic timber arch as a support which, covered with stems and foliage, would make a very attractive porch.

In town

Town houses and formal exteriors usually lend themselves to a more restrained pattern of planting. Box (Buxus) or Sweet Bay clipped back into pyramids, cones, balls or figures and planted in tubs will echo this formality. Tulips, Pinks and Border Carnations, Auriculas, Plantain Lilies (*Hosta albo-marginata*), Irises, the Houseleek, the fragrant white-

You can easily frame your door with tubs and hanging baskets.

Decorative doorways

Front doors and their surrounds are often neglected when it comes to container planting. This is a shame, because they offer a wide scope for decorative and imaginative display which can do much to enhance the entrance to your home.

There is plenty you can do to make a front door stand out. If the door is flush with the house wall you can easily frame it by placing troughs, tubs and urns full of plants on the ground beside it. You can also use hanging baskets on the wall.

flowered Myrtle (*Myrtus communis* 'Tarentina') and Lady's Mantle (*Alchemilla mollis*) are other plants that will flower from spring through to late summer. Lavender and Rosemary make neat grey bushes, and conifers, such as Yew, Juniper and the Lawson's Cypress varieties, will provide elegance all the year round.

Hanging baskets

If you haven't enough wall space for climbing plants or room for large containers, or simply want something a little different, hanging containers always look pretty.

The invention of the pump-can has also made watering them less of a chore. This device enables you to pump water by hand up a long spout to the plants. This removes the necessity of standing on a step-ladder or having to lower the containers every time you want to water them. This is an enormous advantage, as hanging baskets dry out rapidly and need daily watering.

Fill your baskets with trailing plants to cover the sides and base of the basket. This is important as the basket will be viewed mainly from below. Suitable plants include trailing Lobelia, Nasturtiums, *Campanula isophylla*, pendulous Begonias, Ivy-leaved Pelargoniums, *Helichrysum petiolatum*, small-leaved variegated Ivies, the Spider Plant (Chlorophytum), Mother of Thousands (*Saxifraga stolonifera*), *Zebrina pendula* and Fuchsias.

If you want to make the basket a complete ball of vegetation grow *Tradescantia albiflora* (Wandering Jew) which has white-striped, grey-green leaves up to 4in (10cm) long and thick, fleshy stems. It will grow through the compost underneath and completely cover the basket. Take it inside in winter if you want it to flourish for another year.

Railings

Some front doors have railings on either side of the path leading up to the door or a flight of steps similarly adorned. Railings lend themselves beautifully to plant decoration and can make the approach to your home much more attractive. They also provide ready-made supports for climbers such as Honeysuckle, Clematis and also the Russian Vine

(*Polygonum baldschuanicum*) which will quickly cover the railings, making a thick curtain of stems and foliage topped by feathery clusters of creamy flowers all through summer.

Sweet Peas will attach themselves by their tendrils, Nasturtiums will twine. Virginia Creeper (*Parthenocissus tricuspidata*) becomes a

Fill hanging baskets with colourful trailers for maximum effect.

Place tubs full of colourful flowers on your front door steps.

blanket of red in autumn and Grape Vines make excellent cover, especially the purpled-leaved one, *Vitis vinifera* 'Purpurea', which also has edible fruit.

Winter Jasmine (*Jasminum nudiflorum*) often grows better against railings than anywhere else, perhaps because of the protection offered by the walls of the house. It will probably have to be tied to the railings.

If you also have steps, grow plants in containers on the steps themselves backing up against the railings. This way you don't have to stick to climbers but can also grow small upright shrubs or conifers. You could try the Herringbone Cotoneaster (*C.horizontalis*), or the Firethorn, *Pyracantha* 'Fireglow' or 'Lalandei'

Steps always lend themselves beautifully to plant decoration.

with orange berries, the vertical Irish Yew (*Taxus baccata* 'Fastigiata'), or *Juniperus communis* 'Compressa'.

Drainpipes

Finally, don't forget that drainpipes can be decorated. Apart from encouraging climbers to use them as supports (without letting them take over the gutters) you can now buy devices made for attaching pots to them.

Exterior design

Many of the best gardens are never planned but simply develop over the years with the needs of the owner and the discovery of what grows best. The same approach can be applied, to some extent, to container gardening on patios and terraces, but because such areas are so restricted in space, it pays to do a little advance thinking, about both what to grow and the function you want your garden to perform.

The best use of space

A patio or terrace garden is used a lot – for sitting out, perhaps for sunbathing, and for entertaining – so it is important to leave some open space, however enthusiastic you are about growing plants. You will, in any case, want to relax from time to time and admire the results of your work.

Growing plants in containers, using modern composts, can result in such luxurious growth, especially in a hot summer, that plants become over-crowded. They demand a lot of watering and feeding, and may need to be cut back ruthlessly. You can partly get round this problem by spacing out the containers, particularly if you are growing permanent plants like climbers or shrubs.

Annuals grow fast: if you are not sure about their spacing, put them in fairly closely and then take out alternate plants later on if they seem to be getting too crowded. Start by planting the individual containers closely with annuals, bedding plants, bulbs and the smaller herbaceous plants and trailers, and space out the

containers themselves when you can see how well the plants are growing.

What to plant

A bare terrace or patio can be rather intimidating, but even just one or two troughs, an urn and a tub will soon enliven the blank expanse of paving. You can arrange containers in groups, which gives the immediate impression of a mini-garden, using a mixture of plants such as Ageratum and Busy Lizzies in a trough at the front, with Tobacco Plants (Nicotiana) behind them in a deeper con-

Cedrus libani 'Sargentii', *below, extreme left*, forms an attractive mound of foliage, while the Madonna Lily, *Lilium candidum, below centre*, bears white flowers during June and July. Pelargoniums, Lobelia and Petunias, *below right*, form a superb combination.

Lady's Mantle (*Alchemilla mollis*) and Lamb's Ear (*Stachys lanata*), *extreme left*, form a superb foliage and flower combination for summer interest. *Chrysanthemum haradjanii*, *centre left*, also known as *Tanacetum haradjanii*, creates a sea of silvery leaves. Annual Chrysanthemums, *centre right*, form bright, dome-shaped displays, mainly from mid to late summer. Borage, *Borago officinalis*, *extreme right*, flowers from June to September. Borage also has leaves which, when cut young, are used to flavour fruit crops and salads.

tainer, and perhaps a pair of Camellias in tubs, one on either side. This would give you a good summer display, with the Camellias providing evergreen leaves as background; then in the autumn the annuals could be replaced with Polyanthus and spring-flowering bulbs, such as Daffodils, Grape Hyacinths and Scillas, which flower at the same time as Camellias.

Alternatively, you can make a feature of a single container. Use particularly attractive types – such as sculptured Provençal pots, a classical-style Italian trough or an urn on a pedestal – and plant each container with a single striking plant. Try, for example, one of the New Zealand Flaxes; or the tropical-looking Yucca with its rosette of spiky leaves and handsome spike of white bell flowers; or a *Fatsia japonica* – an architectural plant with large, eye-catching, evergreen, fig-like leaves, plus feathery clusters of creamy flowers in the autumn. Other possible plants include a Japanese Azalea, a variegated Holly grown as a standard, a similarly trained Fuchsia dripping with flowers, Canna Lilies, and a pyramid of Sweet Peas or climbing Nasturtiums.

If you have enough space to change containers from season to season, you can grow a succession of different displays throughout the year. Spring, for instance, can be marked in stages: early spring by Snowdrops, Crocus, Scillas and autumn-planted Anemones; then mid to late spring by Daffodils, Hyacinths, Polyanthus, Grape Hyacinths, Wallflowers, Forget-me-nots and Tulips. The gap between spring and full summer can be filled by Pansies, Irises and double Daisies, with the Spider Plant (*Chlorophytum comosum* 'Variegatum') for background foliage. And in summer the possibilities

are endless: plant up with Petunias, French and African Marigolds, Lilies, Begonias, Lobelia, Gazania, Salvia, Heliotrope, Mimulus and Pelargoniums.

Monotone colour schemes offer something a little different from the ubiquitous rainbow mixture. Try sticking to one colour for each container, or even one colour for the whole patio or terrace.

Shades of gold and yellow, for example, make an arresting sight: use Golden Marjoram, the yellow-leaved form of Creeping Jenny (*Lysimachia nummularia* 'Aurea') which has yellow flowers, yellow African Marigolds such as 'Yellow Galore' and 'Inca Gold', yellow Pansies, the yellow-flowered onion (*Allium moly*), a yellow rose called 'Golden Showers', and a yellow-leaved Hosta.

Silver- and grey-leaved plants with

blue or purple flowers provide a cool, elegant look, and here again the choice is very wide. *Pyrethrum* 'Silver Feather' is a lovely, delicate silvery-grey foliage plant; *Cineraria maritima* is a grey-leaved one with white undersides, stronger-growing and with more solid leaves; the softly furry Lamb's Tongue (*Stachys lanata* 'Olympica') and *Tanacetum densum* 'Amani', which has small leaves like miniature ostrich feathers, can both provide the background; while Lavender, Borage, Ageratum, dark and light blue Lobelia, Heliotrope, Rosemary, Campanulas, Love-in-the-mist, blue Nemesias, Pansies, Larkspur and *Echium* 'Blue Bedder' all produce blue or purple flowers, and sometimes grey foliage.

A corner display can be great fun. Such areas are often suntraps where you can grow warmth-loving plants

nobilis) is a good evergreen which can be clipped and trained into various shapes; *Elaeagnus pungens* 'Maculata' is evergreen with gold-centred leaves; Hydrangeas, Fuchsias and Fatsia are all good choices; and the shrubby Hibiscus provides blue, white flushed with pink or magenta flowers from August to October.

Small trees also have the advantage of providing you with shade. Try the graceful False Acacia with golden leaves, *Robinia pseudoacacia* 'Frisia' or a form of Hawthorn called 'Paul's Scarlet' which has double red flowers. The Rowan tree *(Sorbus acuparia)* has orange berries in autumn, while the form 'Joseph Rock' has yellow fruits. The weeping form of the Goat Willow *(Salix caprea)* is most attractive, and grows slowly to about 6ft (1.8m) in a container. Conifers can provide a much more erect habit of growth, such as *Juniperus virginiana* 'Skyrocket' or the upright form of Irish Yew, *Taxus baccata* 'Fastigiata'.

and, if you have a wall or fence on two sides, there will be plenty of space for climbers to spread. It could be worth building a raised bed with a brick or stone surround, either across the corner or along each side, making sure that the compost level is not above the damp-proof course. Plants growing in this sort of position do extremely well, and climbers would be particularly happy. Bougainvillea, for example, would be sensational against a white background; the Passion Flower would thrive in these conditions, and so would a summer-flowering Jasmine or a Grape Vine.

A corner can be made into a tempting sitting-out area with one or two shrubs. Choose Hydrangeas, Azaleas, a Japanese Acer, or a conifer such as *Chamaecyparis lawsoniana* 'Ellwoodii', plus one or two fragrant Roses, Tobacco Plants, clove-scented Pinks and the Curry Plant

(Helichrysum angustifolium) to provide a delicious aroma, especially in sunny weather.

One of the drawbacks of the terrace or patio is its flatness, which is frequently emphasised by the smooth, level surface of the floor, be it paving, brickwork, tiles or plain concrete. The addition of containers full of plants, will, to some extent, relieve this feeling of flatness, but you can give it even more variety and interest by planting shrubs or small trees in large containers.

Camellias are excellent container plants for a slightly shaded site – avoid full summer sun which causes the leaves to turn yellowish-green. Orange trees are ideal in very sunny positions and will, if you're lucky, provide fruit as well as extremely fragrant flowers (they will need winter protection). Sweet Bay *(Laurus*

Trailers and climbers are other plants that help to use vertical space, in all directions. Trailers can be used over the side of a container, whether at ground level or suspended in space, in hanging baskets or wall pots.

The Italian Bell Flower *(Campanula isophylla)*, the Canary Creeper *(Tropaeolum peregrinum)*, small-leaved variegated Ivies, trailing Lobelia, ivy-leaved Pelargoniums such as 'L'Elegante' and 'Mexico', pendula Begonias, Tradescantia, Nasturtiums and *Helichrysum petiolatum* will all flower and cascade down the sides of their containers.

Climbers will not only cover walls and fences but can also be trained up pyramids of canes or poles. Sweet Peas, runner beans, Morning Glory, Clematis, summer-flowering Jasmine, Honeysuckle and *Cobaea scandens* will all climb these.

Heliotrope and Nicotiana 'Crimson Rock', *extreme left*, form a pleasing duo for summer colour, while for spring and early summer colour the Pasque Flower, *Pulsatilla vulgaris*, and the Grape Hyacinth, *Muscari armeniacum*, *centre left*, are invaluable. For clothing steps at the side of patio, the Bell Heather, *Erica cinerea, centre right*, is useful for its June to September flowers. *Salvia horminum* 'Blue Beard', *extreme right*, flowers from June to September, with interesting gradations of colour.

A large room needs a large plant to make any impact.

Displaying plants in a large room

Have you noticed how you can hardly pass a hotel lobby, office reception area or foyer that isn't inundated with masses of plants? They've become part of the essential decorations — just like wall-to-wall carpet and pictures on the walls — and they're not there just to make the place look nice. Part of their intention is to create a relaxed atmosphere, so that people feel welcome, comfortable, and want to come back again — very much the same sort of feelings that you want to create in your own home. The plants you choose can be as important, or otherwise, as you like to the decor, depending on how many you use.

Plants can provide the finishing touches in a room to set off your other decorations, or they can be your main decorative theme, around which everything else revolves. You can even create a major display, using plants along with other 'props', as a dramatic centrepiece to a room.

However 'green' you want to go, there is one basic principle underlying the use of plants to decorate any large room — and that is scale. In other words, the plants *must* be appropriate for the size of room they're in, or they'll just get 'lost'. So it's no good trying to use lots of small plants dotted indiscriminately around the room. Large rooms call for grand features — be they plants or anything else — that create an immediate impact on entering the room.

Specimen plants
Large single specimen plants, or groups of three or five identical plants (for some

45

If you have the room, a Fiddle-leaf Fig is a fine choice for an indoor tree.

Single specimens

Cast Iron Plant (Aspidistra)
Boston Fern *(Nephrolepis exaltata bostonienis)*, grown on a pedestal
Large cacti, such as Opuntia
Castor Oil Plant *(Ricinus communis)*
Coconut, Date and **Parlour Palms**
Fiddle-leaf Fig *(Ficus lyrata)*
Norfolk Island Pine (Araucia excelsa)
Large-leaved Philodendrons, such as Tree Philodendron *(P. bipinnatifidum) P.* 'Red Emerald' and *P.* 'Burgundy'
Large succulents, such as Agave
Swiss Cheese Plant *(Monstera deliciosa)*
Weeping fig *(Ficus benjamina)*

reason any group of plants always seems to look best if it is made up of an odd number), are extremely effective as long as you choose plants with suitably dramatic qualities. So go for plants with architectural shapes, or large, striking

leaves such as those suggested.

Foliage plants are more suitable than flowering plants for use as specimens because they provide a year-round display. And if you opt for a group, create a feeling of unity by standing all the pots in a large basket or other container that harmonises well with the plants.

Plant groups

Arrange a combination of both foliage and flowering plants, grouped together in rather the same way as you would do a flower arrangement. Use the foliage plants to create the basic shape of the arrangement, and use the flowers as highlights.

Be sure to choose plants that harmonise well together. If you are buying new plants specially for your arrangement, it's a good idea to try out several different combinations together in the shop before you buy.

If inspiration fails you, try the following rule of thumb guide, which works well using a variety of plants.

Aim to include:

A large, upright, plain green plant with small leaves as a background, such as Grape Ivy, Heptapleurum, curly-leaved Ivy, or Weeping Fig.

A flattish, spreading plant, such as African Violet, Creeping Moss (Selaginella), Episcia, variegated Ivy, *Maranta tricolor*, and Mind Your Own Business (Helxine).

One or three quite differently shaped plants, such as Cape Primrose (Streptocarpus), Euonymus, Goose Foot Plant (Syngonium), Maidenhair Fern (Adiantum), Scindapsus, and *Philodendron scandens*.

Then, to pull the whole arrangement together, place them all in the same container, perhaps standing the

Here, a group of upright plants acts as a screen to divide up a large area.

individual pots in peat or on dampened gravel in order to maintain a humid environment. Stand the container on the floor if the plants are tall, or raise it up slightly if it needs extra height.

A focal point

Taking the group theme one step further, what about using plants along with other 'props' to make a special feature that will provide your room with a focal point? This is particularly useful in a room that doesn't have a fireplace, which is often a natural focal point. It is also a very helpful way of filling a large empty space in a big room that is somewhat short of furniture — as is so often the case if you've recently moved from a smaller house. Here are a few suggestions for special plant features.

Plant cases. Glass cases make a special feature of a collection of tropical plants.

Incorporate chunks of driftwood draped with Spanish Moss (*Tillandsia usneoides*) and interplanted with creeping Helxine or perhaps strewn with pebbles to link the different plants together.

Cases like this are an ideal way of growing tropical plants, as the conditions inside can be tailor-made to suit the choosiest of plants. They can be heated independently of the rest of the room, using soil-warming cables; and lit

artificially, using special plant lights which allow you to grow plants that natural light would never permit.

The extra humidity that tropical plants need is easy to maintain behind glass. Plant cases like this are sometimes built to quite large dimensions in the USA, and may even take over one wall of a room. On a less ambitious scale, a case can be purpose-built into an alcove, or simply a large fish tank.

Plants for grouping

Angel's Wing (Caladium)
Anthurium
Croton (Codiaeum)
Dracaena
Eucalyptus
Goose Foot Plant (Syngonium), trained up a moss pole

Grape Ivy (*Cissus rhombifolia*), trained up a fan-shaped framework of canes
Parasol Plant (Heptapleurum)
Umbrella Plant (Cyperus)
Umbrella Tree (Schefflera)
Yucca

Air plant trees. These make fascinating features, for which you'll need a well shaped, stripped or bleached and washed twiggy branch to act as your framework. You can either find one of these yourself, or obtain a ready-prepared one from a specialist air plant nursery.

To keep the branch upright, mount it on to a flat board, which can be disguised by standing a chunk of driftwood on it or by covering it with moss, pebbles or bark chippings. Then position a collection of air plants artistically among the branches.

As they don't have roots, they are easily positioned simply by sitting them in place. Group two or three plants of the same variety together rather than dotting several individual ones around the branch.

Plant plaques. Another slightly out-of-the-ordinary feature is to make a wall plaque. Choose a large piece of rough bark and wire a group of three or five Staghorn Ferns (Platycerium) into the centre. Water them by spraying daily.

Still life. This is a more traditional idea. Here a group of plants are turned into something just that bit special by the addition of appropriately sized ornaments — figurines, statues, abstract pieces, or maybe even a lamp. This works very well on a table top or sideboard or, using large plants and ornaments, on the floor in a corner of a room.

Lighting

This can make all the difference to the way plants look in a large room. Use ordinary domestic spotlights to pick out plants from their background, and try playing light from different directions on to your plants to see the difference it makes.

To bring out their colours, light plants from slightly in front — either from above or at ground level. Side lighting can also sometimes give interesting results. Or, for a more artistic effect, choose special uplighters or downlighters which dramatically highlight the shape of architectural leaves and stems — ideal for illuminating your specimen plants.

And, if you want to make a plant feature when natural light would seem to prevent it, just substitute special plant light bulbs in conventional spotlight fittings. Plants need lighting for 12 hours a day and you can plug these lights into an automatic timer, just to be absolutely certain.

Backgrounds

As with any plants, the choice of background is important. And in a large room, working with large plants, you can achieve very dramatic results if you are prepared to experiment a little.

Instead of always going for a 'safe' background, why not strike out and contrast a dramatic specimen plant in an alcove against a brilliant red backdrop? Try using a large mirror to exaggerate the foliar feel in a group of plants. Or create a screen of foliage using deep green plants as the background for a striking display of flowering plants such as Hibiscus and Anthurium, or for a collection of strongly marked, decorative foliage plants such as Caladium and Calathea.

For a dramatic specimen plant a palm is hard to beat.

Small is beautiful

Small rooms may be the natural outcome of having a small home, or they may be secondary rooms in a bigger house — a study or a breakfast room, for example. But just because a room is small doesn't mean it can't be special. You can often create a warm, friendly atmosphere in a small room more easily than in a large one — and the right plants can play an important part. Small areas call for a different approach to plants: you'll want to create points of interest — little 'cameos' — instead of filling up space. A bit of thought and planning will enable you to lift a small room right out of the ordinary.

When space is short, there isn't room to display plants in the same way as you would to make an effect in a bigger room — in groups, for example. There may well only be room for a single plant in any given space, so make the most of a limited resource. But even if you have several places suitable for plants in a small room, you shouldn't necessarily fill them all — if you overdo it, you might end up with a room that looks like a Victorian parlour, so cluttered that it's impossible to see anything properly.

The best rule is to choose plants that have something special to offer in themselves — they may be unusual or exceptionally interesting to look at, or a rare variety, which will excite comment and admiration. But a pleasing effect doesn't depend only on the plants, it also derives from how they're arranged and what containers they're in. If you create fascinating little cameos in unexpected places, visitors will always want to take a second look.

Creating a style

Because you have less space to work in, it's specially important to go for a coherent style in a small room — when decorations and furniture co-ordinate it, it can have the effect of making the room look more spacious. Usually, your style will, to some extent, be determined by the type of home you have: traditional or modern, old or new. Your plants should reflect the style of decor you have chosen in terms of furniture, fittings and soft furnishings.

Some plants do more for particular styles of decoration than others.

● In modern rooms, Bromeliads — such as 'air plants' (Tillandsia) and Cryptanthus — cacti, succulents and any spiky leaved plant can look stunning.

Place your plants where they won't encroach into the room space.

Shapes and styles

Creeping Fig, African Violet and Browallia create a perfect cameo.

ROSETTE SHAPES

African Violets (Saintpaulia)
New double-flowered varieties, and those with variegated leaves, are eye-catching
Air Plants (Tillandsia)
Epiphytic Bromeliads with arching leaves
Earth Star (Cryptanthus)
Low-growing, spiky plants with variegated leaves

ROUND SHAPES

Friendship Plant (Pilea involucrata)
Fleshy, quilted, almost circular leaves, dark green with purple undersides
Peperomia caperata
Slow-growing and compact, with green leaves marked with darker green
Watermelon Peperomia (Peperomia argyreia)
Similar to *P.caperata* with leaves striped with white

ORNAMENTAL LEAVES

Begonia boweri
Emerald green leaves with black edging
Begonia rex
Heart-shaped leaves with stunning red, pink and green variegations

Episcia hybrids
Oval, puckered leaves with silver, white and pink variations
Fittonia argyroneura
Vivid green oval leaves with silvery veins
Fittonia verschaffeltii
Long, dark green leaves with pink veins
Variegated Aspidistra
Tall, upright green leaves with white or cream stripes

FERNS

Button Fern (Pellaea rotundifolia)
Tall, arching fronds with tiny, dark green leaves
Sensitive Plant (Mimosa pudica)
Feathery dark green leaves which close up temporarily when touched

GRASSES

Acorus gramineus variegatus
Dense clump of slender, white-striped leaves
Japanese Sedge (Carex morrowii variegata)
Clusters of tall, slender yellowish-green leaves
Miniature Bulrush (Scirpus cernuus)
Graceful, thread-like bright green trailer

MOSSY PLANTS

Artillery Plant (Pilea microphylla)
Fine green leaves in feathery sprays
Mind Your Own Business (Helxine soleirolii)
Low-growing with masses of tiny leaves
Selaginella martensii
Glistening, fleshy green leaves on low, arching stems

TRAILERS AND CREEPERS

Bead Plant (Nertera depressa)
Matted stems with green leaves and shiny, bright orange berries
Creeping Fig (Ficus pumila)
Heart-shaped, small, thin green leaves
Miniature Ivies
Pointed leaves with white, cream and golden variations

CACTI AND SUCCULENTS

Astrophytums
Globe-shaped, deeply segmented stems with cup-like flowers
Jatropha podagrica
Swollen brown stems crowned by bright red flowers
Living Stones (Lithops)
Pebble-like plants with stunning flowers
Moonstones (Pachyphytum oviferum)
Rosette-like clusters of leaves which are shaped like eggs
Pony Tail Palm (Beaucarnea recurvata or Nolina recurvata)
A 'false palm' with shaggy, grey-green leaves
String of Beads Plant (Senecio rowleyanus)
Tiny green globules on trailing stems

FLOWERING PLANTS

Achimenes
Heart-shaped, velvety leaves with red, purple, blue or white flowers
Cape Cowslip (Lachenalia aloides)
Pale yellow, bell-like winter flowers
Exacum
Lavender flowers with golden centres; treat as an annual
French Marigold (Tagetes patula)
Annual with red, orange or yellow flowers
Lily of the Valley (Convallaria majalis)
Annual with dainty white and very fragrant flowers
Miniature Cyclamen
Variegated leaves and white or pink flowers; treat as an annual
Miniature Pelargonium
Striking flowers in a range of colours and sometimes scented leaves
Petunias
Annuals available in a wide range of colours, single and double blooms, some with frilly petals

With their assertive, dramatic shapes they really function like living sculptures, and are favourites of interior designers for just this reason.

● For colourful, chintzy rooms you could choose country cottage favourites — such as miniature Pelargoniums, Achimenes, Lily of the Valley, Helxine, Pilea and miniature ivies. Go for colours that will enhance your existing colour scheme.

● Traditional rooms, reminiscent of the Victorian style, would favour African Violets, Peperomias, miniature Cyclamen, Begonias and ferns.

These are only rough guidelines, of course — a good many plants will fit in with any style, and you can always aim for the unexpected.

Matching plant to place

In small rooms particularly, it pays to avoid the obvious. A solitary plant in the middle of a windowsill or coffee table entirely lacks the element of surprise. If you think of plants as ornaments, it should help you to find the most interesting places for them. Tuck them away in little nooks and crannies — a gap in a bookshelf, a corner of a hearth, hanging down from a beam or among a group of ornaments. In a bathroom, plants can trail down from the edge of a bath or from a shelf.

Of course, it goes without saying that plants should only be put in positions where they'll thrive and be happy. If available light is low, go for ferns or the mossy Selaginella, which will be happy almost anywhere out of direct sunlight. Other plants will need good indirect light most of the time, while some — such as cacti and Pelargoniums — need sun at least some of the time.

Remember, you can get away with keeping plants in poorly lit places if you only leave them there for a short time, and you can also grow plants under special plant lights. Flowering annuals will always brighten up a dull place, and they'll die after flowering in any case.

Plant containers

If you're aiming for a striking effect, containers are a good place to start. Try to avoid conventional ones, and choose objects that are not usually associated with plants — copper kettles, brass scuttles, ice buckets or old stone jars. The mellow golden colour of brass makes a very good contrast with predominantly green plants, such as ferns.

Strong colours and shapes liven up the plain surroundings.

By using pots and jars that aren't designed for plants you can often create an individual style without great expense — these items can often be picked up quite cheaply in junk shops because no one can think of a practical use for them! Even quite mundane objects can be transformed with a carefully chosen plant — a goldfish bowl, for example, or a modern storage jar.

Small and special

The chart, *left*, listing plants under their major characteristics, will give you some ideas about what to choose. The unusual requirements of small rooms may mean you should go to a specialist garden centre or nursery to get what you want; specialist nurseries also advertise in gardening magazines. And you can always try growing an unusual plant that you fancy from seed.

Plants to look out for include those with interesting shapes or textures, unusual flowers, leaf textures or colourful patterns, or those that particularly suit a space or container that you have in mind.

Any grouping of plants in a small room will probably need to be small itself — miniature gardens, terrariums or bowls of water plants are ideal.

Ringing the changes

One of the biggest problems with a small room is that once you have arranged it, it can be very difficult to change. With bigger rooms you can cre-

ate a fresh look from time to time by moving the furniture around; in a small room, things probably only work well in one position. So to make a change it is the smaller items that you must rearrange or replace: lamps, cushions, ornaments — and plants.

Don't expect to keep the same plants circulating for ever, or you'll soon get bored. Small plants are the cheapest to buy, so you can afford to replace your stock regularly. Try out new combinations of plant and container, and hoard interesting containers for a possible change of scene. And if you choose a plant that outgrows its welcome, don't leave it to spoil your scheme — move it to a bigger room, or donate it to friends with more baronial premises!

A careful blend of shape and colour.

Plants for hot dry rooms

Warm, dry air may be just what the doctor ordered for humans — but it doesn't suit many plants very well! And if you're particularly sensitive to the cold, you're likely to have the heating in your home much higher than most houseplants will happily tolerate.

From left to right: *Sedum morganianum* (in hanging basket), *Chlorophytum comosom variegatum*, *Bryophyllum daigremontianum*, *Ficus pumila*, *Dracaena godseffiana*, *Rebutia miniscula*, *Notocactus ottonis*, *Ficus radicans variegata*, *Aloe arborescens*.

So to have happy and healthy plants, you must choose those that naturally enjoy such conditions, and make sure that you regularly give them any extra care or watering that they need. Under natural conditions, warm or hot, dry air occurs principally in desert regions, where it favours the growth of cacti and succulents or leathery-leaved plants that transpire slowly and are able to withstand considerable fluctuations in temperature and humidity. Thin-leaved exotics from the tropics, on the other hand, which thrive only in a humid environment, cannot tolerate such dehydrating conditions. Our selection of candidates for hot, dry rooms has therefore been determined by their natural habitat and their ability to withstand the loss of moisture from their leaves.

Desert cacti

For the warmest, dryest rooms, the first choice has to be desert cacti. Shaped by nature into moisture-conserving stems with spines rather than leaves, most desert cacti are baked by fierce daytime temperatures in the wild and then severely chilled at night, before receiving a cold douche of morning dew.

There are many species and varieties which we can buy, all of which are ideal for warm dry rooms. They are especially appealing grouped together in a dish garden which shows off their different bizarre forms to advantage. 'Growing cacti' page 675, and 'Designing a cactus garden' page 678, will give you many ideas on which cacti to choose and how to display them.

To get the best out of your cacti, keep them in the sunniest spot available — a south-facing window is ideal — and cool them down every morning with a misting of cold water, which simulates

the dew in their natural habitat. They also enjoy a breath of fresh air, but take care to guard against chilling draughts. Most cacti will flower only on new growth, which calls for summer care and winter neglect — so they need very litttle or no water between mid October and late March — just the time when an overheated room is at its dryest.

Forest cacti

Let us turn next to the forest cacti, which grow in their natural home as epiphytes, attached to trees in wood-

Schlumbergera x buckleyi will add a cool pink note to a hot, dry room.

land and jungles. These include the Rat's Tail Cactus (*Aporocactus flagelliformis*), Christmas Cactus (*Schlumbergera*) and Easter Cactus (*Rhipsalidopsis gaertneri*).

Their natural habitat is the forest regions of tropical America and, not surprisingly, most of them need altogether moister conditions than the desert cacti. Happily these can be provided by misting them daily — or at least as often as possible — with tepid water, to simulate the steam which rises among them in their native tropical jungle habitat. They prefer a position in diffused

rather than bright, hot sunlight so a north- or east-facing windowsill is best. For further details on Forest cacti see pages 675 and 678.

Succulents

This is another group of plants that thrive where thinner-leaved species would turn brown and shed their 'mantle'. There are many attractive forms. The Saucer Plant (*Aeonium tabuliforme*) is a remarkable miracle of nature. Its stems are topped with tightly packed little 'saucers' — hence its common name — which are neatly and symmetrically arranged. Its close relation, *A. arborum atropurpureum*, is tree-like, with stems terminating in sprays of handsome purple, shiny leaves.

The fleshy leaved Aloes are numerous. Impressive, with sharply saw-edged leaves, the Tree Aloe (*A. arborescens*) grows into a fairly sizeable plant. The Partridge Breasted Aloe (*A. variegata*) is much smaller, growing to about 1ft (0.3m). Its sword-shaped leaves, which are patterned with transverse light and dark green bands, form a stiff and arresting rosette. In summer, it sends up a spike of pinkish red, tubular flowers. The Hedgehog Aloe (*A. humilis*) also has upward-pointing, spiky leaves that curve gently inwards to resemble a clutching hand.

We come next to the Crassula family, its most famous member being the Jade Plant (*Crassula argentea*). Mature plants take on the appearance of old, stunted corky barked trees. The leaves, which are deep green, spoon-shaped and very thick, are remarkably resilient to neglect, and happily suffer the driest soils.

The Good Luck Plant (*Bryophyllum daigremontianum*) is a great favourite with children and has a party trick that never fails to amuse: it reproduces itself by forming tiny embryo plants in serried rows along the edges of its leaves. These grow to about ¼in (6mm) across, produce a wisp of roots, and then fall to the ground where they root in the compost on which they alight. The tubular-leaved *B. tubiflorum* is equally appealing; this forms its plantlets at the tips of its leaves.

Rosette-shaped Echeverias are hardy or half-hardy, and some are used as summer bedding plants. The Mexican Snowball (*Echeveria harmsii*) is especially attractive.

Other succulents that can be grown successfully in hot, dry places are the

Increasing humidity

Cacti and succulents need little regular care apart from feeding and occasional repotting, but the other houseplants mentioned on these pages will thank you for introducing a little moisture into the atmosphere. Here are a few ways in which you can do this.
● Fit humidifiers to the radiators.
● Sit pots on a tray of gravel or coarse perlite and keep it wet all the time. Make sure, however, that the base of the pot is not actually standing in a pool of water.

● Put a small plant pot into a larger one and surround it with peat or perlite that you keep damp. You can also group several plants together in a single large pot in the same way.
● Use self-watering containers or other devices so that the plant always has enough moisture to draw on.
● Put a layer of leca — special absorbent clay granules — on the top of the soil and keep it dampened.
● Keep a mist sprayer handy to spray the plants — steamy heat is just what tropical plants enjoy.

Sedums. Burro's Tail (*Sedum morganianum*), for example, is most unusual. Its cascading stems are composed of intricately overlapping, fleshy, waxy leaves that form a beautifully 'sculpted' rope, some 1in (2.5cm) in diameter. This is most successful in a hanging basket.

Another exciting succulent is the Candle Plant (*Kleinia articulata*), which has curious cigar-shaped stems strung together to make a strange little bush topped with fleshy, grey-green, ivy-like leaves. It is easily propagated by sectioning the stems into individual 'cigars' and rooting them in gritty compost.

Thick-leaved houseplants

There are several undemanding leathery-leaved houseplants that will happily withstand the excessively dry air of a centrally heated sunroom or living room, though they will all thank you for introducing a little humidity into the atmosphere — see suggestions below.

All the following will return care with a lavish display of exotic foliage.

The aptly named Cast Iron Plant (Aspidistra) and its pretty cream-striped variety can both withstand long periods of dryness. You can, on the other hand, kill them all quickly by keeping their 'feet' in water for any length of time, so it's better to err on the side of under- rather than overwatering.

The Spider Plant (*Chlorophytum comosom variegatum*) is incredibly long-suffering. Its leaf tips may turn brown in excessively hot air, but its general constitution will remain unaffected either by heat or by fluctuating temperatures. It is particularly effective displayed on a pillar, where its arching stems will cascade in a series of 'waterfalls', each tipped with young plants from which further wiry stems emerge and develop new plants.

A shrubby Dracaena, like the Gold Dust Dracaena (*D. godseffiana*) with gold-spotted green leaves, comes into its own in warm, dry conditions. There it will really thrive, producing a handsome rounded bush, much admired by visitors. Another member of the genus, the Dragon Tree (*D.draco*), is equally undemanding and thrusts forth its shuttlecock rosette of sword-shaped leaves to enhance any decor.

The Australian Eucalyptus can also be successfully grown indoors and is tolerant of warm, dry conditions. Blue Gum (*E. globulus*), which is highly valued for its distinctive, rich blue-green,

No need to limit yourself to cacti — many plants will thrive in dry conditions. Among these are: Philodendron (in hanging basket); *from left to right, back row*, Monstera, Crassula, *Ficus elastica*; *front row*, various Sedums and a Spider Plant (Chlorophytum).

triangular leaves, is best encouraged to form a shapely plant by nipping out the growing tips regularly during the spring and summer.

The Ficus or Ornamental Fig family has for many years been used to decorate draughty reception areas as well as stuffy, very dry, ill-lit rooms. It excels in both capacities and has gained a reputation for its ability to endure many hardships. The common upright Rubber Plant (*Ficus elastica decora*), which is much prized for its large, glossy leaves, also has some creamy variegated forms. *F. e. doescheri* is a particularly splendid example. The Weeping Fig (*F. benjamina*) has long been popular as an indoor tree because of its slender, elegant branches. A very different plant, with its

huge wavy-edged leaves, is the Fiddle Leaf Fig (*F. lyrata*), which is magnificent as the eye-catching centrepiece for a generous-sized room.

Figs can also be grown in hanging baskets. Two contenders for this treatment are the Trailing Fig (*F. radicans variegata*), with creamy yellow-rimmed leaves, and its smaller relation, the Creeping Fig (*F. pumila*), a determined tumbler or sprawler.

Finally, there are three other stalwarts which seem to thrive on virtual neglect. These are the Swiss Cheese Plant (*Monstera deliciosa*), Sweetheart Plant (*Philodendron scandens*), and Mother-in-law's Tongue (Sansevieria) of which the gold-edged (*S. trifasciata laurentii*) is the most spectacular.

Brighten a dull room

Despite all the propaganda on behalf of sunny windowsills, very few plants thrive in direct sun all the time (see page 719 for those that do). More plants than you might think actually prefer a bit of shade. So don't worry if you have a north- or east-facing room that seems rather gloomy, or one that gets good light for only a small part of the day. Plants *will* grow there, so long as you choose the right ones.

The first thing to be aware of is that not all shade-loving plants like the same amount of shade. Start by thinking of a tropical forest, the natural home of many of the plants that we now grow as houseplants. Not many of these grow in bright sunshine — most are found in the shade cast by other, taller plants. There's a progression from the top down, with each layer of plant life growing in deeper shade than the one above. By the time you reach the forest floor, it's really too dark for anything apart from the odd fern to survive.

Much the same thing happens indoors, too — the room gets darker the further away from the window you go. Imagine your room divided into a series of 'zones', each one getting a different amount of light. To get the best from your plants, you should carefully grade them according to the amount of light each one needs, and grow them in the correct zone.

Good indirect light

Most plants in fact do very well in bright light without direct sunlight, provided they get the right amount of warmth and water. Windowsills that get no, or very little, direct sun are a good place for plants that flower, and you can choose from some fairly exotic kinds.

Gesneriads are one of the few groups of flowering plants that will thrive out of sunlight. They include the popular African Violet, as well as less well known kinds such as Streptocarpus,

Most palms and ferns prefer the shade — they are thriving in this rather gloomy bathroom.

Achimenes and Columnea, which have beautiful, delicate flowers in a range of pinks, violets and reds. Then there are Episcia, with unusual dark, variegated foliage, and Aeschynanthus, a long-stemmed trailing plant with strikingly decorative orange flowers, which is perfect for a hanging basket. You should be able to find all of these in a good specialist garden centre or nursery.

All these Gesneriads require much the same conditions as the African Violet — good light, but protected from direct sun, constant warmth and moisture, and a humid, draught-free environment. They should be stood in a bowl of damp gravel so that they get adequate moisture. They dislike lime, so it's best to boil and cool their water, which helps to reduce the amount of lime in it. Feed them once a fortnight in spring and summer when they're growing — this is enough for them because they don't grow very fast. Don't feed them at all in the winter, but keep the gravel just damp. If you keep these plants on a windowsill all the time, but not in direct sun, they will flower even in the winter.

Orchids are becoming fashionable as houseplants, and there are at least a dozen kinds that you can grow in the home. Slipper Orchids (Paphiopedilum) are low-light orchids — they must never be given direct sun and are best kept away from the window. Their bright colours are perfect for shade.

Orchids take a bit of getting used to if you have never grown them before — they have special needs, including unusual compost, and can be rather tricky. We'll be telling you all about how to grow them in Volume 11.

Tropical plants include some unusual and very exciting plants from the family *Araceae*. Caladium, for example, has beautiful heart-shaped paper-thin leaves, ranging in colour from white to very deep red. It needs to be kept warm and humid, and moderately well-lit, but away from direct sun.

Alocasia, also from the same family, is another ornamental foliage plant with huge deeply-lobed leaves. It needs warm humid conditions and good but indirect light — light shade is ideal. You could also try the Tree Philodendron (*Philodendron bipinnatifidum*), which has very large, glossy green, deeply indented leaves, or the even more shade-tolerant Sweetheart Plant (*P. scandens*).

For a really dramatic splash of colour, you could grow the Flamingo Flower

Temporary visitors

Varieties which would not actually *grow* very happily in deep shade may be perfectly suited to such conditions for a short while, when they are near the end of their lives. Some annuals die after flowering in any case, so you needn't feel guilty about them; use them to liven up a shady room when they're in flower. Good choices would be Calceolaria, Cineraria, Cockscomb, Exacum, Prince of Wales Feather and Schizanthus.

Some perennials are often thrown away after flowering because they are not very appealing for the rest of the year; try Ornamental Capsicum, *right*, Pot Chrysanthemum, Primula and Miniature Rose. Bulbs will live happily in a shady room while they are in flower; you can put them in the garden when the flowers are over, and they'll survive another year; try Hyacinths, Lily of the Valley and Pot Lillies.

The Tree Philodendron and Begonias make the most of limited light conditions.

(*Anthurium scherzerianum*) — its huge, scarlet blooms appear from February to July. Needing average warmth, the Flamingo Flower should be protected from the summer sun, and kept in bright light in winter. The Peace Lily (*Spathiphyllum wallisii*) has similarly shaped flowers, but in white — it needs warmth, semi-shade in summer, and bright light in winter.

Bromeliads are a huge family of exotic jungle plants. Some of them, the 'terrestrial' ones, live near the forest floor in their natural habitat, so they're very suitable as houseplants in shady rooms. All of them are, in any case, very slow-growing, so a week or two in shade will do them no harm.

Commonly called Urn Plants, Bromeliads belong to the same family as the pineapple: they grow a rosette of pineapple-like leaves with their own reservoir of water in the middle. Some grow tall and upright, others wide and flat. They should be topped up regularly with water, preferably rainwater or boiled and cooled tapwater. They like warm conditions and high humidity.

Permanent shade

You might think that no plant could grow in dull light all the time, but palms and ferns both do — and there's an enormous number of these to choose from (see page 391).

Palms come in all shapes and sizes, and a variety of leaf shapes — fans, plumes, diamonds and fishtails. Coconut Palms, Date Palms and Parlour Palms have leaves that grow from the top of short stems, while Kentia Palms have reed-like stems that grow in a cluster. All of these love shade and, as a rule of thumb, if it's light enough to read by, it's light enough to grow them.

Palms can be expensive to buy, but they're worth it. They make marvellous centrepieces for groups, and dramatic specimen plants if placed on their own, with their tall, upright, branching growth and their glossy green leaves.

Specialists will have a much more interesting selection, including frilly ferns, trailing ferns, golden, silver and even pinkish-coloured ferns. They all need average warmth and watering, and indirect light.

Specially interesting and unusual ferns to look out for include the Mother Spleenwort (*Asplenium bulbiferum*) with feathery green fronds and offsets along the edges of the older leaves which gradually weigh down the fronds. The Button Fern (*Pellaea rotundifolia*) is a pretty miniature with neat rows of shiny round leaflets, while the Bird's Nest Fern (*Asplenium nidus*) has broad leaves that uncurl from a central boss. The Feather Fern (*Nephrolepsis* 'Fluffy Ruffles') and the Boston Fern (*N.bostoniensis*) have broad leaves with frilly edges, while Rabbit's Foot Fern (*Davallia canariensis*) has tiny leaflets on tall fronds, and enlarged, fleshy stems (called rhizomes) which give it its strange appearance — and its name.

Creeping Mosses (Selaginellas) used to be great favourites, and it is high time that they became popular again. They are low, creeping or mound-shaped plants which come in all sorts of different colours as well as green —bronze and gold are particularly attractive. The Peacock Fern (*Selaginella uncinata*) and Creeping Moss (*S.martensii*) should both be easy to find in shops. Grow them in shallow, well-drained pots well away from the window. Use boiled, cooled water and keep the compost moist at all times — spraying the leaves helps too. They need average warmth and should do very well in a shady room that gets no direct light.

Finally for a really dramatic effect in a high-ceilinged room, you could grow the aptly named Tree Fern (*Cyathea dealbata*). It comes from New Zealand, and can grow up to 10ft (3m) high!

Don't put daffodils, or other tall bulbs, into a shady position until they are in flower — otherwise they grow too tall and flop over.

Some of them grow very tall, which makes them perfect for adding interest to the corners of a room. The Parlour Palm (*Neanthe bella*) and the Kentia Palm (*Howea forsteriana*) are both very easy to look after, requiring cool winters, and summers with average warmth. The Sago Palm (*Cycas revoluta*) is an interesting one, with tall fronds growing out of a ball-like base.

Palms need a moist atmosphere, so it's a good idea to spray them with tepid water every day in summer. This will also help to keep the dust down — if you let dust lie on palms it will literally choke the leaves and kill the plant. Standing them outdoors in a light summer shower is an ideal way to clean them up, or you can wipe them occasionally with a soft, damp cloth. Never be tempted to use a proprietary leaf shiner on palms since it damages their leaves.

🌱 **Ferns** will grow, in the wild, in the shade of most plants, making them very suitable as houseplants. Yet very few members of this large group of plants are commonly found in shops.

Fittonias brighten up a shady spot.

A place in the sun

If you are lucky enough to have a south-facing window-sill, balcony or terrace, you will be able to grow all sorts of exciting, exotic plants; these plants which don't usually do much more than survive in the British climate will suddenly overflow with exuberant growth and flowers under the influence of the sun's concentrated warmth and light. And not

only can you produce some really beautiful displays but, of course, all that heat encourages both flowers and leaves to release their delicate and attractive perfumes.

What to grow

Although gardening in containers or small spaces is obviously to some extent restricting, you can still grow a

The sun is a great encourager of growth and fragrance among plants.

selection of different plants which vary greatly in terms of size, permanence and type, just as you can in the conventional garden in the open ground.

There is actually no need, for example, to restrict yourself to the

Petunias and Verbena can make a spectacular summer display.

Lobelias, Pelargoniums and Petunias all thrive in a sunny spot.

commonly grown bedding plants so often used in summer containers, but you can also stock up with shrubs, rock plants, border perennials, herbs and climbers, and vary the height and size of your plants. Thus you can fill vertical space, you can grow flowers for cutting for the home, and you can provide greenery for the winter.

Bedding plants

The bedding plant that does particularly well, above all others, in warmth and sun, is the Petunia. In cool, wet summers or in dingy, shady places, it is a sad and straggling plant; but planted early in June in a warm place, it will flower lavishly.

French and African Marigolds, too, relish heat and light. There are now so many hybrids in different shades of yellow, orange, cream, mahogany, red and combinations of all these that sometimes it is difficult to make a choice.

Zinnias are other half-hardy annuals which are worth trying and not grown as much as they deserve. These flower from late July to late September. Their strikingly coloured, daisy-type flowers look as though the petals have been painted, in many different colours. Grown from seed, their final height is about 9-15in (23-38cm).

Another easily grown bedding plant which relishes warmth is the Tobacco Plant (Nicotiana), which grows to about 2-3ft (0.6-0.9m) tall and produces tubular flowers in pink, white, lilac, magenta and lime-yellow that are ideal for flower arranging. Their fragrance is delightful, especially in the evening. The one exception to this is the lime-yellow one, which isn't scented. In sunny places, the Tobacco Plant is enormously good value for money.

All these bedding plants can be grown in window-boxes, as well as in larger containers.

Border perennials

Many border perennials enjoy sun. Some are suitable for window-boxes, some for large pots, and some for tubs, planters and paving spaces.

The Geranium, for example – and that is the true Geranium genus or Cranesbill, not the kind which are known botanically as Pelargonium – loves the sun and flowers in July, August and September. Try, for instance, *G. pratense* 'Johnson's Blue', which is 15in (38cm) tall and slightly wider; *G. endressii*, which has pale pink flowers, forms a neat flower-covered mound and grows to about 9-12in (23-30cm) tall; and *G. sanguine* which is an intense magenta colour and flowers for two or three months on 12-18in (30-45cm) stems.

Catnip (Nepeta) has pretty silver-grey leaves and long spikes of lavender-blue flowers from May right through until the autumn. Look for the hybrid *N. x Faassenii*, which grows to 2ft (60cm) or more but tends to sprawl.

The Penstemon has foxglove-shaped flowers in spikes on stems between 1 and 2ft (30 and 60cm) tall. It flowers in June, in shades of blue, rose-pink or red, and needs some protection in winter.

Sea Hollies have striking blue flowerheads rather like Teasels. *Eryngium x oliverianum*, for example, grows to about 3ft (0.9m) and flowers from July through to autumn.

Agapanthus is a beautiful plant which grows well on the terrace or patio and is both large and vigorous. Its common name is Lily-of-the-Nile, and it has clusters of deep blue or white flowers on 2ft (60cm) stems in July and August, emerging from clumps of strap-shaped leaves.

For an intriguing aroma, try the Curry Plant (*Helichrysum angustifolium*). This has grey feathery foliage and small yellow flowers in summer, and grows to about 2ft (60cm) tall. In hot sun, the smell of curry becomes really intense, though its leaves are not used in cooking.

Border Pinks and Carnations are very suitable for warm, light places and, with good compost, make excellent plants both for containers and for spaces in paving. Their silver-grey leaves provide colour in winter, while their profusely produced flowers last from June until well into August, especially if you dead head regularly. 'Mr Sinkins' is white and one of the most heavily scented, but there are also many others, including some older varieties which are currently enjoying a revival.

Shrubs

There are a good many suitable shrubs and sub-shrubs for sunny spots, many of which are evergreen and, once established, need remarkably little care. Lavender and Rosemary are two examples, both evergreen and both highly aromatic.

The Jerusalem Sage (*Phlomis fruticosa*), which comes originally from the eastern Mediterranean, has bright yellow flower clusters and grey-green leaves. It can grow 4ft (1.2m) high and the same in width, but growth will obviously be less dramatic if space restricts its roots.

Hebes, which used to be known as Veronicas, produce spikes of flowers in summer and autumn. These can be blue, pink, white, lavender, purple or rose, depending on the variety, and size can be anything from 9in to 5ft (23cm-1.5m). 'Autumn Glory' is one of the most attractive smaller ones, while the *H. speciosa* hybrids are about 1½-2ft (45-60cm) tall. *H. pinguifolia* 'Pagei' is a low-growing, spreading variety which will trail over the sides of the container; it has silver-grey leaves and tiny white flowers in May.

Sage can have different-coloured foliage. *Salvia angustifolia* is the common one, which produces blue flower spikes in June; 'Purpurascens' has purple-flushed leaves; 'Icterina' has yellow-variegated ones; and 'Multicolor' has pink, white and green markings.

Another good herb to grow in full sun is Thyme, which is evergreen and produces tiny pinkish-purple flowers in June and July. *Thymus x citriodorus* has lemon-scented leaves and flowers in July and August. Both species remain small and slow-growing, to a maximum of about 9-12in (23-30cm).

The smaller versions of the New Zealand Flax (*Phormium tenax*) are also striking patio or terrace plants which like it hot. Their sword-like leaves, which are produced in

Contrast annual Chrysanthemums and Petunias with grey-leaved plants.

clusters at ground level, provide an air of the desert. Look out in particular for 'Maori Sunset', which has pink, orange and bronze leaves; and 'Yellow Wave', which has a yellow central stripe. Their average height, which is slowly reached, is 2½-3ft (0.75-0.9m).

Climbers

Climbing sun lovers which can be used wherever there is sufficient wall or fence space include the Passion Flower (*Passiflora caerulea*) and the summer-flowering white Jasmine (*Jasminum officinale*), both of which can become extremely vigorous and need plenty of space in sunny positions. The Jasmine has the most delicious scent, particularly at dusk. *Eccremocarpus scaber* is another easily grown climber which produces clusters of tubular orange-red flowers starting as early as April and going right through the summer months until the autumn.

Some of the large-flowered Clematis do well in sunny places but need to be chosen carefully, as the colour of some varieties fades in strong sunlight. You should be safe, however, with 'Perle d'Azur' (light blue), 'Etoile Violette' (mauve), 'Jackmannii Superba' (deep violet), 'The President' (deep purple), 'Ernest Markham' (magenta) and 'Miss Bateman' (white).

Fill a wheelbarrow with colourful plants to make a focal point.

Rock plants

These can be very effective in containers – they aren't usually so large that they need a great deal of space – and they can also fit nicely into paving spaces, flowing over the edges and softening them in the process.

Aubrieta is one such rock plant, which produces pretty little lavender or purple flowers in June. And Campanulas will provide bell-shaped flowers later on, in July and August, in various shades of blue; *C. portenschlagiana*, light blue and trailing, and *C. pulloides*, mound-like with dark blue flowers, are two easily grown, free-flowering species.

The Houseleek (Sempervivum) delights in hot sun and starved soil. Look for deep red-leaved rosettes as well as the bright green ones. It's an obliging plant and you can expect it to flourish.

Sun Roses (Helianthemums) are rock garden shrubs which insist on good drainage and make a striking display. They are small but can sprawl and cover quite a large area, about 2ft (60cm) square, with evergreen leaves and profuse flowers in June and July. 'Strawberry Ripple' has striped-white and strawberry-red flowers; 'Wisley Pink' has pink flowers and grey leaves; and there are many other species in various brilliant colours, including yellow, deep red, pink, white, orange and amber.

In the shade

Small areas ablaze with flower and leaf colour can be every bit as attractive as large areas sparsely planted. And even a small enclosed area surrounded by buildings and plunged in semi- or perpetual shade can be made attractive. It's all a matter of choosing the right plants for the right spot, and turning your problems directly to your advantage.

Even in the middle of a city you can have a cool, quiet spot where plants flourish in peace. Plants that thrive in shade help to create tranquility; their gentle blends of colours and textures lead the gardener effortlessly into a theme based on greens and whites and the joys of wild-garden plants.

Use a mixture of plants in tubs and borders, perhaps in odd corners with a backdrop of climbers. But avoid grass as it never succeeds in shade. Instead, use gravel, cobbles, setts or paving, or several different contrasting surfaces, perhaps with a pattern

Foliage plants can really enhance a small enclosed area and, furthermore, they flourish in the shade.

such as herringbone picked out in red brick. To soften the effect it's a good idea to interplant with informal patches of low, evergreen, ground-covering plants which will fill in spaces in a border, or spill over the sides of containers and help to soften their outline. They also help to merge one plant with another.

Fatsia japonica is ideal for filling a large empty corner.

Then, before you buy your plants take a careful look at your site and choose plants to suit. And if you're planning to grow them in a border or large trough, remember that not all shade-loving plants like the same conditions underfoot; some prefer damp soil and others must have it dry, though many are perfectly happy in any soil.

Shrubs for tubs

● *Acer palmatum* 'Dissectum Atropurpureum', one of the small Maples, creates an outstandingly attractive, dome-shaped, deciduous shrub 3-4ft (0.9-1.2m) high and 3-5ft (0.9-1.5m) wide. The finely-divided, deep purple leaves create a dense canopy, and for colour contrast set light-coloured ground-covering plants around it.

● *Andromeda polifolia*, the Bog Rosemary, is a dwarf evergreen shrub that needs acid compost. It rises 1½-2ft (45-60cm), with a spread of about 2ft (60cm), and gladdens the eye with glaucous green leaves and soft pink flowers during May and into early June. For a smaller form try 'Compacter' with bright pink flowers.

● *Aucuba japonica*, the Japanese Laurel, is best grown in the mottled green-and-yellow leaved form 'Variegata' (also known as 'Maculata'). It's evergreen and looks particularly good in spring with a tub or two of golden daffodils in front. It creates a large dome shape, and in a tub grows to about 4-5ft (1.2-1.5m) high.

● *Camellia japonica*, the Common Camellia, is a superb evergreen, with beautiful flowers in spring and early summer. Acid compost and light shade are essential for healthy growth, and remember that even in a large 15-18in (38-45cm) tub it may grow to 6-7ft (1.8-2.1m) high and 5-6ft (1.5-1.8m) wide.

● X *Fatshedera lizei* 'Variegata' creates evergreen, grey-green, hand-like leaves with creamy-white edges. In a tub or large pot it grows to 3-4½ft (0.9-1.4m) high.

● *Fatsia japonica* has a distinctive shape and is ideal for filling a large corner. Its large hand-like, evergreen and glossy leaves create a superb foil for the late summer heads of ball-like white flowers.

● Rhododendrons provide many dwarf forms for containers with acid

Colourful carpeters

Covering the soil with colourfully-leaved plants is like selecting the right carpet for a newly-decorated room. The range of ground-cover plants is wide, some with variegated leaves and others strong with one colour. As well as being used as soil cover they also look good when set around the edges of large containers holding one central permanent plant.

● *Ajuga reptans*, the Common Bugle, has an herbaceous nature and rises 8-10in (20-25cm), with a superb purple-leaved form, 'Atropurpurea'. There are also variegated-leaved forms. 'Burgundy Glow' has leaves marked pink, purple and cream.

● *Pachysandra terminalis*, the Japanese Spurge, has a beautifully variegated evergreen form with green and white leaves, and rises about 8in (20cm) above the soil.

● *Vinca minor*, the Lesser Periwinkle, and its big brother *V. major, right*, the Greater Periwinkle, can be used as spreading and trailing plants. The Lesser Periwinkle reaches only 2-4in (5-10cm) high, while the larger one is up to 10in (25cm). All-green and variegated forms are available.

compost. Small deciduous hybrid types are available, but evergreen ones, commonly called Japanese Azaleas, are best as their foliage remains all year and creates an attractive background for other plants. You can expect them to rise to 2-2¹/₂ft (60-75cm), and slightly wider. Varieties to look for include 'Palestrina' (white), 'Fedora' (pink) and 'Vuyk's Scarlet' (carmine-red). Don't set them in a totally dark corner, but one with a little light for their late spring flowers.

Wall warmers

Gardeners, of course, do not need to heat up walls, but like artists they often need to soften and warm harsh outlines – and even hide unsightly fences. If you have something to hide, choose an evergreen climber for year-through cover. But for seasonal flower power, a deciduous climber in a large pot or tub may be better.

● Of the Clematis suited to growing in shade *Clematis alpina* is deciduous and delightfully delicate, sprawling and rising to 6¹/₂ft (2m). The 1-1¹/₂in (2.5-4cm) long, bell-shaped blue or violet-blue flowers appear in April and May.

● *C.macropetala* with deciduous foliage, and in May to July 2¹/₂in (6.5cm) wide, violet-blue flowers is well suited to spilling out of a large, barrel.

Large-flowered hybrids always create interest with their dominant flowers, some 7in (18cm) wide. Cool roots and sun for their heads is the general prescription for success, but delicately coloured types such as 'Nelly Moser', pale mauve-pink with carmine stripes, tends to fade when in full sun. They are deciduous.

● Ivies (Hedera) are famed for their beautiful evergreen leaves. Many spectacular types are available, with large or small leaves and a range of variegations, but a form you might consider is *Hedera helix* 'Spectre'. This particular variety is not a climber, but will trail its variegated leaves over a low wall or sides of a trough or tub.

Ferns for cool corners

Many hardy ferns are superb on a shaded patio, preferably in a damp border, but in large tubs where their roots remain cool they also create a good display.

Hardy ferns can look superb on a shaded patio.

Soften up harsh lines of walls and fences with Ivies and climbers.

● *Asplenium trichomanes*, the Maidenhair Spleenwort, is hardy and only 4-8in (10-20cm) high; its evergreen nature and diminutive stature make it ideal for paving or damp walls. It helps to soften the appearance of paving and walls around tubs.

● *Phyllitis scolopendrium*, the Hart's Tongue Fern, is evergreen and hardy, with tongue-like, shiny green leaves 1-2ft (30-60cm) high. The crested forms such as 'Cristatum' are much the most interesting types.

● *Matteuccia struthiopteris*, Ostrich Feather or Shuttlecock Fern, is a hardy and evergreen, dwarf tree-fern with tall, feathery fronds up to 4ft (1.2m) high.

● *Athyrium nipponicum pictum* is the hardy Japanese Painted Fern with deep red stems and green fronds with silvery edges.

Herbaceous hustlers

These are those reliable border brighteners that cheekily burst through the soil as soon as spring arrives and create foliage and flower colour that upstage many plants. Some grow well in shady borders or containers.

● Astilbes create lax fluffy flowers from mid- to late summer. For containers select the 9-12in (23-30cm) high *Astilbe chinensis pumila* with rose-purple flowers from July to October. The taller *A. x arendsii* at 2-2¹/₂ft (60-75cm) has many forms in white, pink and red, and likes borders.

● Hostas are famed for their coloured or variegated leaves and certainly earn a place in a shady corner, in or out of a container. The range of leaf colour is wide, from golden-yellow variegations to blue forms. And some have very attractive flowers, often on tall stems.

● *Convallaria majalis* the well-known and fragrantly-flowered Lily of the Valley soon spreads to form a dominant clump up to 8in (20cm) high. White flowers appear in April and May.

Start your own houseplant log book

Why bother to keep a houseplant log book, you may ask. Do it because it gives an instant handy growing guide as well as a precise record of your plants. By noting down their details you can anticipate their needs accurately and closely follow their progress over the years. These notes needn't take much time and they can really help you to improve your plants by reminding you exactly when and how to look after them – rather than in the haphazard way most of us treat them.

All you need to get going is a pen, a tape measure (you'll find out why later) and an empty address book, looseleaf file or some 5×3in (12×7cm) index cards and off you go. Like keeping a diary, it might at first seem difficult to find the time – but just like a diary, once it becomes a habit it's compulsive.

Putting a name to it
In alphabetical order, write down the name of the plant, plus its correct Latin botanical name – do you know it? Find out if you don't and write the names down alongside each other. Latin names are fascinating as they tell you some significant detail about each plant – perhaps its shape, or where it comes from originally.

Now jot down when you bought your new plant and the price, or who gave it to you. Remember to take your log book with you on shopping sprees and compare houseplant prices between shops and garden centres – this can be quite an eye-opener! Then, when you've had the plant for a while, you can look back to see where you got it and go back again if you had value for money.

Once you have a record of your plant's basic details, jot down what you should do to make it grow and flower to the absolute peak of perfection. First and foremost this means noting how much water it needs in summer and winter and how regularly – often there's a special little foible that a particular plant possesses. Add what type of fertiliser it needs, in what strength and, again, how often; when it flowers (if it does) and for how long; when it needs pruning, repotting and staking. All this will give you an at-a-glance guideline so you know how to look after your plant without guesswork or room for error. When you get your latest houseplant home – this is where that tape measure comes in – measure its height, and then, if you can, measure its diameter.

Then, in six months you can go through the process again and know exactly how much your plant has grown. If it should have grown and it hasn't, go to your records – check back over them and you should be able to spot where you went wrong. On the other hand, if your plant has grown

dramatically in all directions, you can feel justifiably proud and congratulate yourself on your wonderful green fingers.

By keeping a note of such points as when you water, you can be sure of giving precisely the right amount at the correct time and so avoid the commonest mistake of all, the dreadful crime of overwatering your plants.

Feeding and fertilisers
It can be even easier to forget when you last fed your plants, especially if you use those solid fertiliser sticks or tablets which last for about six weeks before needing to be replaced. Even a regular 14 day feeding routine can slip past unnoticed if you have been distracted by something like a holiday.

As it is impossible to remember the propagation details of all your plants, this is where a log book is really useful. You'll remind yourself of when a particular plant should be increased and how it is best done. By trying different methods for the same plant you'll get a good idea which is the most successful, both in the time it takes to root and for getting the healthiest plants in the quickest way. Also you can keep a check on the plants you have propagated over the years. Who knows, you might discover how Great Aunt Sally gets the Bizzy Lizzy cutting you gave her to grow into a huge year-round flowering plant, while you are lucky if yours flowers for two weeks!

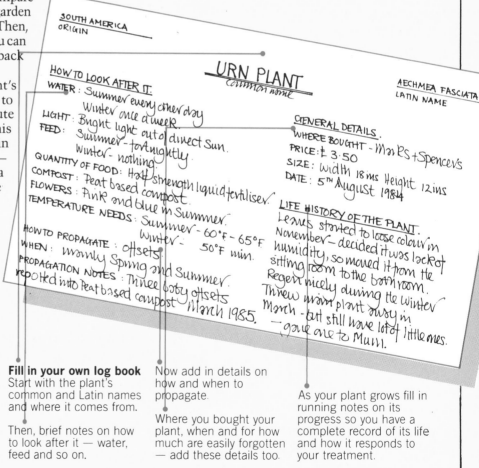

Fill in your own log book
Start with the plant's common and Latin names and where it comes from.

Then, brief notes on how to look after it — water, feed and so on.

Now add in details on how and when to propagate.

Where you bought your plant, when and for how much are easily forgotten — add these details too.

As your plant grows fill in running notes on its progress so you have a complete record of its life and how it responds to your treatment.

CHAPTER 2

Practical Guidelines

Life span of plants— the <u>long</u> and the <u>short</u> of it

Every plant has a built-in time clock that dictates how long it is going to live — which can be anything from a few weeks to many decades. While it's easy to shorten a plant's life through neglect or misunderstanding, it's not possible to lengthen appreciably a plant's life other than by treating it well. It's no use expecting a plant which usually lives 20 years to do so unless you provide the environment and treatment it needs to flourish.

Obviously, a lot depends on your growing conditions, and if these are not met, your plant's life could be short.

Plants such as Cineraria, Christmas Cherry and the Black-Eyed Susan are all annuals, completing their natural life cycle in a year.

Other plants may only have a short houseplant life but can be destined for other purposes than the compost heap. Primroses, sold by their thousands in early spring, are a feast of colour for a few weeks but then start to look a bit leggy and untidy. Rather than dumping them, plant them outside in the garden where they can flower every spring for years to come.

Even the Pot Chrysanthemum, after flowering indoors, can be replanted outside, where it will flower again in future years. But it will grow much taller, because Pot Chrysanthemums are treated with a special dwarfing chemical that wears off after one season. This temporarily reduces a plant which is normally 3ft (90cm) tall to only 10in (25cm) tall.

There are also plants whose colourful life is fairly short and sweet, after which they eke out a healthy but uninteresting life. The Kalanchoe and Poinsettia are just such plants. The problem with these two is that they need a precise amount of bright daylight and long hours of darkness to trigger them into producing buds.

Many Bromeliads die once they have flowered, but not before they have produced a number of baby plants in the form of offsets. The Urn Plant for instance takes two or three years to reach maturity before flowering for about six months. It then stops growing and produces offsets around the base. Once these begin to grow independently the mother plant will start to die, so where you had one plant you'll soon have five or six.

Members of the Fig family, including the Rubber Plant, can live for well over 20 years. Dracaenas live for 10 or more and in general most other houseplants

Long-lived plants
To get the most from your houseplants, feed them fortnightly during the growing season, repot into fresh compost every year and treat any problems as soon as they occur.

Aspidistra
Can live for well over 100 years.

Mother-in-law's Tongue
Lives for at least 50 years.

Cacti
Can last indefinitely.

Croton
Can last for years.

should reach between five and ten years.

Some plants like the Kangaroo Vine, Grape Ivy and Boston Fern grow happily for five or six years and then suddenly collapse and there's very little you can do to revive them.

The little African Violet, Italian Bell-flower and Shrimp Plant get very woody after a couple of years so it's a good idea to take cuttings regularly to have a stock of fresh, young plants. There are a number of bigger plants which live for years but get leggy with age and lose their looks. Cordyline, Dieffenbachia and Asparagus Ferns drop their lower leaves and become very 'stalky'.

Then, in complete contrast, some plants have a limited life-span in the home simply because they grow too big: Philodendrons, the Swiss Cheese Plant, some Agaves, the Banana tree and others are all likely to need new homes after eight to ten years.

At the far end of the spectrum are the plants which live as long or even longer than we do. A number of cacti, succulents and other plants like the Kaffir Lily, Norfolk Island Pine and Aspidistra all live well in excess of 50 years and sometimes beyond 100.

The secret of long life as far as house-plants are concerned is that they need their own ideal growing conditions. You can't expect plants to survive against the odds for any length of time.

Short-lived plants

These plants only flower for one season in the home, after which they are discarded or planted outside. Only the Azalea can be persuaded to flower again indoors, after spending the summer outside.

The Pot Chrysanthemum flowers for eight or ten weeks in the home.

The Poinsettia's colourful bracts last for about three months before fading and disappearing.

Kalanchoe flowers for months, but won't flower again.

A Begonia flowers for about six months then fades and finally dies.

Without a garden Azaleas are difficult to keep happy. Most are temporary plants.

Dragon Tree
Lives about 10 years but gets 'leggy'.

Yucca
Well cared for it will live for years.

Stephanotis
Once settled lasts at least 20 years.

Why plants need light

All plants use the sun's light to make the energy required for growth — which is why you can't get houseplants to grow if you put them in the middle of a gloomy room. The more light you give your plants, the healthier and happier they'll be, with lots of lovely colourful, fresh leaves and flowers. If you can't provide enough light, use artificial light instead — your plants will grow just as well.

Different plants need varying degrees of light, depending on how they have adapted their leaves to get the most from the light they receive in their natural habitat. So, for example, a Swiss Cheese Plant, which grows wild in dimly lit tropical American jungles, doesn't need strong light to grow well; but it does have enormous leaves to catch as much light as it can. However, if you give your Swiss Cheese Plant lots of strong sunlight, thinking to do it a favour, you'll scorch it, because the Swiss Cheese Plant doesn't have natural heat protection in its leaves, as in the jungle such insulation isn't necessary.

The complete reverse is true for desert cacti which are used to extended periods of intense heat; they long ago reduced their leaves into spines as protection against absorbing too much of the baking sunshine. So, if at home you put your cactus in a shady position, it won't grow at all because it's not getting the sheer intensity of light it needs to make it grow and flower.

Judging the light

You can see quite easily which parts of your house have good, bright, light and where it's so poorly lit that you won't be able to grow anything. Unless you have a sunroom, the brightest light is on the windowsills; but it's still quite bright 2-3ft (0.6-0.9m) into a room from the windows and, depending on which way the windows face, and whether the sun is blocked by trees or buildings, the amount of light is bright enough for shade-loving plants for a further 6ft (1.8m). After that the light intensity drops rapidly, no matter what your eyes tell you.

Know your plant

Save your sunniest windowsills for plants that need maximum light. Usually when you buy a houseplant, there is a descriptive label which tells you what amount of light your new plant needs.

Adjusting houseplants to light

Once you find the right spot for your plants, you should still adjust their position slightly from time to time for their comfort. For a start, really strong sun can scorch houseplant leaves through the glass; this is most dangerous in spring, when a sudden burst of sunny weather will damage leaves which normally have time to gradually get accustomed to the higher intensities of summer light.

Never put a new plant straight into bright light, even if it needs it — get it gradually accustomed to brighter light over a week or so — unless you are sure it was grown in bright light.

To protect plants from the fierce sun use net curtains at the windows: they are excellent for filtering the sun, but still let through plenty of really bright light for plants to grow well.

Never spray plants in the bright sun; this is because the water droplets on the leaves act like minute magnifying glasses, and concentrate the sun's rays in one spot, creating tiny scorch marks.

Every three or four days give your plants a 45° turn, because otherwise they lean badly towards the light. Indoor

The Cineraria, in common with most flowering plants, likes plenty of bright, but not burning, light.

plants, unlike garden plants, generally only get light from one direction, which makes a lop-sided plant. The answer is to get into the habit of giving your plants a half turn every two or three days so the stem grows straight and the whole plant is well balanced.

A word of warning about turning plants: some flowering plants must not

How plants use sunlight

Energy for growth comes from the sunlight.

The leaves give off oxygen and take in carbon dioxide

Roots take in water from the soil.

Basically, plants use light to make simple sugars, broadly similar to glucose, which are later turned into the more complex chemicals they need for healthy, vigorous growth. The green colouring of plant leaves — correctly called chlorophyll — absorbs energy from sunlight. This energy is then used to combine carbon dioxide from the air with water to make sugars; the process is called photosynthesis. At the same time the plant is giving off oxygen through its leaves. The sugars are used to form new tissues — which is how a plant grows.

At night when it's dark, plants stop making the sugars. Their 'breathing' reverses and they take in a little oxygen from the air to turn the stored sugars into energy for growth.

Without sufficient light, the amount of chlorophyll in the leaves is reduced, so the plant can't make enough glucose to grow and will be weak with thin stems and pale leaves.

Give your plants good light and they will respond with healthy growth.

be turned while their buds are forming, or they will drop off. By turning the plant you make the flower buds twist towards the light until they drop. Two notorious examples are the Christmas and Easter Cactus — so when you buy such a plant always point the buds and flowers towards the light and don't move them.

Another point to note is that plants with variegated leaves need more light than plants with plain green leaves. If you don't give a variegated plant enough light it will lose its variegation and the leaves will go a plain green. So, while ordinary Ivies put up with poor light, variegated Ivies must have bright light to keep the patterns on their leaves.

If you can, give some of your houseplants a summer holiday in the sun, say between June and early September. Stand them out of doors for a few weeks in good, bright light — it's amazing how much better their growth and leaf colour will be. But be careful not to put them where they get direct, scorching sun — and don't forget to water them regularly as their compost drys out much quicker in the open air.

Sun scorched Dieffenbachia leaf

Using artificial light

If you live in a shady house don't despair of ever growing anything other than Ivies and Aspidistras; use artificial light to brighten up your plants and your decor. Ordinary light bulbs don't emit enough light in the red and orange part of the spectrum for plants to grow, so get a special plant-growing bulb which fits into an ordinary light-bulb socket. These have to be fairly close to the plant — within 3ft (0.9m) to be of much use — and kept switched on for 8-12 hours a day to be effective in a really gloomy spot in the middle of a room.

Fluorescent light is much the best form of artificial light for growing plants. The tubes are not difficult to install, but if you are not electrically minded, get a qualified electrician to fit the units.

Plants for light and shade

Fluorescent light If you are really serious about growing your indoor plants under artificial light, then arrange your set-up as shown above. Use fluorescent tubes — ideally ones that produce a balanced light output — and suspend them 18-24in (45-60cm) from your plants (depending on type). A pebble tray filled with water will help to maintain high humidity.

Mount the fluorescent tubes in pairs, say above shelves, corner units and in alcoves, and position them 18-24in (45-60cm) above the plants, so that the light shines directly down onto them. Choose 40 watt, cool white or daylight tubes and if possible use a reflecting hood to direct and spread the light downwards. Diffusers can be used to hide the tubes, but of course these slightly reduce light intensity.

Another way to provide artificial lighting and a warm, humid, environment for some of the smaller, more delicate and tricky houseplants is to get a fish tank, complete with cover and built-in fluorescent tube. The tank can then be used as a terrarium for extra special plants.

Health and happiness

So, as you now know, your houseplants need light for their health as well as for their growth. It's not enough to buy a plant and put it in the middle of a room and hope for the best. If it is a plant that needs a lot of light, it simply won't grow. For your plant to thrive, you must give it all the light it needs.

● For the sunniest windowsills, where it gets baking hot close to the glass, trust such sun-lovers as zonal, regal, ivy and scented-leaved Pelargoniums (commonly called Geraniums), the Passion Flower, Jade Plant, cacti, Bougainvilleas and Acacias.

● Where there's good sun for part of the day, grow a Shrimp Plant, Spider Plant, Ornamental Peppers and Tradescantia. But even these may need moving away from the burning sun in the hottest weather.

● Bright but sunless positions are ideal for plants needing lots of light, but which would scorch in the direct sun. Grow the magnificent Flamingo Flower, Indian Azalea, the Finger Aralia, all sorts of different Fuchsias, the Dumb Cane and the Christmas Cactus.

Semi-shade

● There are plenty of attractive foliage plants which thrive in semi-shady positions. Some of the finest are the Mother-in-Law's Tongue, Sweetheart Plant, Aspidistra and lots of lovely ferns.

Gloomy positions

● Really gloomy spots are best left to those ardent shade-lovers, the Ivies, especially the small-leaved, plain green varieties, as well as Aspidistra, the Snakeskin Plant and Baby's Tears.

Very few houseplants are as tough as the Bougainvillea, *left*, which can sit safely in the full sun. Most need bright but indirect light, like the variegated Ivy, *above*. Only a few, like the Aspidistra, *below*, are happy in shade.

How much water do plants need?

Of all the different aspects of houseplant care, watering probably presents the most problems. Watering itself is easy, but it takes experience to judge how much water a particular plant needs and when. It is a sad fact that more houseplants die through being overwatered than by not being given enough water. Saturated compost deprives roots of oxygen and cold, stagnant water encourages rot to set in. This is often the result of giving your plants 'just a quick splash' of water every day, regardless of temperature and season. Here we tell you everything you need to know about how to judge the exact amount of water to give to your plants.

HOW PLANTS USE WATER

Energy from sunlight triggers the cells in the leaves to release oxygen to make sugars, which are changed by a series of chemical reactions into all the different 'building materials' for the plant to grow.

Wilting plant: overwatering can cause root rot which in turn leads to wilting leaves. Rot starts when the plant has been standing for too long in cold, stagnant water. The compost gets waterlogged and prevents the roots getting oxygen so they cannot take water to the leaves efficiently. If the soil stays waterlogged the roots start to rot.

Water evaporates from the leaves as a by-product of respiration and of all the chemical reactions taking place. This is why your plant needs most water when it is growing actively. Water also carries all the nutrients and chemicals that have to be taken through the plant to the parts where they are needed.

Check for root rot: get the plant out of its pot and tease the compost away from any brown, unhealthy roots. Pull the root gently; if the outer skin comes away easily leaving an inner core, your plant has rot. All you can do is remove the bad roots, dry the soil and hope that your plant recovers.

A healthy plant absorbs moisture from the soil. This then travels along the roots, up the stem and through the branches to the leaves. From there, water carries the sugars produced in the leaves to the other parts of the plant, which in turn helps more roots and leaves to grow healthily.

Holiday plant care: it's easy enough to take a few simple precautions to avoid the awful let-down of coming home from a lovely holiday only to find that your plants have dried out. One method is to use a self-watering pot, *right*. This is basically two pots, one inside the other, with the lower one filled with water. **1**. Water gets to the plant through a wick, **2**, and the water is topped up via a tube, **3**.
Alternatively capillary matting, *below*, is a good short-term answer. Lay it flat in the sink or bath, dip one end in a bowl of water — such as a washing-up bowl, on a level above the matting. Water moves by capillary action down the mat to where the plants can take it. The capillary matting method works for as long as there is water remaining in the bowl.

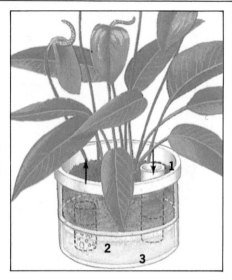

Simple watering tests

● For a plant in a clay pot, fix a cotton reel on the end of a bamboo cane and tap the pot. If you get a ringing sound it means that the clay, and therefore the compost, is dry and needs watering; when you tap the pot and get a dull clunk, then the compost is wet enough already.

● Pick up the plant (whether in a clay or plastic pot): if it feels heavy then the compost is wet; if it feels light, then the compost is dry. This is a reliable test, but it takes a little time to gauge the weights of individual plants and it isn't always practical with large plants.

● Feel the surface of the compost: push your finger down about 1in (25mm) into the compost. If the compost feels dry, then give your plant some water. If it feels damp, play safe and don't water, but test the compost again the following day.

● If you don't feel confident with any of these tests, get yourself a moisture meter. This is a metal probe which is pushed into the compost; on a dial at the top a needle indicates 'wet', 'moist' and 'dry', so you can see at a glance whether to water.

Judging when to water is a skill which comes with practice and appreciation of the way your plants grow. But it's not difficult. There are a few simple rules to remember, and then you'll always be able to get it right.

Plants need most water when they are growing. This is usually during the warm days of spring and summer, especially when they are developing flower buds and blooming.

Give your plants considerably less water in the autumn and winter when the temperature is much lower and the majority of plants are resting. The exception to the rule is when you keep your plants in a hot room, in which case you should water as often as in summer.

A plant which has completely filled its pot with roots needs watering more often than a plant whose roots still have plenty of room for growth.

The type of compost you use affects the frequency of watering; peat-based compost dries out slowly because it's spongy and holds a lot of water. But

Mist sprayers: regular mist spraying is an important part of houseplant care. The decorative brass sprayer emits a good strong spray but doesn't hold much water. The more practical plastic sprayer holds more water and has an adjustable nozzle — but it doesn't look as pretty!

when peat dries out, it shrinks and is almost impossible to re-wet. Soil-based composts such as John Innes don't hold water so well and therefore dry out much more quickly, but soil doesn't noticeably shrink.

Plants in clay pots need watering about twice as often than those in plastic pots. This is because moisture is drawn out of the compost by the porous clay, and then evaporates through the sides of the pot.

Watering tips

Try to water your plants in the morning, when the temperature is rising and when the plant's need is greatest. If you water in the evening, your plants will probably stay damp all night, and if the temperature drops this can make them susceptible to the dreaded grey mould and root rot.

Most plants need a winter rest during which time they require little or no watering. Cacti and succulents are the prime examples. In spring wake

How much water do plants need?

Normal watering: plants such as Busy Lizzie like to dry out slightly. Push your finger about 1in (25mm) into the compost. If it feels dry, then water.

Fill the pot up to the rim with water to thoroughly soak the compost. Wait until water runs out of the pot. Throw the surplus away after 15 minutes.

Constant moisture: some plants, like Maranta, need to have their roots moist. Test the compost with a fingertip — if it's dry, the plant needs water.

Pour in just a little water — but not enough for any to run into the drip saucer. This way you are watering little and often to keep the compost moist.

Watering problems and cures

Compacted soil: sometimes the surface of the compost sets hard and solid. Water then remains on top of the surface and doesn't soak through to the roots.

Cure the problem by gently stirring the compost surface with a small cutlery fork. Try not to damage the roots when you poke the fork into the compost.

Dried compost: peat shrinks if it isn't kept constantly moist. When you apply water, it just runs straight out of the pot without wetting the compost.

Cure the problem by plunging the plant, pot and all, into a bucket of tepid water. Leave for about 15 minutes or until the compost has swelled. Then drain thoroughly.

your plants up with a good drink. Stand the pots to their rims in a bowl of tepid water until the surface of the compost becomes moist, then remove the pots and let them drain. Do the same if any of your plants have dried out by neglect.

Some plants with woolly or hairy leaves, like African Violets and Gloxinias, hate being watered from above as this wets the leaves and leads to rotting and fungal diseases. Be careful with Cyclamen as well, because water in the centre of the corm can start the leaf and flower stalks rotting. Stand such plants up to their rims in tepid water for five minutes, then let them drain thoroughly afterwards.

Urn plants like bromeliads need the centre of their 'vase' filled with fresh water about once a week. Also the so-called 'air' plants (mostly Tillandsias), which are grown on pieces of wood and coral, benefit from a daily mist spray of water in summer and a spray once a week in winter, despite their name!

Using tap water

Ordinary tap water is fine for most plants even if it is hard and contains chalk. But collect rainwater for Azaleas, Heathers, Urn and Air plants which don't like chalk. If you can collect enough rainwater, use it for all your houseplants, otherwise use cold boiled water for chalk-hating plants.

If you spray your houseplants with hard tap water, you'll find that you are left with unsightly white drying smears

on the leaves. These are chalk deposits, but they can be easily removed with a moist soft cloth or sponge.

Providing humidity

Many houseplants must have moist air around their leaves — particularly when it is hot — and for this you may need to create humidity. One way of doing this is to spray the foliage every day.

Another method is to stand pots in trays or saucers containing a layer of gravel or small pebbles sitting in about an inch (25mm) of water.

Yet another way of providing humidity is to stand each pot in a bigger, ornamental container. Fill the space between the pot and the outer container with moist peat up to the pot's rim.

When you're away

A great part of the fun in keeping house-plants is in learning all about them, getting to know your favourites and developing a feel for their particular needs. You'll find that you rapidly become confident about what sort of light conditions and watering they thrive on. But all your patient care may seem to be in vain when you go away for a holiday and are faced with your plants being neglected for several weeks.

You must, of course, make arrangements for your plants while you're away, just as you would for your pets. But don't worry unduly — there are several simple precautions you can take to give your plants the maximum care and attention even while you're not there.

The most important thing — as with everything else to do with holidays — is planning. Provided you think ahead, and allow yourself enough time before you leave, getting your plants ready for their holiday treatment shouldn't present any problems.

First of all, there are certain methods of growing houseplants that are naturally very suited to minimal care and these, of course, are ideal for holiday time. They include growing plants hydroponically, where the water level just needs to be kept within certain clearly defined limits and the plants will naturally take just as much moisture as they need. Any sort of enclosed atmosphere calls for very little attention on your part — bottle gardens, terrariums, Wardian cases all have self-regulating environments, which are highly convenient if you're away, or even if you're just forgetful!

So, if you have plants already well established growing in this way, you're in luck. If not, you'll need to work out how your plants will get the necessary watering while you're on holiday.

Weekend breaks

The sort of precautions you must take will depend on how long you're going to be away. If it's just a weekend or a few days, it'll probably be enough to water your plants thoroughly before you leave. Make sure you protect them from very hot sun in the summer: move them

A little help from your friends

The best way of all to care for your plants is to have someone giving them exactly the care that you would if you were at home. But take care: if your plant-sitter isn't reliable, you would be better using one of the techniques suggested here.

The commonest fault when friends look after plants for you is not, as you might think, that they forget to water them, but that they are so enthusiastic to do the right thing that they *overwater* them. The best protection against this is to take the trouble to leave a brief list, giving details of your plants' particular needs. Suggest how often they should be watered; which of them, if any, should be sprayed and how often; what light conditions they like — and any 'special points' you can think of. It may take an hour or so of your time, but it'll be well worth it. Even if you've talked your plant-sitter through everything, put it in writing, too — people can be forgetful!

Make sure you leave an appropriate watering-can or jug around, a source of water, and a cloth to mop up spillages. If you group your plants together in the kitchen or the bathroom, there will be less trekking about to be done.

Remember, it isn't just you who'll be delighted when you come home to healthy plants — their temporary guardian will be too!

You can rig up your own watering system using lampwick and water raised about 4in (10cm) off the ground.

A sink is an ideal place for capillary matting.

away from windowsills, and partly draw curtains at south-facing windows.

In winter you must protect plants from extreme cold: again, don't leave them on windowsills, where the temperature can drop very low at night, but put them in the warmest room in the house — the kitchen, probably, if motorised appliances such as the refrigerator are left on. If the weather's very cold, you could group your plants on top of the refrigerator, where they will benefit from the warmth of the motor.

Even with a short break, if you have a very thirsty plant, or one that likes very high humidity, you may still need to make other arrangements — like the ceramic mushrooms, *right.*

Annual holidays

Surrounding pots with moist peat or wrapping them in moist paper will help to provide a little more humidity for a few days. For very thirsty plants you may need to use one of the watering methods recommended below.

For longer breaks, more action will be needed. It is probably during your annual holiday that your plants will be at their most vulnerable — and this is likely also to be a hot time of the year, when watering is especially important. As a general guideline, if you're away for up to a fortnight, one of the self-watering methods outlined below will probably be adequate.

If you're away for longer, you really will have to co-opt a friend or neighbour. In this case it's a good idea to put your plants together as it will save time and ensure that none gets overlooked.

The bath or the kitchen sink may seem an obvious place to group your plants while you're away. But make sure you protect your furniture. Line the bath with paper towels so that the bases of the pots do not scratch it — don't use newspaper, as some printing inks leach out and cause irreversible staining, especially to acrylic baths. Newspaper is fine in a stainless steel sink, though.

Loss of water from the surface of the compost can be reduced to some extent by lowering the level of available light. Drawing or partly drawing curtains effectively slows down your plant's life processes, and provided you're not away for more than two to three weeks the plant will not suffer. Substantial reduction of light for a longer period would make the plant spindly and straggly and should be avoided.

Self-watering devices: ceramic mushrooms hold a small reservoir of water and release it gradually into the soil; a permeable holder attached to a tube feeds water to the plants by siphoning.

Self-watering containers

If you have a few large, specimen plants, you may want to invest in some self-watering containers for them. These consist of a reservoir from which water is passed to the compost by means of a wick or a permeable membrane. You'll need to remove the plant carefully from its existing pot and repot it in the new one, but once you've done that, you've got the benefit of a minimum-care container until you need to pot the plant on. All you'll need to do is to check the water level and top it up occasionally — this will be much less often than conventional watering.

Capillary matting

For a large number of plants, a very simple yet useful self-watering technique is to use 'capillary' matting, which you can buy in any good garden shop or centre. It is a material made of man-made fibres, which acts like a wick in drawing water. You can buy any length of it to order, and it isn't expensive.

For capillary matting to work properly — that is, drawing up water in a steady and controlled way — the source of water must be at a lower level than the matting itself (the matting usually comes with instructions giving ideal

water levels). Lay the matting on a flat, water-resistant surface — a piece of Perspex or vinyl would be ideal — and let the end dangle down. Put the plants in their pots on the matting, and immerse the end of the matting in a bucket of water. The matting will act as a wick, drawing up the water as necessary.

What to avoid

● **Don't give all** your plants a good soaking, then leave them standing in water. Even in summer, plants may be overwatered, and leaving them in pools of water easily causes root rot.

● **Don't just leave** your plants and go away with your fingers crossed. Some *may* be tough enough to fend for themselves with no care at all, but it's a big risk to take, especially in high summer or the depths of winter when temperatures can be extreme.

● **Don't despair** if you do have some casualties. If you take care to do the best you can, most of your plants will be fine. But nobody can predict sudden sub-Arctic weather — or heatwaves! If you have any particularly sensitive plants, it's always best if a friend or neighbour can call in and water them regularly.

It is inevitable that, soon or later, one of your houseplants will outgrow its pot and will need to be repotted into a larger one. This is best done during the growing season, between April and September, when plants are at their most adaptable. If the plant is not too big, it is a fairly simple procedure to remove it from its pot and repot it directly into its new one. A large specimen, on the other hand, is a different proposition and the conventional method of repotting may present difficulties, which often result in the plant ending up either off-centre or at an acute angle, both of which problems can be very hard to correct.

What you need

First of all, always select a good proprietary compost rather than using unsterilised soil from the garden. This will provide your plant with the correct texture, a healthy balance of nutrients and a growing medium free from pests and diseases.

Choosing the right pot is also important. Buy one that is 2in (5cm) larger in diameter than the old pot, leaving a space of around 1in (2.5cm) between the root-ball and the new pot. Do not be tempted to use too large a pot as a plant can suffer from being over-potted.

Plastic pots are both cheap and clean but terracotta pots are preferable because they are porous. This helps to prevent a build-up of water which can be detrimental to the roots. Their weight also provides a large plant with a greater degree of stability.

What to do

Having selected both new pot and compost, water the plant evenly and tap the old pot gently all around its rim to loosen it — you may need to run a long knife round the edge of the compost. Remove the plant from its old pot, while holding it gently but firmly in position with one hand placed over the surface of the soil. You may need someone to help you to support the plant while you remove the pot. Once you have done this, gently place the root-ball of the plant on some newspaper, taking care not to damage it. (If you are repotting a large cactus with spines, you will need to protect your hands with heavy-duty

A Dumb Cane in need of potting on.

Potting on a large houseplant

Choose a new pot 2-3in (5-8cm) larger.

leather gloves, or even by wrapping the plant up carefully in several layers of newspaper.)

If you are using a terracotta pot, put a few pieces of broken earthenware pot in the bottom to aid drainage. Next, add some compost so that the rims of both pots are level when the old one is placed inside the new one. Obviously, if the old pot is too low down more compost should be added; and conversely if it is too high some of the compost should be removed.

Now position the old pot in the centre and fill the gap between the two pots with compost, taking care to firm it gently and evenly with your hands as you work and so ensuring that there are no air spaces. Also take care to leave a space at the top of the pot for watering — say, 2in (5cm) for a 10in (25cm) pot and 3in (8cm) for a 12in (30cm) pot or larger. When this space has been completely filled with compost, gently but firmly push the old inner pot downwards and rotate it slightly before removing it. With a bit of luck, this will have created a mould into which the plant will now fit snugly.

Before repotting, examine the rootball of your plant; if it is too tight, gently tease out some of the roots in order to encourage them to grow into their new growing medium — but do take care not to damage the roots.

Now place the plant in its new home, tap the pot in order to settle the compost around the root-ball and water the new compost sparingly. Be careful not to overwater the plant while it is still adapting to its new environment and making fresh root growth into the new compost.

Top dressing

There may come a time when a large plant either grows too big to be repotted or, alternatively, when it is difficult to find a larger container than the one in which it is currently growing. If this is the case, you can improve the plant's situation to some extent by top dressing the surface. To do this gently rake the soil, removing some of the old compost from the surface to a depth of about 1-2in (2.5-5cm), and taking care not to damage the roots. Replace the compost with fresh.

Potting — do's and don'ts

By growing a plant in a pot you limit its size to suit your home by preventing its roots from spreading. In this way indoor favourites like the Rubber Plant and Tree Philodendron, which grow to enormous heights in their native habitat, are restricted to heights of 4ft (1.2m) or so. But there is a limit to the amount of cramping your plant will put up with; sooner or later it will need a larger pot and fresh compost if it's to thrive.

The mistake that many houseplant owners make is to leave their plants in the same pot for too long. With regular feeding most plants will stay happily in the same containers for many months, but eventually the goodness in the compost will be depleted and the amount of compost steadily dimishes as the roots take up more space. As young plants grow, they're potted on into ever larger pots until they reach their 'final size', and even then you'll still need to renew the compost from time to time.

Reading the signs

Growing plants are started in the smallest possible pots and should be moved on as soon as their roots have filled them. This ensures that there's always fresh compost for the plant's roots to penetrate. But don't repot unless it's really necessary — the process *does* disturb the plant and plants aren't at their best growing in pots which are too large for them. 'If in doubt, don't' is the motto for potting on.

A few plants give very clear signals when they're in trouble — the fat fleshy roots of Chlorophytum, for instance, will push up through the drainage holes — but most plants push a few roots through, so don't automaticially pot on until you've examined the roots. Carefully remove the plant from its pot. If the compost is completely packed with roots, the plant needs moving on. But if there's still plenty of root-free compost visible, pop the plant back into the pot.

It's well worth while potting up a number of plants in one go. Find a spot where you will have a large surface to work on, and where all the plants, pots, potting compost, etc, can be collected together. Potting is a messy business, so it's a good idea to spread a large plastic sheet or newspapers over your working area. Protect any nearby furniture, too.

Have a selection of potting composts ready. It's best to pot plants on into the compost that they're used to, but if in doubt consult the guide to potting composts on pages 538-9. The night before start preparing; thoroughly water all the plants you want to repot. This will make it easier to get them out of their pots. Soak any new, unglazed clay pots, too, for at least 12 hours, to rid them of any impurities. Clay pots should always be damp before compost is put in them; this stops them drawing water out of the compost too quickly.

1 Prepare the pots. Scrub your used pots (plastic or clay) with hot water and a household cleaning powder, tackling any lime deposits or other debris with a soft scrubbing brush. Rinse the pots thoroughly in clean water. Leave them until the surface water dries up; if the pots are too wet when you come to use them, the compost may stick to the sides.
Similarly rinse any new clay pots that have been soaking overnight and allow the surface to dry off.

2 Put a layer of drainage material in the bottom of clay pots. (The only exceptions are clay pots that are to stand on any capillary matting or automatic watering tray.) Use broken pot fragments (crocks), if possible. Place one large piece over the hole, and cover it with several smaller pieces. If no crocks are available, use pebbles, but make sure that they don't block the drainage holes and prevent moisture escaping.
Plastic pots, with their numerous small drainage holes, don't usually require 'crocking', but if they are to stand in a saucer or drip tray, it's a good idea to cover the bottom with pebbles. This helps prevent the compost becoming too soggy if water is accidentally left in the saucer.

3 Cover the bottom of the pot with fresh, moist compost and firm it lightly, then remove the plant from its pot.

Some plants may be difficult to examine in this way. Large plants, for example, are not so easily removed from their pots and will be dealt with later. You may find that the plant has become so pot-bound that the projecting roots need to be broken off before you can turn the plant out.

Roughly speaking, annual plants raised from seed and other fast-growing plants will need to be potted on several times in the space of a few months. Usually they start off in a 3½in (9cm) pot and are potted on to a final size of 5in (13cm) — or 6in (15cm) for larger plants. The slow growers — which include most of the permanent houseplants — need potting on only once a year, or even less for very slow growers.

Plants with small root systems — Begonias, Bromeliads, cacti and succulents, many ferns, Pepper Elders, Mother-in-Law's Tongue and Saintpaulias — shouldn't be potted on until their pots are well-filled with roots. And some plants actually prefer to be pot-bound — these include the flesh-rooted Clivias and Hippeastrums, which always flower better when their roots are cramped.

When to pot on your plants

Never move plants during their resting season. The roots won't be able to penetrate the new compost, which will in turn become very soggy and cause root rot. Wait until the spring or summer — preferably April for slow or moderate

step by step

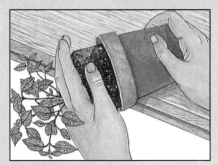

4 Take care when lifting the plant; first slip one hand, palm downwards, beneath the plant's foliage to cover the surface of the compost, with fingers either side of the stem. Turn the pot upside down. Give the bottom some sharp taps, or tap the pot rim on the edge of a table. This should loosen the rootball enough for you to lift the pot away. If there's any difficulty, push a sharp knife down between pot and compost.

Roots coming through the bottom of the pot may stop you removing the plant easily. If you have difficulty, break the pot or cut through it with shears.

Now check the roots. Any that are completely dried up or rotten must be cut off. Gently clear away clinging fragments of drainage material.

5 Not all plants can be dealt with in that way, though. Prickly plants present their own problems. Gloves can help, but the

best way to deal with a cactus, for example, is to 'lassoo' it with a thick band of rolled up newspaper.

6 Large plants, too, need a slightly different approach – and you may need someone to help you. Lay the pot on its side and tap the rim with a block of wood, at the same time gently pulling at the plant. You may need to run a long-bladed knife around the inside of the pot to release the rootball, or, failing that, break the pot. (The repotting of large plants is covered on page 461.)

7 Put a bit of compost on the bottom of the pot then stand the plant right in the centre. Be sure to leave room between the top of the rootball and the top of the pot to allow for watering; the top of the rootball should be between ½-2in (1.3-5cm) below

the rim depending on pot size (see 'Space for water', below. Remember to allow for a light covering of compost then adjust the layer of compost beneath the rootball accordingly.

Take the opportunity to correct any tilt the plant has been suffering from by building up the compost underneath it.

8 Fill in with fresh compost, pouring it down the sides of the rootball so that the plant is firmly supported. Scatter a little over the top; the mixture should completely cover the roots, but shouldn't reach as far as green stem or the lower foliage.

Tap the pot on the table to eliminate air pockets and settle the compost, then push it down with the fingers, gently, just enough to hold the plant secure. But don't firm too much, it may hinder drainage.

John Innes composts need a little more firming than the soilless types.

Space for water

Pot size	Space below rim
Up to 5in (13cm)	½in (13mm)
6-7in (15-18cm)	¾in (19mm)
8-9in (20-23cm)	1in (25mm)
10-12in (25-30cm)	1½in (38mm)
15in (38cm)	2in (5cm)

growers which will just be coming into growth.

Sick plants should never be moved to another pot; the shock may be too much for a weakened plant to bear. So wait until it's on the mend.

Choosing the best pot

Plastic pots deserve their popularity; they are cheap, easy to clean and lightweight. There's a big choice of shape, too. But plastic pots do have disadvantages. Large, heavy plants, may well topple them, for instance, and there can be a risk of waterlogging. Unlike the old-fashioned clay pots, plastic pots can't 'breathe' to allow water (and air) to pass through the sides. So plants in plastic pots need watering less often.

Which pot size?

Existing pot size	Move up by
Up to 4½in (11cm)	½in (13mm)
5-9 (13-23cm)	1in (25mm)
10in (25cm)	2in (5cm)
12in (30cm)	3in (7cm)

For fast-growers, like annuals, double up at least on the above recommendations or you'll be forever potting on. For instance, the usual practice is to move plants from a 3½in (9cm) pot to a 5in (13cm) pot.

Clay pots are ideal for large or top-heavy plants, but they do need a lot more work both in preparation and

when they're in use (see overleaf for more details). Clay pots are more fragile, of course, and being porous the compost in them dries out more rapidly, especially in warm conditions, so plants will need frequent checking. But this does mean there's less chance of plants becoming waterlogged.

The size of pot you choose is important. It's no good potting on into too large a pot. If there's too much compost around the roots, it will become very wet and sour, causing the roots to rot.

Pots are usually measured across the top, inside the rim, either in inches or centimetres. You will usually find the measurement imprinted on the base of the pot. A selection of 2½in (7cm), 3½in (9cm), 5in (13cm) and 7in (18cm) pots

Whether you're repotting a flowering plant, Yucca, fern or trailer, it's important to choose the right pot size. And if using plastic pots take care not to overwater.

should meet most of your needs with a few larger pots for more mature plants. It's probably worth investing in a few half-pots, too. As the name suggests, these are usually about half the depth of normal pots and are useful for shallow-rooting plants like Saintpaulias, Pepper Elders and Wandering Jews. (See page 463 for what size pot to choose.)

Repotting and top-dressing

A plant that's grown as big as you want it — say reaching a final pot size of 12-15in (30-38cm) for large plants — must

still be moved. Every second year it will need repotting to give it a fresh supply of compost. Do this in April, just as growth is starting.

Remove the plant from its pot in the usual way. Using an old kitchen fork, or other similar tool, tease away the compost from around the roots. Cut off any roots that are dead or damaged and trim the rootball by about a quarter.

You can use the old pot again, or select a fresh one; either way, prepare it as you would when potting on. Put the plant back in the pot and fill in with

compost, checking that the level is correct, just as you would when potting on.

In the years when you aren't repotting you'll need to 'topdress' the plant. To do this you simply remove the top 1-2in (2.5-5cm) of compost and replace it with fresh; depending on what compost was used before, topdress with either John Innes No 3, or a soilless compost with extra fertiliser added, if it comes without. Topdress, too, if the surface of the compost has developed a whitish crust — the result of too much lime in the tap water.

Repotting a cactus

The fear of being pricked by vicious barbs is enough to deter the hardiest of us from touching a cactus plant and explains why pot-bound cacti are left in the same pot for years at a time to starve and fall into decline. Sooner or later, if you want your cactus to thrive, you'll need to repot it. By following our instructions, repotting can be a painless experience.

A square pot is an unusual choice.

When to change pots

Young plants — those you've raised from seeds or cuttings — will grow quickly enough each year to need moving up to the next size pot.

In the wild, a desert cactus is obliged to spread its root system as far as possible to make the most of what little moisture finds its way into the soil. A cactus just 6in (15cm) across may have roots spreading for a square yard so, when confined to a small pot, these cacti have a tendency to become pot-bound.

Many desert cacti don't usually exceed 2ft (0.6m) high, with a width of 4-6in (10-15cm), and some of these will have a maximum pot size of 8in (20cm). But others will continue to grow and need bigger pots.

You're likely to notice when the root system is too cramped; growth slows down, despite regular feeding and proper care. If you check, you'll see that the compost has become matted with roots, some of which have pushed their way through the drainage hole.

Forest cacti don't have extensive root systems and probably won't outgrow a 10in (25cm) pot. In years when they don't need potting on, simply topdress the plant by removing the top 1-2in (2.5-5cm) of soil and replacing it with fresh.

The best time for repotting is early spring and you should never change pots in the depth of winter.

Compost

Cacti need a free draining, porous mixture that will retain its open texture through repeated watering. Otherwise, the roots may well start to rot. Either use a proprietary cactus compost or make up your own mixture using two parts John Innes No 1 compost to one part coarse sand or perlite.

Choosing pots

It doesn't matter whether you use clay or plastic pots, as long as they're clean. Just remember that plants in plastic pots require less frequent watering.

Potting on

● **Water the compost,** and leave it to drain for a few hours. This should make it easier to remove the pot.

Manure for cacti

If you can get it, some experts vociferously recommend well rotted or dried cow manure or decomposed leaf mould to guarantee flowering plants. Mix two parts manure or leaf mould to one part potting compost and one part coarse sand or perlite. Those who don't have a ready source needn't despair though! A regular application of fertiliser is a good substitute.

Make sure your hands are well protected with a pair of gloves, or use tongs or a paper collar to handle the cactus.

First grip the cactus and try to lift it carefully out of the pot. If that doesn't work, tip the plant upside down and tap it gently from its pot. If it resists, give the rootball a push with a pencil inserted through the drainage hole.

● **Have the new pot ready;** crock it well with a layer of drainage material and put a layer of potting compost on top.

Remove any loose, crumbly soil and crocks that are clinging to the roots, and set the rootball in the centre of the pot.

● **Trickle the compost** around and over the rootball, and knock the pot gently to get it settled. Avoid pressing it firmly. Make sure you don't fill in deeper than the soil mark on the stem and leave a small gap — about ½in (13mm) — at the top of the pot for watering.

Aftercare

It's best to water from the bottom on the first occasion after potting on a young plant, so that the soil can settle without being disturbed.

Fill a shallow bowl with water and allow the pot to stand in it for no longer than half an hour, then drain well.

Dealing with mature plants

On the whole, cacti prefer to be slightly cramped rather than be potted into an over-large container. And a mature plant in a large pot can certainly be left undisturbed for three or even four years. But it's worth taking the cactus out of its pot each year in spring to see if it's pot-

1. Pot on into the next pot size up.

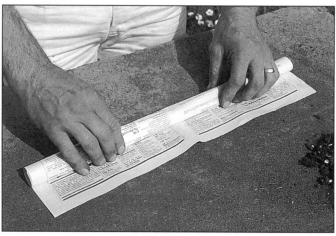

2. A good way of handling a cactus is to roll a paper collar.

3. Wrap the collar round the plant and lift it from its pot.

4. Prepare the new pot with a layer of crocks.

5. Still using the collar insert the cactus into its new pot.

6. After filling with compost, tap the pot to settle it.

bound. If the roots are so densely webbed that the compost is scarcely visible, it's time for repotting.

Instead of potting it into a larger pot, reduce the rootball by teasing away 2in (5cm) or so of compost from around the outside. Scrape a further 2-3in (5-8cm) from the top surface, at the base of the stem. This will make room for a fresh supply of compost.

Clean the old pot, and then replace the plant, potting it up into fresh compost as usual but leaving a little more space at the top — up to ¾in (19mm) — for watering.

If the roots are very pot-bound and some have died, turning black or grey, take a sterile knife and cut them away. This spurs the plant on to develop strong new roots.

Eventually you'll be obliged to move the plant on to a larger pot, unless you're prepared to 'tame' it, by trimming its roots so that it can be repotted into a pot the same size or smaller. After pruning the roots dust the cut surfaces with sulphur powder and then repot.

Don't water for a week or two after root pruning to give the roots a chance to heal and establish themselves.

Potting orchids

After they've finished flowering, or just before they start into new growth — that's the time to think about freshening up your orchids with a change of potting compost and a larger pot, if necessary. You could even consider propagating a new plant — it's surprisingly easy.

One of the things which makes growing orchids different from growing other houseplants is the type of compost used. Most of the orchids we grow as houseplants are epiphytes, growing on trees, shrubs or rocks. Strictly speaking, their roots don't need to be in any growing medium. But when they are, it's vital that the compost is well drained and aerated if there's to be no danger of their roots rotting.

Old compost which has become exhausted deteriorates in texture, and

Orchids put on a striking show — and many are easily grown under home conditions.

83

Orchid compost: 1

one part:	shredded or chipped pine bark (eg orchid grade Cambark)
one part:	peat
one part:	vermiculite
one part:	sphagnum moss
2/3 pieces:	charcoal

plants will not grow well. You can test whether the compost is still firm and sweet by pushing your finger in. If it meets little resistance, it's in poor condition; drainage and aeration will be impaired and it needs replacing.

Compost for orchids

Ordinary potting composts aren't sufficiently free-draining for orchids. You can splash out on ready-made orchid mediums which are available from a specialist nursery (probably made up to their own formula), but it's easy to make your own.

There are as many formulas for orchid compost as there are books on the subject, but there's no great mystery about it. You'll find two very simple, but very good, 'recipes' on this page, suitable for either epiphytic orchids or terrestrials. The trick is to create a mixture which will hold plenty of moisture, yet which quickly rids itself of any surplus. Most important of all, it should allow plenty of air to circulate through it.

Traditionally, osmunda fibre, an extremely porous material, has always been the 'wonder' ingredient in orchid compost. It's the dried root of the Osmunda Fern, chopped fine or coarse across the grain, according to the grade. It has to be imported, usually from Japan — which makes it fairly expensive. Fortunately, there are perfectly good substitutes available.

Orchid compost: 2

one part:	shredded or chipped bark or finely chopped osmunda fibre
one part:	peat
2/3 pieces:	charcoal

Special ways with epiphytes

Epiphytic orchids do tend to do better in special containers. And this is less trouble than it sounds. Your local garden centre will probably have a selection of perforated orchid pots,

and slatted wooden or wire baskets. These are all specially designed for epiphytic orchids, encouraging air circulation round the roots and allowing them to wind themselves around the outside.

Line the basket with a thin layer of sphagnum moss to stop the mixture dribbling through the gaps. Fill with the mixture, and pot the orchid up as you would in a conventional pot.

If you like, you can grow these tree orchids on slabs of bark, *left*, on blocks of osmunda fibre, or even on a piece of wood.

Take the orchid from its pot, shake it gently free of potting mixture and soak its base in water. Allow it to drain for half-an-hour and then carefully remove any remaining compost clinging to the roots.

Press a handful of sphagnum moss under the orchid's moist base, and spread its roots gently over the supportive surface you've chosen. Tie the roots down, very gently, with some nylon fishing line or thin copper wire.

Pine tree bark, for instance, does a very good job of keeping the growing medium well-aerated. It's combined with sphagnum moss and peat, both moisture-retentive materials, which help hold on to water. The more peat there is in a mixture, the wetter it will be, so if you're inclined to overwater rather than underwater, don't be too generous with it when mixing.

It's a good idea to add a few pieces of charcoal to the potting mixture; this will counteract the natural acidity of the peat, and keep the mixture 'sweet' (green algae on the surface is a sign that the mixture has become sour).

There's no need to add any fertiliser, since orchids dislike a rich growing medium. Instead, rely on foliar feeding in the growing season.

When to change pots

You can expect young plants to need potting on annually, to give them more growing space. But don't pot an orchid into a larger pot just for the sake of it—it's far better to wait until the orchid has quite obviously outgrown its current one. The reason is that too much compost around the roots usually means there will be too much water for the plant to absorb. And too much water may lead to root rot, to which orchids are particularly susceptible.

An easy way to tell whether an epiphytic orchid has outgrown its pot is to see if its latest pseudobulb is touching the rim, and there's no room for new growth. And any orchid whose compost is being dislodged by root development needs more room.

Mature plants — those that are in their final pots (usually over 8in (20cm) in diameter) — can be left for two years, or more, before they will need a fresh supply of compost. Put the plants back into the same size pots.

Choosing the container

All orchids — whether or not they are epiphytes — can be grown in either clay or plastic pots. Clay pots are heavier and more stable, and so may be a better choice for very large plants. Special clay epiphytic orchid pots are also available, though they aren't necessary. These have holes round the side which allows the roots to breathe.

Again, beware of choosing too large a pot when potting on young plants. Take a container that will give the plant only enough space for one year's growth (to accommodate one new pseudobulb and its rhizome). In effect, this means moving a young plant on to the next size of pot each time, say from a 5in (13cm) to a 6in (15cm). Don't worry if it looks too crowded.

Potting epiphytic orchids

First wash and sterilise the pots you're going to use. They must then be well 'crocked', so prepare them by putting plenty of drainage material in the bottom. Use broken clay flower pots, if you can, putting large pieces over the drainage holes, and smaller pieces on top of these, to a depth of ½in (13mm), at least, in small pots and 1in (2.5cm) in pots which are 6in (15cm) or more.

1. Clear away any weeds and dead leaf bracts before removing the plant from its pot. Tease away the old compost until you expose most of the roots. Be careful — some orchids have quite brittle roots that are easily damaged. Cut off any that are damaged or decaying — it's quite normal to find one or two dead roots. Trim the longest live roots, if you like, to make potting easier.

You may also remove a few of the oldest back bulbs if they outnumber the leaf-bearing pseudobulbs. Use a sterilised knife, if possible, to sever the short rhizome connecting the back bulbs to their neighbour.

2. Working with care, try to pack some compost between the roots, before potting up the plant.

Position it so that the oldest growth — the first back bulb — is near the edge of the pot, with the newest growth — the youngest pseudobulb — in the centre of the pot. This allows plenty of room for new growth to develop.

3. Place a layer of compost over the drainage material, and sit the plant so that the crown or base of the plant is level with the rim of the pot. Now trickle in more compost, around and over the rootball, working it well between the roots with your fingers. Tap the pot a few times to ensure that it's evenly packed and then firm it only gently. The pseudobulbs should sit, as before, on the surface of the compost, with the top half of the rhizome exposed and the bottom half buried. Remember to leave space at the top — about ½- ¾in (13-19mm) — for watering.

Potting terrestrial orchids

Having a larger root system, terrestrial orchids must be planted in slightly larger containers than the epiphytic orchids, to allow enough room for growth. Use the orchid compost, but otherwise pot the plants up in the same

2

1

3

way you would any houseplant.

Position the stem in the middle of the new container, and leave a ½-¾in (13-19mm) watering space at the top.

Aftercare

Don't water your orchids for at least two weeks after potting, but simply mist spray the leaves to encourage roots to develop. Then start watering, but only moderately (so that compost is always moist to the touch) until the top growth is well under way — a sign that new roots are going strong.

The delightful Papiopedilum thrives in normal room temperatures.

1

2

3

4

5

Dividing pseudobulbs

The time for repotting is also the time for dividing your plants. This is the most straightforward way of propagating epiphytic orchids. But it's worth remembering that the larger the plant, the better the display of flowers; if you reduce it by too much division, you may stop it from flowering for several years. So it's best to wait until it's really necessary — until the orchid becomes otherwise unmanageable, in fact. It's best done in early spring or after the plant has finished flowering.

Division can also be a rescue operation for an orchid in a poor state with much of its root system decayed. Trim back the roots, divide the plant into healthy sections and plant up as the step-by-step sequence shows.

1. Tidy the plant, as you would before changing pots. Now prepare to divide the plant into sections, each containing at least two, but not more than three, pseudobulbs in leaf.

2. With a sterile knife, sever the rhizome that links the groups of pseudobulbs, easing them gently apart to do so.

3. Remove the plant from its container (or support) and disentangle the roots, cutting them if necessary, to separate the new divisions.

4. Trim back any dead or broken roots and remove the leafless back bulbs.

5. Prepare suitable pots with drainage material, and pot up in the usual way (see previous page). Each pot should be large enough to allow for one year's growth. Mist spray regularly until new growth appears.

Dividing monopodials

These are not as easy to propagate as sympodial orchids with their pseudobulbs. But sometimes monopodials produce offsets — known as keiki — round the base of the plant which can be separated from the parent. When these plantlets have developed roots they can be pulled away when you're repotting. Pot up each division separately into a $3\frac{1}{2}$in (9cm) pot of the usual compost, and keep on the dry side for the next two weeks or so to give the roots a chance to become established. Mist spray regularly, until you can see signs of new growth.

Growing plants in water

Although hydroponic houseplants are not very common, they provide an interesting conversation piece as well as a novel technique of indoor gardening which is quite different from that of conventional plant care. The advantages of this approach over orthodox methods are that it saves time and space, is less messy, and makes holiday watering much less of a problem.

Hydroponics, also known as hydroculture, is a method of growing plants in a solution of water and fertiliser rather than potting compost, which is why hydroponics is often referred to as 'soilless' cultivation. The roots are actually submerged, either partially or completely, while the plant is anchored in its pot by granules of expanded clay aggregate which are manufactured expressly for hydroponic culture.

Hydroponic plants have been specially raised to adapt their root structure to this method of cultivation. One of the most surprising things is that a plant that would normally die of root rot if it were standing in waterlogged compost will actually thrive when grown hydroponically, in spite of the fact that its roots are totally submerged in water.

The key to success
The most important thing in hydroponics is to make sure that the correct level of water is maintained. For this you'll need a special hydroponic pot with a built-in gauge which indicates the maximum and minimum water level, or you can buy a separate gauge in which a marker keeps pace with the fluctuating water level, thanks to the action of an inbuilt 'fishing float'. Alternatively, you can mark the maximum water level on the side of the container. This is usually a depth of about 2-4in (5-10cm).

Surprisingly enough, it is actually possible to overwater a hydroponic plant if you keep on topping up the water to the maximum level, as the water may become foul, airless and full of dissolved toxic gases as opposed to

oxygen. This can cause serious damage to the roots which can, in turn, lead to the plant's death. It is preferable, therefore, to allow the water level to drop to minimum before topping it up again to maximum, so that the water always remains fresh and healthy.

Secondly, it is important to maintain an acceptable nutrient balance. Hydroponic plants can be fed either with a specially formulated solution for hydroponic use, which contains all the nutrients the plant will need, or with a slow-release food which may come in solid pill or powder form and releases nutrients over a prolonged period of about six months. Failing this, you could use an all-purpose fertiliser such as Phostrogen, as long as you follow the manufacturer's instructions.

And finally, it is also important to avoid very low temperatures. Although hydroponic plants often grow better than compost-grown ones, they can be surprisingly sensitive to the cold. Never let the temperature fall below 45°F (7°C).

Repotting
If all goes according to plan, your plants will, in time, thrive and grow until they need to be repotted. This will not need to be done as often as with conventional compost-grown plants because hydroponic root systems are much more compact than those of compost-grown specimens. Furthermore, there is no danger of the growing medium becoming nutritionally exhausted if nutrients are regularly added to the water in which the plant is growing; any depletion can simply be corrected by adding more fertiliser as required. To prolong a plant's stay in the same pot, it is also a good idea to siphon off or pour out all the solution and replace it with fresh water and fertiliser, preferably once a year.

Annual repotting is therefore unnecessary. You need to repot only when a plant begins to look uncomfortably large in its container or when it becomes top-heavy and needs a larger container to give it increased stability.

Suitable plants

There is a wide range of houseplants that may be grown hydroponically. These include:

Coleus	**Maranta**
Croton	**Monstera**
Dieffenbachia	**Palms**
Dracaena (as	**Papyrus**
shown above)	**Philodendron**
Ferns	**Sansevieria**
Ficus	**Schefflera**
Hedera	**Tradescantia**

Plants to be avoided include all those with very soft succulent tissue, such as *Begonia rex* and African Violet (*Saintpaulia*), as these do not respond well to hydroponic cultivation.

Choose a watertight container made of plastic or any other material which will neither affect the nutrient solution, nor be itself adversely affected by it. Metal containers, such as those made of copper, for example, are quite unsuitable unless they have been coated with an epoxy resin. The new container need not necessarily be any deeper than the previous one but it should certainly be broader in order to provide greater stability for the plant.

The actual process of repotting is very simple. First gently remove the plant from its old container, taking particular care not to damage the roots. This usually involves removing some of the aggregate in order that the plant may be extracted more readily. You may find that the plant is in fact growing in another, smaller, internal plastic mesh

To convert a compost-grown plant, you need a bowl in which to soak the root-ball, watertight container, water gauge, fertiliser and granules of clay aggregate.

Remove the plant from its pot and soak the roots in tepid water to remove all the potting compost. Place on top of a layer of aggregate alongside the water gauge.

Add more aggregate and water until the water gauge is at maximum.

Enclose the plant in a polythene bag for the first three or four weeks.

pot inside. If so, don't remove this internal pot as you would be bound to damage the roots if you did.

Now cover the bottom of the new container with sufficient aggregate to raise the plant to a similar level as before. To help to ensure that the solution remains clean and healthy, it is probably worth rinsing the aggregate before re-using it. Place the plant on top of the new layer of aggregate and spread the roots out gently. Add more clean aggregate to hold the plant firmly in position. Continue gradually adding aggregate, tapping the container from time to time in order to settle it, until the container is full.

Finally, pour in enough water and fertiliser to fill the bottom third of the container. The roots of the plant will soon explore their new home and adapt to their new environment.

The conversion process

Plants that have been grown conventionally in compost can be adapted to hydroponic cultivation, providing that you take great care and treat the plant with respect. It is not advisable to try to convert too large a plant, as the chances are that it will be too well established to take kindly to change. Start by converting smaller plants of around 12in (30cm) or less before trying your luck with larger specimens, and it is certainly not worth risking a rare or precious plant.

Remove the plant from its pot and submerge the root-ball in tepid water. The roots should then be gently teased apart to remove all the potting compost. Rinse the roots under tepid, slowly running water to remove every possible trace of compost as any compost remaining on the roots may contaminate the nutrient solution.

When the roots have been gently but thoroughly cleaned, pot up the plant into its hydroponic container and keep it at an even temperature of around 68°F (20°C). To conserve moisture, it is worth enclosing the plant in a polythene bag for the first three or four weeks, which are critical to its survival.

Eventually, when the plant seems to be growing normally and is showing no signs of limpness, you can take it that it has recovered from the shock and remove the polythene bag. It may be worth acclimatising the plant gradually to its new conditions by taking the bag away for a few hours each day before removing it permanently.

Keeping up humidity

Most houseplants come from the tropics where they thrive under conditions that the average human finds almost intolerable. It's not just the heat, it's also the humidity — the amount of water vapour in the air — that counts. When the surrounding air becomes too dry, plants begin to shrivel up.

Plants need a moist environment if they aren't to lose too much water from their leaves. Tiny pores (stomata) open to let in vital gases, but at the same time this allows precious water to escape. It's a process known as transpiration. The more water-laden the surrounding air, the less able it is to accept additional moisture from the plants — so the less water they lose.

Cold air holds only a little water vapour before becoming 'saturated'. On an average winter day, the air is usually moist. Indeed it can be so dense with water vapour that you actually see the moisture hanging in the air, as fog.

As the air warms up, its capacity to hold water vapour increases. It needs more moisture to achieve the same degree of humidity or saturation. In the morning, before the

heating system or sunshine has warmed it, a room at a temperature of, say, 50°F (10°C) may be quite humid enough for plants. But, by the time the room is at a respectable 70°F (21°C), it will need twice the amount of water in the atmosphere to achieve the same effect.

Measuring humidity

It's an astonishing fact that a centrally heated room may be drier than the Sahara Desert, when measured on the RH scale. This scale measures 'relative humidity' from 0% (completely dry air) to 100% (completely saturated with moisture). The driest part of the earth, where scarcely any plant life survives, registers only 10%. Many deserts — large parts of Australia, for instance — have an RH value of 20-30%, while on a summer's day in England, the relative humidity will be around 40-50%. At the top end of the scale, humidity in a tropical forest can range from 60-100%.

Plants may enjoy a high humidity, but, on the whole, humans don't. The

happy compromise is an RH of between 60-80%, although some plants can put up with a minimum of 40%. You can easily measure the amount of moisture in the air by using one of the inexpensive humidity meters, or hygrometers. This will save you a lot of guesswork when it comes to meeting your plant's moisture needs.

Broadly-speaking, plants fall into three distinct groups: those that need dryish air, those needing moderately humid air and those which prefer a very high humidity. As a general rule, the thinner and more papery the leaf, the higher its moisture requirements.

On page 475 you will find a humidity table which groups some of the most popular houseplants. The majority of houseplants, especially foliage plants, fall into the second category. Most will thrive in normal warm living rooms, provided the air is kept sufficiently moist around them.

For the desert cacti and succulents that need relatively dry air, you may not have to provide any extra moisture. No plant will grow in completely dry air, but it's safe to say that none of your rooms will be entirely free of moisture. These plants need an RH of only 35%.

Stand pots together on a gravel tray, but not too close, to create a micro climate. Or double plant a pot to increase humidity.

Useful tips

Strange as it may sound, a fish tank fitted with a fluorescent light in its cover provides a guaranteed method of cultivating the most delicate tropical plants — better than a conventional bottle garden or terrarium: Since the compost at the bottom doesn't dry out very quickly, it's really easy to maintain. And it makes a stunning room feature.

Because the cover is removable, the plants can be sprayed as often as necessary, and if it's kept in a warm room, the atmosphere inside will be very humid.

At the other extreme, it's going to be hard to maintain the kind of conditions that plants in the 'high humidity' category flourish in — but not impossible. Give moisture lovers like Angel's Wings (Caladium) a start by putting them in the bathroom or kitchen — both become pretty humid when in use. Then boost the levels, by providing extra humidity locally. You could well achieve tropical rain forest conditions!

Providing humidity

Because we heat our homes in the winter, creating a moist environment is an all-year-round concern. There's nothing quite like central heating for drying out the air. But whatever the source of heat — whether it be fires, convection heaters or sunshine — the warmer the room, the more attention you need to pay to the atmosphere.

The easiest way to increase the moisture in the air is to provide a constant rate of water evaporation. Bowls of water dotted around the room are simple, effective ways of releasing water vapour into the air.

Humidifiers, which can be clipped on to radiators, work on the same principle. Or you could treat yourself to a free-standing electric humidifier. This works like an electric fan, blowing air over a permanent reservoir of water and vaporising it over a period of hours to create a constant, high humidity. Some are self-adjusting and will turn themselves off and on as required.

All these methods increase the humidity of the air in the room as a whole. But you need to be able to take account of the needs of individual plants as well as your own needs — and many will want a moister environment than you find comfortable. The answer is to provide humidity locally.

Gravel trays

Justifiably popular, gravel trays are a good way of creating a local climate around your plants. Any shallow, plastic, waterproof container will do. Fill it, to a depth of 2in (5cm), or so, with gravel, pebbles or a horticultural aggregate like Hortag. Make sure the granules aren't more than ½in (13mm) in diameter.

Add enough water to reach the top of the gravel, but not to cover it, and place the plant pots on top. Don't allow the pots to stand in water; if the compost in the pots becomes waterlogged, the roots will rot. Top the water up regularly.

Use a container whose width is equal to the spread of the plant, if you can; as the water evaporates, all the leaves will benefit from this vapour 'bath'.

This method is especially good for plants standing above or close to a radiator; the gravel tray has the additional benefit of deflecting the heat away from them. But beware, the trays will dry out more quickly too.

Plunging pots

Plunging pots up to their rims in peat (or Hortag) is a highly recommended way of providing humidity. Just choose a container big enough to leave a large gap all around the plant pot — an ornamental pot holder is perfect for a single, specimen plant. Pack a good, thick layer of peat between pot and container — all around it, as well as underneath. The bigger the outer pot, the better. It works particularly well if the outer container is wide enough to provide a moist surface of peat beneath the spreading leaves. The medium should be kept moist, but not absolutely waterlogged.

Double-planting, as this is also called, has other advantages. It provides a reserve of moisture below the pot, and also insulates the plants' roots, protecting them from sudden temperature changes, keeping them cool in summer and warm in winter.

Creating a micro-climate

Plants always seem to grow much better in groups than in isolation. When close together, they create a micro-climate of their own; the water vapour each transpires tends to be trapped in the foliage instead of being dispersed.

You can stand a number of plants together on a gravel tray, but a group

Danger signs

Your plants will give you clear signals if they don't have a sufficiently moist atmosphere around them. The leaves will dry up and shrivel. Or they may turn brown at the edges, making the plants look very unsightly. Flowers and buds may drop, foliage will lack its customary lushness and growth will be altogether poor. Your plants will take on a distinctly jaded air. Take action straight away!

In hot, dry weather mist spray daily; the best time is early morning, and never spray in direct sunlight.

Humidity guide

Plants for dry environments (RH: 35-40%)

Bead Plant (Nertera)
Cigar Plant (Cuphea), *far left above*
Desert cacti and succulents
Dwarf pot Chrysanthemum, *left above*
Geranium (Pelargonium), *far left below*
Ground Ivy (Glecoma)
Hippeastrum
Jacob's Ladder (Pedilanthus)
Japanese Aralia (Fatsia)
Mother-in-Law's Tongue (Sansevieria)
Oleander (Nerium), *left below*
Ornamental Pepper (Capsicum)

Plants for moderate humidity (RH: about 60%)

Asparagus Fern
Begonia (particularly the foliage kinds), *far left above*
Bromeliads, *left above*
Cordyline
Croton (Codiaeum)
Dracaena
Dumb Cane (Dieffenbachia)
Ferns
Forest Cacti (e.g. Christmas Cactus and Orchid Cactus), *far left below*
Palms
Peperomia, *left below*
Philodendron
Prayer Plant (Maranta)
Rubber Plant and **Fig** (Ficus)
Swiss Cheese Plant (Monstera)

Plants for very high humidity (RH: minimum 80%)

African Violet (Saintpaulia), *far left above*
Angel's Wings (Caladium)
Flame Violet (Episcia)
Net Plant (Fittonia), *left above*
Selaginella, *far left below*
Sinningia, *left below*
Sonerila

planting with pots sunk in peat is probably the best way of creating and maintaining a humid environment. The plants can be arranged attractively together in large planters, or you can plant them in a deep trough.

One word of warning. Occasionally, this can produce too moist an environment, especially if the plants are overcrowded. The tell-tale signs are patches of grey mould — or even rot — on the leaves or stems, or flowers covered in grey mould.

Spraying plants

A fine mist spray of water, from an atomiser gun, may be enough to keep the air around your plants moist enough. But the effects of spraying are short-lived and you may find it tedious work having to spray once and often twice a day. During the hotter months, you will probably have to use other methods as well.

Spraying has another drawback. It's important to spray all around the plants, and, however careful you are, this may damage wallcoverings or furnishings unless you're prepared to move your plants before spraying them.

On the credit side, mist spraying keeps leaves clean, and the coating of small droplets has a cooling effect on hot sunny days, It also discourages red spider mite, one of the houseplants' scourges.

Spray in the cool of the morning, before the atmsophere warms up, so that the foliage dries off before the evening. Never spray in direct sunlight, the small droplets will magnify the rays of the sun and brown scorch marks will appear on the leaves. Use tepid water, preferably from a rain butt. Tap water in many homes is hard, and this may leave a white, chalky deposit on the leaves. Should this happen, sponge off the deposit with tepid rainwater.

Don't spray plants with hairy or woolly leaves — the African Violet (Saintpaulia), for instance. Beads of water will be trapped and may cause the leaves to rot.

It's probably a good idea to rely on one of the other methods, and to reserve the mist spray for boosting humidity during the hotter months of the year. Don't be surprised if you end up using all the methods described here, one way or another. Different plants, and different conditions, will always demand a variety of solutions.

Planting a hanging basket

There is no doubt about it — hanging baskets are fast catching on as the latest craze in gardening. And they are not just for outdoors: indoors, too, they are an eye-catching way to make the most of a limited space.

But although a good selection of ready-planted baskets is available from garden centres and nurseries, the range is often limited and the prices can be high. So why not buy containers and plants separately and assemble your own hanging baskets at home? In this way, you will not only get better value for money, you will also have a much wider choice of materials, and you will end up with exactly what you wanted all along, rather than having to 'make do' with somebody else's ideas. And, contrary to popular belief, making up hanging baskets is not at all difficult. Suitable plants will be covered later in Volume 12 ('Hanging gardens', page 706), so now let us look at the baskets.

Types of basket

The range of baskets on the market nowadays is quite extensive, and separate types are available for indoor and outdoor use. The indoor kinds are generally smaller and narrower so as to allow them to be hung in a window without blocking out all the light, and they are also usually more ornamental than outdoor kinds. Baskets that are intended to be hung outdoors are much wider and need more space in which to hang, and they may also drip, so avoid using them anywhere where the floor covering will not withstand splashes.

Hanging containers for indoors. You can often choose container and hanger separately, the most common containers being ceramic and basketware, while the best-known hangers are probably macramé. Plastic flower pots, which come in a range of bright colours, are also available with clip-on hooks and drip trays to convert them into inexpensive hanging pots.

Personalised containers. If you want something a little more out of the ordinary to use indoors or in the conservatory, why not try inventing your own

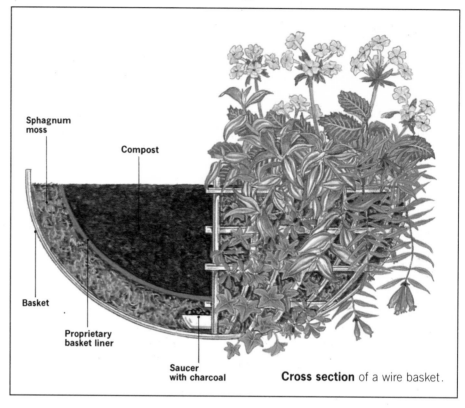

Sphagnum moss

Compost

Basket

Proprietary basket liner

Saucer with charcoal

Cross section of a wire basket.

containers? You can easily adapt pots or jars from junk shops by drilling holes near the top to take picture wires, or by sitting them in macramé hangers.

Alternatively, you can simply look for your containers in slightly different places from everyone else. Orchid growers, for instance, often use slatted wooden baskets, which are also eminently suitable for trailing ferns or other jungle-style plants, though this does mean that they need lining.

Traditional wire baskets. The best-known kind of hanging basket is made of wire mesh. This needs to be lined before use. In the past, moss was always used, but this is not always easy to obtain nowadays. Wire baskets dry out very quickly and can be difficult to re-wet without dripping rather badly, which really restricts their use to outdoors or to rooms with water resistant flooring. They do, however, look most attractive, as their open mesh structure allows you to plant through the sides and base of the basket as well as into the top. A polythene lining will help stem the dripping but this doesn't look nearly

so nice as moss. A good compromise is to use both: a thin layer of moss first, and then plastic sheeting. The plastic should always be pierced with a few holes in the side to draw off surplus moisture after watering and to keep the sphagnum moss moist. Alternatively, you can use a special-purpose basket liner, again inside a layer moss.

Modern plastic hanging baskets are more practical, if not so pleasing to the eye. They incorporate their own drip trays which makes watering very much easier and less messy. Some of the newest designs also feature a series of 'pockets' let into the sides, which allow you to plant them up in the style of an old-fashioned hanging basket.

There are also some pre-formed peat basket shapes with hanging chains attached. These, however, are best regarded as temporary baskets, good for one season only, as the peat will soon disintegrate once it has been kept moist for any length of time.

Designing your basket

Not all hanging containers are designed for you to plant directly into them.

1. To make up a traditional hanging basket, first line the base with a layer of damp sphagnum moss.

2. Add more moss and arrange it carefully around the sides of the container, right to the top of the wirework frame. For using indoors, place a saucer filled with charcoal at the base of the basket in order to catch any drips.

3. Lining complete, you can then follow with a proprietary basket liner or a sheet of perforated plastic.

4. Prepare your compost — adding a water holding gel will cut down on watering — and fill your basket.

5. Insert each plant firmly in position, making sure that there are no air pockets around the roots.

6. Arrange the accent colours with care and leave space around the plants to allow for growth. Make sure that all the plants are firmly in place and trim any excess sphagnum moss to neaten the basket.

7. When planting is completed hang up the basket — preferably at eye level for easy maintenance. The arrangement will look a little sparse to begin with until the plants become established and fill the gaps.

Lipstick Vine — the perfect subject for a hanging basket.

Watering

Traditional hanging baskets tend to dry out faster than conventional pots, so check them daily in very warm weather. This is particularly important when a basket is packed full of plants and flowering vigorously. If you can't reach up to water it, use one of those special gadgets which are sold for watering outdoor hanging baskets, or use a well rinsed-out washing-up bottle. If a porous or wire basket gets very dry, the best way to water it is to lift it down and soak it in a bucket for half an hour. Leave it to drain completely before putting it back in position.

And finally, don't forget to feed your hanging baskets. Stick in two or three houseplant fertiliser spikes per basket a few weeks after planting, and renew them after a couple of months — this should see you through the season.

Compost

There is no special-purpose compost for use in hanging baskets: simply use the same as you would normally use for a particular plant. A peat-based compost holds moisture better than a light sandy type and is ideal for the majority of plants, including the Easter, Christmas and Orchid Cactus. Adding a water holding gel, such as Hydrostock, to the compost while assembling the basket will greatly increase its moisture holding capacity and will considerably reduce the need to water your plants.

Other trailing cacti and succulents, however, require special cactus compost, while orchids need special orchid compost. Both are available ready-mixed from garden centres.

Some of the indoor kinds are meant to take a single plant in a pot, which rather limits your creativity.

As a practical point, though, check first that the container is watertight. If not, put a bowl or saucer in the bottom of it and stand your plant in that to prevent leaks when watering; or, if there is not room to do that, you should at least slip the bottom half of the pot into a plastic bag.

Other containers are designed to be filled with compost, and then planted into directly. Where space permits, a group of plants usually looks better than a single one. Plant several of the same variety to give the impression of a large specimen, or choose a selection of different plants, making sure they all have similar needs in terms of watering, light, and so on.

When you have filled your container with compost, stand the plants in roughly the same position as you intend to plant them, just to see how they look. And, if the basket is likely to be seen mostly from one side, make sure that each plant is turned so as to put its best side forward.

Re-arrange your plants until you are happy with the result — then go ahead and plant. Stand the basket on a bucket while filling it. If plants are growing in plastic pots, knock them out of their containers, taking care not to damage their roots. If they are badly pot-bound, gently tease a few roots out from the base of the root-ball before planting. Plants that have been grown in peat pots should not be removed from their pots: simply plant them pot and all.

Always ensure that plants are set no deeper than they were when growing in their pots. And, after planting, firm the plants in lightly, and give the basket a thorough watering.

Giving support

Most of our houseplants support themselves perfectly well without any human assistance, but some — particularly climbers and straight-stemmed plants such as the Rubber Plant — do need a little help.

If climbers were not supported, they would sprawl all over the place. In fact, with some of them this is a perfectly natural habit but an inconvenient one, to say the least, in the home. That said, some climbers can be grown quite successfully as trailing plants in hanging containers or in pots on a shelf or windowsill — examples being the Goose Foot Plant (Syngonium), Asparagus Fern (*Asparagus setaceus*), Kangaroo Vine (*Cissus antarctica*), Grape Ivy (*C.rhombifolia*) and ordinary Ivies (Hedera).

As for many tall, straight-stemmed plants, if these are not supported their stems will develop kinks and bends. Some people might find this acceptable, but most prefer their Rubber Plants, for example, to have nice straight stems.

Useful tips: I

As you get to know your houseplants you will discover that twining climbers such as Stephanotis and Jasmine — i.e. those which wrap their stems around the supports as they grow — twine either in a clockwise or in an anti-clockwise direction. Loosely tie in the tops of the stems and watch the way in which they want to twine, then train them in that direction. If you train them in the wrong direction, they will simply unwind themselves again!

To avoid root damage, supports are best inserted when potting. This is not always possible, however, as in the case of twiggy sticks and split canes for bulbs, for example, or when the plant has outgrown its original support. Supports should always reach the bottom of the pot.

Stephanotis can be made to twine straight up a single cane or round a wire hoop.

Types of support

There are various ways in which house-plants can be supported — the humble bamboo cane being just one very rudimentary example, and probably the least attractive.

Moss poles. A moss-covered pole is an attractive method of supporting climbing plants which produce aerial roots from their stems. Examples of such plants include the Swiss Cheese Plant (*Monstera deliciosa*), climbing varieties of Philodendron, and Devil's Ivy (*Scindapsus aureus*). Provided the moss is kept moist, the roots will penetrate into it and the plant will therefore support itself.

You can either buy a moss pole from a garden centre, or you may prefer to make your own, which is very easy to do. First of all, you need a broom handle, of the eventual height to which you want the plant to grow. Ideally, a moss pole of the correct height should be inserted when you are potting the plant because the pole is difficult to replace once it is installed and stems have rooted into it, so do think carefully about the eventual height of your plant.

Make sure that the broom handle is long enough to reach the bottom of the pot. Lay out a sheet of ½in (13mm) wire netting on a flat surface and cover it with a 1-2in (2.5-5cm) layer of moss. Then place the broom handle on top of this and roll the whole thing up, securing the edges together with wire.

A refinement is to place a suitably sized plastic pot in the top of the moss pole — with the base resting on top of the broom handle and the rim level with the wire netting, so that it is virtually hidden from view. This device is handy for keeping the moss permanently moist, which is essential if the stems are to root into it. When water is poured into the pot, it trickles down through the moss. Another way of moistening the moss is to mist spray.

Finally, insert your plant in the pot and loosely tie the stems to the pole using soft string.

Wire netting cylinder. A simple cylinder of small-mesh wire netting makes a good support for Ivies. Make up a netting cylinder about half the diameter of a large pot, insert it in the pot and plant three or four young Ivies around it. They will cling to it and soon grow into a thick 'column' of foliage. The cylinder may need to be supported by a few bamboo canes inserted inside it.

A moss pole makes an ideal support for Philodendron with its aerial roots.

Wire hoops. These make ideal supports for some flowering climbers, such as the Paper Flower (Bougainvillea), Wax Plant (Hoya), Madagascar Jasmine (Stephanotis) and Jasmine (Jasminum). It has been noticed that these plants all flower much more freely if their stems are trained in circular fashion rather than straight up.

Wire hoops are easy to make. All you need is a length of thick, heavy-duty, galvanised or plastic-coated wire. Bend this into a hoop, with the two ends acting as supporting 'legs' by being inserted right down to the bottom of the pot.

DIY trellis. It is easy to make your own trellis for climbing plants, including any of those mentioned above as well as Kangaroo Vine, Grape Ivy, ordinary Ivies and Asparagus Fern. Several bamboo canes can be tied together, with some upright and some cross pieces, to form a fan shape.

Pot trellis. If you do not want to construct your own trellis, you can buy a ready-made pot trellis, which comes in various shapes and sizes and is simply pushed into the pot. It is usually made from plastic-coated steel. It is not available in very large sizes, so is recommended only for small climbing plants — such as Asparagus Fern — and Ivies which can be cut back if necessary.

Wall trellis. Really large, heavy climbing plants — such as the Swiss Cheese Plant and Philodendrons — are sometimes trained against trellis panels mounted on the wall. Suitable panels for indoor use are made of plastic-coated

steel and usually come in white. They are available in various shapes and sizes, and are generally supplied with suitable fixing brackets.

Single bamboo cane. A single, thick bamboo cane is an adequate support for tall, straight-stemmed houseplants like the Rubber Plant (*Ficus elastica*), Fiddle-leaf Fig (*Ficus lyrata*) and Dracaenas. Such plants should be supported from an early age.

Split cane. Thin canes, varying in length from 1-2ft (30-60cm), are useful for supporting very small plants and also for bulbs such as Hyacinths. With large-flowered Hyacinths, for example, each stem needs a split cane to support the heavy flower head, and this should be placed just behind the stem.

Twiggy sticks. A good way to support Freesias is to push in branched sticks, known as twiggy sticks, between them before they become too tall. The stems will then grow up through them and be well supported. The sticks could be a bit shorter than the flowering height of the plants.

Tying in

Plants need to be tied into their recommended supports and for this you can use soft green garden string, fine plastic coated wire, or raffia. The latter is a cream-coloured natural product.

Plants are tied in by looping the wire in a loose figure-of-eight around both stem and support (see figure 5) — when using softer ties, make a second figure-of-eight instead of a loop. Never tie in stems tightly — they must have room to thicken. A tight cane can kink or cut into the stem, and can even kill off the part above the knot. Split wire rings are also useful for tying in thin-stemmed plants, as are those paper-covered white ties, the ends of which are simply twisted together to form a loop around both stem and support.

Ways to support your plants

1. A wire hoop is ideal for supporting the twining Stephanotis — it produces many more flowers if trained in a circular fashion rather than straight up.

2. Ready-made pot trellis comes in various shapes and is ideal for small climbing plants, or climbers such as Ivy which can be cut back as much as needed.

3. When making a moss pole the moss should be flush with one long edge of the netting and fall short on the other to allow for the join. Also leave room at the top for a small pot **(3a)**. Secure the edges of the moss pole and plant it **(3b)**. Tie your plant loosely to the pole **(3c)**, and place a small flower pot into the top of the cylinder **(3d)**.

4. A DIY trellis made from bamboo cane is attractive and easy to make.

5. Tall straight-stemmed plants, such as the Fiddle-leaf Fig, need supporting at an early age. Use a thick cane support and tie in the plant at intervals with plastic coated wire **(5a)** making a figure-of-eight as shown **(5b,c, d)**.

Encouraging a plant to flower

An Azalea, *right*, with its buds beginning to open and, *below right*, in full flower.

It is terribly disappointing when a much-loved houseplant fails to flower. However this is more likely to be your fault than the plant's — you may be doing something wrong by failing to supply some vital requirement that your plant needs to develop flower buds. But don't worry, it's very easy to solve this problem of lack of flowers by taking a few simple cultural steps.

Sometimes a particular plant won't flower despite all your loving care and attention throughout the year. If this happens ask yourself the following questions.

Is my plant getting enough light?
Flowering houseplants are essentially windowsill plants; they need maximum light all year, but especially when buds are developing and when the plant is in bloom. If you suspect your plant isn't getting enough light, move it to a bright position shaded from direct sun.

Cacti and Succulents from the dry areas of the world are often reluctant to flower and won't do so at all without plenty of sunlight. Don't keep them anywhere but in the brightest light and in as much direct sun as possible.

One solution to the light problem is to supply artificial light. You can use fluorescent tubes or special growing bulbs or lamps; these are similar to ordinary light bulbs but they transmit light in the frequencies that plants use for growing. African Violets respond well to this treatment but you need to give them between 16 and 18 hours of artificial light a day to make them flower.

Am I feeding my plant correctly?
Many plants need a boost of fertiliser before they can start to form flower buds. Potash is particularly important as it helps plants to form buds and flowers. The other major plant foods, nitrogen and phosphorus, are also needed but in much smaller amounts.

During the growing season — from early spring until early autumn — water your flowering houseplants every two weeks with a liquid fertiliser containing a high proportion of potash. Most of the houseplant fertilisers and Phostrogen are fine for this.

Cacti and Succulents, despite popular belief, need regular feeding with a special Cactus fertiliser, such as Cactigrow, to encourage them to flower.

Is my plant's pot too big?
Some plants need to have their roots fairly cramped before they stop growing roots and start producing flowers. Three popular prime examples are Geraniums, African Violets and Clivia. So if you suspect the pot your plant is in is too big for it, repot the plant in spring or summer into a pot only about 1in (25mm) larger all round than the actual rootball of the plant.

Is my plant too young?
Azalea, Anthurium and Clivia, among others, need to be reasonably large and mature before they can produce flowers; the plant's priority is to grow a good root system first to give it the strength to develop flowers.

Some plants, such as the Shrimp Plant, Cigar Plant and Busy Lizzie, only produce a lot of flowers when they are a nice bushy shape with lots of stems for the flowers to appear on. Pinch out the growing tips when the plant is small.

Do the flower buds drop?
Sometimes plants form flower buds that drop before they open. The Christmas and Easter Cactus are especially notorious for this. With these two plants it's lack of light that causes flower drop; the buds twist themselves off the stems in an attempt to reach the light. Keep your plant in a bright window with the buds facing the light.

Growing herbs for the kitchen

The enjoyment of herbs is nothing new — many Elizabethan houses kept a herb garden for both culinary and medical purposes — but an increased use of herbs in our cooking has become an important aspect of the general trend towards healthier eating. Now that the medical profession is encouraging us to cut down on salt and fat, both of which add flavour to food, herbs are really coming into their own. It isn't always easy, however, to get hold of fresh herbs and those little tubs of dried herbs on supermarket shelves are often stale and musty. So, if you enjoy eating, the answer has to be ... grow your own!

The container herb garden

Don't think you need acres of ground to start a herb garden or even, for that matter, a balcony — there's always the kitchen windowsill to take flower pots or a window-box. As a rule, herbs have no objection to being grown in small spaces and some — like mint, for example — are actually better for having their roots restricted.

What you grow in your container herb garden is obviously going to depend on the amount of space you have available. An average windowsill will hold four or five pots or a reasonable-sized trough. If you plant several herbs together in the same container take account of the eventual sizes of full-grown plants, and avoid planting herbs with different needs together. For example, Thyme isn't a good companion for Basil since the former likes a drier compost.

Although herbs need regular watering, good drainage is equally important. So put a layer of crocks at the bottom of your containers before filling them with John Innes No 1 potting compost for small to medium-sized herbs, and No 2 for larger plants. In general, herbs do not require — or like — feeding.

What to grow where

Like everything else, herbs thrive best in conditions that suit them. Some, for example, need a place in full sun, whereas others are happiest in a shady or semi-shaded position. Take stock of the direction in which your balcony or windowsill faces — south or west is ideal for most plants — and work out how much sunlight or shadow your plants can expect. Basil, Coriander and Rosemary are fanatical sun lovers, for example, while Dill, Sage, Summer Savory, Tarragon and Thyme prefer a

Parsley is often treated as an annual.

Lemon balm has a lemony fragrance.

Borage flowers throughout the summer.

Fennel grows to 4ft (1.2m) or more.

warm, sheltered spot that is not in constant direct sun. And Borage, Chervil, Chives, Fennel, Lemon Balm, Mint and Parsley are all happiest in shade or partial shade.

Fresh herbs through the winter

There are many herbs that can be grown indoors in winter. They won't flourish as vigorously as in the summer months but you should be able to rely on a constant supply until the spring. The warm, humid atmosphere of the kitchen suits some plants very well — put them in pots or troughs that fit your windowsill to ensure that they get the maximum amount of available daylight.

Herbs that shouldn't object too much to wintering indoors are Pot Marjoram, Rosemary and Thyme. And you could sow a fresh pot of Parsley during the summer specially for your winter windowsill.

One way of ensuring a winter supply of Chives is to lift a clump that is growing outside in the open soil in, say,

November, and force it back to growth again in the heat indoors. Then, when your outdoors Chives come up again in the spring, take the indoor clump back out, plant it in open soil and allow it to rest for a while.

Which herbs?

Basic herbs for the kitchen include perennials such as Chives, French Tarragon, Mint, Pot Marjoram, Rosemary, Sage and Thyme; and annuals such as Basil, Chervil and Parsley.

More unusual herbs include Coriander, sometimes known as Chinese Parsley, which is flat-leaved with a pungent, distinctive flavour; Lemon Balm and Borage, both of which are easy to grow and add a delightful, refreshing flavour to summer drinks; Lovage, which is also easy to grow and has sharp-toothed leaves with a flavour reminiscent of celery; and Summer Savory, which strongly resembles Thyme in flavour and is a tasty addition to your soups and pasta dishes.

Fennel

Rosemary

Hints on cultivation

Borage (*Borago officinalis*)
Annual. Sow in March or April directly into pots or window-boxes. Thin plants at four-leaf stage. Use leaves and flowers as desired. Grows vigorously to 3ft (90cm).

Chervil (*Anthriscus cerefolium*)
Biennial treated as an annual. Sow in March and thin out your plants. Snip lightly and, if plants are snipped near the root six to eight weeks after sowing, they will give a second crop. Water well. Eventual height 18in (45cm).

Chives (*Allium schoenoprasum*)
Perennial. Sow in March or April and thin young plants to groups of four to six seedlings. Use shoots when young, cutting close to the base, otherwise they can be tough. Remove flowers to encourage leaf growth. If kept frost-free, they can produce new growth throughout the winter. Eventual height 8-12in (20-30cm).

Coriander (*Coriandrum sativum*)
Annual. Plant seeds in March and thin young plants to 6in (15cm) apart. Pinching out is not necessary. Snip lightly. Water well. A second sowing can be made in July. Eventual height 12-15in (30-38cm).

Dill (*Anethum graveolens*)
Annual. Sow in March or April in permanent position. Does not like to be transplanted. Snip as desired. Sow again in July for a winter supply. Harvest the seed heads and spread them across a sheet of paper where they can be left to dry naturally. When they are dry, shake off the seeds and store in an airtight jar. Eventual height 3ft (90cm).

Fennel (*Foeniculum vulgare*)
Perennial. Sow in pinches in April and thin to strongest seedling in each cluster. Snip as desired and pinch out the flowering stems unless the seeds are required, in which case you can proceed as for Dill. Cut down almost to base in winter, and keep cool and dry until spring. Eventual height up to 4ft (1.2m), so plants need staking.

Lemon Balm (*Melissa officinalis*)
Perennial. Sow in April or May and transplant seedlings in late summer. Snip as desired and cut down to about 2in (5cm) from base in winter, when you should keep just moist and warm. Eventual height 18-24in (45-60cm).

Lovage (*Ligusticum scoticum*)
Perennial. Buy a small plant or sow in March or April and control growth by cutting back. Snip as desired. Cut back in autumn and repot in spring or grow afresh. A strong vigorous plant, it can reach an eventual height of 6ft (1.8m).

Mint (*Mentha*)
Perennial. Many different varieties. Buy a small clump and plant in damp soil in early spring. Keep roots under control by growing in confined space. Snip as desired. Dies down in winter and will come up again in spring. Eventual height of about 12in (30cm).

Chives

Sweet Basil

Parsley

Summer Savory

Coriander

Chervil

Parsley (*Carum petroselinum* 'Crispum'*)*
Biennial. Sow thinly in March, preferably in permanent position as Parsley does not like to be transplanted, and pour boiling water over the soil after sowing to aid germination. Seedlings will appear after four to six weeks. Sow again in July for a winter supply. Snip as desired. To maintain as a biennial, remove flowering stems entirely otherwise discard each winter and sow seeds afresh the following spring. Eventual height 12in (30cm).

Pot Marjoram (*Origanum onites*)
Perennial, but best grown as biennial. Sow in clusters in March or April and transplant to pots when seedlings are big enough to handle. Start with 5in (13cm) pots and pot on to 10in (25cm) pots for winter. Snip until end of second season when you can allow it to die. Eventual height 12in (30cm).

Rosemary (*Rosmarinus officinalis*)
Perennial. Grow from cuttings or sow seeds ½in (13mm) deep in March or April. Many seedlings will appear, so give thinnings to friends. Nip back the main stem to encourage side shoots. Keep out of draughts. Snip as desired throughout year. Eventual height 4ft (1.2m).

Sage (*Salvia officinalis*)
Perennial. Grow from cuttings or sow seeds in April — germination takes about three weeks. A vigorous grower but not long-lived, so it is best to grow afresh every three years. Snip as desired until September when leaves lose their vigour and flavour until new growth starts again in spring. Eventual height 18in (45cm).

Summer Savory (*Satureia hortensis*)
Annual. Sow in early April at ½in (13mm) depth and thin out when young seedlings appear. Cut back to 2in (5cm) when flowers appear to encourage regrowth. Eventual height 12-18in (30-45cm).

Sweet Basil (*Ocimum basilicum*)
Annual. Sow in April and space out in boxes at four-leaf stage, then replant three or four to a 7in (18cm) pot when large enough to handle easily. When two sets of proper leaves appear, pinch out the growing point to encourage bushing. Snip leaves and prevent from flowering to encourage leaf growth by taking leaves as often as you can from the top. Basil absorbs and gives off a lot of moisture, so water regularly. Pick it as you need it, but take care that you don't bruise the leaves, which causes them to lose their aromatic oils. Judicious snipping from the top should keep your plant going until December. A second sowing in July or August will give you a winter crop. Eventual height 12-18in (30-45cm).

Tarragon (*Artemisia dracunculus*)
Perennial. There are two varieties of Tarragon — French and Russian — and you should make sure you buy this one, which is French Tarragon, as the other lacks flavour. Sow in April or buy young plants. When plants are established, you can increase by division. Snip lightly from top throughout year. Eventual height 32in (80cm).

Thyme (*Thymus vulgaris*)
Perennial. Sow in April and thin out seedlings when large enough to handle. Pinch out tips at 2in (5cm) to encourage bushiness. Snip as desired thoughout year. Plants should last five years. Eventual height 10-12in (25-30cm).

Sage

Borage

Thyme

Lovage

Tarragon

Dill

Pot Marjoram

Lemon Balm

Mint

101

All about pruning

Many of our houseplants come from tropical rain forests where they are able to run riot — some sprawling all over the place, others reaching enormous heights. Such unrestrained habits can obviously not be allowed in the home and we therefore have to get rid of bare leggy stems , and to encourage plants to make a bushier, neater growth.

Not all houseplants, however, need pruning. Many of the lower-growing perennials, for example — like the Chinese Evergreen (Aglaonema modestrum) and the Cast-iron Plant (Aspidistra) — will never get out of hand. And neither will most of the flowering pot plants such as the Clivia. The very fact that these plants are growing in pots automatically restricts their size to some extent.

Those houseplants that do require some degree of pruning can be divided into two groups. The one requires nothing more drastic than a simple technique known as 'pinching' which encourages a bushy, compact growth and, with some plants, also ensures more flowers. The other group of plants needs to be more severely cut back, either to restrict their size or to produce a neater, more compact growth, and this is generally done before, or as soon as, plants enter their growing season — in

This Black Eyed Susan would benefit from pinching out to give it a more compact shape.

other words, some time in late winter or early spring.

How to 'pinch'

First of all, let us take a look at the simplest form of pruning, which is known as pinching. This involves removing the tender growing tip — i.e. the top $\frac{1}{4}$in-$\frac{1}{2}$in (6-12mm) — from young plants, around 3-6in (8-15cm) in height. Pinching results in the plant diverting its energy into producing shoots lower down the stem, which results in a bushy growth rather than a single stem with a few meagre shoots at the top. In the case of flowering plants you will also find that more flowers are produced, because each side shoot will carry a bloom.

This technique is so-called because the tip of the stem can literally be pinched out between forefinger and thumb. This is not, however, the best method, and can result in a ragged wound. It is far better to use a sharp knife or razor blade.

For a really bushy growth, the resultant side shoots can also be pinched out, when they are about 3in (8cm) long. With flowering plants, however, do not pinch again after the second pinching,

Fuchsias need cutting back after their winter rest.

Geraniums should be pinched out between finger and thumb.

Plants to pinch

Foliage plants

Aluminium Plant (Pilea)
Beefsteak Plant (Iresine)
Croton (Codiaeum)
Flame Nettle (Coleus)
Ivy (Hedera)
Japanese Aralia (Fatsia)
Parasol Plant (Heptapleurum)
Polka Dot Plant (Hypoestes)
Purple Heart (Setcreasea)
Swedish Ivy (Plectranthus)
Trailing Fig and **Rubber Plant** (Ficus)
Velvet Plant (Gynura)
Wandering Jew (Tradescantia and Zebrina)

Flowering plants

Black Eyed Susan (Thunbergia)
Busy Lizzy (Impatiens)
Cigar Flower (Cuphea)
Fuchsia
Geranium (Pelargonium)
Shrimp Plant (Beloperone)

Plants to cut back

This spindly specimen of Hibiscus would have benefited from cutting back.

Regular pruning of this Hibiscus has produced a bushier, neater growth.

Azalea (Rhododendron simsii and R.obtusum): prune in April by cutting back any long shoots by up to half their length.

Begonia Vine (Cissus discolor): cut back the main stems in February or March by half to two-thirds their length, and side shoots to within 2-3in (5-8cm).

Bell Flower (Campanula isophylla): cut the stems back to their base after flowering.

Fuchsia: prune mature plants after their winter rest by cutting back all the previous year's growth to within one or two buds.

Geranium (Pelargonium): cut back all stems or shoots in March by about half their length.

Hibiscus: prune mature plants in February or March by removing all thin spindly shoots and cut back the main stems by half their length.

Jasmine (Jasminum polyanthum): cut back old stems by two-thirds of their length as soon as flowering is over. In summer, pinch out tips of new shoots.

Shrimp plant (Beloperone guttata): this benefits from regular cutting back as well as pinching. Cut back large established plants by half in February or March.

Zebra Plant (Aphelandra squarrosa 'Louisae'): cut back the stems by half as soon as flowering is over.

---

as this would considerably delay flowering. For example, it takes Fuchsias about six weeks to produce flower buds after the second pinching.

How to cut back

When you prune a plant, always make a clean, smooth cut rather than a ragged one, as the former heals over more rapidly, so reducing the risk of disease. Soft-stemmed plants can be pruned with a really sharp gardening knife, say, or with a safety razor blade. Plants with tougher stems, on the other hand, should be pruned with a pair of secateurs. Generally, only lightweight secateurs are ever needed for houseplants.

When you are cutting back a shoot or stem, always make the cut just above a leaf or bud — in other words, just above a leaf-joint or node.

You will find that some plants — like, for example, the Rubber Plant — exude a milky white sap from the pruning cut. You should try to stop this by dusting the cut with powdered charcoal.

Very tall or leggy plants

Most climbers — like the Kangaroo Vine and Grape Ivy (Cissus), Ivy Tree (Fatshedera), Swiss Cheese Plant (Monstera) and Philodendron — can all be cut

back as required in February or March when they threaten to push their way through the ceiling.

Other plants which are inclined to become too tall — such as the Cordyline, Dracaena, Dumb Cane (Dieffenbachia), Japanese Aralia (Fatsia), and Rubber Plant and other Figs (Ficus) — can all be treated in the same way. These plants often become very leggy, with no leaves at the base. When this happens, try cutting the plant back to within 6in (15cm) of the pot, which should result in new bushy growth. As long as the plant is still a reasonably young specimen — say, up to five years old — there is a fairly high chance that it will produce new shoots from dormant buds. The Velvet Plant (Gynura) also tends to become leggy and this too should be cut back in February or March by at least half to two-thirds.

Dead flowers and leaves

Dead flowers should never be left on plants. They can become infected with the fungal disease grey mould (botrytis), which can then spread to healthy parts of the plants, and they also encourage the plant to waste its energy on seed formation. So always pick or cut off dead blooms, removing the stalks as well.

The same applies to dead leaves. These should be cut off cleanly, including the stalks, with a knife or secateurs.

Variegated plants

These sometimes produce a plain green shoot with no variegated markings. Green shoots are more vigorous than variegated ones and should always be cut right out at their point of origin as soon as you notice them, before they have time to swamp the entire plant.

How to plant

Once you've chosen your containers and the plants you want to put in them, the next step is to do the actual planting. The principles for planting in containers are really very like those for planting in pots for the home, but you must take extra care with drainage to prevent your plants getting waterlogged.

Preparing the container

There's an enormous range of patio containers available, large and small, in all shapes and sizes, and in several different kinds of material. Some materials need special preparation before you can plant them up.

● Wood must be painted with several coats of preservative that is non-toxic to plants.

● Metal (including the hoops on wooden barrels) should be treated with a rust-proofing agent – also, of course, non-toxic. It would probably be best to use a plastic liner inside a wholly metal container, since the roots might be damaged by contact with the metal.

● Clay pots, including the beautiful brownish-red terracotta ones, should be soaked for 24 hours before use if they've been kept somewhere dry. Clay is very absorbent, and will take all the moisture out of the soil if it is dry when you start.

● Plastic, concrete, stone and glazed ceramic containers need no preparation at all.

Drainage

If at all possible, your containers should have drainage holes, but you can use undrained pots successfully if you take the right precautions. The main point to remember is that you should provide a substantial amount of drainage material – as much as half the depth of the tub.

Grade the drainage material, starting with a good layer of coarse rubble, such as large pieces of broken pot, which will allow lots of space for water to run into. Then put in several inches (centimetres) of coarse gravel, followed by finer gravel. Finally, add one layer of coarsely crushed charcoal

about the size of pieces of coal – this will help to keep the soil sweet.

Non-draining pots, if planted directly, should have their compost changed every year to be on the safe side. So stick only to temporary plants, such as annuals, or to plants which will need to be repotted every year in any case. Plants which don't like being disturbed, such as mature shrubs, should never be put in undrained tubs.

You must put drainage material into a pot with holes, but you only need to fill the bottom sixth, or so. Cover the holes with pieces of broken clay pot or tiles, then add a good layer of coarse gravel followed by a thin layer of coarse peat to help prevent any soil being washed down into the drainage level. There must, of course, be room for water to run out, so it's a good idea to raise your tub on blocks of brick, wood or clay.

Staking

If the plant you are going to put in needs staking – either immediately or in the future – you should put the stake or other support in at this stage, before filling with compost.

Compost

🌱 The best compost for contained plants is soil-based. It drains more freely than peat and is suitable for all permanent plants. Usually John Innes No 2 or 3 will be the right choice, but the exceptions to this are plants which hate lime.

🌱 Camellias and Rhododendrons need a special, lime-free compost, or they can be planted in peat. Peat is lighter and therefore may also be the right choice if the surface of your patio cannot bear the weight of a large tub of soil.

🌱 Summer bedding plants and bulbs will do well in peat. Look at the A-Z for each plant's needs.

Getting the size right

In almost all cases, the plant you are putting in your pot or tub will have come from the shop already in a container: you are effectively potting it on, rather than planting it from scratch. If the plant is still quite small, you should pot it on annually into larger containers until it is in, say, a 12in (30cm) pot. Then it may be transferred to a large tub. Don't put a small plant into a pot much too big for it – all that will happen is that the roots will not be able to take up all the moisture and may begin to rot.

Measuring the depth

You should aim to position your plant in the new pot at the same level as it is in the old one.

First you must remove the plant from its existing container. Make sure the compost is fairly damp. If it isn't, water it thoroughly – damp compost holds the shape of the original container, protecting the roots and making the job easier. Strike the pot firmly on the base with the flat of your hand to loosen the soil, then remove the plant together with the compost, holding the stem near to the base.

Hold it upright, with a stake next to it, and mark the level of the soil's surface on the stake. Use the stake as a measure to find out what depth you need to set the plant in the new pot so that the surface level comes right. Remember to allow about $^1/_2$in

(13mm) at the top for watering in pots up to 6in (15cm) diameter, and 1in (2.5cm) for larger ones.

Potting established plants

Fill your new tub up to the top with compost. Using a hand trowel or fork, make a hole where you want the plant to go. If you are potting an established shrub, sprinkle in a fistful of general fertiliser mixed with peat (more if the hole and the plant, are

Planting seedlings: put drainage material into your pot and fill with the appropriate compost.

Make a hole with a trowel or dibber and plant each seedling. Always handle them by their leaves.

Make sure to position the seedling so that the soil level is the same as it was before, and then firm in gently.

very big). The peat will encourage the roots to grow towards it and get settled in the new pot.

Shake any excess compost from the roots of the plant. If they are wound tightly around the outside of the root ball, tease them out a little – again, this encourages them to spread out into the new container. Holding the plant carefully, place it in the hole and check that it is straight.

Add more compost around the sides, making sure there is plenty of soil worked in between the roots and firm it down gently with your fingers, or your fists if there's room. Keep adding compost, firming it in as you go, and checking as you go that the plant is in the right position and straight, and at the correct depth – and don't forget to leave space for drainage. You can finish off with a layer of gravel – this not only looks attractive, but acts as a 'mulch' to keep moisture in.

Planting seedlings

First water the seedlings thoroughly and fill the container with the appropriate compost. Using a wooden plant label, ease out a small clump of seedlings and separate them gently; always handle seedlings by their leaves *never* by their stems. Using a dibber – a wooden tool made for planting – make a hole for each seedling. Place the seedling in the hole, making sure the soil level is the same as it was before. Firm in gently.

Aftercare

Water in your newly potted plant, and keep it in a sheltered spot out of bright light for the first few days. When new growth appears you will know that it is established and rooted well. Then you can start feeding it, according to its individual needs, and treat it as a mature plant.

Tips for tubs

With a little imagination even an old stove can be turned into a container.

It is wise to paint the inside of your tub with a plant-safe preservative, *above*, and when buying terracotta pots, *below*, make sure that they have frost guarantees.

Containerised plants are infinitely more vulnerable to drying out, frost damage and waterlogging than those planted in the ground. The long-term success of large plants like Camellias, Rhododendrons and Hydrangeas in tubs and other outsize containers depends, to a large extent, on correct siting, quality soil, good drainage and your ability to satisfy their needs for regular watering and feeding.

Soil requirements

A good soil-based compost, such as John Innes No 2 or 3, is better than one that is principally made up of peat, which is much lighter and less stable than loam and is much more inclined both to dry out quickly and to be difficult to re-wet.

But proprietary bags of John Innes composts are expensive. There are, however, cheaper and equally effective alternatives.

Home-made compost is the obvious answer. Vegetable plots are by far the richest source of nutritious loam, being manured and fed regularly with fertilisers to help produce and nurture bumper crops.

Use a 1/4in (6mm) mesh sieve to get a barrowful or more of stone-free loam and sterilize it with Jeyes Fluid. This involves spreading out the compost and watering on the concentration recommended on the container. Then mix in a balanced fertiliser, such as Chempak Potting Base, at the rate of eight two-gallon (10 litre) buckets to one packet of Chempak. You now have a perfect pest- and disease-free growing medium in which plants will thrive.

If good topsoil is in short supply, buy some peat in the form of growing bags. These have had the peat in them supplemented with fertiliser but are actually cheaper to buy than bags of peat. Add the contents of the growing bags to ordinary soil, mixing the ingredients in the ratio of seven parts

Camellias will flourish in a container provided you create the right conditions for them to grow.

Make them mobile

Extra large wooden tubs in which frost-tender plants such as citrus trees, Leptospermum or Angel's Trumpet (Datura) are planted need to be moved indoors in late autumn. These will be much easier to move if they have had coasters fitted to them.

Watering and feeding

Large containers tend to dry out quickly in windy weather and therefore need regular watering. Help reduce the frequency with which you need to do this by setting smaller pots inside larger ones and packing the intervening gap with peat. The peat, kept wet, will insulate the compost and keep it damper longer.

Alternatively, you can mix Agrosoke granules into the compost. These, when water is added to them, act as reservoirs for moisture. A regular supply of plant foods is vital for robust growth. Ensure this by inserting Jobes Spikes, specially formulated for tubs and window-sills, into the compost. These nourish growth for up to 60 days.

Frost protection

Large terracotta pots are expensive. The best come with a ten-year frost guarantee. Failing this, protect them from frost damage by painting both inner and outer surfaces with a transparent waterproof sealer: this will stop moisture from being absorbed by the clay, where it would expand and encourage cracks.

Containerised plants have their root systems exposed to relatively low temperatures. Wooden containers should therefore be at least 1in (2.5cm) thick. Thin plastic tubs can easily be protected from severe weather conditions by lining them with some polystyrene ceiling tiles or some of the polystyrene packing that often comes wrapped round particularly fragile wares.

Half-hardy plants should be moved in winter to a frost-free greenhouse or to a sheltered corner of the garden that is not exposed to icy winds. To protect them further from extreme cold, you can then erect some fine mesh netting around the tubs and pack it with some sort of insulating material, such as loose straw. This should ensure that they survive the winter safely.

soil to three parts peat. If the soil is fairly heavy, add two parts of sharp (coarse) sand to improve the drainage.

Preparing tubs

Make sure that tubs and other large containers have 1in (2.5cm) wide drainage holes, about 6in (15cm) apart, in the base. Place a layer of large broken crocks in the base, and cover this with 2in (5cm) of clean gravel. On top of this place a 1in (2.5cm) thick layer of charcoal to keep the compost sweet. Finally, add the compost to within about 1in (2.5cm) of the rim. This allows the

plants to be watered. You should also paint the inside of the tub with a plant-safe preservative, such as Green Cuprinol or Green Rentokil, to extend the life of the container.

Disappointing results often occur when tubs and pots are set directly on a tiled, paved or concrete surface. This gives surplus water little room in which to escape and the resulting airless conditions encourage sickly growth. The solution is to raise the containers on bricks, so there is a gap to allow drainage water to escape. Also, it is easier to move large containers if there is a gap under them in which to place your hands.

Watering: whys and wherefores

Although growing plants in containers – be they troughs, tubs or growing bags – offers enormous flexibility, it has one distinct disadvantage: and that is their overwhelming thirst. Plants grown in open ground have access to a large volume of soil and therefore moisture. Containerised plants, on the other hand, have to adapt their roots to living in a restricted environment, where they have only a limited amount of compost and water at their disposal. Their needs should therefore never be neglected in any way.

The immediate solution to the problem is obviously to water plants regularly – and in hot weather this may mean more often than once a day. This can, however, become quite a chore, so if you have a large patio or balcony garden it is worth looking at ways to make things easier.

Watering methods

Methods of watering range from the traditional use of a watering-can to highly sophisticated, fully automatic irrigation systems. Traditional practices, though effective and inexpensive, can be both time-consuming and backbreaking: trailing backwards and forwards from the nearest tap with heavy watering-cans is a tedious task, particularly if you have a great many containers to deal with. If you do use a watering-can, always fit a rose on it to prevent washing away valuable compost.

● A hosepipe – be it the conventional type or the newer flat sort that is easier to store and takes up less room – will take a lot of the backache out of watering. An outdoor tap is, of course, essential. If you are using a hand-held hosepipe attach a rose with a fine spray – strong jets of water can bruise leaves and stems, compact the soil, and wash away compost.

A good way of watering high containers is to tie a bamboo cane to the end of a hosepipe (see illustration). This will keep the pipe rigid and enable you to reach up and point it exactly where you want it to go.

● The use of capillary watering mats means that the compost acts like a wick, drawing water up to the roots. The capillary watering system can be used for any small plants, though it is less efficient for pots over 4½in (11cm). It is particularly good for plants that do not like their leaves getting wet – hairy-leaved plants, like some alpines, mark or scorch easily and should always be watered from the bottom. A ready-made kit can be bought, consisting of a reservoir tray, another one in which to stand small pots, and a length of capillary matting. It is also possible to improvise your own reservoir, using a shallow dish or bowl, and to buy capillary matting by the metre on which to stand the pots.

● Self-watering planters are one of the simplest solutions: once the reservoir, situated underneath, has been filled the water should last for several weeks. A water level indicator tells you when it needs refilling. Originally designed for indoor use, self-watering planters can also be used outdoors, particularly where an overhanging ledge prevents them from receiving rainwater. Self-watering window-boxes and troughs, are a particularly good idea on a window-sill or semi-enclosed balcony.

● Water-holding granules. A different sort of watering aid is the additives

Irrigation systems

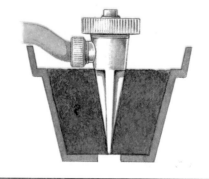

The K2 Dripper from Cameron Irrigation, *above*, is simple to operate yet versatile and effective. It is only 1½in (35mm) long and its tubes really are as thin as spaghetti. You simply attach the required number of tubes and drippers to a hosepipe. The system needs a small water filter near the tap and will prevent water wastage between pots.

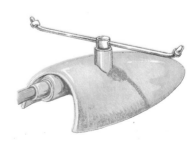

The static sprinkler, *below left*, is the simplest type of sprinkler. Water output is high, but it will cover only a small area. It can be supported on a purpose built stand or stood in a flower pot. With the rotary sprinkler, *below right*, two or three rotating arms produce a circle of fine droplets. Some are adjustable for spray and area covered.

Watering hanging baskets

A self-locking pulley system, *right*, can make watering hanging baskets easier. It can be lowered to the required working height and then simply raised again and locked into place. As an alternative a bamboo cane tied to the end of a hosepipe, *far right*, will help you to reach high containers. It is advisable to bend the nozzle over the end of the cane with some wire to prevent the water running back down your arm.

that can be mixed in with the compost to increase its water-holding capacity or to improve the wettability of the compost. Granules such as Agrosoke increase the water-holding capacity of the soil by soaking up water like little sponges and gradually releasing the moisture as it is needed.

Additives that increase the wettability of compost are not generally available on the amateur market but are sometimes included in proprietary composts, particularly peat-based ones. This type of wetting agent works in much the same way as a detergent and ensures the rapid and even absorption of water throughout the compost.

Irrigation systems

At the top end of the scale, there is a number of relatively simple yet effective irrigation systems with nozzle sprinklers or spaghetti tubes that ooze or spray water into pots in a controlled manner and can be positioned to water strategically placed groups of closely set containers. Their main drawbacks are the wastage of water that falls between container; the fact that they spray windows and outside walls as well as plants; and that they take quite a bit longer to water plants than using a hose or even a watering can.

To make these as efficient as possible, it may be worth installing a timing device which will water plants automatically as programmed. This has the great advantage that you are

not wholly reliant on your memory – which is, no doubt, already sufficiently overburdened without having to keep track of your plants' every need. You will also find the timing device invaluable when you go away on your holiday.

Whatever irrigation system you decide on, it should be used only from May until about September as the action of frost upon the exposed pipework could cause damage. It is advisable, therefore, to rely on a manual system in the early and later parts of the year.

How and when to water

If water is applied in insufficient quantities, it merely moistens the surface of the compost – and this does more harm than good; it encourages roots to probe upwards in search of water, where they are liable to be scorched by strong sun. Water should be applied generously until it just begins to trickle out of the hole at the bottom of the pot, but do not allow plants to become so waterlogged that they are deprived of oxygen.

The interval between waterings varies, depending on season, temperature and wind, as well as on the type and condition of the plant in question. Actively growing, flowering and fruiting plants, warm summer conditions, strong sun and wind all increase evaporation rates and moisture loss, and therefore necessitate more frequent watering. Town patios need particularly frequent watering, as the surrounding

masonry soaks up extra moisture and rain barely penetrates the overhead foliage. In calm, cool, dull or shaded conditions, in drizzle or during autumn and winter when plants are dormant, longer intervals are advised. Always aim to water plants before they start to wilt. In the height of summer, daily watering – or even twice daily during very hot periods – may well be necessary, whereas it can be reduced to only two or three times a month, or even less, in the winter. During cold spells container-grown plants are susceptible to freezing compost and roots, a situation which is made worse when the compost is wet, so keep watering to a minimum during the coldest months.

Early morning and evening are the best times of day to water in the summer months, when transpiration is at its weakest. Water plants and paving alike and spray over the foliage, but do not splash water directly on to the leaves in bright sunshine or they will get scorched.

Mulching

The need for watering in the summer can be greatly reduced by mulching the soil to keep it cool and evenly moist. A mulch is a thickish layer, about 2-4in (5-10cm) thick, of peat, garden compost or leaf-mould which is spread over the surface of the soil. This insulates the roots against the drying effects of the sun, ensures that soil temperatures are kept stable, and helps to retain moisture.

Judging how much water a plant requires is not easy, and is usually gained from experience. Such knowledge may enable you to water all your plants just before you go off on a short holiday, confident that they will be able to last a few days without any attention. This is helped by the plants being in a cool spot.

But for long periods away from home it is best to enlist the help of a friend or neighbour, or it may mean installing an automatic irrigation system. If you do ask your neighbour for help, make sure that all watering equipment is readily available.

Watering systems

If you do not want to bother your neighbour there are several automatic watering systems to consider. These vary greatly in sophistication from simple capillary matting to sprinklers and automatic systems.

Capillary matting is particularly useful for plants in pots up to 8in (20cm) wide. Stand the pots on the matting on a level surface, where they are then watered by continuous capillary irrigation; this means that the compost acts like a wick, drawing water up to the roots.

A ready-made kit can be bought, consisting of a reservoir tray, another one in which to stand the pots, and a length of capillary matting. Or if you prefer, you can rig up your own system, using an improvised reservoir – a shallow dish or bowl – and either capillary matting, which you can buy by the yard (metre), or a moist aggregate, such as sand or gravel, on which to stand the plants. But even if you use aggregate, you still need a strip of capillary matting to conduct the water from one tray to the other. An added refinement is to insert a small wick – available from garden centres – into the bottom of each container to ensure a continuous flow of water.

If you can't rely on a neighbour to check that the reservoir is kept full at all times, invest in an automatic timer, programmed to flood water on to the matting at regular intervals.

It is essential that adequate contact is made between the base of the plants and the matting. This can be done by placing the plants on the matting and then watering them from the top when you first set up the

While you are on holiday it is essential to make some provision for watering plants.

Left on their own . . .

Unlike house plants, which you usually think about before you go away on holiday, patio plants are often neglected. Although they may get some water from natural rainfall – if they are not growing in too sheltered a position – it is essential to make some provision for watering them while you are away. Even a weekend break may result in the untimely demise of some container-grown plants.

The amount of water required will vary greatly according to both plant and container. Some plants, such as tomatoes, need a lot of water and may even require daily watering. Others, like Ivies or Bay trees, can survive on much less.

Plants growing in plastic pots, tubs or urns need less water than those in earthenware or clay containers. This is because the water loss from compost in plastic containers is less.

Sprinklers are ideal for watering plants in large containers.

Trickle irrigation directs water to plants.

It directs water, individually, to the plants through special nozzles that are designed to 'trickle' a controlled flow of water on to the compost.

The amount of water supplied to the plant can be controlled by the flow rate allowed through the system and, in some cases, by the nozzles themselves which can be adjusted to vary the amount of water they deliver. The nozzles are usually attached to fine plastic tubes, known as 'spaghetti tubes' because of their size, which are themselves connected to the main feeder pipe. This is, in turn, connected directly to the tap.

Again, you can either ask a neighbour to turn on the tap, whenever necessary, or leave it in the reliable control of an automatic timer.

Better safe than sorry

Apart from ensuring that great care is taken to connect an automated system according to the manufacturer's instructions, it is also wise to test run it for a few days before you go away to make sure that there are no technical problems or leaks. Check, too, that containers do not become water-logged through lack of drainage, and that water doesn't come into contact with electrical points, which could have disastrous results.

For a few days before you go away it is a good idea to keep a record of the amount of water required by the plants. This will give an indication of the time that needs to be pro-grammed into the system. But even with a fully automated system, it is still worth asking a friend or neigh-bour to check that it is working according to plan.

Finally, even if the watering system is used only for the occasional holi-day, it is worth asking your local water authority whether you need a licence, particularly for sprinklers, or you may be committing an offence. This could result in a more expensive holiday than you had planned!

Feeding

If you are going away for a long time at the peak of the growing season, ensure that the plants remain ade-quately nourished during this period. The easiest way of doing this is to apply a slow-release fertiliser which will make nutrients available over a long period.

system. After that you can rely on capillary action.

Sprinkler systems are excellent if your patio garden consists of large con-tainers which would be impossible to water by a capillary system. They are available in a range of designs, with watering patterns to suit the shape and size of the patio area. The best system for the most common square or oblong-shaped patio is probably the bar type that oscillates backwards and forwards. Circular pattern sprinklers tend to be somewhat wasteful of water unless the area you need to cover is also circular, or a number can be linked conveniently together to suit the particular arrangement of containers on your patio or balcony.

You can either ask a neighbour to pop in and turn on the sprinkler from time to time while you are away, or, if you prefer, it could easily be con-nected to an automatic timer. Set the timer to come on early in the morn-ing or in the evening, but never in the heat of the day, when bright periods of sunshine could all too easily scorch wet leaves.

Trickle irrigation is probably the most effective watering system of all.

How to plant a window-box

A colourful window-box can really brighten up the outside of a dull house.

No matter how limited your scope for container gardening is, a window-box is something you're almost certain to be able to manage. If you've got a wide, flat window-sill, you can simply put a box on it straightaway, but even if your sills are narrow, sloping or non-existent you may still be able to have a window-box. They are the ideal way to brighten up a dull façade, and often the appearance of one in a street encourages the neighbours to follow suit, making a splash of colour which everybody enjoys.

Tips on choice

The range of available window-boxes is extraordinarily wide, and you may be overwhelmed by the choice. They are made in all the following materials: aluminium, asbestos, cement, concrete, fibreglass, lead (including imitation lead, actually fibreglass), plastic, expanded poly-styrene, terracotta and wood.

Wood is the traditional material and is, in some ways, the best. It is relatively easy – and not expensive – to make a wooden window-box your-self; this way you can make sure it is exactly the right dimensions. A

Securing the box

With a flat window-sill at least 6in (15cm) wide, you can have a window-box with no trouble at all. But there are a few points to bear in mind. Window-boxes, when they are full of soil, are pretty heavy. You should ideally provide some sort of restraining brackets to prevent a box being tipped or blown over – apart from damaging the box and the plants, this could cause damage to other property or serious injury to people walking below.

Certainly, if your window-sill is very narrow, or slopes downwards, you *must* provide supports or brackets to keep it immobile. You can sometimes buy a matching iron strip which fits under the rim of the box, and is fixed into the masonry of the wall, *above left*. If you cannot buy one from the same supplier as the box, you may have to have it made. Alternatively, you could have a wooden frame made to go around the box, again attached to the brickwork, *below left*.

If the whole of the bottom of the box is not going to rest on the sill, then you must obviously make sure that you provide a strong frame that actually holds the box up as well as keeping it in position. It is always a good idea, even with a perfectly flat sill, to raise the front of the window-box slightly so that it tips towards the wall – this will make it less likely to fall off.

wooden container must be made of a good, durable hardwood, such as teak or oak; soft woods such as pine soon rot. It must be painted with a non-toxic preservative, such as Cuprinol Green; don't ever use creosote, as it will harm the plants. It is a good idea to empty the box out every few years, clean it and apply a new coat of preservative so that the wood will last longer.

Terracotta must be thoroughly soaked before use, or it will take moisture out of the soil.

Obviously, all these different materials have different weights, and you should bear this in mind before you make your choice. If you're not sure whether your window-sill can support a very heavy container, go for the lighter types, such as expanded polystyrene, fibreglass or plastic. Many of these modern materials are beautifully designed, sometimes in imitation of the more traditional lead or stone. But remember also that if your box is small, a very lightweight material might increase the risk of it being blown or tipped off its sill, so provide good brackets.

Another point to bear in mind is the box's susceptibility to frost. If you know that you live in a part of the country particularly liable to hard frosts in the winter, choose a material that will not be damaged or cracked by frost – such as wood, aluminium, fibreglass, plastic or polystyrene.

The size of your box will, of course, depend largely on the available space for it. A good size for a good display is about 36in (90cm) long, and 6in (15cm) in both depth and height. Avoid a box that is shallower than 6in (15cm); it will dry out far too quickly.

Drainage

As with any container planting, good drainage in a window-box is absolutely essential. If water can't run out freely, your plants will quickly become waterlogged and die. There are two main methods of ensuring good drainage: one is to plant directly in the box and make sure it has adequate drainage holes; the other is to plant in an inner 'liner' with drainage holes – say, a plastic window-box – and place this inside the decorative container.

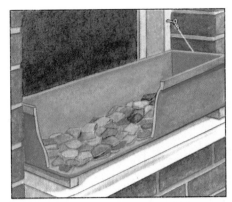

Window-box planting: cover each drainage hole with a large crock, then add a layer of smaller ones.

Using a small trowel, put your plants in the box, carefully firming the compost around the rootball.

You should always raise the window-box (or the inner liner if you are using one) off the surface. Terracotta window-boxes often come with matching chocks to keep them off the ground; otherwise you can use pieces of wood or half-bricks. If you're concerned that your sill might be spoilt you can get plastic or galvanized metal drip trays.

Filling your box

First cover each drainage hole with a large crock, and then add at least 1in (2.5cm) of small crocks or shingle to assist drainage. To prevent any compost washing down into the drainage material, add about $1/2$in (13mm) of peat or leaf-mould.

Next, add your compost. Which you choose will depend on the plants you intend to have – you may, for example, need a lime-free compost. But if not, John Innes No 2 is a good general purpose compost suitable for most window-box plants, particularly those that are permanent.

If you want to reduce the weight of

Fill your box with compost to within about 1in (2.5cm) of the top and firm down as evenly as possible.

As an alternative you can place plants in individual pots in the box and surround them with peat or gravel.

the box, go for a peat-based compost or one mixed in with perlite, a lightweight inert material. These materials are quite suitable for short-term bedding plants, but may not be a good idea for permanent ones.

Fill your box to within about 1in (2.5cm) of the top, and firm it down evenly all over before you start to plant. Remember to leave enough space for your plants to grow. Since contained plants don't grow as large as garden ones, a good rule of thumb is to allow about half as much space as would be needed in a garden.

Always consider the needs of the plants when you are choosing what to put in. Don't, for example, plant a sun-lover on a north-facing wall. Make sure that your plants have the same needs for compost, light, temperature and watering.

Last but not least, be adventurous! You don't have to stick to flowers in a window-box, you can also grow herbs for cooking, small vegetables, such as lettuces – even fruit, like tomatoes or strawberries.

Planning and planting a balcony

With careful planning it is possible to create the impression of a mini garden.

The **balcony's aspect** is important too. Some receive a great deal of sun and become very hot in summer, especially if they face south, in which case you should choose plants which appreciate this kind of climate. Those which are shaded for part of the day – say, west- or east-facing – and those which face north and therefore never receive any direct sun will suit an entirely different collection of plants.

It is very important to make a careful choice here, as growing unsuitable plants for the aspect can turn a potentially pretty space into an untidy eyesore.

Other practical points which you need to consider before you start to plan your balcony in earnest include the following rather tedious but all-important ones. How strong is the balcony, for example, and will it take the considerable weight of containers, composts (usually wet) and plants as well, possibly, as chairs and tables. The peat-based composts are the lightest, as are plastic, fibreglass or polystyrene containers, while lightweight modern garden furniture can be made of cane, glass-fibre or outdoor resin.

How easy is it to carry all this paraphernalia through your home on to the balcony, and to remove the inevitable debris which will result from growing a variety of plants? Have you got ready access to water? This is very important when you consider that plants will need watering daily in hot summer.

Is water likely to drip after watering on to the heads of passers-by below? Is the balcony exposed to wind? High balconies are particularly at risk, and wind not only damages plants but also dries them out.

Balconies on the ground and first floors of buildings in city streets will probably be subjected to pollution from exhaust fumes and all, high or low, may have trouble from pigeons

The first thing you have to consider when you are planting a balcony is obviously its size. Some balconies are large enough to sit out on and some even large enough for open-air meals, while others are not much more than a small rectangular projection jutting out from the house wall.

You will obviously have to tailor your plants to the size of the balcony. However large, it is in any case unlikely to be able to accommodate trees, large shrubs or rampant climbers. Small shrubs, on the other hand, are perfectly possible, as are dwarf conifers, annual climbers, and the less vigorous perennial climbers.

Practical considerations
If the balcony is very small and used for little else than standing on occasionally to admire the view, you should concentrate on quick-growing climbers which will give an instant display and clothe the balcony railings or, if it is surrounded by a solid wall, use window-boxes fixed to the top and sides. Then you can also grow a climber or two up the back wall in pots or tubs and attach a few hanging baskets or wall-pots.

For larger balconies, it should be possible to create the impression of a mini-garden. Cover all the vertical surfaces with climbers and grow a variety of plants in a number of different containers. Make use of as much 'vertical' space as possible by planting up the horticultural equivalent of tower blocks, like tower-pots and upright plant supports.

or seagulls. Have you got somewhere to keep the essential tools of your trade – watering cans, pots, spare compost, pot saucers, secateurs, canes, fertilisers, insect sprays and, if you are really keen, seed trays and propagators?

Choosing plants

When it comes to the choice of plants, remember that each plant will, in effect, be seen under a microscope. They are all at such close quarters and the space in which to grow them is so small, that each plant should give as much value for space as possible.

Ideally, plants should either remain attractive for more than one season, or they should display more than one asset – such as being fragrant as well as flowering, for example, or having coloured foliage in the autumn following a colourful summer show. If you choose flowering plants, their flowering season should be a long one.

Climbing plants can do a great deal on a balcony to provide a feeling of a complete garden and are especially useful for providing privacy where there are side walls or other suitable boundaries at each end of the balcony. For instant results use the quick-growing ones, such as Nasturtiums; Sweet Peas, which are also fragrant; the Golden Hop (*Humulus lupulus* 'Aureus'), which has yellow leaves; Ivy (Hedera); the Cup-and-saucer Plant (*Cobaea scandens*), which has green and purple flowers; and even vegetables like runner beans.

For permanent climbers, choose the large-flowered Clematis hybrids; Honeysuckle; Jasmine (*Jasminum officinale*), which is also heavily fragrant; and climbing Roses such as 'Bantry Bay', 'Compassion', 'Danse du Feu', 'Galway Bay', and 'Golden Showers'. These grow best in a south-, west- or east-facing aspect, except for the Honeysuckle which likes to face north, west or east.

The half-hardy annuals known as bedding plants are extremely effective on a balcony. Trailing Lobelia, trailing Pelargoniums and pendula Begonias, for example, all look good in boxes or hanging baskets. Petunias

come in such an amazing range of colours that you could devote an entire balcony garden to them if it is in a sunny spot.

There are some Nasturtiums known as the Alaska group; try these for their bushy, rather than climbing growth and their creamy-marbled leaves. Try also a short form of Sweet Pea, such as the Cupid or Patio mixed collections. All these revel in sun, as does the biennial spring-flowering Wallflower with its sweet fragrance.

Be careful with Begonias, which prefer a little shade, at least for part of the day, and would grow well alongside the outdoor Busy Lizzies (Impatiens). The fragrant Tobacco Plant (Nicotiana) likes sun, or at least part sun/part shade, as does the dwarf Phlox, Nemesia Carnival mixture and Mimulus Calypso mixture. In spring shade, the mixed collections of Polyanthus or coloured Primrose will flower for many weeks.

Evergreen shrubs provide greenery in winter as well as flowers at other times. The smaller ones include *Hebe* 'Carl Teschner', which has blue flowers in June and July, and the trailing grey-leaved *H. pinguifolia* 'Pagei'; various species of Heather such as the winter-flowering *Erica carnea* and the summer-flowering *E. cinerea*; Japanese Azaleas, which require some shade; aromatic shrubs such as Rosemary, Sweet Bay, Lavender and Cotton Lavender (*Santolina chamaecyparissus* 'Nana').

Deciduous shrubs which lose their leaves in winter but nevertheless deserve a place include the patio Roses; a small version of Mock Orange blossom (*Philadelphus microphyllus*); a small-growing Myrtle (*Myrtus communis tarentina*) which produces fragrant white flowers late in the summer; double Fuchsias which tolerate shade or sun; and, for larger balconies, Hydrangeas.

Winter colour is essential. Dwarf conifers are a good idea from this point of view. They grow slowly and have grey, blue or yellow foliage.

And two trailing plants which provide good winter colour are the Ivies, which can be large- or small-leaved, plain or variegated; and Periwinkles (*Vinca major* and *V. minor*), also

A variety of plants in different colours looks most effective.

large- or small-leaved and plain green or variegated, with blue, white or purple flowers.

Lastly, there is always space for a few essential herbs. Rosemary and Sweet Bay have already been mentioned, both evergreen and therefore good in winter as well; Rosemary also produces pale blue flowers in spring and summer, while Basil comes in a deep purple-leaved form with violet flowers as well as the more common green one with white flowers.

Try to create a careful contrast of colours on your balcony.

Some people think that growing climbing plants on a small patio is tantamount to unleashing a triffid, but they don't know what they're missing. Some of the choicest climbers are some of the smallest.

Often slightly tender, they find the sheltered environment of a small patio suits them far better than wide open spaces. Furthermore, you needn't be restricted solely to small climbers: although giants like Russian Vine and Virginia Creeper are definitely out, it is always possible to find room for one of the slightly less rampant, medium-sized climbers – the trick lies in knowing the best ones to choose to suit your particular situation.

Pick and choose

With limited room at your disposal, you obviously need plants that offer plenty of variety throughout the season. Ideally, you want more than just pretty flowers – so look for plants that also have something else to offer, such as striking foliage, seedheads, fruit or autumn colour.

Don't just grow the obvious 'ordinary' plants that everyone else has got, but go for something special. They may cost a bit more, but as you'll probably have room for only a few you may be able to afford to spend more on each plant. If cost is a consideration, grow some of the striking annual climbers – just for the price of a packet of seeds.

Tropaeolum species not only include the popular Nasturtium, but also embrace some lesser known summer-flowering climbers. Although they don't all look like Nasturtiums, they appreciate much the same conditions and care – dryish sunny spots and regular watering to prevent their roots drying out.

The Canary Creeper *(Tropaeolum peregrinum)* is a fast-growing annual covered in small, frilly, yellow flowers with insignificant foliage. In theory, it can reach as high as 6-10ft (1.8-3m), but doesn't often grow as tall as this, especially in a cool summer.

To see it at its best, let it ramble up a fence – tie a few strings for it to climb up – over a dead tree stump, or even a bird table. It also does well in a hanging-basket.

Choosing and caring for climbers

Climbers thrive in the shelter often offered by the patio.

The Canary Creeper is easily grown from seed. This should be sown in spring, either outdoors where you want the plant to flower, or in pots in a greenhouse.

The Flame Flower *(Tropaeolum speciosum)* looks much more like a conventional Nasturtium, with bright orange, trumpet-shaped flowers. It is a perennial climber and can reach 10ft (3m) high. Although its growth is not very strong and it does not have much foliage, it is ideal for growing up a trellis or fence on the patio. It needs some protection during winter. Cover the compost with a thick layer of peat to protect the roots.

Tropaeolum tuberosum is brightly coloured, with flame-red flowers shaped like a flask with a bunch of yellow stamens sticking out through the end. The individual flowers are not very big – only about 1in (2.5cm) – but grouped together they can look striking.

One of the best ways of growing *T.tuberosum* is over a dark green or blue-green conifer, where the contrast can be best appreciated. Plant so that the roots are 1ft (0.3cm) or so away from the conifer so that they're not fighting each other for water, and train the climber up on to the foliage.

This climber is a half-hardy perennial, so you can grow new plants from seed each spring. It won't withstand frost, and the seed must be sown indoors or in a greenhouse. Plants can be kept from one season to the next, provided you dig up the tuberous root and keep the plants in a frost-free place for the winter. Or, since they are only small plants, growing to no more than 3ft (1m), you may find it simpler to grow them in pots which you can then take inside for the winter.

Clematis forms a large family of climbers containing some very interesting flowers – especially if you opt for the less well-known, more subtle species rather than the gaudy, large-flowered hybrids. Although some Clematis may seem rather large for a small garden, one of the best ways of growing them doesn't require any space at all: simply let the Clematis climb up another plant. Choose a small tree or bush with a completely different flowering time, and you'll end up with two plants for

Clematis is ideal for the patio as it doesn't take up much space.

the space of one. With its feet in the shade and its head in the sun, these are the best growing conditions for Clematis.

C. alpina is a beauty. It flowers in April and May, with nodding little two-tone blue flowers. These are then followed in summer by most attractive feathery seedheads that can be dried and kept for an everlasting flower arrangement (spray them with hairspray to stop the feathery bits flying away). Besides being very

attractive, this is also a most accommodating climber as it suits any aspect, even a north-facing one. Another advantage is that it doesn't grow too big: 10ft (3m) is about its maximum.

C. tangutica is another most attractive species, this time with bright yellow, lantern-shaped flowers produced from July right through until October. Like *C. alpina*, the flowers are followed by feathery seedheads.

It is, however, a slightly larger-growing climber and needs a tree rather than a bush to grow through. It is also good for growing over walls and fences, or an archway where it can spread out.

🌱 *Ampelopsis brevipedunculata* 'Variegata' is a most spectacular climber grown for its large three-coloured leaves variegated with splashes of cream, green and red. Although it is a distant relative of the Virginia Creeper and, similarly, clings to walls without needing to be tied in place, this is a distinctly dom-esticated climber that never outgrows its welcome.

Its brilliant-red stems usually die down to ground level in winter so, without any pruning, you are always assured of a constant supply of brightly-coloured young growth. The flowers are insignificant, but after a particularly warm summer you may be rewarded with small bunches of bluish grape-like fruit. Team it with a late-flowering ruby-red species of Clematis, like *C. texensis*, if you want another climber to share its spot.

Plant climbing **Nasturtiums** in a dryish, sunny position.

Passion Flowers grow best in a sunny spot.

🌱 **Passion Flowers** (Passiflora) are among the most spectacular climbers you can find and, although they are rather tender subjects and definitely candidates for south-facing walls, the toughest will usually survive the winter as long as they are in a sheltered spot. If in doubt, tack a piece of sacking over them during the worst of the winter, or cover the roots with plenty of peat so that, if the top dies down, the roots at least will survive.

Alternatively, grow plants in large pots, sink them in position for the summer, and then in winter prune back the tops to a manageable size and move to a greenhouse.

P. caerulea is the most common Passion Flower; it has large blue and white flowers measuring up to 4in (10cm) across, which during a hot summer may be followed by orange, egg-shaped fruit. These are generally considered to be edible, though they are not as good to eat as some of the better-known passion fruit.

If it's fruit you're after, *P. quadrangularis* is the species to go for. If anything, this has even more spectacular flowers than *P. caerulea*, and large edible fruit just like the passion fruit you buy in the shops. It is, however, a more delicate plant and must be kept in a heated greenhouse or sunroom in winter.

🌱 **Gourds** make very striking plants for a sunny wall, adding a distinctly Mediterranean touch. They are annual plants which are easily grown from seed, sown in spring either indoors or in the greenhouse. Among the varieties on offer are Bottle Gourds, Turk's Turban and the small mixed gourds, which come in various colours and can be varnished for indoor winter decoration.

To be seen at their best, gourds should be grown where the fruit is clearly visible and not marred by competing foliage. They look particularly good against a light-coloured background.

🌱 **Morning Glory** (Ipomoea) is a fast-growing annual with a tropical look to it. The huge, trumpet-shaped flowers come in red, blue, pink, white, lavender or maroon. You can also get bi-colours, such as 'Flying Saucer', which has flowers splashed with blue and white.

Morning Glories look best when grown up a trellis, up canes in pots, up railings, or when they are simply allowed to twine round the stems of other plants – especially those with the type of foliage that would make a good background for brilliant-coloured flowers.

Sow seed indoors in March or April and set the plants out of doors after the middle of May when the risk of frost has passed.

Supporting climbers

Painted trellis can provide an attractive support for climbing roses.

No patio is completely 'furnished' without a few climbing plants. There are several attractive ways of supporting these, including pergolas, trellis and posts.

A few climbers, such as Ivies (Hedera) and Climbing Hydrangea (*Hydrangea petiolaris*), attach themselves without any additional help to flat surfaces like walls and fences by means of little aerial roots that are produced on the stems. Another self-supporting climber is the Virginia Creeper (Parthenocissus), which attaches itself to a flat surface by means of tiny sucker pads. So, apart from a wall or fence, you really don't need any extra support for these varieties of climber.

There is another kind of self-supporting climber which produces tendrils that cling to any convenient object placed in its path. Examples are the ornamental Vines (Vitis and Ampelopsis). So, if you want to grow one of these against a flat surface, you will have to provide some sort of additional support for the tendrils to cling on to, such as trellis panels or horizontal wires.

The majority, however, cannot really support themselves adequately and have to be tied on to suitable supports. Examples of these include climbing Roses, Wisteria, Honeysuckle and Jasmine.

Initial support

A climber should not be planted hard up against a wall or fence as the soil there may well be too dry and the plant will simply not become established. It is better, therefore, to plant it 30cm (12in) away from the wall or fence and to guide it to its support. This is accomplished by tying in the stems to a bamboo cane positioned at an angle pointing towards the wall or fence, up which you want the plant eventually to climb.

Permanent supports

● **A timber pergola** partially covering a patio is a very impressive feature and also provides a shady area for you

119

to sit in hot weather. There is probably no more attractive way of supporting climbers such as Wisteria, ornamental Vines, climbing Roses, Clematis and Honeysuckle. A particularly dramatic and unusual effect can be achieved by training a clematis over a pergola.

Self-assembly pergola kits for your patio are available which are quite easily erected.

● **Free-standing timber trellis**, of a lattice or square grid design, is often used partially to screen a patio – perhaps for privacy, for wind protection or to hide an ugly view – and is probably the most attractive type, but it does require regular painting or treatment with wood preservative. It is an excellent support for climbers such as Clematis, Honeysuckle and Wisteria, which will weave in and out of the trellis and so hold themselves up, and will then add further to the screening effect.

Panels of trellis are easily supported by metal post supports, which are hammered into the ground to hold the posts to which the trellis panels are then nailed. Gone are the days of digging deep holes and mixing concrete! There are several brands of post support, including Met-Posts and Erecta-Posts.

● **Posts** can be erected in beds surrounding the patio or in gaps in the paving, to support climbers like Roses and Clematis. Again, these are easily erected with the aid of metal post supports. A slight modification

Attach brackets above French windows to give support to Wisteria.

Fix trellis panels to railings to give your Clematis extra support.

Dowelling pegs through a wooden post provide additional support.

is to insert lengths of wooden dowelling in pairs through the post, each at right angles to the other, to provide additional support, *see below*.

● **Screen-block walling** consists of ornamental concrete blocks with an openwork pattern. It serves the same purpose as free-standing trellis but is much more expensive. Again, climbers will weave in and out of the openwork pattern, creating a very pleasing effect. Try a combination of Roses and Clematis and allow them to intertwine with each other.

● **Walls and fences** can obviously be put to good advantage. Climbers can be grown up to the house wall bordering the patio, for example, or up timber fencing panels which may be used to screen off the area. Unless you

A **selection of** foliage plants can look very effective on your patio.

Train climbers to weave in and out of screen-block walling and use fan-shaped trellis for smaller climbers.

grow climbers which support themselves by means of aerial roots or sucker pads, you will also need to provide some additional means of support to which you can tie in the stems as they grow.

Trellis panels can be fixed about 5cm (2in) away from the wall using cotton reels or small blocks of wood as 'buffers'. This gap allows air circulation behind the climbers. Panels can be fixed to walls with masonry nails or with wall plugs and screws.

There is a good choice of trellis panels for walls – in timber, plastic-coated steel and strong plastic. Remember that timber while being attractive, requires regular painting or treatment with wood preservative, so the others provide a labour-saving alternative. The plastic types usually come in green or white, the latter being especially good on a white wall. The smaller fan-shaped trellis panels are ideal for climbers of more modest proportions, such as Clematis and the less vigorous climbing Roses. Large square or rectangular panels, on the other hand, are a better choice for growing larger climbers.

An alternative system of supporting climbers on walls and fences is to use horizontal wires. Choose heavy-gauge plastic-coated or galvanised wires and space them about 30cm (12in) apart up the wall or fence. These wires can be supported about 5cm (2in) from the wall with vine eyes – there are different types available for insertion into timber or masonry. The wires should be tight, which can be achieved by using a straining bolt at the end of each wire.

An even simpler way of supporting climbers on walls is to insert nails wherever required, using masonry nails for walls and ordinary nails for wooden fences. Stems can then be tied in to the protruding heads without too much difficulty.

Tying materials

Use soft green garden string for tying in the stems of climbers, making a figure of eight loop around the support and the stem. Never tie in stems too tightly, remembering that they expand as they grow higher, and that tight ties will cut into the stems. Tarred string can also be used and has a much longer life than ordinary soft green string.

121

Growing spring bulbs

Bulbs are among the most accommodating and rewarding of plants, and there is hardly a place where one type or another won't flourish. Even in the shade – next to a north-facing wall or beneath trees, for example – some bulbs such as Snowdrops, Bluebells and Winter Aconites will still thrive.

What to grow where

Most bulbs are suitable for growing in containers and all the miniature varieties look most attractive when grown with Alpines in sink gardens. Tulips flourish in tubs, including both the tall hybrids and the dwarf types, such as the Greigii and Kaufmanniana hybrids. The latter two are also recommended for window-boxes. Tall-growing Daffodils are an excellent choice for growing in tubs, as are Hyacinths, in a variety of colours, and Lilies.

Formal beds around the patio are ideal for tall bedding Tulips, such as the Darwins and Darwin hybrids, the

All bulbs are easy to grow and Daffodils and Tulips can look spectacular when put together in containers.

lily-flowered varieties which have pointed petals bent outwards at the top of the flower, the parrot-flowered varieties which have slightly puckered petals with wavy edges. And both the early and late doubles can also look spectacular.

These Tulips look spectacular when set off by a carpet of the smaller

Daffodils combine well with foliage plants such as Ivies.

species of Wallflowers or Forget-me-nots. It is better to put the Tulips in first because as they are planted deeper you won't damage them when you put in your 'carpet'.

Hyacinths are also suited to formal beds and look particularly good when combined with Polyanthus or spring-flowering Pansies.

There are plenty of smaller bulbs for more informal beds around and in the patio. Examples include Glory of the Snow (Chionodoxa), Crocus, Miniature Cyclamen, Snowdrops *(Galanthus nivalis)*, dwarf Iris, Grape Hyacinth (Muscari), miniature Daffodils (Narcissi), Spanish Bluebells (Scilla) and dwarf Tulips. These are also a good choice for raised beds.

The right aspect

Most bulbs like to be in full sun and indeed some, such as the ornamental Onion family (Allium) and Crocuses, relish a really hot dry spot. Some, however, for example Snowdrops, Bluebells, and Winter Aconite *(Eranthis hyemalis)*, prefer dappled shade. See chart, *opposite page*, for ideal conditions for planting individual bulbs.

The right soil

Bulbs will grow in virtually any soil, and fertilisers should be used only in moderation as too much could cause excessive leafy growth. Bulbs really only need feeding when they are in flower and bonemeal is probably the best fertiliser to use.

Containers such as tubs and window-boxes are best filled with a

When and how to plant

Spring-flowering bulbs should be planted in late summer or early autumn. Tulips can be planted up until late autumn.

When planting containers, the easiest way is to fill them partially with compost, depending on the size of the bulb, firm it, then stand bulbs on the surface and add more compost until it reaches almost the top of the container, firming it between and over the bulbs with your fingers.

During prolonged periods of severe frost, it is wise to insulate containers with straw or bracken to prevent the compost from freezing. If this does occur it can result in the bulbs rotting off.

In beds and borders you can plant your bulbs with a hand trowel or, if you prefer, with a useful little gadget called a bulb planter which takes out a core of soil. Then all you have to do is put the bulb in the bottom of the hole and simply replace and firm the core of soil.

Whichever method you choose, remember that the base of each bulb should be in close contact with the soil. If there is an air pocket below the bulb, it may not form roots and could then rot off. See chart, *opposite page*, for planting depths and distances which really depend on the size of the bulb.

soil-based potting compost, for example John Innes No 1. Remember, though, to place a 1-2in (2.5-5cm) layer of drainage material, such as pieces of broken clay flower pot, broken tiles, or stones in the bottom of the container. Then add a thin layer of moistened granulated peat and finally top with the compost.

If you're planting in a bed around the patio, you can use ordinary garden soil but make sure that there is good drainage as this is most important. Some bulbs, such as Daffodils, Snowdrops and Snake's Head Fritillary (*Fritillaria meleagris*), prefer a soil which will not dry out. You can prevent this from happening by adding some organic material such as peat.

Before planting, prepare the soil well by digging deeply and adding bulky organic matter such as well-rotted garden compost or peat. If the soil doesn't drain well, work in plenty of coarse horticultural sand or grit to open up the texture and to allow excess water to drain away quickly. You could also put some gravel or coarse sand in the bottom of each planting hole. This will ensure that the basal part of the bulbs will not rot.

Lifting and dividing bulbs

Bulbs which are planted in tubs, window-boxes and formal beds all have to be lifted before they have died down in spring so that colourful summer bedding plants can be put in their place.

Remember when flowering is over it is most important to store the bulbs until the foliage dies down. This is the time when the food is produced for next year's bulbs. So heel them in, in a spare piece of ground, until the foliage has completely died down, but make sure they don't dry out – the compost should always be moist. Then lift them, dry them off and store in a cool, dry, airy place until planting time. Make sure that you put them in a vermin-free place.

Snowdrops are the one exception to this rule. They should be lifted and divided immediately after they have flowered and replanted straight away in moist soil. Do not allow them to dry off, because if they do the corms will shrivel. For care of individual bulbs, see A-Z entries.

Planting spring bulbs

Name	Conditions	Planting depth*	Planting distance
Allium	Full sun, free drainage	3in (8cm)	4-6in (10-15cm)
Chionodoxa	Full sun, good drainage	3in (8cm)	3in (8cm)
Crocus	Ideal for hot dry areas	3in (8cm)	3in (8cm)
Cyclamen (miniature)	Dappled shade, peaty soil	1in (2.5cm)	6in (15cm)
Eranthis hyemalis	Moist soil, dappled shade	1in (2.5cm)	3in (8cm)
Fritillaria meleagris	Moist soil, sun or part shade	4in (10cm)	4in (10cm)
Galanthus nivalis	Heavy, moist soil, dappled shade	3in (8cm)	3in (8cm)
Hyacinth	Full sun, good drainage	4in (10cm)	6in (15cm)
Iris (dwarf)	Full sun, very good drainage	3in (8cm)	3in (8cm)
Lilium (Lily)	Well-drained soil, sun or partial shade	6in (15cm)	8-10in (20-25cm)
Muscari	Full sun, good drainage	3in (8cm)	3in (8cm)
Narcissus (miniature)	Moist, fertile soil, dappled shade	3in (8cm)	3in (8cm)
Narcissus (tall)	Moist, fertile soil, dappled shade	4-6in (10-15cm)	6in (15cm)
Pushchkinia	Sun or partial shade, any soil	3in (8cm)	3in (8cm)
Scilla hispanica	Sun or dappled shade, moist soil	4-6in (10-15cm)	4in (10cm)
Tulip (dwarf)	Full sun, good drainage	4in (10cm)	3-4in (8-10cm)
Tulip (tall)	Full sun, good drainage	4in (10cm)	6in (15cm)

* **Note:** planting depth is the depth above the top of the bulb, so the actual holes will be deeper.

Hyacinths look particularly good when planted with Polyanthus.

Flowering shrubs such as Azaleas require little if any pruning.

However, before you go wild with the secateurs or the pruning saw it is wise to consider what tools you are going to use and how you are going to go about pruning so as to get the best results from your plants.

Pruning tools

If you have just a small patio the only tools you are likely to need are a good pair of secateurs. However, if you are growing relatively large plants you may need some other equipment.

Secateurs. There are two basic types of secateurs. The anvil secateur consists of a straight-edged blade which cuts on to a soft metal anvil, gripping the branch securely and making a clean cut. The parrot-bill has one curved blade and a fixed bar against which the blade cuts. In both cases you will get the best results if you cut with the lower part of the blade as opposed to the tip.

Shears. If you are growing bushy plants such as Privet that require reg-

Blackcurrant bushes should be pruned back hard in autumn.

Pruning is necessary to keep a plant healthy, well-balanced and evenly shaped. It will also help the plant to produce the maximum effect required whether flowers, foliage or fruit.

Pruning is an essential part of plant maintenance throughout most of the year, although there are some periods in the year during which it becomes particularly intensive.

ular trimming, a pair of notched hand shears will prove very useful. Their simple scissor-like action will enable you to cut through several stems with a single stroke and to maintain good control of your plant's shape.

Pruning knife. This is a useful tool for light pruning jobs. The blade is usually curved and is ideal for cutting through green to semi-mature tissue.

Vine scissors. These are usually used to trim small, slender-stemmed plants and to cut fruit and flowers. However, they are slightly limited in

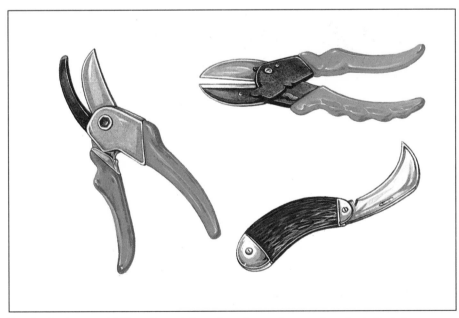

Pruning tools: parrot-bill secateurs, *left,* anvil secateurs, *above,* and pruning knife, *below.*

that they are not strong enough for cutting through thick stems.

Pruning saw. If your patio plants have grown out of control you may need to use a pruning saw. The curved, relatively coarse-toothed blade will remove unwieldy growth from mature shrubs and trees.

Pruning techniques

All plants differ in the type and speed of their growth, and also in how and when they should be pruned. However, here are a few guidelines that will point you in the right direction.

Foliage shrubs. Plants such as *Acer palmatum* (Japanese Maple) and Euonymus require minimum pruning once the plants have become established. However, pruning may be necessary during the early growing stages to ensure a satisfactory final shape. Ideally, you should prune these shrubs during March and April.

Flowering shrubs. Some such as the hardy Fuchsia (*Fuchsia magellanica*), Pieris, Skimmia, Mahonia and many other evergreen shrubs have a relatively compact bushy habit and require little, if any, pruning. Just remove dead flowers and trim away any unwanted growth.

Conifers. These require careful pruning when young, otherwise badly-shaped plants may result. If conifers such as Thuja, Chamaecyparis and Taxus are grown as hedges they will need an annual clipping. However, if grown as specimen plants on the patio or in a small conifer collection, all that is needed is to remove misplaced shoots during their early years, and to cut out awkwardly placed shoots as and when they develop in later years. Others such as Abies, Picea and Pinus don't really need any pruning, although damaged or wayward growth may need the occasional trimming.

Roses. In the first year prune these back to about 4-6in (10-15cm) and cut out any diseased shoots in early

ing years any dead or weak growth removed in February.

Varieties that flower in the early summer, on the previous year's growth, such as Clematis 'Nelly Moser', 'The President', 'Elsa Spath', and 'Niobe' should be pruned back to a strong pair of buds about 12in (30cm) above soil level in February or March. Prune all stems by between a third and a half of that season's growth in the following February. In the following years pruning back to a strong pair of buds to maintain a good habit is all that is required.

Varieties that flower on the new season's growth, in summer and autumn, such as *Clematis orientalis*, *C.tangutica*, *C.texensis*, *C.viticella* and *C.jackmanii* are pruned back to a pair of strong buds close to the bottom of the year's growth in February.

Wisteria is another climber that can grow vigorously and, therefore, requires effective pruning. Once the basic frame of the plant has been

Cut back Buddleia bushes hard each year to avoid ending up with leggy plants.

Dead-head Rhododendrons and trim away unwanted growth.

Dead sections of shrubs such as *Leycesteria formosa* can be removed at any time.

Hydrangea paniculata, *Spiraea japonica*, *Buddleia davidii* and the deciduous *Ceanothus* 'Gloire de Versailles' should be pruned back quite hard each year. This is important, as the flowers of this group of plants are borne on the current season's new growth and if you neglect pruning you will end up with leggy plants and poor flowering. Pruning should be done during March and April.

Other flowering shrubs such as Pyracantha, Choisya, Ilex, Fatsia, Garrya, Azalea, Rhododendron,

spring. Flowers should be removed as soon as they start to fade. In following years prune back plants by about a third by removing old stems.

Climbers. The pruning of climbers such as Clematis varies according to variety. Those that flower in the spring such as *Clematis alpina*, *C.macropetala* and *C.montana* are pruned down to a strong pair of buds about 12in (30cm) above the ground in February. In the second year they should be pruned by about a third of that year's growth and in the follow-

established, the vertical and lateral shoots of the plant should be pruned back by about one third in December or January.

After care

Take care that you don't damage your plant while pruning and make sure that you do it at the right time of the year.

If you accidentally damage your plant or if you prune relatively large stems, a wound sealing compound can be used to protect the plant.

KNOW YOUR HOUSEPLANT TERMS

Acid
Refers to soil/potting mixture/water, with a pH value below 7.0; indicates the absence of lime or other alkaline material (see *pH scale*).

Aerial roots
Roots growing on stems above the level of the soil. They serve a dual purpose: providing support by clinging to tree branches and for extracting moisture from the air. Often seen in Philodendrons.

Alkaline
Refers to soil/potting mixture/water, with a pH value above 7.0; generally indicates the presence of lime (see *pH scale*).

Annual
A plant which is grown from seed to flower within one year, after which it dies. Examples Capsicum and Celosia.

Areole
Peculiar to the Cactus family, a cushion-like sideshoot carrying hair and/or spines. Each areole flowers only once.

Axil
The angle between the leaf and its stem; any new growth from an axil is called an axillary.

Biennial
A plant that completes its cycle within two growing seasons.

Bloom
A harmless powdery or waxy coating on leaves or fruit of certain plants, usually of a whitish or bluish colour.

Bract
A modified leaf backing or surrounding a flower, often highly colourful and long-lasting. Example Poinsettia.

Bromeliads
Relatives of the pineapples, these are epiphytic plants (see *epiphyte*) which can grow supported on tree bark, without the need for soil.

Bud
An immature flower or leaf, often protected by overlapping scales.

Bulbil
A small immature bulb either at the base of mature bulbs or on the stems; a term also loosely applied to the leafy plantlets of certain ferns.

Calyx
The leaves surrounding a flower – usually green.

Capillary action
The natural physical force which causes water to move in narrow tubes, for example from the roots of a plant to its leaves.

Chlorosis
A condition in which leaves become pallid; an indication of insufficient nutrients in the soil.

Compost
Either decomposed plant remains or the mixture of soil and other ingredients used to grow plants in pots.

Compound
A leaf made up of two or more distinct parts called leaflets, or a flower composed of many florets.

Corm
The swollen base of a plant's stem which stores food and protects new growth; it fulfils the same function as a bulb.

Crown
Area at the base or centre of a plant from which top growth and roots emerge. Example Saintpaulia.

Cultivar
A variety of plant that has been artificially bred.

Cutting
A portion of stem or root used to propagate new roots which will develop into a mature plant (see also *leaf cutting*).

Deciduous
Plants which shed their leaves when inactive (usually during winter) producing new ones the following spring.

Division
Method of growing new plants by splitting the roots of a mature plant and potting the sections separately.

Dormancy
A temporary state of total inactivity, sometimes accompanied by a withering away of the top growth.

Drawn
A condition due to inadequate light or over-crowding; the stems become elongated and spindly.

Epiphyte
An 'air plant' generally living on tree branches or shallow moss, and deriving moisture and nutrients from the air and decaying matter, although not parasitic.

Evergreen
A plant that retains its leaves all year round.

Floret
A single flower that is one of many making up a larger compound flower head. Example the Daisy family.

Foliage plant
A plant that is grown indoors to display the beauty of its leaves.

Foliar feed
Liquid fertiliser that is sprayed onto leaves and is rapidly absorbed; it may also be taken up by the roots.

Forcing
The use of heat and/or light to induce growth or flowering ahead of the natural season; a term applied to spring bulbs.

Frond
An alternative term to describe the leaf of a fern or palm.

Fungicide
A chemical used to prevent disease and/or destroy fungus growth.

Genus
A botanical grouping of plants with similar characteristics; each is sub-divided into separate species.

Germination
The earliest stage of plant growth; when a seed begins to sprout.

Grafting
Joining a detached stem or shoot of one plant onto another that is still rooted.

Growing point
The point at which extension growth occurs; usually the tip of a stem or bud.

Hardy
Plants which are tolerant of cool conditions, many capable of surviving frost.

Heeled cutting
A cutting taken by pulling a sideshoot from the main stem with a strip of bark and wood attached.

Herbaceous
A plant that has a soft non-woody stem, and generally loses its top growth during winter.

Hybrid
A plant produced by cross-breeding two plants of different species or genera.

Hydroculture
A method of growing plants without soil; instead the pot is filled with pebbles and the plants are fed nutrients during watering.

Inflorescence
A head, cluster, spike or similar collection of small flowers grouped together on one main stem.

Insecticide	A chemical or organic substance used to combat insect pests.
Leaf cutting	A leaf (usually with stalk attached) used in propagation.
Leaflet	Any segment of a compound leaf.
Leaf mould	A component of some potting mixtures, consisting entirely of rotted leaves.
Leggy	A term describing spindly growth, when the stems are bare towards the base.
Midrib	The central vein (often raised) of a leaf, dividing it into two halves.
Moss pole	A plastic or wooden tube wrapped in moss, valued for its capacity to hold water and for training climbing plants.
Node	A joint or swelling on the stem of a plant from which leaves, buds or side-shoots appear.
Offset	A small plant that grows from its parent. It can be detached and grown separately.
Palmate	Three or more leaflets arising from a single point of attachment on the leaf-stalk, an arrangement resembling a hand. Example Fatsia japonica.
Peat	Partially decayed organic matter, valued in potting mixture for its capacity to retain air and moisture.
Perennial	A plant that lives for three seasons or more, usually indefinitely.
pH scale	A scale measuring acidity and alkalinity.
Photosynthesis	The process by which the leaves of a plant are nourished, requiring water, air and light.
Pinching out	The removal of a stem's growing point in order to encourage bushy growth from the dormant buds lower down.
Pinnate	Refers to a compound leaf with pairs of leaflets carried on opposite sides of the stem; if the leaflets are then further divided the whole leaf is called bipinnate.
Pot-bound	The crowding of roots within a pot which usually prevents healthy growth; some plants however do flourish if slightly pot-bound.
Potting on	The transferring of a plant to a larger container, allowing continued growth of the roots.
Propagation	The formation of a new plant from seed, or by using cuttings from a mature plant.
Pruning	The cutting back of a plant to encourage bushiness, better flowering and a more compact shape.
Repotting	Transferring a plant to a new container or renewing the soil, in order to revitalise growth.
Rest period	A season when a plant is relatively inactive, retaining its foliage but producing little or no new growth – compare *dormancy*.
Rhizome	A fleshy, usually horizontal stem (below ground); it is used as a storage organ and produces new buds and roots.
Rootball	A mass of potting mixture crowded with roots (as seen when a plant is taken from its pot).
Rosette	A cluster of leaves radiating from the centre, either on individual stalks or in an overlapping spiral. Example Echeveria, Saintpaulias.
Runner	An above-ground horizontal stem which roots at intervals to form new plants.
Scurf	Minute scales or particles on the foliage giving it a dusty, or mealy, appearance.
Sharp sand	A coarse sand, free of lime, sometimes used in potting mixture.
Spadix	A particular kind of flower spike (usually in the Arum family); a fleshy column with minute flowers spread over it.
Spathe	A large, often colourful, bract which surrounds and protects the spadix.
Species	A sub-division of a genus of plants, forming a distinct type; they are self-fertilising, and two plants of the same species can produce viable seed.
Sphagnum moss	A spongy bog moss used in the cultivation of houseplants because of its high capacity to hold water.
Spike	A flowerhead in which the flowers are virtually stalkless.
Spore	The tiny, single reproductive cell produced by such plants as ferns and mosses.
Stipule	A sheath which protects growth points, usually drying up and falling off when no longer needed. Example Begonia.
Stolon	A shoot that runs over the potting mixture carrying a new plant at its tip; differing from runners in that runners can root at their nodes and at their extremities.
Stomata	Microscopic breathing pores of plants, mostly found on the undersides of leaves.
Succulent	Plants with fleshy stems or leaves that function as water-storage organs. Example the Cactus family.
Sucker	A shoot that arises from below ground level and develops leaves and roots of its own.
Systemic	An insecticide sprayed onto leaves or watered onto the potting compost which enters the sap killing insects that feed on plant tissue.
Tendril	A thin but wiry organ which twines around a support and holds the plant firm. Leafstalks can act as tendrils.
Top-dressing	Replacing the top layer of soil or potting mixture in order to freshen the plant's growing medium.
Tuber	An underground swollen stem/root which stores food and enables the plant to survive over winter, and produce new growth next year.
Variegated	A term which refers to plants with patterned, spotted or blotchy leaves.
Vein	A strand of thicker tissue in a leaf which distributes moisture and nutrients.
Viviparous	Producing plantlets, without the need for seed, usually on the leaves or stems of the parent plant.
Whorl	A radiating arrangement of three or more leaves or flowers around a node on a plant's stem.
Xerophyte	Plants that are able to withstand very dry conditions. Example Tillandsia, Aechmea, Vriesea (air plants).

CHAPTER 3

Buyer's Guide

Picking a winner

Most people buy houseplants on impulse — especially as tempting new varieties are appearing all the time and there's always something you absolutely must have. But try to restrain yourself a little before you recklessly spend your hard-earned money; give serious thought to where the plant is going to live, as well as, most importantly, how much you can afford to spend.

Very broadly speaking, the larger the plant, the more it costs; confusingly, though, age doesn't equal size as some plants grow enormous very quickly, while others take years to achieve a few inches. Whether you buy large or small plants depends on how much you can afford as well as the effect you want to create — whether you want a really lush, green room full of lots of smallish plants or one or two dramatic large, specimen plants.

Be discriminating: don't just buy the very first plant of the kind you want. Look around shops: the price and quality can vary tremendously. There's nothing more annoying than spending a small fortune on a plant, then walking

around the next corner and finding a bigger, better and much cheaper version of the same in another shop.

Where to buy houseplants

The first rule is to go to a reputable source of supply. In most large department stores plants are usually of very good quality as they are properly looked after, but the range can be limited. However, these plants can be poor if they have been erratically watered and

This cheerful little Polka Dot Plant has all the virtues of a good buy — lots of bright, healthy, nicely-coloured leaves on a well-shaped, sturdy plant.

the air around the plants is so dry that the leaves shrivel. Also shoppers like to feel plants in the same way as they like to touch material and frequent handling bruises tender leaves and shoots.

Market stalls sell a lot of houseplants, especially flowering ones, as they tend to be cheaper than foliage plants and sell quickly because they look so pretty. But sometimes they are not very healthy. Be wary and never buy tropical plants from the pavement if the weather is cold, as the plants will be thoroughly chilled and may already be dying.

A nursery or garden centre can be a much better bet for tropical houseplants as nurserymen are specially geared to the conditions plants need and will usually have a bigger selection to choose from. Also, if you are bowled over by a strikingly beautiful plant the grower will give specialist advice on how to look after it — something you are unlikely to get from a shop.

Choosing a good plant

A number of considerations should go through your mind: Does the plant look healthy? Do its leaves look as crisp as

A good shop will have an interesting range of healthy plants from which to choose.

they should? Is the overall impression a good one? Has it got several new shoots? If it's a flowering plant, in its flowering season, has it got flower buds?

When you buy flowering house-plants such as Azalea, Gloxinia and Cineraria it is always best to choose a plant in bud rather than one in full flower. Once settled down at home the flowers will open quickly and you can enjoy their full flowering time. If you buy a plant in full flower you run the risk of knocking the blooms off while getting the plant home. The flowers may drop off anyway because of the change of environment and that can be embarrassing if the plant is a gift.

Points to check

Leave on the shelf any plant with more than a few yellow leaves — there might be something really wrong with it — unless you are certain that it should have yellow leaves, like a Croton or yellow variegated Ivy. Similarly avoid plants with brown tipped leaves as they haven't been well cared for and are not in a fit condition to buy.

Check to see if the plant is well balanced with a nice shape. If it lurches to one side or has been badly broken the fault may be too basic to correct easily as the plant's shape may be ruined completely.

Look under the leaves and on shoots for pests, whitefly and greenfly are the commonest; and at the leaf joints and stems look for white cottonwool-like mealy bugs and brown, warty scale insects. Give all the plants a wide berth if you find any signs of trouble as the other plants could share the same problem.

Inspect the roots as far as you can. The plant should be sitting firmly in its compost — don't buy a plant that has been knocked about. If it's loose, the plant could be a young cutting which hasn't rooted properly and should not be for sale yet. It is a good sign when there are a few healthy looking roots just beginning to poke through the holes in the bottom of the pot. There's often a mat of roots under the pot. At least this shows the plant is growing well; but it has become too big for its pot and needs repotting. No matter how careful you are you can't help snapping the delicate roots when you transfer it to a bigger pot. Leave it.

Finally, look at the compost; it should be a good colour and

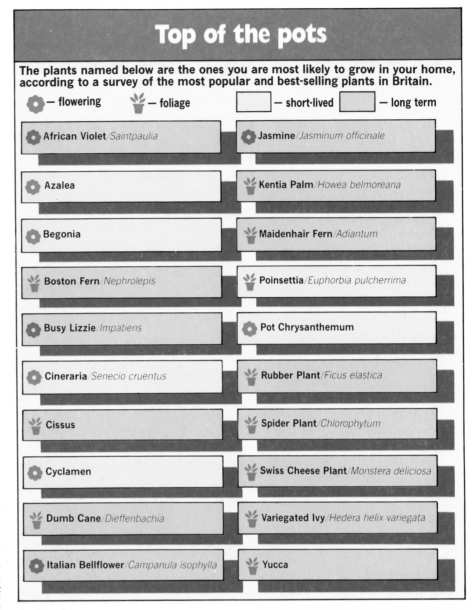

moist. If it has green slimy growths on the surface the plant has been over-watered to the point of being water-logged and could be about to collapse: avoid. On the other hand dry soil is bad too; peaty compost shrinks when it dries out and is then almost impossible to re-wet. Harden your heart, leave the plant in the shop and your money in your pocket. Go to another shop: this one doesn't look after its plants properly.

When buying bulbs, corms and tubers, look over them carefully for any signs of squishy rot or a coating of green powdery mildew, as well as other obvious signs of damage such as worm holes. Similarly avoid any bulbs which have started to sprout in the warmth of the shop.

Getting your plant home

Taking your new plant home safely can be a problem. With a particularly large plant ask to have it delivered. Don't try to cram it into your car, or even worse, onto a bus. After all, you paid good money for it and it is silly to risk damaging your new plant. Also try to transport tropical plants on warm days or, if you must buy one in cold weather, make sure the shop wraps it up well for you. Protect the tender leaves and flowers with a polythene bag or some sheets of newspaper, and seal it at the top to prevent the cold air whistling in. Then get it home as quickly as possible.

Choosing your plants

The secret of success with houseplants is to choose plants which will easily settle down and flourish in the particular environment of your home. We'll help you to sort out exactly what your problems and limitations are so that you can grow the healthiest and happiest possible houseplants

There are so many different kinds of flowering and foliage plants sold as houseplants that the choice can seem overwhelming. Choosing which ones to buy is a process of elimination of the varying factors you can provide, like the amount of light and heat, weighed against the plants you actually want to grow in your house.

There's no point in choosing plants which need extreme conditions you can't achieve — or can only just manage at a pinch. You will do better with your houseplants if you grow ones which are happy with the existing conditions in your home, rather than struggle with

tricky plants which are only hanging on to life by the skin of their leaves.

Narrow the field down by taking a long, cool, assessment of your house; light and heat are the two main controlling factors. Your range is wider if you have good, bright light but there are lots of plants which grow well in light shade and some which even prefer gloom.

Desert cacti, for example, thrive in good, bright light, but this would be fatal for African Violets which need direct sunlight for only part of the day or their leaves turn yellow and they stop growing. Ferns are happiest in subdued light and high humidity — most just

Cool white walls, natural pine and green leaves create a calming atmosphere to sit and relax in.

shrivel up and die if they sit in the sun. Before you buy a plant, read its label to see which plants need plenty of light and which prefer shade.

Then decide which plants you like — shapes and colours have varying appeal to different people. After this, let your home conditions decide which range of plants you can grow, as they all have their own special requirements.

Never be afraid to ask what a particular plant is, especially if it is growing in the sort of conditions you can provide. Houseplant enthusiasts are always happy to talk about their plants and are often very generous with cuttings as well.

Most people can keep tropical species in summer without problems, but trouble starts in winter if plants don't get high enough temperatures. Try not to fall in love with a plant which needs a high temperature if you can't give it a warm room to live in. Buy instead plants that prefer a cooler winter. Fluctuating heat and cold can be harmful and, while the temperature range may not be dangerous, just the fact that the central heating goes on and off can be damaging.

Draughts are another danger which cause houseplants to drop leaves and flowers. Seal all windows well and don't create a through-draught by leaving doors open.

What kind of plants?

Some people treat their houseplants like children, looking after them every day, touching and talking to them; if this sounds like you, get plants which respond well to constant, daily care. Have a look at our room plan for ideas. Flowering plants always want more tending than foliage plants, as they need their dead flowers removed. They also need attentive watering to prevent the flowers and buds shrivelling, which will happen if they've been forgotten for a few days. You'll find that your plants change with the seasons as they come into and out of flower, so there will always be something different to enjoy.

Not all plants need such a close eye kept on them, and if you want beautiful plants without effort, choose plants which don't need much attention. These are, generally speaking, ever-green foliage plants which have tougher constitutions and so are more tolerant of neglect. The famous Aspidistra is the toughest houseplant of the lot, and will put up with a wide range of conditions — though that's not to say that it won't grow much better if you treat it well!

Solving problems

Although most houseplants hail from the tropics, they object to temperatures much higher than 75° F (24° C) because normally they get very high humidity, and our air is too dry, which leads to shrivelled, dry, falling leaves. The answer is to stand your pots on saucers

Dangerous plants

There are a few plants you should avoid or stand on top of a high shelf, if you have children at the 'everything's-worth-tasting' stage. The Dieffenbachia,(**1**), is not nick-named the Dumb Cane for nothing. The sap contains a poison which swells the glands in the throat.
Prickly cacti,(**2**), too, are better not grown if there are small, prying fingers around — similarly, plants like Citrus and Asparagus Ferns which hide vicious spines among their pretty foliage.

Beware of any plant with berries: the ones on Winter Cherry ,(**3**),look like sweets, but are actually poisonous.

1
2
3

of wet pebbles and spray the plants frequently with warm water or install humidifiers to freshen the air.

Other problems occur if you keep plants near fumes from anthracite coal fires, oil heaters, coke stoves and fresh paint. If this is unavoidable, choose leathery-leaved Swiss Cheese Plants, Rubber Plants and Jade Plants, all of which are literally too thick-skinned to suffer at all.

It inevitably happens that despite all this good advice, you'll buy or be given a houseplant which is not suitable for your home. Do the best you can for it; find out what it needs and get as close to the conditions as possible.

If the plant needs lots more light than you can give it, move it to the lightest spot in your home, and buy some fluorescent tubes or special growing bulbs. If it needs warmer winter temperatures, put it in the warmest possible spot; if it's small enough, protect it inside a propagator or glass fish tank, or even warm a room especially for it. If your problem plant needs a cold winter and you live in a warm house, find the coolest spot, well away from all heat sources, and mist spray it frequently. The best solution is to give the plant to someone who can

look after it properly; but, by using emergency measures, you might be able to keep your plant going until spring when you can revive it.

Beginner's houseplants

Some plants thrive on neglect, so here are some you don't need to feel too guilty about if you forget them for a while.

Aspidistra – **Aspidistra elatior**
Asparagus fern – **Aspargus plumosus, Asparagus sprengari**
Urn Plant – **Aechmea fasciata**
Spider plant – **Chlorophytum comosum**
Coleus – **Coleus**
Dragon Tree – **Dracaena marginata**
Castor Oil Plant – **Ricinus**
Baby's Tears – **Helxine**
Swiss Cheese Plant – **Monstera deliciosa**
Sweetheart Plant – **Philodendron scadens**
Swedish Ivy – **Plectranthus oertendahlii**
Grape Ivy – **Rhoicissus rhomboidea**
Mother-in-Law's Tongue – **Sansevieria**
Mother of Thousands – **Saxifraga sarmentosa**
Succulents – **Aeonium. Aloe, Crassula**
Cacti – **Mammillaria, Rebutia, Echinopsis**
Wandering Jew – **Tradescantia**

Easy care plants

All these plants need the absolute minimum of attention. Just remember to water and feed them regularly and they'll be fine.

A mantelpiece is ideal for an Ivy on the darker side, and a Scindapsus nearer the light.

In the direct light, grow a Spider Plant and a Castor Oil Plant.

A Jade Plant likes a lot of light, as does a Yucca.

In a slightly shady spot between two windows, a Mother-in-Law's Tongue will thrive.

An Aspidistra can sit safely in the darkest corner. Make sure it's not in danger of being scorched by the radiator in winter.

The door causes draughts, which are bad for plants. Also the constant flow of people in and out can damage fragile leaves, so keep your plants well away from here.

A Swiss Cheese Plant enjoys bright light but not direct sun. Give it a spot where is has plenty of room to spread.

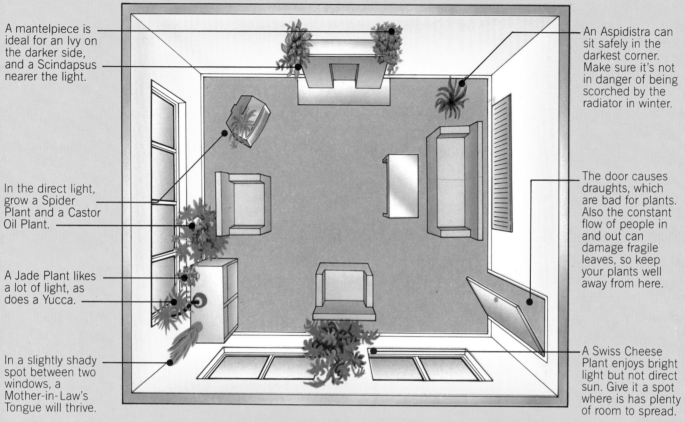

Constant care plants

Most of these plants change with the seasons as their flowers come and go — so there's always something new to enjoy.

Caladium and Croton like warmth, bright light and humidity.

With good light the flowers on Hydrangea and Azalea last a couple of months.

The Dumb Cane needs heat and humidity; and Busy Lizzie should have its dead flowers removed every day.

Put a tender Prayer Plant on top of the mantelpiece where it can get reasonable light.

Grow Ferns in the light shade by the mantelpiece, but block off the shaft to stop draughts.

On a table out of direct light, you can put short-term flowering plants such as Begonias, Italian Bellflower and Cineraria.

A Weeping Fig is easy to grow so long as it is kept warm. But it is much healthier if its leaves are often sprayed and cleaned.

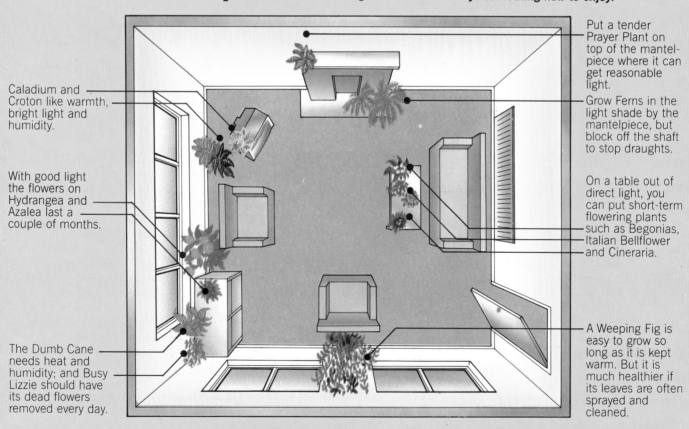

Fabulous flowers

Houseplants that flower — whether in a riot of bright colours or in muted, pastel shades — will give permanent pleasure to any plant lover. They brighten up any room, and count among the most popular and appreciated of presents, both in springtime and in the depths of winter, at Christmas. But a healthy, well-grown flowering plant can often be expensive to buy, so you should know what to look out for to avoid disappointment.

At some time or another, almost everyone must have had the experience of buying a flowering plant and getting it home, only to see it start dying almost immediately. Flowers fall off, buds refuse to open, leaves wilt — and your new acquisition, far from giving you the pleasure you anticipated, is simply a dead loss. But if you check over a plant carefully in the shop before you buy it, you should be able to avoid this sort of disappointment in the future.

When and where to buy

The best time to buy flowering plants is always when they are in bloom and at their most active period of growth. For winter-flowering plants — such as Cyclamen, Azalea and Camellia — this could well be around Christmas time. But when you're not buying such a seasonal plant, it makes sense always to buy in spring or summer. Plants will then be stronger than at any other time of the year, and so better able to withstand the shock of being transported first from a nursery to a retailer, and then from the shop to your home.

It's always very important to get your plant from a reliable stockist. The shop where you buy should be well-maintained, and the retailer and the staff should be knowledgeable and helpful, as well as attentive to the needs of the plants. You are more likely to meet such expertise in a specialist garden centre than in, say, a department store. If you care about your plants — and certainly if you're going to spend a lot of money — you should consider making the extra effort of going to a good garden or plant centre rather than simply buying from the nearest or most convenient

A range of shades, *above*, makes a splash of colour, from the tall pink Begonias to the pink and purple Primulas at the front, complemented by the white and blue of a Cyclamen and a Hyacinth.

What to

It makes sense to buy more than one flowering plant at a time, and to have a colour key in mind. You'll achieve a more decorative effect if you set out to match or contrast flower shades — and don't forget to take into consideration the dominant colours of the room you intend to put them in. Flowers form a definite part of the interior decor of your home, just as wallpaper or furnishing fabrics do — the only difference is that it's easier to change your mind with flowers, and much less expensive to experiment!

Your choice will be affected by what your local shops and garden centres have on offer. Luckily, many of the most popular plants appear in a range of colours — this chart does not attempt to cover all of them, but lists ten of the best in each colour.

Key

E: Evergreen shrub
D: Deciduous shrub
A: Annual
P: Perennial

WHITE	BLUE	PURPLE
African Violet P Year round	**African Violet** P Year round	**African Violet** P Year round
Bleeding Heart Vine E (*Clerodendrum thomsonae*) Spring-autumn, large white bracts with small red blossoms	**Bush Violet** A (*Browallia speciosa*) Winter or summer	**Bush Violet** A (*Browallia speciosa*) Winter or summer
Camellia E Winter-spring	**Campanula** P Summer-autumn	**Cape Primrose** E (*Streptocarpus hybridus*) Spring-autumn
Cape Primrose E (*Streptocarpus hybridus*) Spring-autumn	**Cape Primrose** E (*Streptocarpus hybridus*) Spring-autumn	**Cineraria** P Winter-spring
Cyclamen P Winter-spring	**Cineraria** P Winter-spring	**Cyclamen** P Winter-spring
Gardenia E Summer, fragrant	**Hydrangea** D or E Summer	**Fuschia** D Summer-autumn
Hydrangea D or E Summer	**Pansy** P Summer-winter	**Pansy** P Summer-winter
Jasmine D or E Winter-spring, fragrant	**Plumbago** E Spring-autumn	**Pelargonium** D or E Summer
Stephanotis E Spring-autumn, fragrant	**Primula** D or E Winter-spring	**Primula** D or E Winter-spring
Wax plant (miniature) E (*Hoya bella*) Summer, fragrant	**Yesterday, Today and Tomorrow** E (*Brunfelsia calycina*) Spring-summer, fragrant	**Yesterday, Today and Tomorrow** E (*Brunfelsia calycina*) Spring-summer, fragrant

shop. If you want something a bit unusual, it pays to look at the advertisements in gardening magazines to find specialist nurseries near you: they are bound to have a greater choice than a shop that caters only for casual trade.

The plants in the shop should be on display without any plastic wrappers. Adequately watered and fed, they should be in good positions — neither too shady nor too sunny, and not in any draught from doors or windows. The shop should feel comfortably warm — any severe drop in temperature at night can do a lot of harm. A stockist who seems conscientious is much more likely to provide you with a healthy plant than one who seems ignorant or slapdash.

Points to look out for

● **Do** check the plant for firm and plentiful buds. If the buds are droopy the plant may have been in a draught.
● **Do** check the leaves. They should be firm and glossy. Pick the pot right up, and turn the plant over carefully so that you can see the undersides. This is where any pests will lurk: whitefly, red spider mite, mealy bug. Any blisters or brown areas on the leaves may be a sign of bacterial infection or fungus, while rings or mottling may well be the result of a virus.
● **Do** inspect the flowers carefully. Always choose a plant that has flowers in bloom as well as buds — you can't be sure exactly how the flowers will turn out unless you've actually seen them! Also, if flowers have already come out, you will know the plant is growing vigorously and will be likely to survive the journey home. A plant in bud only may be upset enough by a change in conditions for the buds never to open once you've got the plant home.

Keep an eye out for any flowers that are wilting or withered — this could mean that the plant has not been properly fed.
● **Don't** forget to give the stems a quick look over as well. If they're at all white and powdery it may be a sign of mildew, caused by overwatering.

● **Don't** choose a plant that's already covered with fully opened flowers. It's already past its best, and may be near the end of its life.
● **Don't** buy a plant if the compost in the pot has shrunk away from the sides. This almost certainly means that at some stage the plant has been allowed to dry out, and its subsequent growth may well be affected.
● **Don't** buy a plant that is wilting or that shows any sign of disease.

Asking for advice

Never be afraid of asking for advice. A good retailer should be able to advise you on the best plants to buy if you describe the conditions of your room. Say where you're thinking of placing the plant, and what sort of temperature and light it can expect.

A general rule is that flowering plants demand quite a good light to produce blooms. Many of them — including the popular Azalea, Camellia and Cyclamen — also prefer a rather cool, airy atmosphere to a hot, dry one.

choose

RED

Azalea D or E
Winter-spring

Begonia P
Summer-autumn

Buzy Lizzie A or P
Year round

Camellia E
Winter-spring

Chrysanthemum A or P
Year round

Cineraria P
Winter-spring

Fuschia D
Summer-autumn

Gloxinia P
(*Sinningia speciosa*)
Spring-autumn

Hibiscus D or E
Summer

Pelargonium D or E
Summer

PINK

Azalea D or E
Winter-spring

Begonia P
Summer-autumn

Buzy Lizzie A or P
Year round

Camellia E
Winter-spring

Cineraria P
Winter-spring

Cyclamen P
Winter-spring

Gloxinia P
(*Sinningia speciosa*)
Spring-autumn

Hibiscus D or E
Summer

Oleander E
Summer, fragrant

Pelargonium D or E
Summer

ORANGE

Calceolaria A or P
Spring

Clivia E
Spring-summer

Cytisus D or E
Winter-spring, fragrant

Firecracker Flower E
(*Crossandra undulifolia*)
Spring-summer

Glory Lily P
(*Gloriosa rothschildiana*)
Summer

Goldfish Plant P
(*Columnea gloriosa*)
Spring

Kohleria E
Summer

Lipstick Vine E
(*Aeschynanthus lobbianus*)
Spring-summer

Marigold A
(*Calendula officinalis*)
Summer

Primula P
Winter-spring

YELLOW

Allamanda E
Summer

Cape Cowslip P
(*Lachenalia aloides*)
Winter-spring

Chrysanthemum A or P
Year round

Freesia P
Spring

Hibiscus D or E
Summer

Jasmine D or E
Winter-spring

Kohleria P
Summer

Pansy P
(Viola hybrids)
Summer-winter

Primula P
Winter-spring

Zebra Plant E
(*Aphelandra squarrosa*)
Spring-summer

Getting it home

Many plants, such as African Violets, have leaves and stems that are very brittle and easily damaged. Take care not to crush them when carrying them home; if you have a long journey, it's wise to ask the shop to pack the plant in a cardboard box padded out with newspaper. A good retailer should not mind doing this for you.

If you have to buy plants during very cold weather, then make sure they are very well wrapped and protected from icy winds; screwed-up newspaper between the plant and its wrapping will help to insulate the plant.

You may want to transport a very tall plant — like a palm — in an ordinary car. The best way is to get someone to hold it virtually on its side, but if you're on your own wedge the pot at an angle — don't rest it with the stem taking all the strain.

Finally, when you get home, if you have trouble getting the plant out of its bag, cut it out rather than drag coverings over the foliage, which might damage it.

Plants grown for fragrance

The natural, lingering fragrance of plants adds an extra dimension to a room's decor, and appeals to hitherto untouched senses. Back in the 1890s, Mrs Beaton — everybody's favourite household management consultant — wrote of the inadvisability of using too many hyacinths in floral arrangements for dinner party table centres. The reason she gave was that the ladies — already suffering from the effects of too tightly waisted clothes, a smoky atmosphere, rich food and strong wine — would be so burdened by the heady scent of the flowers that they would probably faint!

Whether anyone took any notice of this particular piece of advice isn't recorded. But fragrant plants and flowers have had their place in the home since much earlier days. In the Middle Ages, for example, when sanitation was poor, herbs and scented flowers were strewn on rush-covered floors to mask any unsavoury smells. And pomanders and posies of sweet-smelling flowers were carried in the streets to ward off the plague.

Nowadays, we are rather more likely to grow fragrant plants for no more devious reason than their straightforward enjoyment. Yet surprisingly few of our most popular indoor plants are scented, and many of the biggest and most flamboyant flowers are disappointingly devoid of any fragrance whatsoever.

So which varieties should you choose with scent in mind? If you want year-round fragrance, then choose plants with scented foliage, such as the old-fashioned scented-leaved Geraniums or aromatic herbs. But if you like to follow the changing seasons round with a succession of different scents, then choose plants with scented flowers.

Where to grow fragrant plants

Just as certain colour schemes suit certain rooms, so there are particular scents that suit some rooms or decorative styles better than others.

Four great fragrances: Oleander, Stephanotis, Gardenia and the scented-leaved *Pelargonium graveolens*.

Plants with scented flowers

The plants listed below are all renowned for their flowers, which are not only decorative but also fragrant.

Citrus	White star-shaped flowers all year round in warmth	***Jasminum polyanthum***	White flowers in spring
Coffee plant (*Coffea arabica*)	Masses of white flowers in summer	**Lily of the Valley**	Forced plants flower in early spring
Exacum	Lavender flowers in autumn, winter and early spring	**Miniature Roses**	Flushes of flowers in summer
Gardenia	Large white flowers in spring	***Narcissus jonquilla***	Yellow flowers in spring
Hyacinth	Flowers from Christmas to spring	**Grape Hyacinth (*Muscari ambrosiacum*)**	Lilac flowers in spring
Heliotrope	Blue flowers in summer	***Nerium oleander***	Large pink, white or red flowers in summer
Hoya	White, pink or maroon flowers in summer	**Madagascar Jasmine (Stephanotis)**	Waxy white flowers between May and October

Herbs, for instance, are best suited to kitchens, largely because people instantly recognise them as culinary plants. But where varieties are not well known, why not consider using them along with conventional houseplants. The red Basil 'Dark Opal', for example, looks most attractive used as a foliage pot plant in the living room.

Scented-leaved Geraniums, with their lovely clean, healthy aroma, are also good for kitchens and, just like herbs, many varieties have culinary uses. But they are eminently suitable plants for a bedroom too — a potted Scented Geranium is a delightful gift for someone who is unwell and confined to bed. Their 'olde worlde' charm also makes them especially well suited to cottage-style homes, where they can be used in virtually any room.

Fragrant-flowered spring bulbs, such as Lily of the Valley, Hyacinths and the miniature *Narcissus jonquilla*, suit any style of house or decor. They are usually grown in bowls and forced, and then brought into the house only after they come into flower. As temporary indoor residents, they won't mind being stood anywhere that allows them to be shown off to best advantage, even if this means slightly less light than that in which you would normally keep a permanently indoor plant. Short-lived annuals, such as Exacum and Heliotrope, will also 'go' quite happily anywhere too.

Miniature Roses are classic flowers that look perfectly at home in any sort of decor, from cottage style to super modern. Although, strictly speaking, they are perennials, they are best treated as temporary plants. Keep them in a reasonably well lit spot, and stand them out in the garden during lulls between flushes of flowers. Better still, keep several plants on the go, so that you can always have one in full flower to scent your room. Take care when choosing miniature roses because, as with full-sized outdoor roses, not all varieties are scented.

Eucalyptus, Citrus and Oleander are all good choices for sunrooms, conservatories and large lounges with patio doors or picture windows, as they grow quite large and need plenty of light. Their exotic scents, their need for light and their rather modern looks probably suit them best to more contemporary-style settings.

The traditional flowery scents of Gardenia and Stephanotis, on the other hand, are better suited to traditional-style rooms. These are smaller plants which dislike too much direct sun, so the old-fashioned cottage, which has smaller windows, is likely to provide them with the best growing conditions.

Useful hints

● Grow scented plants close to doorways, where air currents will carry their fragrance round the house.

● Always keep fragrant-leaved plants a little on the dry side to concentrate their perfume. Stand them where they will occasionally be brushed past or touched; this will make them release more of their scent.

● Keep scented-flowering bulbs as cool as possible to make both flowers and scent last as long as possible.

● Other scented flowers should be kept warm for maximum scent.

Plants with scented foliage

These usually emit a faint fragrance almost continually but, to increase its intensity, you can simply brush the plant lightly with the back of your hand. There is no need actually to damage or destroy leaves by crushing them.

Leaves can also be dried and made into potpourri. The addition of a little orris root — obtainable from some health food shops and herb specialists — will prolong the scent of the blend.

Scented-leaved Geraniums (Pelargonium)

Most varieties have small, rather insignificant, but nevertheless attractive, flowers throughout the summer and early autumn, though plants are grown mainly for their foliage. Both flowers and foliage are quite unlike those of other Geraniums. There are about 50 different species and varieties in cultivation, with a great assortment of scents, ranging from rose and mint to lemon and spice. The strongest-scented is probably 'Mabel Grey', which has a fresh lemon fragrance.

P.'Attar of Roses'	Rose-scented
P.citriodorum	Lemon-scented
P.'Clorinda'	Cedar-scented, large pale pink flowers
P.crispum	Lemon-scented, pale violet flowers
P.crispum variegatum	Lemon-scented, variegated-leaves
P.filicifolium	Balsam-scented, ferny foliage
P.fragrans	Pine-scented
P.fragrans variegata	Pine-scented, variegated leaves
P.graveolens	Rose-scented, magenta flowers
P.'Lady Mary'	Nutmeg-scented
P.'Mabel Grey'	Lemon-scented
P.odoratissimum	Apple-scented
P.'Prince of Orange'	Orange-scented
P.tomentosum	Peppermint-scented, trailing habit

Herbs

For the best of all possible worlds, choose varieties that are not only useful for the pot but also ornamental and scented.

Basil 'Dark Opal'	Attractive dark red form
Lemon Balm, Golden	Strong lemon scent

Herbs, *continued*

Lemon Balm, variegated	Gold-blotched leaves
Marjoram, Golden	Pale gold leaves
Marjoram, Knotted	Stronger-scented
Mint, Eau de Cologne	True eau de Cologne scent
Mint, Curled	Curly form of spearmint
Mint, Ginger	Gold-blotched leaves, faint ginger scent
Mint, Lemon	Strong lemon scent
Rosemary, Prostrate	The best choice of Rosemary for indoors
Sage, Pineapple	Strong pineapple scent, red flowers
Thyme, Doone Valley	Lemon scent, variegated leaves
Thyme (Thymus mastochinus)	Lavender-scented leaves
Thyme, Golden	Pale golden leaves

Other scented-foliage plants

The following plants all make a good choice for house or conservatory. Eucalyptus should be cut back hard each spring to keep it a convenient size; this treatment also encourages the plant to continue producing its attractively shaped, juvenile foliage.

Lemon Verbena (Lippia citriodora)	Strong lemon-scented foliage
Myrtle (Myrtus communis)	Aromatic evergreen leaves
Eucalyptus gunnii	Eucalyptus-scented
Eucalyptus citriodora	Lemon-scented
Eucalyptus linearis	Peppermint-scented

Where to buy your houseplants

YOUR FIRST CALL should be your local garden centre (look in your *Yellow Pages* telephone directory under 'Garden Centres'). If you can't find what you want locally, write for a mail order catalogue from one of the general or specialist suppliers listed below.

Some of these nurseries are open to visitors and for retail sales. Check the opening times by telephone if possible before making a visit. Where the telephone number is not listed, it may mean that the nursery is run singlehanded by someone who is too busy to answer the phone. In that case write, enclosing a stamped addressed envelope for a reply.

General houseplant suppliers

Anmore Exotics   Mail order
4 The Curve
Lovedean
Hants PO8 9SE

Long Man Gardens   Mail order
Lewes Road   Nursery open
Wilmington   weekends
Polegate
East Sussex BN26 5RS
Telephone: (0323) 870816

Newington Nurseries   Mail order only
Old School
Newington
Oxford OX9 8AH

Achimenes

K.J. Townsend   Mail order only
17 Valerie Close
St Albans AL1 5JD

Craig Soil Services   Mail order only
Windermere
Cumbria LA23 2NB
Telephone: (09662) 2818

Stanley Mossop   Mail order only
36 Thorny Road
Thornhill
Egremont
Cumbria CA22 2RZ
Telephone: Egremont 821817

Achimenes longiflora

Azalea indica

African Violets

Eric Beesley's African Violet Greenhouse   Mail order only
12 Alma Road   (please send s.a.e. for
Carlton   list)
Nottingham NG3 2NU

Tony Clements' Nursery   Mail order
Station Road   Nursery open daily
Terrington St Clement
King's Lynn
Norfolk PE34 4PL
Telephone: (0553) 828374

Azaleas

Hydon Nurseries   Mail order
Clock Barn Lane   Nursery open
Hydon Heath   weekdays
Godalming
Surrey GU8 4AZ
Telephone: 048 632 252

Millais Nurseries   Mail order
Crosswater Farm   Nursery open
Churt   weekdays
Farnham   (morning only
Surrey GU10 2JN   Saturday)
Telephone: Frensham 2415

Begonias   Mail order only
Blackmore & Langdon Ltd
Stanton Nurseries
Pensford
Bristol BS18 4JL
Telephone: (0272) 2300

W. Wall   Mail order only
4 Selbourne Close
New Haw
Weybridge

Rebutia pseudodeuminata

Cactus *Mammilaria hahiana*

Bromeliads

Vesutor Ltd
Billingshurst Lane
Ashington
West Sussex RH20 3BA
Telephone: Ashington (0903) 892900 — Mail order only

Bulbs

Jacques Amand Ltd
17 Beethoven Street
London W10 4LG
Telephone: (01) 969 9797 — Mail order / Garden centre open weekdays (morning only weekends)

Avon Bulbs
Bathford
Bath BA1 8ED — Mail order

Walter Blom & Son Ltd
Coombelands Nurseries
Leavesden
Watford
Herts WD2 8BH
Telephone: Garston 673767 — Mail order

Rupert Bowlby
Gatton
Reigate RH2 0TA

Broadleigh Gardens
Barr House
Bishops Hull
Taunton
Somerset TA4 1AE
Telephone: (0823) 86231 — Mail order only

Paradise Centre
Twinstead Road
Lamarsh
Bures
Suffolk CO8 5EX
Telephone: (078 729) 449 — Mail order / Nursery and gardens open in summer weekends and Bank Holiday Mondays only (small admission charge)

Spalding Bulb Company
Spalding
Lincolnshire PE11 1NA
Telephone: (0775) 4436 — Mail order only

Van Tubergen
304a Upper Richmond Road West
London SW14 7JG — Mail order

Cacti

Abbey Brook Cactus Nursery
Old Hackney Lane
Matlock
Derbyshire DE4 2QL
Telephone: (0629) 55360 — Mail order / Glasshouses open afternoons (closed Tuesdays)

Craig House Cacti
56 Ranelagh Drive
Southport
Merseyside — Mail order

Cruck Cottage Cactus Nursery
Wrelton
Pickering
North Yorkshire — Nursery open

Glenhirst Nursery
Station Road
Swineshead
Boston
Lincolnshire PE20 3NX
Telephone: Boston (0205) 820314 — Mail order only

Holly Gate Cactus Nursery
Billingshurst Lane
Ashington
West Sussex RH20 3BA
Telephone: (0903) 892439 — Mail order

Southfields Nurseries
Louth Road
Holton le Clay
Grimsby
South Humberside — Mail order

141

Chrysanthemum 'Redbreast'

Westfield Cacti   Mail order
10 Shillingford Road
Alphington
Exeter EX2 8UB
Telephone: (0392) 56925

Whitestone Gardens Ltd   Mail order
Sutton-under-Whitestonecliffe   Nursery open daily
Thirsk
North Yorkshire YO7 2P2
Telephone: Thirsk (0845) 597467

R. Young   Mail order only
79 Pearcroft Road
Leytonstone
London E11 4DP
Telephone: (01) 556 8048

Carnivorous plants

Marston Exotics   Mail order
Turners Field   Nursery open
Compton Dundon   (telephone to check
Somerton   times)
Somerset TA11 6PT
Telephone: (0458) 42192

Chrysanthemums

Wells (Merstham) Ltd   Mail order
Wells Place
London Road
South Merstham
Surrey RH1 3AS

H. Woolman Ltd   Mail order
Grange Road
Dorridge
Solihull
West Midlands B93 8QB

Charm Chrysanthemum 'Ringdove'

Ferns

J.K. Marston   Mail order
Culag   (catalog 50p)
Green Lane   Nursery open
Nafferton   weekend
Near Driffield   afternoons
East Yorkshire
Telephone: (0377) 44487

Fuchsias

Potash Nursery   Mail order
Hawkwell
Hockley
Essex SS5 4JN
Telephone:

Oakleigh Nurseries   Mail order
Monkwood   Nursery shop open
Alresford   (telephone to check
Hants SO24 0HB   times)
Telephone: (096 277) 3344

C.S. Lockyer   Mail order
70 Henfield Road
Coalpit Heath
Bristol BS17 2U2
Telephone: (0454) 772219

Where to buy your houseplants

Cymbidium Bruges

Impatiens
Brenda Hyatt   Mail order
1 Toddington Crescent
Bluebell Hill
Near Chatham
Kent ME5 9QT
Telephone: (0634) 63251

Ivies
Whitehouse Ivies   Mail order only
Tolleshunt Knights
Maldon CM9 8EZ
Telephone: (0621) 815782

Orchids
Burham Nurseries Ltd   Mail order
Orchid Avenue   Nursery open Monday
Kingsteignton   to Saturday. Closed
Newton Abbot   Sundays and Bank
Devon TQ12 3HG   Holidays
Telephone: (0626) 2233

McBeans Orchids Ltd   Mail order
Cooksbridge
Lewes
Sussex

Ratcliffe Orchids Ltd   Mail order
Chilton   Nursery open daily
Didcot
Oxon OX11 0RT
Telephone (0235) 834385

Wellbank Orchids Ltd   Mail order
Pardown
Oakley
Hants RG23 7DY

Wyld Court Orchids   Mail order
Hampstead Norreys   Nursery open daily in
Newbury   summer
Berks RG16 0TN
Telephone: (0635) 201283

Palms
The Palm Farm   Mail order
Thornton Hall Gardens
Ulceby
South Humberside DN39 6XF
Telephone: (0469) 31232

Pelargoniums
A.P. Elite Plants   Mail order
Vines Cross   Nursery open March to
Heathfield   June (ring to check
East Sussex   times)
Telephone: (04352) 6053

Streptocarpus

Fibrex Nurseries Ltd
Honeybourne Road
Pebworth
Near Stratford-on-Avon CV37 8XT
Telephone: Stratford-on-Avon 720788

Mail order
Nursery open weekday
afternoons (and some
weekends in summer)

Thorp's Geraniums
257 Finchampstead Road
Wokingham
Berks
Telephone: (0734) 781181

Mail order
Nursery open (ring to
check times)

Vernon Geranium Nursery
Cuddington Way
Cheam
Sutton
Surrey
Telephone: (01) 393 7616

Mail order only

Primulas
Genus Primula
Harbour House
Glasson Dock
Lancaster

Mail order

Bressingham Gardens
Bressingham
Diss
Norfolk IP22 2AB
Telephone: (037 988) 464

Mail order
Gardens open on
certain days only (ring
to check dates and
times)

Streptocarpus
Efenechtyd Nurseries
Llanelidan
Ruthin
Clwyd
North Wales LL15 2LG
Telephone: (097 888) 677

Mail order
Nursery open July and
August (please ring
evenings only)

Primula Vulgaris (Coloured hybrid)

Choosing bulbs

There could hardly be a better plant for containers than a bulb: easy-to-plant, hardly needing any after-care and flowering for many weeks. Some bulbs have ornamental leaves, too, and these last even longer. Added to which, there are bulbs for spring, summer, autumn and even winter. They seldom get infested with pests or diseases and, altogether, bulbs seem to have been custom-built for container-growing. Even nature's instant packaging makes them easier to bring home from the garden centre!

When choosing your bulbs, always look for those that are sound and have no brown marks or indentations. Sometimes they can be afflicted with rot, even if they have been sprayed. Always check the basal plate at the bottom – the rounder it is, the more evenly it will grow and the better it will flower. And the larger the bulb, the bigger the plant. With Daffodils, a double-nose (two growing points) will mean two flowers.

Once home, if the bulbs are not going to be planted right away, they can be kept in a dark, cool place in a plastic bag for up to three months. Although they can be planted until February or March, it is advisable to use your bulbs before the spring – ideally between September and December for Daffodils, or from November to February for Tulips. If you are planting in boxes or containers, bulbs prefer a well-drained soil, so a little sand in the planting hole will stop any tendency to rot, especially if you have clay soil and the bulbs are overwintering. Tulips and Daffodils do best in dappled shade; Hyacinths are happy in the sun, as are Crocuses; and Snowdrops prefer a woodland mixture of shade and sun. Another tip for Snowdrops is to dig them up and replant them when the leaves appear: this is known as planting 'in the green', and gives a better show of flowers.

All bulbs should be dug up every four or five years, when you should also divide the offsets – smaller bulbs which will have formed and which will almost drop off. When replanting, bulbs must always have enough depth, and daffodils especially need a good 4in (10cm) of soil, otherwise you will not have a good show of flowers. And, when flowering is over, wait until the leaves have yellowed and died before lifting: there is no need to tie the leaves into knots. In fact, this actually prevents the food from being sent down into the bulb. If you really can't leave them to die down, then dig them up and plant them somewhere else, diagonally in shallow soil.

Springtime is tulip time

For spring-flowering bulbs, the choice is so wide you will be limited only by the size and number of your containers. If their depth is relatively shallow, go for the smaller varieties, such as Squills (Scilla), Glory-of-the-Snow (Chionodoxa) and Grape Hya-

Daffodils have long been known as the heralds of the spring.

In spring fill your window-box with tulips and polyanthus.

Tulips bring colour to a spring patio.

Grape hyacinths like plenty of sunshine.

Summer sunshine

As the Tulips finish, the summer-flowering bulbs can take their place: the white 18in (45cm) tall summer Snowflake (Leucojum), like a giant Snowdrop; the white summer Hyacinth, *Galtonia candicans*; and the elegant Lilies, the cottage-garden Madonna Lily (*Lilium candidum*) and the Regal Lily (*L. regale*), both white and strongly scented. The rainbow-coloured Freesias are another type of bulb with a powerful fragrance, but use the specially-treated summer-flowering kind.

For small bulbs, look among the St Brigid and de Caen Anemones (Florists' Anemones), Sparaxis, Ranunculus and Brodiaeas. Gladiolus is a very special sort of flowering bulb – each flower is exquisite in colour and form.

The mid- to late-summer flowering of the Lilies and Gladioli could be accompanied by the Montbretias (Crocosmia) in yellow and oranges, and these in turn will overlap the first of the autumn bulbs, Meadow Saffron (Colchicum) in pink or rosy mauve, flowering before the leaves. Nerines and Crinums from South Africa flower in September-October.

Winter wonderland

Dwarf Cyclamen can be had for autumn flowering, and their white marbled, dark green leaves will last all winter. *Sternbergia lutea* is an intensely yellow, Crocus-like flower for October, and autumn-flowering Crocus proper include *C. speciosus* (violet-blue) and *C. zonatus* (pink).

Carry on the Crocus theme with Chrysanthus varieties in winter, and mix them with *Iris reticulata*, January-flowering and dwarf, just 6in (15cm) high. Snowdrops will accompany them in sheltered positions, as will the yellow Winter Aconite (*Eranthis hyemalis*). The miniature Daffodils will flower in February: *Narcissus bulbocodium* 'Conspicuus' (the Hoop Petticoat Daffodil) and *N. cyclamineus* 'February Gold' will look delightful alongside the earliest of the spring Crocus.

All these are small, but would not be dwarfed by planting small conifers with them, to give some height and colour when the bulbs are out of flower. Otherwise, you might like winter-flowering Heathers (*Erica carnea*), or small-leaved variegated Ivies.

cinths (Muscari), all with blue flowers between early and late spring. Try the species Tulips, such as the Waterlily *Tulipa kaufmanniana*, *T. greigii* and *T. fosteriana*.

Larger spring-flowering bulbs include Daffodils, Narcissus, Jonquils and Hyacinths, and any specialist bulb catalogue will list an overwhelming number of varieties. Grow them alone or mixed with Polyanthus, Primroses, Primulas, Violets, Forget-Me-Nots or Wallflowers. Or,

try them with the coloured Wood Anemones, *Anemone blanda*, in blue and pink.

Plant the dwarf double-flowered Tulips for a particularly long-lasting, brilliant display from mid-April to mid-May, and continue the season with their larger relatives, such as the May-flowering Darwins. For a change of flower-shape, choose from the parrot and fringe varieties, or the lily-flowered kinds – 'Marilyn' is an especially lovely variety.

The **trumpet-shaped** flowers of *Crinum powelli* are always magnificent.

Bulbs for autumn

The **narrow petals** of *Colchicum autumnale* give it a slightly starry look.

The **fragrant flowers** of *Iris reticulata* usually appear in late winter.

Bulbs are usually associated with spring and early summer but, in fact, there are just as many that will make a show of colour on your patio in autumn and winter. These come in a vaiety of hues and sizes, and all have characteristics that make them particularly good and decorative plants for a patio or balcony.

The autumn collection

Nerines. The graceful blooms of this autumn-flowering species are just as pretty as their name suggests and come in shades of pink, carmine, orange and salmon-pink with strap-shaped petals which are long and curl backwards. *Nerine bowdenii* 'Fenwick's Variety' with deep pink flowers is the type that is normally grown. The flowers start to appear in early autumn and can last well into mid-winter. Give them some protection if the frost is really hard.

They will grow about 2ft (0.6m) high and the leaves should last until midsummer the following year. Plant them in late summer, taking care to keep the tips of the bulbs just above the compost.

Cyclamen. Miniature Cyclamen look delightful when planted in small containers. *Cyclamen hederifolium*, previously called *C. neapolitanum*, is an ideal species for this purpose – its main flowering period being during early to mid-autumn. Rosy-pink flowers with a crimson blotch grow on stems about 3in (8cm) tall, followed by beautifully marbled leaves

and winter

The delicate **Narcissus cyclamineus** are the real heralds of spring.

lasting until the end of late spring. These bulbs should be planted in midsummer, with about 1in (2.5cm) of compost above them.

Crocus. The crocus family has at least one easily grown and common species which flowers at this time – *C. speciosus*. The light to deep purple flowers grow on stems 2in (5cm) long and appear before the leaves. Another species *C. kotschyanus* also flowers in autumn, and it has large, rosy-lilac flowers which appear before the leaves.

Colchicum autumnale. With the common name of 'Naked Boys', this bulb has pink-lilac flowers which grow straight out of the ground without any leaves. It is distinguishable from the more cup-shaped, true crocus by its narrow petals, which give it a starry look. It should be planted towards the end of late summer.

Sternbergia lutea. This native of the eastern Mediterranean has bright yellow flowers which once seen are hard to forget. The leaves appear with the flowers in early autumn, but do not reach full length until the spring. It needs a good baking in dry conditions and summer sun to flower well, and is especially appreciative of a chalky compost. It should be planted in late summer.

Crinum x powellii. The trumpet-shaped, pink flowers of this magnificent bulb are 4in (10cm) long and nearly as wide. They appear in early autumn in clusters on stems which grow at least 2ft (0.6m) tall. The bulbs are large – up to 5in (13cm) wide – and should be planted in a deep container in spring.

Winter blooms

Iris reticulata. The fragrant blooms of this miniature Iris should appear at the beginning of mid-winter, as long as you remember to plant your bulbs in late summer. The flowers, in various shades of blue, and sometimes reddish-purple, grow on stems about 6in (15cm) long.

Snowdrops. These will only appear in winter when planted in sheltered corners and if the weather is very mild. They should be planted in early autumn.

A **combination of** Crocuses and miniature Irises can make a wonderful winter display.

The pretty *Nerine bowdenii* will need some protection if the frost gets really hard.

Winter Aconite (*Eranthis hyemalis*). The golden, cup-shaped flowers of this bulb are delightfully framed in a green ruffle-like calyx, and grow on stems about 4in (10cm) long.

Florist's Anemone (*Anemone coronaria*). This bulb will produce flowers at different times of the year, depending on when it is planted. An early autumn planting will result in flowers in late winter, when their jewel-like colours of purple, scarlet and blue are more than welcome. And, with the help of a cloche or pane of glass to protect the flowers from the worst of the winter cold, you should be able to enjoy them and pick them for at least several weeks.

Daffodils. The miniature Daffodil (*Narcissus cyclamineus*) is the real herald of spring. It grows up to 8in (20cm) high and has narrow petals in deep gold. Once these start to flower you can be sure that winter is nearly over. They look superb when planted in groups – when each flower gives some protection to its neighbour.

How and where to plant

NAME	PLANTING DEPTH AND SPACING	SEASON	CONDITIONS
Anemone coronaria ('St Brigid' and 'De Caen')	2 x 4in (5 x 10cm)	Late winter	Well-drained peaty compost, sun.
Crocus speciosus, C. kotschyanus	2 x 2in (5 x 5cm)	Early autumn	Good drainage, sun.
Colchicum autumnale (Naked Boys)	3 x 3in (8 x 8cm)	Early autumn	Well-drained peaty compost, shade and sun.
Crinum x powellii	6 x 6in (15 x 15cm)	Early to mid autumn	Rich compost, sun, south-facing aspect.
Cyclamen hederifolium	Top of corm just covered, x 3in (8cm)	Early autumn	Well-drained compost, plant low in the container and topdress with leafmould in late spring, dappled shade.
Eranthis hyemalis (Winter Aconite)	1/2 x 1in (1 x 2.5cm)	Late winter	Good potting compost, sun or little shade.
Galanthus nivalis (Snowdrop)	1 x 1in (2.5 x 2.5cm)	Mid to late winter	Good potting compost, little shade.
Iris reticulata	2 x 2in (5 x 5cm)	Mid to late winter	Well-drained compost, sun.
Narcissus cyclamineus	2-3in (5-8cm)	Late winter	Moist compost, well-drained, a little shade
Nerine bowdenii	Tip just above surface x 3in (8cm)	Early to mid autumn	Well-drained compost, sun.
Sternbergia lutea	4 x 3in (10 x 8cm)	Mid autumn	Well-drained compost, south facing, plenty of sun.

Make the most of bedding plants

Twice a year, in spring and autumn, the market is flooded with a sudden rush of plants – first half-hardy annuals and then biennials. Bought individually, they may seem relatively inexpensive, but by the time you've planted up even the smallest patio, you may be surprised to find you've spent a small fortune! It makes sense, therefore, to go for top quality in order to get the best possible value for both your money and your labour.

Annuals

In April and May, garden centres, market stalls and even some local greengrocers are suddenly full of half-hardy annuals, also known as bedding plants. Most of these are highly suitable for patio and balcony containers, such as window-boxes, tubs, urns and hanging baskets and, as soon as they are in the shops, gardeners everywhere are subject to a great urge to buy them.

This is quite understandable, but what follows is a friendly word of warning. You must realise, above all, that half-hardy annuals – Petunias, Lobelia, Marigolds, Wax Begonias (*Begonia semperflorens*), Salvias, Verbena and so on – should not be planted out until all danger of frost is over. In the southern half of the country this means late May, while in northern counties it is early June.

So, unless you are confident that you can give plants frost protection, don't buy them until it is time to plant them out. If, however, you have a cold frame or a small patio greenhouse, you can buy well before planting time and keep the plants under cover while giving them plenty of day-time ventilation to help them become acclimatised to outdoor life.

Then, a few days before they are planted out, they can be given full ventilation, both day and night, to acclimatise them fully to outdoor conditions. If, however, you have to buy your plants, say, a week or more before planting time and you don't have a cold frame or greenhouse, then

Brickwork sets off Petunias and Geraniums.

Mix bedding plants to create a focal display.

Grow Lobelia, Petunias and Geraniums in hanging baskets.

you can stand them outside during the day and bring them into a cool room inside the house at night.

If you buy your bedding plants before planting-out time, you should feed them at weekly intervals – irrespective of where you keep them – with a liquid fertiliser as it is likely that the fertiliser in the compost will be coming to an end. An indication that plants are at risk of starvation is a reddening or yellowing of the leaves. Use a general-purpose liquid fertiliser such as Liquinure, liquid Growmore or Phostrogen.

It goes without saying that plants should be watered regularly. Never allow the compost to dry out, but keep it steadily moist. If the compost

is full of roots – so often the case at this stage – it will dry out rapidly, especially in warm weather.

If you buy plants at planting time, you must try to find out whether they have been well hardened off, or at least acclimatised to outdoor conditions. In a garden centre, plants are usually in an outside display area, perhaps with an overhead cover, which is a good indication that they have been hardened off. If plants are displayed inside a shop, however, they could well still be soft and sappy, in which case they will get a rude shock when they are planted out in the open.

And beware of plants on market stalls – these may have come straight

Viola, Wallflowers and Hollyhock leaves combine well.

Buy Sweet Williams in the autumn.

Grow Myosotis for colour.

from warm greenhouses and still be soft and lush. The safest bet, therefore, is to buy from a reputable garden centre or nursery.

Quality control

There is never any need to opt for second best at a time when so many garden centres and nurseries will be selling summer bedding plants. It makes good sense to shop around until you find top-quality plants.

But how can you recognise quality when you see it? Good quality annuals will be sturdy, with healthy green foliage. Avoid weak, spindly plants with pale or sickly-looking leaves, as these will never grow into strong, free-flowering specimens.

The leaves should not be marked in any way – plants with brown scorch marks caused by hot sun shining on them, for example, are best avoided.

Plants should, of course, be completely free from pests and diseases, so watch out for aphids, mildew and brown spots on the leaves.

Avoid, too, plants that have outgrown their trays or pots. There should not be a mass of roots showing through the bottoms of the containers.

Yellowing or reddish leaves are indications that the plants have exhausted all the fertiliser in the compost. Don't buy these as starved plants never make a really good show later on.

Ideally, plants should just be coming into flower when you buy them, so that you can see exactly what to expect. There should also be plenty of unopened buds.

How many is enough?

It's not always easy to decide exactly how many plants you are likely to need. Bear in mind that the larger bedding plants, like Pelargoniums, need to be planted about 18in (45cm) apart each way. Smaller ones, such as Begonias and French Marigolds, should be spaced about 8in (20cm) apart. One tends to plant closer in smaller containers, so that they are not quite touching each other.

Biennials

Spring and early summer-flowering biennials, such as Wallflowers, Forget-me-nots, Polyanthus, Double Daisies, Sweet Williams and Canterbury Bells, are bought in the autumn, usually October.

Most hardy biennials are sold in trays or strip containers. As regards quality, the only difference between biennials and half-hardy annuals is that the former will not come into flower in the year that they are bought (except, perhaps, for winter-flowering Pansies).

Wallflowers, however, are often sold with bare roots, in bundles, without any soil around them. This works out much cheaper than buying them in trays. But you must check that the roots are well wrapped and are not drying out, as this can delay their establishment in the soil when planted, and they may die.

When you get the plants home, plant them straight away, after standing the roots in a bucket of water for half an hour or so. Make sure that you do not buy plants that have been bundled for a long time, which is indicated by yellow leaves. These leaves will drop when the plants are set out and the plants will look quite bare and never develop into good bushy specimens.

To work out the number of plants you need, bear in mind that Wallflowers, Sweet Williams and Canterbury Bells are planted about 12in (30cm) apart each way, while smaller plants, like Double Daisies, Forget-me-nots and Polyanthus are set about 8in (20cm) apart.

Shrubs and trees for the patio

When buying small shrubs and trees for the patio go to your local garden centre and make sure that they are in containers (pots or polythene bags). This will enable you to plant them at any time of the year you choose.

It is important to bear in mind that there are good and bad garden centres and in the latter, poor quality plants abound – usually because they are not looked after properly. So it is wise to visit a few until you find a good and reliable one which you can trust.

Try to buy shrubs as soon as they come into the garden centre so that you can have the pick of the bunch instead of the leftovers. It certainly pays to look in regularly – say at least once a week.

When to buy

While theoretically, container-grown shrubs can be bought and planted at any time of the year, it is often easier to assess what you are getting if you choose your plant when it's looking at its best.

Buy flowering shrubs such as Camellias, Hydrangeas, Rhododendrons, Azaleas and Roses (the miniature and patio varieties) just as they are coming into flower with a few open blooms and plenty of buds. In this way you can see exactly what you are buying and getting as regards colour and fragrance.

Camellias flower during winter through to spring; Hydrangeas and Roses in summer; and Rhododendrons and Azaleas in spring right through to early summer.

Buy evergreen foliage shrubs, such as dwarf conifers, *Fatsia japonica*, Bay trees, Yuccas, the hardy palm *(Trachycarpus fortunei)* and the hardy Cabbage Palm *(Cordyline australis)* in late spring or summer when they are usually looking at their best. In winter, young evergreen plants standing in a cold, exposed garden centre often become scorched by searing winds and should be avoided for it is unlikely that they will ever recover.

Winter-flowering Ericas can be grown in window-boxes.

Deciduous foliage shrubs should also be bought in spring or summer when they are in full leaf so, again, you can see what you are buying. The Japanese Maple *(Acer palmatum)* and varieties can look very effective when planted in tubs or containers.

Watch out for . . .

● Ensure that the compost is moist. If it has dried out this can result in leaf and flower-bud drop, and could spell death for some plants like Camellias, Rhododendrons, Azaleas and dwarf conifers.

● Shrubs should never be loose in their containers, but rooted and stable, with perhaps just *a few* small roots visible through the holes in the bottom of the pot.

● Avoid shrubs which have a mass of roots showing through the bottom of the container – they have probably been hanging around the garden centre for too long and are past their best. They may also have signs of nutrient deficiency, such as yellowing or red-flushed leaves.

● Avoid plants with brown marks on the leaves, or around the edges of leaves. This could be the result of wind scorch, drying out, or even disease. Conifers with a lot of brown foliage at the base or down one side are almost certainly suffering from a fatal soil-born disease.

● The foliage of lime-hating plants like Camellias, Rhododendrons and Azaleas should be a good green in colour. If it's yellowing they could be suffering from chlorosis – iron deficiency caused by lime or chalk in the compost (this could be the result of watering with limey or 'hard' water).

● Buds of flowering shrubs should be healthy with no signs of browning. And they should certainly not be dropping. If they are it is probably because of cold winds or lack of moisture.

● Avoid shrubs in containers which are full of weeds. You certainly don't want to introduce these to your garden.

● Never buy shrubs with pests on them, even though they may be only aphids such as greenfly. These and some other pests can spread serious virus diseases and a shrub suffering from a virus can never be cured.

● Similarly, never buy shrubs with any signs of disease like mildew (white powdery patches on leaves and shoot tips), grey mould (grey fluffy mould on flowers), and black spot (round black spot on the leaves of roses). These can be eradicated by spraying, but you shouldn't have to do this to a newly-purchased plant.

Make sure that dwarf conifers are always stable in their containers.

Pots and containers

Gleaming copper coal scuttles, teapots, old china potties and hanging baskets — all can make stunning homes for houseplants. Displaying pot plants well is an art form: if you get the effect right, everyone will notice.

When you buy a plant it comes in a standard clay or, more likely, plastic pot **(1)**. The tiniest pot is about $2\frac{1}{2}$in (6cm) in diameter across the inside rim. Sizes increase by about $\frac{1}{2}$in (13mm) at a time, all the way up to 15in (38cm).

Clay pots are thicker and help to insulate plants against the cold better than plastic. But clay is heavier and likely to shatter if it's dropped. Ornamental terracotta containers **(2)**, have the same qualities as clay pots. Glazed terracotta **(3)** is more useful as the glaze stops moisture escaping through the pot and leaving rings on the furniture.

You can grow plants in virtually any ornamental container which will hold soil. Perhaps you have some old china jugs or potties **(4)** you could use. Or even a lovely jardinière **(5)**. Much cheaper and easier to find are stylish modern china containers **(6)** which can be bought at department stores.

An economic alternative but just as pretty are baskets **(7)**. They can be in natural, mellow colours or bright and shiny with paint and varnish. The disadvantages are that baskets tend to be flimsy and they need a drip tray inside to stop water going straight through.

Cheerful, coloured metal and enamel containers **(8)** are particularly useful if you want bright colours to match your decor. But be wary of unsightly rust.

Glass is traditionally used for bottle gardens **(9)** because it lets through plenty of light at the same time as protecting the plants inside from draughts and cold temperatures. Modern glass and lead terrariums are very attractive **(10)** and an effective way of showing off tiny, tender plants.

Gleaming brass **(11)** and copper pots look absolutely splendid holding leafy green houseplants. The catch, of course, is that you need to get the metal cleaning fluid out almost as often as you have to feed the plant inside it! Before using metal containers, line the inside with kitchen foil so the pot doesn't get ruined by water — it is a good idea to do this with all precious ornamental containers.

When planting direct into any container without drainage holes, provide a good, thick layer of pebbles or pea shingle before filling with compost. This is so that excess water can run away from the plant's roots so they are not at risk from rotting.

If your ceilings are a suitable height (and strength) you can broaden your dimensions by using hanging baskets **(12)**. Most useful are the plastic ones with an attached drip tray; with these you won't get water all over the floor. Don't be content with the range of pots and containers offered by your local shops and garden centres. Ingenuity plays an important role in growing plants and it's surprising what you can find if you rummage around in junk shops.

12

Visual mistakes The trick with really effective plant display is to harmonise the pot and the plant so that they go together well. *Top right*, a huge Swiss Cheese Plant in a small pot. This plant is in awful trouble, it is quite obviously far too big for the pot it is living in. Also, having such cramped roots is not doing the plant any good. The plant should be repotted into another pot, half as big again. The delicate Polka Dot Plant, *right*, is drowned in an over-large container.

1   2   3   5

The answer's in the soil...

Compost may look uninspiring, but it's wonderful stuff — it's the source from which your houseplants draw essential nutrients and water through their roots, and without which they cannot survive. Healthy compost, composed of the right ingredients, is vital if you want your plants to flourish. Not only does compost feed your plants, it keeps their roots moist, holds air around the roots and secures the plant upright in its pot.

Garden centres offer a huge range of composts — but don't be overwhelmed;

many of them are much the same thing, but sold under different brand names — just as similar washing powders appear under a variety of brand names in the supermarket. To help you come to the right choice, we'll describe the various ingredients of compost and tell you which particular type is right for your plants.

The most important rule is not to put your houseplants into ordinary garden soil. Not only will this fail to provide the right mix and nutrients — it will also

contain pests and diseases that will attack and harm your plants.

Most composts are composed of either peat or soil (loam), plus fertiliser and sometimes sand as well. Some plants do best in soil-based compost while others prefer one that is peat-based.

Soil-based compost

This is made of sterilised loam (which just means soil), with a smaller quantity of peat and sand, plus fertiliser. The

Compost: What goes in?

The most popular and easily available soil-based composts are the John Innes range, which were researched by the John Innes Institute in the 1930s.

The idea for them came with the discovery that garden soil was not suitable for the artificial conditions in which houseplants are grown. In theory, John Innes compost should be the same wherever you buy it — in practice, of course, it will vary with the quality of the materials.

John Innes potting compost is available in three different types, all carefully designed to promote healthy growth in plants at different stages of their lives. The diagram on the right shows what it is made of. The compost contains seven parts of sterilised loam, three parts of peat and one part of coarse, washed sand. These are measured by volume and mixed together thoroughly. Then a basic fertiliser mix — made up of two parts of hoof and horn meal, two parts of superphosphate and one part of potassium sulphate — is added to the compost by weight: the higher the number of the John Innes compost, the more of this fertiliser mix is in it. Finally, small amounts of chalk or limestone are put in.

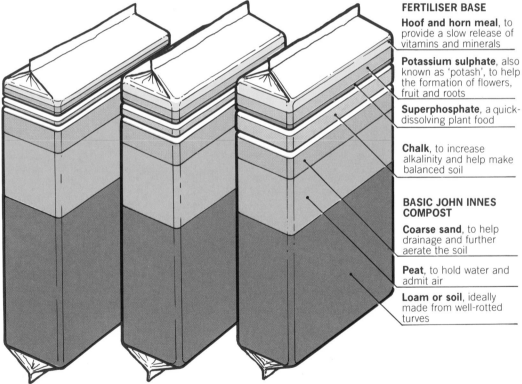

FERTILISER BASE

Hoof and horn meal, to provide a slow release of vitamins and minerals

Potassium sulphate, also known as 'potash', to help the formation of flowers, fruit and roots

Superphosphate, a quick-dissolving plant food

Chalk, to increase alkalinity and help make balanced soil

BASIC JOHN INNES COMPOST

Coarse sand, to help drainage and further aerate the soil

Peat, to hold water and admit air

Loam or soil, ideally made from well-rotted turves

John Innes No 1
For seedlings and cuttings, in small pots up to 4in (10cm)

70lb (32kg) compost
4oz (118g) fertiliser base
¾oz (21g) chalk

John Innes No 2
For mature plants, in medium pots 4-8in (10-20cm)

70lb (32kg) compost
8oz (226g) fertiliser base
½oz (14g) chalk

John Innes No 3
For vigorous and fast-growing plants, in large pots 8in (20cm) and bigger

70lb (32kg) compost
12oz (340g) fertiliser base
2½oz (71g) chalk

widely-used John Innes Composts are based on a mixture — really a recipe — of these four ingredients (see diagram). John Innes Seed Compost is used to give seedlings and cuttings a good start; it doesn't contain any fertiliser, which would 'burn' the tender young roots.

The proportion of each ingredient in the compost is most important: loam is the main ingredient and gives the mixture body and prevents the plant's food from being washed away. Peat holds water well, rather like a sponge does and keeps the roots moist. Sand drains the compost quickly, which prevents waterlogging, and lets air get to the roots. Fertiliser provides the food that plants need for healthy growth.

Soil-based compost holds the fertiliser for about 12 weeks, so you don't need to feed your plant for the first three months after repotting. Don't be tempted to feed repotted plants too soon or to give extra fertiliser to a young plant or a small one; too much of a good thing can kill a plant completely!

Peat-based compost

Peat-based compost is a more recent development, and it's usually the medium your new plant is growing in when you buy it. Nurserymen use it because it's light to carry, and partly because it's cheap to buy and easy to sterilise and unlikely to have weeds or diseases in it.

Most brands of peat-based compost (often also called soilless compost) are a mixture of peat and fertiliser. Or it can be composed of an inorganic material, such as Perlite or vermiculite, mixed in with the peat and fertiliser. Perlite is the brand name for a type of white, irregular shaped granule made from volcanic rock, while vermiculite is expanded volcanic rock — both of them are very light. Fertiliser is released to the plant more quickly from a peat-based compost than from a soil-based one and you will need to feed the plant about six weeks after repotting.

The main disadvantage of peat-based compost is that it can dry out completely if you forget to water the plant in hot weather and be difficult to moisten again thoroughly. The remedy is to stand the pot to over its rim in a bowl of water, until the compost unshrivels, fills out and becomes moist again. If even this doesn't work put a drop or two of Fairy Liquid, or another good quality washing up liquid, into the water, which

If the compost has dried out, immerse the whole pot in water for 15-20 minutes.

coats the peat and helps it to reabsorb water.

It's a good idea to use plastic pots with peat-based compost as plastic is non-porous and doesn't draw out moisture from around the roots and dry out the compost as quickly as clay.

Top dressing

The term 'top dressing' refers to the method of renewing the top layer of compost in a pot without moving the plant or interfering with its roots. Just take off the top 1-2in (25-50mm) of compost and replace it with fresh compost.

Top dress a plant whenever the compost in its pot has developed a crusty surface, or if you have a large mature plant in a heavy container which is too big to repot easily. Water the new compost thoroughly, and don't feed the plant for at least two months.

Wetting agent

There is a special wetting agent available now that you can add to the compost to help it retain moisture — called acrylic copolymer, it comes in granules that you mix in with the compost. You then don't have to water the plant so often. You can get this wetting agent at gardening departments and garden centres.

Fresh is best

Whatever type of compost you choose, try to use it soon after buying it; an open bag of compost loses its goodness within a couple of months after being exposed to air.

Once you have got your plant growing happily in one type of compost (or have bought a plant already in a particular type of compost) try to stick to it. Plants are like some people — they get used to the place where their roots are and don't take kindly to change!

Special composts

Some plants have rather special needs if they are to do really well. Azaleas and Heathers, for example, hate lime — it pushes the soil balance towards alkalinity rather than acidity.

So for those plants you must make sure you ask for a special compost, called ericaceous compost, which has no lime in it. Other plants need particularly good drainage — if their roots are vulnerable to rot, for example, or if their natural habitat is specially light, airy soil. This is provided by extra amounts of coarse sand, charcoal or Perlite.

Most good garden shops or garden centres will have a range of special composts for the most popular houseplants, but if you're feeling adventurous you can always try mixing your own.

The following are just a few examples of 'recipes' that are worth trying — there are probably as many different recipes as there are keen gardeners!

Cacti need specially good drainage. In a pot, where their roots grow more closely together than in the wild, there's a risk that they may develop rot if the soil stays too damp. Many good garden shops, and all specialist Cacti suppliers, will be able to offer you compost specially designed for Cacti and other succulents.

Mix as follows: *or*
2 parts John   1 part loam
Innes No 1   1 part peat
1 part coarse sand   1 part coarse sand

Palms should be grown in a soil-based compost. They need good drainage and lots of fertiliser — you can even use a little manure, provided you don't mind the smell in the house!

Mix as follows:
4 parts loam   2 parts coarse sand
1 part peat   3 parts leaf mould

Ferns can belong to two different types: they can be epiphytic, which means they grow on trees; or terrestrial, growing on the ground. Good drainage is important for both, but especially for the epiphytic ferns.

Mix as follows:
For terrestrial ferns *For epiphytic ferns*
2 parts loam   1 part peat
2 parts peat   1 part coarse sand
2 parts leaf mould 1 part leaf mould
1 part coarse sand
1 part charcoal

Choosing a propagator

Once you've got enthusiastic about your houseplants and about caring for them, it's a short step to wanting to grow your own from seeds and cuttings. But how often have you tried to grow a new plant in a pot on the windowsill and been disappointed? If you've been given a cutting from a friend's plant that you've admired, success will be much more likely if you have a propagator to provide the conditions that new plants need to develop. And in addition you'll be able to grow all kinds of exciting plants from seed that you can't buy as houseplants.

Of all the aids you can buy to help you with your houseplants, a propagator is undoubtedly one of the most useful. It needn't be expensive — even the most basic model, costing no more than a large bag of potting compost, is an improvement on nothing. You'll use it most in spring, when you want to sow seeds and root cuttings, but in fact it is useful throughout the year — for an ailing plant that needs intensive care, for example, or a delicate plant that needs extra protection during the winter. The enclosed environment improves humidity and keeps the plants free from draughts, sudden changes of temperature and attack by pests. The basic choice you'll need to make is between an unheated and a heated model — the latter cost about three times as much as the cheapest unheated types. More expensive propagators can provide thermostatically controlled heat and even automatic mist-spraying.

Tips on buying
The range of propagators is enormous, making selection rather difficult unless you know what you're looking for. As well as making sure that you're buying a reliable model, you should also think beforehand about what facilities you require — there's no point in spending a lot of money on gadgets you won't use.

At its simplest, a propagator consists of a solid base tray and a transparent top. The bottom may be just a plain tray, or it may come complete with an inner, removable seed tray or individual pots. The top allows sunlight and warmth in to the growing plants.

Good ventilation is important for developing plants. These propagators have adjustable ventilators to regulate the humidity and air circulation.

There are some general points to look out for whatever type you're buying.
● The top must be made either of glass or a strong, durable, clear plastic that will not break or scratch easily or become discoloured in bright sunlight.

Traditional propagators with glass lids are generally considered better, since they let through the greatest spectrum of the sun's rays. But against that there is the disadvantage of their greater weight and fragility; glass may not be a good idea if you have small children in the home. Good quality plastic is much lighter and less easily broken.

Lids must be at least 6in (15cm) high, to allow the young plants room for growth, and preferably domed or gabled,

Decorative cases

If you want to use your propagator all year round, and keep it somewhere where you'll see it constantly, you may want to buy a more decorative model. You can get very attractive ones which are as pleasant to look at as pots or terrariums and are obviously ideal for display purposes. Some heated propagators are also suitable for growing hothouse plants all the year round — orchids, for example — and obviously you will want them to be an attractive complement to the plants, as well as practical. Go to a good garden centre, or look at the advertisements in gardening magazines, to get the best choice.

so that condensation runs down the sides into the tray and does not drip directly on to the plants. You should be able to remove the lid completely when the time comes to 'harden off' your seedlings before transplanting them to their own growing pots.
● The base tray must also be made of a durable material that will not become brittle with age or during prolonged exposure to sunlight. It may be worth avoiding the cheapest models, since they're likely to be of poor quality.
● A ventilator of some sort is extremely useful, so that you can control the level of humidity inside the propagator. The simplest propagators have none, but their lids can usually be propped open. Though you aim to keep up the humidity when growing young plants, you must be able to let some fresh air circulate or there's a risk of 'damping off' diseases attacking the plants. These include pythium and grey mould (botrytis), which thrive in dank, airless conditions, and can lead to the total collapse of the young plants.

Your propagator might have miniature windows that can be opened and closed by hand; a circular vent similar to those used in the home, with a variable aperture instead of a fan, usually in the top of the lid; or louvres that are a miniature version of the best sort of greenhouse ventilation and allow a through air flow. Ask your retailer exactly how they all work, and make sure you're happy with the system on offer before you commit yourself. Remember that if you're out of the house during the day, it would be worth paying for a propagator with a ventilator, preferably a self-adjusting one — a few hours without fresh air in bright sunshine could finish your plants off in one afternoon.

What to choose
Although the range of propagators is diverse, they can be slotted into three distinct types — basic, heated, and heated with a mist-spraying unit. Higher up the range you can even get propagators with built-in lighting for pushing plants on during winter and early spring when natural light levels are low. But you'd have to be very keen

indeed to use one this expensive!

Unheated propagators are the simplest and most popular. This type is essentially a seed tray with a high, transparent lid. Look for one that is well made and has an adequate ventilator in the lid. If there's no ventilator, you'll have to prop the lid open several times during the day, or even take it right off occasionally, which might be a nuisance. Internal, removable seed trays or individual pots in the base are a useful facility, since they enable you to remove seedlings or plants separately when they are ready, providing you with space for more. If you just want to raise a few cuttings or seedlings every year on a windowsill or in a greenhouse, then this is probably all you'll need.

An unheated propagator should be placed where it will get the maximum warmth — a south-facing window-sill is ideal in early spring. As the days get hotter, move it to an east- or west-facing sill, or provide shade from the hottest sun.

The heated propagator opens up new horizons for the keen gardener. It allows you to grow more delicate plants at all times of the year, and you don't have to worry about young plants not getting enough warmth. The top will probably look similar to a basic model, but in the solid base of the unit there is a heating element that provides an even warmth for the seedlings from below. This in turn, of course, increases the air temperature and encourages faster germination. Young plants really benefit from 'bottom heat', as it's called, and will be healthier and more vigorous as a result.

Heated propagators that work on electricity are the most popular and convenient to use, but if you want to use your propagator in a greenhouse that doesn't have electrical power, you can get models in which a galvanized (not plastic) tray is heated by oil or paraffin.

Heated propagators can either raise the temperature to a predetermined level and keep it there by thermostatic control, or allow you to adjust the temperature to suit different plants. If you're thinking of keeping delicate plants in a propagator over the winter, as well as growing seedlings in the spring, you'll want the adjustable temperature control, since the temperatures needed in each case will be markedly different. But if you're only going to grow new plants in spring, a fixed temperature model

A heated propagator is invaluable for raising delicate or exotic plants.

that keeps the plants at about 70°F (21°C) will be sufficient.

When you're comparing different models, check that all the electrical parts, especially the thermostat, comply with British Standards for electrical safety. Another point to bear in mind is that they might vary in the amount of power they use, and it makes sense to go for the model that's cheapest to run, even if it might cost a bit more to start with. A good propagator will last you many years and you'll easily recoup the extra outlay.

An added refinement is a heated propagator with a built-in mist-spray unit. These are expensive and will only be necessary if you want to go in for raising new plants in a big way — to sell, perhaps. You can raise plants throughout the year, because the temperature will be controlled, and keeping up humidity will be made easier. The misting unit can be applied manually whenever necessary or, for an extra cost, it can be switched on automatically by an electronic trigger mechanism that measures the dampness in the air, so that the young plants are never allowed to dry out. Professionals use such devices in greenhouses so that they don't have to

worry about plants drying out during prolonged hot weather, but you're unlikely to need one in the home.

Looking after your propagator

Propagators are simple to care for and with a little attention should be useful for years — just make sure that you follow the manufacturer's instructions at all times. It's a good idea to clean them out occasionally, between batches of plants, by washing with a liquid detergent. Rinse it thoroughly and let it dry. If you're not going to be using it, put it away with the lid propped open so that it will not become musty inside.

Take care!

As well as checking that all electrical equipment complies with the relevant safety standards, be sure to use it strictly in accordance with the manufacturer's instructions. A mist-spraying model, which involves water, should be installed by a competent electrician. Make sure that you never get any part of the power elements wet — remember that electricity and water don't mix.

Lighting-up time

This attractive pendant Growlight — the Saturn 160 — looks much like any other domestic lamp; it is modestly priced and needs no special electrical fittings.

With artificial lighting you can make even the very darkest nooks and crannies into a home for healthy, thriving houseplants. It can be used as the main source of light or to supplement the natural light that's in such poor supply in the winter. Artificial light will also speed up the growth of cuttings and seedlings indoors.

What to choose

What you choose to buy in the way of equipment depends on whether you want simply to supplement natural daylight or to do without it altogether. And that can depend on how much money you're prepared to spend — from just a few pounds to over £100.

Some bulbs will fit conventional bayonet or screw cap light fittings. But the more powerful systems need lamps with special fittings.

LIGHTS FOR CONVENTIONAL FITTINGS

The two types mentioned below are both widely available and fairly cheap to buy. And they're not too bright for the home. Though you can use them with existing light fittings, there are several that are purpose-built fittings with reflectors, which disperse the light more efficiently over a wider area.

These lamps aren't able to light as large an area as the more sophisticated discharge lights in the same wattage (see below). And you'll need to place the plants quite close to the lights, while still taking care that they don't get scorched — the lamps give out quite a lot of heat. Nor can they take the place of natural daylight entirely.

Filtered incandescent lamps are just ordinary filament lamps with an internal coating which filters out the harmful warm red rays. Unfortunately, they also filter out some of the other non-harmful light, at the same time. However, as long as you buy them in a suitable voltage (no more than 100 watt if you want to use them in an ordinary light fitting), they're certainly a relatively cheap and easy way to give plants a boost.

A 75 watt bulb, set 1ft (30cm) above the plant, will light an area up to 2sq ft.

Mercury blended lamps, known as MBTF/R, are one up on the filtered incandescent lamps. They give a better balanced light, with less heat, but they are twice or three times the price of the incandescent lamps, on average.

SPECIAL LIGHTING UNITS

Fluorescent lights (or low-pressure mercury discharge lamps) are hard to beat, and are the best type of artificial lighting for indoor plants. They're efficient, give a good spread and are widely available. They also produce much more useful light and less heat. What's more, the fittings they need are much cheaper than for the other sorts of mercury discharge lamp.

Tubes come in a choice of 'colours', determined by the coating on the inside of the glass. Some let through too little warm red light, but too much of the light at the other end of the spectrum. But there are several suitable 'daylight' fluorescent tubes which are suitable for growing plants, such as 'Warm White', ' Northlite' or 'Cool White',

which give a relatively well-balanced combination, although the Warm White can make plants look too red.

It's best to buy tubes on adjustable stands, so that they can be raised or lowered according to the plants you're growing. You can also buy plant containers — display cases, tiers or troughs — that incorporate fluorescent tubes.

As a general rule, it's unwise to use less than two tubes. With one tube, only 25-30 per cent of the light provided is usefully employed; with two, the percentage is increased to 40 per cent.

The tubes come in a choice of lengths, with wattage varying according to the length. In effect, though, they all give out more or less the same amount of light per 12in (30cm).

Two tubes, placed parallel to each other about 4-6in (10-15cm) apart and suspended about 2ft (60cm) above the plants, will suit a single row of foliage plants. By putting in more tubes, you can increase the distance from the plants; four tubes would mean you could hang them up to 4½ft (1.35m) above the plants. Or, alternatively, it could mean increasing the depth of the area you want to light, and including another row, or two, of plants.

Flowering plants, and others that like higher light intensity, need to be nearer the lights — a distance of 6-12in (15-30cm) instead of 1-2ft (0.3-0.6m).

High pressure mercury and metal halide lamps are two other types of mercury discharge bulbs. Both systems are much more expensive to buy, initially, but have cheaper running costs and last longer than other types. Because they aren't so common, you may find it difficult to buy replacement bulbs.

Their great advantage is that they can be used as a sole source of light for plants. Most are really more suitable for large-scale and commercial use, but you can find lower wattage versions, some with reflectors, which are suitable for houseplants in the home.

These mercury discharge lamps produce a bright beam of light, which does tend to be a bit bright in the home. The metal halide types are marginally more efficient and give plants a slightly better colour.

For the ordinary high pressure lamps, choose a 125 watt bulb, with a reflector. For the metal halide, an 80 watt lamp is adequate. Suspend them about 3ft (0.9m) above the plants, and they will light an area with a diameter of about 18in (45cm).

Fittings that combine lamps and plant containers can provide charming displays. These are best used with shallow rooting plants that enjoy additional light in the evenings — African Violet is an ideal candidate. But you'll need to keep an eye on the compost which will tend to dry out rapidly.

A well-placed lamp or spotlight can highlight the colour and shape of an attractive plant — but unless you know what you're about, you could do it harm. With the right equipment, you can give your plants a beneficial boost, and cultivate plants you wouldn't otherwise be able to. An indoor herb garden, to keep you supplied summer and winter alike, is one good idea.

What's in light

To imitate natural daylight and the good effects of sunlight, an artificial light has to produce the right balance of different light rays. Get the balance wrong, and plants will become stunted and deformed or weak and leggy.

Natural daylight is made up of a wide spectrum of coloured rays ranging from violet through indigo, blue, green, yellow, orange to red; mixed together, they come out as 'white' light.

Unfortunately, the easiest and most convenient artificial light source is the ordinary light bulb (known as an incandescent or filament bulb) which won't do. It gives off too many rays from the 'warm' red end of the spectrum and too much heat. If placed too close (it doesn't have to be touching, even), it will scorch the leaves and rupture the plant cells.

Even spot lights, including the newer type which runs on a lower voltage, aren't much help. To do the job, you need special lamps.

Supplementary lighting

There are few spots where absolutely no natural daylight can penetrate, and most people will want artificial lighting to supplement rather than to replace the natural light.

In winter, for instance, plants may only get 8 hours of light. But if you can reproduce the 12 hours of light many of them would find in their natural habitats (the tropics or sub-tropics), they'll go on growing all year round. Remember, though, that they'll need to be kept warm and fed all year as well! And, of course, not all plants can be treated like this — many do need a winter rest.

There are other benefits, too. Artificial lighting can give winter-flowering plants — like orchids — the vital extra hours of light they need to come into flower. And it will also let you grow light-loving plants in the murkier depths of a room.

Flowering plants usually need about 13-14 hours of light daily, foliage plants 9-10 hours. To calculate how much extra light to give each plant, take away the number of good daylight hours it actually receives from the total amount it should receive. Use this as a starting point, and make any adjustments as the plant requires.

Artificial light only

If you've got a dim, dark hall, which is otherwise inhospitable, a small lighting system — a bowl full of plants lit with a single light — can bring it to life.

In theory, you can grow absolutely any plant under artificial lighting — there need be no difference in the quality of the light needed. But you would have to give them just as long an exposure, and just as good a light, as they would experience normally. So plants requiring long hours of bright, direct sunlight might be an impractical proposition as you'd have to be prepared to spend an awful lot of money on the necessary lighting equipment. Cacti and other succulents, Joseph's Coat (Crotons), Zebra Plants (Aphelandra), Cyclamens, Busy Lizzies (Impatiens) and Azaleas, for instance, would be out.

But there are plenty of less demanding plants to choose from — Marantas, Calatheas, Philodendrons, some brom-

Creating a fluorescent growing unit

A fluorescent light fitting may well look out of place suspended from the ceiling in some rooms. But tubes can be tucked neatly and almost invisibly beneath a shelf, especially if you fix a lip along the edge of the shelf. A white shiny surface, or some aluminium foil, can make a good reflecting surface, increasing light levels by 10 per cent.

eliads (Cryptanthus and Vriesea), African Violets (Saintpaulias), Creeping Figs (Ficus pumila), members of the palm family and ferns. The green of the ferns looks particularly good, and their feathery fronds throw interesting patterns of light and shade.

Time clocks

Timing devices will relieve you of the chore of switching the lights on and off again each day — and time clocks don't forget, either. To use them, your light will have to be wired to a plug rather than to the lighting circuit.

160

A **lighted display** of Ivy, Hibiscus, Caladium and Fern in a disused fireplace provides a good focal point for a room.

While **many plants thrive** in the humid conditions of a bathroom, if you want them to be illuminated you should have the lighting installed by a qualified electrician — and be sure to position the light switch outside the bathroom.

Monitoring your plants

If you notice that the plants are not doing very well, try adjusting their distance from the light. If they aren't close enough to the light, plants will be tall and spindly, new leaves will be smaller and mature leaves will turn yellow or fall. And variegated plants will produce all-green leaves.

Plants can become distressed if placed too close; foliage becomes scorched, growth is stunted and leaf colour fades.

Don't be in a hurry to blame the lighting for all ills, however. Do check that humidity, watering and other factors are all in order.

What to consider

Whatever system you choose, artificial lighting is going to cost money. You will have to estimate the costs not only of the equipment, the fittings and any timing devices, but also the cost of the electricity they use. You may also need to get a qualified electrician to fix it up for you, unless you're more than a layman.

Don't forget that there'll be a lot of water usage in this environment — in the form of condensation, as well as in mist sprayers, etc — and water and electricity don't mix! So take care when fitting any lights and always follow the manufacturer's instructions. And take their advice, too, on positioning your plants to best advantage.

They are particularly handy for the flowering plants that will bloom only in response to a certain number of hours of alternate light and darkness (see individual plant guides for details). Poinsettias are a case in point, and show you just how sensitive a plant can be to barely discernible changes of light. Poinsettias are 'short day responsive' plants, which means they aren't 'triggered' to flower until the days are short enough. If a plant doesn't get just the right amount of light — and no more — it won't produce its wonderful bracts in time for Christmas.

Reflectors

Many of the lights and fittings mentioned come complete with 'reflectors' which direct the light more efficiently. Some bulbs have part of their inside surface silvered, others have silvered shades to do the job.

A herb garden

You can have fresh herbs throughout the year — where you want them, and whenever you want them.

Mount a parallel pair of 2ft (60cm), 40 watt fluorescent tubes (Warm White or Cool White) — under a kitchen cupboard which has first been painted white to give extra reflection. Position the lighting tubes not more than 2ft (60cm) above the pots, and if you can organise a reflector, as well, above the tubes you will be making even more effective use of the light.

For the best results, you should aim to give plants between 14 and 16 hours of artificial light a day, but if you have a bright sunny kitchen, you can cut this down to just six or eight hours in summer, switching lights on in the late afternoon, when natural light is beginning to fade.

Tools for the patio

It can hardly be said that growing plants in containers on the patio is in any way a back-breaking task and, fortunately, none of the necessary tools requires very much effort in its use. One of the secrets of successful patio gardening is the effective use of space, and it is equally important to take some care in selecting the right tools that will be of most help in caring for your plants without cluttering up whatever storage space you have available for them.

Cultivating tools

With container gardening the amount of soil cultivation is minimal, but it is useful to have a couple of basic tools, like a small hand trowel and fork, which will serve various purposes. They can be used for planting up any containers, including growing bags and troughs, as well as for lightly forking the surface of the compost to improve its aeration, taking care of course not to damage plant roots. A narrow trowel may be particularly useful for interplanting a container with bulbs when working within a confined space and where a larger tool, like a hand bulb planter, could prove to be more of a hindrance than a help.

A small hand rake is also useful to rake the surface lightly, both to improve aeration and to prevent the problem of 'capping'. This is when the compost forms a hard crust, sometimes with algae on top, which reduces the effective absorption of water and oxygen and encourages some of the harmful gases produced in the compost to be retained rather than being released into the atmosphere.

Depending on the size of the container, a small hand hoe may be useful for weeding, as well as for scraping off accumulated algae, moss, lichens or liverworts. And finally, a dibber is useful for making holes to plant tiny plantlets or seedlings and for gently firming the compost around tender roots.

Rather than purchasing all these tools separately, you may find it better in terms of storage to take advantage of a new type of tool system, consisting of just one handle which fits into several tools. A further advantage of this kind of system is that individual tools can also be fitted on to longer handles by the same 'click-fit' system – for use in the garden if required – and all the tool heads can be stored away tidily on a special wall rack which is out of the way and doesn't take up much space.

Pruning tools

The most useful pruning and trimming tool is a good quality stainless steel pruning knife, which is not only ideal for most trimming purposes but is also useful for cutting string used for supporting plants and various other miscellaneous tasks in both patio and garden. A pair of secateurs or vine scissors will prove to be very useful for trimming wayward stems on woody shrubs, although a pair of ordinary general-purpose scissors may be all that is required for most trimming purposes.

Unless you also have some open ground or you are growing a containerised box hedge (which, it must be said, is unlikely), it is probably not worth investing in a pair of shears. If, however, you do need some, try to select as compact a pair as you can with a notch at the base of the cutting blades. Their compact shape will enable more controlled trimming of your plants, while the notched blades are useful for cutting away any heavier branches that you may come across.

Providing support

As your plants grow, so it will be necessary to provide them with adequate means of support. It is therefore a good idea to keep a supply of canes, stakes and plant ties ready to hand in order to prevent any top-heavy plants from becoming damaged and wrecked during periods of high wind and rain.

Any plants such as tomatoes which are growing in growing bags will need rather more than just canes for support. These will benefit greatly from the use of a support frame, which will provide plants with a stable anchorage as they bear their heavy trusses of fruit.

Apart from the obvious ball of soft garden string which you can use to tie plants to their support, you may prefer to use the more sophisticated adjustable plastic or toggle ties. Another useful item is a reel of plastic-covered wire which comes complete with built-in cutter; this can be hung up on its reel and appropriate lengths simply pulled from the reel and cut off with the wire snipper as you need them.

Water, water everywhere

Even if you have a sophisticated automatic irrigation system with which to water your plants, you will find it useful to have a watering can to hand in order to top up a dry plant or to water in plants or seedlings. In the latter case, make sure that the can that you choose can be fitted with a fine watering rose – preferably brass which will not rust – in order that all your seedlings and young plants can be watered safely without any damage being caused.

You will almost certainly have to spray your plants from time to time. A small mister is useful for applying water to foliage in order to reduce water loss through transpiration during dry periods and, if you can afford it, it is also a good idea to have a second sprayer for applying pesticides to control both insects and diseases. Although the two sprayers may, for economy's sake, be combined as one to serve a dual purpose, it is probably better to buy two and to keep them separate.

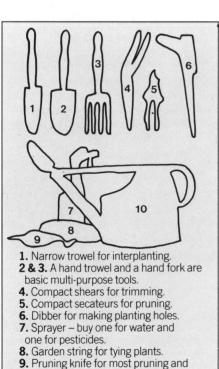

1. Narrow trowel for interplanting.
2 & 3. A hand trowel and a hand fork are basic multi-purpose tools.
4. Compact shears for trimming.
5. Compact secateurs for pruning.
6. Dibber for making planting holes.
7. Sprayer – buy one for water and one for pesticides.
8. Garden string for tying plants.
9. Pruning knife for most pruning and trimming purposes.
10. Watering-can with brass rose.

Pots and containers

Pots and containers come in a vast range of shapes and sizes.

Growing plants in containers is fun and is actually a lot easier than growing them in the garden. One big advantage of containers is that they allow you complete control over the plants' conditions: you can give them all the food and water they want, at exactly the times they need them; you can move them in or out of the shade; and you can keep them sheltered and warm, or cool and airy, depending on what suits them best. Another big advantage is that you can create a garden – even if you haven't got any open ground – by using containers full of plants to decorate areas that would otherwise have been dull and dreary, so making them colourful and inviting to sit ' 1.

Containers have improved out of all recognition in the last few years. They add a great deal to the attractiveness of plants, setting off their colours and emphasising their foliage and habits of growth. There is now an enormous variety of design, size and material – a vast improvement on the rather dull choice of the past.

164

Wood is acceptable material, but it should be treated with preservative.

Spoilt for choice

🌿 Terracotta pots are still around, but now come in beautiful sculptured designs – in the Italian style, for example, or with lilies, swags of fruit and ribbons, Acanthus leaves, Tudor roses and many others. Pots no longer come in only the conventional pot shape, but now have waists, lips, banding and decorative basketwork. Some of the larger ones come with pedestals attached, some are urn-shaped for use on separate pedestals, and the French Provençal pots are a different style again, lending an authentic Mediterranean warmth to a patio or courtyard.

🌿 You may, on the other hand, prefer the look of the old lead containers, cast in a foundry with beautiful classical mouldings. You can still buy the real thing – in the form of urns, square Regency or Georgian boxes, rectangular window-boxes and cisterns – or use the simulated kind, made of fibreglass and suitably coloured in grey, which are such convincing copies that it is only their weight which gives them away.

🌿 Stone, or what is known as reconstituted stone (i.e. stone which has been crushed and then put together again), is a marvellous medium in which to grow plants, both for its looks and for the health of the plants. Urns, wall-mounted half pots and large planting pots in various shapes and sizes are all supplied in this material.

Terracotta pots and urns add interest to any patio.

🌿 Where there is not enough space for these large containers, or where the support does not permit their weight – as,. for example, on a window-ledge or balcony – various types of plastic have been manufactured to produce a wide range of pots, boxes and urns. Some are unashamedly plastic and make use of its ultra-modern, shiny quality – such as the French containers made of synthetic resin which mimic square wooden tubs in brilliant white.

🌿 Others, even lighter in weight, look as though they are made of stone and, in the shape of shallow or vertical urns, are totally convincing. Straightforward shiny, plastic pots, shaped like the conventional clay ones, come in green, white, black and terracotta colour, with saucers to match for every size of pot, and there is now also a range with an attactive matt surface. Plastic window-boxes in similar colours also have their own trays, which are essential for use on window-ledges and balconies; lengths can be anything from 1-2¹/₂ft (30-75cm).

There are moulded, rigid, cellular fibre containers or planters, which come in a pleasant brown colour and various shapes, including round, square, rectangular and hexagonal, again with their own saucers. These last for about two years after which they will break down and can be mixed into the compost.

Wood is a most acceptable, natural material for containers. It can be plain timber, or coloured with paint, stain or varnish – but whatever the finish it should first be treated with several coats of wood preservative that is harmless to plants. Window-boxes and tubs – the latter sometimes cut-down half barrels – are the most common containers in wood. Wooden window-boxes are occasionally made with an ornamental bark covering.

Half pots, or baskets for attaching to walls, to cheer up a large, blank expanse, are available in clay, plastic or stone. And then, of course, there are hanging baskets of various kinds – made of wire, plastic-coated wire, or plastic with drainage holes or saucers attached. Cellular fibre liners can be used in wire baskets to prevent dripping. And, incidentally, there is now a useful gadget, called a pump-can, for watering these baskets without having either to lower them or to stand on a chair.

Vertical planters provide yet another dimension. There are terracotta strawberry barrels as well as a diminutive version for parsley, and tower pots in moulded plastic which stack and have a series of side pockets for various plants. Cluster pots are made in much the same style but can be combined either vertically or horizontally, and there are even some self-watering tower pots.

A newcomer to the vertical container scene is the portable garden, which can be either stood or hung. This consists of a square-shaped vertical tube, made of polypropylene, which is filled with compost and has openings all the way up into which plants can be inserted. Flower, herb, fruit and vegetable gardens can all be planted in this way, and in time the plants will entirely cover the container.

Some containers are made of fibre and will last for about two years.

Use your imagination and construct your own container.

Make your pot a focal point.

A traditional strawberry pot.

Container composts

Garden soil is rarely suitable for use in containers. It either holds too much water and packs down into an airless mass which results in the roots being unable to breathe and rotting, or it contains pests and diseases that will attack your plants. For best results you need to use a high quality potting compost. Either buy a good proprietary potting compost from a garden centre or make up your own.

Basically, there are two types that you can use in containers: the traditional soil-based John Innes mixes that are made up of loam (soil), peat (organic material that has been partially decomposed under water), sand and base fertiliser such as John Innes, or modern soilless composts consisting of peat (and maybe other ingredients like sand, perlite, or vermiculite) plus a base fertiliser.

Soilless composts
Pros
● They don't weigh much, so are easy to handle.
● They are especially good for plants, such as Camellias, Rhododendrons and Azaleas, which hate lime. Make sure, though, that you always use a compost which is made up with lime-free base fertiliser.
● They encourage good root growth

With the right ingredients it is easy to make up your own compost.

as long as you follow the instructions for firming as specified by the manufacturers on the back of most packets of compost.

Cons
● They must be firmed lightly and may not have enough support for large or heavy plants.
● They don't retain nourishment for long, so plants have to be fed quite soon after repotting.
● They have a tendency to hold water and if you apply too much, or water too often, the compost can become too wet.
● If you allow the compost to dry out completely it can be difficult to moisten again thoroughly.

Soil-based composts
Pros
● They are heavy and able to support large and heavy plants.
● Drainage of surplus water and circulation of air are usually excellent.
● They retain nourishment, so you don't have to start feeding too soon after potting.
● They are easily moistened if they dry out.
● If you tend to overwater your plants, you are less likely to saturate the compost.
● They are excellent for plants, like Alpines, that thrive in well-drained conditions.
● They are suitable for most plants.

Cons
● Some are of poor quality because of the use of heavy loam. If this is the case, you can add to a given volume of compost one third extra of coarse sand or grit to improve the drainage and aeration.

Buying composts
You can't go wrong if you buy John Innes potting composts: Nos 1 and 2 are ideal for most container plants and No 3 for potting on large specimens. If you are growing Camellias, Rhododendrons, Azaleas and other lime-hating plants, use a lime-free, soilless compost or a lime-free John Innes compost.

Soilless composts are also perfect for hanging baskets where minimum weight is essential, and they are suitable for short-term planting like spring and summer bedding displays.

Remember to mix all components thoroughly.

Mixing your own

If you have a number of containers to fill, or several large ones like double walls and raised beds, it will work out cheaper if you mix your own compost. There are many different ways of doing this, but the following 'recipes' may help you. All parts are measured by volume and should be mixed together thoroughly.

Basic John Innes Mix together seven parts of sterilised loam, three parts of peat and two parts of sand. The loam should be light or medium and can be bought in bags from garden centres or in larger quantities from local suppliers of topsoil. Use sphagnum-moss peat, sold in bales, and lime-free, sharp horticultural sand, available in bags from garden centres or in larger quantities from local horticultural suppliers. Sharp sand is often sold under different names such as Bedford.

To make John Innes potting compost Nos 1, 2 and 3 follow the instructions given on pages 538 and 539.

Soilless potting compost Mix together 3 gal (13.5l) of peat and 1 gal (4.5l) of sand (or perlite or vermiculite), then add a proprietary potting compost base fertiliser, for example Chempak (lime and lime-free), as directed by the manufacturer. If you can

get hold of them, you can add a small amount of acid or lime-free loam and well-rotted leafmould (exact proportions are not critical) instead of the base fertiliser. **Lime-free compost** Follow the 'recipe' for John Innes No 1 (given on page 538) but use acid or lime-free loam, and don't use chalk or ground limestone.

How much compost do you need?
One of the easiest ways to measure small amounts of compost at home is in a large plastic bucket with a capacity of 2 gals (9l). Block up the hole at the bottom of your tub with plasticine or putty and, using your bucket as a measure, fill up your tub with water to find out how much compost you will need. Here are several examples.
● A round tub 17in (43cm) wide and 10in (25cm) deep needs 7 gal (32l) of compost.
● A round tub 21in (53cm) wide and 12in (30cm) deep needs 12¼ gal (56l) of compost.
● A square tub 2ft (0.6m) wide and 2ft (0.6m) deep needs 43 gal (195l) of compost.
● A trough or window-box 3ft (90cm) long, 9in (23cm) deep and 10in (25cm) wide needs 10 gal (45l) of compost.

Always buy well-known proprietary brands of compost from a good garden centre. Compost is usually measured in litres and is sold in a wide range of bag sizes. If you find that the compost is wet because the rain has got in through a hole in the bag, take it straight back to the garden centre. Sometimes the compost may seem to be compacted because the bags have been stacked in the garden centre. If this is so, simply crumble it up with your hands. Compost in bags should be moist, so there is no need to water it before use.

Remember, compost will keep in good condition for only six to eight weeks after the bag has been opened, so finish up the bag as soon as possible after opening.

Buying seeds

Seeds are those near magical gems of life that for many plants are the blueprint for the next generation. They are not cheap to buy, as anyone who has recently visited the seed display at a local garden centre or shop will agree. Anything from 40p to well over £1 for a packet is not unusual, and it is not without reason that gardeners question whether it is better to raise your own plants from seeds or to buy established plants.

Seeds are good value if you have the space and equipment to sow and raise plants. A packet of French Marigolds might cost up to 60p and yield many plants, while a tray of thirty or so established plants will be well over £3. If you buy F1 seeds expect to pay about £1. F1 plants result from seed specialists crossing two pure-bred varieties or closely related forms to create a generation of plants which is exceptionally uniform and robust.

Buying seeds

The golden rule when buying seeds is to select the best you can afford. Nothing is more irritating than having economized on seeds then to be disappointed by the sparse display in your garden during summer. You can buy your seeds in several forms.

Ordinary seeds are the types that have been known to us for many years, and do *not* include those now raised as F1 hybrids.

F1 hybrids are a more recent development where seed specialists have created seeds that develop into uniform, large and often very abundantly flowering plants. In the flower garden they are superb for creating a uniform display.

Pelleted seeds are, like their name suggests, seeds encapsulated in a pill to make small seeds easier to handle.

Vacuum-sealed seed packets exclude air and so reduce the speed at which seeds lose their powers of germination. The sealed packet prevents both air and moisture reaching the seeds and activating them.

Seeds for patios

On a patio, it is plants for flowering in window-boxes, tubs and troughs that are usually grown from seeds. These include summer-bedding plants, which are raised under glass early in the year and ready for planting out into a container in the garden as soon as all risk of frost has passed – late May and early June. They are sown, pricked out into boxes and eventually hardened off so that they are accustomed to garden conditions. When they fade and die during early autumn frosts they are removed and the containers planted with spring-flowering bulbs or plants.

Spring-flowering plants for containers are usually biennial – sown one year for flowering the following season – and include Wallflowers (*Erysimum x allionii*), Daisies (*Bellis perennis*) and Sweet Williams (*Dianthus barbatus*). They are sown in shallow drills in a spare piece of ground during May and June, thinned to the healthiest seedlings and planted into containers after the summer-bedding plants have been removed, during autumn.

Saving your own seeds

It always sounds so easy to collect and save your own seeds – but is it?

It is possible to save your own seeds from bedding plants, instead of buying them fresh each year. Non-F1 seeds are well worth keeping as the offspring will resemble the parent, but seed collected from F1 types will not be like the parent. Seeds collected from them produce a mixed bag of seedlings, most inferior to the parent.

Sowing seeds

There are several key elements to success.
● **Selecting the right plants** is essential – non-F1 types.
● **Gathering the seeds at the right time** is critical. Leave the pods and their seeds on the plant as long as possible. An indication of the right time is when the pods and capsules turn from green to brown. They will also become brittle and dry.
● **Drying the seeds** is another critical stage. Place the pods and capsules on newspaper and allow them to dry naturally, with a good circulation of air. Once dry, crush the seed containers to remove the seeds.

The whole job can be made easier by cutting off the seed-heads with several inches of stem attached and placing the flower heads in large paper bags. Hang them upside down in a light and airy place. If seeds do escape from the pods before you are ready, they will fall into the bag.

Pop the seeds into small envelopes, labelled with the name and the date of collection.
● **To store seeds** you need a cool, dry position. Small packets can be put into airtight jars, together with a small quantity of silica gel to absorb moisture. The jars can even be placed in a refrigerator.

If you have bought seeds and not used them, these can also be stored in air-tight jars – but don't try storing them for more than a year.

Under glass on the patio

A greenhouse is always an asset to a gardener and is perfectly suitable for erecting on a patio, terrace, balcony or roof garden. Indeed, the range available for this purpose is quite wide.

The majority of small greenhouses are lean-to structures which have to be placed against a south or west-facing wall, although some are free-standing. Most have an aluminium framework, which means they don't weigh much and are therefore perfect for balconies and roof gardens where excess weight could be a problem. Some are clad with plastic or polythene – instead of glass – which also helps to keep down the weight. Traditional timber mini-greenhouses and lean-to types, usually with a cedarwood frame filled with glass, are also obtainable.

As a general guide, when we refer to small greenhouses we are talking about structures which are 4-6ft (1.2-1.8m) or under. Many models are smaller, especially the mini lean-to types which are often only about 2ft (0.6m) wide and 4ft (1.2m) long. Obviously, you have to work from the outside of these structures, gaining access through sliding or hinged doors at the front.

Small, free-standing greenhouses can be equipped with staging similar to that of larger models, and most mini lean-to types also have shelving. The smallest lean-to will take a full-size growing bag (some will take two) which is proof that 'buying small' can still provide plenty of growing space. Shelves and staging are also often removable if you want space for tall plants like tomatoes.

How to heat

A small greenhouse is comparatively cheap to heat and there are several ways of doing it. A small paraffin heater will keep it frost-free during the winter, but remember you must provide ventilation to allow fumes, which could harm plants, to escape. Also, ensure that your fuel burns efficiently. Keep the heater clean and the wick neatly trimmed.

As an alternative, install a small, electric, tubular heater, or fix electric air-warming cables around the inside

Small greenhouses are usually lean-to structures which should be placed against a south or west-facing wall.

walls. If you just want bottom heat for germinating seeds or rooting cuttings you could install soil-warming cables, either on staging or on the floor.

Greenhouses are normally heated from late September through to the middle of May.

Plants for a greenhouse

Summer. A small heated greenhouse can be used for raising summer bedding plants and summer flowering pot plants from seed. You should also be able to raise tomatoes, sweet peppers and egg plants, and perhaps a few spring-flowering pot plants such as Primulas and Cinerarias. You could try to force some spring bulbs like Daffodils, Hyacinths and Tulips into early flower. They should be planted in bowls in autumn and put in the greenhouse only when the roots are well developed and the young shoots display an inch or so of growth.

If you don't heat your greenhouse you can still grow tomatoes, sweet peppers and egg plants, but you may have to buy young plants and plant them in mid-May, when the risk of frost is over. At the same time you could also buy Fuchsias and Regal Pelargoniums for summer colour.

Spring. If you have sufficient headroom for tomatoes you will be able to grow a few pots of greenhouse Chrysanthemums. These can be grown outside in summer and put in the greenhouse in autumn when you have cleared away the tomatoes.

Winter. A small heated greenhouse is an ideal place for over-wintering tender plants such as Dahlia tubers, Gladiolus corms, Begonia tubers and so on. It is also worthwhile trying to make room for a few winter-flowering pot plants such as Cyclamen, an Azalea, a winter-flowering Begonia, Winter Cherry and ornamental peppers.

Autumn. This is the time for planting winter lettuces, and for making small sowings of radishes, spring onions and mustard and cress. Plant hardy bulbs for spring flowering and pot up Polyanthus for winter or spring colour. Pans of alpines or rock plants will also flower in spring.

Slatted staging will help the air to circulate around the greenhouse.

Greenhouse care

Greenhouses tend to heat up very quickly in spring and summer, when the sun is shining. Temperatures can soar and cause serious damage to plants and it is therefore essential that adequate ventilation is possible. The entire front on many models of small lean-to types can be opened and this gives excellent ventilation.

From April to September some form of shading is essential to keep temperatures down and to prevent plants being scorched by the sun. Roller blinds are ideal, or you could drape your greenhouse with some proprietary shading netting available from garden centres. Another alternative is to paint the outside of the glass with a proprietary liquid shading material. However, if this is applied it also prevents light entering the greenhouse during dull weather.

Good air circulation is also necessary. You can achieve this partly by using slatted staging or shelves, and also by opening the ventilators.

Where to position

A lean-to greenhouse should ideally be sited on a south or west-facing wall, whereas the best possible pos-

Tomatoes are ideal for growing in small greenhouses.

ition for a free-standing greenhouse is in a warm spot on your patio or your balcony which receives full sun for the best part of the day.

Where to buy

You can either write to mail-order greenhouse manufacturers advertising in gardening magazines, or make a visit to a garden centre that you know has a greenhouse display site.

Plinths enable you to give height to what could otherwise be a rather flat arrangement of plants on your patio. What you decide to put on the plinth is up to you, but urns, shallow pans or pots can all be used to good effect.

Before choosing your containers, it is wise to consider the benefits of the various shapes and the types of materials of which they are made, as these factors influence the types of plants that may be grown.

Types of containers

Shallow containers tend to dry out quickly because the surface area is relatively larger than the depth, which speeds the evaporation of water from the compost, so they are really suitable only for plants that will tolerate drier soil.

Deep containers will generally retain water longer and are therefore more suited to plants that prefer a moist environment.

Materials

The material from which the container is made will also affect the success of your planting.

Plastic containers, although readily available, can pose a few problems: the light weight of the container can make it unstable during windy periods, and when the compost is on the drier side the pot may topple over; exposure to sunlight and weather extremes can make the plastic brittle causing it to crack. The pots can also look out of place on a traditional, well-designed patio.

Pottery containers are more suitable – they are stable, have a longer life and look more pleasing on the patio. Although most glazed containers sold for outside use are durable, it is important to ensure that the container is weatherproof and, more specifically, frostproof. Some unglazed terracotta pots are not frost resistant and these tend to crack if the weather becomes really cold.

The shape of the container can affect its survival through the winter. If the top of the pot is narrower than the middle there's a good chance that, when the temperature drops and the soil freezes and expands, it will break. When choosing a container for your plinth go for one that has a wider circumference at the top.

Grouping plants together on plinths of various heights makes an interesting display.

Stoneware, concrete, wooden and metal containers all look very effective on the patio, although the wooden and metal ones require greater maintenance.

Drainage

When possible, all containers should have adequate drainage to avoid the danger of waterlogging, both in summer and winter.

If a container doesn't have any pro-visions for drainage you may have to drill a few holes in the bottom, though great care must be taken with some materials as they may be easily damaged. You can grow plants in containers without drainage holes, but care must be taken with the watering – any surplus water should be drained off by gently tipping the container to one side.

Where a container is drained by only a small hole, drainage can be

The base of an old Victorian cast-iron table makes an unusual and attractive plinth.

This imposing stone urn on a plinth is an arresting feature in a flat garden.

Plants for containers

The range of plants that can be grown on plinths is enormous, varying from summer season bedding plants to shrubs and conifers.

When planting annuals in a shallow container ensure they can tolerate dry conditions. Livingstone Daisies (Mesembryanthemum) prefer a dry soil; 'Yellow Lunette' makes a colourful display around the edge of the container.

For a trailing effect there is nothing to match the various shades of blue, white and cerise-red Lobelia. Petunias will also grow well in a shallow container; while they cannot tolerate such dry conditions as the Livingstone Daisies, they will provide spectacular colour. Nasturtiums will also provide summer colour.

Apart from the more usual annuals, and plants such as Fuchsias, Geraniums and pendulous Begonias, it is worth considering perennials.

Variegated Ivies look attractive throughout the year when trailing from a container on a plinth, and many other perennials, alpines, shrubs and conifers will also produce dramatic effects.

Campanulas can provide a blaze of cascading colour, and even some varieties of Saxifrage and Thyme give a 'creeping' effect. The Rock Rose (Helianthemum) can also be useful with its mass of brightly coloured flowers which appear from May to September, according to the variety and when the plant is propagated.

Shrubs such as Potentillas, with varieties like 'Princess' and 'Red Ace', and the golden Spiraea 'Golden Princess' provide a good compact display with a long season of colour.

Grasses such as *Hakonechloa macra* 'Albo-aurea' are superb, with magnificent foliage; some Hostas can look spectacular and are particularly good for shady situations.

Conifers, such as *Thuja orientalis* 'Aurea Nana' and *Juniperus* x *media* 'Golden Sovereign', will provide colour all year round.

Combinations of plants, including mixed plantings of bulbs, herbaceous plants and shrubs, can look effective in large containers provided they are not overcrowded.

With thought and imagination, the amazing effects that can be produced by planting on plinths are endless.

Stone troughs on a plinth have added another dimension to this small roof garden.

improved by placing pieces of broken clay pot or crocks in the bottom of the container.

Compost

Peat-based composts are ideal for growing a wide range of plants and there are specific composts for growing lime-hating and acid loving plants. For plants that prefer a soil-based compost, the John Innes range of composts contain a percentage of loam which helps to provide slightly greater stability, and even when dry they are heavier than peat-based types.

Where possible, select a compost that contains a proportion of sand, as this helps to improve drainage.

Garden soil is not suitable for containers; as it is unsterilised, soil-borne pests and diseases will take their toll in a very short space of time, giving poor results.

A natural effect

Small brick paths are easy to construct between gravel beds, *far left*. Special paving bricks are easily obtainable, *above*, and can be laid to form decorative patterns, *left*.

ONE OF THE MOST IMPORTANT ELEMENTS of a patio garden is its paving. The pattern, colour and texture of the floor covering of your outdoor room will determine the tone and feel of this area just as much as the planting.

There is a bewildering variety of paving materials on the market in all kinds of colours and shapes. But do remember that in a small outdoor area (just as in a small room indoors) too much pattern and colour can be confusing and distracting. The most restful effects will be achieved by using traditional materials in their traditional colours. And the smaller your patio is, the less inclined you should be to think about using more than one material, or more than one pattern.

Paving in natural stone slabs always looks good and wears well, but tends to come expensive. Concrete slabs are much cheaper, and are produced in many shapes and colours. A restful and 'well-worn' effect can be achieved right from the start by using plain concrete slabs with the exposed aggregate side uppermost. Traditional brick paving achieves a lovely warm, homely effect.

Other materials that can be used to good effect to pave a small area are quarry tiles, ceramic tiles, granite setts and cobblestones. Cobblestones are not very comfortable to walk on, but they can be used to make a contrast in texture to the main area of paving, or to fill awkward spaces that would otherwise be difficult to pave. Other materials that have been used to make unusual floor coverings for patios include round timber discs, timber slats, and old railway sleepers.

There are other kinds of paving available from garden centres that are basically concrete slabs manufactured to simulate natural stone of various types. In some cases they may incorporate crushed aggregate of the natural material, and many of them are quite attractive. It is important not to be misled by some of their names. 'York Paving' which, say the manufacturers, 'captures the character and charm of traditional riven faced Yorkshire flags' is essentially concrete paving imitating stone. Such pavings are of course much cheaper than the real thing, but in a very small area the greater outlay involved in using natural materials may be worthwhile.

Whatever material you choose, it should be laid on a properly prepared, stable base and, in most cases, bedded in mortar. Always take professional advice.

Some useful addresses

Atlas Stone Co., Harbour Road, Rye, East Sussex TN31 7TE, telephone (0797) 223955. Supplies paving slabs of reconstituted stone (a mixture of stone aggregate and cement) in various guises, such as Etruscan paving.

Brick Advisory Centre, The Building Centre, 26 Store Street, London WC1, telephone (01) 637 0047. Will give advice on the types of brick suitable for paving.

Cement and Concrete Association, Wexham Springs, Slough, Berks SL3 6PL. Publishes a useful booklet *Concrete round your house and garden*, available free from the publications department.

ECC Quarries Ltd, Okus, Swindon, Wilts SN1 4JJ, telephone (0793) 28131. Supplies the Bradstone paving, various styles imitative of York stone, Cotswold stone, red sandstone and brick.

Haddonstone Ltd, The Forge, East Haddon, Northampton NN6 8DB, telephone (0604) 770711. Produces various decorative slabs with layered relief.

Marshalls Mono Ltd, Southowram, Halifax HX3 9SY, telephone (0422) 57155. Produces paving generally composed of stone aggregate mixed with cement to achieve the effect of natural stone.

Sitting pretty

WITH THE ADDITION of just a few pieces of patio furniture – chairs, loungers, table and parasol – you can add new life to your patio, transforming your patio into an extra 'room' in which you can dine and relax.

Patio furniture should blend with both the house and the patio and generally look part of the overall plan. Cane, for example, with its near wispy-like form looks pleasing on a light and graceful patio. It can be moved without effort, but does need to be stored somewhere when not in use. Wooden furniture looks its best on a more substantial patio, while collapsible furniture is a good idea if your patio is small as it can be easily stored.

Most garden centres make a feature of the many different styles of patio furniture and a browse among them on

The addition of elegant furniture can transform the appearance of your patio.

a quiet day, comparing prices, materials and designs, can be rewarding. Don't decide until you've consulted the catalogues, tried out those on display and are absolutely sure that what you like at the garden centre will look equally fetching on your patio.

Luckily, with the advent of synthetic resin chairs and tables and those made from painted aluminium, furniture can be kept outside without any fear of it deteriorating or discolouring. Wicker tables and chairs – light, handsome and durable if protected from the elements – need a home in winter, so make sure you've somewhere to store them.

Imparting a permanent look to the patio, stone seats, made from reconstituted stone that mellows more quickly than quarried stone, are virtually indestructible. Sited in a sunny corner, they warm up quickly and retain the sun's heat after dusk, making them ideal for enjoying a chat when shadows lengthen. Make sure that the seat is positioned on a level surface, preventing pivoting and twisting, which can strain the seat. Designs range from utilitarian to positively sumptuous, and prices vary accordingly.

Superb – and pricey – white expanded resin furniture is the stylish hallmark of Sommer Allibert's range. Their Tangor armchairs are made for relaxing, offering positions from upright for dining to tilted back for snoozing.

If you need to take it really easy then settle back in a Cormoran wheeled lounger. Their handy Balcony folding table and Dalgoria folding armchairs are a delight to assemble and so convenient to pack away.

Geeco's polypropylene patio furniture is both handsome and weatherproof. It has an ultra-white finish with detachable table legs for storage and plastic-coated, tubular steel chair frames to prevent rusting.

Brambley Garden Furniture produce superb reproduction aluminium alloy furniture, finished in bright-white polyester powder paint, which is baked on for a weatherproof finish. They specialise in benches, which are fitted with cast seats or aluminium slats, with matching chairs, large and small tables, round, square and rectangular tree seats. All fixings are in stainless steel.

Without doubt, teak seats, benches, tables and chairs are good value, offering durable qualities, coupled with a light-brown hue that complements the patio and garden. Barlow Tyrie have been making teak furniture since 1920. Their range includes a rectangular Windsor table in four sizes, and a circular Monaco – parasol holes are drilled on request. The Balmoral and Edinburgh tables come with holes already drilled.

The same company also specialises in recliners and their Commodore with recliner cushion is a joy to lie on. Circular and rectangular parasols are made from 100 per cent natural cotton.

Constructed from beautiful beechwood, Triconfort's Leisure range includes the Riviera 2000 sun couch and the clever six-position Monaco armchair, with base and seat backs made from wide-arched horizontal slats, with head, back and seat cushions.

Rustic seats and tables have much to commend them, too. In a suitably rural setting the natural lines of timbers used in the construction blend harmoniously with background trees and shrubs. Barnaby Smith's seats, benches and tables are made from durable timbers.

Rectangular – straight or curved – stone seats are mostly sold with sturdy scrolled supports. Haddonstone's selection can be combined and extended in various ways to suit the site in question.

At the less expensive end of the market are loungers with elegant polyester-coated steel frames, clad with foam-filled cushions, and fully adjustable back rests. What about a box-sided airbed on the lawn? Just the thing for soaking up the sun while engrossed in a good book.

Arbours, beloved by the Victorians, take on many forms, but essentially an arbour is a bower embraced by

Wooden tables and benches can look most effective.

fragrant climbing Roses, sweet-scented Jasmine, protected from wind and summer showers, and forming a concealed feature. Within there is a wooden, stone or metal seat made comfortable with cushions providing a perfect setting where you can unwind and relax, savour enigmatic scents and chat with friends or enjoy secluded solitude. Many arbours are recessed into hedges for extra protection and to trap the sun's warmth.

Ponder carefully the many forms of furniture available. When you're sure, and you've sited it to advantage, you'll be delighted by how much it improves your patio.

Suppliers

PLASTIC, PVC, EXPANDED RESIN

Allibert Garden Furniture, Berry Hill Industrial Estate, Droitwich, Worcs WR9 9AB. Tel. 0905-774221

Nova Garden Furniture, The Faversham Group, Graveney Road, Faversham, Kent ME13 8UN. Tel. 0795 535511

Fair Plastics Ltd, Kingsland Grange, Woolston, Warrington, Cheshire WA1 4RW. Tel. 0925-811636

Geeco Products Ltd, Gore Road Industrial Estate, New Milton, Hants BH25 6SE. Tel. 0425-614600

ALUMINIUM

Aldridge Garden & Leisure Supplies, Unit 32, Empire Works, Brickyard Road, Aldridge, Walsall. Tel. 0922-55580

Jardine Leisure Furniture Ltd, Rosemount Tower, Wallington Square, Wallington, Surrey SM6 8RR. Tel. 01-669 8265

Brambley Garden Furniture, 4 Crittall Drive, Springwood Industrial Estate, Braintree, Essex. Tel. 0376-20210

WOOD

Barlow Tyrie Ltd, Springwood Industrial Estate, Braintree, Essex CM7 7RN. Tel. 0376-22505

Barnaby Smith Ltd, 10 High Street, Stonehouse, Glos. Tel. 045-3822100

R.V. Branson & Co Ltd, East Road, Sleaford, Lincs NG34 7EH. Tel. 0279-32151

Triconfort Ltd, 96b Oak Street, Norwich, Norfolk NR3 3BP. Tel. 0603-625287

Nightglow patio lights from Hozlelock are easy to install.

WHETHER YOU'RE ENJOYING a dinner for two in the garden on a warm summer's night or entertaining friends with a barbecue, the right lighting can create an evening to remember. Light is one of the most important elements in a patio garden.

Spotlights and floodlights have many uses. Spotlights enhance single objects, such as sculptures or trees and shrubs with distinctive leaves, while a bed of roses or a tub of luminous pink Livingstone Daisies (Mesembry-anthemums) can look stunning if highlighted with a spotlight; and freshly fallen snow can look even more pure and dramatic. Floodlights, because of their diffuse light, can be used to illuminate large areas. Statues and shapely trees, such as the Weeping Birch or Ash, look very dramatic when lit with back lights. If you have a Lily-pond and a fountain, coloured lights create a dream-like vision and a Christmas tree planted in the garden can be decked with lights and switched on at party times.

Garden lighting can also be functional: downlights are best for picking out potentially hazardous steps or paths because they don't shine directly in your eyes (and if situated close to the road they should always be glazed with some sort of shatterproof polycarbonate).

Installations involving mains electricity should always be carried out by a qualified electrician. Cables have to be buried and all connections must be watertight, so it is vital there are no mistakes. Similarly, when gaslights are assembled ensure that a properly trained gas-fitter carries out the work.

Most garden centres have a reasonable stock of garden lights, but there are specialists who can offer something a little different. For example, the Emess die-cast aluminium lantern in antique finish with amber glass can be wall mounted or free standing and takes a 100W light bulb. The same company stocks white aluminium lanterns, set on columns of different lengths, made from attractive polycarbonate globes that won't shatter if stones are thrown at them. Emess also make single or double spotlights in plastic, double insulated and wired to a junction box, to highlight paths, flowerbeds and other decorative features.

Equally appealing are the gas and electric lights created by Sugg Lighting, many of which are replicas of street lights dating from 1860 to post 1930. The Camberwell, introduced by William Sugg in 1865, was considered a great improvement on the ordinary square lamp of the day. The replica is handmade from copper with a hinged door and sliding brass wire catch. It is lit by gas, oil or electricity and can be fixed to a lamp-post, or on a wall.

Other old-fashioned creations are the Westminster and Windsor lamps. The columns – fluted and barley sugar – are wonderfully ornate and give these standard lamps great character.

Nightglow patio and garden lights from Hozelock are quick and easy to install – all you need is a screwdriver. They are sold as a four- or two-lamp kit, complete with step-down transformer to reduce mains-electric current to a safe voltage. The mushroom-like heads on short poles can be positioned anywhere along the length of cable.

Hozelock's Moonglow garden lighting is equally safe to install – kits are sold in two- or four-lamp sets with spike bases, brackets, transformer and cable – and can be stuck in the ground or wall mounted. A screwdriver is the only tool you need to assemble the lights. In addition to clear lenses, the four-lamp set comes with green, amber, blue and red lenses.

Aquaglow pool lighting transforms a water garden into a magical feature. Low-voltage lights are designed to float or submerge – you sink them by weighting the cable. When combined with a fountain, the droplets are richly coloured blue or amber, depending on which colour lens you use. Other coloured lenses are available from Hozelock, who make the lamps. Each lamp set comes complete with blue and amber lenses, transformer and low-voltage cable.

Lotus Water Gardens are equally inventive. Their Pool Glow, Rainbow Fountain, Aqua Floodlighting and Light Fountain kits are wonderful – colours float to the surface and fountains become multi-coloured plumes.

An evening barbecue calls for good lighting. Add a carnival atmosphere by stringing lamps over the patio or from tree to tree. Especially cheerful are Coronet Outdoor Lanterns made by Stapeley Water Gardens, available in yellow, green, blue, red and clear. Each set comprises 10 old-English-style lanterns with bulbs and 47ft (14.25m) of cable. Decorlamps are similar, consisting of coloured 25W light bulbs and can be bought from Lotus Water Gardens and Stapeley Water Gardens. They are sold in kit-form comprising 10 light bulbs and 16ft (5m) of cable. They are completely weatherproof and easy to install.

There are many ways to accentuate the beauty of your garden; but with strategically-placed lighting you can create different atmospheres for different occasions.

Suppliers

Emess Lighting (UK) Ltd – All products are available from garden centres and other lighting outlets. The company does not deal with personal or written inquiries.

Hozelock–ASL Ltd, Haddenham, Aylesbury, Bucks., HP17 8JD.

Lotus Water Garden Products Ltd., 260-300 Berkhamsted Road, Chesham, Bucks., HP5 3EY.

Stapeley Water Gardens Ltd., Stapeley, Nantwich, Cheshire, CW5 7LH.

Sugg Lighting Ltd., 65 Gatwick Road, Crawley, Sussex, RH10 2YU.

Use garden lights to highlight steps and paths.

With careful lighting your can create different atmospheres.

Many different types of ornament can be used to give interest to a tiny garden.

STROLL ROUND THE MANICURED grounds of any great garden and your eyes will focus on the subtle juxtaposition of classical statues with trees, shrubs and border plants. But these objects of beauty needn't be confined to large, famous gardens. There are ornaments galore for patio gardens, including scaled down versions of those seen in the grand gardens.

A lion's head looks splendid when gushing water from a retaining wall, but there are also smaller ornaments, such as miniature windmills, water wheels, Chinese cranes or herons, and even painted wheelbarrows planted with summer bedding or spring bulbs in rainbow hues that make fetching features.

As well as being decorative, ornaments can also help to create an illusion: you can divert attention from the confining boundaries of a garden with the help of strategically placed columns, obelisks or pieces of sculpture, creating the impression that the garden is larger than it really is. Huge terracotta jars give character to a terrace or patio, and when overflowing with golden ivy or white-flowered Clematis they can be objects of great beauty.

Introducing humorous or unusual ornaments brings a relaxed atmosphere to a garden. An old pair of leather gardening shoes, planted with silver-leaved helichrysums would make an amusing and interesting feature.

Shopping around for ornaments

Trips to antique and junk shops or car boot sales are often rewarding, but if you're seeking something special, then you'll need the help of those who specialise in garden ornaments. Haddenstone is one such company whose reproduction lead figures – an 18th-century gallant and his lady, both 45in (114cm) high and 14in (36cm) wide at the base – are made by craftsmen using traditional methods.

In finely sculpted, reconstituted stone, Chilstone's charming French Figure, circa 1740, is wearing breeches, large-collared jacket, and a floppy hat with two feathers. His expression is pensive and restful. Equally appealing is Chilstone's Classic Figure, circa 1800, in the neoclassic revival style. The lady is draped, and she is holding a shell in one hand and her drapery in the other. Both figures are around 50in (125cm) high.

From the same company, the Goddess Flora at 39in (97cm) high and Boy Warriors dressed as Romans, holding shields and swords, at 37½ (95cm) high look magnificent when mounted on pedestals.

Figures such as these look best when they are positioned in wall alcoves, hedges or shrubs that partially embrace them, or in the centre of a raked gravel circle fringed with low Box hedging.

A well placed piece of statuary will give your patio a touch of mystery.

Columns such as fluted Doric pedestals and obelisks in stone, made by Haddonstone and Chilstone, can make arresting features, particularly if they are topped with, say, a bust of a Roman emperor, or the figure of a satyr.

Urns and vases are a speciality of Knight Terrace Pots and they have a fascinating collection. Their Thistle Vase, 20in (50cm) high, the shape of a thistle flower, is elaborately worked round the bulbous base; and their ivy vase is the same shape but etched with ivy leaves. They also make classic Italian vases.

Ornamental stone troughs are made in many patterns, such as scroll and ropework. Set on fluted supports, a trough makes a feature that commands attention.

A sundial, positioned perhaps at the end of a vista or where two paths cross, makes a superb focal point. Whether mounted on a fluted or scrolled pedestal or set in a wall, sundials are objects of riveting interest, and a powerful reminder of the great gardens of the past.

Ornamental sundials

There are many ornate forms of sundial. Haddonstone's Jacobean Figured Sundial, including the pedestal, consists of a round table supported on a sculptured shaft of three cherubs, enriched with fluting and other ornamentation.

Brookbrae's sundials are ingenious and also work well. Their Butterfly Wall Dial, Cat Dial and Dandelion Clock Dial are intricately wrought and attractive to look at.

Of all the garden sculptures, bird baths are probably the most popular. Viewed from a window, the sight of garden birds preening themselves while splashing water over their wings is most enjoyable.

Harcostar's blow-moulded plastic bird bath is inexpensive and shapely – 24in (60cm) high, with a 15in (38cm) bowl. Wide-bowled, pedestalled bird baths in stone are also available from Knight Terrace Pots, Chilstone Garden Ornaments and Haddonstone Ltd.

W. R. Farman's delightfully constructed Tit and Robin nesting boxes can be secured to the trunks of trees or tall posts. They also supply attractive bird tables thatched with Norfolk reed, and five designs of dovecote, all pleasingly roofed with reed.

A carefully chosen piece of statuary, thoughtfully placed, can give your patio that special touch that is the mark of your own individual style.

Suppliers

Chilstone Garden Ornaments, Sprivers Estate, Horsmonden, Kent TN12 8DR. Tel: (089272) 3553.
Haddonstone Ltd, The Forge House, East Haddon, Northampton NN6 8DB. Tel: (0604) 770711/365.
W. R. Farman, Cherry Tree Lane, North Walsham, Norfolk, NR28 0HR. Tel: (0692) 403022.
Harcostar Ltd, Windover Road, Huntingdon, Cambs PE18 7EE. Tel: (0480) 52323.
Renaissance Casting, Dept CFS/86, 102 Arnold Avenue, Styvechale, Coventry CV3 5NE. Tel: (0203) 27275.
Brookbrae Ltd, 53 St Leonard Road, London SW14 7NQ. Tel: 01-876 4370.
Tempus Stet Ltd, Acell House, Stockley Close, West Drayton, Mddx. Tel: (08954) 46624.
Knight Terrace Pots, West Orchard, Shaftesbury, Dorset SP7 0LJ. Tel: (0258) 72685.

All about pesticides

The subject of pesticides is a complex one and can baffle even the keenest gardener. Gone are the days when there was only the one chemical, DDT, which could be used for everything. A highly sophisticated armoury is now available to tackle all the different possible fungal infections and other garden pests.

Chemical activity

The term 'pesticide' in fact covers a wide range of chemicals that have a number of different uses. As far as houseplants are concerned, pesticides include all the following.

Insecticides. These include many different chemicals and are applied to the plant or compost to control pests such as aphids (greenfly and blackfly), caterpillars, whiteflies (above), fungus gnats and other insects.

Acaricides. These are specialised chemicals used for controlling members of the spider family which are particularly dangerous to houseplants and can be difficult to eliminate, such as red spider mite and tarsonemid mite. Specific acaricides tend to be restricted to commercial use, but examples of those that also have wider insecticidal properties include pirimiphos-methyl, malathion and dimethoate.

Nematicides. These chemicals are even more specialised and have been specifically designed to control nematodes (worms) such as eelworms. Eelworms are microscopic worms which live inside the affected plant tissue and, in order to deal with these pests, nematicides are inevitably highly toxic. They are not therefore generally available to members of the gardening public and their use is usually restricted to professional growers.

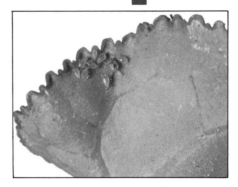

Aphicides. These are targeted at aphids, such as greenfly (above) and blackfly. Some are specially formulated to kill only aphids; these are particularly useful for plants in flower that are likely to be visited by perfectly harmless insects such as butterflies and bees or, for that matter, useful ones such as ladybirds that are doing their best to rid your plants of aphids. The best specific aphicide is probably pirimicarb, which acts selectively against only aphids. There are, however, many other aphicides that also act as general insecticides and will control many pests; these include malathion, dimethoate, permethrin and pyrethrum.

Molluscicides. These are used to control pests such as slugs (above) and snails. They are not usually a major threat to houseplants, but some small slugs and snails that seek refuge in crevices in the compost in the daytime and then feast on the plant in the evening can be problematic. Molluscicides, either in the form of a poisonous bait or in liquid form which is coated on to plant tissue, control these particular pests very effectively. Chemicals such as metaldehyde and methiocarb are very efficient.

Fungicides. These are a very useful group of chemicals that prevent and, in some cases, control and kill fungal disorders. The wide range of fungal disorders that affects houseplants includes leaf spot, stem and root rot, mildew and rust. Not all fungi actually kill plants — indeed some will only survive on living tissue — but they can seriously reduce plant vigour and deform growth. Fungicides are generally best applied as a preventive measure.

Methods of application

Although the effect of any particular pesticide depends to a great extent on its actual chemical activity and mode of action, it can also be influenced by the way in which it is applied.

Sprays. These are probably the most common formulation and come in concentrated form, either as a liquid or as a wettable powder, which is diluted according to the manufacturer's instructions and then applied to plants by means of a hand sprayer. Water acts as the chemical carrier and conveys it to the plant in droplets of chemical solution. The water then evaporates, leaving the chemical behind to act on the pest. It is always best to apply pesticidal sprays out of doors.

Drenches. Some chemicals are applied as a drench or watering to the compost. These are used to control soil-borne pests and diseases, unless it is a systemic pesticide, in which case it will be absorbed by the plant. Chemical solutions for use as drenches are usually the same formulations as those used for sprays, as water is once again used as the chemical carrier.

Granules. These are chemicals packed in a granular form and are used in the control of certain soil-borne pests. The granules can either be mixed into the compost or simply added to the surface. On wetting the soil the chemical is leeched out into the compost and will start to take effect on the pest or fungal disease. Chemical granules are not often used for the pest control of houseplants and tend to be more widely useful in the garden, where they are regularly wetted by rainfall and thus more easily absorbed, first by the soil and then by the pest.

How they work

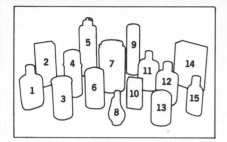

1 Murphy Liquid Copper Fungicide
2 Bio Sprayday
3 Corry's Yellow Sulphur
4 Py Spray Garden Insecticide
5 Murphy Malathion Dust
6 Corry's Green Sulphur
7 Fisons Slug and Snail Killer
8 Bio Flydown
9 Py Powder
10 Baby Bio House Plant Insecticide
11 Murphy Liquid Malathion
12 Murphy Systemic Insecticide
13 PBI Slug Mini-Pellets
14 Benlate
15 Bio Long-Last

Pesticides are complex chemical formulas that may either be derived from a natural source — such as pyrethrum which comes from a plant and will appeal to those gardeners who prefer to use products of natural origin — or they may have been developed by chemists after many years of research.

Although the effect of each chemical varies according to the particular group of chemicals to which it belongs, it can also work quite differently according to how the insect actually receives the poison.

● **Contact pesticides.** These are applied directly on to the pest, which means that good coverage of the infected plant is absolutely essential. The insect may then be poisoned either by the direct effect of the chemical on it, or by eating — or walking over — poisoned plant tissue to which the chemical has been applied. Many of these insecticides have special wetting agents, or surfactants, added to them — as,

indeed, they are to many pesticides — in order to improve the chemical's ability to stick to plant tissue. Some contact insecticides also contain fungicides.

● **Preventive pesticides.** The term 'preventive' is applied to those fungicides which help to control fungal diseases such as mildew, grey mould fungus and leaf spot. Preventive fungicides have been in use for many years and may be sulphur- or copper-based. The effect of these chemicals on a plant is to inhibit the germination of fungal spores, which helps to reduce the spread of the disease. Preventive treatment should not, therefore, be applied at too late a stage, when the plant may already be at an advanced stage of infection.

● **Systemic pesticides.** These include both insecticides and fungicides and are a relatively recent innovation in the history of pesticides. They are extremely effective and greatly facilitate the control of many pests.

Systemic pesticides may be sprayed or even watered on to plants and then rapidly enter the plant tissue where they are able to move freely to all parts of the plant and thus provide comprehensive protection from pests and fungal diseases — unless, of course, the pest or fungus in question has developed a resistance to that particular chemical. An insect only has to eat some of the poisoned plant tissue to be killed as sap is absorbed into its body. And a fungus may suffer the same fate as it attempts to draw nutrition from the plant carrying the fungicide in its tissue. Products that combine a systemic insecticide with a systemic fungicide are now widely available. Systemic pesticides are a superior alternative to contact pesticides because they do not depend on total coverage of the foliage.

> **WARNING**
> Remember to take full account of all the safety precautions recommended by the manufacturer as regards the mixing, use and storage of pesticides.

Dusts. Instead of being diluted in water, a chemical dust uses an inert carrier dust or powder to transport the chemical. Chemical dusts can simply be 'puffed' on to plants in order to control pests or diseases, but they tend to leave an unsightly deposit on foliage which devalues their use indoors.

Aerosols. These are a particularly convenient way of applying a chemical to a plant. The aerosol transports it in minute droplets which provide an effective coverage. Another advantage is that

aerosols come in an easy, ready-to-use form.

Misters. Hand mist sprayers containing ready-to-use solutions have recently been introduced to fill the gap between the convenient aerosol and the dilute-yourself concentrate. This combines the advantages of the aerosol with those of the re-fillable mister and is therefore a useful additional pest control system.

Chemical baits. Some pests, such as slugs and snails, cannot easily be sprayed and are therefore more easily

dealt with by chemical baits. These both attract their victims and then poison them. They are widely used in the garden and can also be used, in a smaller version, on houseplants.

Chemical vaporisers. These work on the same principle as those chemical vaporising strips that are sometimes hung from the ceiling to control insects such as mosquitoes. They take the form of small plant 'labels' or tabs which are impregnated with a special chemical and which you simply insert in the soil.

Know your pesticides

CHEMICAL NAME	BRAND NAME	TYPE OF PESTICIDE
Benomyl	Benlate (ICI)	Systemic fungicidal spray/drench
Copper compound	Murphy Liquid Copper Fungicide	Fungicidal spray
Copper sulphate and ammonium carbonate	Cheshunt Compound (PBI)	Fungicidal spray/drench
Derris, see Rotenone		
Dimethoate	Murphy Systemic Insecticide	Systemic insecticidal/acaricidal spray
Dimethoate and permethrin	Bio Long-Last (PBI)	Systemic and contact insecticidal/ acaricidal spray
Malathion	Malathion Greenfly Killer (PBI) Murphy Greenhouse Aerosol Murphy Liquid Malathion Murphy Malathion Dust	Contact insecticidal spray Contact insecticidal/acaricidal aerosol Contact insecticidal/acaricidal spray Contact insecticidal dust
Mancozeb	Dithane 945 (PBI)	Fungicidal spray
Metaldehyde	Fisons Slug and Snail Killer ICI Mini Blue Slug Pellets Murphy Slugits Murphy Slugit Liquid Slug Mini-Pellets (PBI)	Molluscicidal bait Molluscicidal bait Molluscicidal bait Molluscicidal spray Molluscicidal bait
Methiocarb	Slug Gard (PBI)	Molluscicidal bait
Permethrin	Baby Bio House Plant Insecticide (PBI) Bio Flydown (PBI) Bio Sprayday (PBI) Fisons Whitefly & Caterpillar Killer Picket (ICI) Boots Caterpillar & Whitefly Killer	Contact insecticidal spray Contact insecticidal spray Contact insecticidal spray Contact insecticidal spray Contact insecticidal spray Contact insecticidal spray
Permethrin and heptenophos	Murphy Tumblebug	Contact insecticidal/systemic spray
Permethrin and malathion	Crop Saver (PBI)	Contact insecticidal spray
Pirimicarb	Rapid Greenfly Killer (ICI) Rapid Aerosol (ICI)	Contact aphicidal spray Contact aphicidal aerosol
Pirimiphos-methyl	Sybol 2 (ICI) Sybol 2 Dust (ICI)	Contact insecticide/acaricide Contact insecticidal/acaricidal dust
Pirimiphos-methyl and synergised pyrethrins	Sybol 2 Aerosol (ICI) Kerispray (ICI)	Contact insecticidal/acaricidal aerosol Contact insecticidal/acaricidal aerosol
Pyrethrum and piperonyl butoxide	Py Powder (Synchemicals) Py Spray Garden Insect Killer (Synchemicals) Py Spray Garden Insecticide (Synchemicals)	Contact insecticidal dust Contact insecticidal spray Contact insecticidal aerosol
Rotenone (derris)	Abol Derris Dust (ICI) Liquid Derris (PBI)	Contact insecticidal/acaricidal dust Contact insecticidal/acaricidal spray
Rotenone and quassia	Bio Back to Nature Insect Spray (PBI)	Contact insecticidal spray
Rotenone and sulphur	Bio Back to Nature Pest and Disease Dust (PBI)	Contact insecticidal/fungicidal dust
Sulphur	Green and Yellow Sulphur (Synchemicals)	Contact fungicide
Thiophanate-methyl	Fungus Fighter (May & Baker) Murphy Systemic Fungicide	Systemic fungicidal spray Systemic fungicidal spray

How fertilisers work

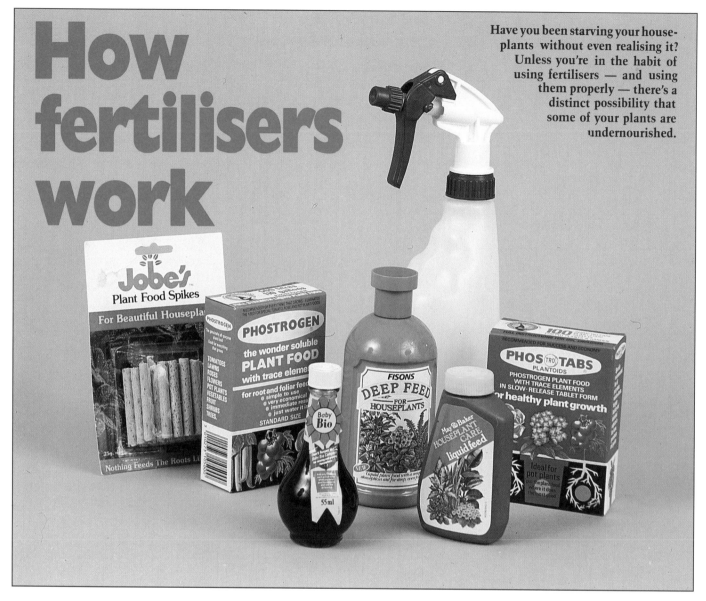

Have you been starving your house-plants without even realising it? Unless you're in the habit of using fertilisers — and using them properly — there's a distinct possibility that some of your plants are undernourished.

You'd be forgiven for assuming that houseplants can rely on their compost for the nourishment they need, and up to a point that's certainly true. But watering alone will not do; within a matter of weeks, a perfectly healthy specimen may start to decline in vigour, as the natural goodness in its compost is used up, or washed away.

For young plants that have to be moved on to ever bigger pots in the natural course of events, renewing the compost every three to six months is perfectly practicable. Indeed it's actually unwise to add fertiliser to a young plant for fear of burning its root system. But for established plants, it makes more sense to use a fertiliser to replenish the plant's food supply.

Used with a little know-how as part of a good plant-care routine, a fertiliser will keep plants in the best possible shape, ensuring well balanced growth and, for flowering plants, a splendid display. And the joy is that you will be able to direct improvements towards each individual plant's weakness — by choosing the right fertiliser for its needs.

Fertilisers need to be treated with respect; plants may be killed by too much interference far more easily than by too little, so it's wise to err on the side of caution and to add less rather than more.

Remember, too, that more than plants may be at risk. Fertilisers can be dangerous in the hands of children and the unsuspecting. Keep all packets well out of reach and make sure they are clearly labelled. Avoid transferring fertilisers into discarded food containers or bottles.

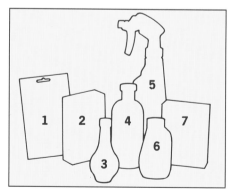

1. Jobe's Plant Food Spikes.
2. Phostrogen, root and foliar feed.
3. Baby Bio, liquid.
4. Fison's Deep Feed, liquid.
5. Spray for applying foliar feed.
6. May and Baker Houseplant Care, liquid.
7. Phostrotabs, tablets.

Choosing and using a fertiliser

Fertilisers come in a wealth of forms, from solutions to powders, sticks or granules. The choice can seem intimidating, but a brief profile of each will put you in the picture.

Whichever you choose, always ensure that the compost is thoroughly damp before applying any fertiliser. Water the plants first, and let the moisture drain right through the compost. Unless the compost is properly dampened in this way, the fertiliser may burn the roots.

Liquids, powders and crystals

If you're in the habit of regularly checking over your houseplants, you'll probably find it easy to establish and stick to a feeding programme using a liquid fertiliser. As these must first be diluted with water before use, they can easily be incorporated into your watering sessions.

The great advantage of liquid feeding is that it gives you far more flexibility than the other methods; you can control exactly when you feed and how much you give your plants. On the other hand, you will have to spend time mixing up the formula, and if you are at all forgetful, you may end up inadvertently neglecting your plants.

These minor shortcomings apart, products like Baby Bio (solution) or Phostrogen (powder) produce very good results, provided you follow a few simple dos and don'ts:

● Do dilute the fertiliser adequately, following the manufacturer's instructions. A plant will *not* grow faster if you feed it with a stronger solution. If you do, you may damage your plant's roots quite severely and scorch its leaves.

● Always use the weakest solution specified on the label if the manufacturer has not specified a strength for houseplants.

● Try not to let fertiliser come into contact with the foliage unless, of course, you are using a foliar feed (see below). This is especially important in sunny weather when

An under-nourished *Pittosporum tenuifolium.*

leaves may be scorched by the sun's rays coming through the window. Wipe off any droplets with a damp cloth.

How often you feed will vary from plant to plant, but as a rough guide you can expect to give each one a minimum of three or four applications of a standard fertiliser during one growing season. In practice, you may find that you need to feed some plants once a fortnight, and really fast-growing plants, like Busy Lizzies and Spider Plants, once a week. Never exceed the manufacturers' recommendations, and if you notice that growth is becoming lush and rather floppy, chances are that you should cut down on the feeding. Another sure sign of overfeeding is poor flowering, although plenty of leaves are produced.

Fertiliser sticks and tablets

If you want as little trouble as possible, these 'solid' fertilisers are ideal. Just poke them into the compost as recommended and your work is over for the next few weeks, as the goodness slowly seeps into the growing mixture.

Although sticks can't give you the flexibility offered by the liquids, individual manufacturers are at last beginning to offer a choice of formulas (like the Jobe range, for instance) to suit different types of plant.

Tablets work in the same way as sticks.

Granules

Fertiliser granules are really only useful when you are making up your own potting mixtures.

Controlled release fertiliser pellets

These can be an absolute boon because they provide long-term nourishment for as much as a year, but, once again, they are designed to be mixed in with a made-up potting compost. Osmocote and Ficote are both well-known, reliable brands.

Foliar feeds

Foliar feeds have revolutionised feeding techniques by breaking the rules. The only fertilisers that can be sprayed directly on to leaves, they make the perfect plant pick-me-up, as they are absorbed into the plant sap and quickly assimilated.

Because of this characteristic, they're marvellous for plants which can't absorb much through their roots — like air plants, for instance, whose roots are surrounded by moss rather than compost.

Use these sprays with a little caution and don't spray near any furnishings.

Don't rely on foliar feeds exclusively. Use a foliar feed as a trouble shooter, then return to the more conventional methods of your regular feeding programme.

When to start a feeding programme

Feeding plants at the wrong time is more than wasteful — it's positively harmful. The golden rule is: only feed plants during their active growing season (which is, roughly speaking, between April and September); for the rest of the time, stick to water.

🌱 It's a mistake to try and 'force' growth during the dormant period. All you'll achieve is a spindly specimen with small, pale leaves, for the untapped nutrient salts build up around the roots and actually hinder the plant.

🌱 Any plants that have been repotted recently into fresh compost will have enough goodness to last them quite a while. As a rule of thumb, soil-based mixtures like John Innes will hold their fertiliser for up to 12 weeks, while a peat-based variety is likely to be

exhausted inside six to eight weeks. Once that time limit is up, you should start feeding.

🌱 Where shop-bought plants are concerned, be prepared to start feeding immediately. It's very likely that their supplies will be used up by the time they reach your home.

🌱 The tell-tale signs to watch out for are a crop of duller, smaller leaves and, in the case of variegated plants, new leaves without the usual markings. Start feeding at once!

🌱 Don't expect any miracles, though; fertilisers are a food, not a medicine. Before stepping up on the feeding, do check for any other possible causes if a plant is failing to respond. Is it being overwatered, or does it prefer a different location? Make sure that it hasn't outgrown its pot, either.

Making the right choice

You can't go wrong with a 'standard' fertiliser — a sort of chemical cocktail of the nutrients which plants require for healthy growth. The nutrients, dissolved in water, are absorbed via the plant's roots.

The 'big three' plant foods are nitrogen, phosphorus and potassium (abbreviated, by international agreement, to the letters N, P and K, respectively). Besides these *macronutrients* (which also include calcium, magnesium and sulphur) are a host of *micronutrients*, otherwise known as trace elements, since only a 'trace' of each is needed. Turn to the chart overleaf to see what part each of these plays in your plants' lives — and what can happen to your plants if there's a deficiency of any of them.

Stick fertilisers cut work down to a minimum; push the recommended number into the soil and for the next few weeks the nutrients will slowly seep into the compost and all you'll need to do is water the plant.

Tablets work in the same way as stick fertilisers and are equally clean and simple to use. In both cases it's important to follow the manufacturer's instructions to the letter.

Liquid feeding is probably the most popular method and gives good results; it's slightly more time consuming but has the advantage that you can control exactly how much food your plant gets.

What's in the fertilisers

	What it's for	Signs of deficiency	Source	Special notes
NITROGEN	The most important element for healthy growth, and also for maintaining leaf colour.	Small, pale leaves lacking vigour and lustre.	Can only be absorbed in nitrate form such as ammonium nitrate, potassium nitrate or the more inferior sodium nitrate. Also supplied by organic products like bonemeal and hoof-and-horn.	Always useful for leafy plants, but especially important at the start of the growing season.
PHOSPHORUS	Essential in helping plant metabolism (process of converting nutrients into living matter), it's present in relatively high levels in the growing parts of the plant and is very important in root growth.	Poor root growth; poor plant development; immaturity.	Many different forms. Examples include superphosphate and mono-ammonium phosphate.	Good for plants just before or during flowering. Especially good for roses.
POTASSIUM	Vital to the development of flowers and fruit. Potassium helps stimulate flowering and maturing of fruit.	Plants produce poor show of fruit and flowers, or none at all.	Potassium sulphate, or sulphate of potash, and potassium nitrate.	Especially good for plants that have just finished flowering; helps them in the rebuilding process.
CALCIUM	General growth and development.	Disrupted rate of growth and development; may result in death of developing shoots.	Usually available in most fertilisers.	
MAGNESIUM	Helps to make chlorophyll, the green pigment that absorbs sunlight as an energy source.	Poor, weak foliage and chlorosis (loss of colour in leaves and stems; see also iron, right).	Epsom salts, magnesium sulphate.	
SULPHUR	Needed for photosynthesis — the conversion of carbon dioxide into the sugars the plant needs.	Small, pale leaves, or leaves with a reddish tinge. May make the plant vulnerable to disease.	Sulphates such as potassium sulphate.	

All the main and trace elements, *above,* are vitally important to healthy plant growth, the basic distinction being that the main elements are needed in larger amounts than the trace elements.

Knowing which elements are affecting which aspects of plant growth and development will help you select the best fertiliser for your needs. Consult the A-Z guides for further information on individual plants and also follow any suggestions you get from the shop or nursery.

There are plenty of natural, or 'organic', sources for these elements — bonemeal, fishmeal, hoof-and-horn, dried blood, woodash, seaweed, etc., are all familiar names to the outdoor gardener. However, these organic fertilisers are all very slow-acting because their chemicals have first to be released by the actions of micro-organisms in the compost.

Synthetic products tend to be a better bet for houseplants. They are quicker acting and can be absorbed more or less directly by the root system.

You can buy either 'simple' fertilisers, containing just one or two chemicals, or the more versatile 'compound' or standard fertilisers which provide a balanced mixture of plant foods. All the major elements are usually present, together with

What's in the fertilisers (trace elements)

	What it's for	Signs of deficiency	Source	Special notes
IRON	Vitally important for the production of chlorophyll, the green pigment in plants.	Chlorosis: leaves become blotched with pale green or yellow. Particularly noticeable on young, green growth. Results in poor, stunted growth.	Iron is not readily available to plants and has to be given in the form of iron sequestrene or sequestered iron.	Deficiency affects acid-loving plants in particular.
BORON	Assists in tip growth of roots and shoots.	Unsatisfactory development of roots and growing points, and even of flowers. However, deficiency of this kind is very rare.	Normally present as a trace in standard fertilisers. Directly available from borax (sodium tetraborate).	It is very unlikely that your plants will lack boron, so use with very great caution; it can be toxic if added in excess.
ZINC	Important for satisfactory growth.	Loss of vigour and lack of growth.	Zinc salts in plant compost.	Plants are very unlikely to suffer from lack of zinc. Add with caution; it is toxic if applied in excess.
MANGANESE	Important in photosynthesis (see sulphur, left).	Similar to, though less common than, iron deficiency, but leaves become more mottled.	Manganese sulphate.	
COPPER	General growth.	Growth defects.	Usually available in fertilisers with a quantity of trace elements added to them.	Copper deficiency in plants is very rare and usually confined to plants in a peaty compost.
CHLORINE	Important in photosynthesis.	Any deficiency is most unlikely.	Present in most tap water and most fertilisers.	
MOLYBDENUM	Important in helping plants to use nitrate.	Similar to lack of nitrogen.	Sodium molybdate or ammonium molybdate. Usually available as a trace element in certain fertilisers.	Poinsettia (*Euphorbia pulcherrima*) is one of the few houseplants susceptible to molybdenum deficiency; the leaves turn mottled and yellowish with brown edges.

If fertiliser is accidentally splashed on leaves, carefully sponge it off — unless, of course, it's a foliar feed!

Do check the individual A-Z guides for feeding information on your houseplants, as their requirements will vary.

Special purpose fertilisers

Standard fertilisers are perfectly adequate for most houseplant needs, but there may be occasions when a special purpose fertiliser could be worth a try. There is a number of such products on the market, and of these the tomato fertiliser is probably the best known. Don't be put off by the name! When used at a more dilute rate (as recommended on the pack for flowering plants) a tomato fertiliser can be very beneficial to flowering plants and cacti, promoting sturdier growth and a fine show of flowers.

If you want to grow any lime-hating plants — Miniature Orange, Gardenia or Indian Azalea, for example — you could find that some iron sequestrene comes in handy. Plants can find it difficult to get iron from a chalky or limy soil, and lime-haters will be unable to get sufficient supplies if there's the slightest hint of these alkalis in their compost. They may develop a sickness called chlorosis, in which they lose the green pigment in their leaves and stems. Old wives' tales about adding rusty nails to the soil are quite unfounded — the iron must come in an easily soluble form, as in 'sequestered' iron.

Incidentally, there are certain fertilisers that acid-loving plants must steer clear of — bonemeal, hoof-and-horn and superphosphate all contain alkaline calcium salts. You'll find that there are special 'acid reaction' fertilisers available from which any offending alkalis are banished.

a few trace elements, and the finished product is often a combination of synthetic and organic products; Baby Bio and Liquinure, for instance, both have a seaweed base.

Each manufacturer makes his product to his own recipe, so if you can learn to read the coded labels on the pack, you will have an advantage.

Reading the labels

Manufacturers are obliged to include a three-number code on their brands. It will look something like this: 6:10:6. The numbers stand for the nitrogen, phosphorus and potassium content in the product concerned, and always in that order. The content is shown as a percentage, so in our example, the nitrogen and potassium content is, in each case, 6 per cent, while the phosphorus is a higher 10 per cent. The chart above reveals that a high phosphate content is good for plants in bloom, or just starting into flower.

Try to avoid those fertilisers with a very high nitrogen content — in a ratio of more than four parts nitrogen to one part each of phosphorus and potassium (written 4:1:1). High nitrogen fertilisers are not suitable for indoor use and will make growth far too lush and soft.

Finding a fertiliser

If you want to get the best from your patio plants you must make sure that they are adequately nourished. Watering, although essential, is simply not enough. You must also feed your plants to enable them to grow and produce healthy foliage and, where appropriate, flowers and fruit.

It is important to remember that patio and container-grown plants are unlikely to obtain as many natural nutrients and water as those plants grown in ordinary garden soil. In fact, on the patio, nutrient supplies can be depleted quite rapidly – even within a few weeks of repotting during the growing season – and therefore regular feeding is especially important. You must take care, however, not to overfeed as too much fertiliser can lead to excessive leafy growth at the expense of flowers and fruit.

Choosing the type

Which type of fertiliser you choose depends on the type of plant you are growing on your patio. In general, ornamental plants that are grown for their foliage only, such as Hedera species, require less nutrients than flowering plants like Hydrangea, or fruiting plants like tomatoes.

For ornamental foliage plants, a fertiliser with a higher ratio of nitrogen to phosphorous and potassium will help to encourage good healthy growth. A higher level of potassium, however, is required for flowering and fruiting plants. In this case a tomato fertiliser can be used, but at a lower level than that recommended for tomatoes, otherwise too much foliage could be produced and scorching might occur.

Choosing the form

When you have decided what nutrients you require you will have to decide which form of fertiliser will best suit your purpose.

Controlled release fertiliser. This comes in pellets and is worth considering for use on ornamental foliage-type plants that you don't

Nutrient sticks are easy and convenient to use – simply push them into the compost around the plant as far as they will go.

want to spend too much time looking after. The pellets, which should be buried in the soil, are made up of fertiliser mixture contained in a resin coat which will release the nutrients according to the temperature and the moisture level of the compost. The standard formulation available will provide enough nutrients for a plant's growing season as long as you use it as directed.

Watch out for . . .

● An excess of nutrients can cause damage. Too much fertiliser can lead to a high concentration of salt in the compost which often means the plant can't absorb enough food and water. If you think you have added too much fertiliser it can be leached out with clean water applied over the surface of the compost. This will help to rinse the high concentration through the compost, diluting it on its way, and out through the bottom of the container.
● Excessive rain or watering can actually deplete the nutrients in compost and your patio plants may need a 'top-up' if you suspect that this is a problem.
● Don't feed for at least three weeks after potting. The compost should contain sufficient nutrients, and the roots need some time to get established.

Top dressing. A compound fertiliser such as a basic John Innes compost can be added as a top dressing. Simply sprinkle the fertiliser on to the surface of the compost and rake it in before watering. When using this form of fertiliser take care not to let it come into contact with any leaves or roots, because if it does, it could cause scorching. During the growing season you may have to repeat this top dressing according to your plant's nutrient requirements and also to the type of fertiliser you choose.

Nutrient sticks or tablets. These are very convenient and safe and can be used to nourish plants over a prolonged period. All you have to do is to push them into the compost around the plant. The number required and the nutrient type depend on the size of container and species of plant.

Liquid feeding. The great advantage of this form of fertiliser is that you can decide exactly when you feed and how much to give your plants. In fact, a solution of plant nutrients applied regularly throughout the growing season will probably give very good results.

Organic fertilisers. These can be used for the long-term feeding of foliage plants as they are slow-acting. Bonemeal is probably the best for patio plants but make sure that it has been approved and sterilised and that you use it according to the manufacturer's instructions.

When to feed

To be effective, fertilisers must be applied at the correct time, which is during the plant's growing season – usually between April and September. One application every seven to 14 days is normally sufficient. In most cases no fertilisers should be given between October and March. Feeding plants during their time of rest can, in fact, be detrimental to their health because they can't absorb the chemicals and toxicity builds up in the soil.

Insecticides

The enormous choice of insecticides available to the gardener nowadays can make selection quite difficult, particularly when there are so many that seem to do much the same job.

It is important, however, to remember that, as far as the choice of any chemicals is concerned, the first thing to consider is always their safety. Not only are they likely to be used in very close proximity to the home, where people and pets will come into contact with treated plants, but some of the plants you are treating may be edible, or bear an edible crop, which may retain pesticidal residues even after thorough washing.

Fortunately, the majority of chemicals now available have been cleared for use by the government's Pesticide Safety Precaution Scheme. It is extremely important that the manufacturer's recommendations are always followed closely.

The following chemicals should solve most patio pest problems (for details of brand names and forms of application see pages 565-7).

Types of insecticide

Malathion: this is a contact insecticide effective against a very wide range of insects, including aphids, caterpillars, red spider mites, thrips and whitefly. Its slight systemic activity also helps in the effective control of pests, although its somewhat pungent smell may deter you from using it too frequently.

Malathion is available either as a chemical dust or as a liquid concentrate, which is made up into a solution and sprayed on to the foliage or watered on to the compost to control such soil-borne pests as fungus gnat larvae or root mealy bugs.

Metaldehyde: slugs and snails can be quite a problem, especially during wet weather when they will come out from under pots and other areas of cover to consume your plants at night while you are asleep. They are therefore somewhat difficult to deal with using a spray, and are best controlled with a chemical bait.

The use of metaldehyde pellets is usually the most effective way of controlling these pests, provided that the bait does not become wet as it then soon ceases to be effective.

Always follow the manufacturer's instructions when using insecticides.

Many baits containing metaldehyde are coloured blue to act as a deterrent to birds and other wildlife that might otherwise be attracted to eat the poison. Their colour will not, however, deter young children – in fact, it will have quite the opposite effect – so it is important to take extra care to place the poisoned pellets carefully away from anywhere where children, as well as pets or wildlife, could find and consume them.

Methiocarb: a more recent insecticide that has been introduced to control slugs and snails is methiocarb. This is again incorporated into a bait, which is also stained blue, and is usually available as a smaller pellet.

The advantage of this one is that its effectiveness is not significantly reduced when it gets wet, which makes it more appropriate for outdoor use. The same precautions should, of course, be taken to protect children, pets and wildlife as with metaldehyde.

Permethrin: this is another relatively new chemical that has been refined from the naturally occuring pyrethroid insecticides. It is a contact insecticide with a particularly fast 'knock-down' effect on all flying insects and is very useful for the control of aphids, whitefly, fungus gnats and thrips.

Permethrin is available· either in

189

aerosol form, to be applied as a fine mist, or as a liquid concentrate, to be diluted in water and applied to any food crops growing on the patio. This means that the interval that needs to be observed between spraying and eating is likely to be considerably less (24 hours) than with a chemical such as malathion (for which there is a seven-day interval).

Although its level of toxicity is less than that of many other chemicals, it is still important to realise that some harmless insects may be adversely affected if great care is not taken when you apply the product.

Pirimicarb: this is a useful contact aphicide for the control of all aphids (greenfly and blackfly). It is particularly useful when certain food plants are in flower on the patio and the services of bees and other insects are required in order to pollinate the flowers and thus set the fruit. Unlike many insecticides, including some of the 'safer' types which are still a hazard to bees and butterflies, pirimicarb is active exclusively against aphids.

The effect of pirimicarb is extremely rapid and all the aphids on a treated plant will usually die within about half an hour. Although it may appear to be relatively safe, it is still important to observe all the manufacturer's recommendations, including instructions relating to the safe interval between treatment and harvest. Pirimicarb is available either as a liquid concentrate or in a ready-mixed aerosol formulation.

Pyrethrum: this is a naturally occuring chemical of plant origin that has been in use for many years. Although it has been used for a long time, it is still a worthwhile insecticide for such pests as aphids, whitefly, fungus gnats and thrips.

Pyrethrum is a contact insecticide similar to permethrin in that it is extremely rapid in its action and has an efficient 'knock-down' effect. Although it is extremely toxic to flying insects, it has a low level of toxicity in humans and animals, and is therefore a common ingredient of many fly sprays for domestic use and for the control of animal pests such as fleas, when it is often formulated as a fine dust.

As with permethrin, pyrethrum

has a relatively short life and therefore needs to be applied regularly in order to gain complete control over your local pest population. It is available as an aerosol, a dust, or a liquid concentrate for dilution as a spray.

Rotenone (Derris): this is derived from a natural plant source and is an effective insecticide for the control of such pests as red spider mite, thrips, caterpillars and aphids. It is a contact insecticide, available either as a dust formulation which can simply be 'puffed' on to the plant's foliage, or as a spray which can be applied through a small hand sprayer.

Rotenone is probably best used to control red spider mites and thrips, and should be used for aphids (greenfly and blackfly) only when there is no alternative specific aphicide available. This is because it is such a broad spectrum product that it will also kill many other insects, including attractive and beneficial ones such as butterflies and bees.

Types of application
The choice of insecticides obviously depends to a large extent on the pest in question, but convenience of application is also an important factor to be taken into consideration.

Chemical dusts: puffer packs containing a powder impregnated with

the chemical are convenient for small localised infestations, but the deposit which the powder leaves on the plant may prove to be too unsightly for use on the patio.

Liquid concentrates: chemical concentrates are available either in liquid form or as a wettable powder, which is then made up into a solution and sprayed through a hand sprayer. They often offer the most economical solution, although you do have to measure them out accurately. If, however, you have a large number of plants on your patio, this type of formulation may be the best for you.

Aerosols: these are very convenient, though their convenience is now matched by some of the new products marketed in ready-to-spray formulations in a sprayer. Aerosols are ideal for small numbers of plants of moderate size, but could be costly if you have many large plants that require a great deal of coverage.

WATCHPOINT: all of the insecticides can be used on edible crops. However, the interval between spraying and eating varies between 24 hours for insecticides such as rotenone and permethrin and a minimum of seven days for malathion. Be sure that you check the manufacturer's instructions on the packet.

Which insecticide?

	Aphids	Cater-pillars	Fungus gnats	Red spider mite	Slugs and snails	Thrips	White-fly
Malathion (Aerosol, dust or liquid concentrate)	✓	✓	✓	✓		✓	✓
Metaldehyde (Pelleted chemical bait)					✓		
Methiocarb (Pelleted chemical bait)					✓		
Permethrin (Aerosol or liquid concentrate)	✓	✓	✓			✓	✓
Pirimicarb (Aerosol or liquid concentrate)	✓						
Pyrethrum (Aerosol, dust or liquid concentrate)	✓	✓	✓			✓	✓
Rotenone (Derris) (Dust or liquid concentrate)	✓	✓	✓	✓		✓	✓

Fungus and fungicides

The range of fungal disorders is wide and sooner or later you are going to have to use fungicides on your patio as a preventative or curative measure.

Many plant diseases are caused by fungi – parasitic organisms that can live only by weakening or actually killing their hosts – and therefore fungicides are of utmost importance.

Fungal problems, however, are not easy to control, especially if you apply fungicides when the plant may already be in an advanced state of infection. If you think that infection is likely to occur it is much better to apply fungicides at recommended intervals as a preventative measure.

Fungal problems on indoor plants and plants grown under glass can be controlled by varying the temperature, watering and ventilation to help the recovery of the plant. This is more difficult to do on the patio, although careful watering can reduce the risk of root diseases as fungi flourish in very wet conditions. Dead, decaying or infected tissue should also be removed immediately, as they could become a dangerous source of infection.

Types of fungicide
Fungicides can be put into two categories – preventatives which help to stop infection in the first place and

curatives which kill the fungus when it has actually started to attack. Unfortunately, there are not many curatives available which makes the careful use of preventative fungicides all the more important.

Preventative fungicides
Some older types of fungicide based on copper or sulphur and, more recently, zinc and other chemical compounds are still effective in stopping the spores of fungi from germinating on the foliage of plants and from spreading once the disease has taken hold.

Diseases such as mildew and rust are best controlled by preventative-type fungicides, used if possible before the plants become infected. Even when a heavy infection is evi-

A fungicide such as benomyl will cure a botrytis infection.

dent, it is worth using fungicides containing copper, sulphur and zinc-based compounds on any nearby plants as, hopefully, this will stop the infection from taking hold.

Curative fungicides
Fungicides such as benomyl will kill fungi, such as botrytis, and some root diseases like rhizoctonia. To be totally effective, however, they must be applied as soon as the fungal disease is first identified.

Formulations
Fungicides are available in various formulations based on liquids, wettable powders or dusts to be applied according to the appropriate situation.

Liquids and wettable powders. The chemical is diluted in water which then acts as the carrier. These can be sprayed directly on to the foliage or applied as a drench or watering to the compost, and are usually used to control soil-borne diseases. By their very nature wettable powders tend to leave more of a deposit on foliage than liquid formulations.

Dusts. Instead of being diluted in water, a chemical dust such as sulphur uses an inert powder as a carrier. These are usually used in localised situations to stop the spread of fungal diseases such as mildew. Unfortunately, they tend to leave a deposit which may prove too unsightly for patio plants.

Take care...
Whatever chemicals you choose, make sure that you use them according to the manufacturer's instructions, especially when treating plants bearing fruits, such as tomatoes. It is always a wise precaution to wash treated produce.

Pick and choose

The following are a selection of commonly-available fungicides that can be used to control most diseases that you are likely to find on patio plants.

Benomyl. This has a broad spectrum activity against many fungal diseases, including botrytis (grey mould fungus), powdery mildew, some stem and root infections and leaf spot fungi. If applied early enough, it may also have some activity against Clematis wilt, which is best treated by spraying or watering the stems with a solution of the fungicide.

Benomyl is usually available as a wettable

powder to be diluted in water and applied as a spray or drench treatment. It is both preventative and curative.

Captan. This can be used as a preventative treatment for a number of leaf spot fungi and other organisms, such as some of the root and stem rot fungi. It is available as a wettable powder.

Copper compounds. These can be used as a preventative treatment for leaf spots and some other fungi. Clematis wilt can also be controlled if the chemical is applied early enough. Copper compounds are usually

available as a liquid to be applied as a spray or used as a drench.

Sulphur. This preventative fungicide is useful for the control of mildew and some leaf spot organisms. It is applied as a dust.

Thiram. Used as a spray or a dust, thiram helps to control downy mildew and some fungal spots. It is most active when used as a preventative treatment.

Zineb. This may also be applied as a spray or a dust to help to prevent and control downy mildew and some fungal spots.

Talk to your plants

LUTHER BURBANK, a famous nurseryman from California, developed the spineless cactus (*Opuntia ficus-indica*) in the early years of this century. He spoke to the plants as they were growing: 'You have nothing to fear,' he would tell them, 'you don't need your defensive thorns. I will protect you.' How much influence Burbank's soothing comments had upon the development of the spineless cactus is difficult – if not impossible – to estimate. But like many plant owners, he was convinced he had to win the trust of his plants – and that talking to them was the best method.

Many people talk to their plants just as they do to their household pets or, indeed, their children. House-plants are regarded and treated by many people in much the same way as dogs, cats or birds. And people's reactions to the health or otherwise of their plants is often out of all proportion to the cost of replacing the plants involved. We really do get upset when our plants are not growing as they should.

Do *you* talk to your houseplants? Do you regularly chat them up, giving them words of encouragement to grow lustily or to start to flower, or do you offer threats of banishment if they don't mend their ways? And do you think your plants take any notice of your words of praise or your warnings?

Some eminent interest

A number of very eminent people deeply involved with plants (Darwin was one) have thought of plants in human terms and over the last few decades extensive research has been carried out into the idea that plants are not indifferent to human beings.

Former CIA employee Cleve Backster connected the electrodes of a lie detector to a Philodendron, and claimed to have evidence that the plant was able to react to his *intention* to maltreat it in some way: he called this seemingly supernatural ability 'primary perception'. In the late 1960s, a student named Mary Retallack in Denver, Colorado, subjected a group of plants to the notes B and D played

Can plants hear? Those above seem to thrive in a musical environment, while the one on the right below suffered badly when continually exposed to loud rock music.

loudly over and over again 12 hours a day. At the end of three weeks, all the plants had died – except for some African Violets, which flourished. A 'control' group of the same plant types grown at the same time in normal sound conditions all grew in a healthy manner.

Fact or fancy?

Whatever the results of this scientific (or pseudo-scientific) research, there is one thing that we can probably say about talking to plants: the specific needs of each plant must always be considered, and the person who talks to his or her plants, treats them as individuals and is concerned for their various states of development is by far the most likely to get good results. The single-minded decorator, concerned only with instant effect, placing plants in corners without light or in draughts merely because it suits the room is unlikely to get anything like the same healthy, growing specimens.

Interestingly enough, while the scientific research on plants responding to humans is inconclusive, it has been established over the past few years that humans respond positively to caring for plants. Several major American universities offer degrees in horticultural therapy, a treatment whereby patients with physical or mental problems can find some relief in a close interest in plants. And in this therapy, patients are actively encouraged to talk to plants!

So talk to your plants by all means – it's good for them, and it may be even better for you.

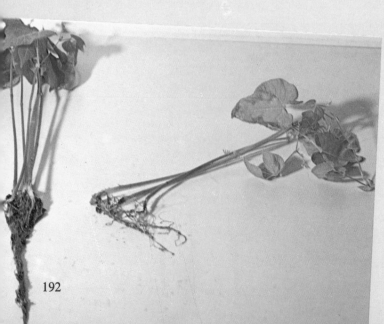

192

CHAPTER 4

Living with Plants

Seasonal spring care

Plants seem to sense the coming of spring long before we do and, just as the first spring bulbs burst into flower on even the coldest, dampest spring mornings, houseplants have also noticed the increasing hours of daylight and have started to put on fresh growth, so signalling a change in care from that required in the long, cold, dark winter months.

The appearance of new growing shoots, new leaves or even flowers are the most common signals to watch out for, all of which herald the change in season. And with this seasonal change comes the need to adjust the care of your houseplants.

Watering

As houseplants start to put on new growth, so their need for water increases. And as daylight hours increase and temperatures rise, so plants become more active in producing plant foods and will lose more water from their leaves, thus increasing their need for water.

Care should nevertheless be taken not to overwater, but only gradually to increase the amount of water supplied. Apart from certain plants — such as Azaleas and Ferns — which should always be kept moist, it is a good practice to allow the compost to dry out a little before re-watering it. Surprisingly enough, houseplants are very susceptible to being overwatered in the spring — particularly as the onset of spring is not always all that it is romanticised to be: a sudden return of a cold snap can slow plants down again and reduce their need for water. Plants can only be overwatered by watering them too often, so it is always a good idea to let them use up most of the moisture they have available before giving them any more.

Feeding

The increase in a plant's growth in the spring necessitates the addition of extra plant nutrients to sustain healthy development. Whatever type of plant food you use, you must give your plant somewhat less at the onset of spring than it will require later on, when at the height of its growing season. Overfeeding

Spring clean foliage by spraying it with tepid water, but take care not to overwater the plant in the process.

encourages lush growth with no stamina in the stems and discourages the production of flowers, and too high a concentration can also damage the plant's root system.

If you are using a liquid fertiliser, for example, do not feed at full strength for the first few weeks but use in a more diluted form, at half or even one-third of the normal recommended rate. It is particularly important not to feed the plant when the compost is dry. It is also important not to feed for six to eight weeks after repotting as the fresh compost will have all the nutrients the plant needs. Then, as the season progresses and the plant's rate of growth increases, so the amount of fertiliser may be increased to the normal recommended dilution rate. The frequency with which you need to feed depends on the type of plant in question: feed those plants that produce a lot of new foliage, such as Ivy (Hedera) or Grape Ivy (*Cissus rhombifolia*) once every one to two weeks; while those plants which produce less foliage, such as Dracaena, Cordyline and Maranta, usually need to be fed only once every three or four weeks.

Repotting

Towards the end of spring, it is time to consider repotting your houseplants. It is important, however, not to repot them too soon, or you might run the risk of losing them.

Plants that are still in a relatively dormant condition after their annual winter rest should not be repotted until they have started into active growth, as the shock of being repotted too soon can kill them. The sudden increase in the amount of water available when a plant has been potted on may prove too much and the plant may be damaged or even killed by this excess. As its need for water increases through the season, however, it will be more tolerant and better able to withstand being moved to a larger pot.

The benefits of repotting are not only that the plant has more room to spread its roots but also that it has an increased amount of plant nutrients available to it during the growing season, more water, and greater stability.

Temperature

As outdoor temperatures rise during the spring, so houseplants become less dependent on central heating. It is, however, important to try to avoid sudden fluctuations in temperature, which can result in leaf drop and may even be fatal.

Houseplants need to be gradually weaned off artificial heating at this time of year in order to enable them to survive the late spring and summer without any artificial heat at all.

It is also important to avoid subjecting your plants to draughts during the early part of the season, particularly if they have grown accustomed to a warm, stable environment. You may find it refreshing to allow a breath of cool fresh spring air to ventilate your home, but your houseplants may not be quite so enthusiastic!

Pruning, training, staking

As houseplants start to grow anew, it is important to ensure that they grow in the way you want them to. Climbers such as Ivy (Hedera), for example, will probably need some sort of additional support in order to guide them in the right direction from the very start of the growing season.

Other plants may need to be trained to ensure a good compact growth. Plants such as Jasmine, for example, need to be trained regularly — around and up a cane, say, or around a hoop — or their growth will soon become

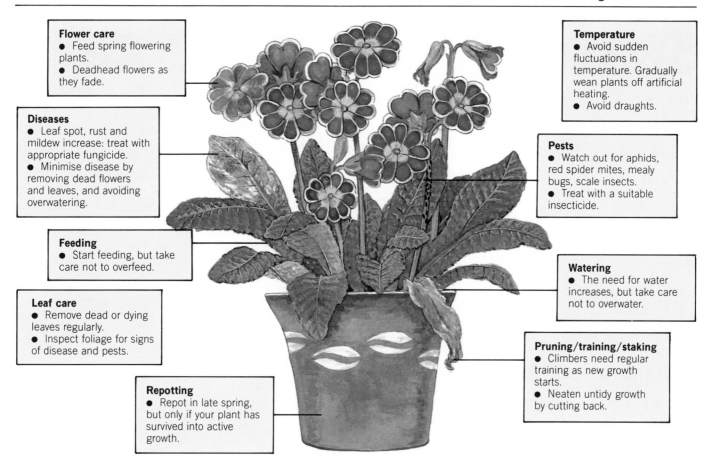

Flower care
- Feed spring flowering plants.
- Deadhead flowers as they fade.

Diseases
- Leaf spot, rust and mildew increase: treat with appropriate fungicide.
- Minimise disease by removing dead flowers and leaves, and avoiding overwatering.

Feeding
- Start feeding, but take care not to overfeed.

Leaf care
- Remove dead or dying leaves regularly.
- Inspect foliage for signs of disease and pests.

Repotting
- Repot in late spring, but only if your plant has survived into active growth.

Temperature
- Avoid sudden fluctuations in temperature. Gradually wean plants off artificial heating.
- Avoid draughts.

Pests
- Watch out for aphids, red spider mites, mealy bugs, scale insects.
- Treat with a suitable insecticide.

Watering
- The need for water increases, but take care not to overwater.

Pruning/training/staking
- Climbers need regular training as new growth starts.
- Neaten untidy growth by cutting back.

tangled and untidy. While others, like the Shrimp Plant (*Beloperone guttata*), benefit from being cut back in order to encourage a neat compact habit rather than allowing them to become leggy and unsightly.

Flower care

Some houseplants flower in the spring. Jasmine, Easter Cactus (*Rhipsalidopsis gaertneri*) and Primula, for example, are all at their best during this season. It is important with these plants, therefore, to ensure that they are correctly supplied with the right balance of plant foods, with a higher level of potash or potassium, in order to help the development of flowers.

And finally, when the flowers have faded, remove them by regular deadheading in order to make sure that no debilitating disease can set in, and to prevent the plant from wasting its energies on seed formation.

Leaf care

The accumulation of winter dust on your houseplants can suddenly look unsightly when the sun begins to shine on them, and it is worth 'spring cleaning' the foliage at this time of year. Do be

wary of oil-based cleaning products, however, as these can sometimes damage more delicate foliage — so use with caution and always read the manufacturer's instructions carefully.

Towards the end of spring, many houseplants will benefit from a light shower of tepid water to remove accumulated dust, but be careful not to overwater the plant during this process.

Pests

Many pests hibernate during the winter, though some — such as scale insect, mealy bug and red spider mite — seem to keep going all year round. But as spring arrives, a new-found energy seems to hit the insect world.

Pest infestations that had up until now been at a low level will suddenly and quite dramatically explode, causing immense damage to houseplants in a relatively short period. Watch out in particular for aphids (greenfly and blackfly), as their rate of reproduction is alarmingly rapid.

Inspect the foliage of your houseplants regularly and look out for aphids on any new shoots and flower buds; red spider mites on the underside of leaves; mealy bugs on the undersides of leaves

and in the leaf axils; and scale insects on leaf stems and veins. As soon as you have identified a problem, be sure to deal with it promptly with a suitable pesticide and repeat the treatment as recommended by the manufacturer.

Diseases

Although some diseases, like pests, cause problems throughout the year, spring will bring a new surge of activity in the fungal and bacterial world, though that said, certain diseases such as grey mould (botrytis) and some of the root rots tend to be more prevalent during the late autumn, winter and early spring. But there are some diseases, on the other hand, such as leaf spot, rust and mildew, which will increase as the improved climatical conditions favour their growth and spread.

Care should be taken to control all plant diseases, both by chemical and physical means. Their effect can often by minimised by careful plant management — for example, by removing dead or dying leaves or flowers, and by avoiding overwatering. A close watch should be kept at all times and, at the first sign of disease, appropriate remedial action should be taken as soon as possible.

Seasonal summer care

Although summer is the most active time of year as far as houseplants are concerned, it is also the time when they are usually at their best and probably their healthiest. It is nevertheless a time when their care is vitally important.

Watering
Surprisingly enough, the amount of water required by houseplants can vary dramatically, according to the weather. During periods of prolonged warmth and sunshine, a plant may need to be watered as often as once a day. But during cool wet periods, on the other hand, the amount of water it requires will be much less, and that same plant may not need to be watered more often than once or twice a week. It is therefore important to take note of climatic conditions when watering, as houseplants can just as easily be overwatered during the summer months as they can during the winter.

It is particularly important to ensure that a plant is carefully watered for the first few weeks after repotting, in order to allow the new roots to penetrate the compost. Too much water may prevent this from occurring and can, at worst, kill the plant.

As far as holiday care is concerned, it is important to make special provisions for the care of your houseplants when you are away. Try to ensure that all your plants are adequately watered before you go away and, when necessary, make plans for their continued care. This may mean moving plants to a location where their water requirements are reduced, or finding some alternative method of supplying them with water in your absence, such as capillary matting. Alternatively, it may be worth calling on the services of a friend or neighbour to 'plant sit' (see also 'When you're away', page 459).

Feeding
Houseplants require additional nutrients during the summer months, when they are at their most active. Most houseplants should be fed weekly or fortnightly, according to their rate of growth. Use a proprietary liquid fertiliser and follow the manufacturer's instructions. Do not be tempted to feed

Climbing and trailing plants will benefit from a light trim.

more often or at a higher concentration than recommended by the fact that the plant seems to be growing so well that you want to encourage it. Overfeeding can cause severe damage to the root system — which can, in turn, lead to the plant's untimely demise. And always water well before feeding a 'dry' plant.

Do not feed for six to eight weeks after repotting, as the fresh compost will contain all the necessary plant nutrients. When you do start feeding, do so at a reduced rate. It may not be necessary to feed at all if the plant is repotted late in the season, or if the compost contains a long-lasting fertiliser.

Repotting
The best time to repot your houseplants was in the late spring, so any plants that have not yet been repotted and would benefit from a bigger container should be potted on now. It is best not to wait until the season is too far advanced.

Temperature
Fortunately, the indoor temperature is probably one of the last things that you will need to worry about during the summer months, as the majority of houseplants will tolerate normal house-

hold temperatures during this period. If, however, the temperature drops during cold wet periods, it may be necessary to provide some additional, artificial heat for the more tender plants, such as Angel's Wings (Caladium).

Conversely, during warm dry spells it is essential that some ventilation be provided for many houseplants, such as Ivy (Hedera), Grape Ivy (*Cissus rhombifolia*), Kangaroo Vine (*C. antarctica*) and Cyclamen, all of which prefer more temperate conditions.

Pruning, training, staking
As their rate of growth increases, it may become necessary to prune your houseplants to maintain a tidy shape. Climbing and trailing plants, for example, will clearly benefit from a light trim, which can be carried out with a sharp pair of scissors or secateurs. Plants with softer tissue, such as Pilea or Wandering Jew (Tradescantia), can simply be pinched into shape by the careful use of thumb and forefinger, while pinching out growing tips will encourage bushiness. Climbing plants also need staking to give them adequate support, otherwise their stems may get broken.

When you are tying stems to the support, make sure the ties are not applied so tightly that they could cause damage or restrict growth. Also inspect existing ties to ensure that they too are not causing any damage.

Flower care
Houseplants which produce flowers throughout the summer will benefit from special-purpose flowering plant fertiliser when they are in bud and bloom. Many plants will produce more foliage when they have finished flowering and will then require further nutrition in the form of a conventional houseplant fertiliser.

Dead flower heads should be removed immediately after they have started to fade to ensure that they do not rot and cause subsequent disease, and to prevent the plant from diverting its energies into seed formation.

Leaf care
Certain houseplants benefit from extra humidity throughout the summer. This

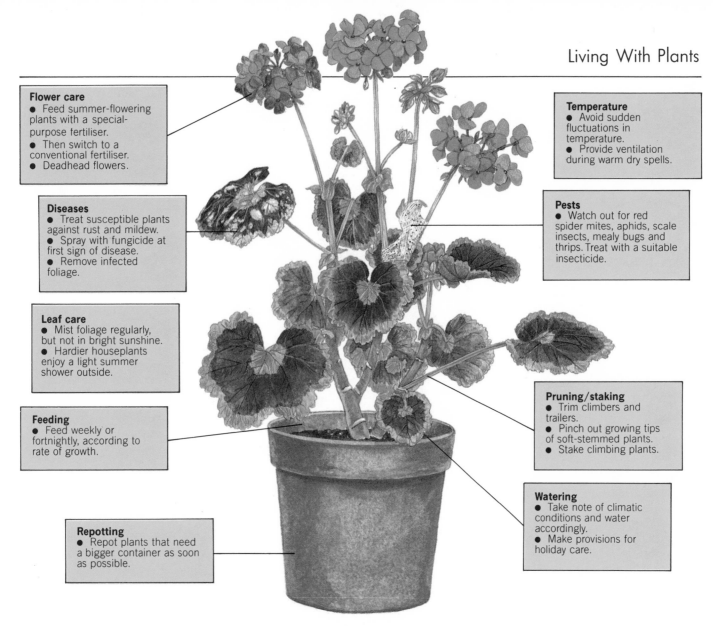

Flower care
● Feed summer-flowering plants with a special-purpose fertiliser.
● Then switch to a conventional fertiliser.
● Deadhead flowers.

Diseases
● Treat susceptible plants against rust and mildew.
● Spray with fungicide at first sign of disease.
● Remove infected foliage.

Leaf care
● Mist foliage regularly, but not in bright sunshine.
● Hardier houseplants enjoy a light summer shower outside.

Feeding
● Feed weekly or fortnightly, according to rate of growth.

Repotting
● Repot plants that need a bigger container as soon as possible.

Temperature
● Avoid sudden fluctuations in temperature.
● Provide ventilation during warm dry spells.

Pests
● Watch out for red spider mites, aphids, scale insects, mealy bugs and thrips. Treat with a suitable insecticide.

Pruning/staking
● Trim climbers and trailers.
● Pinch out growing tips of soft-stemmed plants.
● Stake climbing plants.

Watering
● Take note of climatic conditions and water accordingly.
● Make provisions for holiday care.

is particularly beneficial to African Violets (Saintpaulia), Prayer Plants (Maranta) and Ferns.

Most plants will benefit from a regular misting on their foliage with tepid water, applied through a fine mist sprayer. Care should, however, be taken to ensure that water droplets are not allowed to remain on the foliage in bright sunshine as they will act as tiny magnifying lenses and may result in scorched leaves.

You should also avoid applying water to those plants, like African Violets (Saintpaulia), which do not like water on their foliage. For plants such as these, it is better to improve the humidity in the immediate atmosphere by surrounding the plant with moist peat or dampened stones in a saucer.

The foliage of many houseplants, including Ficus, Monstera, Palms, Hedera, Philodendrons and many others, enjoys a light, tepid shower to remove any accumulated dust and dirt. This is

particularly useful for plants with leaves that are difficult to clean by hand. Some of the hardier houseplants, such as Ivy (Hedera), may even be placed outside during a light summer shower. It is important, however, not to allow the compost to become too wet as a result.

Always remove any damaged, diseased or dead leaves in order to discourage any disease.

Pests

These are particularly active during the summer months and a close watch should be kept at this time of year to ensure that the appropriate remedial action is taken at the first sign of infestation. Red spider mite and whitefly are particularly troublesome now and it is essential to control them by using the appropriate insecticide.

Red spider mites thrive in hot dry conditions, so their activity can be reduced somewhat by regularly misting both surfaces of the foliage with tepid

water. Plants which benefit particularly from this treatment include Ivy (Hedera) and Croton (Codiaeum).

Other major pests which you should look out for are aphids, scale insects, mealy bugs and thrips.

Diseases

Rust and mildew are two particularly problematic fungal diseases at this time of year, and control is often best effected by prevention rather than cure. Applying fungicides to prevent these diseases from infecting susceptible plants is better than waiting for the first sign of disease to occur.

With other diseases, however, it is probably better to save spraying all your plants until a problem actually manifests itself. Many fungal and bacterial diseases are localised and can quite easily be controlled by the removal of all infected foliage, which should then be hygienically disposed of to prevent the spread of disease.

Seasonal autumn care

The change in seasons can often be quite difficult to detect. This is particularly true of the critical transition from summer into autumn, as houseplants put the brakes on their rate of growth in readiness for the onset of the long, dark, cold winter months.

Watering

The amount of water your houseplants require will steadily decrease to a minimum at this time of year. Great care should therefore be taken to ensure that you reduce the quantity you give them in line with their needs, which you should follow closely. As the weather deteriorates, so most houseplants automatically reduce the amount of water they can make use of, and it is therefore all too easy to overwater them, which can result in damage either to the root system or to the stem.

Feeding

It is important to discontinue feeding most houseplants from the end of September, as their growth rate slows down and their need for nutrients diminishes. The application of any fertiliser during this period may result in the accumulation of excess fertiliser salts in the compost. This can, in turn, lead to severe root damage and may even be fatal.

Slow-release fertilisers come into their own at this time of year, because the release pattern of nutrients is governed both by temperature and by moisture content. As ambient temperatures decrease and you give your plants less water, so the amount of fertiliser which is released into the soil reduces automatically. Generally, however, most houseplants are now preparing themselves for a condition close to dormancy, with little if any sign of growth, and don't therefore need any fresh supply of fertiliser.

There are, however, some exceptions. These include Poinsettia, Azalea and Cyclamen, which flower late in the autumn, or even later in winter. These do need to be fed, using a fertiliser that is relatively well balanced in its nitrogen, phosphorus and potassium content, with a slight bias — if anything — towards a higher potassium content for good flower development and quality.

Dead or dying leaves and flowers are breeding grounds for botrytis, to which African Violets are very susceptible.

Repotting

It is inadvisable to repot houseplants at this time of year. The shock could seriously damage or even kill them.

Temperature

It is important to try to maintain a stable, constant temperature at this time of year as houseplants acclimatise to colder conditions. Severe damage may be caused by sudden fluctuations in temperature, particularly if the weather suddenly changes dramatically from a warm Indian summer's day to a cold, frosty night.

Sudden low temperatures, coupled with excessively wet compost, are the principal hazards for houseplants during this season. It is also important to avoid draughts.

Flower care

Continue to remove any dead or dying flowers on those houseplants that are still producing flowers at this time of year. Late autumn and winter flowering plants, such as Azalea and Cyclamen, need to be adequately fed and watered as their flowers develop, otherwise the results will be a great disappointment at a time of year when many houseplants are not at their best.

It is particularly important to note the special care of those plants that are sensitive to day length and, in particular, short-day responsive plants such as the Poinsettia *(Euphorbia pulcherrima)*. In order to obtain a well-coloured display of bracts, the plant must not only be adequately fed and watered but should also be allowed only a natural quota of daylight. Any exposure to artificial light after the natural hours of daylight during the key months of September to November will prevent the plant from producing its colourful bracts.

Leaf care

Little needs to be done to houseplants in the way of leaf care at this time of year — apart, of course, from the continued removal of any dead or damaged leaves. And it is advisable to stop mist spraying plants, or at least to reduce it dramatically. Not only does the atmosphere tend to be more humid at this time, just before the central heating is turned on, but any water which is allowed to remain on foliage may actually be detrimental to a plant's well-being.

Pests

As their peak of activity during the summer passes, many pests will slow down their reproductive rate and become less of a problem. They should not, however, be ignored and remedial action should be continued if necessary.

Aphids may continue to be a nuisance during the early part of the season, particularly if the plant is still flowering. Towards the end of the season, however, they will probably disappear until the spring, when you will see a new upsurge in their activity.

Take particular care to control red spider mite at this time of year, as they will continue to feed quite happily on your houseplants throughout the year, albeit at a reduced rate in line with lessening day length and temperature. Mealy bugs and scale insects will also continue to be active, though again less so than at the height of summer.

Whiteflies will remain a nuisance throughout the winter, in much the same way as red spider mite, and may be particularly difficult to control. Thriving as they do in warm, dry conditions, they delight in the comfortable environment produced by central heating. As they go through several stages of development — from egg to larva and then finally to adult — they are rather difficult to eradicate, especially as they can only really be effectively killed at the adult moth stage. Their control is in

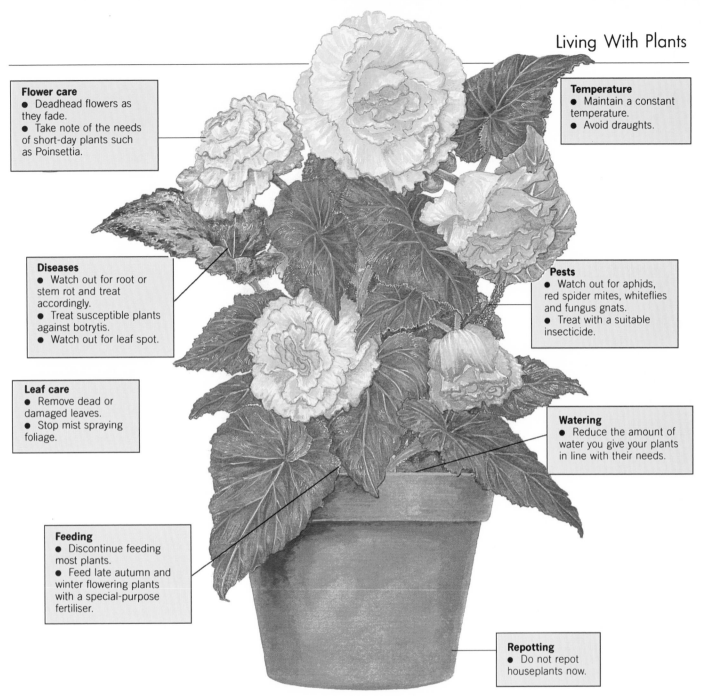

Flower care
- Deadhead flowers as they fade.
- Take note of the needs of short-day plants such as Poinsettia.

Temperature
- Maintain a constant temperature.
- Avoid draughts.

Diseases
- Watch out for root or stem rot and treat accordingly.
- Treat susceptible plants against botrytis.
- Watch out for leaf spot.

Pests
- Watch out for aphids, red spider mites, whiteflies and fungus gnats.
- Treat with a suitable insecticide.

Leaf care
- Remove dead or damaged leaves.
- Stop mist spraying foliage.

Watering
- Reduce the amount of water you give your plants in line with their needs.

Feeding
- Discontinue feeding most plants.
- Feed late autumn and winter flowering plants with a special-purpose fertiliser.

Repotting
- Do not repot houseplants now.

fact more difficult during the autumn and winter months because their life cycle is spread over a longer period, which means you need to treat them regularly over a long period of time to catch the adults as they emerge. A watchful control of whitefly during the autumn will reduce the likelihood of a continuing winter problem, especially on plants like Poinsettia.

Fungus gnats may also be a problem at this time of year. These little insects lay their eggs on the surface of the compost and the larvae then eat dead and decaying organic matter, such as peat and dead leaves and roots. Not only can the insects be a nuisance when they fly up in your face every time they are disturbed, but the larvae are also suspected

of aiding the demise of an ailing plant by eating damaged root tissue. With the increased likelihood of this happening in the autumn under the relatively dank conditions that so often exist at this time of year, this pest may be particularly troublesome.

Diseases

Pay close attention to the possibility of root or stem rot, both of which can easily set in at this time, particularly when plants are at risk of being overwatered. If root or stem rot does occur, it will be necessary to use an appropriate fungicide.

It is also important to ensure that any dead or dying leaves or flowers are removed promptly as these are ideal

breeding grounds for diseases such as grey mould fungus (botrytis), which produces a fluffy, greyish-brown growth. Having exhausted the food available in dead tissue, the fungus then rapidly multiplies and attacks healthy living tissue, particularly on susceptible plants such as African Violet (Saintpaulia) and Cyclamen. Apart from continued good husbandry, it may also be worth using a fungicide to help prevent the disease from occurring in the first place, rather than waiting to treat a plant that is already affected.

Leaf spot may also be a problem if foliage is allowed to remain wet or if the atmosphere is dank. A general improvement in regular cultural care should reduce the likelihood of the problem.

Seasonal winter care

The winter is a very trying time for houseplants as well as houseplant enthusiasts. Although many plants will by now have slowed down their rate of growth to a virtual halt until the spring, they are nevertheless exposed to an increased risk of damage from a variety of seasonal factors, including low temperatures, overwatering and draughts.

Watering

Great care should be taken throughout the winter months to ensure that houseplants are not overwatered — something to which they are particularly vulnerable at this time of year, probably more than at any other. In general, it is better to keep the majority of plants on the dry side rather than to allow them to get too wet. Even moisture-loving plants such as Ferns and Azaleas can easily be given too much water in winter when drying conditions are slow, and plants that are allowed to sit in cold, wet compost will rapidly fail, though central heating will have a very drying effect.

Some plants, such as cacti and other succulents, can get by with very little water indeed in winter. Depending on the variety, certain cacti actually prefer not to be watered at all in winter and this, coupled with lower temperatures, should in fact encourage the plant to flower the following spring.

The temperature of tapwater will obviously be lower at this time of year and care should be taken not to shock plants by giving them water that is too cold. It is therefore better to allow water to stand in the can for a few hours until it has reached room temperature, or to add just a little hot water from the kettle to the cold tapwater in your can. Do take care, however, not to go to the other extreme and to water with hot water: water that is barely tepid is just right.

Feeding

The majority of houseplants should not be fed at all during this period: being in a dormant state, the plant's nutritional needs are low and any accumulation of fertiliser salts in the compost will probably result in root damage and may even be fatal. There are, however, certain plants that should be fed in winter,

Provide your Cyclamen with a humid atmosphere by placing it on a saucer full of moist pebbles.

including Cyclamen, Azalea and Poinsettia, all of which produce their flowers at this time of year or, in the case of Poinsettia, their showy, colourful bracts.

These plants should be fed with a dilute feed of a special-purpose liquid fertiliser for flowering plants. A tomato fertiliser may also be used, as long as it is well diluted. The frequency of feeding should not, however, be more than once every two to four weeks, in order to avoid the problem of excess fertiliser salts accumulating in the compost.

Temperature

The temperatures that houseplants have to tolerate in the winter can cause them problems. It is best to aim for as stable a temperature as possible. Sudden fluctuations, from the cosy warm environment during the hours when your heating is on to the inhospitable cold temperatures while you are out at work or overnight — can easily be detrimental to a plant's well-being.

Draughts can be particularly damaging to houseplants and can cause much the same problems as sudden fluctuations in temperature. Rapid leaf drop, for example, can occur with plants such as Croton (Codiaeum) and Weeping Fig (*Ficus benjamina*). Try to ensure that plants that are sensitive to draughts and

temperature fluctuations are kept away from windows and doors where problems are likely to be most severe.

Humidity

The humidity level tends to be rather low in centrally heated houses at this time of year because of central and other forms of modern heating which encourage a dry atmosphere. Kitchens and bathrooms tend to be relatively more humid and provide a welcome refuge for plants such as Prayer Plant (Maranta), African Violet (Saintpaulia) and *Begonia rex*, all of which appreciate a humid environment. The use of a humidifier helps to some extent, but not enough to meet the requirements of many plants, while frequent misting can sometimes encourage fungal diseases. It is therefore more practical, if possible, to improve the general level of humidity.

A good way of providing localised humidity is by placing the plant on a large saucer containing dampened pebbles, which will then release evaporated water into the surrounding atmosphere. Alternatively, sink the pot into a container filled with moist peat. This is of particular benefit to relatively low-growing plants, such as Prayer Plant (Maranta), African Violet (Saintpaulia), *Begonia rex* and Creeping fig (*Ficus pumila*). Larger plants will benefit to a lesser degree from this technique, so you may find that you have no alternative but to resort to misting with tepid water. If this is the case, however, you should take care not to overdo it and remember not to spray mist close to furnishings or any electrical equipment.

Flower care

Although there are relatively few houseplants that flower during the winter, it is important for those that do to ensure that they are given a little extra care.

Try to avoid getting water on to the flower petals, which could encourage rot, remove flowers as soon as they start to fade and before they have a chance to rot. This is particularly important for Cyclamen and African Violet — though even Azalea flowers, which tend to be somewhat hardier, can also be affected. It is also advisable, where possible, to

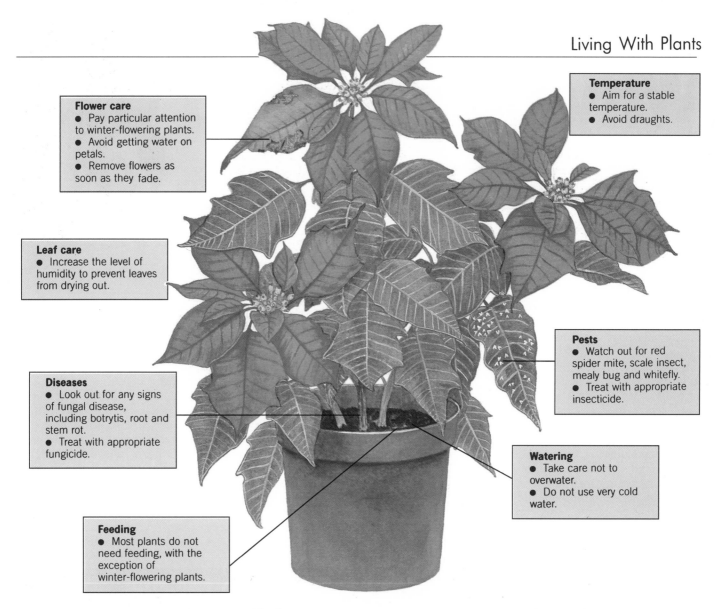

Flower care
● Pay particular attention to winter-flowering plants.
● Avoid getting water on petals.
● Remove flowers as soon as they fade.

Temperature
● Aim for a stable temperature.
● Avoid draughts.

Leaf care
● Increase the level of humidity to prevent leaves from drying out.

Pests
● Watch out for red spider mite, scale insect, mealy bug and whitefly.
● Treat with appropriate insecticide.

Diseases
● Look out for any signs of fungal disease, including botrytis, root and stem rot.
● Treat with appropriate fungicide.

Watering
● Take care not to overwater.
● Do not use very cold water.

Feeding
● Most plants do not need feeding, with the exception of winter-flowering plants.

avoid dank conditions for flowering plants as these too can encourage fungal problems and may necessitate treatment with a fungicide, either to prevent or at least to eradicate problems.

Most plants will probably 'rest' after flowering, or at least slow down their growth rate, before bursting into growth again in the spring. Cyclamen will actually die back down to the corm and remain dormant for several weeks.

Leaf care

Something that commonly affects foliage in winter is a brown dessication, or drying out, of the edges and death of leaf tissue. It is usually caused by too dry an environment. Those plants that are most commonly affected are ones with thin leaves such as Maranta, Ferns and Dracaena, although thicker-leaved plants such as Monstera may also suffer the same fate. The problem may be alleviated by increasing the level of humidity in the atmosphere.

Pests

Fortunately, pests are not generally a great problem during the winter, although red spider mite, scale insect and mealy bug will remain relatively active, though less so than in the height of summer. In general, the warmer the temperature the more active the pests. Whitefly can also be a nuisance on some plants, such as Poinsettia, and again this is especially likely if temperatures are fairly high.

In spite of their relatively reduced activity, the control of pests is nevertheless important at this time of year, as it may well help to lessen the problem in spring.

Diseases

Look out for the signs of grey mould fungus (botrytis) which can cause immense damage at this time of year, especially on flowering plants. Look, too, for any signs of fungal disease on the leaves: the tips and edges are often the first place

where a fungal infection will take hold, especially when they are grown in a dank environment with fairly high humidity levels. At the first sign of a brown softening of the leaf extremities, treat the plant with a fungicide and, if the infection is limited to only a few leaves, remove these to help avoid the spread of infection.

Also watch out for root and stem rot, both of which can occur at this time when it is all too easy to overwater houseplants. Should you overwater them, you'll need to be prepared to take drastic action to save a seriously ailing plant. The symptoms of overwatering, which can eventually lead to root and stem rot, include limp, wilting foliage.

If the plant is not too wet at the root it may be watered with a fungicide. But if it is too wet, gently remove it from the pot, lay it on its side on some newspaper to absorb the excess moisture and leave for a few days to dry out a little. Then repot and water with a fungicide.

Why plants need a winter rest

If you overwater a *Ficus elastica* at rest, you can expect wilting leaves.

For many plants, the arrival of winter heralds a period of rest. As light intensity decreases and day length shortens, so most houseplants put the brakes on their rate of growth, thus slowing it down or even calling a complete halt to it.

The care of plants during their rest period is crucial, and it is particularly important to avoid extreme fluctuations in temperature and excessive amounts of water, both of which could damage their health. Plants are at a very susceptible stage at this time of year, in spite of their relative inactivity.

If you encourage a tropical or subtropical plant to grow actively during periods of low winter light, it will eventually suffer, becoming spindly and pale.

Instead of being encouraged to grow in winter, therefore, most indoor plants should be forced to rest. This slows down the plant's growth, until conditions are again right for renewed growth. 'Rest' usually means, quite simply, the restriction of watering, the cessation of feeding, and a lowering of temperature.

Although many houseplants appear to be quite dormant at this time of year, most do continue to require some water — albeit in much lesser quantities. Evergreen plants, which retain their leaves, should still be watered moderately, whereas deciduous plants, such as Fuchsia and Caladium, which lose their leaves, need just enough water to keep the potting compost barely moist.

The benefits

Indoor Jasmine (*Jasminum polyanthum*) will be encouraged to flower in the early spring after a cool winter, with just sufficient water to prevent it from wilting. If it is denied its winter rest and the plant is kept too warm and watered too frequently, it will become lank and will not flower nearly so profusely, if at all. African Violets also benefit from a rest period.

Cacti and succulents have a pronounced rest period, during which watering must be greatly reduced. Water them only when the surface of the soil feels dry and crumbly and the pot feels light when you pick it up, which may happen as rarely as once a month in the winter. They are also more likely to produce flowers if they are kept dry from October until March or early April. They should be watered only very little — perhaps just a couple of times throughout the winter — to prevent total dehydration. With the advent of longer days and increased light, watering may then be resumed. If cacti are deprived of this rest period, they will flower less prolifically — if at all.

Another benefit that plants should reap during their winter rest is that they are not forced into the production of lank, unhealthy foliage, which would be particularly vulnerable to disease. Any new foliage which is produced at this time is also sensitive both to very low temperatures and to temperature fluctuations, which makes it important that plants remain in a stable condition during their rest period.

Following this rest period, houseplants will sense the increase in day length, temperature and light, and will suddenly break into new growth, producing both fresh foliage and, where appropriate, flowers. At the first signs that the winter rest period is drawing to a close it is important to start increasing the amount of water applied — still taking great care, of course, not to overwater — and to resume feeding.

Exceptions to the rule

Not all plants need a winter rest period — some are in fact actively growing during what is, for them, their normal growing or flowering period.

● The Poinsettia (*Euphorbia pulcherrima*) is probably the best-known plant that is active during the winter months. Having developed new foliage between April and September, the plant then produces coloured bracts, which are usually bright red but can also be pink or white. These are produced as soon as the plant senses the shorter day length, from September on. It also produces tiny insignificant flowers over the Christmas period and then ceases to develop any further until the spring.

● The Pot Chrysanthemum or, as it is sometimes called, the All-year-round Chrysanthemum, flowers naturally in the autumn and early winter, and the Christmas Cactus is another example. Similarly, the Silver-leaved Cyclamen also flowers quite naturally in the latter part of the year before taking a rest, when the foliage dies back to the corm for several weeks before being started into growth again — usually by increasing the plant's watering.

● Another plant which is well known for its long period of late colour is the Indian Azalea (*Azalea indica*) which, although it is in active growth from May through until about August, comes into bud in October or November to flower over the Christmas and New Year period. After flowering, the Azalea then rests briefly for just a few weeks at the end of the winter before breaking into renewed growth as fresh foliage develops. Even though it may not be growing actively after flowering, it should nevertheless be kept watered and not allowed to dry out completely.

● It is important to remember that all plants need some sort of rest period. Care that is taken at this time will help to ensure that the plant's transition from dormancy into activity is as smooth as possible, with a better chance of a healthy, vigorous growing period.

Inside outside

In the heat of even a mild summer, a cooling breath of fresh air can work wonders for certain houseplants. And it could be most important to their welfare.

Azalea and Amaryllis grown indoors look out on to a window-box filled with flowering Polyanthus.

Most bonsai, such as this Spirea, are outdoor plants, so keep them indoors for short periods only.

We're all accustomed to treating some of our houseplants — bulbs, for instance — as temporary residents, to be planted out once they've finished flowering. Without this period of banishment into the garden, the bulbs couldn't thrive.

What we often don't appreciate fully, is how many other plants would benefit from a spell out of doors. And how many more would happily tolerate it. The point is that there is no ruthless distinction between houseplants and garden plants. It's simply a matter of their growing conditions. What makes a houseplant a houseplant is the fact that it can put up with the sort of conditions that we enjoy living in — *and* look good for most of the year. But that doesn't mean that low light levels, high winter temperatures and a dryish atmosphere are ideal. For various reasons, you may do your houseplants a very good turn by putting them outside during the warmer months of the summer. Some of them, if you like, can be left even longer.

But don't rush to put your whole plant collection out, willy nilly. Not only will you cause irreversible damage to the most tender species, you may also harm those that would actually be suitable candidates, once correctly hardened off. It's important to know which plants can safely be given an excursion and how to go about it.

Outdoor/indoor plants

There are many plants, like hardy bulbs for example, which need never come indoors at all. We bring them in because we want to. Often, it's so that we can encourage them to bloom early during the winter. The Indian Azalea (*Azalea indica*) is one such hardy plant. All too often, it's mistakenly thrown away once the flowers have faded. If they are to prosper, they benefit enormously from spending a part of the year outdoors.

Place the Azalea outside on warm May days, once all danger of frosts have passed, hardening it off gently (see below). To produce flowers in time for Christmas, bring it inside in September, when the warmth will trigger it early. With this treatment, Azaleas will become sturdy and compact while those left inside are inclined to develop rather soft, straggly foliage. There's a host of other flowering plants that are brought indoors to flower in just the same way — Passiflora, Hydrangea, and Polyanthus, to name just a few.

Outdoors and indoors

Other plants must avoid a winter outside if they are to survive. The charm of tender perennials like Pelargoniums and Busy Lizzies is that by careful management they can be encouraged to flower all year round. They'll flower outside in the summer months, and can then be brought indoors to continue growing and flowering.

Indoors and outdoors

On the other side of the coin are the houseplants that cannot stay outdoors for too long, but need to be put out occasionally in the fresh air when rooms indoors are hot and stuffy. The importance of the fresh air is that it lowers the temperature — and the humidity — around the plants. And this is vital for the hardier indoor plants, like Punica or Jasmine, which suffer if temperatures rise too high.

Cacti and succulents, and plants like the Norfolk Island Pine (*Araucaria heterophylla*) or Piggyback Plant (*Tolmiea menziesii*), prefer to stay indoors, but appreciate a little ventilation.

Summer's an opportunity for a 'wash and brush up' for the hardier, thicker-leaved plants, like the Rubber Plant (*Ficus elastica* 'Decora'), Swiss Cheese Plant (*Monstera deliciosa*) and Canary Island Ivy (*Hedera canariensis*). Rain water is much better than tap water for

any plants, and a summer shower is a good way of cleaning your plants.

Fruit setting

There are plants which need to be put outside for a period of time if they are to be useful as houseplants. The Winter Cherry (*Solanum capsicastrum*), for instance, needs to be outside from May to September, to allow insects to pollinate the flowers. The Bead Plant (*Nertera depressa*) requires the same treatment.

Hardening off

Even hardy plants need to be hardened off. The trick is to get the plant used to these new conditions gradually.

Put the plant outside on a warm day in late May, when the temperatures won't fall below 45°F (7°C). Make sure it's not in full sun, and that it's sheltered from any wind. Bring it in at night. Keep this up until June, when you should be able to leave it out overnight, as well.

Seasonal airing

OUTDOORS AND INDOORS
Plants that must winter indoors
Begonia
Black-eyed Susan (Thunbergia)
Busy Lizzie (Impatiens)
Fuchsia
Geranium (Pelargonium)
Schizanthus
Winter Cherry (*Solanum Capsicastrum*)

OUTDOORS OR INDOORS
Hardy plants to enjoy indoors
Azalea
Bay tree (*Laurus nobilis*)
Bulbs
Fatshedera
Fatsia
Hydrangea
Ivies (Hedera)
Passion Flower (Passiflora)
Polyanthus
Spotted Laurel (Aucuba)

INDOORS AND OUT
Indoor plants needing some fresh air
Cacti
Citrus
Jasmine (Jasminum)
Kentia Palm (*Howea forsteriana*)
Norfolk Island Pine (*Araucaria heterophylla*)
Piggyback Plant (*Tolmiea menziesii*)
Plumbago
Punica
Rubber Plant (*Ficus elastica*)
Succulents
Swiss Cheese Plant (*Monstera deliciosa*)
Yucca

A suitable place

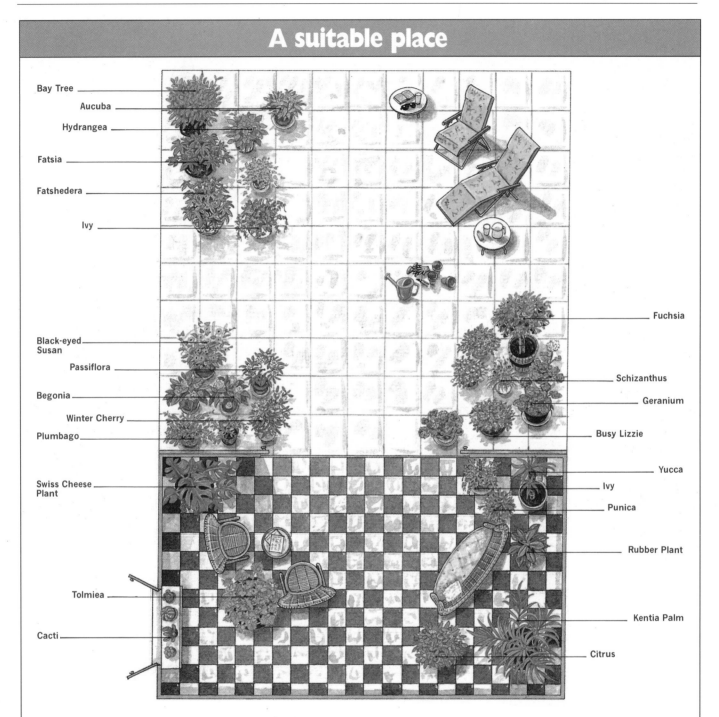

Bay Tree
Aucuba
Hydrangea
Fatsia
Fatshedera
Ivy
Black-eyed Susan
Passiflora
Begonia
Winter Cherry
Plumbago
Swiss Cheese Plant
Tolmiea
Cacti

Fuchsia
Schizanthus
Geranium
Busy Lizzie
Yucca
Ivy
Punica
Rubber Plant
Kentia Palm
Citrus

WHAT TO WATCH FOR

1. Light
Because light outside is so much more direct, and comes from all around, even plants that enjoy bright light indoors will actually need to be shaded outside. A shady spot in the garden will be much brighter than a bright spot inside.

2. Watering
Indoors there's usually much more danger of overwatering plants than underwatering them. Outdoors, the reverse is true.

Outdoors any excess water can drain freely away. In fact, the plants may lose too much water through evaporation, as wind and sun take the moisture away from the foliage — just as they do from washing hanging on a line. You may find you need to water twice a day, if there's no rain, instead of once. Do check regularly, to make sure that plants are getting enough.

Guard against heavy rainfall, though. It may actually damage delicate plants.

3. Pests
Outdoor plants can put up with a certain amount of infestation, which

might well overcome a houseplant. Being outside will toughen a plant up, gradually, making it stronger and more resistant to pests. Until it is tougher, though, you'll have to take extra care — watch out, particularly, for pests it wouldn't normally encounter, like slugs and snails.

4. Wind
Apart from too much sun, a plant's main problem between June and September out of doors is likely to be the wind, which may be too cold for the plant, or may even knock it over. Be sure to choose a sheltered spot.

Welcome spring with a container full of daffodils.

An instant patio for spring

There's nothing like the first signs of spring for dispelling the gloom of a winter that has perhaps gone on for too long. One of the best ways of getting winter out of your mind is to put it out of sight, and on the patio you can do this instantly by simply replacing one set of pots with another.

Design ideas

It would be only too easy to leave your winter display intact and to merely season it with a sprinkling of spring-flowering bulbs. But that would be doing only half the job and it's worth making the effort and starting afresh.

So clear away the pots, tidy up the patio, and make sure that there's not a dead leaf or patch of moss in sight to remind you of winter. Then treat your patio to a new look that shouts 'spring'!

Containers. Start by splashing out on a new set of containers. You can use the same troughs and tubs that you will be using later to house your summer display, but different spring and summer containers help to emphasise the seasonal changes more dramatically. Wooden containers – either smart and varnished or rough and rustic – are perfect partners for spring flowers.

Flowers. A good selection can usually be bought, already coming into bloom, from garden centres. The choice of flowers includes spring-flowering bulbs, small plants like Polyanthus and Primroses, as well as larger shrubs. Try and combine a mixture of each, with the larger shrubs giving height to the display and forming a backdrop for the smaller plants.

If you have a garden as well as a patio, don't be afraid to include some shrubs that will eventually grow quite large. You can buy them in flower. Use them to decorate and give colour to the patio until they have finished flowering and then plant them out in the garden to bloom again the following year.

When choosing your flowers and deciding where to put them, aim for a display that frequently changes, so

Plants for spring colour

The following plants are listed in order of flowering.

FEBRUARY

Bulbs
Galanthus nivalis (Snowdrop): white, 6in (15cm).
Crocus: white, yellow, mauve and purple, 3in (8cm).
Eranthis (Winter Aconite): bright yellow, buttercup-like flowers, 5in (13cm).
Iris reticulata (miniature Iris): blue or purple flowers, 6in (15cm).
Narcissus cyclamineus 'February Gold', 'Tete-a-Tete': 6-8in (15-20cm).

Shrubs
Daphne mezereum: purple flowers, 5ft (1.5m).
Daphne petraea: rose-pink flowers, 3-6in (8-15cm).
Daphne retusa: rose-purple flowers, 3ft (0.9m).

MARCH

Bulbs
Narcissus 'Jack Snipe': 8-15in (20-38cm).
Narcissus triandrus albus: 3-4in (8-10cm).
Anemone blanda: star-shaped flowers, 4in (10cm).
Anemone 'De Caen', 'St Brigid': Florist's Anemones, 6-12in (15-30cm).
Chionodoxa (Glory of the Snow): blue flowers, 4in (10cm).
Cyclamen repandum: lilac-pink flowers, 4in (10cm).
Leucojum vernum (Snowflake): white flowers like a snowdrop, but tipped with green, 6in (15cm).
Scilla sibirica (Squill): blue flowers, 4in (10cm).
Tulip species, especially low-growing kinds such as Kaufmanniana hybrids, 4-10in (10-25cm).

Shrubs
Camellia japonica: flowers from March onwards, according to variety, 6-7ft (1.8-2.1m).
Salix lanata (Woolly Willow): dwarf form, with yellow-green pussy willows, 2-4ft (0.6-1.2m).

Tulips look especially good when mixed with purple Hyacinths.

Bring colour to early spring with a *Camellia japonica*.

You can buy shrubs such as *Daphne mezereum* already in flower.

APRIL

Bulbs
Fritillaria imperialis (Crown Imperial): large heads of flowers, 2-3ft (0.6-0.9m).
Muscari (Grape Hyacinth): short spikes of blue flowers, 6in (15cm).
Hyacinth: in white, cream, red, pink, blue, 8in (20cm).
Convallaria (Lily-of-the-Valley): strongly-scented flowers, 6in (15cm).
Chionodoxa gigantea (Glory of the Snow): blue flowers in spring, 7-8in (18-20cm).

Fritillaria meleagris (Snake's Head Fritillary): spring, purple checkering, 1-1½ft (30-45cm).

Flowers
Primrose, 4in (10cm).
Primula auricula, 5in (13cm).
Polyanthus, 6in (15cm).
Wallflowers, 9in (23cm).

Shrubs
Rhododendron 'Bow Bells': pink flowers, 3-4ft (0.9-1.2m).
Rhododendron 'Elizabeth': orange-red flowers, 2-3ft (0.6-0.9m).
Rhododendron 'Benigirl': crimson flowers, 2-3ft (0.6-0.9m).

creating the sensation of spring gradually unfolding. This is easy to achieve by using a number of plants that flower at different times and by arranging them in order of flowering.

On a large patio you can virtually guarantee a continuous display of flowers from a single 'one-off' planting – put the various subjects close together and use plenty of containers. On a smaller patio, however, you'll have to re-plant 'little and often'.

By concentrating so many flowers together in a small area they will make much more impact, which is always important on a patio where you are striving for a continual show of interest and colour.

Points to remember . . .
● Regularly remove flowers that are over – a mass of fading heads and dying foliage harks back to winter.
● Don't forget 'scent' when planning your spring patio – a few Hyacinths or Lily-of-the-Valley among your display will work wonders in encouraging spring fever.

Main picture: **The positioning** of seating is an important part of patio planning and requires a considerable amount of thought. Inset: Hanging baskets overflowing with plants make a colourful and decorative display.

Summer is the season for outdoor living and the patio becomes the perfect place for entertaining, relaxing, sunbathing, or just lounging about with a good book. It is transformed into an open-air living room and plants, although of prime importance in other seasons, must now share the stage with these leisure activities and the 'set' has to be laid out accordingly.

Furnishings

When planning your layout, pride of place must go to seating. If possible, put it in a spot which receives the most sun but still has easy access to the shade. Also, try to position your chairs where you will get the best view of your garden.

Barbecues should always be sited with safety and convenience in mind. They need to be far enough away from fences and furnishings so as not to cause a fire risk or make black, smoky marks on walls and yet close enough to the house to enable you to make frequent trips to the kitchen.

Placing plants

When you have decided on suitable locations for your furnishings it is time to plan what plants you are going to put around them.

Summer on a patio calls for annuals –also known as bedding plants – growing in containers of all kinds. Use tubs, troughs, hanging-baskets, individual pots as well as 'specials' such as strawberry planters, old stone sinks, or even a wheelbarrow.

Annuals are the perfect fillers for your containers. They are colourful, cheerful, relatively cheap and best of all – instant.

Start to buy them in the middle of May when they are just coming into flower and ready to plant. And, if looked after properly, they should flower until the end of summer. Just remember to water and feed them regularly and to snip off dead flowers as soon as they appear.

Design tips

The key to a successful summer patio is co-ordination. And this doesn't just mean furnishings and fittings. Containers and plants should also match.

Containers don't have to be identical. Indeed, a mixture of shapes and sizes looks much better. Just make sure that the materials they are made of are in harmony with each other and also with the patio surface. Stick to all natural materials, or different designs in stone, synthetics or wood.

Containers can look especially effective when filled with just one type of plant such as Lobelia.

Group containers together to make individual displays that will form a good spectacle from where you are planning to sit. Three tubs, identical in design but different in size, can look effective, as can hanging baskets suspended at different heights.

Then link the different elements of the design by carefully repeating one or two particular plants throughout some or all of the containers in the scheme – maybe dark blue Lobelia, or you could stick to one particular colour such as peach.

When planting your containers, vary the heights of the plants you choose. Place one or more tall plants towards the centre and try to achieve the correct visual balance by relating the height of the plants to the size of the container. As a rough guide, the height of the tallest plants should be two and a half times the width of the tub or one and a half times the length of the trough.

Containers are usually filled with a mixture of different plants, but they can look incredibly effective when planted with just one type of flower, either all the same colour or mixed. Or you could create a two-tone effect by using two colours such as orange and maroon or green and white. Plain foliage plants used as a background in a container of mixed flowers create a perfect foil for the variety of colours.

Finally, make the best possible use of space. Most patios have at least one or two sunny walls or fences and these are ideal for growing fast annual climbers. Fix either trellis or netting for them to ramble up.

Plants for Summer Colour

Name	Height	Description
CLIMBERS		
Gourds	9-12in (23-30cm)	Grown in various shapes, sizes and colours.
Humulus japonicus variegatus (Variegated Climbing Hop)	5-6ft (1.5-1.8m)	Most attractive fast-growing climber, grown for its cream and green – splashed foliage.
Thunbergia alata (Black-eyed Susan)	6-10ft (1.8-3m)	Bright orange flowers with black eyes in centre.
Tropaeolum peregrinum (Canary Creeper)	8-12ft (2.4-3.6m)	Lots of small, frilly, bright yellow flowers.
FOR HANGING BASKETS		
Convulvulus tricolor (Dwarf Morning Glory)	12-15in (30-38cm)	Large saucer-shaped flowers in shades of pink, blue and purple.
Fragaria indica (Mock Strawberry)	6-8in (15-20cm)	Small, ornamental, strawberry-like fruits.
Fuchsia	18in (45cm)	Choose trailing varieties.
Impatiens	6-12in (15-30cm)	For striking results, plant into sides of basket as well as on the surface.
Lobelia	10-15in (25-38cm)	Choose trailing varieties.
Pelargonium	12-15in (30-38cm)	Choose ivy-leaved varieties.
Petunia	9-15in (23-38cm)	Large trumpet-shaped flowers in various colours, single or double; also striped and frilly versions.
PLANTS FOR CONTAINERS		
Begonia	6-12in (15-30cm)	Go for tuberous-rooted species for large, flamboyant flowers.
Fuchsia	12in (30cm)	Choose upright varieties.
Marigolds	4-24in (10-60cm)	Choose French or African varieties.
Mesembryanthemum (Ice Plant)	3in (8cm)	Creeping plants with brilliantly-coloured daisy-like flowers that open only in the sun. Good for dry sunny spots.
Ocimum basilicum 'Dark Opal'	10in (25cm)	Ornamental version of Basil, grown for its dark red foliage, a useful foil for red- or orange-flowering plants.
Osteospermum ecklonis (Star of the Veldt)	12in (30cm)	Large single daisy-like flowers in orange, salmon pink, or cream shades.
Salvia	6-12in (15-30cm)	Brilliant-red flower spikes.
Senecio maritima	8-12in (20-30cm)	Foliage plant grown for silver leaves which make an effective foil for brightly-coloured flowers.
SPECIMEN PLANTS FOR SINGLE POTS		
Canna (Indian Shot Plant)	4-5ft (1.2-1.5m)	Exotic, tropical-looking blooms grown from a tuber planted indoors during spring.
Eucalyptus globulus	4-5ft (1.2-1.5m)	Foliage plant with silver-blue leaves.
Ricinus communis (Castor Oil Plant)	3-4ft (0.9-1.2m)	Foliage plant with large, five-lobed leaves in red, bronze or mahogony shades.

Autumn patio

A patio can be every bit as colourful in autumn as it is in spring.

Once the summer flowers start to come to an end on your patio, don't just leave it empty and uninteresting. It is much better, instead, to refurbish it in autumn colours. Whatever the weather, you'll want a view that you can be proud of, and – who knows? – we could get an Indian summer yet!

So be ruthless: pull out the old bedding, take down the hanging baskets, clean up the containers, scrub the paving, and treat yourself to a trip to the nearest garden centre to stock up. It takes only a moment to clear away the fading remnants of your summer plants and to give your patio

a bright, fresh new look for autumn.

Autumn is every bit as exciting to plant enthusiasts as spring. The backbone of your autumn display – including shrubs and conifers – will probably already be in place. Shrubs, like Japanese Maple, will take on blazing autumnal colours, gradually giving over their star roles, as they shed their leaves, to evergreens and conifers. And many plants choose the autumn to produce flowers that might have been overlooked during the more colourful summer months.

There's plenty of scope for the creative patio planner to create something very special. Don't be in too much of a hurry to buy the first things that take your fancy. There's a lot to choose from, so spend some time planning what is going to suit your particular patio and the style of your house, and then pick a selection of plants that really do something for each other, too.

Don't expect to end up with an autumn version of your summer scheme. You'll be using very different sorts of plants, so expect to use them in different ways. And from the purely practical point of view, remember that there is a completely different set of growing problems in the autumn from those that you encountered in the summer, and you'll need to make allowances for these, too.

Designing your display

After the gaudy summer flowers, the autumn look is a lot more restrained, relying not on short-lived annual plants but on perennials for its colour. Flowers still play a part in highlighting areas of interest, but for the mainstay of the scheme you'll have to rely on evergreen foliage in a variety of different colours and different textures.

Small shrubs, conifers, autumn flowering heathers, rock plants and bulbs can all be used, but rather than treating them like bedding plants, make them into displays in much the same way as you might arrange indoor plants. Use the conifers and evergreens as the background to your display, and add smaller variegated or coloured foliage plants and flowers to provide colour and interest. Remember, though, that tiny flowers must always be planted in reasonably sized groups to have any real effect.

The combination of conifers with Heathers or rock plants is a particularly attractive one, and you can also experiment with groups of Bamboo, Ivy and various autumn-flowering bulbs. And make good use, too, of strikingly shaped specimen plants such as Yucca and Phormium.

Growing considerations

🌺 Buy only container-grown plants when an instant effect is wanted – in full flower if you like.

🌺 'Double-plant' everything by plunging pots inside larger containers of peat. Otherwise, as soon as the weather turns rough, plants will blow over, get waterlogged from standing in puddles, or suffer frozen roots without a layer of soil to insulate them. And in very cold weather, you can provide extra protection by tying newspapers or sacking round the outsides of the containers.

🌺 Use potting compost rather than peat. Add gravel to the compost to provide extra drainage for rock plants, and if you're planting Heathers or other lime-haters, use special-purpose ericaceous or another lime-free compost rather than the standard John Innes or peat-based soil mixtures. Avoid breaking up the root-ball when you plant your autumn plants especially if they are in flower at the time.

🌺 All tender plants, such as Nerine, most Agapanthus and Zephyranthes, must be moved inside into a cold or slightly heated greenhouse, porch or sunroom before the first severe frost.

🌺 When the time comes to replace your autumn display, you can either keep plants in their pots to re-use next autumn (repotting if necessary), or plant them permanently out in the garden. Only naturally small or dwarf plants are suitable for being kept permanently in containers.

Evergreen foliage plays a large part in the autumn patio display.

Flowers for autumn colour

Bulbs

African Lily (Agapanthus), 4ft (1.2m), large blue or white flowers from July through to September, the 'Headbourne' hybrids are handy.

Autumn Crocus (*Colchicum autumnale*), 6in (15cm), pink crocus-like flowers, September.

Crocus medius, 3in (8cm), violet flowers with red stamens, October to November.

Cyclamen neapolitanum, hardy cyclamen, 2in (5cm), pink flowers, September to November.

Guernsey Lily (*Nerine bowdenii*), 3ft (0.9m), large pink flowers, tender.

Zephyranthes robusta, 8in (20cm), pink flowers, tender.

Cyclamen neapolitanum.

Erica cinerea.

Heathers

Bell Heather (*Erica cinerea*)
Cross-leaved Heather (*Erica tetralix*)
Cornish Heather (*Erica vagans*)
Ling (*Calluna vulgaris*)
Irish Bell Heather (*Daboecia cantabrica*)
Tree Heather (*Erica arborea* 'Estrella Gold' and 'Gold Tip')

Colchicum autumnale.

Chrysanthemum hosmariensis.

Herbaceous and alpine plants

Acaena 'Blue Haze', carpeting plant, blue-bronze evergreen foliage.

Acaena pulchella, carpeting plant, light bronze evergreen foliage, red flowers.

Chrysanthemum hosmariensis, 12in (30cm), white flowers, finely indented silver foliage.

Ice Plant (*Sedum spectabilis*, 12in (30cm), pink flowers attract butterflies.

Sedum pulchellum, mat-forming plant with pink flowers.

Erica arborea 'Gold Tip'.

Crocus medius.

Nerine bowdenii.

Erica tetralix.

Sedum spectabilis.

An instant patio for winter

Bergenias are good low-growing plants which flower in late winter.

Just because it's winter you don't have to forget about your patio garden. In fact, winter can be every bit as exciting as summer and because the patio is the one part of the garden you can always see it is worthwhile spending some time on it.

Evergreens will probably form the backbone of your display and by using plants in pots you can create an instant winter patio and you can also restyle your display to keep pace with the seasons.

Design ideas

There is no point in trying to create a summer patio in the middle of winter, so forget about garden furniture, barbecues and bedding plants and start to plan your winter scheme from a different angle. The most successful winter patios are not based on vivid colours but on striking shapes and contrasting foliage effects. And, as you probably won't be spending much time outside, don't go for small

Heathers

For winter foliage
***Calluna vulgaris* varieties*,** 6in (15cm), 'Orange Queen', orange foliage; 'Robert Chapman', golden orange foliage; 'Sir John Charrington', orange foliage with red tints; 'Wickwar Flame', flame red foliage; 'Ruth Sparkes', golden foliage.

Erica arborea*, 'Estrella Gold', 3-4ft (0.9-1-2m). Tall golden tree useful for adding height to collection of heather. *These are not suitable for growing in alkaline soils.

For winter flowers
***Erica herbacea* varieties*,** 6in (15cm), 'January Sun', pink; 'John Kampa', deep pink; 'King George', rose-pink; 'Springwood Pink', bright pink; 'Springwood White', white.

***Erica darleyensis* varieties*,** 6in (15cm), 'Ada S. Collins', white; 'Arthur Johnson', pink; 'Furzey', deep pink; 'Ghost Hills', deep pink; 'J W Porter', purple-mauve.

Erica erigena*, 'Irish Dusk', 6in (15cm), attractive light-grey foliage with pink flowers that flower throughout winter.

*All varieties are lime tolerant.

Erica herbacea 'King George'.

Calluna vulgaris 'Ruth Sparkes'.

plants that need to be seen at close quarters, but go for larger ones to create an impression from a distance.

The most interesting displays are often achieved with very few plants – the trick lies in making a little say a lot. So don't just dot plants around, but group them together for a contrast of shapes and colours.

You can accentuate the shapes of plants by contrasting them with other natural accessories. Paving stones make a good background to evergreen foliage and you can increase their decorative value by adding areas of raked gravel, Hydroleca granules (lightweight, man-made, terracotta-coloured pebbles), and even beach pebbles.

It is important to decide your theme before you start so that you end up with things that combine well. Here are some suggestions.

Garden schemes

Conifer garden. A contrast of different shapes and foliage colours makes a striking show – choose one columnar plant and one horizontal ground hugger with one or more block-shaped varieties. Try to include at least one golden conifer and a blue among the more usual green and grey-greens. A particularly good combination is: *Juniperus horizontalis* 'Turquoise Spreader', *Chamaecyparis pisifera* 'Filfera Aurea', *Chamaecyparis pisifera* 'Boulevard', *Taxus baccata* 'Standishii' and *Chamaecyparis lawsoniana* 'Minima Glauca'.

Mediterranean garden. Plant evergreen plants with exotic foliage in large terracotta pots for an eye-catching display. Suggested plants are *Fatsia japonica*, Phormium varieties and *Yucca filamentosa*.

Traditional garden. Aim for a cottage garden look made up of flowering heathers, a mixture of different evergreens and Bergenias which flower in late winter.

Formal garden. Fill areas of wall adjacent to the patio with clipped and trained bay trees in pots. These look especially effective when placed between windows and doorways. Fill troughs or tubs with trimmed Rosemary or other plants with well-defined shape such as *Euonymus*. Alternatively, go for colour and fill your tubs with heathers.

Other plants to choose

Shrub/tree	Height	Description
Evergreen		
Bambusa or *Arundinaria viridistriata*	3-5ft (0.9-1.5cm)	Variegated bamboo
Euonymus fortunei varieties	2ft (0.6m)	Low, bushy plants, variegated, silver or gold
Fatsia japonica	3-4ft (0.9-1.2m)	Low, rounded bush with large shiny leaves
Laurus nobilis	5ft (1.5m)	Bay tree that can be bought already trained and clipped into ornamental shapes
Phormium varieties	3ft (0.9cm)	Long, leaves growing from a central crown, red, purple or yellow striped
Rosmarinus (Rosemary)	3ft (0.9m)	Can be trained into spires or left to grow naturally
Yucca filamentosa	5ft (1.5m)	Tropical looking plant, long, narrow leaves with short trunk
Conifers		
Chamaecyparis lawsoniana 'Ellwoodi'	5ft (1.5m)	Loose, open-topped, grey-green spires, needs a large container
'Minima Glauca'	2ft (0.6m)	Globular sea-green plant
Chamaecyparis pisifera 'Boulevard'	3ft (0.9m)	Flame-shaped, blue-grey plant
'Filifera aurea'	2ft (0.6m)	Shaggy, weeping conifer with yellow, thread-like foliage
Juniperus horizontalis 'Turquoise Spread'	3-4ft (0.9-1.2m)	Ground-hugging spreader with bright turquoise foliage
'Glauca'	3-4ft (0.9-1.2m)	Ground-hugging spreader with feathery, blue-grey foliage
Juniperus media 'Gold Sovereign'	1ft (0.3m)	Low-spreading conifer with bright golden foliage
Picea glauca 'Albertiana Conica'	3ft (0.9m)	Densely-packed pyramids of bright green foliage
Picea pungens 'Hoto'	4ft (1.2m)	Brilliant blue pyramidal conifer with silver-frosted foliage
Pinus leucodermis 'Compact Gem'	3-4ft (0.9-1.2m)	Miniature pine with attractively tufted foliage, mid-green
Taxus baccata 'Standishii'	4ft (1.2m)	Yew variety that forms a tall, narrow column of golden foliage

A window-box of evergreens can look most effective.

Many hardy evergreen shrubs will survive the winter outside.

Many gardeners frequently confess that they have just two types of plants in their garden borders – those that are hardy and strong enough to survive winter outside without any protection, and those that die through being too tender!

Patio, terrace and roof-top gardeners, however, cannot be so careless and blasé about plants in pots, as many straddle the difficult line of being too tender for growing outdoors and having full hardiness. It is only by protecting them during winter that they will survive.

Winter survival

Protection levels

Not all patio plants need winter protection. By their very nature the relatively short-lived summer-bedding annuals will not survive winter, and are raised from seed sown each spring. Neither are spring-flowering bedding plants such as Wallflowers (Cheiranthus) or Daisies (*Bellis perennis*) any problem – they are planted in autumn and, as long as the

compost does not become waterlogged, survive to flower from April to June the following year.

Spring-flowering bulbs such as Tulips – also planted in autumn for flowering during April and May – do not need any protection. Daffodils and most other spring-flowering bulbs are also winter hardy. The main plants that need protection are tender container-grown shrubs, trees and climbers, and these are indicated throughout this series of features of plants to grow on patios, terraces and roof-tops.

The dangers to your plant vary from region to region. In the South and South-west, most susceptible plants will survive with only a small amount of help, mainly preventing the compost becoming too wet. In the Midlands, and progressively going North, the amount of protection needed increases and includes both keeping the compost relatively dry and the plants and compost insulated from bitingly cold, low temperatures.

Cold winds are a particular danger in areas bordering the North Sea, especially when Russia and Scandinavia are exporting blizzards. Snow is another problem, and the weight of an overnight fall of several inches soon breaks branches and bends over leading shoots. But there are ways of living with these problems.

Facing the problems

Waterlogged compost. This is susceptible to freezing during exceptionally cold periods and is, perhaps, one of the main problems. Well-drained compost, a good layer of crocks in the base of the container, and drainage holes not blocked by compost, all contribute to warm, problem-free compost. Also, if the container has drainage holes in its base, stand it on three bricks to ensure they do not become blocked. Wooden tubs especially benefit from being placed on three – not four – bricks, as the air space beneath the tub greatly reduces the rate of decay of the container's base.

Preventing excessive water reaching the compost during winter is essential in wet areas, or if the plant is tender. If the container is small enough to handle, and the plant's size allows, move it to the shelter of an overhanging roof – preferably in a wind-sheltered spot against a south- or west-facing wall. If this is not sufficient to keep the compost moderately dry, it will need covering, either with two large tiles if the pot is not too large or with a piece of polythene.

The use of two tiles – resting against the plant's stem and tilted to form a tent – is an old method, but

In very cold weather some protection for your plants is often necessary.

the tiles can become dislodged during winter. Cut semi-circular holes out of the top of each tile to accommodate the plant's stem.

A better method, however, is to tie a piece of polythene over the compost and to secure it with string around the pot or tub. However, from time to time you must check that the compost is not bone dry, and in late winter or early spring remove it entirely. If the polythene sags towards the centre of the pot you must give it support, otherwise water will drain into the compost.

Low temperatures. These are especially dangerous if the compost is badly drained and waterlogged and, as a consequence, the water freezes. Many near tender plants can survive the winter quite happily outside in containers, as long as there is no risk of the compost freezing and damaging the roots.

Plants grown in a border in the garden have their roots surrounded by a mass of soil that during summer has warmed up and acts as a reservoir of warmth during early winter. However, plants in pots have such a relatively small amount of compost that it reacts quickly to extremes of temperature – in winter it is extra cold and in summer can become nearly cooked if placed in a warm, sun-soaked position.

Wrapping straw or hessian around the container, then encasing it in a layer of polythene, will give some protection. Don't allow the hessian or straw to become soaked with water, because if it freezes it will keep the temperature around the plant low for quite a long time. It assumes the role of a refrigerator until spring and better, warmer weather arrives.

Cold winds. These soon 'burn' leaves, causing their edges to become dry, brown, crisp and eventually to fall. The Bay Tree, *Laurus nobilis*, so often grown in large tubs and displayed either side of an entrance or French window, soon presents a bedraggled appearance if exposed to cold, searing winds.

There are several ways to protect your plant from cold winds. The easiest method is to position it in a

Snow can damage branches so always brush it away if possible.

Keep compost dry by resting two tiles against the plant's stems, tilted to form a tent, *left*, or put some polythene over the compost and tie it around the pot, *right*.

sheltered spot, away from biting winds and cold draughts. Avoid especially those places where wind becomes funnelled between buildings and rushes along, buffeting plants, and causing untold damage.

A long-term wind-reducing plan for the whole garden, as well as a patio, is to plant a hedge on the windward edge of your garden. The protective benefit of this screen will be felt for many yards on the lee side, depending on the height of the hedge. For instance, a 6ft (1.8m) high hedge

reduces the wind for 18-36ft (5.4-11m) on the lee side.

Hedges are much more useful than walls in reducing wind speed, as they tend to act as a filter. Walls and border fences only redirect the wind, causing buffeting and strong, circular eddies on the lee side that do more damage than if the wall was not there.

On exposed patios – and especially where wind whips around corners – a wattle-hurdle type screen will provide some protection, as it has a fil-

tering effect. It can even be made as a temporary structure – secured in a concrete box – that can be removed as spring and, hopefully, better weather and sunshine arrives.

Newly-planted or tender plants benefit from a winter overcoat formed from a wigwam of stout rustic poles clothed with hessian or straw. Don't make it so wind-proof that it stops air from circulating around the plant, as this may encourage an onslaught of diseases and pests. Take care that the structure isn't so high and unwieldy that it blows over in the wind.

Snow. Heavy falls can weigh down branches, splaying them out and eventually tearing them from the main stem. Conifers with several leading shoots are quickly damaged in this way and upright types become spreading and unattractive. Lightly brush off snow and if branches splay out tie them together to create a natural shape.

Severely damaged plants will need pruning to shape in spring, and leading shoots should be tied to a central support securely.

Seed sowing step by step

The cheapest way of getting a large collection of houseplants is to grow them from seeds — and one of the nicest things about doing this is the satisfaction you get from growing plants from scratch. Many seeds germinate very easily and the seedlings pop up out of the soil within a couple of weeks. Other seeds can be trickier; start with the easy ones and progress to those that are slightly harder. Be guided by the seed packets; most of them say how easy or difficult the seeds inside are to germinate and grow.

Where to start
The time to start thinking about seed sowing is in the spring; this is because the weather is beginning to warm up and the summer stretches ahead to give your plants plenty of time to grow and gather strength before the rigours of winter. You can buy seeds and equipment at garden centres and department stores.

Ideally you need a little bit of extra warmth to encourage seeds to germinate; one way to achieve this is to invest in a small, inexpensive propagator. You can get a propagator small enough to sit on a windowsill and progressively bigger sizes up to one that will take three seed trays. Propagators can be unheated or electrically heated, depending on how much you want to spend. An electric propagator will provide a temperature of around 65-70°F (18-21°C), which is warm enough for raising most seeds.

If you only want to grow a few plants or don't want to spend any money, you can still germinate a wide range of seeds on a warm windowsill. Cover the seeds with a clear polythene bag and seal it with a rubber band or piece of string to

An electric propagator provides the ideal environment for germination and the early stages of seedling growth.

keep the moisture and warmth inside, or use a piece of glass. Or put the seeds in the airing cupboard to give them the initial warmth they need to germinate; if you do this remember to move the seedlings out into the light as soon as they show.

Don't try to economise on compost by using garden soil; it has too many other seeds and bugs in it that will overwhelm your seeds. Buy a good seed compost like John Innes Seed Compost or one of the soilless composts, such as Levingtons or Arthur Bowers, or a multi-purpose compost.

Growing houseplants from seed is a very simple process — just follow our step by step guidelines, *right*, and you will be rewarded with lots of healthy plants of your own — and much cheaper than in the shops!

● **Preparing the compost.** If you only have a few seeds you can sow them into a small pot, say 3-4in (7-10cm). But use a tray if you have a lot of seeds. Fill the pot or tray to within ½in (13mm) of the top and lightly firm it. Level and smooth the compost with a flat piece of wood or the bottom of another pot.

● **How to sow the seeds.** Space out large seeds individually, roughly ½in (13mm) apart, across the compost surface. Sprinkle smaller seeds evenly over the surface using your finger and thumb. Tiny, dust-like seeds can be mixed with a small amount of fine, dry silver sand before sowing to make them easier to handle.

● **Cover the seeds with compost.** Use a fine-mesh kitchen sieve to sift the compost to a fine texture and cover the seeds with an even layer of compost equal to twice their diameter. This helps the seedlings to germinate evenly. Don't cover very small, dust-like seeds with compost or they may not appear at all. Instead, press them into the compost surface using a flat piece of wood.

Primula seedlings — before and after
You can have hundreds of plants for less money than you would pay for one in a shop! Sow Primula seeds in spring/summer to flower the following spring. The result should be healthy, fresh green seedlings, *left*.
The following spring you should have lots of lovely, colourful, mature *Primula obconicas* like this one, *below* !

● **Watering the seeds.** Seeds can't swell and germinate without water so the compost must be nice and moist. To avoid the devastating seedling disease known as 'damping off', which causes seedlings to keel over and die, add some Cheshunt Compound powder fungicide, as directed on the tin, to the water. Use a hand mist sprayer and thoroughly dampen the compost, or stand the container up to its rim in tepid water until the surface of the compost becomes moist. Remove the container from the water and let it drain.

● **Germinating the seeds.** Put the pots or trays in a propagator or cover them with a polythene bag. This gives the seeds warmth and prevents the compost drying out too quickly. Mist spray the compost whenever it looks in danger of drying out.

The time seeds take to germinate varies considerably depending on the plant. Busy Lizzies can appear within a week or two, but Palms can take six months or more.

● **How to treat the seedlings.** As soon as the seedlings appear move them to a spot where they will be in good natural light, but not in direct sun or they will shrivel and die. If seedlings don't get sufficient light they will become very pale, drawn and spindly.

● **Thinning out the seedlings.** When lots of seedlings germinate they can become too overcrowded to grow properly. So keep the seedlings healthy and give them air and room to spread by thinning them out a little. Starting from one end, work over the tray removing the weaker seedlings by pulling each one gently out between your thumb and forefinger, until there are no leaves touching each other. This gives the remaining seedlings plenty of room to grow without the danger of the roots becoming too cramped.

| Some plants to grow from seed ||
Easy	Difficult
Asparagus Ferns	African Violet
Busy Lizzie	*Begonia rex*
Cacti	Calceolaria
Castor Oil Plant	Cape Primrose
Coleus	Cineraria
Myrtle	Ferns
Philodendrons	Figs
Polka Dot Plant	Italian Bellflower
Sensitive Plant	Palms
Silk Oak	Primula
	Umbrella Plant

● **Pricking out the seedlings.** When the seedlings are large enough to handle easily, and before they become overcrowded again, they must be transplanted to other containers.

● **Transplanting the seedlings.** Use a soilless peat-based compost or John Innes No 1 and put a little compost in the bottom of a 3in (7cm) pot and firm it gently. Using a plastic plant label or tiny kitchen fork, loosen a few seedlings at a time from the compost. Insert the label well under the roots and gently lift the compost up trying not to snap too many roots as you do so.

Always handle a seedling by its lower two fleshy leaves — in other words the first two leaves that appear. Never touch

One to two year old Silk Oak seedlings.

the stem or you'll strangle and kill the seedling, or the upper leaves, as you may damage the growth point and again kill the seedling.

Lift and gently shake one seedling at a time away from the compost. Hold the seedling over the centre of the pot so that its roots dangle straight down, and the lower seed leaves are more-or-less level with the pot rim. Trickle compost into the pot up to the rim; give the pot a sharp tap on the table to settle the compost and gently firm it with your fingers. By the time you finish, the compost surface should be about ½in (13mm) below the rim of the pot to allow room for watering and the lower leaves should be just above the compost surface.

● **Establishing the seedlings.** Mix a little Cheshunt Compound fungicide powder into some water and, using an indoor watering can, water the seedlings. Keep them in a warm, light place for a week or two to help them get established in their new compost. Each one can be moved to a position with a temperature suited to that particular plant.

Where to buy seeds

Houseplant seeds can be bought from garden centres and most department stores around the country. They are also available mail order from the major seed companies. You can get seeds in colourfully illustrated paper envelopes as well as foil wrapped. The seeds wrapped in foil will keep for much longer because oxygen won't be able to get at them.

Some packets only contain a few seeds while others contain lots; this depends on the type of plant concerned. If a flower produces hundreds of seeds, then that's what you'll get; at the other extreme, with some Palms and very rare plants there'll only be perhaps three or four seeds in a packet. This regulating of contents also helps the seedsman keep most packets at around the same price.

A very convenient method of raising seeds are the so-called starter packs; these consist of a plastic tray filled with sowing compost or a sterile material called vermiculite. In some packs the seeds are already sown. In many packs the clear plastic lid is lifted off and turned over to make a mini propagator for the seeds. Full, fairly straightforward instructions are always supplied with the packs.

Take your cut

After you've grown and loved your houseplants for a while, you'll find yourself itching to try your hand at propagating them. The easiest way to increase your favourite plants is to take cuttings in spring and summer. It's a quick, cheap and almost foolproof method and you're guaranteed to get a plant identical in every way to the parent.

Stem cuttings are the easiest cuttings to take but there are other methods which we shall explain later on. Select the plant that you want to take cuttings from and put it on a clean table or surface where you can see it properly. Choose the cuttings from fresh, healthy young stems that don't have any flowers or flower buds; cut the stems from the middle and crowded top of the plant or from a point where you won't ruin the shape of your plant.

To give your cuttings the best possible start buy a small bottle or tube of hormone rooting powder; it contains growth hormones that encourage a cut shoot to grow strong healthy roots.

You can get ready-made peat-based or John Innes Seed Compost or, if you prefer, you can make your own by mixing equal amounts of moist peat and horticultural sand.

Always place your cuttings in small, shallow pots to root — a 3in (7cm) pot is usually right for a few cuttings. Fill the pot with compost then make holes in the compost round the edge of the pot using a sharp pencil or knitting needle.

Warmth and light

Keep your cuttings in a reasonably warm place, well away from draughts, to give them every chance to root. Most cuttings root best when they are kept in a warm, closed environment in good light — but not in direct sunlight where they might get scorched.

A heated propagator is helpful as cuttings will root quickly in its constant warmth and humid atmosphere. An electrically-heated propagator giving a temperature of 65-70°F (18-21°C) is perfect. But if you don't have one, you can improvise successfully by putting a clear polythene bag (not one with holes punched in it) over the pot and sealing it with a rubber band.

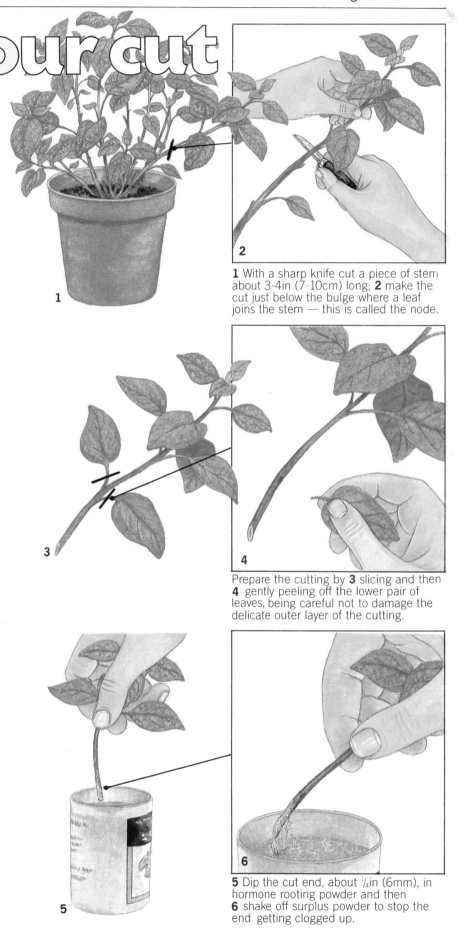

1 With a sharp knife cut a piece of stem about 3-4in (7-10cm) long; **2** make the cut just below the bulge where a leaf joins the stem — this is called the node.

Prepare the cutting by **3** slicing and then **4** gently peeling off the lower pair of leaves, being careful not to damage the delicate outer layer of the cutting.

5 Dip the cut end, about ¼in (6mm), in hormone rooting powder and then **6** shake off surplus powder to stop the end getting clogged up.

221

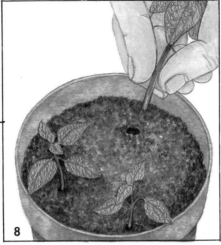

7 With a pencil make a hole for each cutting in the compost, near the edge of the pot. **8** Drop a cutting into each hole and firm the compost with your fingers.

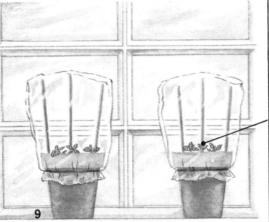

9 Improvise your own propagator with a clear polythene bag secured at the pot rim by a rubber band. **10** Use short canes to hold the polythene clear of the cuttings.

11 When the cuttings have grown for about four weeks and are starting to produce shoots, they should have developed a healthy root system **12**.

Watering and rooting

You must check a heated propagator every day to see if the compost needs watering as the heat dries it out very quickly. With cuttings under polythene, or in an unheated propagator, the moisture in the compost will be enough for the cuttings until they root, as the condensation will run off the sides back into the compost.

Open a heated propagator every day to change the air and to wipe away any condensation with a tissue. At the same time check for dead leaves and any sign of black, soggy or rotting stems. Throw away any cutting that looks unhealthy as it can contaminate the others.

Once the cuttings have grown roots they are ready to be moved into individual pots. Wait until you can see that the tips of the shoots have started to grow — then you can be fairly sure that the roots are also growing under the compost. When you think the cuttings have 'taken', lift one up to see if it has good white roots.

Start each rooted cutting in a small 3in (7cm) pot. Don't be too ambitious for it by putting it in too big a pot; young plants grow best when their roots don't have too much room to explore.

Alternative methods

With a plant that has a rather woody stem, such as a Fuchsia, you can take cuttings with a heel of bark. This gives the cutting a head start on rooting. In this case you simply peel off the shoot taking with it a slither of bark from the main stem. After that you treat the cutting in exactly the same way as an ordinary stem cutting.

Some cuttings will root in water as well as compost; try this with Busy Lizzies, Tradescantias, Zebrinas, Coleus, Fuchsias and Crotons. Prepare cuttings in the same way as already described. Use a jam jar with about 1in (25mm) of water in the bottom and stretch a piece of clingfilm across the top; make holes in the clingfilm with a sharp pencil to hold the cuttings. Push each cutting carefully through its hole so that the bottom of the stem just enters the water. Put the pot in a warm, bright place, but not in direct sunlight, and inspect it daily to see if the roots are growing.

When the roots are about 1in (25mm) long they are ready to go into pots of compost. Be extra careful when handling water-grown cuttings as the roots are particularly brittle.

Taking leaf cuttings

Making new plants from leaves is fun: they root easily and quickly and give you more new plants than you could ever expect from stem cuttings. Only a small range of plants is eligible for this treatment, but they include very popular and pretty ones such as the African Violet and Begonias. Because you get so many new plants for so little trouble, leaf propagation would be an enjoyable and inexpensive way to make presents for other people.

The plants with the ability to propagate from their leaves are those in the Begonia, Crassula and Gesneriad groups — these plants all have slightly fleshy leaves. The best time to take leaf cuttings is in early summer, when leaves are strong and mature. In spring they are putting all their energy into growing, while late in the summer their capacity to propagate is reduced. But when leaves are just mature, their surface area is at its maximum, they're at their best in terms of producing food, and they're strong enough to withstand the period during propagation when they are severed from the parent plant. You should always choose a complete and undamaged leaf that has finished growing and that looks completely healthy.

What you need
🌱 The most common problem when taking cuttings from a leaf is that it rots before the new plantlets have developed — so make sure that the materials you start with are the best you can get, and that all the equipment you use is completely clean. In the enclosed atmosphere necessary for propagation any disease will develop very rapidly and pests will multiply.

🌱 You can root some leaves in water, but most go straight into compost and the right mix is essential. Plants won't establish roots in very packed soil where air and water can't circulate easily, so good drainage must be provided. Use equal parts of good fresh peat, coarse Perlite and Vermiculite, or a proprietary brand of seed and cuttings compost, such as Levingtons or Arthur Bowers, with some extra coarse sand, Perlite or Vermiculite added. Fill a shallow seed

Plants to choose

Leaves with stalks
Begonia boweri (Eyelash Begonia)
Peperomia argyreia (Watermelon Peperomia)
P.caperata (Emerald Ripple)
P.griseo-argentea (Silver Ripple)
Saintpaulia ionantha (African Violet)
Sinningia speciosa (Gloxinia)

Whole leaves
Begonia rex, above
B.masoniana (Iron Cross Begonia)
Crassula arborescens (Chinese Jade)
C.argentea (Jade Plant)
C.lycopodioides (Rat Tail Plant)

Echeveria glauca (Blue Echeveria)
E.harmsii (Mexican Snowball)
E.setosa (Firecracker Plant)
Sedum adolphii (Golden Sedum)
S.morganianum (Burro's Tail)
S.rubrotinctum (Jelly Bean Plant)

Leaf sections
Begonia masoniana (Iron Cross Plant)
B.rex
Sansevieria hahnii (Bird's Nest Sansevieria)
S.trifasciata or *S.zeylanica* (Mother-in-Law's Tongue)
Sinningia speciosa (Gloxinia)
Streptocarpus hybridus (Cape Primrose)

tray or individual, wide pots, with this mixture.

🌱 For best results you should have a propagator, to keep the temperature warm and constant — 70°F (21°C) is ideal. But you can also get good results by enclosing the pot or tray in a clear polythene bag or covering it with glass, and rooting the cuttings on a lightly shaded windowsill so that they get warmth but not bright sun.

🌱 Always water in the leaves with a dilute systemic fungicide containing benomyl, such as Benlate, before

you cover them. This will help reduce the chance of pests and diseases damaging the leaves or new plantlets.

Using leaves with stalks
Whole leaves, with a spur of stalk, can be used to propagate several very attractive plants — African Violets (Saintpaulia); all the Peperomias, including the glorious silver and green striped Watermelon Plant *(Peperomia argyreia)*; small-leaved Begonias, including the Eyelash Plant *(Begonia bowerii)*, and Gloxinias *(Sinningia speciosa)*.

1. Remove the entire African Violet leaf.

Whether you have rooted your new plantlets in water or compost, the cluster that usually forms from each leaf or section needs to be split up as soon as the plantlets are about 1in (2.5cm) tall.

Pot each new plant separately in a 2in (5cm) pot, using a peat based compost, such as Arthur Bowers or Levingtons. Grow them in bright but not direct light, and feed them at every other watering with a fertiliser high in phosphate and potassium, but low in nitrogen – this is the right mix to encourage new, healthy roots. A tomato fertiliser would be ideal (see page 568).

When the young plants are well established, you can treat them as mature plants – see individual details in the 'A-Z of Plants' section.

2. Trim the leaf stalk and dip in a rooting powder.

3. Insert the stalk into prepared compost, firm and water in.

4. The leaves should root in about six weeks.

Slice a leaf from the plant, together with ½-1in (13-25mm) of stalk, using a razor blade or a very sharp knife. Dip the end of the stalk in a hormone rooting powder or gel (such as Fisons Clear Cut) and then insert it into your prepared pot or tray of compost.

Do this with as many leaves as you like, but bear in mind that each leaf will produce several new plants. Firm them gently and water them in, and they will root in about six weeks; shoots will appear in about ten.

You can also root African Violets in water — fill a small jar nearly to the rim with water and cover it with aluminium foil. Make holes for the leaf stalks and pop them through so that the ends are in water. When the shoots have appeared, transplant them into compost.

When the plantlets are about 1in (2.5cm) tall, plant them out in separate pots and treat them as mature plants. It's likely to take about nine months to get to this stage.

Using whole leaves

Succulent plants are easily propagated directly from the leaves. Echeverias, Sedums and Crassulas (which all belong to the *Crassulaceae* family) are all good candidates for this treatment. You simply detach whole, fleshy leaves by slicing them off the parent plant, and allow the gummy sap to dry for a day or so. Then insert them up to a quarter of their length in the compost and water them in, remembering to add the fungicide. Cover the tray or pot with clear polythene or glass, making sure it doesn't touch the leaves, and rooting will start within two to three weeks.

Whole leaves are used in a different way to propagate *Begonia rex* and its

You can raise several new African Violets from a single leaf.

1. *Begonia rex* is easily propagated from leaf cuttings.

2. Trim the edges of the leaf, then cut up in squares.

3. Lay the squares on compost, with leaf undersides down.

4. In five to six weeks the new plants will be ready for potting.

handsome cousin *B.masoniana*. Slice off a whole leaf (remember that one leaf will give you several new plants) and lay it on a flat surface with the underside facing up. With a razor blade, make cuts through each vein where it joins with another — you'll have half a dozen or more cuts, depending on the size of the leaf. Water the prepared compost so that its surface is slightly damp, and lay the leaf, cut side down, flat on top of the compost, anchoring it firmly in place with one or two wire staples pushed through it. You may need to use more staples with *B.masoniana* to keep it in good contact with the soil.

Water in, and cover the pot or tray with polythene or glass or, even better, put it in a propagator. Keep it at a steady 70°F (21°C), and plantlets will begin to form from each of the cut veins after five to six weeks.

Using leaf sections

To make even more plants at one time, you can cut one leaf of *Begonia rex* or its

Increase *Begonia rex* from leaf cuttings.

related species into several small sections. Then you'll get several new plantlets from each section. The principle is just the same as using a whole leaf.

Choose a big Begonia leaf and cut it into squares about 1in (2.5cm) across. This will automatically make the neces-

sary cuts through the veins. You then lay each section flat on the compost as for whole leaves. Because *B.masoniana* leaves are too wrinkled to keep in good contact with the compost when lying flat, it's best to insert each section upright in the compost to about half its length, as you would when using leaves with stems attached. Make sure that the biggest severed vein in each section is inserted in the compost.

This is also the best way to propagate succulents like Sansevierias, which have long leaves with parallel length-wise veins, and Streptocarpus, which has a single, central vein in each leaf. Gloxinias can also be propagated in this way. In these cases, slicing each leaf into sections straight across its whole width will ensure that you get the necessary cuts in the veins from which new plants will root. However, if you want to try Sansevierias, stick to the green-leaved types — variegations will not come through in the new plants, which will always be plain green.

225

Air layering

Do yourself a good turn: neaten up that straggly, unkempt Rubber Plant and gain a new one — for scarcely any effort. And all for the price of a bag of sphagnum moss, a tray of gravel and a little potting compost.

Is your Rubber Plant touching the ceiling? Stiff-stemmed plants like the Fiddleleaf Fig, Dumb Cane and Swiss Cheese Plant easily get out of hand. They can become tall, ungainly and increasingly unattractive as they get older and lose their lower leaves. When they reach that stage, they don't really deserve house room.

Air layering offers you a chance to grow a fresh new plant, by encouraging part of the stem near the top of the established plant to produce roots. The top is then severed to make a new plant — and the parent plant usually benefits from the trim.

This is one of the oldest methods of raising plants, probably pioneered in China over 4,000 years ago, hence its other name — Chinese layering. It's particularly useful for woody plants, because they can't be 'layered' in the usual way — by bending the stems down to soil level and allowing roots to

develop where stem and soil meet. But air layering is also easier and more reliable than taking cuttings — and Rubber Plants and other Ficus species, Crotons and False Aralia are notoriously tricky to raise in that way. Air layering leaves the parent plant fairly undisturbed, so you use this technique without risk of harming your plant. When working with younger plants that are still in good shape, it's best to leave the main stem untrimmed and to use a side shoot.

Don't think of starting until late spring or early summer, though, when plants are in their active growing season and will be more efficient at producing roots. The warmer the weather, the quicker the rooting.

You'll need nothing more sophisticated in the way of equipment than a bag of sphagnum moss obtainable from your local garden centre or florist. Before you begin, check the box, *right*, for what you need.

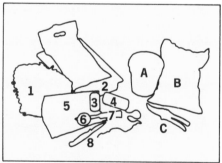

For the layering you will need:
1 sphagnum moss
2 a gravel tray (see text)
3 hormone rooting powder
4 some strong thread (optional)
5 a piece of clear polythene about 2ft (0.6m) × 1ft (0.3m) — a plastic bag cut down the sides will do
6 waterproof adhesive tape
7 a paintbrush (optional)
8 a sharp knife

In addition, for potting up:
A suitable-sized pot
B John Innes No 1 Potting Compost
C sharp secateurs

1a

2

Air layering step-by-step

1a Begin preparations the day before you're going to begin layering, by soaking the sphagnum moss in water overnight.

The following day, select the stem you're going to use, whether it's a main stem or a large side shoot. Near the top, say between 6in (15cm) and 12in (30cm) down, cut away a few of the leaves to give you a clear space of 4-6in (10-15cm) or so to work in.

Now prepare to cut a wound in the section of stem you have cleared, about 3-4in (7-10cm) below the top leaf; it is from the wound that the new roots will grow.

Using a really sharp knife, make a slanting upward cut, about 2-3in (5-7cm) long, but not penetrating more than halfway through the stem. Food and hormones will now begin to build up in the area of this 'tongue', as the plant responds to the wounding.

1b A less risky way of making the wound is to remove a girdle of bark from around the stem. This method leaves the tissues inside the plant undisturbed and therefore means that the stem is not weakened as much.

Scratch out two fine rings in the bark, about ½in (13mm) apart and peel off the area between the lines.

2 To encourage fast rooting and a strong root system, coat the wound with a hormone rooting powder or liquid; use a paintbrush to apply the rooting hormone, and prise the tongue open gently.

3 It is important to keep the wound open, to stop it from healing instead of putting out shoots. So pack the cut with a small, moist wad of sphagnum moss. Some experts suggest using a small pebble, or a matchstick, but these have no advantage and may be trickier to insert without risk to the weakened stem.

3

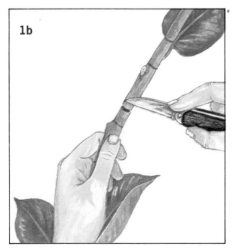

1b

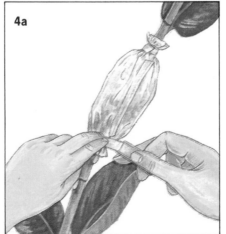

4a

Good candidates

Cordyline
Croton (*Codiaeum*)
Gold Dust Dracaena (*see above*)
Dumb Cane (*Dieffenbachia*)*
False Aralia (*Dizygotheca elegantissima*)
Fiddle-leaf Fig (*Ficus lyrata*)
Philodendron
Rubber Plant (*Ficus elastica*)
Swiss Cheese Plant (*Monstera deliciosa*)
Weeping Fig (*Ficus benjamina*)

* WARNING
Be careful when dealing with the Dieffenbachia; the sticky liquid it exudes is poisonous so wash your hands thoroughly afterwards.

4a The wound is now wrapped in sphagnum moss; this is the best rooting medium because it holds water well, is well aerated and easy to handle.

Take a thick pad of the moss (about two handfuls), squeeze out the excess water and work it into a ball so that the fibres are interwoven. Once the ball is about 2-3in (5-7cm) in diameter, divide it in half and press half to either side of the stem, where the wound is. Knead the moss together again at the sides, and secure it firmly with strong thread or sticky tape.

Wrap the polythene sheeting around the stem like a bandage, and seal it, top and bottom, with a few rounds of waterproof, adhesive tape. Seal the overlapping edge with tape, too, so that as little moisture as possible can escape.

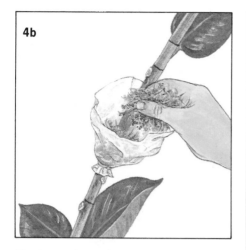

4b

4b As an alternative, you may find it easier to make a 'cup' of polythene first, and then pack the moss in afterwards. Fix on the polythene sheet, securing it at the base and side. Now fill the 'bag' with moss and, finally, seal it at the top.

5 Try to create a warm and humid atmosphere for the plant. If possible, stand it on a dish or tray filled with gravel, pebbles or Hortag (a proprietary gravel) which should be kept moist. If you can, put the plant in your warmest room and spray the foliage daily with a mist sprayer.

5

Now all you can do is wait. Inside the sealed polythene, the environment will be warm, dark and moist, and a new root system will begin to develop. How long this takes will depend on the plant — some root more quickly than others — but on average, it will be about eight weeks or so before you'll see any white roots appearing. Not until they are visible should you think or removing the polythene bandage.

When you see that the time is right, choose a suitable-sized pot for the young plant — one that is at least 4in (10cm) in diameter. Because you'll have to make a guess, have one or two larger

Caring for your new plant

The young plant will need some special attention until it establishes itself. Encourage it to root into the compost as quickly as possible, by keeping it in a warm place until the tip of the stem is starting to grow. Until then, use the gravel tray described earlier to keep the atmosphere humid, and make sure the plant is shaded from sunshine. Water just enough to keep the compost moist, not sodden.

You may find the young plant needs some extra support until it develops more roots; tie it temporarily to a stick pushed in the potting mixture — but take care to avoid the young roots. Once new growth appears, treat the plant like a mature specimen, watering and feeding accordingly. In the following spring it will be ready for repotting.

As to the parent plant, now's the opportunity for some radical reshaping. Don't be nervous — cut the old stem back to a point where new growth will make a more compact, respectable specimen. You can get away with trimming it by as much as two-thirds and you'll be well rewarded with a rejuvenated, bushy plant.

Air-layer your old, leggy *Ficus elastica* to gain a fine, new plant, *left*.

pots ready, just in case. You will need one that is just a bit larger than the plant's root system, by about ½in (13mm) all round. Half fill it with John Innes No 1, or a similar potting mixture.

6 The rooted stem may now be cut away from the parent plant. First remove the polythene wrapping then make a horizontal cut just below the ball of moss, clear of the new roots, using a pair of sharp secateurs. On no account allow the new roots to become dry; once the plant

is separate from the parent, it must be potted up straight away.

7 Leave the sphagnum moss in place. If you try to remove it, you may damage the new roots, whereas putting it into the pot with the young plant can do no harm at all.

Put the young plant into its pot immediately, working more potting mixture in around the sides of the mossy root ball and on top. Firm it down very carefully to avoid damaging the brittle roots. Now water it well.

6

7

Cuttings made easy

There is a wide range of houseplants which it is possible — indeed easy — to propagate by rooting in water. This method could not be simpler. Cuttings can be taken indoors at virtually any time of year, because they are in an artificially controlled environment. The best time of year, however, is in the spring and summer, when there is plenty of light and plants are in active growth.

Getting ready

All you need is a jam-jar, filled to within ½in (13mm) of the rim with water and covered with a sheet of kitchen foil, which should be held in place with a rubber band. Cuttings are then inserted through small holes in the foil, so that about a half to two-thirds of their length is immersed in water. Roots form quickly in a warm, light place and will soon fill the jar.

A special gel, called Clearcut, has recently been developed, which is a clear, thick jelly and is sold in containers a bit like little yoghurt pots. It works on much the same principle as the foil-covered jam-jar of water, and cuttings are inserted through the lid. But, unlike water, the gel stays pure and uncontaminated and is very successful in rooting a much wider range of cuttings — even leaf cuttings — than is possible in water. And, when the pot is filled with roots, transplanting is less hazardous, as the soft roots — which are so often damaged when moved from water to compost — are thickly coated in a protective layer of gel which cushions them from damage when they are being packed around with potting compost.

Taking the cutting

Cuttings should be 4-6in (10-15cm) long. Prepare them by removing the lower leaves with a very sharp knife or razor blade and make the bottom cut just below a leaf joint. Make small holes in the foil lid — one for each cutting — and insert the cuttings. These can be spaced quite closely together, but should not actually touch one another.

When roots begin to form in water, which can take anything from a week to eight weeks depending on the plant, add a little dilute liquid fertiliser, such as

Suitable candidates

Among the many houseplants which can be propagated in this way, the list below includes some of the easiest. This is also a good way of propagating some of the perennial herbs, such as Sage and Thyme.
Don't forget that an even larger range of plants will root in gel — and it's always fun to experiment.

African Violet (Saintpaulia)
Aluminium Plant (Pilea), *top left*
Begonia
Blood Leaf (Iresine)
Busy Lizzie (Impatiens)
Cape Leadwort (Plumbago)
Chrysanthemum
Freckle Face (Hypoestes)
Fuchsia
Geranium (Pelargonium)
Ivy (Hedera)
Night Jessamine (Cestrum)
Oleander (Nerium)
Ornamental Pepper (Piper)
Persian Violet (Exacum)
Pink Allamanda (Dipladenia)
Shrimp Plant (Beloperone), *below left*
Shrub Verbena (Lantana)
Spider Plant (Chlorophytum)
Swedish Ivy (Plectranthus)
Umbrella Plant (Cyperus)
Wandering Jew (Tradescantia)
Yesterday, Today and Tomorrow (Brunfelsia)
Zebra Plant (Aphelandra), *below right*

half-strength Phostrogen, to encourage growth. In time, the water may turn green, which is caused by algae feeding on the fertiliser; this does not matter, and the roots will continue to grow quite normally. Wait until the container is reasonably full of roots and the plant has a good 'shaving brush' on the end before moving it. Then pot it up into any good proprietary compost, to which the addition of a quarter part by volume of perlite will give a better texture and will allow more air to circulate around the delicate little roots.

229

Living With Plants

At the back Tradescantia is being rooted in Clearcut, left, and water, right. A Chlorophytum plantlet can also be started off in water but you'll have to dispense with foil because of its awkward shape.

Palms from seed

You've got to be dedicated to grow a palm from seed, and it will be no mean achievement when you succeed. But the satisfaction you'll feel will make all the trouble worth while, and you'll have saved the not inconsiderable expense of buying a shop-bought plant. You could even find yourself growing a palm few others have in their collection.

Palms take a long, long time to develop. A Kentia Palm, for instance, will take up to two years to grow to any size and six years before it really comes into its own. Rarer palms may take up to two years to germinate! And that's why commercial growers concentrate on just a few varieties. This leaves the stage clear for the botanical seedsmen who do stock a remarkably wide range of rarer palms as well as the most popular — the Fan Palm (Livistonia), Canary Date Palm *(Phoenix canariensis)* and feathery leaved *Cocos plumosa*, for instance.

The problem lies in getting the seeds to germinate at all — and the vital factor is temperature. The seeds should be kept at a sustained, humid 80°F (27°C) if they are to germinate, though you may get away with 75°F (24°C).

If you have an efficient, heated propagator, this shouldn't be a problem. Even if you haven't, you may still succeed with a bit of improvisation. An airing cupboard can be just the warm, dark spot these seeds need. You may even get away with a snug perch above the boiler or radiator, provided you don't sit the seeds right on top; rest them on a cake stand, or something similar.

Moisture is, of course, another factor. Instead of watering the seeds, which tends to disturb them, the idea is to provide a humid atmosphere by enclosing them. A propagator will have its own top, but putting the seed tray inside a plastic bag will do just as well. Either way, the moisture condenses on to the inner surface and trickles off to keep the mixture moist.

Total darkness isn't vital, although the seeds will be perfectly happy in an airing cupboard until they germinate. But seeds must be shaded from bright sunlight. If this is unavoidable, use a black plastic bag to cover the seeds.

Getting started

The best time to sow is in early spring. Palms need a spongy, well-aerated mixture, so make one up of equal parts peat-based seed compost and coarse-grade Perlite (or coarse sand). A gritty mixture like this will ensure good drainage and speed germination.

Use small peat pots, 1¾in (4½cm) square. This cuts down on the amount of handling the seedlings will have to endure later on, and so increases their chances of surviving.

Make sure you have fresh seeds; the seeds of tropical plants do not keep well. All will benefit from soaking in cold water for a day or two prior to sowing, to help encourage germination. Date stones, from the Date Palm, can be cracked slightly, to allow room for the seedling to push through. Just put them in a vice and squeeze gently.

Sowing step-by-step

1. Fill peat pots with the prepared mixture. There's no need to line them with drainage material because the mixture is so gritty.

Sow the seeds, one to a pot, to three times their depth — about ½-1in (13-25mm) — and cover them with the seed compost. Firm it, and water the pots carefully with a watering can fitted with a fine rose.

Should you come across a sprouting coconut, don't throw it away. Fill a large pot with John Innes No 3 and lay the coconut on top with the three black eyes lying near the compost. Keep warm, moist and humid — and be patient.

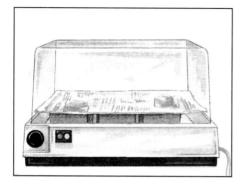

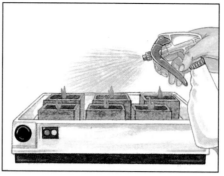

2. Pack the sown pots close together in your propagator, or in a seed tray, as this helps to keep the peat pots moist. Cover them with a propagator dome or enclose the seed tray in a clear polythene bag to retain the moisture.

It's a wise precaution to put a sheet of newspaper over the pots to absorb any condensation. Otherwise, you'll have to wipe condensation off the inside of the top or cover each day, so that the germinating seedlings don't fall victim to fungus or rot.

3. Put a heated propagator in a shady spot, out of bright sunlight. If you are using an unheated seed tray, choose a warm, shaded position where you can achieve a temperature range of between 75-80°F (24-27°C) — such as an airing cupboard.

4. Now forget about them for two weeks. After that it's important to check up on them daily. Open up the dome or plastic cover and lift the newspaper to check on progress. It's after the first couple of weeks that there's a danger of the pots drying out. Keep a mist sprayer handy, and watch for signs that the compost is beginning to shrink away from the edges of the pots. If so, soak the top ½in (13mm) of compost.

Be vigilant. Once germination occurs, and the first grass-like leaves push their way through the compost, the seedlings shoot up very quickly. If left too long at a very high temperature, they will become leggy.

5. With luck, seedlings will emerge within one or two months of sowing — but they may take longer. As soon as they emerge, begin to harden them off, very slowly. Move them into good light, but not bright sunlight. Remove the polythene cover or dome, but be careful to keep them steadily warm — at least 70°F (21°C) to begin with, gradually reducing to normal room temperatures over the next few weeks. Mist them frequently with tepid water to keep them damp, but don't overwater.

6. When the plants have two or three leaves, and have filled their peat pots with roots, pot them on. This may mean waiting for a month or two.

Prepare a peat- or loam-based potting compost by adding a one-third part of coarse-grade Perlite (or coarse sand). Select some plastic pots, 3in (8cm) square, large enough to take the plants, peat pots and all. Put a little of the mixture in the bottom.

Water the peat pots well, so that they are fairly soggy, otherwise the roots may have difficulty in penetrating through them into the fresh mixture. Place them inside the plastic pots, and adjust the level of potting mixture beneath, so that the plants sit at the right level. Fill in all around with mixture, but cover the roots only. Take care to keep the base of the stem above the surface. If this is covered, it may become too wet and start to rot.

7. During this period, when plants are very small and vulnerable to draughts, fluctuating temperatures and pests, keep them close together in a warm place and water them frequently enough, with tepid water, to keep the leaves damp. Again, don't overwater; it's better to keep the potting compost damp and aerated rather than wet and airless.

8. After two years, or so, when the plants are about 12-18in (30-45cm) high and filling their pots with roots, it will be time to pot them on. Mix three parts of John Innes Potting Compost No 2 or No 3 with one part Perlite. Take a 6-8in (15-20cm) pot and pot up the young palm in the usual way, filling in with the mixture and pressing it firmly around the plant. Take care not to break the thicker roots as you go.

9. Parlour Palms and Kentia Palms look best when planted two or three to a pot, so that they quickly create a handsome, feathery clump. Choose a container which will allow you to space the plants 6-8in (15-20cm) apart, and pot them up.

Your palm can now be treated as an established plant. Remember, most palms enjoy light shade — a spot away from bright sunlight. Water only when the surface of the compost looks dry.

Don't be impatient! Palms do take a long time to develop, but this can be to your advantage. Why not plant them up in a bottle garden, or in any spot which will benefit from a plant that won't outgrow its position in a hurry!

Raising ferns from spores

Since ferns are not flowering plants, it follows that they do not produce seed for propagation. Instead, ferns reproduce themselves by means of millions of minute, dust-like spores.

A surprisingly beautiful range of tender ferns may be propagated from these spores to be found in symmetrical rows of roundish or kidney-shaped, brown spore cases — which look like little bumps on the undersides of the fronds. Types of fern that can be grown from these almost invisible specks include the glorious Tree Fern (*Dicksonia antarctica*); a range of Ladder Ferns (*Nephrolepis*); the curious Staghorn Fern (Platycerium); and the Button Fern (*Pellaea rotundifolia*) with its fascinating coin-shaped leaves.

Propagation from spores is not usually recommended for amateur growers, as it takes so much patience and special care. But it is a highly gratifying procedure for anyone who is prepared to wait several months before anything even vaguely resembling a young fern emerges to reward their efforts.

It is best to start with a seedsman's mixture, such as that offered by Dobies, Unwins or Thompson & Morgan.

Technique

🌱 Start with a well scrubbed 4-5in (10-13cm) half pot. Fill with a mixture of equal parts John Innes No 1 and peat, mixed with a quarter part fine perlite. Use fresh, sterilised compost which is free from weeds, seeds, pests and disease — proprietary brands usually are — and firm it gently before sowing.

🌱 Mix the spores with a little very fine sharp sand, and sprinkle this mixture evenly on to the surface of the compost. Then water from below to avoid disturbing the spores. Remove the pot from the water when the compost surface changes colour.

🌱 Put the pot in a propagator or cover with a pane of glass to keep the air moist within , keep it in a warm place at around 70-80°F (21-27°C), and provide plenty of bright filtered light. Make sure that droplets of condensation do not fall on the compost to wet it further. This can be avoided by placing a sheet of newspaper between glass and compost.

1. Mix spores with very fine sand to help you sow them evenly.

2. Continue to keep the pot covered and warm after the prothalli appear.

3. Make sure the fronds are growing strongly before transplanting.

4. When plants are ½-1in (1.3-2.5cm) high, prick them out into a seed tray.

Collecting spores

Spores can easily be gathered for sowing. Cut a ripe frond and place it on a large sheet of paper, covering it with another sheet. Within a week or so, spores will be ejected from the spore cases. Hold your breath and tap the spores into a greaseproof bag. Sown as described here, they will give you thousands of plantlets. Select the strongest and grow them on.

🌱 It is essential to maintain a very warm, moist environment for at least three months — the time most ferns take to develop a prothallus, or a tiny heart-shaped 'leaf', upon which male and female organs develop and then fuse to produce a fern. You have to be patient: nine months can elapse before the fronds develop strongly.

🌱 The moment plants are about ½-1in (13mm-2.5cm) high, prick them out about 2in (5in) apart into a seed tray containing the same growing medium as

5. In about six to eight weeks the tiny ferns will be ready for potting up singly.

you used for the spores. Cover the tray with a pane of glass to retain essential humidity and encourage robust fronds to form. Within six to eight weeks, the tiny ferns will have grown to about 4-6in (10-15cm) high and are ready for potting on singly in 3in (8cm) pots of peat-based potting compost.

Something for

Tropical plants grown from pips or roots are no more difficult to care for than any other kind of houseplant; and because many of these plants have luxuriant, exotic foliage a successfully grown specimen can make a distinctive feature for your living room. It's fun to experiment to discover what you can grow, but you'll need lots of patience, since some of the large stones take up to four months to germinate. Remember, too, that it's very unlikely you'll ever get any edible fruit from your plants.

Always use fresh fruit and vegetables. If the fruit has been processed in any way, by being canned or frozen, the seeds will probably be sterile. Don't worry if you have difficulty getting the pips or roots to germinate; try growing a number at the same time and some of them will sprout. The seedlings will need warmth, water, humidity, bright light, good compost and fertiliser.

PIPS

Many kinds of tropical fruit can be grown from their pips so long as plenty of warmth is provided.

The pips of citrus fruits, including those of grapefruit, oranges, tangerines, limes and lemons, all grow into attractive small trees with glossy green leaves and sweet-smelling white flowers. Some of these pips are sterile

Many unusual and attractive houseplants can be yours for virtually nothing: all you need is a little ingenuity and a lot of patience! Almost every tropical fruit or vegetable that you can buy at your local greengrocer's — avocados, lemons, pineapples, sweet potatoes and many more — can yield pips, stones or roots capable of germinating and growing into a dramatic plant that will thrive in your home.

and won't germinate, but if you grow a number of pips of different types you are bound to get some seedlings.

Plant five or six pips to a 3in (7cm) pot of John Innes Seed Compost. Provide a temperature of 70°F (21°C) until the seedlings are about 3in (7cm) tall, then let the temperature drop a bit. Pot up each seedling into John Innes No 2.

Provide the young plants with good light and plenty of fresh air, and feed them every 14 days during the growing season with a tomato fertiliser. Every two months dissolve some sequestred iron powder (a type of fertiliser that prevents mineral deficiencies) into water and water it into the soil: this prevents lack of iron in the plant, which shows as yellowing between the leaf veins.

Protect your plant from the cold in winter. If you are lucky, after a few years pretty white flowers will appear in summer. You can hand pollinate these

with a small paint brush if you wish — but don't expect the resulting fruit to be fit to eat. The fruit will be small and misshapen due to the plant's restricted root growth, but it will look very pretty!

Coffee

Sow unroasted coffee beans ½in (13mm) deep in moist John Innes Seed Compost, in a temperature of 80-85°F (27-30°C) and in semi-shade. Keep the compost moist until the seeds sprout, then provide good light and less warmth. Pot into John Innes No 3 when the seedlings are large enough to handle.

nothing

The attractive green kiwi fruit is also known as the Chinese Gooseberry and is a vigorous climbing shrub. It has creamy white flowers about 1½in (4cm) across in summer and occasionally, under the right conditions, produces edible fruits. Collect some of the shiny black seeds from fresh fruit and sow them as described earlier.

The pomegranate is a lovely bush with light green leaves and,

in summer, 2in (5cm) scarlet flowers. Sow the dry seeds in spring.

The coffee plant has very handsome glossy, dark green leaves but rarely grows more than about 4ft (1.2m) tall in the home. To grow your own specimen, sow fresh unroasted coffee beans into seed compost. It takes several years before it is mature enough to produce its sweet-smelling, small white flowers which are followed by red berries.

ROOTS

Lots of interesting plants can be grown from roots.

If you keep a sharp eye open at the greengrocer's you can often find fresh ginger with a few pale green growth buds beginning to sprout from the roots — though the shoots don't have to be showing to grow a plant. The ginger plant, which comes from the East Indies, grows up to 3ft (90cm) high with dark green, strap-like leaves. It produces a thick, aromatic root.

To grow your own ginger plant, take a ginger root and plant it about 2-4in (5-10cm) deep in a large 10in (25cm) pot of John Innes No 2. Keep the pot at about 68°F (20°C) while the root is sprouting and in the growing season. Feed your plant every 14 days with liquid fertiliser and keep the compost moist. In winter your plant will die

Growing a pineapple
Some crowns can be reluctant to root, so be prepared to try a couple of times. Slice the top of a pineapple off 1in (2.5cm) down from the crown. Let it dry for two or three days.

Remove the bottom layer of the leaves and plant firmly on top of the compost. Cover it with a clear polythene bag and stand the pot in a light, warm position with a night temperature of no less than 65°F (18°C).

From these raw peanuts you can grow lovely green plants. Just pop them, with their shells on, into a pot of John Innes No 2 and keep them warm and moist.

Sweet Potato

Plant a sweet potato with the narrow end pointing downwards, halfway into John Innes No 2. Keep it moist and warm and long tendrils will grow out of the top. Train the tendrils up a frame of bamboo canes.

Avocado Pear

1 Suspend a cleaned avocado stone over a jar of water so the rounded end just touches the water.
2 Roots and a shoot should appear.
3 Plant two thirds into John Innes No 1 and keep warm and moist.

Date

Roughen the date stones with sandpaper. Sow the stones in John Innes Seed Compost, keep them moist and very warm.

A mature date palm is an attractive houseplant.

down and you should keep it cooler, about 45°F (7°C) and rather drier; let the compost dry out on the surface before watering again. In spring you can divide your plant to make two plants or simply let it stay as one large plant.

The sweet potato is a type of Bindweed related to Morning Glory. It looks like a large, elongated, fairly smooth-skinned potato with a red or yellowish skin. Plant one in John Innes No 2 in a pot about 10in (25cm) wide with the narrow end of the tuber pointing down. Eventually long tendrils will emerge which you can stake.

A yam root will produce a dramatic large plant with huge leaves. The root has a skin that looks a little like tree bark. It needs a very big container so its roots can spread. Give your yam plenty of light and keep it cool during winter. When the plant gets too big, just cut the tuber in half — you can plant one end and eat the other!

STONES

Some fruit stones, such as those of the avocado, mango, lychee, date and coconut, can be grown into attractive plants. Always carefully wash the stone and remove all fruit before planting.

Almost everyone has had a go at growing an avocado stone, though with varying degrees of success. Properly grown, an avocado is a lovely plant which, in its native habitat of the West Indies, grows to 60ft (18m), but luckily it won't reach anything like that at home!

An avocado has large, elongated oval, dark green leaves on a tall, slim plant. Use a firm, ripe stone (if the brown skin sticks stubbornly to the fruit the stone is not mature enough). You can either suspend the stone over a jar of water, using matchsticks to hold it upright with the base just touching the water surface, or plant the stone in a 3in (7cm) pot of John Innes No 1, leaving one third of the stone above the surface. Give it a temperature of 70°F (21°C). Once it germinates pot your avocado up into a 7in (18cm) pot of John Innes No 2.

When your plant is 8-10in (20-25cm) high, cut off the top 2in (5cm); this will encourage it to make branches. Prune your avocado back in this way whenever the stems get too leggy and you will encourage a nice, bushy shape.

A mango has a flat, oval, almost bearded stone that can be persuaded to sprout in time. It will grow into a dark green, large-leafed tree but it needs a lot of humidity to do well. As with all tropical plants, if the leaves turn brown at the edges it is a sign of dry air or overwatering, so watch out for this and act accordingly.

The lychee is an evergreen tree with attractive long, hanging leaves; it is a native of Southern China. Use seeds taken from the fresh fruit; they are about 1in (25mm) long, hard, black and oval shaped. They take a while to germinate.

Sometimes you can be lucky enough to find a coconut that is sprouting; this can grow eventually into a large and handsome palm tree. Put the coconut into a large pot of John Innes No 3 and lay it on its side, so that the three black 'eyes' are lying near the compost. Provide light, heat and humidity.

Date stones require more patience than most as even after sprouting they can take up to two years before they produce a leaf that even looks like a palm! Until then they have just a narrow green spike. Eventually a date palm will grow to 5-6ft (1.5-1.8m).

Wash the stones, then lightly sandpaper or file them to help moisture get in and the stone to germinate, which can take months.

An alternative method is to put the stones together in a polythene bag of moist peat, seal it tightly and leave them in a warm, dark airing cupboard. Look at them after about six weeks to check for signs of growth. As soon as any start to sprout, pot them up in John Innes Seed Compost. Keep them moist and at a temperature of 60°F (15°C).

NUTS

All sorts of nuts can be grown into plants but the most successful are fresh peanuts. They are very easy to grow in a warm and sunny position. Sow them still in their shells in John Innes No 2 in a 3in (7cm) pot. Give them a temperature of around 80°F (27°C) to germinate; then keep them on a warm, sunny window. When the pot is full of roots, pot each plant singly into a 10in (25cm) pot. Keep the compost moist and mist spray the foliage every day in warm weather. As your plant grows, long green shoots will appear from the yellow blooms; these will bend over and disappear and burrow into the compost where they will start to form peanuts below the compost surface. You can harvest your peanuts at the end of the growing season.

Citrus

You can grow either orange or lemon trees from pips. Plant a few fresh pips in moist John Innes Compost and keep them warm. Give young seedlings good light and feed every two weeks until they are about 3in tall. Pot them on individually into 3in (7cm) pots of John Innes No 2.

Help your citrus produce fruit by brushing the pollen from one flower to the next.

Growing plants from seed

Don't be taken in by the mass of small, brightly coloured plants produced by nurserymen for summer bedding displays and put on sale in garden centres during spring.

All too often these plants, and also small vegetables and herbs, are put on sale too soon when it is still not warm enough for them to be planted outside. Moreover, they are probably only in flower so early in the season because they have been started off early in artificial conditions and have been forced on into the flowering stage to make them more attractive. They will have finished flowering by early summer and all you will be left with in July and August are blank, empty spaces which you won't find at all easy to fill.

If you have the time and the right facilities it is much better to start off your own plants from seed. This way you can make sure that they won't die of cold when they are planted out and that they are grown slowly and don't become weak from forcing. You will also be able to choose your own varieties and colours.

When to sow

Most seeds are sown in spring, between March and May, depending on how much space you have in which to bring up the seedlings after germination. Half-hardy annuals shouldn't be planted outside until late May or early June so if you do sow them in March you will need plenty of space, warmth and light to keep them healthy and growing well for about six weeks.

Sowing in March does produce the earliest-flowering plants, but if you sow in May and plant out in June your plants should start to flower in late July and continue right through to September, and you won't have to set up artificial conditions to start them off.

Hardy annuals and vegetables, and the hardy herbs don't need artificial warmth and so can be sown outside in March without any problem, unless it is unseasonably cold.

Where to sow

Annuals, some vegetables and some herbs are usually sown where they will eventually grow, and then thinned after germination, but this is not really practical for small-space gardening. Among the disadvantages are the fact that potential planting spots on the patio are often awkward to get at, and also slugs and snails can present a problem. You can put down slug bait, but then you will have the continual problem of trying to keep away children and pets.

So when starting off plants for the patio it is better to sow seeds in small 2in (5cm) diameter pots or cellular propagating trays in a propagator or on a window-sill so that you can give individual care to each seedling and so that they can grow into small plants before being put into their flowering containers.

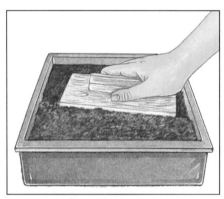

How to sow. Fill seed tray and press compost gently down with a wooden firmer.

Cover seed tray with some glass and a plastic sheet to keep compost moist.

There are several types of pots you can use, such as plastic pots, peat pots (these are especially good as you don't have to transplant the seedling but can just plant the pot), yoghurt cartons, Jiffy 7s (compressed dry discs of peat bound in a fine nylon netting, which expand to 1½in (4cm) when wet), and soil blocks, which you can make yourself with a special tool obtainable from garden centres.

Alternatively, you can use seed trays, full, half or quarter size, or cellular trays which come in many sizes with square or circular cells.

Preparing the compost

Composts for sowing seed can be obtained ready-mixed, the peat-based ones being especially good. If the seedlings are to be grown on for several weeks, use a potting compost instead, as this contains more nutri-

Sprinkle seeds over compost as gently and evenly as possible.

When seedlings have grown two small leaves transplant them into pots.

ent, but take out the larger lumps of peat before sowing.

How to sow seeds

Fill containers to within 1/2in (1.5cm) of the rim, pressing the compost gently down. Sow seeds thinly and evenly; it is wasteful to sow thickly and can lead to weak, leggy seedlings. It is easy to space out the larger seeds, but some, such as Begonia and Tobacco Plant seeds, are almost dustlike; try mixing these with a little silver sand to make even sowing an easier job.

Fine seed doesn't need to be covered with compost, but just firmed down gently with a 'firmer' (a flat-surfaced piece of wood will do). Larger seeds should be covered with a fine layer of sieved compost, also firmed gently into place.

Then moisten it either by watering from the top or by standing the container in a shallow tray of water and allowing the water to soak up through the compost. The latter method is preferable as it makes sure that the base of the compost really has been watered and the compost shouldn't need watering again until after germination. However, if you do have to water, use a light spray so that the seeds are not washed in too deep, or all to one side. Then cover seed trays with glass and a plastic sheet to keep the compost moist, and put in the dark.

Germination. For successful germination plants must have moisture, food and oxygen, and many need warmth as well. Temperatures of 60°F (16-18°C) are necessary for tender and half-hardy plants. Most home temperatures are of this level or even higher during the day, but if you are in a place where they tend to drop at night you can keep your seeds warm by keeping them in an airing cupboard. A special propagator, with an electric base plate and a rigid PVC lid to keep them warm and moist is also ideal. For more information on growing seeds in a propagator see page 602.

Proprietary seed composts will contain nutrient and be structured in such a way so that air is always present unless they become waterlogged. You can make sure that the seeds have moisture by watering before sowing and by covering them with glass and a black plastic sheet.

Pick and choose

Pansies, *above left,* vegetables such as marrow, *left,* and Lobelias and Petunias, *above,* can all be grown from seed.

Where gardening space is at a premium, as it usually is on a patio, plants that are easy to grow from seed include: hardy and half-hardy annuals, vegetables, herbs and biennials. You can, in fact, raise most plants from seed, but shrubs and trees can take a long time to germinate and are usually too large, even for a terrace or patio. Suitable plants include:
Hardy annuals – Aster, Candytuft, Chrysanthemum (annual), Clarkia, Cornflower, Echium, Godetia, Larkspur, Limnanthes, Love-in-a-mist, Mallow, Mignonette, Nasturtium, Pansy, Poppy (Iceland and Shirley), Pot Marigold (Calendula), Sweet Pea.
Half-hardy annuals – Ageratum, Begonia, Busy Lizzie (dwarf variety), Love-lies-bleeding (Amaranthus), Marigold (French and African), Nemesia, Petunia, Stocks, Tobacco Plants.
Biennials – Canterbury Bells, Foxglove, Honesty, Sweet William, Wallflower. Strictly speaking these plants should be put into a nursery bed, but as they don't eventually grow into large solid plants you can put them straight into their flowering containers.
Herbs – Basil (half-hardy), Borage, Caraway (biennial), Chervil, Chives, Coriander, Dill, Fennel, Lemon Balm, Lovage, Parsley, Savory, Sorrel (French), Sweet Marjoram (half-hardy).
Vegetables – Beans (all types), Beetroot, Carrots, Cucumber, Fennel, Lettuce, Marrow, Peas, Radishes, Spinach, Tomatoes, Turnips.

Germination can take from four days to more than three weeks, depending on the plant and freshness of seed, so keep an eye on your pots from day four, and remove the plastic sheet as soon as the first seedlings appear. Put them in a light place, but take care to shield them in periods of strong, hot sun.

Looking after seedlings

When your seedlings have grown two seed leaves and one tiny true leaf, either transplant each seedling with its roots intact from the seed tray into 2in (5cm) pots or another tray of potting compost, 2in (5cm) apart each way. Always handle seedlings by their leaves – never by their stems.

Keep your seedlings watered, and protect the outdoor ones from cold by bringing them inside if necessary.

The half-hardy seedlings may outgrow their 2in (5cm) diameter pots before it is safe to plant them outside. If so, transplant them into 3 1/2in (9cm) diameter pots.

Seedlings raised inside will need hardening off before being planted outside. So about a week before planting, introduce your seedlings to outdoor life by putting them on a window-sill, balcony or patio during the day and just before planting, leave them out at night protected by newspaper or a plastic sheet.

When seedlings have become well established in their seed trays or their roots have filled the pots it is time to plant them on into their final pots, boxes and tubs. And you can sit back and look forward to a fine summer display at a fraction of the cost of ready-bought seedlings.

Divide and multiply

Increasing your stock of plants by propagation can produce an arresting mass display.

Raising sturdy plants from cuttings or offsets is a stimulating and challenging part of patio gardening. You can accumulate more of your favourite plants and build up a reserve that you can swap with coveted specimens on your neighbour's patio.

Propagation – by soft or semi-ripe cuttings taken in early spring or summer; by hardwood cuttings struck in autumn; by root cuttings taken during the autumn and winter; by offsets removed in autumn or spring; by layering in late spring or summer – is easy provided you follow the rules.

Softwood cuttings

These are soft young shoots that root easily in a mixture of equal parts peat and sharp sand in a propagator at a temperature of 61°F (16°C).

Chrysanthemums are usually propagated by this type of cutting as are many other border plants, such as Anchusa, Delphinium, Anthemis, Lupin, and Scabious.

Cuttings should be 2½-3in (6–8cm) long, with the lower leaves trimmed off and the stem cut cleanly just under the lowest leaf-joint. Dip the cut ends in a rooting hormone powder and insert them 1-1½in (2.5-3cm) deep in the compost, 2in (5cm) apart and about ½in (12mm) in from the edge of a 3-4in (8-10cm) diameter pot. Keep them shaded from bright sunshine and they should root within three weeks.

Take Delphinium cuttings from the base of the plant, making sure that they are solid at the bottom as hollow-stemmed shoots won't root. The same advice applies to Lupins.

Rock plants such as Sedum, Thyme and Alpine Phlox may also be increased in this way. Similarly Dahlias can be propagated from shoots 'nicked' out from the parent tuber.

Semi-ripe cuttings

These are shoots with soft tips that are starting to harden at the base. They should be taken in late July and August, and many shrubs, such as Forsythia, Buddleia, Broom, Caryopteris, Clematis, Cornus, Ilex, Choisya, Potentilla, Viburnum and Weigela are increased in this way.

The best method is to take 'heeled' cuttings. These are side shoots tugged from the main stem with a small piece of older wood attached. The torn edges of the detached portion should be trimmed to within 1/8in (3mm) of the base. Remove the lower leaves, dip the cutting in rooting compound and insert it into a firmed mixture of equal parts peat and sharp sand.

Semi-ripe cuttings can be rooted outdoors in a lightly shaded frame. No artificial heat is necessary. If you have taken lots of cuttings prepare a bed of the rooting mixture in a strip across a sheltered patch and cover with a frame or cloche. Keep your cuttings healthy with regular watering, and protect from hot sun.

Roots should start to form within a month and you can then transfer the

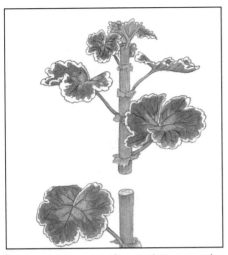

Border plants such as Chrysanthemums and Delphiniums are easy to propagate from softwood cuttings.

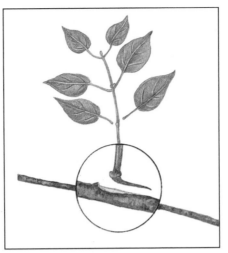

Late summer is the time to think of taking semi-ripe cuttings of shrubs such as Viburnum and Forsythia to root outdoors.

Roses, blackcurrants and gooseberries can be propagated from hardwood cuttings in late October or early November.

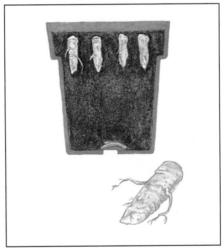

Root cuttings are an excellent way of increasing your stock of thick-rooted plants such as Peonies and Globe Thistle.

Shrubs and climbers such as Clematis and Honeysuckle can be increased by layering. Layered shrubs usually flower within two years of being planted out.

young plants to a nursery bed in a protected part of the garden for the winter. If bad weather threatens, cover with cloches.

Hardwood cuttings

Most shrubs, including Roses and fruits such as blackcurrants, gooseberries and red and white currants can be raised from woody cuttings in late October when leaves have fallen and growth is dormant.

Choose pencil-thick shoots, 9-12in (23-30cm) long, and cut them cleanly below the lowest joint and above the highest bud. The top cut should slope gently up in the direction in which the bud is pointing. When taking cuttings from gooseberries, and red and white currants remove all but the top three buds to create a short stem.

Insert cuttings to half their depth, 6in (15cm) apart, in a slit trench dug in a sheltered, well-drained part of the garden. Line the base of the trench with sharp sand. Make sure you push the cuttings well down into the sand as this will irritate the tissues and initiate rooting.

By winter a thick callous will have formed at the base of the cutting and roots will form in the following spring. Leave the cuttings to grow in the summer and move them to a nursery bed in the autumn.

Root cuttings

Many herbaceous plants are raised by root-cuttings. Thicker rooted plants such as Verbascum, Anchusa, Poppies, Statice and Cupid's Dart (Catananche) are prepared by sectioning roots into 2-4in (5-10cm) long pieces.

Insert the cuttings vertically, 1-2in (2.5-5cm) apart, in 3-5in (8-13cm) diameter pots of gritty compost, so that their tips are just below the surface of the compost and covered with it. Put the cuttings in a cold frame. New roots will form and young shoots will appear in the spring.

Border Phlox (Phlox paniculata) and Primulas are also raised from root cuttings. However, these have string-like roots, thinner than cuttings from fleshy and woody plants, and should be placed horizontally in pots and covered with a 1/2in (1cm) layer of compost. Root cuttings should be taken in the autumn and strong new plants will appear in the spring.

Division

Border perennials and alpines are normally increased by division. This should be done in autumn, when flower stems are dying back to the crown, or in early spring before new shoots are more than 2-3in (5-8cm) long.

Clump-forming plants can easily be divided into well-rooted portions by inserting two garden forks, back to back, and levering the clump apart. Michaelmas Daisies, Dicentra, Geraniums and Chrysanthemums can all be propagated in this way.

Alternatively, if the clump is small prise away soil from the fringe, cut off shoots with roots and plant them out in well-prepared soil.

Bulbs such as Daffodils, Crocosmias and Crocuses are also increased by division when the leaves have died back and the plant is resting. Daffodil offsets – the tiny bulbs that form at the side of the parent plant – are best pulled away and planted in a nursery bed, where they should be left to grow to flowering size before being put in their final positions.

Layering

A sizeable plant can be produced by pegging down and rooting a branch while it is still attached to the parent plant. Shrubs and climbers such as Clematis, Wisteria, Honeysuckle and Jasmine can easily be propagated by layers. July and August are the best months for doing this.

Select a thin young shoot close to the ground. Make a 1/2-1in (1-2.5cm) sloping cut into the shoot, but make sure you don't weaken it too much. Wedge open the cut with a sharp stone or some sharp sand and sprinkle the wound with hormone rooting compound.

Prepare the ground by adding a mixture of Perlite, or sharp sand and peat in equal parts, and peg the shoot down. Pieces of heavy wire bent to form hooks make ideal pegs. These should be at least 9-12in (23-30cm) long – it is vital that the layer doesn't become dislodged from its position.

Tie the tip of the shoot to a vertical cane to ensure a shapely plant. Roots should form within six to twelve months, when the layer can be removed from the parent plant and planted in its flowering postion.

You can create a mass display of Lupins from softwood cuttings.

This attractive Forsythia 'Minigold' was rooted from a semi-ripe cutting outdoors.

A patch of cultivated Blackberries is easily grown from hardwood cuttings.

These beautiful *Phlox paniculata* can be propagated by root cuttings.

Wisteria sinensis is a suitable climber for layering.

Know your enemy

Have you ever wondered why your Poinsettia seems to suffer from flying dandruff, why your Busy Lizzie feels sticky, or why your Joseph's Coat looks decidedly shabby? The answer is probably that some nasty pest and all its relatives are feasting on your beloved plant. Don't ignore signs that all is not well; if these pests are not dealt with promptly, drastic remedies may eventually be necessary.

Your immediate response should be to identify the pest so you know how to deal with it effectively. But prevention is better than cure, so it is only sensible to inspect your houseplant regularly for pests, checking for the first signs of trouble, and to give preventative sprays of insecticide two or three times a year.

When pests are just beginning to trouble your plant you can usually wipe them off with your fingers or wash them off with a sponge and a drop or two of washing up liquid in a bucket of tepid water. For more severe trouble and also as a preventative, use chemicals. Generally these come as liquids, or as dry powder which dissolves in water. There are lots of brands formulated for different pests. Usually a good all-purpose pesticide suffices, but sometimes a particular active ingredient is called for, so look for a product containing that specific chemical. For more information on pesticides see Volume 11.

ALWAYS READ THE CHEMICAL MANUFACTURERS' INSTRUCTIONS BEFORE USING ANY PESTICIDE. PAY PARTICULAR ATTENTION TO CHILDREN, PETS, WILDLIFE AND FOODSTUFFS WHICH SHOULD BE KEPT WELL AWAY FROM THE CHEMICALS AND ANY TREATMENT.

Thrips

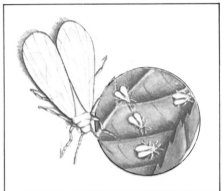

Thrips fortunately only attack a few plants. They cause most damage to the flowers of plants such as Cyclamen by streaking and spotting the petals. Look for tiny, long black insects nestling among the flower petals.

Control by spraying with a pesticide containing permethrin, pyrethrum, derris or malathion and repeat if necessary.

Whitefly

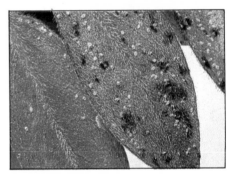

You know your plant has got whitefly if a cloud of tiny flying insects rises from the plant when the leaves are disturbed. They can be a real nuisance and a problem to control. Whitefly thrive in warm, dry conditions but they can still be a problem in the cold — the only difference is that their life cycle takes longer. The flies leave behind eggs and larvae on the undersides of the leaves. The larvae don't cause serious damage, but the presence of the adults, and the fact that the larvae can clearly be seen as tiny, white oval 'scales' that excrete 'honeydew' and encourage sooty mould, makes them a real nuisance. Eventually, masses of larval scales will make the leaves mottle and the plant lose its vigour.

To control whitefly you have to commit yourself to a concerted campaign for up to six weeks. Spray the plant twice a week with permethrin, pyrethrum or malathion.

Aphid

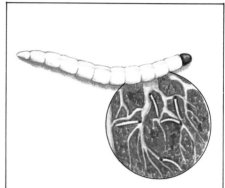

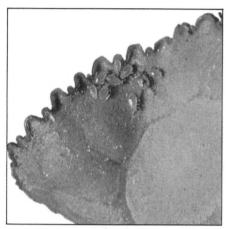

Aphid is the blanket term for the different kinds of black, yellow, pink and greenfly. They all breed prolifically and hundreds can appear almost overnight. They are winged or wingless depending on maturity. Once aphids start to multiply your plant can be severely damaged very quickly. They attack new growth by stabbing a pointed feeding tube into the young cells and sucking out the plant juices. This makes new growth curl with damage until it's severely deformed. The plant may take several weeks to recover.

Aphids also excrete the sticky substance known as honeydew. This drops down onto the lower leaves leaving a sugary deposit. After a short time a fungus called sooty mould may develop and disfigure your plant even more.

A small attack of aphids can be easily rinsed off with tepid water, otherwise spray with permethrin, pyrethrum or malathion once a week for three weeks.

Remove honeydew and sooty mould by lightly sponging the leaves with tepid water containing a few drops of washing-up liquid.

Mealy bug

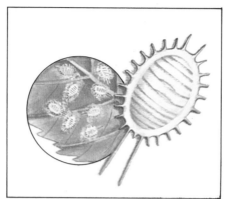

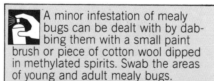

An adult mealy bug looks rather like a flattened wood louse with a white powdery coating that acts as a protective covering. The first sign of mealy bug is little white cotton-wool blobs at the leaf joints and under the leaves near the veins. This is the protective home for the young mealy bugs. When the infestation is really bad they are found in large numbers on young growth, and the damage they cause can be quite severe.

Root mealy bugs are not quite as active, but they are just as destructive. If your plant's growth seems stunted, suspect root mealy bugs at work. Remove the plant carefully from its pot, and look for the bugs clustering around the roots, particularly at the base of the root ball.

A minor infestation of mealy bugs can be dealt with by dabbing them with a small paint brush or piece of cotton wool dipped in methylated spirits. Swab the areas of young and adult mealy bugs.

Treat serious attacks of mealy bug with a spray of malathion or dimethoate, which is a systemic insecticide.

Control root mealy bugs by watering or dipping the root ball into a solution of malathion. For complete control repeat the treatment two or three times at 10-14 day intervals.

Fungus gnat

Also called scarid fly; these are not a major problem but they can be a considerable nuisance and damage the roots of plants grown in peat compost. They thrive in warm, moist, humid conditions and can increase to almost plague proportions. The gnats look like tiny mosquitoes and live in the surface compost where they eat dead and decaying matter. They only become obvious when the compost is disturbed and the adults fly up — but it's the small, maggot-like larvae that cause damage. They eat plant roots and succulent stems at, and just below, soil level.

To control them you have to carry out a two-pronged attack. The adults can be effectively dispatched with a spray of permethrin, pyrethrum or malathion. Then, deal with the larvae by watering a solution of malathion into the compost. Give two or three treatments at seven to ten day intervals.

Red spider mite

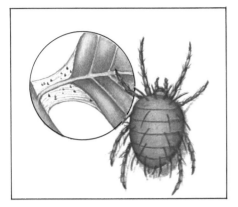

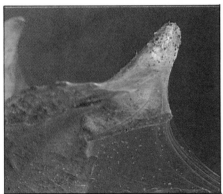

These are one of the most difficult pests to see and one of the most tricky to eradicate. The minute mites are almost invisible to the naked eye and live on the underside of leaves, biting and tearing the leaf tissue. In severe attacks the adult mites are visible as pale, straw-coloured creatures, several of which could fit on a pin head. The mite only turns red when temperatures drop and it prepares to hibernate, but it rarely does this indoors. The damage done to the leaves by the mite causes a distinct loss of green pigment and a dull, yellowish, mottled appearance.

Severe attacks occur when the air is warm and dry, making the leaves curl and turn brown at the edges and then progressively all over. When the damage is this severe the underside of leaves and new shoots show the minute webs.

Discourage red spider mite by regularly misting the foliage — particularly the undersides — with water, but this doesn't kill the mites totally. To kill them you have to use an insecticide such as derris, malathion or dimethoate applied regularly at seven to ten day intervals for about a month in order to catch all stages of the pest.

Scale insect

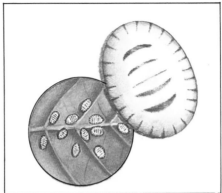

Scale insects are an unusual-looking plant pest. They look like tiny, dark brown blisters or warts on the stems and leaves, and are generally to be found on the underside of the leaves, clustering close to the veins. These blisters are really egg cases; the eggs hatch out inside the case, which then serves as an incubator for the young scale insects and protects them from attack by other insects and chemicals.

The young scale insect is tiny, flat and a pale straw colour, almost to the point of being transparent. When it crawls out of the protective blister, the young scale insect searches for its own feeding position; each one attaches itself to the surface of a stem or leaf and starts to excrete honeydew and consume the plant's fluids.

As scale becomes severe, new growth is deformed and young shoots may be killed off completely. The growth of sooty mould on the honeydew excretion can also become a major problem in bad infestations.

Scale insects are difficult to control, especially as the eggs and very young are protected by the egg case. Deal with it in two ways: firstly, scrape off visible scales with a fingernail or nail file, then spray three times with malathion or dimethoate at 10-14 day intervals.

Slugs and snails

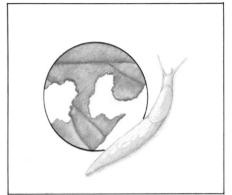

The types of slug or snail that attack houseplants are very different from the garden kind; they are quite tiny and hide during the day in any little crevice they can find, only coming out for a nocturnal feast. They cause severe damage in localised areas where they eat large chunks of leaf. If you can't find the culprit in the pot, look for the tiny tell-tale silvery streaks of slime that slugs and snails leave behind.

Slugs and snails are easily dealt with by a light sprinkling of metaldehyde pellets on the compost surface. The slug or snail will then be poisoned when it eats the pellets.

What's wrong

KEY
- Symptom
- Cause
- Cure

However hard you try, at some point you are bound to have a houseplant that will, completely out of the blue, wilt, drop its leaves or be attacked by nasty mites or bugs. But don't despair — just identify what's wrong with your plant by checking the picture below; look for your problem, see what the cause is and then you can follow our recommended cure. If you catch the trouble quickly you will be able to stop the problem spreading and help your plant recover fast.

NO FLOWERS
- **Lots of leaves and no flowers.**
- Too much fertiliser.
- Stop feeding for six weeks and then only feed in the growing season.

- **Buds shrivel.**
- The air is too dry.
- Provide humidity by regular spraying.

- **Falling flower buds and leaves.**
- Due to warm, dry air.
- Spray regularly and stand the plant on a tray of moist pebbles.

WILTING PLANT
- **The leaves on a plant kept on a windowsill turn yellow.**
- Frost damage.
- Move the plant inside the room where protected by curtains at night.

- **Unnaturally deep green leaves. Old and new leaves turn yellow and drop off.**
- Too much water.
- Water less often and in less quantity.

DAMAGED LEAVES
- **Bronzy mottled leaves and webs at leaf joints.**
- Red spider mite.
- Spray with insecticide and mist spray regularly.

- **Leaves creamy yellow and poor, stunted growth.**
- Lack of nitrogen.
- Regular feeds with high nitrogen fertiliser.

- **Holes in the leaves.**
- Slug, snail, caterpillar or insect damage.
- Spray with a good all-purpose insecticide.

DISEASE
- **Grey 'fur' at leaf joints and stems which then spreads to entire plant.**
- Grey mould.
- Pick off affected parts, spray with benomyl, improve air circulation and don't crowd your plants.

WILTING PLANT
- **The leaves turn yellow.**
- Plant has been sitting in a draught.
- Move it to a more sheltered position.

NO GROWTH
- **Tight mass of roots and little compost.**
- Plant is pot-bound.
- Repot.

STUNTED, DISTORTED GROWTH
- **Masses of fleshy, bright green insects clustering on new growth.**
- Greenfly are sucking the sap and distorting the leaves.
- Spray with insecticide.

- **Clouds of white, moth-like insects rise when the plant is disturbed.**
- Whitefly.
- Spray with insecticide.

with my plant

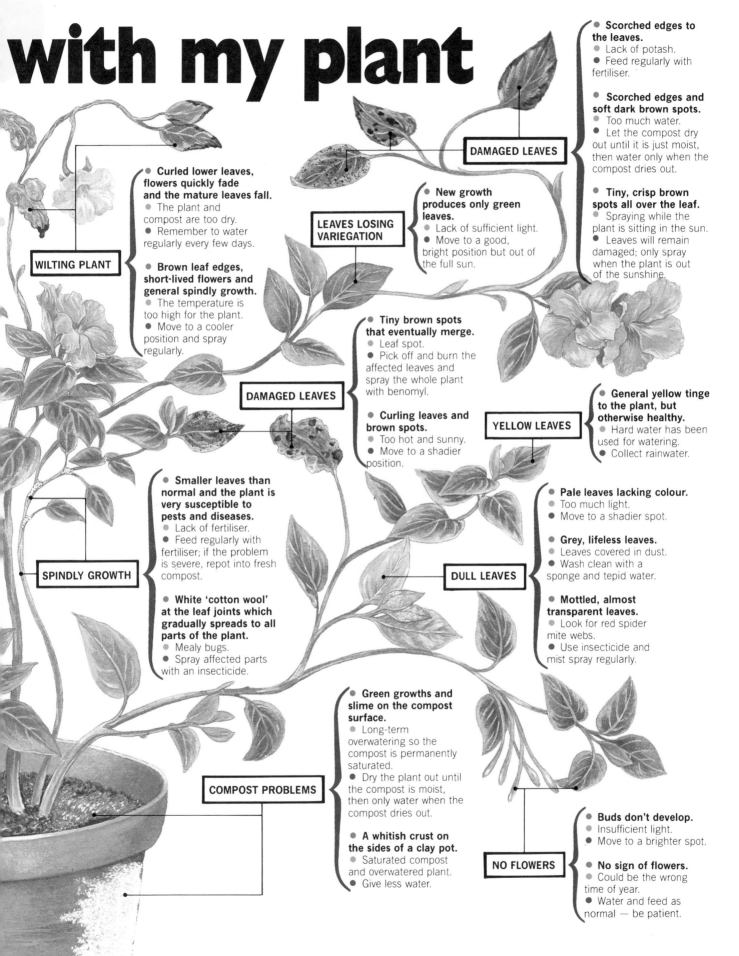

- **Scorched edges to the leaves.**
- Lack of potash.
- Feed regularly with fertiliser.

- **Scorched edges and soft dark brown spots.**
- Too much water.
- Let the compost dry out until it is just moist, then water only when the compost dries out.

- **Tiny, crisp brown spots all over the leaf.**
- Spraying while the plant is sitting in the sun.
- Leaves will remain damaged; only spray when the plant is out of the sunshine.

DAMAGED LEAVES

- **Curled lower leaves, flowers quickly fade and the mature leaves fall.**
- The plant and compost are too dry.
- Remember to water regularly every few days.

- **Brown leaf edges, short-lived flowers and general spindly growth.**
- The temperature is too high for the plant.
- Move to a cooler position and spray regularly.

WILTING PLANT

- **New growth produces only green leaves.**
- Lack of sufficient light.
- Move to a good, bright position but out of the full sun.

LEAVES LOSING VARIEGATION

- **Tiny brown spots that eventually merge.**
- Leaf spot.
- Pick off and burn the affected leaves and spray the whole plant with benomyl.

- **Curling leaves and brown spots.**
- Too hot and sunny.
- Move to a shadier position.

DAMAGED LEAVES

- **General yellow tinge to the plant, but otherwise healthy.**
- Hard water has been used for watering.
- Collect rainwater.

YELLOW LEAVES

- **Smaller leaves than normal and the plant is very susceptible to pests and diseases.**
- Lack of fertiliser.
- Feed regularly with fertiliser; if the problem is severe, repot into fresh compost.

- **White 'cotton wool' at the leaf joints which gradually spreads to all parts of the plant.**
- Mealy bugs.
- Spray affected parts with an insecticide.

SPINDLY GROWTH

- **Pale leaves lacking colour.**
- Too much light.
- Move to a shadier spot.

- **Grey, lifeless leaves.**
- Leaves covered in dust.
- Wash clean with a sponge and tepid water.

- **Mottled, almost transparent leaves.**
- Look for red spider mite webs.
- Use insecticide and mist spray regularly.

DULL LEAVES

- **Green growths and slime on the compost surface.**
- Long-term overwatering so the compost is permanently saturated.
- Dry the plant out until the compost is moist, then only water when the compost dries out.

- **A whitish crust on the sides of a clay pot.**
- Saturated compost and overwatered plant.
- Give less water.

COMPOST PROBLEMS

- **Buds don't develop.**
- Insufficient light.
- Move to a brighter spot.

- **No sign of flowers.**
- Could be the wrong time of year.
- Water and feed as normal — be patient.

NO FLOWERS

247

First aid

Healthy plants — like healthy people — tend to shrug off disease. But if you detect any sign of disease on your houseplants you should move to the rescue quickly, before the trouble spreads to the rest of the plant or to other plants near by.

The problem with an ailing houseplant is that it's difficult to tell at first whether it is suffering from an illness, or whether it is just weak and listless and very unhappy about the conditions in which you are growing it.

If you are worried about the health of any particular plant, ask yourself whether the plant is getting too much light or warmth, or too little of either. Is the plant waterlogged — or perhaps completely dried out? Is it sitting in a draught?

A plant sitting in the wrong environment for it won't be completely healthy, and will therefore be much more susceptible to disease. And, once it has succumbed, it will go downhill rapidly. Act quickly, both by improving the plant's surroundings and by giving it the appropriate treatment for the disease.

All the chemicals we recommend are available from good gardening shops and garden centres. The chemical ingredients of each product are clearly set out on the packet — read the instructions before you buy to check whether the manufacturer warns you not to use the product on certain plants.

TAKE GREAT CARE WHEN YOU ARE USING ANY CHEMICAL TO KEEP IT WELL AWAY FROM CHILDREN, PETS AND FOOD. READ THE MANUFACTURER'S RECOMMENDATIONS CAREFULLY, AND MAKE SURE THE TREATMENT IS SUITABLE FOR YOUR PARTICULAR PLANT.

Leaf spot

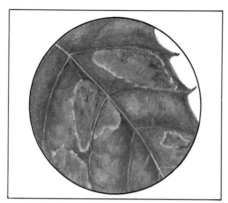

Bacterial spots are rather uncommon and not easy to recognise; they sometimes have a translucent margin and they may occasionally ooze little globules of bacteria. You might find them on Ivies; if so, it's important to remove all the infected leaves.

Fungal spots vary from tiny spots to large patches spreading all over the leaf (the Rubber Plant sometimes suffers from this). The entire leaf may turn yellow and then brown as the cells are destroyed.

To control bacterial leaf spot, spray the plant regularly with a liquid copper fungicide. You can treat fungal leaf spot with a fungicide containing benomyl, such as Benlate, and products containing copper. Remove the affected leaves and burn them. However, by the time you have noticed the spots the fungal spores may already have been released and it may be too late to save your plant.

Root & stem rot

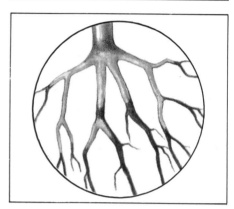

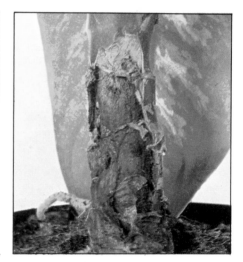

If your pot plants are kept too dank and wet, organisms that live on decaying matter may suddenly attack.

Most houseplants don't like their roots being constantly wet — except for Ferns and Azaleas, which should always be moist. You should suspect that fungal organisms are attacking the root or stem of your plant if the leaves turn yellow, wither and fall off prematurely. Rotting roots are easy to pull apart (healthy roots are usually white and brittle). The stems may also be turning black, and becoming soft.

Watering with a chemical such as benomyl may help if the affected plant is treated early enough. But if the treatment is too long delayed your plant may be beyond saving. To avoid root and stem rot, make sure your plants don't become waterlogged, particularly in cold weather. When watering a plant by placing the pot in water, don't let it sit there longer than 15-20 minutes.

Damping off

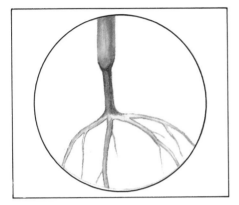

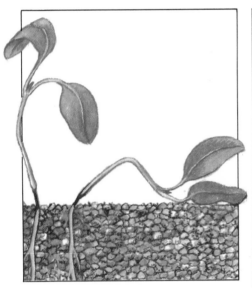

Damping off is a fungal disease caught by seedlings and cuttings. Suddenly, without warning, what you thought was a perfectly healthy cutting or seedling may topple over and die. If you pull the victim up you will see that the base of the stem has withered and gone completely black.

The problem is caused by a minute fungus living in a dirty pot or tray, or possibly in unsterilised or contaminated compost. It might even have come from the water you have been using.

Whatever the cause, there is nothing you can do to save the affected cutting or seedling. Pull it out and throw it away — if possible, burn it. To save the rest of the cuttings or seedlings spray them all immediately with a liquid copper fungicide, or Cheshunt Compound (a fungicide powder that you dissolve in water and spray on to your seedlings).

Mildew

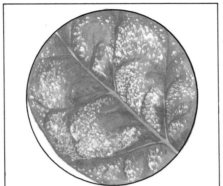

Powdery mildew is a disease that shows up as a fine white powdery dust mainly on leaves but sometimes also on the flowers. It doesn't have fluffy growths like grey mould but it can stop the plant growing healthily. There is also a less common kind of mildew called downy mildew, which has spore-bearing bodies that are easier to see.

Spray the infected plant with a fungicide containing benomyl or triforine at two or three week intervals during the season when the plant is very dry and the fungus is particularly active. You can prevent mildew by dusting the plant lightly with flowers of sulphur every 10 or 14 days — but check the label to see that sulphur won't cause any damage to your plant.

Grey mould

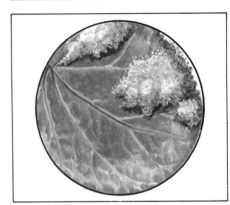

Grey mould, or Botrytis, is a particularly nasty disease that attacks fleshy plants such as African Violet, Cyclamen, Begonia and Gloxinia when they are kept too damp.

The fungus looks greyish-brown and is rather fluffy. It normally starts by infecting pieces of dead and decaying plant tissue, such as old leaves and withering flowers, and when it has used up that source of food it then attacks healthy living tissue.

Grey mould is dangerous and must be treated urgently as soon as you notice it.

First cut away all withering or damaged leaves and dying flowers using a clean sharp knife or tweezers. Don't leave any jagged or broken stems behind; try to remove dead flowers and leaf stalks cleanly, as near to the base of the plant as possible. Make sure that the plant isn't waterlogged and that it has enough fresh air. To prevent the problem occurring again, spray the plant with a fungicide containing benomyl.

The first thing to look out for is the *position* of a sick plant. The natural habitats of your plants are almost certainly very diverse, so it is important that you try and match, as much as possible, their natural growing conditions with those available within your house; the A-Z guide will help you decide the most suitable position for each of your plants. Generally, green foliage plants thrive much better than flowering plants in poor light. So for these areas, Aspidistras and palms are ideal, while the colourful African Violets (*Saintpaulias*) should be given the brightest light that windowsills can afford. Your Cyclamen or Cissus may be suffering from higher temperatures that are more suitable for plants such as Cotyledon or Dieffenbachia. By putting your Araucaria in a hot sunny position it will not only have to endure leaf scorch, but the compost will dry out rapidly, leading to dehydration — and a very sick plant. Be very wary of heat sources such as radiators or stoves; avoid them at all costs — the same is true of draughts.

If the positioning seems right, the next thing to look at is watering. In fact, of all the things that make plants start to lose condition, the most common are problems with watering.

Plants obviously need more water during the periods of active growth, but knowing exactly how much water to give and how often is not easy. Although the plastic pots most commonly used today retain moisture, they are not as porous as the clay ones, and can prevent roots from receiving the aeration they require. Evaporation often takes place unevenly, so while the surface of the compost appears dry, the roots of your plant may still be very damp. You may find yourself tempted to give your plant daily waterings in the belief that it has dried out. But beware — waterlogging beneath the surface of the compost can prevent vital air from getting to the roots. This waterlogging can cause root rot; the roots then cannot take up moisture properly, and so, even though it has been receiving plenty of water, your plant will begin to look dehydrated.

The simplest way of discovering whether your plant needs water is to test the compost by scratching it with your fingertips; provide water if the compost is dry for about 1-2 inches (2.5-5cm) below the surface. For a few foliage

Kiss of life

One of the most disheartening experiences for any houseplant owner is to find a favourite plant developing limp, lifeless leaves, or foliage dying when there is no apparent pest to blame. The tendency is to blame yourself — but although you may not have been providing the right living conditions, you shouldn't despair. Look carefully at the situation of the plant and try to assess the likely causes of the problem. Sometimes the treatment will be quite small-scale — merely changing the plant's position or giving it less water — sometimes it will be more drastic, and you may have to use ruthless surgery to trim off dead foliage or branches. Remember, plants that have been sick need time to convalesce, just like people.

The Joseph's Coat Croton is especially vulnerable to cold — below 60°F (15°C) its leaves will droop and go brown, *above*.

plants the compost can be allowed to dry out more — to one-third or even one-half of its depth.

It is important that you never guess your plant's watering requirements. Look them up in the A-Z guide, and, as a simple rule of thumb, when in doubt, don't water. Your plants will probably thank you if you follow this rule!

Overwatering

The symptoms of overwatering are many: rotten areas of foliage; brown and mushy roots; leaves that are limp, curled or prone to dropping off. Try to avoid overwatering at all times, especially during the resting period; watering one to three times a month is generally quite sufficient. However, if you find that one of your plants has been overwatered, you must give it the chance to dry out completely. Carefully ease the whole plant out of the pot and stand it on a sheet of newspaper to help absorb excess moisture.

Underwatering

To confuse matters, *under*watered plants generally have the same symptoms as *over*watered ones. Modern peat-based composts can dry out very quickly and these composts can also be extremely difficult to re-wet. They often will not retain moisture and the result is dehydration. If you think this has happened, take the plant gently out of its pot; a very dry mixture that falls away readily from the roots indicates that your plant has not received sufficient water from the compost. To remedy this, first of all plunge the rootball into a bowl of tepid water for half an hour — or until bubbles stop rising from the potting mixture. Doing all this in a cool place will give the foliage every opportunity to recover properly; if you spot the warning signs early enough there is every chance that your plant will regain its vitality.

One way of helping the compost to absorb moisture more effectively is to add three or four drops of a good quality washing-up liquid to a pint of tepid water, and soak the rootball in this for 20 to 30 minutes. This is not such a surprising method — some leading producers of peat-based composts add a kind of detergent called a wetting agent to their compost.

Correct watering

To water a plant properly, place it on a saucer and water the surface of the compost, allowing the water to drain through the compost into the saucer below. Leave the plant on the saucer for 20 to 30 minutes and then throw away any remaining water. If the surface of the compost is 'caked', preventing the water from draining through, prick the surface gently with a fork. If the moisture has still not been absorbed after 20 minutes or so, the soil is probably so compacted that the plant will have to be repotted in a more porous mixture; remove any rotted brown roots and don't water again until you see signs of renewed growth.

For plants such as Saintpaulia, Gloxinia and Cyclamen, which do not like water on their leaves or crowns, a different technique is necessary. Immerse the pots in tepid water to just below the level of the compost, and allow them to soak for about half an hour, or until the surface glistens.

Summertime

During the hot, dry summer months plants lose much of their moisture through evaporation, and it is important that you provide an adequate supply of water, both to replace the water lost and to enable new growth to appear. Always check the guidelines for each individual plant, however; it is more difficult to correct overwatering than to compensate for underwatering. If any of your plants have suffered a shock to their system caused by either too much, or too little, water they will need considerable care and attention if they are to be nursed back to full health.

A wilting plant has probably been overwatered with the result that the roots have been partially damaged. One solution is to place it inside a temporary mini-greenhouse to aid recovery. You can easily rig this up using a clear polythene bag, supported by a few short canes long enough to keep the polythene clear of the foliage. Before placing your sick plant inside, spray it well with a fine mist of tepid water. Try to avoid direct sunlight (to prevent leaf scorching) and place the mini-greenhouse in as cool a place as possible so that the plant does not completely dry out. (Be careful, of course, to keep polythene bags away from children.)

When your plant begins to look fit again, you can start to wean it away from its protective covering, but remember that it is still in convalescence — try to avoid placing it near draughts and keep a watchful eye out for badly damaged or dead leaves. These have to be cut away cleanly before they rot and cause further problems.

To cure a plant, wrap it in a polythene bag and keep it warm. A healthy plant, *above*, has a strong upright growth.

Wintertime

In the winter months it may take even longer to persuade your plant to pick up again due to the fluctuating temperatures caused by central heating. If you use a mini-greenhouse during this time, keep it at a temperature of 60-65°F (15-18°C), and do not give the plant any water.

Chances of survival

The watering requirements of your houseplants will obviously vary. Those with fleshy or succulent leaves (whose natural habitat is in dry conditions) can stand up to drought more effectively than thinner-leaved plants. Similarly, semi-aquatic plants such as Cyperus can not only endure waterlogging — they actually thrive on it. With the majority of plants, however, be very careful when watering: try not to succumb to either pitfall of under- or overwatering. But if you do miss the early warning signs, it's always worth trying to revive any plant that you're fond of.

Drastic measures

Many plants can recover well after the initial shock of over- or underwatering Others, however, may lose a lot of leaves, or some of their shoots may die back. You might find it necessary to prune your plant quite severely, back to the point where new growth looks likely to appear. In an extreme case, where all the leaves have died, try cutting right back to the base of the plant. Unfortunately, if your plant has reached this state, there is only the slimmest chance of recovery unless you are dealing with a fern. The Maidenhair Fern can become a dreadul mess if it's allowed to dry out, but by watering it thoroughly and cutting away the dead or dying fronds, you can help it recover.

A few tips

Aspidistras	Moderate light; room temperature; moderate watering
Begonias	Bright but indirect light; room temperature; moderate watering
Busy Lizzie (*Impatiens*)	Bright light; room temperature; frequent watering when growing
Dieffenbachia	Good light; warm; frequent watering
Ferns	Indirect light; warm; frequent watering
Fittonia	Shade essential; warm; moderate watering
Geraniums (*Pelargonium*)	Direct sunlight; room temperature; moderate watering
Ivies (*Hedera*)	Moderate light; cool moderate watering
Kaffir Lily (*Clivia miniata*)	Bright but indirect light; cool; moderate watering

Patio pests and diseases

Pests and diseases are often more of a problem on the patio than they are in the garden. This is partly because some pests, like whitefly, which fly up as soon as they are disturbed, can be more of a nuisance and also because great care has to be taken when using chemicals near the house. There are, however, several chemicals available which are particularly suitable for use on the patio. They are safe to use and do not have objectionable smells.

Pests

The number of pests that you may encounter on your patio can be rather daunting. But as with houseplant pests (see 'Know your enemy', page 627) they can be quite easily controlled.

Ants

Ants tend to live on or close to the patio, but are easy to control.

Although not a major nuisance, ants tend to like living on, or close to, the patio, and if the weather becomes very hot and dry they may invade the house where their presence quickly becomes unbearable.
Control. The smell of Lavender or Marigolds will help to deter ants, so you could plant these flowers on your patio. Alternatively, use one of the proprietary ant killers based on borax dissolved in a sugary solution. Put the liquid in a small tin lid and, hopefully, the ants will carry this back to their nest where it should kill the whole colony.

Aphids

Aphids such as blackfly thrive on the young growth of vegetables.

Aphids is the general term for greenfly and blackfly, which can often be spotted on the tender young growth of many plants during spring, summer and early autumn. These somewhat pear-shaped insects multiply at an alarming rate and can cause considerable damage to your plants as they attack new growth and suck out the plant juices with their stabbing mouthpieces.
Control. Aphids can easily be dealt with by using insecticides based on pyrethrum. However, if you are worried about the effect a broad spectrum insecticide could have on beneficial insects such as ladybirds or bees, you could try a specific aphicide called pirimicarb, which is known to control only aphids.

Caterpillars

Caterpillars can cause considerable damage to patio plants.

Most caterpillars are extremely destructive on your patio and should be controlled as quickly as possible.

Cabbage white and tortrix caterpillars, especially, can have a severe effect on your plants and so need to be dealt with at the earliest opportunity. Cabbage white butterflies attack members of the Brassica family, such as wallflowers, causing massive loss of leaf tissue as they consume everything except the plants' leaves and stems. Tortrix caterpillars spin silken webs which are used to draw leaves, especially those of carnations, into a protected cover within which they can feed.
Control. Although several general-purpose chemicals such as derris or pyrethrum are effective, a specific insecticide based upon a bacteria that kills the caterpillar is the most rapid.

Red spider mites

Red spider mites flourish in the warm, dry atmosphere of the patio.

These tiny spiders are normally straw-coloured, rather than red. Thriving in the warm, dry environment encouraged by the patio, the pests rapidly multiply. The tiny mites feed and breed on the undersides of leaves, causing a fine, light mottling of the upper surface. In severe attacks this can lead to yellowing and bronzing.
Control. Spray the undersides of leaves with general-purpose chemicals such as derris, dimethoate or malathion.

Earwigs

These fascinating insects with fierce-looking pincers at the end of their bodies usually live under containers on the patio, where they scavenge an existence on dead or decaying organic matter. However, they can cause a lot of trouble to the blooms of Chrysanthemums, Clematis and Dahlias, especially at night, leaving ragged holes in petals and leaves.

Control. Chemicals such as derris and pyrethrum will poison these pests, and you can also trap them. Place inverted flower pots filled with straw among the infested plants to trap the insects as they emerge from their midnight feast. Remove the pots the following morning and dispose of the contents onto the compost heap.

Scale insects

It usually takes several weeks to totally eradicate scale insects.

Scale insects are often a problem on plants such as Bay trees, where it can be difficult to distinguish the oval-shaped insects, looking as they do like small, round blisters.

Control. An insecticide with a systemic activity such as dimethoate can be used. However, several applications will be necessary.

Slugs and snails

Slugs can be troublesome as they move around by night.

These nocturnal feeders can become very troublesome, as they eat holes in leaves, stems, buds and flowers and cause considerable damage to roots below ground. They hide during the day, but you can tell the extent of

their presence by the slime trails they leave by night.

Control. Slugs and snails can be controlled chemically by various means. Poisonous baits containing metaldehyde are effective, provided they do not become wet, as are baits containing methiocarb, or try using a 'beer trap'. A saucerful of beer will attract slugs and snails and hopefully they will drown in the liquid.

Whitefly

Whitefly live on the undersides of leaves, where they lay their eggs.

These tiny white moths fly up as soon as the foliage of the infected plants is disturbed, and can be most annoying. Adult moths live on the undersides of leaves where they lay their eggs, which then develop into larvae and start to feed on sap, and excrete honeydew which makes the plant sticky and could encourage attacks of sooty moulds.

Control. Pyrethrum or derris are effective in controlling the pest, but the insecticide must be applied every seven to 10 days to catch the emerging whitefly before they start to lay any eggs.

Diseases

Fortunately, patio plants are not prone to too many diseases and are all quite controllable using similar methods to those you followed when caring for your houseplants. See 'First Aid' page 632.

Botrytis

Botrytis, or grey mould fungus, usually affects the fleshy parts of flowers or fruit. The fluffy, brownish-grey spores are present in the air and the disease tends to spread very rapidly. It should, therefore, be

treated as soon as it is identified.

Control. Damaged tissue should be removed and the diseased plant sprayed with a chemical such as benomyl.

Leaf spot

Some plants can become infected by fungi or even bacteria, which results in discolouration or brown spots on the leaves. These can vary from tiny spots to large spreading patches.

Control. Although you can control the effects of the infection, the damage caused will never disappear. It is, therefore, important to treat the plant as soon as possible, using a spray of either a broad spectrum fungicide such as benomyl or a liquid copper fungicide.

Mildew

There are two major forms of mildew – powdery mildew and downy mildew. Powdery mildew is the most common and appears as a whitish powder on leaves, and sometimes the flowers. As it spreads the plant's growth becomes dramatically impaired. Downy mildew usually occurs in cool, dank conditions and appears as fluffy blotches on the under surfaces of leaves.

Control. Regular spraying of susceptible plants with a fungicide such as benomyl helps to prevent the problem of powdery mildew. Fungicides containing thiram or zineb will help to prevent downy mildew from spreading, or even from appearing, in the first place if applied early enough. You can also dust the plant slightly with flowers of sulphur every 10 to 14 days – but check the label to make sure the sulphur won't cause any damage to your plants.

Watch out

Always read the instructions before using any pesticide. Pay particular attention to children, pets, wildlife and foodstuffs which should be kept well away from the chemicals and any treatment. When spraying food crops make sure that the chemical is safe for use on foods and that the appropriate interval is left between spraying and harvesting.

Off with their heads

Deadheading is the removal from a plant of flowers that are fading, dead or damaged. Its main function is to prevent plants from setting seeds, which saps their strength perhaps more than anything else, and thus diverts their energy away from producing new flowers.

It encourages energy to be channelled instead into some other, more important, process which varies from one plant to another. It may, for example, help it to develop strong new flowering shoots and produce larger blooms. It may also prolong the plant's flowering season – as with Roses and many annual bedding plants, such as Petunias, Pansies, Bellis, Calendula, Impatiens and Salvia – while on some early flowering perennials, such as Delphiniums, Lupins and Violas, it will encourage a second show of flowers. With some shrubs – such as Lilac, Rhododendrons and Azaleas – and most bulbs, it may build up a plant's energy reserves for the following year and so lessen the possibility of flowers appearing only in alternate years.

Deadheading also has two other important functions. First, it prevents plants from looking unsightly. And second, it reduces the risk of disease: dead flower heads, if left on a plant, will eventually rot – especially in wet weather – and will then encourage attack by fungi.

Exceptions to the rule

Some plants, however, do not produce seed, so deadheading these has no effect on their growth. This applies, for example, to double-flowered varieties of Chrysanthemum and Gypsophila, and some of the newer varieties of Marigold. In cases such as these, you should be guided by your instincts and remove the flower heads only if you find them unsightly.

Some plants, such as Clematis, Achillea and Sedum, produce rather attractive seed heads which will add to their interest and can therefore be left on. Deadheading is also not usually done if fruit, seed or berries

Use sharp secateurs when deadheading your roses and cut back to the nearest leaf, making a clean cut.

are required, nor on Roses that are grown for their autumn hips.

Hydrangeas produce their flowers on the tips of the previous year's growth, so you should never cut off these tips and the old flower heads should be left on the plant in winter to provide protection for the dormant buds. These can then be removed when pruning is carried out in the spring.

How to deadhead

This depends to a large extent on the plant in question.

Hybrid Tea Roses should have their flowers cut off as soon as they wither. Using a good pair of secateurs, cut just above the topmost leaf, making a clean cut with no bruising or tearing that might allow disease to enter. This will encourage a second flowering. Towards the end of the season its a good idea to deadhead lightly – to prevent your plant putting its energy into the production of seeds.

Large blooming perennials, such as Peonies and Dahlias, should also have dead flowers cut off just above the uppermost leaf.

Bulbous plants, such as Daffodils, Tulips and Lilies, should just have the flower heads snapped off with a quick twist.

Clusters of sizeable blooms, such as Floribunda Roses and Spray Chrysan-

themums, should be deadheaded in two stages. First, pick off the individual flowers as they fade and then, as the last flowers in a cluster die, cut off the entire cluster just above a leaf. Similarly, with the large-flowering Gladioli and Lilies, remove individual flowers as they fade and then, as the spike ends its flowering life, cut it off completely just above the topmost leaf.

When Delphiniums and Lupins have finished flowering, cut out the main spikes promptly and smaller, secondary spikes may be produced. When the flowers on these too have faded, cut down all the spikes right down to ground level.

Profusely flowering annuals, such as Sweet Peas, Pansies, Petunias and Marigolds, should be deadheaded often – if possible daily – or picked for the house. Snap off the blooms between finger and thumb, with a twisting motion.

If you want to save some seed for the following season (though this will probably be inferior to commercial seed), allow one or two blooms to wither on each plant. Then harvest the seed when ripe.

With rock plants, like Alyssum and Aubretia, the individual flowers are too small and too numerous to be picked off singly, so clip them over lightly and carefully with a pair of shears or scissors to remove faded flowers and old seed heads.

When deadheading Azaleas, take care not to damage the following year's buds.

Winter- and also spring-flowering Heathers should have dead flower heads removed with scissors immediately after they have faded. Cut the growth just below the faded flower spikes. The dead flower heads of summer- and autumn-flowering heathers often provide attractive colour during the winter months, in which case deadheading can be postponed until the following spring.

The healing plant

THE HISTORY OF MEDICINE is inextricably linked with Man's discovery that infusions, lotions, potions and ointments made from plants had amazing healing and curative effects on injury and illness. The herbals of the ancient world that described plants and their qualities were not botanical or culinary manuals but medical reference books. The great physicians of ancient Greece and Rome – Hippocrates, Dioscorides and Galen – researched and recorded a great mass of information on the healing properties of plants, much of which is still valid today.

The pretty little wild flower Eyebright, for instance, has been valued for centuries for its properties as an eye medicine capable of preserving and improving eyesight. For many herbalists of the 16th century Eyebright was regarded as the specific cure for all eye diseases – and even today it is still recommended by modern herbalists for eye complaints. A simple preparation of 1oz (28g) of its leaves infused in 1 pint (0.5 litres) of boiling water makes a lotion that can be used (when cooled) to bathe the eyes three or four times a day – helpful in cases of tired or inflamed eyes.

The 17th-century physician and herbalist Nicholas Culpeper esteemed Eyebright so highly that he wrote in his famous *Herbal*:

> If the herb was but as much used as it is neglected, it would half spoil the spectacle maker's trade and a man would think that reason should teach people to prefer the preservation of their natural before their artificial spectacles . . .

Culpeper maintained that taking 'the juice or distilled water of the Eyebright . . . inwardly in white wine, or both, or dropped into the eyes for several days together helpeth all infirmities of the eye that causes dimness of sight.' He also believed that it 'strengthens the weak brain or memory'.

The traditional belief that Eyebright was good for the eyes was based on the ancient Doctrine of Signatures, which maintained that a plant carried on it signs of the affliction, or part of the body, that it would cure. 'The purple and yellow spots and stripes which are upon the flowers of the Eyebright,' the author of one ancient reference book tells us, 'doth very much resemble the diseases of the eye, as bloodshot, etc., by which signature it has been found out that this herb is effectual for the curing of the same.'

Lungwort good for lungs

According to the Doctrine of Signatures another common plant, Lungwort, was said to be an excellent remedy for lung disease – since the pale blotches on its leaves were thought to resemble diseased lungs. Even today a modern herbalist might prescribe an infusion of the leaves as a remedy for coughs and congested lungs.

A preparation from the Aloe plant is a very ancient purgative medicine that has been used since the time of ancient Greece. It was certainly in use in the UK in Anglo-Saxon times (it was recommended to Alfred the Great by the Patriarch of Jerusalem), and by the 19th century it formed the basis of many common domestic proprietary medicines. It is still used in several preparations that appear in the official pharmaceutical list in the UK and US, and is widely used in veterinary practice as a purgative for horses.

A preparation from *Aloe Vera, below,* has long been used as a purgative. Lily-of-the-Valley, *right,* yields a drug that regulates the heart.

The flowers of the Lily-of-the-Valley yield a drug used in modern medicine to stimulate the heart. Safer than some other drugs used for the same purpose, the Lily-of-the-Valley drug regulates the action of a weak or disturbed heart, and at the same time strengthens it. Traditionally, Lily-of-the-Valley has been recommended as a remedy for many ailments, and water distilled from its flowers was known as 'Golden Water' and was thought to be imbued with very special properties. After describing how to steep the flowers in 'New Wine for the space of a month' one 17th-century writer claimed that the resulting wine was:

> more precious than gold, for if any one that is troubled with apoplexy drink thereof with six grains of Pepper and a little Lavender water they shall not need to fear it that month.

The 16th-century herbalist Gerard claimed that Lily-of-the-Valley water cured gout, and Culpeper recommended it for inflammations of the eye. He also believed that it 'strengthens the brain and renovates a weak memory' and that:

> The spirit of the flowers, distilled in wine, restoreth lost speech, helps the palsy, and is exceedingly good in the apoplexy, comforteth the heart and vital spirits.

The Violet is another attractive little wild flower that has a long medical history. A syrup made from its flowers was a popular laxative given to infants in the 19th century. Earlier herbalists maintained that Syrup of Violets was effective for a wide range of ailments, including jaundice, epilepsy, pleurisy, sleeplessness and ague. And, according to Gerard, Syrup of Violets 'has power to ease inflammation, roughness of the throat and comforteth the heart, assuageth the pains of the head and causeth sleep.'

Although many of these herbal remedies may seem quaint to us now, modern medicine is nevertheless based on the knowledge amassed by the old herbalists. A surprising number of medicines in the present-day official British Pharmaceutical list include extracts drawn from plants. And even where new drugs have been synthesised, in many cases they imitate, and were inspired by, the action of a traditional natural drug supplied by the plant world.

The purple and yellow blotches and stripes on the flower of Eyebright, *right*, were thought to be signs of diseases of the eye that the plant would cure. A syrup made of Violets, *below*, used to be a popular laxative.

CHAPTER 5

Something Different

Caladium

Plants with

Indoor plants are available with a huge selection of different leaf markings. So, if there is any particular pattern you fancy, just take your pick. But remember, if you grow plants especially for their patterns, you must take extra care of those beautiful leaves. Keep plants out of strong sunshine and draughts, and make sure you never give them too much or too little water — all of which can result in browning.

And if you spray your plants to increase their humidity, always use previously boiled water otherwise you may end up with unsightly calcium deposits on those pretty leaves. To keep leaves clean, wipe smooth-leaved plants over periodically, and blow the dust off velvety or hairy leaves.

STRIPES

Blushing Bromeliad
(Neoregelia carolinae 'Tricolor')
Green leaves, yellow longitudinal stripes

Dracaena fragrans
Varieties
Green leaves, yellow vertical stripes

Flaming Sword
(Vriesea splendens)
Green leaves, horizontal purple-black stripes

Peperomia
Varieties
Many varieties in a colourful range of stripes

Pilea

Peperomia

SPOTS

Gold Dust Dracaena
(Dracaena godseffiana)
Green leaves, yellow spots

Polka Dot Plant
(Hypoestes sanguinolenta)
Green leaves, pink spots

Spotted Angel's Wing Begonia
(Begonia lucerna)
Shiny green leaves, cream spots

HERRINGBONE PATTERN

Dumb Cane
(Dieffenbachia amoena)
Green leaves, white pattern

Mosaic Plant
(Fittonia verschaffeltii)
Green leaves, red pattern

Snakeskin Plant
(Fittonia argyroneura nana)
Green leaves, white pattern

Flame Violet
(Episcia dianthiflora)
Bronzy-green leaves, silver pattern

Herringbone Plant
(Maranta leuconeura tricolor)
Green leaves, red and yellow pattern

ZONED LEAVES

Begonia rex
Green, pink, red, yellow and cream zones, also marked with spots

Zonal Pelargonium 'Distinction'
Frilly green leaves, narrow black zone

Zonal Pelargonium 'Marechal MacMahon'
Yellow-green leaves, red zones

Zonal Pelargonium 'Mrs Henry Cox'
Yellow leaves, red and green zones

patterned leaves

COLOURED VEINS

Angel's Wings
(Caladium hortulanum candidum)
White leaves, green veins

Caladium hortulanum 'Lord Derby'
Pink leaves, green veins

Blood Leaf
(Iresine herbstii)
Dark red leaves, pale red veins

Croton
(Codiaeum variegatum pictum)
Red and green leaves, yellow veins

Crystal Anthurium
(Anthurium crystallinum)
Large green leaves, white veins

Friendship Plant
(Pilea involucrata)
Silvery leaves with purple undersides,
brown or green veins

Zebra Plant
(Aphelandra squarrosa)
Dark green leaves and yellow veins

CHEVRON PATTERN

Aglaonema modestum 'Silver Queen'
Green leaves, silvery pattern

Never Never Plant
(Ctenanthe oppenheimiana tricolor)
Green leaves, dark mauve-green pattern

Rattlesnake Plant
(Calathea insignis)
Bright green leaves with reddish
undersides, purplish-green pattern

Calathea zebrina
Bright green
leaves, mauve-
green pattern

COLOURED LEAF MARGINS

Cordyline terminalis 'Rededge'
Green leaves, red edges

Dieffenbachia picta 'Rudolph Roehrs'
Green leaves, white edges and midrib

Mother-in-law's Tongue
(Sansevieria trifasciata laurentii)
Green leaves, yellow edges

Ribbon Plant
(Dracaena sanderiana)
Green leaves, white edges

OTHER PATTERNS

Iron Cross Begonia
(Begonia masoniana)
Green bouclé-look leaves with distinct
greyish-brown central cross

Peacock Plant
(Calathea makoyana)
Cream leaves with green flushed
edges and pattern like blades of grass

Prayer Plant
(Maranta leuconeura kerchoveana)
Pale green leaves, regular brownish-green
blotches

Stromanthe amabilis
Bright green leaves with grey-green
undersides, deep green pattern like
blades of grass

Peperomia

Hypoestes

Aphelandra

Caladium

259

▲A thin dark blue tracking line runs down the centre of each Plumbago petal.

▲Only a tiny hummingbird can reach the nectar deep inside a Datura flower.

Flower power

One of the great delights of flowers lies in their infinite variety of shape, colour, size and scent. The range — as you can see — is enormous, and these have been selected only from plants that are capable of flowering indoors.

Flowers are not produced by plants simply for us to admire; they are actually an important part of the plant's reproductive system. The shape, colour and scent of flowers have evolved over thousands of years to attract pollinating visitors.

▲ The daisy-like flowers of Lithops are typical of many Cacti.

▲The Cyclamen has unique petals that fold right back on themselves.

◀ Cheerful Cineraria flowers all open at the same time for maximum impact.

The Echinopsis Cactus opens its flowers just after dusk and fills the air with perfume. ▶

▲ One of the simplest flowers of all is that of the long-lasting African Violet.

◀ Waxy Cymbidium flowers last for ages but, sadly, have no scent.

▲ *Allamanda neriifolia* — what else could this be but the Golden Trumpet?

Pretty little Persian Violet uses colour for its main effect.▶

Animals, birds and insects come looking for nectar and, in doing so, they help the plant complete its fertilisation process. The result is that seeds and fruit can develop to enable further generations of the plant to follow. Plants such as grasses, which have inconspicuous flowers, are pollinated by the wind or passing animals; so these plants have never needed to evolve elaborate and attractive flowers.

Some of the most unusual and attractive pollinators are the tiny hummingbirds that use their long beaks to reach a drop of nectar at the bottom of a trumpet-shaped Datura. Generally, you can safely assume that tube-shaped flowers are pollinated by insects, such as butterflies and moths, that have long mouth parts that can reach the nectar. Some plants have evolved so closely with their pollinators that they can only be pollinated by one type of insect or bird.

Hoya bella holds a rich sugary nectar in its porcelain-like clusters of small star-shaped flowers.▼

▲ The Hippeastrum has huge individual flowers the size of a stretched-out hand.

Something Different

The bright throat of
a trumpet-shaped
Dipladenia attracts
insects straight
to the pollen.▶

Typical of Bromeliads are
the tiny bright flowers and
colourful bracts of Billbergia.▶

▲ The Odontoglossum Orchid often
has brightly coloured and marked
petals on a flat, open flower.

Surprising though it seems, the
brilliant colours that we see in
flowers appear very different to
insect eyes. Research has discovered that
bees and butterflies don't see red — they
cannot distinguish it from green. This
may perhaps explain why relatively few
natural species have red flowers.

However, insects can see ultraviolet
light, along with other colours from that
end of the spectrum such as blue, violet
and purple; again, this may explain why
there are so many wild flowers to be
found in those colours.

The smell given off by plants may also
be perceived differently by humans and
insects. The odour of rotting meat given
off by Stapelia seems foul to us — but is
attractive to blow flies!

Simple yet effective,
a single Begonia
flower only has four petals.▲

◀ These Nidularium buds are
ready to open in the centre
of colourful, water-holding
Bromeliad bracts.

◀ Gorgeous crocus-shaped flowers
make the Clivia irresistible
to both insects and people!

▲ Busy Lizzie nods its pretty head in even the lightest breeze to attract attention.

▲ Polyanthus flowers clearly show insects where to find the nectar with their bright throats and tracking lines.

Ultra violet tracking lines have been discovered on some flowers which show the insects the way to go to find pollen and nectar. Such tracking lines can be visible to the human eye, but more often they only become obvious to us when shown under ultra violet light.

Some 'flowers' are not really flowers at all. The attractive red 'petals' of the popular Poinsettia are actually a type of leaf, properly called a bract. These bracts fulfil the same function as the petals of real flowers — they entice insects to visit the insignificant flowers found in the centre. This is also the case with most Bromeliads, Bougainvillea and the Shrimp Plant, and many other — especially tropical — plants.

The spectacular Strelitzia is actually a horizontal bract from which three-petalled flowers rise in turn.▼

One of the simplest flower shapes is the concentric arrangement of petals around the centre of a Chrysanthemum flower.▶

The flowers of an Anthurium are the tiny bumps along the yellow spike, not the bright red surrounding bract. ▶

Grow a palm

It may seem odd that palms, which thrive in intense sunlight in their natural habitat, should have a reputation for enjoying dark hotel foyers and dim corners. The answer is very simple. The palms we grow as indoor plants are youngsters which will probably never come to full maturity. Like any young plants, they need to be protected from the full ravages of the sun and are happiest in diffused light, away from the window. That's why they excel as indoor plants.

Palms suffered a long eclipse after their Victorian heyday. Nowadays, their unique appeal has been recognised once again. But the great, specialist palm nurseries have long since disappeared, and today's plant growers find it uneconomic to offer the wide choice of palms that were once available. High heating costs, and the length of time they take to rear are to blame.

Palms can be a bit expensive for just those reasons. Despite this, the ones listed here have so much to offer that no other plant can quite take their place. Gracious, elegant, majestic are the kinds of adjective these plants deserve.

They're really not very fussy plants, as long as you keep them moist all the time, and will happily grow in conditions found in the average room. They can put up with poor light for several months, although they'll make very slow growth and will gradually deteriorate. But even if you can only find a poorly lit location for your palm, by moving it to a sunnier spot for two or three hours every other day, you can do much to compensate.

Water plants freely in spring and summer — so that you can see water running out through the drainage holes at the base of the pot or tub. Don't let them stand in water for more than half-an-hour at a time, though. Palms need less water in autumn and winter when they should be encouraged to rest for two or three months. Keep the mixture barely moist, until new growth appears sometime in mid-spring.

Feed palms with a controlled release fertiliser, such as Jobe's Spikes, or ICI Keri-sticks, or water in a liquid fertiliser especially formulated for leafy plants.

Feeding every two to three weeks in the main growing season — May to September — should ensure robust growth.

In mild, rainy weather your palm can be put outside for an hour or two, so that the rain can wash the fronds free of dust. Failing this, you can rinse the leaves with the aid of a bathroom shower or a spray gun. Or simply use a sponge to wipe them. Don't be tempted to clean the leaves with a proprietary leaf-shine product — it may well kill them.

Repot or pot-on every three years, or so, when roots mat the compost and push through the drainage holes. Take care not to break the roots, as these are fleshy and liable to die back, affecting leaf growth for the worst.

Make sure they have a free-draining, soil-based potting compost — ideally John Innes No 2 or 3. To improve the texture and keep the mix spongy and aerated, add a quarter part, by volume, of coarse sand. A good layer of crocks, or a 1in (2.5cm) layer of coarse gravel at the bottom of the pots will help.

Do choose a plant that won't become too big for your purposes. You can expect new palms to produce one, two, or at most, three new fronds a year.

Individual leaves can be removed, but plants can't be cut back in any other way. Each stem has only one growing point, from which *all* the leaves develop. If the terminal bud is damaged or destroyed, it isn't replaced and the plant will eventually die.

Selecting your palm

As a family, palms are very versatile – some are small enough for a bottle garden, others will grow to fill a corner alcove from floor to ceiling. If you've never grown a palm before, start with the elegant, broad-leaved Kentia Palm – it happily tolerates a degree of neglect – and you'll soon want to expand your collection. Here are some of the most popular palms with brief cultivation details on each, to help you choose the right palm for conditions in your home. The 'A-Z of Plants' section gives more details on how to care for the individual species.

The Parlour Palm. A miniature delight, the Parlour Palm (*Chamaedorea elegans*, also called *Neanthe bella*) is perfect for bottle gardens, dish gardens, or smallish rooms. One of the easiest, as well as one of the smallest of the palms to grow, its feathery leaflets radiate from a central stem.

It's a quick starter, too. Within three years a seedling will turn into an attractive plant that may produce a spray of tiny, greenish-yellow, ball-like flowers. It's one of the few palms to flower indoors; most never develop sufficiently.

This is also one of the few palms to tolerate being dried out in winter, and cheerfully accepts a dry, centrally heated atmosphere. It also thrives in light shade. Potted on regularly, it will eventually reach a height of 2ft (60cm).

The Parlour Palm likes warm nights, with temperatures never falling below 50°F (10°C).

Canary Date Palm
(*Phoenix canariensis*)

Sentry Palm and Kentia Palm. Tall, feathery-leaved cousins to the Parlour Palm, the Sentry Palm (*Howea belmoreana*) and the Kentia Palm (*Howea forsteriana*) have remarkable constitutions, growing well when conditions are far less than ideal.

Both need siting in light shade — they resent hot sunlight — but will tolerate being in a room too dark for many other plants. They need to be warm at night, with temperatures over 55°F (13°C).

The older the plants, the droopier their dark-green leaves, and while a young specimen, with leaves still quite erect, looks good in a pot, older ones bowed with age will look more attractive standing on the floor in a tub.

The Canary Date Palm (*Phoenix canariensis*). This palm is more robust, by far, than the others already mentioned, but make sure you allow it plenty of headroom. Its very handsome, stiff leaves, radiating from impressive midribs, can reach 6ft (1.8m) long, leaving little space for other houseplants.

This palm actually enjoys a bit of direct sun during the summer (put it outside from time to time) and prefers to be in good light in winter. It doesn't mind the cold, and can survive temperatures as low as 40°F (10°C) during the coldest months.

The Pygmy Date Palm.
A miniature plant, the Pygmy Date Palm (*Phoenix robelenii*), is altogether more demanding than its hardier big brother, the Canary Date Palm. This graceful palm is decked with arching, feathery, dark-green leaves some 1ft (30cm) long.

What's the trouble?

● **Underwatering**, *above*, and a too dry atmosphere will do permanent damage. Palms can be exposed to slightly dry air occasionally, without dire consequences, but if the environment becomes too arid, the leaf tips turn brown — an effect that's permanent, unfortunately. Often, central heating is the culprit; counteract it by fitting humidifiers to the radiators or by misting leaves regularly. If this doesn't make much difference, sit pots on trays of moist gravel.

● **Brown spots** on leaves are usually due to a sudden chilling. Most palms like airy conditions, but can't tolerate drafts — or extreme heat or sudden changes in the intensity of light. So, if you're putting them outside for a while, help plants to get used to breeze and brighter lights gradually. And bring them back in before the weather turns cooler. Brownish spots could also be the result of using hard water — water that's got too much lime in it.

Once the damage has been done, cut off affected leaves and try to provide your palms with more even conditions. And if your water is too hard, use water which has boiled for a few minutes.

● **Yellowing fronds** or, worse still, fronds which become bronzed, *below*, and netted with webs, mean the palms are probably under attack from red spider. Mist spray regularly to keep the atmosphere moist, and water in a liquid malathion-based insecticide to control the infestation.

Sticky, white and fluffy patches of the sap-sucking mealy bug are also controlled with malathion, while greenfly fall victim to permethrin.

◀**Kentia Palm** (*Howea forsteriana*)

◀**Sentry Palm** (*Howea belmoreana*)

Parlour Palm
(*Chamaedorea elegans*)

The European Fan Palm is almost hardy and enjoys normal room temperatures.

Adding an elegant finishing touch are: *Howea belmoreana* and *Phoenix canariensis*, *above*, and *Chamaedorea elegans* and *Howea forsteriana*,*right*.If you keep your palm in poor light move it to a brighter spot for an hour or two a day.

They rise from a very characteristic stem that is no more than 2ft (60cm) tall, and thickened with the old leaf bases along its length, which give it a swollen look. It rarely grows taller than 3ft (90cm). This palm needs a minimum winter temperature of 50°F (10°C).

The Coconut Palm. Fascinating indeed is *Cocos weddeliana*. Its much admired, slender, upright stems are clad with feathery leaflets, which burgeon with just a little cosseting. But a higher winter temperature is vital, and this shouldn't drop below 65°F (18°C).

The European Fan Palm. Bearing large, deeply-segmented, fan-like leaves — of great beauty — the European Fan Palm (*Chamaerops humilis*) needs space to show off its 'fans'. Greyish-green leaves are felted with silvery-grey 'wool' when they first emerge, creating a delightfully 'soft' effect, but this fine hair falls off as the fronds open. Each fan, with its many sword-shaped segments, grows to about 18in (46cm) long, 12in (30cm) wide, and is set on 4ft (1.2m) stems.

It's the only palm which grows wild in Europe, mainly in Spain and Italy. Not surprisingly it's almost hardy, actually preferring full light, and putting up with temperatures as low as 45°F (7°C).

The Chinese Fan Palm. Now making a come-back, the Chinese Fan Palm (*Livistona chinensis*, also sometimes referred to as *L.borbonica*) was a great favourite of the Victorians, back in the 1860s. It's similar to the European Fan Palm, but stemless, and young plants have impressive, shiny, bright-green leaves, up to 2ft (60cm) wide. The fans aren't split into segments all the way down to the stalk, however, and at the tips the individual fronds droop slightly.

Feed them well in summer to ensure the finest leaves, and make sure that winter night temperatures do not drop below 45°F (7°C).

The Little Lady Palm. The elegant Little Lady Palm (*Rhapis excelsa nana*) is a tufty dwarf plant that reaches scarcely more than 18in (45cm) in height. Its fingered leaves form on short stalks up the main stem.

Reasonably amenable, this miniature palm prefers temperatures around the 65°F (18°C) mark in summer, and enjoys a winter minimum of 50°F (10°C) and maximum of 55°F (13°C).

Focus on ferns

Gently arching, frothy green ferns provide a romantic appeal that few other houseplants can match. They add a feeling of luxury and friendliness to a room — whether it's to add a softness to an angular modern design or to emphasise an informal, relaxed mood. Ferns grow in all sorts of lovely shapes and sizes so there's a huge range to choose from.

Because ferns can thrive in the shade, they come into their own in rooms where there isn't a great deal of natural light. This makes them a handy solution to poorly-lit corners, where their grace and soft lines can brighten up a dull spot.

Ferns are not extreme in their needs, and once these are understood they are among the easiest of plants to keep. The secret of success is to keep the air around their fronds warm and moist.

Remember that most ferns prefer a stable temperature of about 65°F (18°C), although some species will be healthier at slightly higher or lower temperatures depending on where they come from.

Ferns are happiest in dappled light, where they are in no danger of burning in the sun; the deep green colouring of the fronds helps them to make the most of whatever light is available, and because ferns don't flower, they don't need the extra light that other plants need to form flower buds.

Growing a healthy plant

When repotting put a good layer of pebbles or stones in the bottom of the pot. The stones let the water drain away freely. Then add some peaty compost which you can make by using John Innes No 2 with an equal amount of peat.

Keep the compost moderately moist at all times and always water your fern with tepid water long before the compost is in danger of drying out. If you overwater and saturate the compost the fronds will turn brown and drop, or the plant may die altogether. Feed your ferns with a half-strength liquid house-plant fertiliser every two weeks or so throughout the growing season.

Underwatering makes a fern dehydrate — especially a species like the Maidenhair, which has very thin, delicate fronds that dry out quickly. If this happens trim back the damaged and dead fronds. Keep the compost moist and the atmosphere humid, and nurse

Boston Ferns grow well at a window provided they don't have to sit in the sun.

atmosphere for too long. You can solve this problem in two ways: either don't grow those ferns with thin fronds — concentrate on species with fleshy leaves, or improve the condition of the atmosphere around the plant.

By mist spraying your ferns twice a day in warm weather you will help to ease the problem of dehydration, as this helps to reduce water loss from the plant by covering the fronds with a film of water. Also, grouping your ferns together helps to produce a moist micro-climate around the plants. You don't even have to plant them in the same container — just stand them close together to get the same effect.

When growing a fern on its own as a feature plant stand it on a tray or saucer with a surface area roughly similar to the spread of the fronds. Put small pebbles or shingle in the tray and then fill it with about an inch (25mm) or so of water. Don't let the bottom of the pot actually sit in the water or the compost will get saturated and the roots rot. When it's warm the water evaporates and moistens the air around the fronds; but remember to top up the tray with water as it evaporates.

the plant back to health. Not all ferns react as badly to underwatering as the Maidenhair. Species such as the Bird's Nest Fern and Stag's Horn Fern have fleshier leaves and seem to be able to recover well from drought and so are much more reliable for the absent-minded fern lover!

Creating humidity

By far the biggest problem when growing ferns is due to the effects of a warm, dry atmos-phere.Generally most ferns have fairly thin fronds that are not able to store much water. This makes the fronds very susceptible to dehydration when exposed to a dry

Maidenhair Fern *(Adiantum)*

Delicate, light fronds make the Maidenhair Fern one of the prettiest and most popular houseplants of all. But it needs plenty of moisture in the air around its fronds. There are lots of lovely Adiantiums to look for from tiny, fragile little plants to enormous, arching specimens. *A.tenereum* has glossy, black-stalked fronds, and *A.scutum roseum* produces each new frond with a beautiful pinkish colour before changing to green as it matures.

Bird's Nest Fern
(Asplenium)

The Bird's Nest Fern has shiny, strap-like, apple-green fronds

Above, Maidenhair Fern.
Above right, Holly Fern.

Left, Bird's Nest Fern.

which unfurl from a central tangle of brown scales. The fronds form a rosette of arching leaves which in time can grow quite long. Generally hardier than most houseplant ferns, the Bird's Nest Fern will tolerate more exposure to light than most ferns.

Holly Fern (Cyrtomium)
This is a really easy fern to grow and can stand quite low temperatures, so keep it in cool rooms which aren't warm enough for other plants. The most common species is *C.falcatum* which has shiny fronds with almost holly-like leaflets. New fronds have an interesting whitish-brown covering of scales.

Boston Fern (Nephrolepis)
The Boston Fern, *N.bostoniensis*, is an improved version of the Ladder Fern. Both this and *N.exaltata* are popular ferns which grow very large and full given the right conditions. Grow the Boston Fern in a hanging basket or on a pedestal where its lovely arching, feathery fronds can be properly admired.

Button Fern (Pellaea)
The *P.rotundifolia* is a beautiful little fern with downward arching rather wiry stems which then lie flat out from the base of the pot. These delicate stems have small, almost circular, dark green leaves. It is easy and undemanding to grow, but it does not like cold water being left on its leaves.

Stag's Horn Fern (Platycerium)
The Stag's Horn Fern is a most unusual plant with strange, fleshy, grey-green leaves that look just like antlers. Both *P.alcicorne* and *P.bibifurcatum* are tough houseplants that can tolerate low temperatures, a dry atmosphere and even the occasional missed watering.

Above, Boston Fern.
Above right, Button Fern.

Left, Stag's Horn Fern.

Easy indoor orchids

If you think you can't grow orchids — think again. Modern plants — hybrids produced by the experts in plant breeding — can be surprisingly undemanding. And the new easy-grow orchids are often even more alluring than their predecessors. They're still exciting and exotic, but, fortunately, they're no longer necessarily expensive to buy or tricky to keep.

The orchid family is vast — probably the largest flowering plant family in the world, with over 100,000 species and hybrids, divided among 750 genera. The figures are staggering. But only a handful of genera have been able to produce tolerant plants which will grow in a variety of surroundings, with a minimum of attention. They can bring flamboyant blooms to your home — often in the darkest, most cruel months of the year.

With its tapering, outstretched petals, the striking *Paphiopedilum rothschildianum* 'Mont Milais' resembles a fleet of outlandish aircraft.

Autumn-flowering *Paphiopedilum hirsutissimum* from Northern India.

271

Stunning *Phalaenopsis* Solvang 'Portland Star' can produce up to 15 blooms.

Temperatures

	NIGHT		DAY	
	Winter	**Summer**	**Winter**	**Summer**
Cool	50°F (10°C)	55°F (13°C)	55°F (13°C)	65°F (18°C)
Intermediate	55°F (13°C)	65°F (18°C)	65°F (18°C)	75°F (24°C)
Warm	65°F (18°C)	75°F (24°C)	75°F (24°C)	85°F (29°C)

Orchids grow wild all over the world. The tree orchids, called epiphytes, are native to the tropics, where they cling to trees and shrubs, even rocks, for support, with the aid of their aerial roots.

They aren't parasites, despite popular belief, but are true air plants. Their needs are slight and they get all their water from the moisture in the air, via their aerial roots. Extra nourishment comes from animal and vegetable debris collected amongst the cluster of their leaves. Most of the orchids grown as houseplants are tree orchids. They are ideal for growing on slabs of bark, but most of them grow perfectly happily in pots. Potting will be covered separately.

A few houseplants belong to the other group of orchids — the ground-growers or terrestrials. Terrestrials come from the more temperate climes. They are much less adaptable and usually less attractive than epiphytes and only one type — the Slipper Orchid (Paphiopedilum) — has become relatively common as an indoor plant.

Where to shop

Surprisingly, orchid plants can be bought from chain stores and supermarkets, where they're excellent value. Garden centres and florists also stock them, of course, but for the best choice, contact a specialist orchid nursery.

No orchid is cheap. But remember, most have been carefully nurtured for anything between five and 15 years before they're ready for sale. Hybrids are the best buys, usually. If you stick to those that have a proven track record, you can't go far wrong, and choosing by colour is as good a way as any. Species tend to be a bit more expensive.

There's a guide to the five easiest and most rewarding types given overleaf, but there are a few others you can look out for. They include Cattleyas, Brassias, Dendrobiums, Laelias, Miltonias and Vandas.

Lighting needs

In the wild, orchids prefer bright, but dappled light. They need good light to

Orchid structure

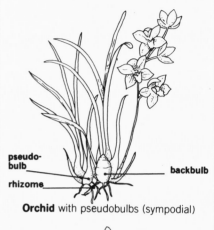

Orchid with pseudobulbs (symapodial)

pseudo-bulb
backbulb
rhizome

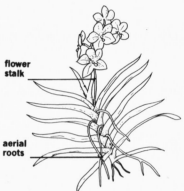

flower stalk

aerial roots

Single-stemmed orchid (monopodial)

Orchids are unusual in more ways than one. Most of those grown as houseplants produce pseudobulbs, or false bulbs, which are like swollen stems. They come in all shapes and sizes, and their job is to carry the new growth. But they have one other important function — to store enough water to get the orchid through a drought.

A long time after their leaves have emerged, the pseudobulb continues to survive. Once its flowers have opened, the pseudobulb, now known as a 'back bulb', begins to die. But its life span can be as long as five years. A plant may carry many pseudobulbs and back bulbs at any time, for new ones develop every year. These are joined to each other by a length of rhizome (stem).

Not all orchids grow in this way. Some epiphytes have just one main stem, which rises from a tuft of roots at the base, and carries leaves (and sometimes aerial roots) along its length. It grows upwards, and can reach 2ft (60cm) or more before producing flower stalks at the top.

The typical terrestrial orchid also has a single stem, rising from thick, fleshy roots or tubers. The terrestrials may rest for a time during the winter months.

Flowers and leaves

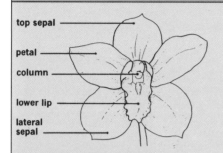

top sepal

petal

column

lower lip

lateral
sepal

The orchid flower is quite unique. It always follows the same basic design. But no two have quite the same shape: colour and size vary enormously, too.

The characteristic lower lip can be spectacular, often spurred or frilled, and often in colours that startle by their contrasts. Fleshy, waxy blooms may be scented or scentless, noxious or fragrant. They come singly or in clusters, drooping or erect. And they are very enduring. Whether on the plant or in a vase, a flower may last for as long as 12 weeks — though some may last no longer than three weeks.

Foliage can be a bit disappointing. Most leaves are in a single shade of green, and either thick and leathery or thin and papery. Some even fall occasionally. But there are some orchids which make very attractive foliage plants with mottled, two-tone leaves to compensate for the lack of flowers once they have died down.

Orchids fit into temperature categories, as you can see on the chart. Most of those featured here enjoy cool to intermediate conditions. And although they enjoy some fresh air, they don't like cold draughts. If they're on a windowsill, make sure the windows are well-sealed, and move plants away from the windows on frosty nights. In summer months, when temperatures outside are reliable, open the windows, or better still put the orchids outside in a shady spot for a few hours.

A moist atmosphere is vital at all times. To achieve it, fill a dish or gravel tray with pebbles or shingle, which should be kept topped up with water, and put the pots on top.

Gravel trays help to protect the plants from a radiator, too, as these plants can't tolerate too much direct heat.

Mist spraying with a water gun will help keep the atmosphere moist, too, and most orchids will benefit from having their leaves sprayed during the growing season when temperatures rise.

Watering

Orchids prefer rainwater to tapwater, since they dislike lime. If you aren't able to provide this, add one teaspoon of vinegar per gallon (4.5 litres) of tap water, and use this instead.

Never let an orchid stand in water or its roots may rot. The free-draining mix-

ture in which they're grown helps prevent this sort of problem. When watering an epiphytic orchid, soak the mixture thoroughly, making sure the water can drain away. Then leave the plant until the mixture begins to dry out before watering again. This means you probably won't have to water it more than once a week.

During the resting period (see below), water sparingly, giving only enough to stop the compost and the pseudobulbs from drying out completely.

Plants grown in baskets or on bark can be watered by immersing them in a bowl of water for some minutes. Drain them thoroughly before returning them to their usual position. Don't water again until the plant base begins to feel dry.

Terrestrial orchids like more water than tree orchids, so keep their compost steadily moist.

Resting

Some orchids — Odontoglossums, for instance — grow throughout the year, though they'll slow down in autumn or winter. Others, like the Laelias, have a resting phase, when growth all but stops, and some of the leaves may even fall off. This resting period, which follows flowering, lasts no more than a matter of weeks as a rule and during this time plants shouldn't be fed. Water requirements are also minimal.

---

develop flowers, but they shouldn't ever be exposed to direct sunlight, even through a window. Direct sun can burn them — the foliage becomes yellow and can develop brown or black patches.

The answer is to protect orchids with net curtains and place them, ideally, near an east- or west-facing window. Here the plants will get three or four hours of filtered sun every day.

In winter, good light is even more important for plants about to flower. Unless you can provide them with 10 hours of light a day (and preferably 12), you can't be sure of a good display. Obviously this can present problems. But if weather conditions don't permit, don't give up — an artificial lighting system is a good alternative to natural daylight.

Temperature and humidity

To grow and flower successfully, orchids also need enough (but not too much) warmth and moisture. But getting the temperature right to the last degree isn't crucial.

***Cymbidium* Annan 'Cooksbridge'** flowers between late winter and spring.

The superb yellow *Cymbidium* Mary Pinchness 'Del Rey'.

Name and type	Description	Temperature and humidity	Watering	Resting	Varieties
Odontoglossum Very showy plants, mainly epiphytic, producing pseudobulbs. Includes some of the best modern hybrids.	Large, attractive flowers 3-4in (8-10cm) across, often in several colours which form dramatic designs, usually in the form of spots. Plants can produce up to 30 flowers, carried in sprays at the top of several arching flower stems. Flowers are sometimes fragrant, lasting up to 8 or even 10 weeks. They are produced irregularly, every nine months or so, but usually between late autumn and spring.	Cool or intermediate, depending on plant. High humidity; mist spray daily in temperatures over 60°F (15°C). Ensure some fresh air occasionally.	Allow the compost to dry cut to half its depth between waterings.	Hybrids have no definite resting period, but slow down after flowering in autumn/winter. Some species have a short rest.	Plants available are mainly hybrids in a wide range of colours. Many are the results of breeding Odontoglossums with more robust relatives. The most popular are Odontiodas, Odontonias, Wilsonaras and Vuylstekearas. Recommended species include: *Odontoglossum bictoniense.* (yellow-green spotted with brown, with a white or pink lip). *O. grande* (Tiger Orchid). (Bright yellow with brown stripes and a creamy yellow lip.) *O. crispum* (white or rose-tinged, or blotched with red).
Moth Orchid *(Phalaenopsis)* Single-stemmed epiphytic orchid which produces aerial roots that may cover surface of compost. Can do well in wooden or wire baskets.	Flowers appear on long, arching stalks, up to 30 at a time, looking like a flight of moths (hence the popular name). Flowers can be 1-5in (2.5-13cm) across, and can appear at any time of year, lasting up to three weeks each. These produce only a few leaves, which are wide and fleshy but not very large. Strong aerial roots.	Intermediate temperatures. High humidity; mist spray daily.	Allow top ½in (13mm) of compost to dry out between waterings. Water in mornings if possible, and wipe off any water that drops on to foliage at once; these plants are particularly vulnerable to fungus and rot.	Growth practically ceases in winter.	Species are naturally either white or pink. Hybrids, which are superior, come in a range of colours and may be striped or spotted. Popular species include: *Palaenopsis amabilis* (white with red-spotted lip and yellow tinge). *P.schilleriana* (pale pink with reddish brown spots). *P.stuartiana* (white, heavily speckled with purple; yellow lip).
Lady's Slipper or Slipper Orchid *(Paphiopedilum)* Terrestrial orchid in an immense range of sizes, shapes and colours. Flowers usually require staking.	Owes its popular name to the pouch-shaped lip. Each flower stem carries just one flower, which may last over 10 weeks, appearing between autumn and spring. Flowers have a waxy, almost artificial look, and the top sepal is often in a contrasting colour to the rest. Thick, fleshy leaves may also be attractively mottled with purple and maroon, though plants of that type tend to need slightly higher temperatures.	Both cool and intermediate growing plants. Mist spray daily in temperatures over 70°F (21°C).	Allow top 1-2in (2.5-5cm) of compost to dry out between waterings.	No resting period, but plants make little growth for six weeks after flowering.	Many colours and combinations available; most plants on offer are hybrids. It is possible to buy species from specialist growers. Recommended species include: *Paphiopedilum fairieanum* (white, veined with purple; green lip with reddish-purple tinge). Flowers in summer and autumn. *P.spiceranum* (yellow-green petals with crimson stripe; white top sepal; crimson lip). Spring flowering. *P.villosum* (glossy, rich bronze). Flowers in winter and spring.
Lycaste Includes some of the easiest of orchids to grow indoors. Those used as houseplants are epiphytic and produce pseudobulbs.	Arching stems each produce one 3in (8cm) flattish, waxy flower. These may be fragrant. Usually spring and summer flowering, but some varieties bloom in winter. Dark green leaves are narrow at base and tip, but very wide in the middle.	Cool growing plants	Allow compost to dry out almost completely between waterings.	Most have long winter rest periods.	Available species include: *Lycaste aromatica* (yellow with reddish spotting). *L.cruenta* (shades of yellow with its lips flushed red). *L.deppei* (green and white with red-streaked lip). There are many hybrids, some of which produce very large flowers.

grow at home

Name and type	Description	Temperature and humidity	Watering	Resting	Varieties
Cymbidiums Easy-to-grow 'beginner's orchid'. Best in miniature form, though standard sizes are also available. Those suitable for growing in the home are all epiphytic and produce pseudobulbs.	Flowers 3in (8cm) across appear along stems, often with as many as 15 flowers per spike. Plants may bloom for up to 12 weeks. Many varieties are autumn and winter blooming. Very wide choice of colours; boat-shaped lip may harmonise or contrast with rest of flower. Leaves are leathery, strap-shaped, about 15in (38cm) long.	Intermediate growers. Plants will survive up to 80°F (27°C). They like high humidity, so mist spray daily in temperatures over 65°F (18°C).	Allow top 1in (2.5cm) of compost to dry out before watering.	Plants may rest briefly in autumn.	Many hybrids and one or two species worth trying. The following are worth considering: *Cymbidium* Annan 'Cooksbridge' (deep pink). *C.* Aviemore 'Lewes' (pale pink). *C.* Stonehaven 'Cooksbridge' (yellow). *C.* Evening Star 'Pastel Princess' (rich cream, with pink lip). *C.devonianum* (olive green, crimson and purple).

Feeding

It's a good idea to give plants a little extra nourishment during the growing season, but take care not to overfeed them — it's harmful. Foliar feeds are ideal for air plants like tree orchids, although liquid feeding is perfectly acceptable — especially for the terrestrials.

Use any general fertiliser, like Phostrogen, at a quarter strength, or buy a special orchid fertiliser from an orchid nursery. These may come in various strengths — for young plants, adult plants or plants approaching flowering.

Give a liquid feed once every two weeks or so, or use a foliar feed at every third or fourth watering.

Caring for your plants

Orchids enjoy a clean, tidy environment. So sponge the leaves of your orchids from time to time, to keep them free of dust. Nip out any black tips that appear — these are just a sign of old age. If a plant loses the odd leaf from time to time, don't be alarmed — it's quite normal. Dead and dying leaves should be removed, in case they cause blemishes on otherwise healthy parts.

When a flower dies always remove it, and at the end of the flowering season cut off the flower stem at the base. Watch out for pests like scale insect or mealy bug, which may be lurking at the base of the old flower stalks, beneath the leaves or on the pseudobulbs. If the atmosphere is not kept sufficiently humid red spider mite can be a problem.

If you look after your plants, you can regard orchids as permanent features of your home which will go on flowering successfully, year after year.

Some of the startling patterns produced by breeding Odontoglossums with other related genera. Mature plants will produce up to 15 flowers on arching stems.

Planning a miniature garden

Miniature gardens can be a lot of fun. Basically, the idea is to group plants in such a way as to create a suggestion of landscaping. This is what sets a miniature garden apart from any other arrangement of plants in a bowl.

This delightful garden in miniature is arranged on a serving dish and comes complete with model ducks and a pond made of slate.

Plants include: Armeria, Saxifraga, Sempervivum, Sedum and Selaginella.

Properly done, a miniature garden is far more interesting to look at than a single plant, or even a group, because there is so much more detail to absorb. It can be as realistic — or otherwise — as you like, ranging from a miniaturised replica of your garden outside to something one step removed from a Japanese flower arrangement. As you might expect, there is a definite technique for creating a successful miniature garden. And, in just the same way as full-sized landscape gardening, it all starts with careful planning.

First things first

Designing and planning the miniature garden begins by looking carefully at the place in which the finished garden is to go. It is most important to get the relationship between the garden and its surroundings right from the start.

Plants

Choose these with care. Plants should remain small and keep their shape well. Remember to decide on your theme before you start buying new plants, and choose only those which contribute to it.

Go for varieties which replicate the shapes of larger, outdoor plants if you want a realistic miniature garden, or choose ones that represent scaled-down tropical landscape gardens, alpine gardens, or even stylised Japanese gardens.

SMALL AND SLOW

Dwarf Pomegranate **(Punica granatum nana)**
Earth Star (Cryptanthus)
Episcia
Lachenalia
Palm seedlings
Snakeskin Plant **(Fittonia argyroneura nana)**
Look out too for bonsai trained versions of shrubby houseplants or trees.

FERNS

Button Fern **(Pellaea rotundifolia)**
Dwarf Maidenhair **(Adiantum pedatum subpumilum)**
Rose Maidenhair **(A. hispidulum)**

MINIATURE IVIES

Hedera helix 'Ambrosia' — small crimped leaves, variegated

H. helix 'Arran' — mini version of plain green wild Ivy
H. helix 'Aurea' — variegated, lime green leaves marked with dark green splashes
H. helix 'Jubilee' — notable dense variety with tiny vareigated leaves
H. helix 'Spetchley' — stiff upright stems, densely packed with tiny leaves

PLANTS MIMICKING SCALED-DOWN OUTDOOR PLANTS

SHRUBBY
Box **(Buxus sempervirens)** — can be clipped into miniature topiary shapes
Bead Plant **(Nertera depressa)** low hummocks covered with small red berries
Euonymus
Miniature Rose
Myrtle **(Myrtus communis compacta)** — can be clipped and trained into shape
Resurrection Plant **(Selaginella lepidophylla)**

SPIKY
Mondo Grass **(Ophiopogon japonicus)**
Sweet Flag **(Acorus gramineus)** 'Variegatus'

CREEPING
Creeping Jenny **(Pilea depressa)**
Indian Strawberry **(Duchesnea indica)**

ALPINE AND ROCK PLANTS

These are best grown in a sunny porch before being brought into a cool room for flowering, and then returned outdoors after flowering.
Armeria caespitosa — a mini hillock-forming Thrift, pink flowers
Arenaria purpurascens — mat forming, pink flowers
Cobweb Houseleek **(Sempervivum arachnoideum)**
Dwarf Lavender **(Lavandula spica** 'Dwarf Munstead')
Lewisia cotyledon — rosette-shaped plant, short spikes and stripy pink flowers in summer
Raoulia australis — spreading yellow carpet
Saxifraga aizoon — silvery mounds, pink flowers in spring
S. oppositifolia — bright green mats, purple flowers in spring
Shooting Stars **(Dodecatheon dentatum)**

Spend a few moments really studying the place you have chosen — its shape, whether or not it is enclosed, and so on. Make a mental note of the maximum height the garden can go up to, its width, the background against which the garden will be seen and, most important of all, whether it will be viewed from only one side or all round.

Containers

Now turn your attention to the choice of container. This is the most important single feature of a miniature garden, because it acts as a link, pulling together all the various elements that go to make up the garden. The style of the container sets the scene for the garden more than anything else. Terracotta, glazed porcelain and stoneware are all ideal materials for your container, though good quality plastics may also be used. Neutral colours such as beige, earthy greens and browns look most natural, though there is, of course, no reason why you shouldn't choose another colour if it happens to tone in with your room's colour scheme. Bright colours, though, do not somehow look quite right in the context of a miniature garden. Patterned containers are also difficult to work with.

Containers for miniature gardens need to be wide and relatively shallow. And, since the garden will probably be stood on a polished surface, you'll need a container without any drainage holes in the bottom. You may find something suitable at a garden centre, but the best choice is often found in a florist's shop specialising in unusual vases — the shallow kind used for Japanese flower arrangements is ideal.

Ornaments and other 'props'

This is an area where you are allowed a certain amount of artistic licence. Try to choose tasteful items that pursue the theme of your garden, while remaining on the same scale. The sort of ornaments you might like to use include small figurines, miniature pagodas, models or abstract pieces.

Cut flowers

Another useful way of adding to the illusion of a real-life garden is to use cut flowers or foliage. Then, when you are designing the layout, leave a space for a small water container (such as the containers that rolls of film come in), which should be sunk into the compost. This can then be used for an ever-changing selection of fresh seasonal materials.

Soil and surface cover

Because your container has no drainage holes you'll need to provide an adequate drainage layer and ensure that the soil doesn't go sour. See 'Planting a terrarium' page 669 and 'Growing plants in a fish tank' page 722 on how you can achieve this.

Finally, the finishing touch that completes any miniature garden is its surface cover. Like the container, this acts as a link, pulling plants and props together, so that they no longer look like a lot of separate items. It also provides a common background against which everything in the garden can then be seen.

Choose a background appropriate to the type of garden you are making. For example, alpine plants suit a fine gritty background, whereas a tropical garden looks better against a mossy background. And if you are trying to recreate a very realistic garden, use a bit of both to suggest lawns and pathways. Gravel surfaces are in fact best suggested not by gravel itself, but by a scaled-down alternative — sharp sand or the sort of fine grit often sold for cacti. Both are available from garden centres.

Mossy surfaces are best achieved using Helxine or one of the creeping Selaginellas such as *S.denticulata*, which is green, or *S.d. aurea*, which is gold. Alternatively, for a hummocky surface, try *S.krausseana brownii* , which forms bright green mossy mounds, about 4in (10cm) high. Or for a pale, greeny-blue mossy finish, use dried Reindeer Moss, which is available from florists.

Planting a bottle garden

Creating a beautiful plant arrangement inside a container is not only challenging and great fun — it's also a very practical way to give plants an environment in which they'll thrive and be happy. And glass containers, plain or tinted, look lovely in themselves, as well as providing the perfect setting for a miniature garden.

A range of containers: carboys often have attractively tinted glass, but plain storage jars will do just as well.

Bottle gardens have a lot of plus points, and virtually no disadvantages. Obviously you must take care not to have them somewhere where they might be knocked over and broken, so don't put them on the floor near doorways or in parts of the house which get a lot of traffic, and don't risk them on shelves unless they're going to be left undisturbed and are out of the reach of small children.

A bottle garden acts like a miniature glasshouse — its main advantage is that it provides an enclosed, self-regulating atmosphere for the plants to live in. Not only will they do very well, but they require virtually no care or maintenance — essential if you're forgetful or very busy! They are also a boon if you go away frequently, since you needn't worry about the plants drying out, provided the container is sealed properly. They're protected from fumes, draughts and sudden changes of temperature, and can't be knocked or damaged. Pests and diseases won't be a problem either, since there is no way that they can get in from the outside.

Bottle gardens may seem to work by magic, but actually the principle is very simple. Once the compost has been watered and the bottle sealed, water is just recycled inside. It is taken up by the roots of the plants and given off by the leaves; it then condenses on the sides of the bottle and runs back into the compost. There's no risk of underwatering or overwatering your plants, because they'll take just the amount of moisture they need.

The best plants to choose for a bottle garden are those that like moisture and warmth, and that grow fairly slowly. If you plant fast-growing varieties in a bottle you'll be spending all your time pruning them back so that they don't run out of space! On the whole, flowering plants don't do all that well — their petals are vulnerable to mould in the humid atmosphere, and that encourages disease. So it's best to stick to the prettier foliage plants. The one exception to this, however, is the African Violet: all the varieties, with their lovely colours, do very well in an enclosed atmosphere. On the opposite page we give you some

ideas about what to choose and what plants look good together.

What container?
Almost any glass jar or container can be used, provided it is large enough for you to plant it comfortably and has a tightly fitting lid or stopper that you can remove easily. Carboys, wine demijohns, sweet jars, bulbous wine bottles — the possibilities are endless. You can buy specially made jars in garden centres, but it's more fun — and cheaper! — to experiment with other containers. You can often pick up lovely things in junk shops. Tinted glass looks pretty, but make sure it isn't *too* dark, or it will stop the light getting to your plants.

If you buy a bottle from a garden shop, it'll probably be ready to plant straightaway. But if you are using a container from any other source, do be sure that you clean it very thoroughly — it could have had something in it that might be damaging to your plants. Wash it with mild, soapy water and rinse it and, just to be on the safe side, sterilise it with a solution such as Milton.

A variegated ivy, some creeping moss, a Silver Lace Fern and a palm provide a wide variety of textures.

A pretty jar with a fittonia around the edge and a bromeliad to fill out the centre.

Bottle beauties

Acorus gramineus variegatus **Sweet flag**	Fan-shaped tufts of white-striped grassy leaves
Adiantum raddianum **Delta Maidenhair Fern**	Filmy pale green fronds on dark brown stems
Begonia rex	Leaves marked with red, green and russet
Calathea insignis **Rattlesnake Plant**	Leaves with reddish undersides and dark brown bands
Calathea makoyana **Peacock Plant**	Green and white herringbone-striped leaves
Calathea ornata	Leaves with narrow pink or ivory stripes
Calathea zebrina **Zebra Plant**	Dark stripes and a velvety surface
Cryptanthus **Starfish Plant**	Striped with white, brown or red
Cyperus alternifolius **Umbrella Plant**	Tiny umbrellas of slender leaves
Dracaena sanderiana **Ribbon Plant**	Vivid green leaves with white rims
Ficus pumila **Creeping Fig**	Small oval green leaves and wiry stems
Fittonia argyroneura **Snakeskin Plant**	Leaves intricately netted with white
Fittonia verschaffeltii **Mosaic Plant**	Leaves netted with red
Hedera helix **Glacier Ivy**	Creamy variegated leaves
Hedera helix **Little Eva Ivy**	Small leaves rimmed with cream
Hedera sagittaefolia **Needlepoint Ivy**	Leaves with a long pointed lobe
Maranta leuconeura **Prayer Plant**	Broad green leaves blotched with purple
Maranta tricolor **Herringbone Plant**	Red veins and a yellow midrib
Neanthe bella **Parlour Palm**	Elegant and tiny palm with arching stems
Pellaea rotundifolia **Button Fern**	Button-like leaves on slender stems
Pellionia daveauana	Tiny plant with brown-edged golden leaves
Pellionia pulchra	Green leaves with dark brown veins
Peperomia argyreia **Rugby Football Plant**	Heart-shaped leaves with green and silver stripes
Peperomia caperata **Emerald Ripple**	Quilted green leaves and whitish-green flowers
Pilea **Moon Valley**	Greenish-yellow leaves with black veins
Pilea cadieri **Aluminium Plant**	Quilted leaves patched with silver
Pilea involucrata **Friendship Plant**	Reddish leaves with dark veins
Saxifraga sarmentosa tricolor **Mother of Thousands**	Cream and green leaves edged with pink or red

Tools for the job

You'll need some rather unusual tools to plant a bottle garden, but don't worry — you don't need to buy them specially because they can be very easily made up from ordinary household and gardening things.

You'll need a few lengths of thin cane or some supporting stakes, long enough to reach comfortably to the bottom of the jar and leave you enough to hold on to. Tie to the end of three of them:

A a spoon.
B a kitchen fork.
C an empty cotton reel, flat end down.

These will be perfect for making holes for plants, and for loosening and firming the soil.

You'll also need:

D a small sharp knife or a razor blade on the end of a stick for removing

dead leaves and pruning back growth.
E some tweezers to help position your plants, and you can make these by splitting the end of a cane.
F two sticks held together can serve as tongs.

1 First funnel in a 2in (5cm) layer of gravel, to provide good drainage. Then add 3-4in (7-10cm) of potting compost.

2 Starting from the outside of the bottle, put your selected plants gently into prepared holes.

3 When you've positioned each plant, firm the soil around it gently using the cotton reel tied to a cane.

1

Arrange your plants in size order. *From left to right* (this page): Snakeskin Plant, Button Fern, *Peperomia rotundifolia*, Peacock Plant.

Preparing for planting

Because you don't want your bottle plants to grow too fast, the soil in your container must not be too rich. Also, to make sure you don't introduce any pests or diseases, buy the soil ingredients from a supplier who sells them in sealed plastic bags — they ought to be quite sterile. First of all, put in a 2in (5cm) layer of gravel, to provide good drainage. The best method is to pour it in through a funnel made from stiff paper or thin card, so that it goes neatly to the bottom of the jar and does not mess up the sides. Then add ½in (13mm) of charcoal to help keep the soil free from impurities — it will absorb the excess mineral salts and decaying plant matter that can build up in an enclosed atmosphere.

For compost, you could use John Innes No 1, Levingtons Multi-Purpose or Baby Bio Seed and Potting mixture. It's an excellent idea to add one part of Perlite to every two parts of compost — these granules of very light rock help the soil to drain well. You can buy all of these products easily in garden shops. When you've mixed up your compost, funnel it carefully into the jar to a depth of about 3-4in (7-10cm). If you like, you can then use the spoon and fork to make a few little 'hills' in the soil to add interest to the plants and help to set them off. It's a good idea also to bury in the soil a few tablets or spikes of solid fertiliser. This is a convenient way of releasing nourishment to the plants over the next few months.

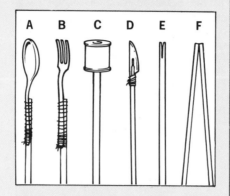

6

Planting the garden

After all the preparation, you're now ready for the exciting part! Lay out some sheets of newspaper on a table, and experiment with arranging the plants you've chosen. Aim to put taller plants in the middle where they'll have the most space above them; but otherwise just move them round until you're pleased with the effect.

When you've decided where they'll go, use the spoon to make the first planting hole. Always start with the plants on the outside of the jar; if you plant the middle first, you won't be able to reach the outside easily. Put the plant carefully into the cane tweezers (or between the tongs) and lower it into the hole and, with your other hand, pack the soil around the roots with the fork. When the plant feels firmly positioned, ease the tweezers away gently, and then press the soil down firmly around the plant with the cotton reel.

5

When all your plants are in, water them carefully. The best way is to let the water trickle slowly down the side of the jar and seep into the soil, so that it doesn't splash the plants with mud. Add just enough water for the surface of the soil to become dark — if you're in any doubt, go for too little water rather than too much. If there are soil particles or mud splashes on the inside of the jar,

4 When the bottle garden is full, water it carefully, directing the water down the inside of the glass.

5 Clean the inside of the glass of soil or water by wiping with a piece of sponge or cloth.

6 Put the stopper on your completed garden, and position the bottle where it will get lots of light.

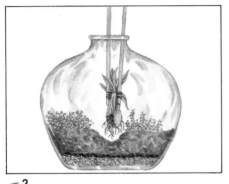

2

From left to right (this page): Parlour Palm (centre), Ribbon Plant, Delta Maidenhair, Prayer Plant, Creeping Fig.

Arrangements to try

There are dozens of exciting permutations when it comes to arranging plants in a bottle garden, and you can be as artistic as you like, provided you don't crowd the jar. Try and choose plants with different coloured leaves, so that they contrast with each other. You could have a Ribbon Plant as a centrepiece, set off by an equally tall Parlour Palm, the two of them contrasted with a selection of much smaller plants, such as Ivy (right). Or for smaller plants you could choose the golden-leaved *Pellionia daveauana*, a Starfish Plant and a Friendship Plant. Another pretty group of small plants would be the Aluminium Plant, the Mother of Thousands and the *Peperomia* Emerald Ripple.

3

Caring for your bottle garden

Put your bottle garden somewhere where it will get lots of light, but not in direct sun — glass concentrates the sun's rays and the result could be scorched leaves inside the bottle. A north-facing windowsill is ideal. You may find that condensation forms on the inside of the bottle after a few days. This is nothing to worry about — just take off the lid or stopper for a few hours to let the compost dry out a little, then replace it.

Once a week or so, you should have a look at your bottle garden, to check whether it needs any attention. If you see any dead leaves or decaying matter, prune it away carefully. Also remove any leaves the moment you see them becoming discoloured — they'll attract disease spores if they are left to decay further and would eventually ruin the other plants in your arrangement. You may also need to cut away occasional

4

clean them off with a piece of sponge or damp cloth attached to a wire — a bent wire coathanger is perfect for the job. Apart from making your bottle garden look attractive, you should keep the insides clean so that water is not trapped by soil particles as it trickles down the sides of the jar into the compost. Now replace the stopper on your bottle and make sure it is a tight fit.

shoots if a plant is growing very vigorously, in case it begins to take up too much room in the bottle.

If all goes well, you shouldn't need to do anything more — your plants will literally look after themselves. Just add a few more fertiliser tablets or spikes every few months to encourage healthy growth. If a disease or pest does manage to get into the garden, it should be quite simple to deal with. If it's a minor problem — such as greenfly, for example — spray a little insecticide into the bottle. But any infestation by mealy bug or red spider mite calls for more drastic action, and it's safer to deal with it outside the bottle. Repeated spraying of strong insecticide into an enclosed atmosphere may be too much for the plants, because it will remain in the atmosphere for a long time, unable to disperse.

Using your tongs, gently prise the affected plant out of the soil and remove it carefully from the bottle. Clean it and dip it in an insecticide solution containing malathion, and then return it to the garden. Repeat the process if necessary.

You'll probably find that your bottle plants don't grow so much in the winter, when light levels are low. This is perfectly normal, but there is a way round it. If you have a bottle with a wide enough neck, and can manage to get a lamp holder to fit it, you can shine a low wattage light bulb (say up to 60 watts) directly into the garden. This will help the plants to grow, as well as make the garden a very pretty feature.

Beautiful bromeliads

Named in honour of Bromel, a seventeenth-century Swedish botanist, bromeliads make up an enormous group of plants, tremendously varied and full of surprises. The best known one is the pineapple. Originally from the humid regions of tropical America, they make excellent houseplants, with stunning flowers, brightly coloured bracts and ornamental foliage. Because they are so exotic and because the way they grow is most unusual, many people assume they are difficult to keep — but nothing could be further from the truth!

Bromeliads can be divided into two categories: the 'epiphytic' ones, which grow on the branches of trees, and the 'terrestrial' ones, which grow rooted in the ground.

Most bromeliads grown as houseplants are epiphytic, although many are adaptable enough to be happy in a pot — except for most Tillandsias. However, their natural method of getting sustenance remains: they draw moisture and nutrition through their leaves directly from the air, and not through their roots, which serve mainly to anchor them. You can arrange to grow them on a piece of bark or tree branch, instead of in a pot, if you prefer!

To assist them in collecting water, bromeliads have developed a little 'cup' at the heart of each rosette of leaves. It is into this cup, if it is big enough, that you pour their water rather than into their compost, although that too should be kept moist. If the cup is very small — as it will be with a young plant, for example — overhead mist spraying is sufficient, because the water will drip down and collect in the cup.

Not only are the leaves of most species thick, glossy and attractively patterned, but some kinds produce magnificent, waxy-textured and startlingly beautiful flowers. The bromeliads that do flower will only do so when they are mature — say, after two or three years — so if you have started with a young one you may have to wait a while.

The flowers sometimes grow half-hidden inside the leaf rosettes, sometimes at the end of long, dramatic spikes. The blooms themselves are in fact no more than $\frac{1}{2}$in (13mm) across,

The leaves of the Blushing Bromeliad are suffused with scarlet when it flowers.

but they grow among brilliantly coloured leaf bracts, usually red or purple. Bromeliads can flower at any time of the year and although the blooms themselves only last a few days, the coloured leaf bracts can survive for much longer, and some varieties produce colourful berries as well.

How to care for them

Apart from the decorative indoor form of the edible pineapple, *Ananas comosus variegatus*, and Earth Star (Cryptanthus), both of which are terrestrial bromeliads which revel in hot, bright sunlight, the rest of the family are happiest in diffused, almost subdued light. This most closely resembles their natural jungle habitat.

They like an average to warm temperature — not less than 55°F (13°C) — but may need extra heat, up to 75°F (24°C), in order to flower. Once the leaf bracts start

to deepen in colour, it is a sign that flowering is getting near, so it's a good idea to put them somewhere specially warm for a few weeks and make sure they get constant, very good light, but not direct sunlight. Guard them carefully against draughts and extremes of temperature.

Watering

The best water for bromeliads is soft. If you don't have naturally soft water, use rainwater, water that has been boiled and cooled, or the water you collect when defrosting the refrigerator — but make sure it's come up to room temperature first! You can also add a few drops of vinegar to every pint (0.5 litre) of tap-water to soften it.

With epiphytic bromeliads, the main watering is by filling the leafy cup at the centre of the rosette of leaves. Check this regularly in summer and always keep it topped up and, in addition, replace the water completely once a month. You can do this easily by turning the whole plant gently over to tip out the old water. Every other month you should add liquid fertiliser to the new water. If the plant is in a pot, keep the compost just moist.

With terrestrial bromeliads, such as Ananas and Cryptanthus, you should keep the potting compost fairly moist, but never let the soil get waterlogged.

Mist spray leaves regularly from overhead in spring and summer, and occasionally in the winter. If the leaves ever look pale it's a good idea to spray them with a foliar feed, such as PBI Fillip.

Displaying bromeliads

Because epiphytic bromeliads don't need to be rooted in soil, you can grow them in fascinating ways, such as clinging individually to a piece of bark, cork or driftwood. Or you can arrange several of them on a nicely shaped tree branch about 3-4in (8-10cm) in diameter.

Anchor the branch in a decorative bowl or pot, by packing it round with stones and pebbles and cementing it in with plaster of Paris. Choose half a dozen or more epiphytic bromeliads, such as Tillandsia, Guzmania, Neoregelia and Aechmea. Remove them from any pots, wrap their roots in thick wads of fresh sphagnum moss, and fix this to the branch with loops of plastic-coated wire. Water them and mist spray them regularly just as usual.

With complementing colours and shapes, an arrangement like this makes a stunning feature in a conservatory, where frequent mist spraying can be done without risking any damage to furniture. And if you'd like the branch to be covered with moss, you can make it grow quickly by spraying the branch with milk!

Potting on and propagation

Each rosette of a bromeliad will only flower once and then die, though the bracts will remain attractive for several months. During this period, new offsets will grow up around the base of the plant. When the parent plant has died, you should cut it down to leave room for the offsets to grow up.

With terrestrial bromeliads, the best plan is to leave one, or perhaps two, offsets in the original pot, and remove any others to make separate plants. You'll need to pot the original plant on every year to allow for more root growth, and also more room for the new plants. A pot size of 10-12in (25-30cm) should be the biggest you'll need. Use a peat-based compost, such as Levingtons, mixed with a quarter part of coarse sand or perlite to improve drainage. The compost you use must be lime-free.

To make new plants, remove the offsets carefully and pot them singly in 3-4in (8-10cm) pots, using an open, lime-free, peat-based compost as described above. Keep them in a warm place — at least 55°F (13°C).

You make new epiphytic bromeliads in much the same way: after cutting down the parent plant, separate off a few new offsets, and attach them to separate pieces of bark or wood. You can then treat them as mature plants.

Ananas comosus variegatus is the decorative Pineapple Plant.

Tips on care

One reason why bromeliads make excellent houseplants is that they are remarkably free from pests. They might suffer from scale insects or from mealy bugs, but both of these can be easily wiped away with a sponge or cloth soaked in a malathion-based insecticide. Always make sure that you keep the central cup filled with water, or your bromeliad will lose strength and die (*above*).

Which ones to choose?

● **The Urn Plant** *(Aechmea fasciata)* is justly popular. It has grey-green, arching leaves, banded with white, from the centre of which appears a long flower spike with a large cone of rosy red bracts around small, pale blue flowers. The flowers gradually turn red, then die, but the bracts remain colourful for several months.

● **The Blue-Flowered Torch** *(Tillandsia lindenii)* has a rosette of long, narrow leaves and a flower stalk up to 1ft (0.3m) long, bearing royal blue flowers inside pink bracts. It looks really exotic, and can bring gasps of amazement from people who see it for the first time.

● The increasingly popular 'air plants', sold on pieces of cork or bark, are members of the Tillandsia group. **Spanish Moss** *(Tillandsia usneoides)* is a curious one, forming long, greyish-green strands that gather into trailing 'beards' several feet long.

● There are others worth seeking out. Specially fine is the **Blushing Bromeliad** *(Neoregelia carolinae tricolor)*, whose rosette of green leaves, striped with white or rose-pink, becomes suffused with scarlet at the centre as the plant is about to flower.

● The aptly named **King of the Bromeliads** *(Vriesea hieroglyphica)* is prized above all for its intricately patterned leaves. They grow up to 2½ft (0.75m) long and 3in (8cm) wide, and are bright green with bands of purple. **Flaming Sword** *(Vriesea splendens)* is similar in foliage, but has in addition a long flower spike of brilliant red bracts, from which yellow flowers emerge.

● The plants in the Guzmania group are very beautiful, and usually flower in the winter. *Guzmania lingulata* has several forms, usually with smooth green leaves and a flower spike bearing crimson bracts and yellow blooms.

● There are low-growing kinds too, notably **Earth Star** *(Cryptanthus)*, a terrestrial bromeliad, which makes a fascinating plant in a terrarium or bottle garden. The leaves, in star-shaped rosettes, are strongly patterned, striped and banded with cream, and often with attractive wavy edges. *Cryptanthus zonatus* has brownish-green leaves, cross-banded in white, brown and green.

A good garden centre should stock quite a range of bromeliads. Go along and see what you can find. You certainly won't be disappointed.

The Urn Plant has a stunning bloom.

Flaming Sword sums up this flower.

The colourful stripes and spiky shape of Earth Star make it a striking plant.

Planting a terrarium

Many people are fascinated by terrariums, but nervous at the prospect of owning one themselves. They imagine that they must be both complicated to construct and tricky to look after. As it happens, both these fears are quite unfounded. A terrarium is simply a miniature indoor garden made of glass which, once you've planted it, virtually looks after itself. One of the most attractive and original ways of displaying a selection of houseplants, you'll find it is a constant source of enjoyment for yourself and admiration for your visitors.

The original name for a terrarium was a Wardian case — a purpose-made, brass-framed, glass container rather like a small indoor greenhouse. It was developed by a nineteenth-century biologist, Dr Nathaniel Ward, to transport plant specimens — especially ferns — in safety from one country to another. Ferns rapidly became among the most popular of all houseplants and Wardian cases were soon found in many elegant Victorian drawing rooms.

Choosing a terrarium

Garden centres and shops nowadays often stock a range of metal and glass terrariums, based on the design of the earlier Wardian cases. These are extremely decorative (and often quite expensive), but are by no means the only suitable receptacles. Almost any glass container can be used as a terrarium, and will offer a perfectly suitable environment for your plants. Ideally, it should have a door or lid that closes fairly tightly, and the top should slope so that condensed water runs down it gently rather than dripping in large drops on to the plants beneath. However, many modern terrariums have a more open structure, making them a half-way stage between a real Wardian case and an elaborate pot.

How they work

If they can be completely sealed, terrariums work just like bottle gardens (see page 662), countering the hot, dry atmosphere common in centrally heated homes by creating a humid microclimate. Combined with adequate heat,

A traditional Wardian case filled with a selection of ferns which all enjoy the same moist, semi-shaded environment.

this admirably suits the more tender houseplants whose native habitat is the steamy, tropical jungle.

A sealed terrarium is almost completely self-sufficient. Water in the compost at the bottom of the container is taken up by the plants and given off as vapour from their leaves. This condenses in droplets on the glass walls and roof and, together with water evaporated directly from the soil, runs back into the compost. The whole process then starts again, enabling the plants to thrive with almost no attention.

If the case has an opening to the air, you will have to water the plants occasionally, though probably far less than conventionally potted plants. Some terrariums, however, are almost entirely open-topped; while the container does increase the humidity around the plants to some extent, the result is not so much

The tall Asparagus Fern A. plumosus is best grown in a case with open sides.

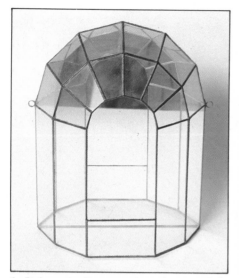

1. Before planting up a terrarium, wash it well with detergent and rinse carefully.

2. Underneath the compost you'll need a layer of gravel and some charcoal.

3. When planting, start from the back and work forwards.

4. When planted fill in around the plants, making sure they are firmly in place.

5. A Parlour Palm at the back balances a Fittonia to the fore.

a terrarium as a particularly attractive type of plant holder.

Planting the container

Having decided on your container, the next step is to make sure it is scrupulously clean, so that no harmful mould can get a foothold later on. Give it a good wash in liquid detergent, rinse it carefully, and let it dry completely before you start to fill it.

First you should put in a drainage layer of gravel, a minimum of ½in (13mm) deep, but up to 2in (5cm) if your container has sufficient depth. Follow this with a layer of lightly broken charcoal of the same depth — this keeps the compost from going sour. The final layer should be 2-3in (5-8cm) of a weak potting compost, such as John Innes No 1 or a peat-based compost mixed with a little sand.

Make a small hole in the compost for each plant, drop it in gently and firm the compost around the roots. Remember not to put the plants too close together so that they have room to grow. When they are all in, give them some water, letting it trickle slowly down the inside of the container if it is narrow-necked or watering with a sprinkler if you have room. Then move your terrarium to a lightly shaded position and close the door or lid if it has one.

Water, feeding and light

A sealed terrarium will rarely need watering — perhaps only every four to six months. Test the surface of the soil occasionally with your fingers — if it feels dry, water carefully until it becomes just moist. Be careful not to overwater — the compost should not be saturated and the surface should not look wet. Open terrariums will need proportionately more watering, depending on how quickly the surface of the compost dries out.

You don't need to feed plants in a well-established terrarium, since they are constantly manufacturing their own food through the atmosphere. And resist the temptation to use chemical fertilisers: they are far too rich for terrarium plants and will only encourage harmful parasites and mould.

A terrarium needs between six and eight hours of light a day in order to keep the plants flourishing. It is not advisable to keep it in direct sunlight, however, as this would soon cause condensation inside the glass and possibly scorching of the plants' leaves. Aim for good light at all times of the year in a lightly shaded position.

Pruning

In the sheltered and humid conditions of your miniature greenhouse, even plants carefully chosen to be slow-growing may eventually get too large. It is important to keep a check on plant size, since over-enthusiastic growers can damage their smaller companions by choking them or cutting off their light.

Either remove the big plants temporarily and prune them back into shape before returning them to the terrarium, or remove them completely (transferring them to pots if you like) and replace them with new, young plants.

Dealing with problems

From time to time you should inspect your plants carefully to make sure they have not been attacked by any pests. Drooping or wilting leaves can be signs of infestation. Try washing the infested plant with a weak solution of soapy water. This isn't a difficult operation: simply wipe the leaves with a small sponge or piece of cotton wool. In more severe cases, swab the leaves and stems with methylated spirit.

Never use chemical pesticide sprays in a terrarium, as the chemicals cannot disperse quickly and may build up in the atmosphere, causing damage to the plants. If you do have to use a spray, remove the plant from the container first, and don't replace it until you are quite sure that it is healthy again.

If your plants lose their colour or droop, and you're sure they have not been infested by insects, the problem may be insufficient water or light. Experiment by moving the container to a brighter spot and, if that fails, by giving the plants a bit more water. Remember not to use any chemical fertilisers.

Excessive condensation may be another problem with sealed containers, but not a serious one. Simply open the door or lid, or remove the covering, and leave it open to the air until the glass has cleared. Replace the cover when there is no further sign of steaming up — the plants won't come to any harm.

Having outlined the worst, don't expect your terrarium to suffer from all, or any, of these problems. As a rule, these delightful miniature gardens are surprisingly trouble-free. The plants love them — and so will you!

Many modern terrarium designs are only partially glassed in and will need to be regularly watered.

Choosing your plants

The main thing to avoid in a contained garden is any rampant grower that will try to take over all the soil and space. So, unless your terrarium has an opening like the one featured above, you should steer clear of Tradescantias, Zebrinas and Mind Your Own Business (Helxine). Plants that like lots of fresh air are also unsuitable, so avoid succulents and desert cacti. And make sure you go for plants that don't have extensive or deep rooting systems — the container won't provide sufficient space for them.

Small ferns, mosses and some of the bromeliads are the best choice. You'll find lots of suggestions for suitable plants in the article on bottle gardens (page 662) — with a terrarium, you can afford to concentrate on quite tall plants if you prefer to.

In addition, the small Earth Star (*Cryptanthus acaulia*) makes a good ground cover, while Japanese sedge (*Carex morrowii variegata*) is an excellent tall plant, with arching green-and-white striped leaves. The Bead Plant (*Nertera depressa*) will bring a splash of brilliant colour with its bright orange berries on a mat of tiny leaves. Its foliage is similar to one of the creeping Pileas, Creeping Charlie (*Pilea nummulariifolia*), which is another good choice. If you've got a fairly open terrarium, you can go for flowering plants (they're not happy in sealed containers because their petals are liable to mould). The trailing Episcias, which hail from the same family as the African Violet, will contribute pleasing foliage as well as attractive flowers: try the Flame Violet (*Episcia cupreata*), with silver-veined coppery leaves and orange flowers, or the Lace Flower (*E.dianthiflora*), with velvety leaves and delicate, frilled white flowers.

Killer plants

A fly buzzes in through your window one fine sunny day, circles, then lands on a strange-looking plant with toothed leaves. Suddenly, two hitherto motionless leaves snap shut like a pair of jaws, and the fly is trapped behind two rows of interlocking teeth. One of nature's most extraordinary creations, a carnivorous plant, has just secured another meal.

This may sound as if it has come straight out of science fiction, but it could be happening on your windowsill if you keep a Venus Fly Trap (*Dionaea muscipula*). This is just one of many insect-eating plants which make an unusual change from more run-of-the-mill houseplants. They're not difficult to keep, and they're certainly exciting to have around — one thing they'll do is keep down the fly population in your kitchen! Quite apart from their bizarre habits, many of them are very beautiful to look at, especially when they flower.

How do they work?

These aberrations of nature have evolved over many thousands of years through living in places where the soil is very short of nutrients — such as marshes and bogs. They have gradually become modified so that they can attract and trap insects, which they digest to supplement their meagre diet.

They don't all work in the same way. The Venus Fly Trap is one of the most spectacular, which probably accounts for its popularity as a houseplant. Just inside the edges of its leaves it has sensitive bristles — if you look closely you can see them. When these bristles are touched they trigger the 'trap' mechanism, making the pair of leaves snap shut. The teeth along the outer edges then interlock, so that the prey cannot escape, and the plant secretes juices that dissolve it.

If you want to watch the trap work, you can put minute pieces of meat or fish on a lower leaf — the plant will love this, especially if insect life is scarce. But

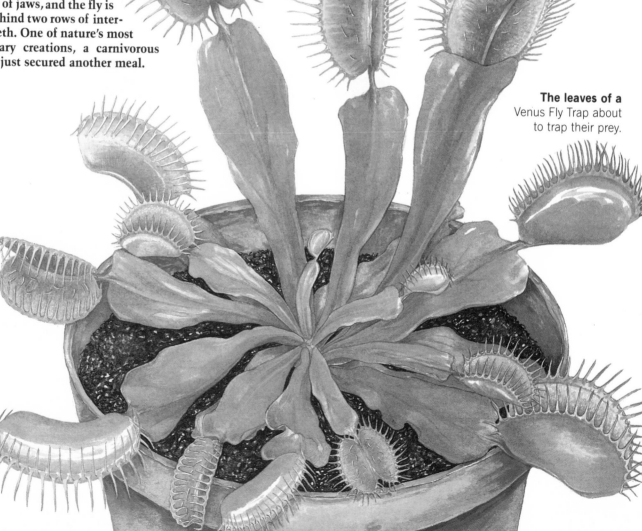

The leaves of a Venus Fly Trap about to trap their prey.

288

don't do it too often — it's all too easy to overfeed the plant, and each pair of leaves can only 'swallow' five times before they die.

Pitcher Plants (Sarracenia) don't move to trap their prey — they don't have to. Instead they attract insects by the smell of the liquid they produce. These plants have tall, pitcher-shaped pouches, up to 3ft (0.9m) high, which are open at the top, although sometimes they have a slight hood. At the bottom of the pouch is the liquid; when the insect crawls down inside to find it, it slips and drowns in the pool. The liquid, which is a digestive juice, then dissolves its prey to provide nutrition for the plant.

A third group of carnivorous plants, called Sundews (Drosera) are related to the Venus Fly Trap but operate differently. Their leaves are covered in tentacles that produce a sticky substance; when insects land on the leaves they become stuck fast and the leaves slowly wrap themselves around the trapped insect. These plants are sometimes called 'Living Flypapers' — it's easy to see why!

What do they look like?

● The Venus Fly Trap is small and compact, and can be grown from a small bulb. It won't outgrow a 3-4in (7 - 10cm) pot, where it will flourish happily for years. It is light green in colour, but if you keep it in a really bright natural light it it will become flushed with red. In spring or early summer it bears white flowers.

● Pitcher Plants are much more beautifully coloured, and flower in the spring or summer. Sarracenia x catesbaei, which is among the easiest to keep as a houseplant, bears pinkish pitchers and bright red flowers. Huntsman's Horn (S.flava) has tall pale green pitchers contrasting with yellow flowers, while S.leucophila has tall white pitchers, beautifully veined with green or red, and red flowers. Huntsman's Cup (S.purpurea) is the lowest-growing of these — it has short, fat, red pitchers and pink or red flowers. Although Pitcher Plants grow quite tall they won't need a final pot size bigger than 5in (13cm).

One truly spectacular Pitcher Plant is the Cobra Lily (Darlingtonia californica). Its yellow-green pitchers, veined with red and mottled with white at the top, grow up to 2ft (0.6m) high — they look like cobras poised to strike. And in April or May the plant bears pale green flowers with crimson veins on unusual, arching stems.

● Sundews are not quite so dramatic as Pitcher Plants to look at, but are still very attractively marked and are easy to keep. Drosera binata has forked green leaves with conspicuous bright red tentacles and contrasting white flowers, while D.capensis is similar but with purplish flowers. Both of these grow to about 6in (15cm) high and will flower in early to mid-summer.

Looking after them

● **Water** is very important to carnivorous plants. They are very sensitive to any chemicals, and ordinary tap water from a public supply will, quite literally, kill them, because it contains chlorine. If you have a fresh source of water — from a spring or a well, for example — you could use it, but if not you must collect rainwater for your carnivorous plants. If you can't manage that, the only course is to use distilled water.

It isn't only the purity of the water that matters, but also its degree of alkalinity. Carnivorous plants hate limy water (often called 'hard' water), so if you have a fresh source of water that is high in lime, you must take steps to neutralise it. You can do this by adding vinegar — about a teaspoon to every gallon (4.5 litres) of water should be enough. An alternative is to boil your water for several minutes and cool it before use — this helps to remove some of the lime.

Water carnivorous plants very freely — they grow naturally in very wet places. If you make sure that these plants have a lot of water and a humid atmosphere they should do very well in the home. You should grow them in plastic pots, which retain moisture better than clay ones, and stand the pots in a shallow tray — no more than 2in (5cm) deep — kept half full of water.

● **Compost** requirements for carnivorous plants are slightly different from normal — getting the right compost will make all the difference to your plants' health. The compost must be able to drain well, so that the roots don't get waterlogged, but must also hold moisture. Also it must be fairly loose so that air can circulate freely through it.

A good choice of compost for the bigger and more vigorous plants is pure live sphagnum moss. Or you could use a mixture of equal parts of sphagnum-based peat and silver sand.

Because carnivorous plants are so expert at getting their own nutrition, it can be easy to overfeed them. The safest course is not to add any extra fertiliser to the compost — they'll manage to get quite enough food from insects.

● **Potting on** is done in the spring. Only pot on the plant if the present pot is full of roots. This is also the time to propagate new plants by dividing existing plants. Each division should contain some new growth buds and some roots. Put the new plants in small pots, just big enough to hold their roots comfortably.

● **Temperature** for carnivorous plants isn't a problem. Normal room temperature, without extra heating, is fine for them in summer — anything between 50-70°F (10-21°C) — and about 40°F (5°C) in winter. They like fresh air, so open the windows when the weather is warm. Bright light is essential, but really strong sun might scorch the leaves and flowers, so shade them from the sun's glare if the weather's really hot or move them to a windowsill that doesn't face south.

The Cobra Lily, in particular, needs to keep its roots cool in summer, so it's a good idea to water it frequently — several times a day if the weather's very hot. Use cool water and pour it into the top of the compost.

● Winter is when carnivorous plants rest. They'll start to die back in the autumn, when you should prune off any dead leaves or flowers. Take the pots out of the tray of water in the winter, and water them just enough to keep the compost slightly moist. Keep them on a windowsill, in a cool room if possible.

Pests and diseases

Carnivorous plants have a distinct advantage when it comes to insect pests! However, it *is* possible for them to become infested with greenfly in the summer. If you see any greenfly on your plant that it doesn't seem able to destroy itself, then gently rub them off. Don't use an insecticide, because it could be harmful to the plant. If you see any sign of grey mould or rot, cut away all the affected parts and spray with a systemic fungicide containing benomyl. Unlike insecticide, this is safe to use on carnivorous plants.

The flowers of the Venus Fly Trap appear in spring.

Sarracenia psittacina has leaves veined with purple.

Drosera glanduligbria has neat, compact growth.

Huntsman's Horn can grow up to 2ft (0.6m) tall.

Drosera capensis bears out its nickname of 'Living Flypaper'.

Growing cacti

Cacti are among the easiest of houseplants to keep, and among the most rewarding. They come in amazing and bizarre forms — thin columns covered in silky hair, barrel shapes studded with spines, fleshy rosettes and starry shapes. They are always full of interest, and their flowers can be truly breathtaking.

It is a popular idea that cacti thrive if they are neglected — this isn't strictly true! Like all plants, they'll do best if they're looked after properly, but equally they're tough enough to survive being forgotten occasionally. Most of them can tolerate long periods without water or fertiliser, and then, perhaps, repay us with a dazzling display of brilliant, brightly-coloured blooms.

Two kinds of cacti

Cacti belong to a group of plants called succulents. Their main characteristic is that they have managed to adapt to very harsh conditions that would kill other plants; they can withstand extremes of temperature, for example, and go for long periods without water. Cacti have a structure in their leaves, stems or roots which stores water, so that in drought conditions (or if you forget to water them!) they have a source of nourishment to draw on.

Opuntia aciculata bears purple seed pods on flattened leaves.

Desert cacti (easily raised from seed)

Acanthocalycium
Globe-shaped flowers ranging from white to pink and violet

Ariocarpus
Gnarled rosette shape with pink flowers

Azurocereus hertlinglianus
Unusual sky-blue stems with branches

Cephalocereus senilis Old Man Cactus
Beautiful silky-bearded column

Cleistocactus pallidus
Thin columns with yellow flowers

Blossfeldia campaniflora
Globe-shaped with starry yellow flowers

Echinocactus grusonii Barrel Cactus, *above left*
Enormous globes up to 2ft (0.6m) across with yellow spines

Ferocactus, above: F.townsendianus
Globe-shaped family with hooked spines and red, yellow or orange flowers

Gymnocalycium bruchii
Globe-shaped with shell-pink flowers

Lobivia backbergii
Columnar with ribbed stems and crimson flowers

Lophophora williamsii
Globe-shaped with no spines; blue-green with light pink flowers

Mammillaria Pincushion Cactus, *above*
Vast family, globe-shaped with pink flowers

Opuntia
Large family, most with flattened, branching leaf pads

Parodia sanguiniflora Tom Thumb Cactus
Globe-shaped with hooked red spines and red flowers

Rebutia miniscula Mexican Sunball Cactus
Globe-shaped with flowers in a vast range of colours from scarlet through gold to white

Turbinicarpus Hatchet Cactus
Distinctive with a ruff of white spines and semi-double cream, pink or magenta flowers

What makes cacti different from other succulents is that their spines and flowers grow from a round or elongated 'cushion' of hairs called an areole. Almost all cacti come originally from the Americas, where they exist in two habitats — deserts and rain forests.

● **Desert cacti** have adapted to growing under an arid, burning sun during the day, and surviving nights that are freezing cold and heavy with dew. The Pincushion *(Mammillaria)* and Bunny Ears *(Opuntia)* are examples — it goes without saying what these look like! Most desert cacti are globe-shaped or cylindrical and have masses of prickles or hooked spines — these are in fact leaves that have adapted to the dry conditions by becoming very thin and hard so that the minimum amount of water is lost from them.

● **Forest cacti** (sometimes called jungle cacti) thrive in completely the opposite extreme, in the rich leaf debris found in the rain forests of tropical America. They have a flatter shape than desert cacti and some of them trail. Christmas Cactus *(Schlumbergera truncata)* and Easter Cactus *(Rhipsalidopsis gaertneri)* are popular types that will do well in the home — their names come from their

traditional flowering times, but as houseplants they'll flower any time in spring.

The real king of the forest cacti is undoubtedly the Orchid Cactus *(Epiphyllum)*. A dull plant out of flower, it is a thing of wonder when it blooms, treating you to a marvellous display of brightly coloured, cup-shaped blooms, up to a dozen at a time, each of them as much as 6in (15cm) across. Hybrids are available in a range of colours; the white ones have a ravishing scent.

Find the best conditions

Not surprisingly, given their different habitats, desert and forest cacti require rather different treatment if they are to do well as houseplants. To put it simply, you must aim to copy their natural conditions as closely as possible.

● **Desert cacti** are happiest in full sunlight; a brightly lit, south-facing windowsill is ideal, but they can face north or east, too, provided you feed them with a fertiliser high in potash — such as Phostrogen, Cactigrow or any fertiliser sold for tomatoes — to compensate for the lack of light. If you have double-glazing, you may find that a cactus in a sunny position needs a little

shade in high summer, since the sun's rays may be too concentrated by the double thickness of glass.

Most desert cacti enjoy temperatures of 50-55°F (10-13°C) from autumn through to spring, but they can tolerate dropping down to 45°F (7°C). But two types — Old Man Cactus *(Cephalocereus senilis)* and Peruvian Old Man Cactus *(Espostoa lanata)* — like it warmer, and are best kept at around 60°F (15°C). If the night threatens to be particularly cold, you should move your cacti away from the windowsill.

Water cacti only when the surface of the soil is crumbly and dry, and the pot feels light when you pick it up. This is likely to be about once a week in spring and summer, and once a month in winter (when they are not growing actively), but if you have central heating, winter watering may need to be a little oftener.

Desert cacti hate stuffy conditions. Try and give them plenty of fresh air in summer by putting them near an open window on a fine day. But, like all plants, they don't like draughts, so try to avoid putting them in the path of a concentrated blast of cold air — such as you might get from a badly fitting window or an open door.

Pests and diseases

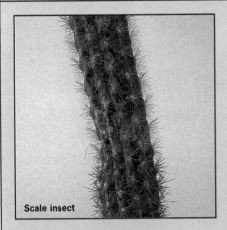

Scale insect

Basal rot

On the whole, Cacti are very easy to keep. But there are a few problems that might cause trouble.

● **Mealy bugs** can be very troublesome if your Cactus gets them. Watch out for the sticky, whitish blobs that look like cotton wool — these are tiny insects that live on the sap of your plant and stop it from growing properly. You should wipe the bugs off with a piece of cotton wool dipped in an insecticide containing malathion or dimethoate.

● **Red spider mite** is a minute pest that also distorts growth; it lives in patches of whitish webbing and discolours your Cactus, turning it a bronze colour. Red spider mite hates humidity, so the first step is to spray the Cactus thoroughly

with water. If that doesn't do the trick, try spraying with a solution of malathion or dimethoate.

● **Scale insect** is a tiny, limpet-like creature that sucks sap and weakens growth; it makes the plant turn yellow. You'll have to scrape off the brown scales with a fingernail first, then give the Cactus a good spray with an insecticide containing malathion to protect it for the future.

● **Basal rot** occurs when the base of the plant above the soil begins to rot. If this happens, you have overwatered your Cactus and the roots are already rotten. But you might not have lost the whole plant — if the upper stems still look healthy, cut them off and use them to propagate another plant.

● **Forest cacti** don't like the intense heat enjoyed by the desert variety, so a west- or east-facing windowsill is ideal for them. They like moderate warmth, and they love humidity — so spray a fine mist over the leaves from time to time, or stand the pot on damp gravel so that the plant has a constant supply of moisture to draw on.

Your forest cacti will flower regularly, except during their natural resting periods after flowering, when the temperature is best kept at around 55-60°F (13-15°C) and water withheld. Water them at other times quite frequently, about twice a week.

Propagation

There are two ways you can raise cacti — from seeds and from cuttings. Using seeds is easier but of course you'll have to wait much longer for results. You can get cactus seeds at most good garden shops and garden centres as well as from specialist cacti suppliers. You should have no difficulty growing them provided the seeds are reasonably fresh. Fill 3in (7cm) pots with compost: a good mixture is two parts John Innes Seed Compost to one part of Perlite. The Perlite improves the texture and drainage.

Leave a depth of ¾in (19mm) between the surface of the soil and the rim of the pot. Now give the mixture a good soaking by watering the pots thoroughly and letting all excess water drain away.

Scatter the seeds thinly and evenly over the surface, pressing big ones in

gently, but do not bury them. To encourage the seeds to germinate, you need to provide them with lots of moisture. The best thing is to cover the pots with a sheet of glass or clingfilm, or put clear polythene bags over them to prevent water loss.

Put the pots in a warm place — about 80°F (27°C) — or in a propagator, if you have one. Germination can take anything from three to eight weeks or longer, so don't worry if nothing seems to happen for a while. At first the seedlings do not need light, but because the seeds may germinate at different times, it's safest to provide moderate light from the beginning. When the seedlings have started to appear — they'll look like little green balls — uncover the pots so that they can get fresh air to help them to grow.

The next stage is to prick them out into individual tiny pots, called thumb pots, which are about 1-1½in (2.5-4cm) across. You do this when they're big enough to handle, say about 1in (25mm) high. But cacti grow very slowly, and it can take between six months and a year before they'll get to this stage. During this time, keep them at room temperature with the right amount of sun depending on their type, and make sure the compost is always slightly moist.

We'll be giving you all the information you need for raising new cacti from offsets and cuttings later, when we'll also tell you in detail how to pot on your cacti when they need bigger pots.

Forest cacti

Aporocactus flagelliformis Rat's Tail Cactus
Slender trailing prickly stems; pink flowers

Ephiphyllum hybrids Orchid Cacti, *above*
Leaf-like stems with flamboyant shuttlecock flowers in a range of reds, gold, purple and white, some richly scented

Rhipsalidopsis gaertneri Easter Cactus
Leaf-like stems with scalloped edges and double scarlet flowers

Rhipsalis cassutha Mistletoe Cactus
Thin, branching stems with mistletoe-like fruits following white flowers

Rhipsalis paradoxa Chain Cactus
Branching, triangular winged stems which narrow and twist at intervals

Schlumbergera truncata Christmas Cactus, *above*
Toothed, leaf-like stems; flowers ranging from white through magenta and pink to crimson

Designing a cactus garden

First decide where you want to put your cactus garden. If it's going against a wall, place tall species at the back.

When choosing plants look out for complementary shapes and colours, and choose species with different flowering times.

Spaces between plants can be filled with pea gravel which looks most attractive and aids drainage.

Place your finished garden in a sunny spot and it should delight you throughout the year.

Cacti and other succulents come in such strange shapes, and are so unlike other houseplants, that they usually look their best when grouped together. This enhances their sculptural qualities, and also ensures that the smaller ones, which would look rather odd alone, are well set off in the company of similar or complementary plants. Cacti gardens are also practical: you can keep together all those plants that require the same, rather unusual, conditions.

There are dozens and dozens of cacti to choose for the house (see 'Growing Cacti' page 675, for suggestions on suitable species for growing indoors). Grouping them together to make a suitable landscape – perhaps using small stones and pebbles to suggest a desert scene – is a challenge to bring out the artist in you. But the main thing is to use the tremendous variety of shapes, sizes and colours of the plants to make the most attractive presentation.

Choosing a container

Almost anything will do for a container, new or old — brass troughs, soup tureens, casseroles, even goldfish tanks for larger plantings. However, good drainage is essential for cacti, so the container should have drainage holes. If making holes in an old container would spoil it, cover the base with at least 2in (5cm) of drainage material — crushed charcoal is best because it mops up any impurities in the soil.

Get the compost right

Most cacti thrive in a free draining soil-based compost, but it should not be too rich — two parts John Innes No 1 mixed with one part coarse sand is ideal. Alternatively you could use a proprietary cactus compost.(For more details, see the article on cacti on page 181.)

Making a landscape

Whether you're making a small or a big garden, the first thing to create is a focal point, using a tall, dramatic cactus. Then you can fringe this with smaller ones, and plant trailing cacti around the edges, which will in time grow over and conceal the sides of the container.

With a bowl 4-5in (10-13cm) deep and 12in (30cm) across, you could choose a Prickly Pear (Opuntia) with its branching pads as a dramatic centrepiece, with a column-shaped cactus next to it, such

Be adventurous!

Always arrange your chosen plants on a piece of newspaper first, to check that they'll look right before you commit yourself to planting them — and always leave enough room for them to grow. Make sure that you put together only those plants that enjoy the same conditions.

Once you're familiar with the many cacti and succulents available, there's no limit to the variety and number of the arrangements you can make.

as the Silver Torch Cactus (*Cleistocactus straussii*).

Plant around it little groups of smaller cacti, chosen for their exciting shapes. The Goat's Horn Cactus (*Astrophytum capricorne*) is globe-shaped with prominent ribs and wavy spines, while the Pincushion or Powder Puff Cactus (*Mammillaria bocasana*) is prized for its green globe, hooked spines and ring of starry white or red flowers. Choose others from the same type if you have room, bearing in mind their shapes and flower colours. You could intersperse these bigger plants with Living Stones (Lithops) — not cacti but succulents, which look like pebbles, until they burst into flower. To unite all these plants, spread shingle over the compost, and scatter a few real pebbles around.

For the edges of the container, the Rat's Tail Cactus (*Aporocactus flagelliformis*) really comes into its own. It is in fact a forest cactus, but is unusual in that it looks and should be treated just like the others listed above, which are desert cacti. It has prickly green stems with brown spines, which will trail down over the sides of the container, and beautiful bright pink flowers. Burro's or Donkey Tail (*Sedum morganianum*), another succulent which enjoys the same conditions as desert cacti, can keep it company; this has fascinating, tassel-like, waxy, green stems, made of symmetrical 'scales', which trail downwards.

Hanging baskets

You don't have to have your cacti at table or windowsill level. Many varieties are suitable for planting in hanging baskets, trailing from pedestals, or cascading down from flat-backed pots fixed to the wall at any height. These would make a striking feature in a warm, well-lit room — remember that most cacti like as much sun as they can get.

The extraordinary Saucer Plant (*Aeonium tabuliforme*) would make a good centrepiece — with a stem so short that it's scarcely noticeable, the rosette appears quite flat. It should be planted on the slant so that water can run off its packed foliage. It will produce a flower spike that can grow as high as 18in (45cm), with yellow flowers on branches at the tip. Blue Echeveria (*Echeveria glauca*), with its waxy, bluish leaves, would also make an excellent rosette-shaped centrepiece.

One succulent show-stopper is String of Beads (*Senecio rowleyanus*) — an

Pebbles and stones add colour and interest.

amazing plant with bright green leaves in the shape of tiny globes that trail in strings like necklaces. The strings can grow as long as 3-4ft (0.9-1.2m), so you would need to set the basket pretty high!

The Money Plant or Jade Plant (*Crassula argentea*) would also be a good choice for the focal point of an arrangement, with its shiny dark green leaves on branching stems. It would be beautifully set off by the tree-like *Aeonium arboreum* 'Atropurpureum', with branching stems and lovely deep purple leaves in the shape of little umbrellas. The Tree Aloe (*Aloe arborescens*) is another good upright, tree-like succulent, with striking, toothed leaves.

For a fringe choose the trailing Rosary Vine (*Ceropegia woodii*), with delicate, white-veined leaves on purple stems, interplanted with the Partridge Breast Aloe (*Aloe variegata*) and the Rat Tail Plant (*Crassula lycopodioides*).

A succulent dish garden makes a handsome table centrepiece.

盆栽

The art of bonsai

A **Crab Apple**, *left*, gives a fine spring display.

Bonsai, in Japanese, *top left*.

The ancient art of growing trees and shrubs in miniature is currently enjoying a great increase in popularity. Bonsai — which has been practised for hundreds of years in China and Japan — actually means 'plant in a container', and that is exactly what these fascinating 'doll's house' trees are.

It isn't known for certain how bonsai first originated. It could have been accidental. Deprived of good soil and nutrients, a tree will grow small and stunted — you may have seen one yourself like this growing on a mountainside, for example. If such a tree were brought indoors in a container as a decoration,

looked after and given nutrition, it would then start to grow to its normal size, and would need drastic pruning of both roots and shoots to keep it small. What is certain is that the art of miniaturising plants in this way has been known in China and Japan for at least six hundred years.

Many kinds of tree and shrub lend themselves to this treatment. Majestic deciduous trees such as Maple (Acer) and Beech *(Fagus sylvatica)* are chosen for their shape, colour and the variety they afford as they pass through the seasons, with spring blossom, summer fruits and autumn leaf fall. Evergreens such as Juniper (Juniperus) and Japanese Cedar *(Cryptomeria japonica)* are ideal subjects, while shrubs such as Azalea, Cotoneaster and Pyracantha are interesting not only on account of their leaf form but because they flower. The chart describes some more varieties.

You can keep bonsai trees successfully in your home provided you remember a few very important rules. The first one is that most bonsai are not genuine houseplants. They love fresh air, and will not survive if kept indoors all the time. Unless they are tender species which have been specially raised as indoor plants, you should keep them in a sheltered garden, or on a balcony, as a permanent home and just bring them indoors from time to time for short periods as a splendid and unusual decorative feature. If you keep several bonsai trees, you should be able to have one on a table indoors most of the year by moving them around — but it's not a good idea to leave any one specimen indoors for more than a few days at a time. Lack of fresh air and light will make its leaves pale and straggly.

Buying a bonsai

The best thing to do if you are a beginner with bonsai is to buy a good, healthy specimen from a reliable garden centre or specialist. It may be a genuine Japanese specimen — grown in Japan and exported — or one grown in this country. Either way, it will be much more expensive even than an exotic houseplant — in Japan bonsai are regarded as heirlooms! But the expense will be worth it: if you take proper care of your tree it should live for more than a hundred years.

When you buy a bonsai tree, you should first establish that it is genuine — there are dwarf conifers now available which, at three to five years old, can look confusingly like bonsai of about ten years old. Look out for a good shape, with no signs of damage, pests or disease. There should be no evidence of crude cutting back of branches, leaves should be glossy and green and any flower or fruit buds should look plump and firm. The older the tree, the better established it is — look out for moss on the trunk which is a sign of age.

Day-to-day care

Bonsai trees should be grown outside most of the time. Choose a semi-shaded position in summer, and protect them from hard frost in the winter by moving them to a shed or frost-free, but cool, place indoors — this is particularly important for citrus trees. Bonsai are especially vulnerable to sudden changes of temperature, so don't move them from a cold outdoor position straight to a centrally heated room in winter.

A Pomegranate is a good choice for growing indoors.

Traditional bonsai styles

The Japanese shape their bonsai trees in certain specific styles. These are the most common:

Chokkan: upright.

Group plantings: arranged with the tallest trees at the front to create a perspective that suggests a forest grove. (See Spruce and Elm forest, *left.*)

Hankan: gnarled and growing in one direction, to suggest a tree on a windswept cliff.

Ishi-tsuki: tree growing out of a stone, as may be seen on a cliff or mountain.

Kengai: cascade, grown on a tall stand and trained to grow downwards.

Shakan: slanting trunk, or semi-cascade.

The fruits of *Cotoneaster horizontalis* last for several months.

A Japanese Maple *(Acer palmatum)* about 80 years old.

Transfer them in stages through several positions, each one slightly warmer than before, and do the same in reverse when returning them outside.

While they're indoors, they should be given a fairly cool position, free from draughts and with as much natural light as possible. Don't put them in front of a south-facing window, as the direct sun could scorch the leaves.

Water your trees regularly — the compost must never be allowed to dry out completely. Rainfall will usually be sufficient for most of the year while they are outdoors. In summer, and during their stay indoors, water them every few days and spray them with soft water several times a day to reduce the loss of moisture from the leaves. Rainwater is ideal, but if you use tapwater, let it stand for a day first to get rid of toxic gases.

During the growing season in spring and summer it is important to provide the tree with nutrients. Use a liquid fertiliser every two to three weeks, applying it either with the water, or when the plant's roots are well moistened (giving fertiliser when the roots are dry can scorch them). The fertiliser should be a standard one, with equal proportions of nitrogen, phosphorus and potassium. Don't feed the trees after the end of the summer or during the winter.

Potting on

Don't be frightened at the idea of repotting a bonsai tree — it's just the same as with any houseplant. You'll need to repot your tree every one to two years while it is up to ten years old; thereafter repot anything between two and ten years, depending on how fast it is growing. If you don't repot it regularly, the roots will gradually fill the pot and push out all the compost.

With bonsai, there is another reason to repot: it gives you the opportunity to prune the roots, which is necessary to keep the plant small. You may find that some years you don't need to put the tree in a bigger pot, but that after pruning you can replace it in the same one.

The time to repot is in very early spring, before the plant starts into new growth — don't ever repot a plant while it is actively growing because the shock could severely damage or even kill it. Remove the plant from the pot, carefully tease open the root ball and spread the roots out. Using a sharp, sterilised pair of scissors or secateurs, trim off up to a third of the roots.

Prepare the new pot with a few pieces of broken earthenware in the bottom to cover the drainage holes. Then add a sprinkling of sharp horticultural grit to help drainage. Don't be tempted to use garden soil for your bonsai, even though it is a tree. Its roots are contained in an unnaturally small space and it must have a balanced compost to grow in. Partly fill the new pot with John Innes No 2, and put the trimmed plant in, firming it gently with more compost round the roots. Water in thoroughly and leave it to continue growing.

Growing your own

If you want the challenge — and have a lot of patience! — you can try growing your own bonsai from seeds or from cuttings; good indoor specimens can be raised from fresh olive, pomegranate or date pips. You will need to shape and control the growth of the tree's branches — an art calling for some skill. We'll be telling you in detail how to do this later.

Pots for bonsai

Containers for bonsai specimens must be very carefully chosen from a point of quality, shape and size. Because they'll spend most of the year outdoors, they must be able to withstand rain and a degree of frost. This means, in practice, that they are usually made of very good quality pottery, which has been highly fired to make it strong. They should be shallow — as little as 1½in (3.75cm) in depth — in order to keep the root growth down, and must have good drainage holes.

Traditionally, Japanese containers are oval or rectangular, and often very old. They are without any ornamentation, and come in beautiful muted colours — blues, greys, browns, greens and cream. Artistically, they are like frames to pictures — the container should enhance the single tree or group, but not distract attention away from it.

Keeping bonsai in shape

Even with a ready-grown bonsai tree, you'll have to prune it regularly to keep its growth compact and its shape neat and attractive.

Pruning of the tree above the soil is done in early spring, just before the plant starts into new growth — it's best to do this at the same time as you prune the roots. It involves removing any branches or stems that look as though they may overcrowd the plant with foliage, that are beginning to grow in completely the wrong direction or are crossing each other, or that are growing too low down the main trunk. Also any branch that shows signs of disease or damage should be removed.

Using sharp, sterilised secateurs, cut back stems close to the main branch, or to the nearest bud, so that as little as possible of a stump remains. As well as keeping the plant looking attractive, this will help the wound to heal rapidly. It is traditional to cut off alternate branches from the main stem to make the plant well balanced in growth. Once the main shape is assured, you'll just need to prune the tree once a year to keep it nicely shaped.

With deciduous trees, such as Maple, or very young pine trees, the tips of the growing shoots should also be pinched out from time to time to encourage bushy, dense growth. And it's a good idea to remove some whole new leaves in early summer — the tree will then put out more leaves, but they will be finer and smaller. Do this only with the larger-leaved trees.

With flowering trees, such as those in the Prunus group, you should prune back about two thirds of the branches after flowering. We'll be giving you more precise details on the needs of each type of tree in a later article.

With younger specimens, experts twist wire round the branches and bend them to make them grow in the right direction; this is a skilled job and part of the bonsai art. Mature trees will have already been trained to shape and you should only need to prune the top growth and roots. This will keep them looking beautiful and growing healthily for many years.

Varieties to choose

Deciduous trees	Evergreen trees	Flowering and/or fruiting shrubs and trees	
Beech (*Fagus sylvatica*) Oval, wavy-edged leaves with round clusters of green flowers in spring.	**Fir** (Abies) Pyramid-shaped with glossy dark green needles.	**Almond, Cherry, Peach** and **Plum** (Prunus) Lovely blossoms in spring and miniature fruit in season. Deciduous.	**Herringbone Cotoneaster** (*Cotoneaster horizontalis*) Herringbone-shaped leaves and scarlet berries. Deciduous.
Elm (Ulmus) Leaves turn golden in autumn.	**Japanese Cedar** (*Cryptomeria japonica*) Delicate bright green leaves turn crimson in winter.	**Azalea** (*Rhododendron lateritium*) An evergreen with dark pink flowers in June.	
Maidenhair (*Gingko biloba*) Attractive foliage turns yellow in autumn.	**Juniper** (Juniperus) Pyramid- or bush-shaped with narrow needles.		**Pomegranate** (*Punica granatum nana*) Vivid orange flowers in May/June, followed by fruit. Semi-evergreen indoors.
Maple (Acer) Red-veined leaves turn crimson in autumn.	**Pine** (Pinus) Dark green needles and erect cones.	**Crab Apple** (Malus) Rose-pink or white blossom in spring, fruit in autumn.	
Oak (Quercus) Rather rare as bonsai, because leaves stay large.	**Spruce** (Picea) Pyramid-shaped with hanging cones.	**Firethorn** (Pyracantha) White blossom and yellow, orange or scarlet berries most of the year. Evergreen.	**Winter Jasmine** (*Jasminum nudiflorum*) Bright yellow flowers between November and March. Deciduous.

Plants for windowsills

A pretty windowsill acts like a magnet to the eye, and there's no better way of welcoming visitors to your home and making a cheerful impression on the passing world than a windowsill full of healthy, vibrant houseplants. You'll need a bold display if it's to be noticed from the outside, so choose something with strong form and colour — bulbs in full bloom or a display of pelargoniums as seen above would be ideal.

What is surprising is that people don't make more of what can be a ready-made micro-climate ideal for many varieties of indoor plants. All too often the only thing you see — if there's anything at all

— is a few boring pots and an equally dull selection of plants, with no attempt to display them attractively.

The windowsill is the biggest asset you have for growing your plants —

with all that wonderful natural light, it's the obvious place. If you are lucky enough to have wide sills, then your choice of which plants to grow is delightfully difficult — the range is enormous!

Which plants for which window?

The first step is to check the aspect of your various windows and choose plants that either enjoy the brightest

An eye-catching and varied display — *Maranta*, *Canna* and *Crassula lycopodioides*.

Check the aspect of your window; while the *Nephrolepsis* fern is best sited on a north or east-facing sill, Black-eyed Susan (*top right*) needs bright light for best results.

sun or relish the shade. Remember that north-facing windows receive little sunlight, especially in winter, and you will need to find plants that actually dislike the sun, such as Ivies or Aspidistras.

South-facing windows are just the opposite — the hot midday sun in the summer months can even be strong enough to scorch tender plants, so it may be worth placing them behind a translucent white roller blind to diffuse the harsh rays. Of course, this is the ideal environment for succulents and cacti. For a sunny windowledge, a low wide dish can be turned into a garden of desert cacti, which thrive on bright sunlight. Or, in a south-facing kitchen, try a scented Geranium like *Pelargonium* 'Mabel Grey'. This plant has a lovely lemon scent which it gives off when you touch its leaves.

East and west windows will suit most plants, if you also remember the conditions of the particular room. A bathroom windowsill, for instance, is best for growing humidity-loving plants such as *Sedum*, *Ficus*, *Fittonia*, Philodendrons, *Caladium*, some orchids, ferns or Wandering Jew.

If you have patio windows, frame them at either side with Ivy trained up a support, or use large floor to ceiling plants to provide you with privacy without the need for curtains! Where you do have curtains, however, you should be careful at night not to trap the plants in a pocket of cold air. They would be much happier brought into the room on chilly winter evenings.

Traditional or modern?

Perfect plants are the first ingredient. You should regularly replace any plants that are past their best. Whether you buy new ones, or grow your own, it's a good practice to follow. From the design point of view, choose plants that follow a theme, rather than mixing widely different kinds together. For example, if yours is a traditionally furnished room, choose traditional plants like *Stephanotis*, *Clivia* (Kaffir Lily), *Streptocarpus*, Foxtail Asparagus, *Pilea*, *Beloperone* (Shrimp Plant) or *Peperomia*.

Alternatively, you might want to grow traditional flowering pot-plants — *Cyclamen*, Begonias, Azaleas, Poinsettias and African Violets are ideal.

Old-fashioned cottage windowsill plants like *Gloxinia*, Primroses, *Kalanchoe* (Flaming Katy), Lily-of-the-Valley, Cockscomb, *Coleus*, *Achimenes* (Hot

Water Plant), *Fuchsia* or Geraniums add a homely touch to cottage rooms.

For very modern rooms, go for strikingly shaped plants. Succulents are among the most sculptural looking — *Euphorbia, Jatropha podagrica, Echevaria, Cotyledon undulata, Pachyphytum oviferm* (Sugared Almonds) or *Lithops* (Living Stones). Then again, there are hairy cacti like *Cephalocereus*, or dramatic tropical plants — *Anthurium, Spathiphyllum, Hibiscus rosa-sinensis, Syngonium, Maranta, Calathea, Fittonia*, Croton, *Dieffenbachia, Aralia, Cycas revoluta* (Sago Palm), *Aechmea* (Urn Plant) and other Bromeliads.

When you come to put your display together, you'll find it's difficult to get away from the 'straight row', particularly if yours are narrow windowsills. But try to introduce changes of level by using plants of different heights, or raising some plants up in tall containers. And, if the window is big enough, grow hanging plants down from the top too, perhaps in baskets. Besides looking better, this enables you to pack a lot of plants in without looking cluttered.

Finishing touches

One dramatic way to improve your window display, providing there is enough depth, is to build shelves across the window opening (see page 389). Glass shelves are ideal as they won't block the sunlight, and the plants allow light to filter through into the house in a lovely dappled way. This kind of racked plant display is very common in the Netherlands, where everyone is plant mad and growing plants is an art.

The whole country is a riot of flowers — growing in the fields, cheering up every window, spilling out of window-boxes and in gardens everywhere. But where the Dutch really excel is with their large windows that seem to have been specially designed with plants in mind! They have even done away with their curtains. All that's left is a lace fringe along the top of the window — the plants take over by filling the frame with foliage.

A deep window can even be turned into a special 'plant window' by constructing a trough along the sill, and sealing the plants between the outside window pane and a permanent inner pane, rather like a terrarium.

In a small space, accessories can make all the difference, particularly white china, which contrasts beauti-

Keep things moving

There's no need to keep the same old display for ever and a day. Give your window a new look from time to time. If you grow annual flowering plants, you've got the perfect excuse, as they need replacing after they've finished flowering. You could change from summer annuals like *Fuchsia* and *Calceolaria* to winter Azaleas and Pot Chysanthemums, Christmas Poinsettias, a display of spring flowering bulbs or Arums for Easter.

Just enjoy yourself and have a go. Don't be afraid to move things around until you feel happy with the effect. And, whenever you feel like a change of scene, re-think the whole idea and try your plants another way.

fully with green leaves. Floral patterned or brightly coloured containers are not so good for windowsills — when you have lots close together the effect is rather overwhelming. Plain containers or basketwork, neutral coloured pottery or wood look much better and allow your plants to dominate the scene.

You may also want to incorporate various ornaments into a window display. If you have chosen plain white containers for displaying your plants in they could

be intermingled with plain white ornaments, carefully chosen to contrast in shape and size with the surrounding pots. You could easily do the same thing with a display based on pottery or basket pot-covers.

Or dream up a few ideas of your own. How about adding a collection of polished stones and rock crystals to a windowsill full of grotesquely shaped succulent plants — or some small antique objects to a traditional window?

Patio rose garden

You don't need an open garden to be able to grow roses. The patio rose garden can be every bit as pretty and interesting and you can grow some delightful miniatures in containers or in spaces in the paving to great effect. If you follow these easy guidelines your roses will flourish and will give you the best possible display.

Making your choice

Choice of variety is important. There are hundreds of different types of rose, but you should limit your choice by concentrating on the low-growing kinds, some of which have been bred especially for patio cultivation. These are short but vigorous and have masses of flowers in clus-

Miniature roses can be grown in tubs and containers to great effect.

ters, often covering the whole bush and flowering throughout the summer months.

Look in the rose catalogues under the headings 'Patio' and 'Miniature' for plants which are between 12 and

18in (30 and 45cm) high. You can grow the taller varieties, preferably the cluster-flowering (floribunda) kind, but anything above 3ft (90cm) is likely to be too vigorous for a container and could grow to be unwieldy, even if planted in spaces between paving stones.

Choosing your site

Most roses like the sun and a south-facing patio or terrace with a wall at the back is an ideal spot for your rose garden. Some shade during the day won't do any harm and you could even provide it by the strategic positioning of larger plants. Avoid a windy spot, but if this is impossible a good way of providing shelter is to erect a screen of plate glass.

Containers

These should be at least 9in (23cm) deep, even for miniature roses, otherwise the roots will be cramped and won't be able to spread out enough to ensure strong top growth. Large pots, planters, deep window-boxes, vertical urns, tubs and cisterns are all suitable; wooden tubs, boxes and barrels are also ideal, and the classical sculptured lead containers can set off the flowers superbly.

Planting

Use a soil-based compost such as John Innes Potting Compost No 3. You could use a peat-based type, but this needs more frequent feeding during the summer and is not suitable for lightweight plastic containers. Cover the base of the container with drainage material such as broken pieces of clay pot or brick, mortar rubble,

Group a number of pots together for a spectacular display of colour.

expanded polystyrene or even small stones, and stand the containers on bricks to allow the water to drain away easily.

Roses can be planted in containers at any time of year, although spring is best when new growth is just starting. Start off with a container which is about 9in (23cm) in diameter. Position the root-ball about 2in (5cm) below the rim of the container. Sit the root-ball on a bed of compost and pack in more compost around it, firming it well, all the way down. Continue to add more compost until it is about 1in (2.5cm) above the root-ball, so allowing a 1in (2.5cm) watering space between the top of the compost and the rim of the container. Firm it down well and make sure that it is level.

Spacing will depend to some extent on the depth of the container. If you are using a comparatively shallow, long box, allow about 12-15in (30-38cm) between plants. For tubs it will depend on the variety of rose and how much it is likely to spread – if in doubt allow as much space sideways

Grow climbing roses up the wall adjacent to your patio.

Watch out for . . .

Pests and diseases can be a problem with patio roses.
● They seem to attract greenfly and leafhoppers in particular, so be ready with your spray gun as soon as these pests start to gather on buds, tips of shoots and undersides of leaves.
● Watch out, too, for red spider mite – a minute sap-sucking creature which lives and feeds on the under surface of leaves and produces webbing in bad attacks.
● Regular spraying against mildew and another rose fungus disease – black spot – is almost obligatory from the time the leaves unfold.

as the rose is high. Roses usually need repotting every four years.

If planting roses in paving spaces, fork up the soil and, about three weeks prior to planting, mix in a general compound fertiliser such as Growmore. Just before planting, mix in some soil improver based on composted seaweed such as Garotta Soil Builder. This will help the roses to get established and keep the soil in good condition. Whether in containers or in the ground, the plants must be watered in after planting.

Watering and feeding

During the growing season, watering and feeding will be necessary, and in summer your containers will need watering every day. Water well so that the compost is thoroughly soaked; any surplus water will drain through the holes in the container base. Roses grown in paving spaces will need less watering.

Use a proprietary dry rose fertiliser for peat-based composts about 10 weeks after planting, or whenever the manufacturers instruct, and water it in. Roses planted in John Innes compost and paving spaces will not need feeding until early the following spring and should be fed again in early summer. Use a proprietary rose fertiliser which has a high potash content. Alternatively, you could combine a liquid feed with your watering every few days.

Plant care

Patio roses should always look immaculate, so deadheading is essential throughout the flowering season, and it also encourages the plants to produce more flowers. Broken stems and torn or discoloured leaves should also be removed.

Pruning

Only a little pruning is necessary, and it should be done in early spring. Remove dead or badly-diseased wood on which there may be peeling or cracking bark, and cut off any weak shoots that you can see.

If the bush is still crowded with shoots, remove a few to give some light and air – the centre should always be fairly open. As the plants age, cut one or two of the oldest shoots right down to ground level to encourage new, strong growth.

Pick and choose

'**Angela Rippon**', *top*, salmon-coral pink, 18in (45cm)
'**Baby Masquerade**', *centre left*, pink, orange, yellow, 15in (38cm)
'**Anna Ford**', *bottom left*, orange-red, semi-double, 18in (45cm)
'**Bianco White**', 15in (38cm)
'**Bright Smile**', yellow, 2ft (60cm)
'**Darling Flame**', *centre right*, light red, 15in (38cm)
'**International Herald Tribune**', violet-purple, fragrant, 1 1/2-2ft (45-60cm)
'**Little Buckaroo**', *bottom right top*, red, fragrant, 12-15in (30-38cm)
'**Meteor**', red, 18in (45cm)
'**Red Sprite**', deep red, 18in (45cm)
'**Topsi**', *bottom right*, orange-scarlet, 15in (38cm)
'**Yvonne Rabier**', double, fragrant, 18in (45cm)

Containing rockeries

A sink filled with alpine plants can look most effective.

A rock garden can be the most enchanting feature of a garden, and one which is confined to a container can be just as pretty, in spite of its limited space. Most rock plants are very small, usually because they grow in soil which is extremely short of nutrients and, often, water. They also often grow in their natural habitat, high up in mountainous areas where the weather is cold and quite dry.

There is an enormous choice of suitable plants, some of which are so easy to grow that, if you are not careful, you could end up with a riotous jungle! Fortunately, however, many rock plants are slow to spread, and there are plenty that grow only into neat little mounds, miniature trees and small-scale shrubs.

Before you start to arrange the rocks and plants, a quick sketch on squared paper will help you get some idea of the amount of space you have available. It is often disappointing to discover that there is much less space than you originally thought, but knowing this in advance does at least save you from buying too many plants, only to dig them up two or three years later when you will have no option but to discard them.

If, to begin with, you have empty spaces between plants – as indeed you should have if you are going to allow them to develop properly – you can temporarily fill these with small annuals, such as Ageratum, Candytuft or one of the dwarf varieties of Busy Lizzy (Impatiens).

Some rock plants will flower in their first year and it doesn't take long for a newly-planted rock garden to look as though it has been growing for years. Part of the art in encouraging this is the way in which stones and rocks are positioned; the choice of rocks helps, too, as old weathered pieces obviously contribute to the well-established look.

Good drainage

Containers can be as large or as small as you like, but they should be at least 6in (15cm) deep – preferably more – and they must have a drainage hole in the bottom. You can have a wooden container especially made – don't forget to treat it with a plant-safe wood preservative; or use a shallow, conical concrete planter; or put an old kitchen sink into service – either one of the deep, white porcelain ones or the biscuit-coloured stone type.

Alternatively, you can have a trough specially built in bricks or paving stone, to be a permanent feature on the patio, supported on brick or stone pillars; always include a drainage hole in the bottom of one of these, too. Whatever type of container you use, it should be sited so that it slopes very gently towards the drainage hole.

A permanent rock garden should contain soil-based compost. John Innes No 1 is suitable. Good drainage is vital, so the compost will be improved by the addition of gritty sand, added in the proportion of three parts sharp sand to six of compost. Plants needing acid compost grow well in John Innes compost that has not had chalk added to it.

When filling the container, put a disc of perforated zinc over the drainage hole to prevent compost being washed out. It also prevents worms or woodlice getting in. Spread a 2in (5cm) thick layer of crocks in the base of the container, then add a 1in (2.5cm) thick layer of peat. Finally, fill up with compost to within 1in (2.5cm) of the rim.

Positioning the rocks

After filling and firming the compost, water it and leave to settle for a day or two, then put the plants and rocks in position. You can position the rocks either before or after planting, but before is probably easier and enables you to get the pattern right without having to disturb the plants.

You can get small pieces of limestone or sandstone from nurseries, garden centres or specialist rock garden nurseries. Alternatively, use tufa – a lightweight porous stone, volcanic in origin – again from specialist alpine nurseries. Don't use too many pieces and place them with the stratum lines running naturally, which usually means horizontally, and bury the best part of each piece below the surface.

When and how to plant

Now position the plants according to your plan, at such a depth that their crowns are level with the surface of the compost. Make sure that the roots have enough space in which to spread. It is better to remove some compost, very gently, from the rootball rather than planting it in its entirety; this gives the roots a better chance to spread into the compost.

The best time to plant is in the early spring, though rock plants can

be put in at any time, as long as the weather is neither too hot, too dry, nor freezing. Firm and water plants, then put a layer of clean stone

chippings on the surface of the compost, which will both provide coolness and help to retain moisture in the compost.

Sempervivum species are easy to look after and will flourish when planted in a stone trough, *above*. A container filled with a selection of rock plants will make a delightful and attractive feature on your patio, *right*.

What to plant where

Most rock plants like a sunny position. This applies to all the following rock plants: *Campanula garganica*, which has large blue or white bells; the creeping Wild Thyme (*Thymus serpyllum*), which has lilac-pink flowers on evergreen mats; *Armeria caespitosa*, an alpine form of Sea Thrift, with whitish-pink flowers; Edelweiss (*Leontopodium alpinum*), which has white flowers with felted petals; two Sedums – 'Cappablanca', which has yellow flowers, and 'Purpereum', with purple-flushed leaves; Pinks, such as 'Little Joe' which is pink, 'Oakington', which is deep rose, and 'Spark', which is red; the Pasque Flower (*Pulsatilla vulgaris*), which produces purple flowers in spring; *Geranium* 'Ballerina', which is lilac-pink with dark veins; *Gentiana ornata*, which produces beautiful deep-blue trumpets in August; *Allium cyaneum*, an attractive blue-flowered dwarf form of ornamental onion; *Cheiranthus* 'Moonlight', a delightful tiny yellow perennial Wallflower; and the Cobweb Houseleek (*Sempervivum*

arachnoideum).

There are also a few rock plants which prefer shade, such as the Alpine Phlox, mossy Saxifrages, dwarf Cyclamen, a miniature Daffodil called *Narcissus cyclamineus* and the Hoop-petticoat Daffodil (*N. bulbocodium*).

Dwarf conifers do best in the sun, but will also grow in the combination of part sun and part shade. These include *Picea glauca* 'Albertiana Conica'; the dwarf *Juniperus communis* 'Compressa'; a miniature form of the Scots Pine called *Pinus sylvestris* 'Beuvronensis', and *Chamaecyparis lawsoniana* 'Ellwood's Pillar'.

The smaller bulbs all do well in container rock gardens and like to have their faces in the sun. Miniature Daffodils have already been mentioned, and others include Snowdrops, Crocus, Winter Aconite (*Eranthis hyemalis*), the tiny winter-flowering *Iris reticulata* with deep blue or violet flowers, Scillas and Grape Hyacinths.

Dwarf conifers

Dwarf conifers are splendid for growing in a variety of containers to give your patio a furnished look all the year round.

Prized for their alluring shapes and vivid hues, dwarf and slow-growing conifers have much to commend them.

In silver-blue, bright green, golden yellow and marbled white, use them to camouflage manhole covers to soften your patio or just to colour a window-box, tub or trough.

Garden centres stock a wide range of conifers and they're not expensive. Furthermore, once planted – whatever the weather and time of year – they demand little attention. Provided you water them freely during dry spells and remember to feed them occasionally, these beautiful, statuesque plants will reward you with lustrous foliage.

Pick and choose

There are many types from which to choose and all are hardy and will survive extreme cold.

Dwarf firs (Abies). *Abies balsamea* 'Nana', compact, dark green and rounded, is especially suitable for growing in a tub or container. *A.*

koreana, which is taller with silvery undersides to its deep green needles, is valued for its bright blue cones that sit vertically on stiffish shoots. The form 'Horstmann's Silberlocke' has blue-grey foliage.

Cedars. There are some wonderful tiny species of cedar that will flourish in a container. Take your pick from *Cedrus deodara* 'Golden Horizon', semi-prostrate when young but rising to form a golden cascade when mature; *C.deodara* 'Nana Aurea', which is more robust, grows to around 6-8ft (1.8-2.4m) and resembles a yellowish-green waterfall; and 'Sargentii' which is a trailing form of the Cedar of Lebanon and looks superb when planted to cloak a retaining wall.

Cypresses. There are some amazing conifers to be found among the genus Chamaecyparis, the Cypresses from North America and Japan.

Chamaecyparis lawsoniana 'Albospica' makes a roundish, cone-shaped bush with shoot tips flecked with white. 'Little Spire' makes a slender green column, while *C.lawsoniana* 'Minima Aurea' is a broad, squat pyramid of golden leaves which stay richly coloured all the year round.

Among the Sawara Cypresses of Japan (*Chamaecyparis pisifera*) is the outstandingly attractive 'Filifera Aurea', a whipcord-leaved species that forms a broad dome of gold.

Junipers. The selection of junipers available for growing on a patio is wide and ranges from the tiny cigar-shaped *Juniperus communis* 'Compressa', perfect for window-boxes, rock gardens or small pots, to the handsome blue and yellow columns of *J. chinensis* 'Pyramidalis' and 'Aurea', respectively.

The slender *J. scopulorum* 'Skyrocket' is one of the most spectacular species and is ideal for bringing height to a sheltered border or for growing among paving slabs.

Spruce. Picea and its varieties are strikingly beautiful. In its *P. pungens* 'Hoto', 'Moerheimii' and 'Globosa' forms it will bring shades of grey and blue to your patio in shapes that are perfectly symmetical. Two varieties of *Picea glauca* – 'Alberta Globe' and

'Albertiana' – form neat bright green pyramids and are also very endearing.

Yew (*Taxus*) has several superb forms, such as 'Standishii' with an upright stance and 'Summergold' with a prostrate habit.

Pines. The dwarf forms of pine are usually bun or ball-shaped and they can create great impact with their ground-hugging habit. *Pinus mugo* 'Mops' and *P.sylvestris* 'Aurea' are a couple of varieties that will give character to any patio.

Thuja. This is particularly valued for its *T.occidentalis* 'Sunkist' form which is ideal for containers, and 'Rheingold', with its brilliant, golden yellow foliage.

Tsuga. This is another conifer suitable for any balcony. *T. canadensis* 'Cole' forming a bright green, soft-leaved curtain is perfect for clothing a retaining wall or large urn.

The right setting

When planted in tubs, window-boxes or troughs, dwarf conifers seldom become embarrassingly large. A restricted root run slows down growth.

Potting compost

Conifers grow best in acid soil. Use John Innes potting compost without any chalk added to it, or a proprietary ericaceous compost. Feed subsequently with a conifer and shrub fertiliser.

Watering

Conifers are survivors and will tolerate dry spells for several days without showing any signs of stress. However, in summer it is advisable to water them regularly.

Repotting

This is only necessary if the compost becomes netted with roots and frequent watering becomes essential to keep it moist. Tap the plant from its container, trim away some of the roots and then repot.

Winter care

Container-grown plants should be positioned in a sheltered spot, away from the blast of east winds which can scorch leaves.

Small but good

SITUATION	NAME	SHAPE	HEIGHT	COLOUR	COMMENTS
Window-boxes and rock gardens	*Junipeus communis* 'Compressa'	Cigar	1-1½ft (0.3-0.5m)	Greenish grey	Very slow growing, slim
	Juniperus media 'Gold Sovereign'	Bun	1¼-1¾ft (0.38-0.53m)	Vivid golden	Feathery; striking in winter
	Juniperus squamata 'Blue Star'	Ball	1-1½ (0.3-0.45m)	Steel blue	Very compact, impressive
	Picea albertiana 'Conica'	Neat cone	1-1½ft (0.3-0.45m)	Green	Bright green in spring
	Thuja occidentalis 'Hetz Midget'	Globe	¾-1ft (0.23-0.3m)	Green	Slowest growing of all
Tubs, planters, large troughs	*Abies koreana*	Pyramid	2-2½ft (0.6-0.75m)	Green and silver	Statuesque; handsome cones
	Cedrus deodara 'Nana Aurea'	Pyramid	7-8ft (2.1-2.4m)	Golden yellow	Waterfall of feathery shoots
	Chamaecyparis obtusa 'Nana Gracilis'	Pyramid	2-3ft (0.45-0.6m)	Dark green	Shell-like formation of leaves
	Picea pungens 'globosa'	Bun	1½-2ft (0.45-0.6m)	Silvery blue	Rigid 'unreal' symmetry
	Thuja occidentalis 'Sunkist'	Pyramid	3-4ft (0.3-1.2m)	Brilliant yellow	Layers of leaves
	Taxus baccata 'Standishii'	Pencil	3.4ft (0.3-1.2m)	Bright yellow	Slender column, sturdy, elegant
Low hedges	*Thuja occidentalis* 'Smaragd'	Pyramid	4-5ft (1.2-1.5m)	Emerald green	Narrow, neat; doesn't need trimming
	Juniperus communis 'Gold Cone'	Column	3-4ft (1.2-1.5m)	Bright yellow	Slim, elegant, plant closely
	Juniperus chinensis 'Pyramidalis'	Pyramid	5-6ft (1.5-1.8m)	Steel blue	Bushy, neat, no trimming necessary
Camouflaging	*Juniperus horizontalis* 'Glauca'	Carpeter	3-5ft (0.3-1.5m) spread	Silver blue	Rapid ground coverer
	Juniperus x media 'Gold Coast'	Carpeter	3-4ft (0.3-1.2m) spread	Golden	Tipped leaves. Dense, bushy habit
	Juniperus virginiana 'Grey Owl'	Carpeter	5.6ft (1.5-1.8m) spread	Smoky tinged green	Rapid grower, effective ground coverer
Statuesque features	*Cedrus deodara* 'Nana Aurea'	Pyramid	7-8ft (2.1-2.4m)	Golden yellow	Waterfall of feathery shoots
	Abies koreana 'Horstmann's Silberlocke'	Pyramid	2½-3ft (0.75-0.9m)	Green and silver	Rigid, sculptural form
	Picea pungens 'Hoto'	Pyramid	7.8ft (2.1-2.4m)	Intense blue	Symmetrical – quite beautiful

A terrace herb garden

Growing herbs in containers on a terrace, balcony or patio is, in some ways, not only easier but also better for the plants than planting them in the open garden. You can keep rampant herbs under control; you can move containers about so that the plants get the shelter, sun or shade that they enjoy most; you can arrange them as you like; and you can alter the arrangement at will to get the best possible combinations of colour and form.

A terrace herb garden is also a superior alternative to growing your herbs indoors. They do better outside and, for some strange, inexplicable reason, they also seem to taste better. It also allows you to grow some of the taller herbs like Bay and Fennel, which may be too large to be accommodated on the kitchen window-sill. Not everyone, however, is lucky enough to have somewhere outside where they can grow herbs, and these people should read about growing them indoors in 'Growing herbs for the kitchen' on page 483.

All sorts of herbs can be grown in containers – not necessarily only the culinary kinds – and they can be extremely ornamental. With a judicious choice of both plants and containers, you need not grow anything else *but* herbs on your terrace – they will be more than adequately decorative without any other plants.

Some herbs are native wild flowers, many of them Mediterranean in origin. And some are now used mainly as border plants, but were nevertheless once important culinary or medicinal herbs. The red-flowered Bergamot (*Monarda didyma*) is one example, and the white-flowered Florentine Iris (*Iris germanica* 'Florentina') is another, the root of which – Orris root – supplies a strong violet perfume, which used to be the main reason for its cultivation. Indeed, in the days when sanitation was poor, many herbs used to be grown purely for the fragrance of their flowers or leaves, which were then incorporated in pot-pourri mixtures and put to household use. Some

Rampant herbs are more controllable if grown separately in containers.

had especially pungent aromas, which helped to keep clothes moths and other insects at bay.

Window-boxes, pots, tubs and urns will all be appropriate for one herb or other, whether in depth, colour or design, and you can have great fun tracking down just the right container and pairing it with exactly the right varieties of herbs. Shrubby and woody herbs will usually need the larger size pots and tubs; herbaceous border herbs can be small, medium or large; some are bulbous; and some have little root growth so can survive in quite shallow containers.

As you build up your collection of herbs, you will find that grouping the containers together usually makes the most effective display. You can, of course, keep pots, boxes and tubs apart – which may suit your needs and the space available to you better – or you may like to try arranging them in some formal design, like a cross, a star or the spokes of a wheel. You can also plant some in the spaces between the paving stones, so that you make a chessboard design, perhaps, or some other kind of regular geometric pattern. Exactly what you choose to do will depend, to a large extent, on how often you use the terrace and what you use it for – be it relaxation or entertaining.

Choosing herbs

Most of the low-growing herbs have correspondingly shallow root systems and don't need more than a few inches of compost, so do well in smaller pots and boxes. But these also make a good edging for a taller display in a large container. Small herbs include golden-leaved Marjoram, which spreads to form good ground cover without swamping other plants; Chives, which are especially pretty if allowed to flower and, with age, will grow to about 1ft (0.3m) high; moss-leaved Parsley; plain and variegated Thymes, such as 'Doone Valley' and 'Silver Queen' (lemon-scented), and the Creeping Thyme – another good ground cover plant with tiny pinkish-purple flowers; Salad Burnet, which has delicate frond-like leaves that taste of cucumber; and Chamomile, the true version of which is annual but which seeds itself so readily.

Of the other annuals that can be grown from seed, Borage is one of the most ornamental, with clusters of intense blue, star-shaped flowers all summer that are much loved by bees; be prepared for it to grow as tall as 4ft (1.2m) in conditions it enjoys. Basil matures into a bushy plant 2-3ft (0.6-0.9m) tall, with spikes of white flowers or, in the cases of the purple leaved 'Dark Opal', violet ones. Another herb with a highly individual aroma is the tender little Sweet Marjoram, which is best used as an edging plant and is also a marvellous culinary herb.

Shrubby herbs supply the backbone of a terrace herb garden and continue to be decorative in winter, as several are evergreen. Lavender does well in containers and is surprisingly hardy; so is Rosemary, which has pale blue flowers that appear as early as April and go on through the summer in a warm position.

Sage has purple-blue flowers in its

Thymes have a shallow root system and flourish in smaller pots.

Sages are a good choice for warm and sheltered terraces.

The right aspect

What herbs you choose will depend to a large extent on the direction in which your terrace, balcony or patio faces because, like everything else, herbs will do best in the conditions that suit them. Some, for example, like a sunny position, others prefer semi-shade, and some like a warm, sheltered spot.

	Full sun	Semi-shade	Warm, sheltered
Basil	✓		
Borage		✓	
Chamomile	✓		
Chives		✓	
Curry Plant	✓		
Dill	✓		✓
Fennel	✓		
Feverfew	✓		
Hyssop	✓		
Lavender	✓		
Lemon Balm	✓		
Marjoram	✓		
Mint		✓	
Oregano	✓		
Parsley		✓	
Rosemary	✓		
Rue		✓	
Sage	✓		✓
Salad Burnet	✓		
Sorrel	✓		
Sweet Bay	✓		✓
Tarragon	✓		✓
Thyme	✓		✓

narrow-leaved form (*Salvia angusti-folia*), which provides the best flavour; there are also varieties with coloured foliage, such as 'Pur-purascens' (flushed purple), 'Icterina' (with golden variegated leaves), and 'Tricolor' (with creamy-white, pink and purple markings on grey-green leaves). There is also a slightly tender species called *S.rutilans*, which has bright scarlet flowers and soft, strongly pineapple-scented leaves and is a good choice for really warm, sheltered terraces.

Sweet Bay is, strictly speaking, an evergreen tree, but also does well as an informal shrub, a trained form or a standard in a tub or large planter. Two small deciduous shrubs, which were originally regarded as herbs but are now grown largely for their highly decorative qualities, are hyssop, which has blue (occasionally pink or white) flowers in summer; and the strongly purgative Rue, which has a blue-green leaved form called 'Jackman's Blue'.

If your terrace herb garden is to be confined to containers, this is a great opportunity to go in for Mints, as this is an ideal way to keep them under control. Garden or Spearmint (*Mentha spicata*) is the most common but there are other good varieties: these include Eau de Cologne Mint (*M.piperita citrata*), which has dark green, purple-flushed leaves and stems; Apple Mint (*M.suaveolens*), with round felty leaves; and Peppermint (*M.piperita*), of which there is a handsome, almost black-leaved form called Black Peppermint that is the one used to make peppermint tea. Then Pineapple Mint (*M.suaveolens variegata*) has soft, cream-variegated, pointed leaves, and the so-called Ginger Mint (*M.gentilis*) has green leaves with yellow stripes along the veins.

No herb collection is complete without Dill, French Tarragon (*Artemisia dracunculus sativa*), French Sorrel (*Rumex scutatus*) and the Italian form of Marjoram called Oregano. Golden variegated Lemon Balm also provides a striking display, as does Feverfew, which has lacy leaves and white daisy-like flowers that keep going throughout the summer. And finally, for real aroma, plant a Curry Plant (*Helichrysum angustifolia*) which in hot sun will announce your herb garden in no uncertain manner.

Grow flowering Chives, Parsley, Thyme and Marjoram in a herb pot.

No herb garden is complete without some Sage and Tarragon.

Fruit and vegetables in containers

Fruit and vegetables picked fresh from the garden seem to taste better than those you buy in the shops and, furthermore, they are richer in minerals and vitamins. Even if you have no garden, it is still possible to grow a good selection of vegetables in containers, which provide you with something to pick, cut or dig up all year round. You can also grow your own fruit, though this will need a little more care and attention.

The choice of container

This is crucial for both fruit and vegetables. Its depth is obviously of the utmost importance, though growing bags are an exception. Some vegetables will grow in a comparatively shallow amount of compost; others demand more; and a few greedy feeders with far-reaching roots need a really good depth and are, therefore, best planted in tubs.

The diameter of the container is also important. In general, the larger the container, the better the vegetable is likely to grow. In the case of the shallow-rooting varieties, such as

broad beans, french beans, chicory, some lettuces and small tomatoes, these all require a 6in (15cm) diameter pot for each plant, whereas carrots, garlic and radish can be grown several to a pot – the actual number depending on the particular vegetable variety concerned. Chinese artichokes can, in theory, be grown two or three tubers to a pot, but in practice they produce a good deal of top growth and one per pot is much better. They are not very often grown, but are so easy to grow and so delicious in stir-fries that they are worth having a go at.

In the second, 'moderate' category, aubergine, cabbage, potato and tomato require one 9in (23cm) diameter pot per plant; cucumber, courgette and marrow prefer a wider diameter, though still a 9in (23cm) depth; and all the remainder can be grown several to a 9in (23cm) pot.

Vegetables that are not at all suitable for container cultivation include Jerusalem and globe artichokes and sweetcorn, which are too tall; and asparagus and Brussels sprouts, kale

Courgette and marrow require containers of moderate diameter.

and sprouting broccoli – which are fairly large and take up space unproductively for too long; note that this also applies to cabbage, cauliflower and leeks, but these are not as tall and do provide welcome greens at an otherwise difficult time of year. Vegetables that are not commonly grown and which you might like to try include celery and celeriac, Chinese cabbage, endive, fennel, kohlrabi and swede.

On roof gardens, in basement areas and on some balconies, beds can be made up on the ground: line the beds with plastic sheeting and confine the compost with old wooden beams, peat blocks or wire netting and provide a drainage layer – about 1-2in (2.5-5cm) thick of expanded polystyrene chips, mortar rubble or pieces of broken clay pot.

Growing bags are a convenient form of container in which the specially blended compost overcomes the lack of depth. Their horizontal shape

313

A question of depth

Below is a list of vegetables suitable for various depths of container

Shallow: 6in (15cm) minimum	Moderate: 9in (23cm) minimum		Deep: 12in (30cm) minimum
Broad bean, dwarf var. 'The Sutton' Carrot, small vars. 'Early French Frame' 'Amsterdam Forcing' Chicory red Chinese artichoke French bean Garlic Lettuce 'Tom Thumb' Radish Tomato 'Tiny Tim'	Aubergine Beetroot Cabbage Carrot Cauliflower Courgette, bush Cucumber, bush Leek Lettuce, var. 'All the Year Round'; 'Continuity' (red flushed); 'Salad bowl'(no heart, continuous picking);	'Webbs Wonderful' (Iceberg type) Marrow, bush Onion Pea 'Little Marvel' Potato Ruby chard Spinach	French bean, 'Climbing purple podded' Parsnip Runner bean Spinach, perpetual

Chicory 'Red Verona' grows well in shallow containers.

provides more compost area in relation to their depth than conventional containers.

Where space is a serious problem, try a vertical alternative to pots or tubs, such as long boxes in stepped tiers on an A-frame as illustrated below, or hang similar boxes on a wall.

The right conditions

Vegetables are grown most successfully where there is plenty of sun. This is especially true when they are grown in containers, in which case they need all the help they can get! If you cannot provide a great deal of sunshine, try spinach, radish, Swiss and ruby chard, and lettuce. The others are all unlikely to grow well, and will tend to be attacked by pests.

Composts can be either peat-based, in which case you should be prepared to liquid feed regularly throughout the crop's life from an early age; or soil-based, such as John Innes No 2 or 3 depending on the size of the container; use No 2 for the shallowest containers, No 3 for deeper ones. Vegetables growing in this latter type of compost may not require any additional feeding, depending on the quality of the soil; if they do, however, start halfway through the life of the plant.

Most vegetables are sown from seed; those that you can buy from small plants, tubers or sets include Chinese artichokes, garlic, onions and potatoes. If it is difficult to start your own from seed, many can be bought as young plants in the spring.

Look out for them from April to July in the garden centres and chain stores, though you may not, of course, be able to find exactly the varieties that you would like.

The most difficult part of successful container vegetable growing is starting them off. Slugs and snails will devour seedlings as fast as they appear, and you may find it necessary to sow in small, individual pots and to transplant when the small vegetables are well beyond the seedling stage; even then, they will still need

vigilant guarding. Seeds germinate best in warm, moist conditions – preferably in the dark if you are sowing indoors or in a propagator.

Regular watering is vital throughout. Vegetables which run short of water end up tough, stringy, bitter, cracked and small – so the vegetable gardener can rarely go away on holiday in the summer months!

Pests to watch for include greenfly, blackfly on broad beans, leafhoppers, red spider mite, and caterpillars on the cabbage family; use a permethrin

Where space is at a premium, use long boxes in stepped tiers on an A-frame.

Purslane will grow well if planted in a container on the patio.

Sweet peppers grow best in a spot where there is plenty of sun.

A collection of vegetables in containers can look most attractive.

greater need for more care and attention. The easiest fruits to grow are strawberries and melons; blackcurrants, redcurrants and gooseberries are not difficult to grow but they need more room; raspberries need a good deal of space – a long, deep box is the best kind of container and it is a good idea to choose a small variety such as 'Malling Jewel'; blackberries and loganberries need at least 10ft (3m) of wall space for support and are really too large; apples, pears and plums can be grown in tubs; and so, too, can oranges, though they do need protection in winter.

On the whole, tubs – with a diameter of at least 12in (30cm) and a similar depth – are the best containers for individual specimens. Strawberries, on the other hand, can be grown individually in 6in (15cm) pots or strawberry barrels, and can be grown in growing bags, as can melons.

All fruits require a sunny position and good compost – preferably a soil-based one, which is longer-lasting and ensures good anchorage for what is often a lot of top growth.

Planting is done, ideally, in October or November. Strawberries are one exception to this and are usually planted in August, or in the spring if you are planting one of the perpetual fruiting varieties. Melons are sown from seed in March in heat, potted on and planted out when frost is no longer a problem but with some protection.

Drainage is important, and tubs should be stood on blocks so that surplus water is certain to drain through freely. Watering and feeding are the same as for vegetables; and in winter the tubs should be lagged to protect the roots from frost.

Pests and diseases to watch for include caterpillars, greenfly, leaf sucker and leafhopper; red spider mite can be a problem on tree fruits, scale insect on oranges. Grey mould is likely on soft fruits, mildew on tree fruits, and scab on apples and pears: use benomyl to control these.

Correct pruning will ensure the heaviest fruiting and is usually done in late November and December when the plants are dormant. The subject of pruning fruit trees is a complicated one, depending both on the exact fruit in question and on the shape you want to achieve.

insecticide. Slugs and snails will attack anything, but can easily be collected and disposed of in the evening when they start feeding, just after darkness falls. Grey mould can be a problem in a cool, damp summer,

mildew in a drier one – treat both with benomyl, a systemic fungicide.

Fruit

Where fruit in containers is required, the range is not so good and there is a

Growing strawberries

Terracotta strawberry pots add an interesting feature to any patio.

Strawberries always grow extremely well in Ken Muir Towerpots.

Convert a wooden beer barrel into a container for strawberries.

Growing strawberries in a strawberry barrel or pot has great advantages. Not only is it the perfect solution to obtaining a weighty yield of fruit when there's not enough space to grow them in the open garden, but you also have the freedom to choose the warmest, most sheltered part of the garden.

Choosing your container

There are several types of container which are popularly used for growing strawberries on a patio or terrace. Traditional terracotta strawberry pots are a pretty and dainty way of growing strawberries and are readily available but are quite expensive.

Ken Muir Towerpots are an effective alternative in plastic. They are stacking modules – both self-watering and very stable – which have been specially designed for growing strawberries and provide a highly efficient modern alternative. A set of four pots takes 12 plants and forms a column 23in (58cm) high. Strawberries grow well in these and maintenance is minimal.

Another possibility is to convert a used, full-sized beer barrel, which can easily be done at home *(see right)*. Barrels – both wooden or plastic – are available from some garden centres, though they are gradually becoming rather more difficult to get hold of. They, in any case, do not provide the most economical way of growing strawberries – they take a lot of compost for a comparatively low yield – but they do make an attractive display with an old-fashioned feel.

Planting

You can use either gritty and nourishing loam-based compost such as John Innes No 2, or a peat-based potting compost such as Verdley, Arthur Bowers or Levington. For it to succeed, it must remain cool and moist in hot dry spells, but it must not become waterlogged should you be too generous with the hosepipe.

Whatever you use, its texture will be much improved by the addition of a quarter part, by volume, of Perlite. This will ensure that air spaces are retained, even after repeated watering, and that the compost stays spongy and 'life-giving'.

Early planting, in July and August, will yield the heaviest crop the fol-

Converting a beer barrel

A 40-gallon barrel is the ideal size. Using a brace and bit and a keyhole saw, take out 18 staggered holes, 2in (5cm) in diameter, in three evenly spaced rows around the barrel. Holes should be 6in (15cm) apart and start 6in (15cm) from the bottom.

Protect the wood from rot by painting both inside and out with Green Cuprinol or Rentokil wood preservative, both of which are harmless to plant life.

Drill a couple of holes, 1in (2.5cm) apart, in the base of the barrel and set it on bricks so that surplus water is allowed to escape unimpeded. If you don't, the base of your barrel is likely to rot. Then cover the barrel floor with a 2in (5cm) layer of gravel crocks. This will facilitate good drainage.

It is important, too, that water which is poured in the top of the barrel seeps evenly through the compost to water the lowest level of plants: failing this, they will soon show their dissatisfaction by wilting. The answer to this problem (which can also be used in strawberry pots) is to insert a length of plastic drainpipe 4in (10cm) in diameter, through the middle of the barrel before filling it with compost and to fill the pipe with drainage material such as gravel or crocks. Then, when the barrel has been filled with compost, the pipe should be removed, leaving a central drainage channel.

Plants should then be planted at the same time as the compost is filled in. Ease the plants through the holes, spreading the roots out gently in the compost. Then add more compost, firming it as you go and planting carefully as you reach each successive row of holes.

Finally, stop adding compost when you are within 1in (2.5cm) of the barrel rim, and plant a further six plants evenly on the surface layer of the compost. Now is the time to withdraw the piece of drainpipe, so leaving a central core of gravel or broken crocks which provides a lifeline to the very lowest plants. Water in your plants, directing the water into the drainage core from where it will spread out evenly.

lowing year. If this is left until the autumn or late spring, the return in the first year will be far less. Never plant between November and late February as the roots are liable to be killed by frost.

Water in your plants after planting and keep the compost moist at all times. Take care not to overwater, particularly when the fruits are swelling, as this may lead to rot.

Aftercare

In the first year after planting, there should be sufficient nourishment in the compost to sustain robust growth and weighty yields. But in the second year, or when leaves take on an unhealthy pallor which indicates nitrogen deficiency and a possible shortage of some other vital element, you should feed every two weeks with a solution of general-purpose fertiliser such as Phostrogen, from early April until about late July when the fruit starts to form. Thereafter, make a point of feeding again in the autumn after fruiting, and then stop until the following spring.

With luck, your plants should fruit

well for two or three years, after which they will probably decline. In the third year, therefore, you should spur on robust growth by feeding a little more frequently – say weekly – with Phostrogen. If the leaves turn a very deep green and grow abnormally large, this is a sign that they have been overfed. If you notice this, stop feeding immediately.

When runners form – usually in June – cut them close to the crown. Left in, they will deprive the plants of energy and crowd their space.

After fruiting, cut away all the old leaves of summer fruiting varieties; this will encourage a further flush of foliage which will, in turn, invigorate the plant. Burn all the discarded leaves as they are likely to be diseased. But don't, on the other hand, remove all the leaves of the perpetual fruiting kinds, such as Gento and Ostara, as these will help fruit to develop later in the year. Plants need to be renewed every third year.

Netting the crop

One of the joys of growing strawberries in a container is that it is easy to deter birds from pecking the fruit. You can either drape fine mesh netting over the container – supported and held away from the crop with a few lengths of wood stuck in the soil and topped with jam jars – or you can create a mini fruit cage which you can use every year.

What to buy

Because you want to maximise cropping in a small area, choose only high-yielding varieties. Happily, there are many of these from which to choose. A good midsummer selection might consist of Cambridge Favourite; the giant-fruited Grandee – berries can attain a diameter of 3in (8cm) and weigh as much as 3oz (85g); Cambridge Favourite; Hapil, which crops well in dry conditions; and Tenira, acclaimed to be one of the finest-flavoured of modern strawberries.

Among the perpetuals – varieties which start fruiting in summer and continue right through until the autumn – are Ostara, which has a red skin and orange flesh; Aromel; and Gento, which is probably the biggest-fruited perpetual and, even if it is planted in the early spring, a full crop can be anticipated the same year.

Reach for the sky

Always consult a builder before planning a 'garden in the air'.

A roof garden can change your life: it provides you with extra outdoor space, invaluable if you haven't already got a garden; somewhere where you can grow plants, relax and catch the sun; an attractive view from inside the house; and, most important, privacy. All you need is a flat roof and planning the garden can be a challenge.

It's important before you start to consult your builder or surveyor. A 'garden in the air' can be surprisingly heavy: containers, soil, screening materials, tiles, leisure furniture, barbecue, and so on – it all adds up. So it's vital that load-bearing areas provide sufficient support. The average roof is capable of bearing just 20-30lb (95-145kg) of soil per sq ft (sq m). The weight may be much greater than this if the soil is soaked with water.

It is also important, when you choose your roof surfacing, to get professional advice as to its suitability and drainage. Planning permission may be required too, so do check with your local authorities.

Containers

Here the choice is yours but bear in mind, first, that you want to add as little as possible to the weight on your roof; and, secondly, that roof gardens tend to be subject to strong winds. Material and shape are therefore both important considerations. The lightweight materials such as fibreglass and plastic really come into their own on the roof and there are also some moulded, rigid cellular fibre containers which are exceptionally lightweight and last for only about two years, after which they will break down and can simply be mixed into the compost. As for shape, wide-based pots, troughs or urns which won't be blown over in windy weather are all ideal. Position them over or near load-bearing walls which can take the weight, and close to walls for wind protection.

Make sure that drainage is good by filling the containers first with a 4in (10cm) layer of gravel and topping this with porous John Innes compost to within 2in (5cm) of the rim. You may like to construct permanent brick-built troughs, in which case you should leave 'weep holes' at roughly 18in (45cm) intervals, positioned 6in (15cm) above the base for efficient drainage.

Getting the wind up

Wind can be a problem on an exposed roof garden, drying out soil and playing havoc with your plants. Its effects can be much reduced by erecting screens. Effective screening includes wattle hurdles, close-mesh trellis, or Rokolene Windbreak netting which is both weatherproof and tear-resistant. The latter is available in 100ft (33.3m) rolls and several widths, from 3ft (1m) to 6ft (2m).

Year-round colour

First of all, you can welcome spring with a wealth of Daffodils, Tulips, Grape Hyacinths, Crocuses and Snowdrops to brighten the lengthening days. These will all thrive in low, wide pots or tubs.

Then follow the spring bonanza with a summer display of exotics, such as Cannas, Geraniums, Fuchsias, Petunias, Zinnias and Lobelias. Or, for something really exciting, just as you can plan for an overhead screen of summer flower-

Add colour with a mass of flowering plants in containers.

Terraces are ideal for relaxation.

ing climbers such as Honeysuckle, Clematis and Jasmine to enhance a ground-floor patio, so too you can for a roof garden. Indeed, the height provided by a pergola of tub-grown climbing Roses, or a trellis draped with annual climbers such as Nasturtiums and Morning Glory, will add greatly to the charm of your design.

Make autumn more exciting with *Crocus speciosus*, Nerones, Kaffir Lilies and the lovely *Colchicum speciosum* 'Waterlily'. And winter will be much more cheerful with odd splashes of variegated foliage. Try, for example, a golden variegated evergreen shrub such as *Elaeagnus pungens* 'Maculata', or one of the variegated Ivies. They'll certainly brighten your view of the world. Other examples of suitably low-growing evergreens which provide good permanent planting and are not vulnerable to wind include Sea Pinks *(Armeria maritima)*, Vinca and Euonymus.

Watering

This is always a vital task but it may be required even more frequently on a roof top if it is subject to strong sun and wind, both of which will have a drying effect. In midsummer, a roof garden may need watering as often as twice a day.

The first thing you can do to reduce watering to a minimum is to use a good loam-based compost, such as John Innes potting mixtures augmented with something like Vermiculite or Agrosoke. The latter resembles granules of coarse sand which absorb water and expand into a jelly-like substance. When mixed in with potting compost this water is gradually released over a period of time so reducing frequency of watering. It also pays to mulch the compost with a layer of peat, say, or a shredded, composted tree bark, such as Forest Bark to insulate the roots from a blazing sun, which is inevitably more concentrated at roof level than on the ground.

Your life will be much improved by the presence of a hosepipe, so do consider installing an outdoor tap on the roof. A particularly efficient way of watering long troughs is with a seep hose – a length of tubing perforated with tiny holes. If you place it 'face' downwards on the soil, moisture seeps directly down to the roots without any waste. Alternatively, some form of trickle irrigation may be devised, whereby each container receives a controlled drip of water to keep the compost moist at all times. See also 'Watering: whys and wherefores', page 492.

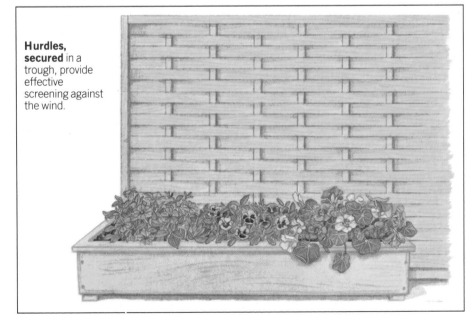

Hurdles, secured in a trough, provide effective screening against the wind.

319

WATER USED AS A FEATURE brings a sense of peace and tranquillity to a garden. A lily pond built into a patio, for instance, looks enchanting, and with some goldfish it can be a source of fascination all the year round.

Ponds

There are several attractive ways to design your pond. You can make the rim of the pond level with the paving; or raise it in a circle of bricks; create a cascade by constructing the pond in two or more tiers; or, if you have the space, make a stepped, slow-flowing stream that discharges into a pool.

Construction

The simplest type of pool consists of a hole 18in (45cm) deep, with a marginal shelf measuring 9in (23cm) wide and 9in (23cm) deep to take edging plants. Line the excavation with a durable material such as double laminated PVC (Duralay) or one reinforced with nylon (Wavelock). Butyl rubber (Stapelite) has an even longer life, sometimes lasting up to 20 years. If the soil is stony the lining could tear so, for protection, line the sides of the excavation with soft sand or polyester matting.

Plants

For a pond with a surface area of about 15sq ft (4½sq m) and not less than 15in (45cm) deep you will need: one Water-lily, choosing from such varieties as white tipped, glowing red 'Attraction', salmon pink 'Amabilis', free flowering white 'Candida' or bright yellow 'Moorei'; six oxygenating plants, such as ferny-leaved Water Milfoil (*Myriophyllum verticillatum*), Hornwort (*Ceratophyllum demersum*), Hair Grass (*Eleocharis acicularis*), Willow Moss (*Fontinalis antipyretica*), Canadian Pondweed (*Elodea canadensis*) or its curled cousin *Elodea crispa*.

For the edges of the pool, there are four ideal bog plants: Double Marsh Marigold (*Caltha palustris plena*); Flowering Rush (*Butomus umbellatus*), a magnificent plant with bright rose-pink starry flowers; *Iris laevigata variegata*, with cream and green striped leaves; and Water Forget-me-not (*Myosotis palustris*).

You will also need two floating plants, such as Fairy Moss (*Azolla caroliniana*) – a tiny fern that is green in early summer and changes to a bright russet-red in late summer – and white-flowered Frogbit (*Hydrocharis morsus ranae*), which should be left to float and colonise on the water surface.

With the exception of the floating plants, all others should be placed in perforated polythene crates instead of directly into the soil to avoid the water being polluted by soil; this will also prevent inquisitive fish nosing the plants. First, line the crate with sacking or hessian and place a layer of fairly heavy soil in the bottom. Nestle the plant's roots in the soil, then pack more soil around the plant. Draw the hessian up around the soil and roots, and tie it loosely at the neck of the plant.

A Water-lily should be elevated on bricks when first introduced to the pond, so it is just a few inches below the water. Then, as new leaves form, gradually lower the plant to the bottom of the pool, making sure the leaf pads are, at all times, lying flat on the surface of the water.

Water can turn your garden into a haven of peace.

Introducing fish

After about two weeks your new plants will have started to effect changes in the water and this is the time to introduce fish to your pond.

Allow 1sq ft (0.33sq m) surface area for each 2in (5cm) fish; a 15sq ft (4½sq m) pool could therefore support 15 2in (5cm) fish or seven or eight double the size. Too many fish in a well planted pond could prove fatal because the plants give off carbon dioxide at night and the fish could therefore die from oxygen starvation.

CHAPTER 6

Special Effects

Hanging gardens

The key to success is to choose the right plant for the container.

The hanging gardens of Surbiton may not have quite the same ring to it as the original Babylonian version, but hanging baskets are nevertheless enjoying a popularity boom unrivalled since the days when hanging gardens were the main attraction as one of the seven wonders of the world. And it isn't just outside that hanging baskets are taking off. Indoors too, they can give a tremendous 'lift' to a room, as well as adding a whole new dimension to the way in which you grow your houseplants.

Making the most of hanging baskets in the house means using the right plants, the right containers, and plenty of imagination. For example, instead of always falling back on the usual range of trailing plants which you can find in every high street florist, why not spend a little time seeking out more unusual varieties from specialist nurseries, or perhaps you could even try growing your own from seed?

And don't restrict yourself to trailing plants: try climbers too. Self-twining varieties look particularly good because they wind themselves up round the basket's supports, as well as cascading down over the edges. Finally, don't be afraid to use plants that neither trail nor climb. Some of the best hanging baskets are planted with upright plants that you would normally expect to find in a more conventional growing situation.

Campanula isophylla is a rich blue.

The Achimenes 'Cascade Evening Glory' needs a well lit spot and regular watering.

Begonia pendula 'Orange Cascade' is a pretty trailer.

But do make a definite decision as to whether you want a formal look, with a single variety in a basket of its own, or a crowded, flamboyant effect with lots of different plants all growing together in riotous profusion.

Specimen baskets

The idea here is to use only one kind of plant — either a single specimen or several all the same. Growing plants in a basket can shed a totally new light on the most ordinary plants.

But the plants are only half the battle. With a specimen basket in particular, the container is just as important. Take time to find both plants and containers

that really do something for each other. If necesary, take the plants with you when you shop for the container, or *vice versa*. And, for a really professional finish, use a creeping mossy plant like Mind Your Own Business (Helxine) as a 'filler' to cover bare compost and hide the edges of the basket.

Here are a few suggestions that should spark off some ideas of your own.

Staghorn fern (*Platycerium bifurcatum*): plant three 'back-to-back' in the centre of a large hanging basket. Alternatively, do away with the basket entirely and make a 'mobile' by simply wiring the plants on to a chunk of driftwood or bark (in which case they don't need any soil), and hanging it from a wall or ceiling. The ferns will eventually cover it entirely, with their long, ribbon-like fronds forming a fringe all round. This is a particularly effective arrangement in a conservatory.

Busy Lizzy (*Impatiens*): this takes a lot of beating if you want to create a perfect ball of flowers. Use mixed colours or all one colour, as you prefer, and pack in as many plants as you can. This will need frequent watering and a bright, well lit spot.

Christmas Cactus (*Zygocactus truncatus*): plant three cuttings round the edge of a small basket — or five in a larger one. Instead of growing into the

sort of one-sided plant that you so often see, this should give you a perfect umbrella-shaped effect. It looks great even when it is not in flower, and in full bloom it is sensational.

Boston or Ladder Fern (*Nephrolepsis exaltata* 'Bostoniensis'): plant one per basket, bang in the middle for a pretty cascading effect. The Boston Fern, with its feathery leaves, is one of the most popular ferns and is seen at its best grown in this way.

Fittonia: the striking green and white net-patterned Snakeskin Plant also has a red-patterned cousin — the Painted Net Leaf. The stems are slightly trailing but rather slow growing, so plant three or five per basket for a quick cover-up.

Kangaroo Vine (*Cissus antarctica*) **and Grape Ivy** (*C.rhombifolia*): these two foliage plants are usually thought of as climbers and are often trained up canes, but you'll soon appreciate their trailing qualities when you plant three in a hanging basket — a treatment which will transform a fairly ordinary plant into something really special for a shady spot.

Shrimp plant (*Beloperone guttata*): this is in fact rarely grown in a basket, which is surprising because it is seen at its best in one, with its long salmony bracts dropping down all round.

323

Plant one large or several small plants per basket, and prune back by half each winter to maintain their shape.

🌱 **Herringbone Plant** (*Maranta tricolor*): this is a low-spreading plant with large leaves picked out in a conspicuous, brilliant red herringbone pattern. Although it is not a true trailing plant, it makes a stunning specimen plant when grown in a basket. Plant three together so that the leaves fan out deeply over the edges, and hang it fairly low down — ideally below eye level — so that you can appreciate its full effect.

🌱 **Creeping Gloxinia** (*Maurandia erubescens*): you'll have to grow this unusual plant yourself from seed. It has beautiful purple, trumpet-shaped flowers reminiscent of the Gloxinia — hence its name. The plant twines up as well as dangling down, so you'll get an imposing specimen in record time.

🌱 **Mind Your Own Business** (Helxine): try a rustic-style basket planted with this plant in a really dark spot where most things refuse to grow. There's a yellowish variety as well as the usual plain green one.

A mixed basket

However smart a specimen basket can look, it takes a lot to beat the straightforward exuberance of a mixed basket. There's an enormous difference between a riot of colour and a downright mess, and the trick lies in finding that difference. It's a good idea to experiment with different combinations and arrangements of plants on a table top before committing yourself to planting.

You can mix together virtually any colour — few flowers actually clash. And if you do decide to opt for this mass of colour, remember that it sometimes pays to break it up with a little plain green or silver, so keep a few plain foliage plants in stock. Once again, that old stand-by Mind Your Own Business (Helxine) comes in very handy to fill in odd gaps, in rather the same way as you would use moss in a conventional outdoor hanging basket.

Alternatively, if you prefer a more thought-out co-ordinated look, you could aim instead for a two-tone effect — say, pink and silver, green and gold, or indeed whatever you fancy.

A summer flowering basket

Try to exploit every possibility to the full by including plants in your basket that grow up, out and down. Use

A trailing Lobelia 'Colour Cascade' provides a mass of colour.

A pot of *Pelargonium violareum* looks good hanging in a window.

twining uppers — such as Black Eyed Susan (*Thunbergia alata*), which has orange or yellow flowers with a dark purple centre, or Morning Glory — both of which will grow up the basket supports; dangling downers like trailing Fuchsia, trailing Lobelia, Basket Begonia (*Begonia pendula*), Livingstone Daisies (*Mesembryanthemum criniflorum*) or, for something very unusual, the Indian Strawberry (*Duchesnea indica*), a trailing plant with small strawberry-like fruits; and inner fillers such as Busy Lizzy, a rich blue trailing Bell Flower called *Campanula isophylla*, or Hot Water Plant (*Achimenes*).

Then to add foliage interest, choose from the Polka Dot Plant (*Hypoestes sanguinolenta*), which has pink-splashed leaves, Cudweed Everlasting

The Boston fern is a popular species which is seen at its best in a hanging basket.

(*Helichrysum petiolatum*), which has trailing stems and silver-grey or gold-green felted leaves, or an ornamental Basil called 'Dark Opal' which has deep red leaves.

A permanent mixed basket
Choose a mixture of flowering and foliage plants for year-round interest, and do check that all the plants you want to use enjoy similar conditions.

Good combinations to try include Creeping Fig (*Ficus pumila*) with trailing African Violet; *Asparagus densiflorus*, 'Sprengeri' with the Firecracker Plant (*Manettia inflata*), which is an unusual trailing and twining plant that produces bright yellow, waxy, tubular flowers with scarlet bristles at their base all summer; or a curly-leaved ivy such as Crispa or Fluffy Ruffles with Duchesnea. And for bigger baskets, try a combination of the purple-leaved Velvet Plant (*Gynura*), Lamb's Tail (*Sedum morganianum*), the Bead Plant (*Nertera granadensis*) which has bright orange, bead-like berries in autumn, and Black Eyed Susan (*Thunbergia alata*). Or, for an easy to maintain, neglect-tolerant foliage basket, plant the greeny-gold version of *Helichrysum petiolatum* with Ivy Goldheart, which has a bright gold splash in the centre of each leaf, and Mind Your Own Business.

A collector's basket
Another idea is to make up a basket using a specialist selection of plants that, although different, are all on the same 'theme'. If you are an avid collector of something like Bromeliads, for example, this is an effective way of displaying your collection.

A Bromeliad basket: plant several small varieties, choosing those with grassy leaves and a tendency to grow in clumps, such as Tillandsia and Billbergia, both of which flower easily and colourfully, along with the greeny-grey, trailing Spanish Moss. Spray frequently with tepid water, as these plants take in most of their moisture through their leaves. This basket needs a shady position.

A herb basket: try planting prostrate Rosemary, a selection of variegated and creeping Thymes, and aromatic Greek Basil. This works particularly well in a sunny kitchen window. If you want more colour, add a few dwarf French Marigolds which will pick out the gold tones of the variegated Thyme.

Practically speaking

● **Baskets**. Make sure you choose a suitable basket that will enhance the plants. Look around for unusual containers that can be turned into hanging baskets — junk shops are a particularly good source. Most pots and jars can be suspended in a macramé hanger, or converted into a hanging basket by drilling holes near the top edge and suspending it with picture wire.

Don't overlook the benefits of containers that allow you to plant into the sides as well as the top; the type of open-mesh wire basket that is commonly used outside can also be used indoors, and allows you to plant up through the bottom by pushing plants through the gaps. It does, however, tend to drip badly when it is watered.

Alternatively, you can look out for those solid-sided containers with holes cut in them — like strawberry or parsley pots — and plant each pocket with a different little plant.

● **Compost**. Use exactly the same compost in a hanging basket as you would use for that type of plant if you were using a conventional pot.

● **Planting up**. Pack plants close together for an effective, immediate display, but in the case of a permanent mixed basket you should be prepared to thin them out later as the basket becomes overcrowded, removing the plant that seems to be doing least well.

● **Watering**. This can be a real problem with hanging baskets indoors. If you can't reach up to water, use one of those special gadgets sold in garden centres for watering outdoor hanging baskets, or take careful aim and squirt from an old washing-up liquid bottle which you have rinsed out well beforehand. Porous or wire baskets that could well drip on to the carpet below, as well as those plants that are growing wired on to pieces of driftwood or bark, are best watered by taking the whole thing down and soaking it in a bucket for about half an hour. Leave it to drain completely before putting it back in place.

Climbers and trailers

If you've already filled all your rooms with houseplants and have to resist the temptation of buying any more — think laterally — look upwards! Why not use all that empty space? Fill this wasted area with climbing and trailing plants, which are ideal for growing into awkward nooks and crannies where nothing else will fit. What's more you can add a totally new dimension with a dramatic feature of a lush, green waterfall of glossy leaves to make an unusual focal point in your home.

Pots and plants: brass pot: Hearts Entwined; clay pot: Ivy on a branch; old potty: Jasmine; china bowl: Creeping Fig.

Space savers

Climbers and trailers are perfect if you only have limited space at your disposal; by growing plants up and down instead of outwards and side by side, you can achieve large impressive displays without losing valuable floor space. Indeed, however short of space you are, there will always be room for a few trailing plants in hanging containers, growing apparently in thin air!

You can grow climbing plants in all sorts of oddly shaped corners where normal plants wouldn't have room to spread, because you can train them into any shape you choose; simply grow them over a supporting framework or lines of twine arranged to fill the space — alcoves, fireplaces or even corners under stairways.

Lighting

Don't worry about lack of natural light; you can still grow foliage plants so long as you illuminate them for 12 hours a day with special 'plant lights'. These are available from garden centres and fit into standard spotlight fittings. Strategically placed, these lights enable plants to grow where it would otherwise be too dark for them to grow.

You can achieve some stunning effects with artificial lighting too; by directing a beam of light up from the floor through the leaves, you can throw dramatic shadows across the ceiling; and by placing the light behind your plant you will bring out the shape of the leaves and intensify the colour of variegated or unusually patterned foliage.

Dramatic plants

One of the most effective ways of finishing the decor of a room is to use a single, large plant in a strategic position where it immediately catches the eye. Such plants can stand alone and form a dramatic focal point in your room, really lifting it out of the ordinary. Climbing and trailing plants are particularly effective used this way as they are generally vigorous plants that can quickly assume vast proportions.

A large plant can be expensive to buy, so if you can't afford the outlay, grow your own. Use a professional grower's trick and put three or four of the same plant together in a large pot. This way the 'plant' immediately looks more impressive and will grow bigger and fuller much more rapidly than one left to grow on its own.

Climbing plants need to be given some support to grow successfully. For large-leaved plants, such as the Swiss Cheese Plant and Philodendrons, a

moss covered pole is very useful. Tropical plants like these grow aerial roots which they like to insert into the moss for support and moisture. You can buy moss poles at garden centres or make your own: simply cut a narrow strip of plastic covered wire mesh into the length of pole you require, bend the mesh into a cylinder with about a 3in (7cm) diameter and wire it together down the side. Pack the tube with some moist sphagnum moss — and you've made a pole for a fraction of the price a shop-bought one would set you back!

Put the moss pole into the pot at the same time as you repot the plant, firming it in well so that it doesn't lurch at an angle. Water the pole to keep the moss moist every time you water the plant. As the plant grows tie it to the moss pole with garden twine.

Bamboo canes are useful for thinner stemmed, more wiry climbers. Small leaved plants, like Grape Ivy or Kangaroo Vine, look most effective when planted so that one side trails over the edge of the tub and the rest is trained up a fan of canes in the middle.

Another display idea is to cut the canes so the tallest are at the centre surrounded by a circle of shorter canes; this gives the climbing plant an elegant, rather pointed triangle shape. Alternatively train these climbers onto one of the cane spirals or trellises you can get in garden centres. Whichever method you choose, simply tie the shoots to the supports with soft string or twine as they grow — don't tie too tightly though as you may strangle the stems.

Flowering climbers such as Stephanotis and Jasmine, on the other hand, look most attractive trained into circles, resulting in a spectacular concentration of bloom — and scent! To do this, wind the stems round a hoop of wire pushed into the pot, and secure the stems in place with plant ties. As the plant grows add another, bigger hoop above and around the existing one and train the plant onto it.

It's possible to ring the changes by making other shapes with wire, such as hearts or ovals, or even write your name in big, bold letters and grow the plant along it! For something else a bit different, train your favourite climbing plant to completely encircle a small window.

Pick and choose

Climbing plants for moss poles

SCINDAPSUS: variegated plants with large, attractively marbled leaves.
GOOSEFOOT PLANT, *Syngonium*: variegated arrowhead-shaped leaves.
CLIMBING PHILODENDRONS, *P.seandens*, 'Red Emerald', 'Red Burgundy'.
SWISS CHEESE PLANT: large, spectacular, dramatically shaped leaves.
GRAPE IVY: lots of small dark green leaves, very vigorous.
KANGAROO VINE: very enthusiastic climber with masses of leaves.
IVY: will tolerate low temperatures and poor light.

Trailing foliage plants

CREEPING FIG, *Ficus pumila*
VARIEGATED IVIES
ASPARAGUS
BURRO'S TAIL, *Sedum morganianum*
STRING OF BEADS PLANT
HEARTS ENTWINED, *Ceropegia woodii*

Flowering plants for hoops

PASSIONFLOWER
STEPHANOTIS
BOUGAINVILLEA
JASMINE
HOYA

Flowering plants for baskets

LIPSTICK PLANT, *Aeschynanthus*
COLUMNEA
PENDULOUS BEGONIAS
HOT WATER PLANT, *Achimenes*
BLACK EYED SUSAN, *Thunbergia alata*
WAX FLOWER, *Hoya bella*
CHRISTMAS CACTUS
ORCHID CACTUS, *Ephiphyllum*

Short trailing plants

BABY'S TEARS, *Helxine*
ITALIAN BELLFLOWER
SWEDISH IVY, *Plectranthus*
FITTONIA
EPISCIA

Room features

Study the individual style in which your climbing and trailing plants grow so you can exploit the full potential of each one. For instance, with dense, leafy plants, grow a trailing curtain to screen off a window with an unattractive view.

Or use your plants to give the impression of a completely bogus view; make a false 'window' using a poster, or if you're artistic get your paints out and daub yourself a mural — a formal garden, a vista of mountains, even a moonscape, anything you want! To complete the illusion fill a windowbox with trailing plants arranged so that the dangling foliage breaks up and softens the straight line of your container.

Room dividers

If you live in a bed-sit one of the best ways to use climbing and trailing houseplants is to grow them as a natural screen to split the room into two. All you have to do is grow a row of climbing plants up a framework of thick bamboo canes or rustic poles.

For something even more out of the ordinary, grow climbers up and through fishing net.

It is up to you to decide how formal or informal you would like your screen to be; for a formal one, grow a row of the same upright growing plants; for an informal one, a mixture of foliage plants which you can let ramble and scramble.

Growing conditions

When you choose your climbing and trailing plants always remember to work out where they will be placed and what growing conditions they will have.

Check the care label to see how much heat and light they need and whether they have any special requirements.

If you choose the plants which suit your home best they will thrive and provide you with a glorious display.

An old sewing table with an effective arrangement of Ivies, Maidenhair Fern and Cissus, *above*.
Antique scales make a good home for a Boston Fern, *top left*.
A Needlepoint Ivy and an Italian Bellflower make an attractive pair, *above left*.

A leafy green Maidenhair Fern and Cissus liven up a hallway.

A bathroom windowsill full of Ferns plus a Fig!

Climbing and trailing plants present one of the biggest challenges of all for the houseplant grower, but successfully grown they also provide one of the very best and most spectacular ways of displaying houseplants.

Caring for climbers and trailers

Due to the way climbing and trailing plants grow and the often rather inaccessible places they climb into, these plants can present you with special care problems.

Browning lower leaves

This is a normal sign of ageing; the oldest leaves have finished their useful work and are being discarded by the plant. However these brown tips look very unsightly and are especially noticeable in hanging containers when you look at them from below. Check your plants regularly and trim off the brown leaves to keep them always looking their best.

Sometimes the leaf tips go brown because the plant receives too much heat or is sitting in burning sunlight. Apart from moving the plant altogether all you can do is try to shade it from the sun.

Watering

Don't forget about watering your plants just because they are above eye level; the poor things need just as much caring for as your other more accessible plants. To reach hanging pots high up you can get a special gadget designed for outdoor hanging baskets; it looks like a washing up liquid bottle with a long curved spout attached to the nozzle. Simply hook it over the edge of the pot and squirt!

Alternatively, rig your plant up with a pulley, so you can raise and lower the plant for watering, as well as all the other jobs you need to do at close quarters, such as pruning.

Feeding

Hanging plants also tend to get neglected when it comes to feeding. Again the danger is that plants in high places will go for long periods without food because they are difficult to reach. If you water as suggested it's a good idea to add a few drops of a liquid fertiliser, such as Baby Bio, to the water to feed them at the same time. Otherwise climb on a chair or a ladder and give them a slow release plant feed like Jobes Spikes or Long Lasting Feed; both of these dissolve slowly.

Humidity

Your climbing and trailing plants suffer particularly from problems arising from dry air; this is because hot air rises and these plants tend to have large leaf areas. If your house is particularly warm or dry, plants are bound to get dried out. The leaves often get brown before they are old and fall off. To prevent the plant shedding leaves, mist spray it every day, and if you can leave a pan of water under the plant the water will evaporate and bathe the plant's leaves with the moisture they need.

Cleaning

Inevitably a plant grown in one place for some time gathers dust. Clean large-leaved plants by hand with a moist pad of cotton wool or a proprietary leaf cleaning product.

If your plants have lots of small leaves and you can manage to move them fairly easily, stand them outdoors on the outside of the windowsill in a light summer shower. But plants with hairy or downy leaves must not be washed; give them a light blowing over with a hair-drier set on 'cold', held about 18in (45cm) away, or gently brush them clean with a soft paintbrush.

Highlight a simple, rustic room with a trailing Ivy.

Hoya carnosa **'Variegata'**, *right*.

A dramatic, cascading *Plectranthus* gives this room character.

Alive with colour... all year round

Colourful foliage houseplants should be the highlight of any plant collection. They are valuable because they remain attractive all year round, rather than relying on a short-term display of flowers. You must give these plants good light: this plays a big part in how effective they look, as the intensity of leaf colour and variegation increases with the amount of light they get. This is why shade-loving plants, which require less light, have duller leaves with a greater depth of green pigment — such as you see in Ferns. Colourful leaved plants have adapted so that they don't need as much green pigment in their leaves to absorb energy from the sun, and brighter leaf colours appear. This explains why variegated plants lose their markings and go greener when they are placed in a poorly lit spot and, similarly, why plants with yellow and red leaves tend to go greener during the lower light intensities of winter.

Coleus blumei **hybrids** are the most colourful of all houseplants. They are easy to grow from seeds and there's a vast range to choose from.

The Begonia family is a treasure house of dramatic foliage. *B.rex*, *right*, has an amazing range of colour; while *B.masoniana*, *below left*, has remarkable iron cross markings. Fittonia, *left*, is a creeping plant with leaf veins picked out in pink.

Small plants

There are many small, jewel-like plants which simply glow with warmth and colour. Use them on their own or mix one or two in with a group of ordinary green-leaved plants to highlight their colourful charms.

The *Begonia rex* really is the king of this plant kingdom with an enormous range of bright, distinctively shaped leaves. Another bright little family is the Peperomias with their small, round, fleshy leaves and cheerful colours.

Completely different are bromeliads: Cryptanthus are all tiny, attractively cross-banded, starfish-like plants, while the somewhat larger Neoregelia turns a bright, blushing rosy-red just before it flowers and stays like that for months.

The central rosette of *Neoregelia carolinae*, *below*, turns bright red immediately before flowering, then lasts for months.

Cryptanthus, *above*, have striking cross-banding on their thick, fleshy leaves.

Marantas and Calatheas have particularly exotic foliage. *Top right*, *M.leuconeura*, 'Kerchoveana'; *above*, *M.l.* 'Erythrophulla'; *right*, one of many attractive Calatheas.

Large plants

Grow a large plant on its own as a dramatic feature plant, or group a number together using their different heights and shapes to get an effective arrangement.

There's quite a choice of large plants with colourful leaves. The Codiaeum, for example, is well named Joseph's Coat as it is the most colourful of houseplants and grows in a wide range of leaf shapes. A large plant is quite expensive, but you can always start with a smallish one and feed and repot it regularly every year. Acalyphas also have remarkable leaves and, like the Codiaeum, need good light and warmth to grow well.

Acalypha wilkesiana needs good light to bring out the beauty of its leaves, *left*.

Dieffenbachias, *above*, have beautifully marked leaves, while few plants beat Iresine, *below*, for intensity of colour.

Draceana terminalis, *left*, has gently arching, spear-shaped leaves which start green then turn a brilliant pinky-red with age.

Aglaonema treubii, *left* has characteristic mottled leaves.

Bright light and warmth are needed for success with Codiaeums, *above*.

Make a feature of colourful hanging plants. *Tradescantia blossfeldiana*, *left*, has attractive leaves and all the many kinds of Ivy, *below*, give a lovely effect.

Hanging and climbing plants

Plants which can clamber up an inviting wall or cascade down into an open space present the greatest challenge of all when it comes to displaying houseplants. With imagination, plus a good eye for form, the effect is absolutely magnificent.

Some of the best plants for climbing are Ivies. Use them where you can't provide much support as they can cling tenaciously to almost any surface. A mature Spider Plant (*Chlorophytum*) has a waterfall of small 'spiders'. Give it room and it will look wonderfully different from your other plants.

For something really unusual, try a

purple arrangement — grow together a dark purple Setcreasea, a violet-purple Tradescantia and a reddy-purple Gynura. Give them plenty of light and food and set them off against a white wall. The effect will be amazing.

Take the time to experiment with your plants and you'll be rewarded with a truly personal and pleasing display!

Hanging plants are apt to get leggy without bright light, but these need light for their colouring as well. Gynura, *left*, has unique velvety-purple leaves. Setcreasea, *centre*, goes a fantastic deep purple and Scindapsus, *above*, loses its mottled variegation without enough light.

Plants and Places

	Bathroom	Bedroom	Centre of room	Hall	Kitchen	Lounge	Porch	Windowsill	Central heating	Low temp.
Acalypha	✓	✗	✗	✗	✓	✓	✗	✓	✓	✗
Aglaonema	✓	✗	✗	✓	✓	✓	✗	✗	✓	✗
Begonia	✓	✓	✗	✓	✓	✓	✗	✗	✓	✗
Calathea	✓	✗	✗	✗	✓	✓	✗	✗	✓	✗
Coleus	✓	✓	✗	✓	✓	✓	✓	✓	✗	✓
Codiaeum	✓	✗	✗	✗	✓	✓	✗	✓	✓	✗
Cryptanthus	✓	✓	✓	✓	✓	✓	✗	✗	✓	✓
Dieffenbachia	✓	✗	✗	✓	✗	✓	✗	✗	✓	✗
Fittonia	✓	✓	✗	✓	✗	✓	✗	✓	✓	✗
Gynura	✗	✓	✗	✓	✓	✓	✗	✓	✓	✗
Hedera	✓	✓	✓	✓	✓	✓	✓	✓	✗	✓
Iresine	✓	✗	✗	✗	✓	✓	✗	✓	✗	✗
Maranta	✓	✗	✓	✗	✓	✓	✓	✓	✗	✗
Neoregelia	✓	✓	✓	✓	✓	✓	✗	✗	✓	✓
Scindapsus	✓	✓	✗	✓	✓	✓	✓	✓	✓	✓
Setcreasea	✓	✓	✗	✗	✓	✓	✓	✓	✓	✗
Tradescantia	✓	✓	✗	✓	✓	✓	✓	✓	✗	✓

A really bright, sunny room may be heaven for us, but hell for houseplants if they're not carefully chosen to suit the unusual conditions. Many houseplants don't respond at all well to scorching, direct sun; equally, some of those that do may also require long hours of sunlight, which isn't easy to provide except in greenhouse conditions where the sun is let in from all directions. A south-facing room, with windows also on the east or west, may be very bright to our way of thinking, but it still isn't likely to come near conditions in the Mediterranean!

Sun-loving plants come in roughly four groups. There are the desert plants, which are mainly cacti and other succulents — these can delight us with the oddest shapes and also produce breathtakingly beautiful flowers. There are the plants that grow naturally in sunny, tropical conditions — these need bright light and heat. And then there are bulbs and the annual flowers, which can fill your room with masses of colour and fragrance. If you choose these carefully, you can arrange to have brilliant flowers all the year round.

Desert plants

The main group of plants that live naturally in desert conditions are the succulents, which have developed over thousands of years so that they can store water in their stems or leaves.

The best known succulents are undoubtedly cacti (see page 675). For a sunny room it's the desert type that you'll want — these thrive in bright conditions, and many produce stunning flowers. Even when they're not in flower, some of them have such extraordinary shapes and bright colours that they make a splendid design feature, especially in a modern room. The chart *overleaf*, will give you some ideas.

Other succulent desert plants are equally good for sunny rooms, and you can choose them for their shape or colour, to set off an arrangement of cacti, for example. Living Stones *(Lithops)* are tiny plants consisting of a single pair of thickened leaves that look just like beautifully marked and coloured pebbles. In late summer lovely yellow or white daisy-like flowers emerge from between the two halves, looking for all the world as if they are coming straight out of stones! For a particularly effective setting try planting them in a bowl among real pebbles.

Flowering plants are perfect for very sunny rooms. Here, Geraniums and Marguerites help to make a riot of colour.

Silver Ruffles *(Cotyledon undulata)* is a plant with unusual crinkly-edged leaves in a subtle shade of grey-blue, while *Echeveria* also has beautiful leaves in shades of pink, apricot, purple and mauve as well as green, usually with a whitish bloom and sometimes with wavy edges.

Aloes and Agaves come in a variety of shapes and sizes, in compact rosette shapes or with interesting striped or spotted leaves. Look out for *Aloe barbadensis (A.vera)*, which is the one used in cosmetics — its juice, which you can easily squeeze out, is an excellent home remedy for burns.

Tropical plants

Exotic and exciting, tropical plants will add a dash to your decor, whatever the setting. They are generally fast growers and need plenty of water and feeding in the summer, and dead flower heads should be removed to keep them looking their best. In winter you should reduce their water, but keep them moderately warm and dry — don't, whatever you do, leave them behind curtains on frosty nights.

Rose of China *(Hibiscus rosa-sinensis)* is becoming very popular as a houseplant. Its large flowers only last for a day or two, but if you care for it properly it

Rooms with lots of light suit the Grape Ivy, Monstera and, of course, the ever-popular Spider Plant.

Cacti for sunny rooms

 Cacti that flower freely

Cereus
Tall, thin columns, unlikely to flower indoors

 Cleistocactus
Tall columns, bright red or orange flowers

Echinocactus
Globe-shaped with golden-yellow spines

 Echinopsis
Globe- or barrel-shaped with brown spines, pink or white sweetly-scented flowers

Ferocactus
Barrel-shaped, deep yellow and bright pink spines

Gymnocalycium
Globe-shaped with pink flowers

 Lobivia
Globe- or barrel-shaped, yellow or brown spines, bell-shaped red or yellow flowers

Mammillaria
Globe- or barrel-shaped with hooked spines and white hairs, purple-red or cream flowers

Notocactus
Globe- or barrel-shaped, yellow or red spines, orange-yellow flowers

Opuntia Prickly Pears
Branching pads, with tufts or spines. *O.basilaris cordata* has purple heart-shaped pads and creamy flowers

Oreocereus
Thick column, yellow spines and long white hairs

Parodia
Globe-shaped, yellow or red spines, red flowers

Rebutia
Barrel-shaped with white spines, golden, orange, red or purple flowers

Turbinicarpus
White spines and cream, pink or magenta flowers

should produce blooms all the year round. White, yellow, orange and pink varieties are now available, as well as the more familiar red, and the blooms can be single or double. Prune your Hibiscus bush back well every year in February so that it stays small. It needs frequent watering and good light and heat — don't let the temperature drop below 50°F (10°C). If you look after your Hibiscus well, it could last for up to 20 years!

You can even try growing citrus trees, though you'll need lots of room to let them grow tall (they're really at their best in greenhouses or conservatories). But there's a lovely miniature orange, Calamondin Orange *(Citrus mitis)* which bears fragrant white flowers and tiny orange fruit most of the year (don't try to eat the fruit, though — it's far too bitter). Small citrus plants, such as Kumquats and Tangelos, grow up to 4ft (1.2m) and will produce edible fruit, and you might be able to find these in a specialist garden centre. What makes citrus plants particularly interesting is that they bear pretty flowers and fruit, ripe and unripe, all at the same time.

Angel's Trumpets *(Datura)*, with their huge trumpet-shaped flowers up to 6in (15cm) long, would be a most exotic choice. It's best to stick to the annual varieties —the shrubs really need to be grown in a greenhouse. Good choices would be *D.ceratocaula* with white, blue-tinted flowers and a sweet scent, and *D.metel* with red stems and creamy flowers — both of them flower in July. Be careful handling Daturas because their leaves and flowers are poisonous.

Shrub Verbena *(Lantana camara)* looks fairly unremarkable when it isn't in flower, but its blooms are wonderful. Its large flower heads — borne throughout the summer — are actually clusters of smaller flowers, which start out pale yellow, and gradually turn red as they open, giving an unusual two-tone effect. Other colours are also available. Their strong fragrance attracts whitefly, so spray them frequently in summer with insecticide.

Cape Leadwort *(Plumbago capensis)* makes a marvellous houseplant if you train it to climb around a sunny window. It has pale blue star-shaped flowers carried in flat clusters at the tips of the stems (white if you buy the *alba* variety). You should cut it back hard every spring to keep it bushy, and it will reward you with a long flowering period. In winter keep it cool — about 45°F (7°C).

Bulbs for sunny rooms

WINTER FLOWERING
Hippeastrum
Enormous flowers, white, pink, orange or red.

SPRING FLOWERING
Clivia miniata **Kaffir Lily**
Up to 20 red or orange flowers on a single stalk.
Freesia
Many different colours and a ravishing scent. Choose greenhouse varieties and plant in August.

SUMMER FLOWERING
Agapanthus africanus
Blue African Lily
Large round heads of blue flowers on a long stem.
Eucomis comosa **Pineapple Lily**
Greenish-white flowers on a long pineapple-shaped head.
Haemanthus katharinae **Blood Lily**
Single huge round head of bright red flowers.
Nerine sarniensis **Guernsey Lily**
Flowers range from warm pink to red.
Vallota speciosa **Scarborough Lily**
Flaming red heads of trumpet-shaped flowers.

Tulips and Narcissi announce the arrival of spring.

Bulbs

Bulbs are a must for sunny rooms. You can grow very pretty varieties of the commoner ones, such as *Tulipa clusiana* and *Narcissus* 'Flower Drift', *above*. A brightly lit interior provides a perfect home for a much more interesting range than you could possibly grow under more usual conditions. A careful choice will give you an ever-changing sequence of flowers in all shapes, sizes and colours, lasting virtually the whole year round. Look at the chart, *above*, for some ideas.

Bulbs of all kinds are bought while they are dormant — plant them as soon as possible after you've got them home. Use ordinary potting compost in pots with drainage holes — special compost and undrained bowls are only suitable for forcing spring bulbs.

Other flowering plants

If you want traditionally pretty flowers, rather than unusual exotic ones, there are lots to choose from. To get the best selection, try growing your own from seed. Choose plants from a catalogue described as suitable for pots indoors — if you stick to the dwarf varieties, you shouldn't go far wrong. Most of these are treated just like annuals, so you'll need to buy or raise new ones every year.

Amaranthus is a whole family of eye-catching houseplants, including the well-known Love Lies Bleeding (*A.caudatus*) with its drooping scarlet flowers. You could also try Joseph's Coat (*A.tricolor*), which has brilliantly coloured variegated leaves as well — scarlet or crimson, overlaid with yellow, bronze or green. 'Molten Fire', another variety of *A.tricolor* has deep copper leaves. Carnations are now available in dwarf annual varieties with flowers just like the traditional tall ones. You might be able to buy ready-grown plants — but they're very easy to raise from seed.

Petunias can be really spectacular, especially in big, double-flowered grandiflora types. Grow them from seed, then propagate your favourite colours from cuttings for the following year.

Stocks have lovely flowers in winter and spring, as well as a ravishing scent. Look out for a new variety called 'Stockpot', which flowers only nine weeks after you've planted the seeds. Like all stocks, it will produce a mixture of single and double flowers.

Transvaal Daisies *(Gerbera)* make good houseplants, but you must make sure you get a compact strain — sometimes if you grow Gerbera from seed they will revert to their natural height, which is up to 2ft (0.6m) tall! With large, daisy-like flowers in brilliant reds and oranges, new dwarf varieties like 'Happipot' and 'Frisbee' make ideal houseplants.

Indoor eatables

For something really unusual, why not try growing something you can eat? It'll be fun, and decorative, as well as saving you some money! There are dwarf varieties of fruits now that will grow perfectly well indoors provided they get lots of light and warmth. Grow them on a windowsill, spray them regularly with malathion in the summer to protect them from greenfly, and wash the fruit well before eating it.

'Minibel' is a dwarf tomato plant that grows only about 9in (23cm) tall, yet produces perfect tiny tomatoes that you can eat. 'Fembaby' produces half-sized cucumbers — and, of course, there are always herbs. They are happy with lots of sun and no sunny home should be without a few pots of herbs on a windowsill. Parsley, chervil and marjoram grow very well indoors, while the dark red leaves of 'Dark Opal' basil would make a specially ornamental foil near a brightly coloured plant.

Growing plants in a fish tank

A fish tank is a less expensive alternative to the traditional, purpose-built terrarium or Wardian case; and a more practical one to the bottle garden, which can be difficult both to plant and to maintain. Fish tanks closely resemble Wardian cases and are, of course, very easy to plant, thus offering an exciting opportunity for interesting and natural-looking planting schemes.

To brighten up a gloomy corner with plants it's an easy matter to fit a fluorescent tube to the lid of the tank.

They come in a wide range of sizes and are relatively inexpensive to buy. Another great advantage is that a tank can be equipped with fluorescent lighting and can therefore be placed in a gloomy corner which would otherwise be unsuitable for plants. A fish tank can be provided with a lid or cover, with a built-in fluorescent tube mounted

underneath it. When the tank is being used for plants, it is best to use a cool white or daylight tube.

It is a good idea to reserve a fish tank for your most delicate and difficult tropical plants which would not survive — or would at least not grow too well — in normal room conditions. These plants need steady warmth and very high

humidity. The humidity will automatically be kept at a very high level inside the tank as long as it has a lid, and placing the tank in a warm room — say at about 65-70°F (18-21°C) — will take care of the temperature requirements.

An artistically planted glass tank can make a stunning room feature. It can be stood on the floor, in a disused fireplace,

General care

● **If your fish tank** is in a dark spot, to ensure that plants grow and flower well, a fluorescent tube should be fitted and left on for about 16 hours a day. To be on the safe side, it can be controlled by an electric timer switch.

● **The tank will need** very little care and attention. Do not allow the compost to dry out, however, but keep it steadily moist. This will not be difficult in the tank's enclosed conditions, in which the compost will dry out only very slowly. If you need to provide more humidity, mist spray the plants as required — but not, however,

African Violets, which do not enjoy contact with water.

● **Give them a** weak liquid feed every two to four weeks between May and September, using half the recommended strength.

● **Regularly remove** any dead or dying leaves and flowers, which not only look unsightly but also encourage the fungal disease botrytis, or grey mould, which can easily spread rapidly in these warm, humid conditions. If the disease does appear, spray the plants with a benomyl fungicide.

on a low table, on a shelf or even on a wide windowsill. But don't position it where it will receive direct sun.

Preparations

The tank should first be thoroughly washed out with water and soft soap to ensure that the glass is really clean. Rinse well to remove all the soap, then allow it to dry thoroughly.

The next stage is to place a layer of shingle or horticultural aggregate in the bottom, which will act as a drainage layer. This need be only about 1in (2.5cm) deep.

Next add a layer of potting compost, about 3-4in (8-10cm) deep. Most of the plants recommended for tanks like plenty of humus or organic matter in the compost, so a peat-based or soilless kind is ideal. It is a good idea to improve the drainage of these, however, by including some perlite or vermiculite, adding one part in volume to three parts of compost. Now you have everything ready for planting up.

Planting

Most of the plants grown in fish tanks are low-growing varieties which will, when established, form a lowish carpet of growth reminiscent of the 'floor' of a tropical rain forest. This is highly appropriate, since most of the plants recommended here do in fact originate from tropical rain forests.

Set the tallest plants at the back of the tank, and maybe a few at the ends. Then grade down towards the front of the tank, using shorter and shorter plants. Finally, add a few pieces of tree branch, bark, or the attractive dark brown or black mangrove root which is available from tropical fish dealers.

Choosing plants

Some of these are easily available from garden centres, while others have to be purchased from specialist suppliers of tropical plants.

African Violet (Saintpaulia). Any variety of African Violet is ideally suited to being grown in a tank. As well as the usual, standard-sized plants, try the new micro-miniatures, which come in a great variety of colours, such as 'Pip Squeek' (pink); 'Tinkerbell' (blue); 'Elf' (lilac); 'Sprite' (white); 'Twinkle' (pink); and 'Blue Imp' (blue). The trailing varieties are also highly recommended for tanks, like 'Breezy Blue' (blue), 'Trail Along' (pink), 'Snowy Trail' (white), and 'Easter Trail' (deep lilac). Micro-miniatures and trailers are available only from specialists in African Violets.

Club Moss (Selaginella). Low, ferny or moss-like hummocks are formed by these attractive foliage plants, which will not survive under normal room conditions. There are several species available, such as *Selaginalla kraussiana*, which has green foliage and a creeping habit; *S.k.* 'Aurea', which has yellow-green foliage; *S.apoda*, which has mossy, light green foliage; *S.emmeliana*, which has light green ferny stems up to 12in (30cm) high; and *S.martensii*, which is of upright habit with finely divided green stems.

Flame Violet (Episcia). This is not really suited to normal room conditions and can only be grown successfully in the steady warmth and high humidity provided by a glass tank. It is a low-growing, creeping or trailing plant and, given sufficient artificial light, freely produces

If you want to keep the plants in individual pots, rocks and small pebbles on the tank floor will provide cover for the containers.

tubular flowers. Most of the plants on sale are hybrids of the species *Episcia cupreata* and *E. reptans*, and have attractively coloured leaves. Some good hybrids to look out for include 'Acajou', which has red-orange blooms, and silvery-green and coppery leaves; 'Chocolate Soldier', which has red blooms and deep brown leaves with silver veins; and 'Cleopatra', which has orange-red blooms and patterned leaves in pale green, white and pink. *E.lilacina* has large lilac flowers with a yellow throat, and bronzy-green leaves.

Frosted Sonerila (*Sonerila margaritacea*). This is a low-growing creeping foliage plant, with red stems and dark green leaves, heavily speckled with silvery-

white and with purple undersides. It is a most attractive plant that revels in being grown in a glass tank.

Gloxinia (Sinningia). Miniature Sinningias, most of which are hybrids of the species *Sinningia pusilla*, are particularly recommended for tanks. These plants produce flat rosettes of leaves and tiny Streptocarpus-like flowers, ranging from lavender to violet. Named hybrids, which have to be bought from a tropical plant specialist, include 'Cindy', 'Dollbaby' and 'Freckles'.

Net Plant, Lace Leaf or Snakeskin Plant (*Fittonia verschaffeltii*). A very low-growing, carpeting foliage plant, which does far better in a tank than in normal

room conditions, this has deep green leaves with red veins. Varieties include 'Argyroneura', which has silvery veins, and an extra dwarf form called 'Argyroneura Nana'.

Other, taller-growing plants which you might like to grow in your tank include Achimines, Columnea, Kohleria and Peperomia, but you need to be careful with some of these more vigorous plants which could virtually fill a fairly small tank in a relatively short time. Another way of providing height without resorting to too fast-growing plants is to bank up the soil towards the back of the tank.

Other suggestions for plants that can be grown in a fish tank are shown in the photographs on these pages.

Recreating a tropical climate

Philodendron, Dumb Cane and Boston Fern thrive in a humid bathroom atmosphere.

Many houseplants originate from the tropics and most of these are surprisingly adaptable and flourish in normal room conditions. There are some, however, which are decidedly delicate and much more demanding and these do need special loving care if they are to survive.

Most of these are found in tropical rain forests, which have very subdued light, high temperatures which do not vary much between day and night, and extremely high humidity. The conditions found in their natural habitat are the best clue as to what these plants require under cultivation.

Suitable rooms
The chances of success are greatly improved if you choose the right room. Rooms with the most atmospheric humidity, for example, are the bathroom and kitchen.

These plants also need a reasonably steady temperature all year round — preferably around 65-70°F (18-21°C) by day, with a drop of no more than about 5°F (3°C) at night. Remember that these are *ideal* conditions; plants may well survive in lower temperatures but they are unlikely to thrive. There should definitely be no draughts — which are

notoriously lethal to delicate plants — and no noxious fumes from paraffin heaters or gas fires.

How easy it is for you to maintain such constantly high temperatures — summer and winter, day and night — obviously depends on what sort of heating you have in your house — and, indeed, on whether or not you are prepared to pay for the extra fuel bills this will entail. But remember that you need to heat only the one room for this purpose, and that these conditions will not necessarily agree with any other, less delicate plants that you may have. So choose the warmest room in the house (obviously not your bedroom because you wouldn't want such high night-time temperatures there), and group together enough tropical plants to make a worthwhile display which will warrant the additional expense — it's hardly worth going to all this trouble for one plant!

An easy — and economical — way of maintaining all the required conditions is to grow plants in a terrarium, a glass fish tank, or a bottle garden (see **Planting a terrarium**, page 669, and **Planting a bottle garden**, page 662). The temperature behind glass is steady and the humidity high. There are also some decorative, electrically heated propagator cases which act like miniature greenhouses and perform much the same sort of role as a terrarium.

Aspects of care
The humidity in a bathroom or kitchen will still not be high enough for many of these plants without some additional help, so stand pots on a layer of pebbles or special expanded clay granules, which should be kept permanently moist. Alternatively, plunge the pots up to their rims in peat in suitably large ornamental containers and keep this permanently moist. Daily mist spraying of the leaves will also help, particularly in very warm conditions or for plants in hanging baskets, and may even be necessary twice a day in very hot weather.

These plants enjoy good light but should not be subjected to direct sunshine which may scorch the leaves. Keep the leaves clean by regularly sponging them with tepid water. If your tapwater is hard, it is better to use rainwater instead for watering, spraying and sponging these plants, which hail from tropical rain forests where they are used to plentiful supplies of lime-free water.

Tricky tropicals

The following are amongst the most delightful plants you could choose for your tropical indoor garden. While they are considered to be tricky subjects and are in need of special care, given the right conditions they should flourish in your home.

Angel's Wings
(Caladium hortulanum)
Plants are available in summer and have large, paper-thin leaves, finely patterned in various colours. They grow from tubers, which should be dried off for the winter and kept warm. They require a fairly bright light but must not have direct sunlight.

Croton
(Codiaeum variegatum pictum)
These shrubby plants, with their highly coloured leaves, are particularly sensitive to draughts, to noxious fumes, and to dry air.

Firecracker Flower
(Crossandra infundibuliformis).
This shrub produces spectacular salmon-pink blooms in spring and summer if it is given really good light, though not direct sun. Grow in John Innes No 2, to which you should add one in four parts of peat.

Flame Violet (Episcia)
These creeping or trailing plants have colourful foliage and — as long as they are in adequate light — red or reddish-orange tubular flowers. They are best grown in a terrarium, fish tank or bottle garden. Alternatively, grow in shallow pots or hanging baskets, using a peat-based compost with one in four parts perlite or vermiculite.

Goldfish Plant (Columnea)
This has a trailing habit, which is ideal for hanging baskets. Large tubular flowers are produced in good indirect light — say, sunshine filtered by net curtains. Grow in a well-draining compost — either a peat-based potting compost with extra perlite or John Innes No 2 with some added sharp sand. Keep compost only slightly moist at all times. Well-known species are *C. banksii*, with scarlet blooms; *C. gloriosa*, with scarlet and yellow blooms; and *C. microphylla*, with orange-scarlet blooms. There are also several hybrids available with equally colourful flowers, including the excellent Cornell hybrids.

Lipstick Vine (Aeschynanthus)
A trailing plant with large tubular flowers, it is best grown in a hanging basket using peat-based compost with added perlite or vermiculite. Species include *A. lobbianus*, which has bright

Caladium

Columnea

Aeschynanthus

Episcia

red flowers; *A. marmorata*, which has greenish-yellow blooms; and *A. speciosus*, with yellow-orange flowers.

Monkey Plant (Ruellia makoyana)
An attractive trailing plant, it has deep green velvety leaves netted with silver and with purple undersides. Trumpet-shaped, rose-red blooms appear in winter. It is an excellent plant for a hanging basket, or can be grown in shallow half-pots in an equal mixture of John Innes No 2 and soilless compost.

Net Plant, Lace Leaf, or Snakeskin Plant (Fittonia verschaffeltii)
This creeping foliage plant, with its deep green, red- or silver-veined leaves, is ideal for a terrarium, a glass fish tank or a bottle garden. Otherwise, it should be grown in a small pot of peat-based compost. Overwatering causes stem rot while underwatering results in the leaves shrivelling, so keep it slightly moist all year round.

Painter's Palette
(Anthurium andraeanum)
The shield-shaped, waxy red spathes of this rain forest plant are spectacular. There are also other varieties with differently coloured spathes, including pink, salmon and white. It relishes a peat-based compost, and enjoys the addition of equal parts of leaf mould or chopped up sphagnum moss. Each brilliantly coloured spathe can last for eight weeks or even longer.

Temple Bells (Smithiantha)
Perennials with large velvety leaves and highly coloured tubular flowers in summer and autumn, *S. cinnabarina* has red blooms, while *S. zebrina* has red and pale yellow flowers and purple-veined leaves. Plants should be grown in soilless compost with the addition of one part of perlite. They should be allowed to dry out after flowering, when they take a complete rest. Repot in early spring and resume watering.

Bulbs in the home

Golden daffodils, delicate stripy crocuses and hyacinths with their ravishing scent are among the most attractive heralds of the spring. In bowls indoors, their bright colours will cheer up any room after the dreariness of winter. You may think that the only way to enjoy bulbs indoors is to grow the sort specially sold for 'forcing' over the winter. But there are many other beautiful bulbs that grow permanently indoors, and flower over and over again every year.

A bulb is in fact a modified leaf bud. It produces roots from its base, and leaves and flower stems from its top, and can store food and water for a long period of time. It is this storage capacity that allows a bulb to be quite dormant for several months during its annual rest period, needing neither light nor water, only to burst into new growth again as soon as watering is recommended at the appropriate time of year.

Bulbous plants are often put in the same category with corms and tubers, but the latter two are, strictly speaking, rather different: they store their water and food in modified stems. Tubers, in addition, produce stems of their own, as rhizomes do. Corms produce no stems, and are closer to bulbs, although their structure is distinct. The commonest corm is the crocus — and, just to make matters even more complicated, it is treated exactly as if it were a bulb!

Two types of bulb

There is a vast range of bulbs, and most of them are hardy — that is, they can withstand frost and need to live outside once they have flowered. A much smaller range, including some really beautiful houseplants, are tender bulbs, and these must live indoors all the time.

'Garden' bulbs won't survive a second season if kept indoors, where it is too warm. But if you have a garden or a bal-

The magnificent flowerheads of Hippeastrum may need staking.

cony, you can keep your hardy bulbs going year after year by putting them outdoors during their dormant season, and bringing them in to enjoy their flowers. If you have a very cool place indoors, such as a cellar, for example, you might try to keep garden bulbs over the winter and see if they will flower again the next year — if the temperature doesn't get too warm, you may be lucky. Otherwise, you might as well stick to the type sold for early forcing, which lasts only one season.

Tender bulbs need higher temperatures than hardy bulbs during their dormant season, and must be grown indoors all year round. Ideally, you'll need a dry, coolish place for their dormant period — about 50°F (10°C), but this will depend on the species. They won't need light, and since there is nothing to look

343

A few

	African Blood Lily (Haemanthus)	Amaryllis (Hippeastrum)	Easter Lily (*Lilium longiflorum*)	Freesia (prepared corms)	
When to plant	Sept or Mar	Aug or Mar	Late Oct-Nov	Aug-Sept	
Compost	John Innes No 2	John Innes No 3	John Innes No 1	John Innes No 1	
Depth of planting	top just exposed	half exposed	1in (2.5cm) deep	2in (5cm) deep	
How many to a pot	1	1	1	7-8 to a 14in (36cm) pot	
Light	full, direct sunlight	full, direct sunlight	full, direct sunlight	full, direct sunlight	
Feeding	every 14-21 days	every 14-21 days	every 14-21 days	every 14-21 days	
Flowering period	Aug-Sept	Dec-Mar	Mar	Jan-Feb	
Scented	no	yes	yes	yes	
Colours	red, white	white, pink, red	creamy-white	very wide range	
Temperatures: dormant / flowering	50°F (10°C) / 60°F (16°C)	50°F (10°C) / 65°F (18°C)	40°F (5°C)* / 60°F (16°C)	** / 45-50°F (7-10°C)	
Eventual height	12-24in (30-60cm)	18-24in (45-60cm)	36in (90cm)	18in (45cm)	

* cold temperature during dormant period essential   ** warm temperature during dormant period inevitable in summer

at during this period, it makes sense to store them out of sight.

We'll be telling you later all about growing forced bulbs indoors over the winter; here we concentrate on the lovely, and rather rarer, tender bulbs that you can only grow indoors. The chart (above) gives you the necessary basic information on their needs and their flowering season.

How to grow them
Tender bulbs do best if kept in their potting mixture all year round, so you don't need to worry about removing them from their pots and storing them dry over their dormant season. In fact, a few roots do sometimes persist, in which case the bulb will be better off left in the compost during the rest period.

For tender, indoor bulbs it is essential to provide good drainage, so avoid using the undrained bowls you would choose for forced bulbs. Use ordinary pots or bowls with drainage holes and crock them well. Indoor bulbs do best in a good, soil-based compost, such as John Innes, which should be fairly closely packed and evenly moist throughout. The chart gives details about each bulb's cultivation needs.

Water your newly potted bulbs sparingly for the first two weeks or so, until they're settled in, then gradually bring

Crinum looks most attractive grown in groups of 2-3 to a 10in (25cm) pot.

them up to the recommended level of watering for each species.

To get the best out of your bulbs, you should feed them regularly with a high-potash, tomato fertiliser from the start of their growth period. This will ensure that the plant grows well and that it will produce well-developed, healthy flowers. After flowering, you can dead-head the plant by removing the spent flower,

but don't touch the foliage or flower stalk at this stage. The plant will continue to produce leaves, and should be fed for as long as it does so. This is the time that the bulb builds up nutrition for the next year.

Eventually the foliage will start to wither, and feeding and watering should be discontinued. If the plant needs any water during its rest period, the residual

of the best

Freesia (unprepared corms)	Kaffir Lily (*Clivia miniata*)	Scarborough Lily (Vallota)	Spider Lily (Crinum)	Veltheimia (Forest Lily)
late Mar-Apr	Feb-Mar	June-July	Feb-Mar	Sept-Oct
John Innes No 1	John Innes No 2	John Innes No 2	John Innes No 2	John Innes No 1
2in (5cm) deep	1-2in (2.5-5cm) deep	half exposed	half exposed	half exposed
7-8 to a 14in (36cm) pot	1	1	1 to an 8in (20cm) pot 2-3 to a 10in (25cm) pot	1 to a 5in (13cm) pot 3 to a 10in (25cm) pot
full, direct sunlight	direct sunlight but shade when very hot	full, direct sunlight	full, direct sunlight	full, direct sunlight
every 14-21 days	every 21-28 days	every 14-21 days	every 21-28 days	every 21 days
Sept-Oct	May-June	Aug-Sept	June-Aug	Nov-Mar
yes	no	no	no	no
very wide range	yellow, orange, red	white, pink, red, apricot	white, pink, red	white, pink
50°F (10°C) 65°F (18°C)	50-55°F (10-13°C) 70°F (21°C)	50-55°F (10-13°C) 65°F (18°C)	50°F (10°C) 65°F (18°C)	** 50°F (10°C)
18in (45cm)	24-28in (60-70cm)	24-28in (60-70cm)	24-36in (60-90cm)	12-18in (30-45cm)

Haemanthus katherinae.

A variety of *Clivia miniata.*

Lilium longiflorum.

Vallota speciosa.

moisture in the soil should be enough. When the leaves and stalks have completely dried out, and not before, cut them down, and put the pot away with the bulb in its winter quarters.

Repotting and propagation
Most indoor bulbs will be quite happy staying in the same pots for up to four years, but remember that it's essential to keep up their feeding. It's a good idea to topdress them every year, before they start into new growth, by replacing the top 1-2in (2.5-5cm) of soil with fresh.

Bulbs propagate by division, so after a few years you'll find that there are clumps of new bulbs growing around the main one. When the time comes to repot, remove the bulb carefully from its pot and tease away as much as possible of the old potting mixture — you may find that holding the bulb under running water helps.

If it has developed several new bulbs, prise these off carefully and pot them up separately. New bulbs don't need feeding until after their first flowering, which will probably take a couple of years. Repot the main bulb in one size larger pot if necessary, but it probably won't be if you've split the clump up.

Staking
Bulbs that produce tall flower stalks will need to have some support if the stalks are not to break. Support single flower stalks, such as Amaryllis and Scarborough Lily, with individual stakes, and use a circle of stakes with thread around them to provide support for smaller flowers, such as a cluster of Freesias.

Flower stalks will always tend to grow towards the light, so make sure you give your pots a quarter turn every day during their active growth season. This is especially important for heavy, single blooms on tall stalks: if the stalks lean too much in one direction, the plant won't just look unsightly — there's a danger that the stalk might break under the weight of the flower head. So make sure also that the stake you put in with the compost is tall enough for the eventual height of the plant.

Large Hyacinth heads may need staking.

Forcing bulbs for Christmas

Bulbs which are forced into flower for Christmas are always a welcome sight, largely because they give the feeling that spring cannot be far away. Bulbs are used which flower naturally in the spring, and it is important to buy bulbs which have been specially treated by the growers if you want blooms over the festive season.

Before these bulbs are offered for sale — usually in September — they are given a cool winter period by refrigeration at controlled temperatures. Once these treated bulbs are in the shops and garden centres, they are ready to burst into rapid growth and must therefore be planted as soon as possible, otherwise the beneficial effects of the treatment will wear off. Forced bulbs usually take at least three months between planting and flowering.

Planting bulbs

Special bulb bowls — which are usually plastic or pottery, round in shape and have no drainage holes — are the most commonly used containers, but there is nothing to stop you using any favourite bowl or dish you happen to have in the house. The bulbs should be planted in proprietary bulb fibre, which is basically peat with added crushed oyster shell and charcoal. The bulbs do not need any fertiliser in the compost.

Narcissus, Hyacinth and Tulip bulbs can all be made to flower for Christmas.

Take your pick

Hyacinths: these are the most popular of the spring-flowering bulbs for forcing into early bloom indoors. They are available in a wide range of colour and most of them are highly scented. Among the many popular varieties are 'Bismarck', pale blue; 'Jan Bos', red; 'King of the Blues', indigo-blue; 'L'Innocence', white; 'Myosotis', sky blue; 'Ostara', deep blue; 'Pink Pearl', deep pink; and 'Yellow Hammer', creamy yellow.

Buy the largest possible treated bulbs, which should feel firm and heavy for their size. A 6in (15cm) diameter bowl will comfortably hold three large Hyacinth bulbs, which should be planted so that the top third of each bulb is exposed.

Daffodils: these are also very popular for Christmas flowering. Good varieties which have been specially treated for forcing include 'Golden Harvest', a trumpet type in golden yellow; 'Peeping Tom', same colour but with a long trumpet and reflexed petals; 'Grand Soleil d'Or', deep yellow clusters of fragrant flowers; and 'Paper White', white clusters of fragrant flowers.

Buy large Daffodil bulbs with two or three 'noses' or growing points, as these produce the most flowers. A 12in (30cm) diameter bulb bowl can be expected to hold six bulbs, which should be planted so that their tips are just exposed.

Tulips: good varieties for forcing include 'Brilliant Star', bright scarlet; 'Christmas Marvel', carmine; 'Marshall Joffre', yellow; 'Princess Margaret', pink; and the double-flowered 'Scarlet Cardinal'.

Choose large bulbs for the maximum number of flowers. It does not matter if some of these have lost their brown skins. Plant them so that their tips are exposed.

Hippeastrum: this bulb, popularly known as Amaryllis, has large, trumpet-shaped blooms in spring or summer, but it is also possible to buy specially prepared bulbs for Christmas flowering.

Some good varieties are 'Apple-blossom', pale pink; 'Belinda', deep red; 'Hecuba', salmon; 'Minerva', red and white; 'Picotee', white, edged in red; and 'Rembrandt', deep red.

Pot one bulb in a 6in (15cm) pot, using John Innes No 1, and leave the upper part exposed. Keep the compost slightly moist, provide maximum light and a temperature of 60°F (16°C).

Liquid feed fortnightly after flowering. As the leaves die down, allow the compost to dry off to give the plant a rest. Store dry in frost-free conditions over winter. Restart into growth in late winter and do not try to force again. It should then flower again at its 'normal' flowering time — which is in late spring or summer — and will take a rest during the following winter. Repotting is necessary only every three or four years in spring.

Crocus is another favourite for forcing.

You'll probably need to tie the stalks of Daffodils with soft green twine.

Ensure that the fibre is moist before use, and place a layer in the bottom of the bowl. Stand the bulbs on it and fill in with more fibre, firming lightly with the fingers. Ensure that there is enough space at the top for watering, and that the tips of the bulbs — say, up to about a third of their height — are exposed. Then water in the bulbs and tip off any surplus water by gently tilting the bowl to allow excess water to run out.

When the bulbs have been planted, they must be given a period — usually about eight weeks — in cool conditions and complete darkness. During this period, roots will grow and shoots will start to be produced.

The traditional method of providing these conditions is to stand the bowls in the garden in a north-facing position, and then to cover them with a 6in (15cm) deep layer of peat, sand or weathered ashes. Inspect them from time to time to make sure that the bulb fibre is not drying out.

If you do not have a garden, perhaps the bowls can be placed in a cupboard in an unheated room. Alternatively, enclose each bowl in a black polythene bag and place it in an unheated room, or perhaps on a balcony or in a porch. In any event, the bulbs must not be subjected to a temperature higher than 45°F (7°C). Again, check occasionally to make sure that the fibre is not drying out.

Forcing

When shoots reach about 1in (2.5cm) high, place the bulbs indoors, at a temperature of around 50°F (10°C), and provide maximum light. The best place is on a window-sill. When flower buds are well formed, the temperature can be increased to 60°F (16°C), which is usually achieved quite simply by moving the bulbs to another, warmer room.

Bulbs do not need any extra humidity and normal room conditions are quite suitable. Keep the fibre steadily moist.

If flower stems need supporting, use thin canes and raffia or soft garden string. This is particularly likely for heavy flower heads such as Hyacinths or the tall, thin stems of Daffodils.

Liquid feed the bulbs fortnightly after flowering until the foliage dies down, but do not be tempted to feed them before they flower or you will get very bushy, weak growth. They are best off during this time in a cold frame, if you have one. Do not force the bulbs again, but plant them out in the garden.

A lasting impression

Whether you buy them yourself, receive them as a gift, or take them from your own garden, cut flowers require as much care as living plants. It takes patience – and time – to arrange flowers, which is why a few extra minutes spent caring for blooms is time well spent if it means that your arrangement will last longer.

This doesn't just mean topping up your vase once a week with water. You need to begin from the minute you pick your flowers or get them indoors. With careful treatment, most should last for several weeks in a vase, with some varieties, such as Chrysanthemums and Orchids, still looking good six weeks after cutting!

Water alone is not good enough. Imagine a flower stem as a drinking straw. While it is growing, a flower is constantly sucking up water from the plant beneath. Once it is cut, the flower doesn't stop sucking, so air starts being drawn into the stem instead. The longer the flower is out of water, the higher up the stem the air rises. And when it is put back into water, the liquid cannot rise because the stem is blocked by its own air-lock.

When you buy flowers from a shop, the florist will have already given the flowers some special treatment to get rid of the air that has risen in the cut stem, enabling them to absorb as much water as possible. This is a fairly involved business, but it needs to be: those flowers may have been travelling for two or three days before reaching the shop. But, though the florist has done most of the work for you, flowers still need a little attention back home – as do flowers from your own garden. A simple plan of action will yield remarkable results.

Ten tips for long-lasting flowers

1 Unwrap bunches as soon as you get home, and start work on them straight away. Alternatively, pick your garden flowers early in the morning or in the evening. Only choose those flowers at the right time of their life-cycle – cut Roses, Poppies, Peonies, Irises when the buds are just beginning to unfold, and Dahlias and Chrysanthemums when they are fully out.

2 With shop-bought flowers, cut one or two inches (2.5-5cm) from the bottom of the stems with secateurs or sharp kitchen scissors. Cut the stems on a slant – that way they can take up water faster. If you are cutting the flowers from the garden, take a bucket of tepid water with you, and put them straight into it. Slit the base of woody stems, such as Roses or Lilac, to one or two inches (2.5-5cm), or crush with a small hammer or mallet, and singe the ends of stems that exude milk (such as Euphorbia) in the flame from a match or lighter.

3 Always strip away foliage from the lower half of the stem, otherwise it will rot and foul the water later.

Loving care and attention can prolong the life of an arrangement of cut flowers considerably.

4 Stand flowers in a bucket containing several inches of tepid water for between two and 12 hours before arranging them. Any flowers that are limp can be freshened up by laying them in a bath of cool water for a few hours.

5 Make sure everything you use with flowers is completely clean: buckets, vases, pinholders, wire and water. If you don't do this, green sludge can form which blocks flower-stems and prevents water being taken up. Use diluted bleach to clean vases and utensils when not in use, then rinse thoroughly.

6 If you use Oasis foam inside vases to hold flowers in place, give it a 30-minute soak in water before use.

7 Add a sachet of proprietary cut-flower food to the water when arranging flowers. It costs only a few pence, and really does work.

8 After arranging, stand vases of flowers somewhere out of direct sunlight and away from radiators or fires.

9 Check daily to see if the vases need topping up. Provided you have cared for flowers properly before arranging them, you will not need to change the water, as it won't get dirty.

10 In hot or overheated rooms, flowers will last better given a daily spray-over with tepid water.

Pots, stands and jardinieres

Jardinieres — exquisitely fashioned porcelain containers, usually on matching stands and elaborately decorated — were used in the 17th and 18th centuries to display bulbs and other plants. Today, we tend to regard any handsome container as a jardiniere. From brass coal scuttles to chimney pots, anything goes — as long as you adopt some sensible ground rules.

A cascade of foliage from the Boston Fern is the perfect complement to this unusual, and delightful, elephant pedestal.

350

Strictly speaking, an authentic jardiniere is an 'ornamental pot or stand for the display of growing flowers in a room' — the pot may come with or without a matching stand or pedestal. What makes it special is a little ledge running round the inside, 1in (2.5cm) or so above the bottom. The plant, in its own pot, stands on this ledge, so that any surplus water can drain into the reservoir beneath. At the height of their popularity, jardinieres were often quite outrageous in their design. One French version of about 1800 was decorated with nude figures, and also accommodated an aviary and an aquarium. The actual plant pots were supported by sphinxes! In the Victorian era many a potted palm was set in an ornate, scrolled and beautifully glazed container.

These days we are much more adventurous about containers. Troughs, cubes and cylinders in plastic, clay or earthenware are widely available, in all sizes and colours. But exciting and appealing old containers can still be picked up for a song in junk shops. Soup tureens, chamber pots, ornamental tubs and old-fashioned cooking pots can all be used as 'cache-pots' to hold plants in separate pots, or as containers to be filled with soil for direct planting.

Pots within pots

If your jardiniere is large enough, you can use it as a 'cache-pot' — that is, an outer, decorative container within which plants are arranged each in their separate pots.

There are several advantages to this approach. The plants can be treated separately, and individual ones removed if they are beginning to fail or need to be treated for pests or diseases — or if you just want a change!

Even though the inner pots will have drainage holes, it's still important to prevent waterlogging in the jardiniere. Prepare a base of charcoal, coarse perlite or broken crocks — up to 3-4in (8-10cm) deep, depending on the size of the container. Put a layer of peat on top. When you have arranged your plants inside, pack peat around and over the pots, so that they aren't visible — this creates a natural effect as well as keeping the plants securely in place. By 'stepping' the supporting layers of peat, you can lift up small plants to provide height.

Turn the individual plants round fairly frequently, to prevent any roots that may emerge from the drainage

Interesting shapes

● **A centrepiece of** African Violets, blue Browallias and white Streptocarpus, fringed with trailing, small-leaved Creeping Fig (*Ficus pumila*) (*right*).

● **The flaming** Dragon Tree (*Dracaena terminalis*) next to a Spider Plant, Wandering Jew, Delta Maidenhair Fern (*Adiantum raddianum*) and *Begonia rex*, (*below left*).

● **For really dry,** centrally heated rooms and poor light, try *Sansevieria trifasciata laurentii*, with its stiff, sword-shaped, golden yellow edged leaves, contrasted with the spotted, Laurel-like foliage of *Dracaena godseffiana* and the Desert Privet (*Peperomia magnoliaefolia*), with fleshy, white-edged leaves. Swedish Ivy (*Plectranthus australis*) and its white-edged form (*P.coleoides marginatus*) can provide a fringe (*below, right*).

holes from anchoring themselves in the surrounding peat.

Direct planting

You can also put your plants directly into soil in your jardiniere. You'll need to make sure that you reduce the risk of waterlogging by putting in a deep layer of drainage material — at least a fifth of the container's depth.

Expanded clay aggregate is ideal for this purpose, because it can absorb water and thus 'mop up' excess, to release it later when it's needed. But small pebbles or gravel will also do. It's a good idea to add a few lumps of charcoal

to help prevent any standing water from becoming stagnant. Cover the drainage material with a layer of potting compost, and you're ready to start.

Group planting

With any group planting, you should always work out your design before you start. It makes sense to stick to plants that will have a fairly long life, so avoid flowering annuals. And unless you're prepared to have a rather sparse arrangement to start with, don't include very young plants, because they won't have enough room to grow and will have to be removed when they start getting over-

Which plant, which pot?

Plants and containers must suit each other, and suit the environment in which they'll be seen.

🌱 Don't use a multi-coloured pot for a multi-coloured plant. Colourful, patterned containers should on the whole be reserved for plants with strong, dramatic foliage forms — preferably plain green — unless, of course, you can manage to match the blooms of a flowering plant with the colour of a container.

🌱 Always remember that your plants have a style of their own. An old-fashioned jardiniere or wickerwork basket calls for an 'old-fashioned' plant — a Boston Fern (*Nephrolepis exaltata*), for example, or one of the palms.

🌱 More 'architectural' plants — Swiss Cheese Plants, Rubber Plants and the like — look good in modern containers made from stainless steel, plastic, earthenware or wood.

🌱 When planting a group display, choose a container that harmonises with the dominant plants in the arrangement.

🌱 On a practical level, a 'cache-pot' should always be taller than the pot it's destined to hold, with an allowance for drainage material in the bottom, and wide enough for a packing of peat. It should also be in keeping with the size of the plant. A single plant in a decorative pot could be easily overwhelmed, either by the pot or by its surroundings. So choose a good-sized, mature plant that can hold its own. The list gives you some ideas for plants with enough charm or impact to stand by themselves.

Planting in groups

Smaller plants have much more impact if they're arranged together than they do if displayed individually. Give rein to your creativity by 'mix and matching' your plants in a group display, but be sure to always choose plants which have similar needs.

At its simplest, a mixed group is usually made up of tall plants, which give height to a display, medium-sized plants which give the basic framework, and trailing plants which soften the hard edges of the container itself. Try and plan a group so that some of the plants, at least, share a characteristic which will help to bind them together visually as a group. Patterns, colours, leaf size or shape — you can choose any of these as your 'theme'.

Plants on pedestals

Tall pedestals or stands make a perfect basis for trailing plants which can cascade down from the top. But don't restrict yourself to these. Branching, erect plants can also look stunning when raised from the ground, and this is especially true of palms. Stylish and elegant, they are surprisingly adaptable plants. Try growing the Feather Palm (Howea), European Fan Palm (Chamaerops) or Sago Palm (Cycas) in moderate light and a temperature of 55-66°F (13-19°C). But make sure your pedestal or stand is sturdy enough to take the weight of a possible 8ft (2.4m) tall plant in a large container.

The upright form of Aspidistra (*top*) and a trailing Cissus (*above*) are equally effective on a pedestal.

crowded. Even mature plants will need some room to grow and spread.

Put each plant in individually, firming it in position before introducing its neighbour. Don't try to squeeze in too many plants — overcrowding reduces the air between plants and opens the way to attack from pests and diseases.

With a group planting, the plants you choose must have similar requirements for light, humidity and water if they are to live happily together.

Single specimen plants

With a small jardiniere, or if you have a well-grown specimen plant, you may want to display one plant on its own. The same principles of planting apply as with groups — if you plant directly, make sure you allow for good drainage. Obviously, you won't have to worry about plant compatibility, or overcrowding. A splendid specimen plant can look really stunning in a carefully chosen, complementary jardiniere.

Smaller plants make more impact when arranged together in a 'cache-pot'.

One way to build up a group is to base it on shape — create a triangle, rectangle or circle, complemented by a similarly shaped container. Another way is to mix a group of plants with leaves of different textures — hairy or corrugated leaves against smoother, glossier ones. Don't go for too many contrasts in one group — decide on one theme, based on colour, shape or texture, and stick to it.

The delicate, trailing Ficus pumila contrasts well with a bold, upright Solanum.

Some ideas to try

SINGLE SPECIMEN PLANTS

Weeping Fig (Ficus benjamina), prized for its handsome, highly polished, willow-like branches and shiny, oval leaves. It can grow up to 6-9ft (1.8-2.7m) tall.

Fiddle Leaf Fig (Ficus lyrata or Ficus pandurata), massive and arresting with huge, outstretched, violin-shaped leaves.

Rubber Plant (Ficus elastica decora), a single-stemmed column up to 10ft (3m) tall, perfect for a high alcove.

Black-Gold Philodendron (Philodendron melanochryson), with long, heart-shaped leaves of velvety, blackish-green, can grow up to 6ft (1.8m).

Crystal Anthurium or Strap Flower (Anthurium crystallinum), a single beauty with long, pointed, shield-shaped leaves, attractively netted with white veins, each up to 2ft (0.6m) long.

FLOWERING PLANTS

Oleander (Nerium oleander), up to 6ft (1.8m) tall, has heavy heads of bold, saucer-shaped flowers — in pink, red, yellow or white — and blooms throughout the summer.

Shrub Verbena (Lantana camara) has scented flowers that change from pale yellow to rosy red, lasting from late spring to late summer. Prune to keep to 10-15in (25-38cm) tall.

Camellia (Camellia japonica) has flowers that will open to perfection indoors, but it needs exactly the right conditions to thrive. Grows up to 6ft (1.8m) tall.

Madagascar Jasmine (Stephanotis floribunda) bears fragrant, creamy white blossoms with a scent of citrus. Train it round a trellis or hoops, because the stems can grow 12ft (3.6m) long.

Indian Azalea (Azalea indica) is a Christmas-flowering dwarf shrub — up to 18in (45cm) tall — in all shades of pink and red, with white and many bicolours.

Poinsettia (Euphorbia pulcherrima) is a bushy plant up to 15in (38cm) tall. The flowers have vivid scarlet, pink or white bracts lasting for between two and six months during the winter.

PEDESTAL CASCADES

Devil's Ivy (Scindapsus aureus), with pendulous stems, bears aerial roots and is clad with gold-mottled leaves. **S.aureus 'Marble Queen'** has leaves which are splashed with white.

Spider Plant (Chlorophytum) has green and white striped, arching leaves with wiry stems bearing baby developing plants.

Italian Bellflower or Star of Bethlehem (Campanula isophylla) is summer-flowering with a profusion of star-shaped pink or white flowers.

Cupid's Bower or Hot Water Plant (Achimenes hybrida) is a good trailer with white, blue, purple, pink or yellow blooms.

Basket Begonia (Begonia pendula) has slender, drooping stems and downward-hanging scarlet flowers.

Trailing cacti include **Rat's Tail Cactus (Aporocactus flagelliformis), Easter Cactus (Rhipsalidopsis gaertneri)** and **Christmas Cactus (Schlumbergera 'Buckleyi')** — all are trailers with double, telescoping pink or orange flowers.

Plants for patio paving

Large areas of paving on the patio can look monotonous and are greatly improved when offset by something with a contrasting texture. Patches of cobblestones or gravel are ideal, as of course are plants. And you don't have to grow these in pots – they will look just as effective if you put them actually among the paving stones.

Paving plants must always be chosen carefully. The conditions are hot and dry, and plants will have to stand up to being trod on occasionally. They will also have to look good in their own right, as well as providing an effective contrast with the paving around them.

Surprisingly, there are more plants than at first you might imagine that will thrive in these conditions. Here are some suggestions.

Herbs
Herbs are always a good choice and those with scented foliage are generally preferable to the culinary variety

for growing on the patio. The scent released by aromatic plants should never be overlooked when you are planning your patio as there's nothing like plant fragrances for creating a relaxing atmosphere. Herbs are a good choice from the growing point of view too, as most flourish in a hot, dry environment as found at patio paving level.

Go for evergreen plants so that your patio paving never looks entirely bare, even in winter.

Thymus serphyllum with its naturally low, creeping habit and tough wiry stems is perfect for places which will be walked over quite regularly. These plants will gradually form a 'carpet' which in midsummer will burst into bloom, producing hun-

Watch out for . . .

All the plants suggested are highly tolerant of the conditions they will encounter at patio level, such as heat and dryness, but these tips should help plants to get established.
● Any crack that is more than 1/2in (1cm) wide should be large enough for a plant, although you will probably have to lift one of the paving slabs before you plant it. Larger gaps between slabs can be planted without removing the slabs by gently squeezing the plant's rootball to flatten its shape to fit. Always make sure that there is enough depth for the roots by removing the compost

about 2-3in (5-8cm) down with a fork or, if you don't have one a small piece of metal.
● The ground under paving is frequently poor and stony, so always remove a handful of soil from the planting crack and replace it with good garden soil.
● Paving plants shouldn't need feeding, but if the soil is very poor you could add a Jobes houseplant spike when you are putting in each plant. Renew the spikes every spring.
● Watering should not usually be necessary, either. However, during long dry spells it is advisable to water plants once a week.

dreds of tiny, pale pink flowers.

There are several other creeping varieties of Thyme which look decorative among paving stones, but always try and go for those which, like *T. serphyllum*, are evergreen so that you can benefit from them all the year round.

Thymus 'Doone Valley' is an especially attractive variety which has variegated leaves, a sharp lemony scent and purple flowers. *Thymus herba-barona*, with its caraway-scented leaves and mauvish flowers, is another delightful choice, and there are plenty more.

Oregano, or Wild Marjoram as it is also known, is worth considering. The compact form, *Origanum vulgare compactum*, with its rose-purple flowers which appear in August is by far the best choice when it comes to a paving plant.

Chamomile *(Anthemis nobilis)* is another herb that is well known for its ability to survive heavy wear. *A. nobilis* 'Treneague', the variety usually used for Chamomile lawns, is unusual in that it doesn't flower, but if this characteristic appeals to you it can certainly be grown in paving. If, however, you prefer flowers there are plenty of other varieties that produce wonderful daisy heads in summer.

Creeping Savory *(Satureja hortensis)* is a good choice if you are after something a bit different. With small white flowers, this evergreen perennial grows about 2-3in (5-8cm) high and has quite a strong scent.

Rock plants

This is another group of plants that thrives under paving conditions. There are varieties that flower effusively as well as some that are mainly grown for their shape or leaf colour. Again, try to pick evergreen plants so that your paving never looks entirely naked, even in winter.

For foliage

Festuca glauca and **F. amethystina** are two dwarf ornamental grasses that are well worth including. Both are a bright blue-grey and grow to about 6in (15cm) high. To ensure continual bright colour, trim plants back hard every other autumn, so that the oldest foliage is replaced as soon as it starts to dull. If you want to create a carpeting effect, plant several plants

Break up the monotony of gravel with plants of a contrasting texture.

Thymus serphyllum with its tough wiry stems is extremely hard-wearing.

The low-growing Euonymus is an excellent carpeting plant.

Herbs tend to flourish in the hot, dry atmosphere of patio paving.

Phlox subulata 'Crimson' always looks most effective and colourful.

Grow Erigeron to help to soften the hard edges of paving slabs.

close together , and you can easily increase your own stock as these plants certainly benefit from being split up periodically.

Acaenas are another good group of carpeting plants which are grown mainly for their foliage. Several different varieties are available, mostly with grey, blue, bronze or bronzy-purple leaves. They hold their colour well in winter, too, which is a rare trait in coloured-leaved evergreens. Acaenas do flower, in late summer, but the flowers are not decorative.

Ajuga reptans is usually grown for its foliage which comes in red, purple, green/cream variegated and a most colourful variety called 'Multicolor' which has red, white and cream leaves. The plants have low creeping stems that form a loose carpet and, if these become untidy, they can easily be pruned back to the base in autumn or early spring. Ajugas have dark blue flowers that appear in summer.

For flowers

Alpine Phlox, especially *Phlox douglasii* and *P. subulata* species, and Dianthus, especially the *D. deltoides* species, all of which come in pink, white and red are the most suitable for growing in paving. They can look very effective when grown checkerboard fashion. Simply miss out alternate paving slabs and fill the space with flowers. This way you can walk among the flowers instead of over them.

Crane's-bills are another good family of flowering rock plants. The smaller types which make nice neat rounded hummocks are perfect for growing in cracks. Look especially for *Geranium cinereum* varieties, such as 'Ballerina', with beautiful pink flowers with red veins, and 'Apple Blossom', with pale pink flowers and dark pink veins, or any of the *G. subcaulescens* varieties, all with pinkish flowers.

G. sessiliflora, with its chocolate-coloured foliage growing in mats and white flowers which appear in summer, looks stunning when set against pale-colouring paving.

The Wild Strawberry (Fragaria vesca) looks most attractive when grown among dark coloured foliage like that of some of the purple Ajugas. Plant it somewhere in the shade close to a wall where it won't get trampled on too much.

Trailing plants on display

Trailing plants and patios make perfect partners. With plenty of walls, balconies, door and window frames to which hooks can be attached for hanging baskets, patios offer a mass of potential spots for plants that trail. And trailing plants often grow faster than the average, and so quickly add a feeling of maturity to the newest of patios, softening the hard edges with a gentle fringe of flowers and foliage.

Where to plant

🌿 **Hanging baskets** are the obvious first choice. Styles can vary, but the final effect will depend on the plants you put together and the type of basket you choose. However, because of their limited size, hanging baskets are most suitable for annual bedding plants and are usually used for adding a cheerful splash of summer colour.

Add colour to your patio with a basketful of cascading plants.

Circular wire baskets, suspended by chains from a bracket or hook are the most popular. These look particularly good beside a door or hanging from the corner of a low roof, and you can also hang them from a bracket on the wall or from especially-made frameworks – this is a useful way to add height to an otherwise flat garden. In a more formal patio, a row of hanging baskets can be suspended from the ends of pergola poles.

🌱 **Half baskets** filled with cascading plants will brighten up a short stretch of plain wall, though they tend to get lost if the space is too large. These sit flush to the wall and are secured with masonry nails.

You can also convert an ordinary flower pot into a hanging container by slipping it inside a special wall mounting bracket. And although this is suitable only for a single plant, a collection of suspended pots filled with similar plants, or plants that combine well, can make a very attractive display.

🌱 **Terracotta and standard plastic pots** are also perfect for trailing plants and are certainly the cheapest way of housing a large collection. If you decide to grow lots of plants in small pots you can increase their decorative value by placing them in a spot where the plants can dangle down freely – on a shelf, along the top of a wall, or perhaps beside a flight of garden steps. For extra height, place individual pots on bricks, or even on other pots turned upside down.

A single large pot, bursting with plants, makes a good focal point. In this case, you could go for something more ornamental, such as a strawberry pot which, with its pockets around the sides, makes an ideal container. You don't have to stick to strawberry plants as the same pots look equally good when planted with a collection of trailing herbs or colourful annuals.

🌱 **Low walls** are often overlooked as areas where trailing plants will flourish. From a design point of view trailers are very useful as they help to soften the harsh straight lines of the brickwork and to blend it in with the garden.

🌱 **Hollow walls** – two layers of bricks laid a few inches apart with the gap in between filled with soil – make a good place where virtually any trailing plant will grow as there is plenty of room for the roots to spread. A container or group of containers placed in a nearby corner will help to break up the monotony of the straight line of plants on the top of the wall.

Use hanging baskets to brighten up a dull patch of wall.

Try dotting about a selection of plants in a dry stone wall.

Dry stone walls offer a more rarified environment where only alpine and rock plants will thrive because of the dry conditions. They also lend themselves to a far more informal style of planting than hollow walls. For a natural or cottage-garden look, try dotting about a selection of plants at different heights of the wall and choose plants that will flower in succession over the longest possible period. To enable plants to grow and flourish, press a small handful of garden soil or compost between the stones before planting.

Perennials

This group is planted permanently and therefore needs more root space than annuals. Trailing shrubby plants like to ramble over fences, paving, low walls and the edges of steps, while alpine and rock plants can be planted in walls or reasonably large containers.

Shrubby plants

● *Cotoneaster dammeri* – medium-to-large prostrate shrub with bright red berries.
● *Rosa* 'Nozomi' – medium-sized trailing plant with pale pink, single flowers.
● Clematis – although it is usually grown as a climber it can also be grown as a trailer. Plant to trail down a low wall or over the edge of steps or paving. All varieties are suitable, though species such as *C.montana rubens* are best grown in this way.
● Epimedium (varieties) – small plants grown primarily for their foliage, often heart-shaped, display as for Clematis.
● Ivies – all trailing types are suitable.

Alpine and rock plants

● Aubrieta – mauve and purple flowers.
● Campanula – blue and white flowers.
● *Gypsophila repens* (also known as *G.prostrata*) – pink and white flowers.
● Helianthemum (varieties) – yellow, white, red or orange flowers.
● Alpine Phlox – pink, red and violet flowers.
● *Cymbalaria muralis* (Kenilworth Ivy) – small violet and white flowers.
● *Nepeta hederacea* 'Variegata' (Ground Ivy) – lilac-blue flowers.

Pick and choose

Annuals and tender summer brighteners

This group is primarily grown for summer and early autumn colour and includes not only genuine annuals but also hardy and tender perennial plants, normally grown as annuals to create summer colour. Grow them in hanging baskets, tubs, pots or along the top of hollow walls, from which they can trail. Good ones to try include:
● *Helichrysum petiolatum* (now called *H.petiolare*) foliage plant with silver or lime-green leaves.
● Fuchsia – make sure you choose trailing varieties.
● Lobelia – make sure you choose trailing varieties.
● Begonia – select trailing versions, such as 'Pink Avalanche'.
● *Lantana camara* – yellow flowers that turn orange as they open.
● Nasturtium (*Tropaeolum majus*) – make sure you choose trailing and semi-trailing varieties.
● Petunias – available in single, double and giant frilled, double flowered versions, striped or plain coloured.
● Sweet Pea – choose bushy varieties such as 'Snoopea'.
● *Gazania* x *hybrida* – large orange-red, daisy-like flowers.
● *Portulaca grandiflora* (Sun Plant) – large red or yellow flowers, likes a dry position.
● *Sagina subulata* – small, lime-green, low creeping plant, useful for filling in space between flowers.
● *Mesembryanthemum criniflorum* – multicoloured, daisy-like flowers that open only in the sun.

Fuchsias, *above*, **and** Lobelias, *below*, make an effective display.

A large single pot bursting with plants makes a good focal point.

Trailing Aubrieta looks spectacular on old brick walls.

Add a blaze of colour to your patio walls with hanging baskets filled with trailing plants.

Gardening the vertical way

Do you often bemoan the lack of space on your patio? If the answer is yes, relax: you can double the size of your patio at a stroke simply by making better use of the walls. Gardening vertically as well as horizontally means you instantly have that much more space for your plants.

Walls form the natural backdrop to the patio, so make them as interesting as possible. Choose plants that, between them, provide some colour all year round. Since space is always finite, pick those that have more than one thing to offer – colourful autumn foliage, say, or fruit as well as flowers. And for a patio that appeals and delights in every sense of the word, don't forget to include some sweet scented plants.

Don't be afraid to use slightly tender plants. Many plants which are too delicate for life in the open garden thrive in the shelter of a patio wall. And for additional highlights, how about some hanging-baskets or wall pots spilling over with a riot of colourful trailing plants? There is a huge variety of trailers available.

Climbing roses can look sensational, especially the scented varieties.

Try growing Clematis 'Perle d'Azur' for dramatic effect.

Fruits such as redcurrants flourish in the warmth of patio walls.

Climbers

First of all, start your planning with climbers. These will take up the most space, thanks to their rambling, meandering habit, and you therefore need to decide carefully how many to grow and how much space you need to allow for them. It is probably best on patio walls – unless you want to be swamped – to use the smaller climbers, such as Passion Flower, Clianthus, Akebia or, on a north-facing wall, small-leaved Ivies.

Don't grow climbers only on existing walls – use them to 'grow' your own wall wherever you need an additional one. If your patio lacks privacy, for example, or if it would benefit from extra shelter from the wind, erect a light framework of trellis and grow climbers up it. You can also train climbers along pergola poles to help blend house and garden.

Roses

Climbing Roses can look lovely trained round a patio, but they do take up a lot of room. Get two plants for the space of one by training a spring-flowering Clematis up the Rose's stems. This harms neither plant and looks sensational.

Like all wall plants, Roses are best trained on to trellis that can be lifted away from the wall whenever you want to repair the brickwork or to give the wall some paint.

Any climbing varieties of Rose are suitable for patio walls. The best are scented ones, some of which can even be grown against a north-facing wall. These include 'Zephirine Drouhin' (pink), 'Golden Showers' (yellow) and 'Danse du Feu' (orange-red).

Wall shrubs

Many shrubs can be grown in virtually any situation, but you shouldn't forget they can certainly be grown against walls. The best kinds to grow in this way are those rather 'special', tender types that don't do well elsewhere, such as Ceanothus, Fremontodendron, Moroccan Broom (*Cytisus battandieri*), Myrtle (*Myrtus communis*) and Dwarf Pomegranate (*Punica granatum* 'Nana'). A wall-trained Ornamental Quince (Chaenomeles) and a Firethorn (Pyracantha) can also look most attractive planted against a wall.

Annuals

Annual bedding plants can be used in all sorts of imaginative ways to add a series of focal points to a wall, providing seasonal splashes of colour just where you need them.

Hanging-baskets, for example, are one of the most attractive ways of using bedding plants. They can be planted with naturally trailing varities such as Lobelia, Ivy-leaved Geranium or trailing Fuchsia, with compact upright plants such as Impatiens, or even with small climbers like Black-eyed Susan (*Thunbergia alata*). Hanging-baskets look attractive when suspended from a wall bracket next to a door.

As well as the usual kinds of hanging-baskets, you can also get half-baskets which are meant to be fixed directly up against the wall. A series of these, placed at regular intervals and at different heights, makes a most attractive display on a wall. Similar half moon-shaped containers, available in terracotta, look particularly striking in the summer when planted with tender trailing plants like Ceropegia, *Senecio rowleyanus*, *Sedum morganianum*, or with the hardier Livingstone Daisy (*Mesem-*

The attractive *Camellia Japonica* 'Elegans' is easy to look after.

Liven up a stretch of trellis with trailing plants in pots.

A dry stone wall makes a perfect home for an *Alyssum saxatile.*

bryanthemum criniflorum). Give them a sunny spot and you'll think you're in the Mediterranean!

Trailing plants in pots can also be used to liven up a stretch of trellis. Just slip the pots into a noose of wire and hang them between climbers. Choose brightly coloured plants that will really stand out against the foliage. And if you have an archway leading off the patio, a large pot of trailing annuals looks most effective standing over the top with flowers cascading down.

Fruiting walls

Fruit trees or bushes can be most attractive, covering the walls with blossom in the springtime, followed by ripening fruit in the summer. It is, however, essential to start with ready-trained plants. Cordon-trained apples are ideal as they can be planted very close together – as little as 18in

(45cm) apart. Redcurrants and gooseberries can also be grown as cordons. Peaches, nectarines, cherries, are usually fan-trained.

Growing fruit on the patio has several advantages: the warmth of the walls makes this a very productive method; the fruit is easily accessible and therefore easy to pick; and it is not difficult to provide protection from birds. It does, however, necessitate rather more work than purely ornamental gardening. It is vital, for example, to continue the training process once the trees have been planted – and this means regular pruning, in both summer and winter. Patio fruit also needs lavish feeding and generous watering.

Low walls

These offer all sorts of opportunities for growing interesting plants in unusual ways. Dry stone walls, for

example, make perfect homes for rock plants such as Aubrieta, Sedums and Sempervivums, all of which thrive in hot, dry conditions. Simply push a handful of earth into the cracks before planting; or plant them in hollow-topped walls, filling the gap between two rows of bricks with soil to make a shallow bed. Try growing Wallflowers in this way for spring flowering, for example, and watch them live up to their name!

Another idea for something really different is a 'wild wall', naturalised with things like the Ivy-leaved Toadflax, Wood Sorrel (*Oxalis acetosella*), Fumaria or a climbing Corydalis planted in the cracks. And for shady areas, ferns such as the Maidenhair Spleenwort (*Asplenium trichomanes*), Wall Rue and Rusty-backed Fern all thrive in dry walls, while most other species of fern will do well in damp walls.

Frame your patio or balcony with a mass of climbing and wall shrubs and quickly transform it into a secret retreat – a secluded spot where you can relax and unwind.

The selection of climbers to choose from is wide: twining types that need suporting and self-clinging species that don't need any help; wall shrubs that benefit from the night heat released from brickwork; roses prized for their scent and colour range; conifers and cane fruits such as blackberries and loganberries.

Climbers

Clematis is among the finest of climbers which will twine and drape over trellis and wires. The large-flowered varieties that bring colour to spring and summer are ideal.

Choose from the violet and carmine 'Barbara Dibley' which flowers from May to June and again in September; the blue-violet 'Beauty of Worcester' blooming from May to August; the petunia-red 'Ernest Markham', decking walls with colour from June to September, and the carmine-red 'Ville de Lyon' which brightens gardens all summer.

Honeysuckle is another twiner not to be ignored. There are many varieties, but the deciduous *Lonicera periclymenum* 'Belgica', the Early Dutch Honeysuckle, and *L.periclymenum*, the late Dutch Honeysuckle, 'Serotina' will fill your patio with scent and a profusion of reddish-purple flowers from May to October. If you want to create an evergreen screen your best choice would be *L.japonica* 'Halliana'. The fact that its sweetly-fragrant, biscuit-coloured flowers appear in late summer, when few other climbers are at their best, is an added advantage.

The Passion Flower, *Passiflora caerulea*, always prized for its blue and white blooms, will need warmth and winter protection if your patio is in a chilly position. In a warm summer its flowers are followed by a profusion of yellow, plum-shaped fruits which, although pippy, are sweet-fleshed and can be made into a preserve.

Summer Jasmine (*Jasminum officinale* 'Grandiflorum') is another sun lover and will reward you with its richly-perfumed white blooms from June to September, as will the climb-

The beautiful *Carpenteria californica* is best planted against a warm wall.

Patio framework

ing member of the potato family, *Solanum crispum*. *S.c.* 'Glasnevin' is one of the finest varieties – its rich purple-blue, yellow-centred blooms are borne on twining stems which brighten summer and winter.

Self clingers

Give self-clinging plants a rough brick wall and up they go, sticking firmly to the brickwork with their aerial roots.

Ivy is probably the best example, and all species are adept at completely clothing walls, fences, garages and sheds.

Hedera colchica 'Dentata Variegata', the Persian Ivy, with its large leaves, imparts a touch of gold to a wall or fence. *H.helix* 'Goldheart' is more demure, while 'Buttercup' will cover the side of your house with a mantle of bright yellow.

Warm walls can be draped with the orange-scarlet trumpets of *Campsis radicans*, the Trumpet Vine, a beautiful climber with finely divided leaves which bring glowing autumn colour.

The Climbing Hydrangea (*Hydrangea petiolaris*) enjoys cold spots on north walls and this emerald green beauty will delight you in early summer with its cartwheel blooms.

Roses

The modern climbers are probably the best value for money. Choose low-growing varieties that flower repeatedly throughout the summer for draping over the uprights of a covered patio or a low fence or wall.

Take your pick from apricot-pink 'Breath of Life', salmon-pink 'Compassion', rich scarlet 'Copenhagen', yellow 'Golden Showers' and pink 'Parade'. Most have a pleasing scent and all flower profusely.

The old-fashioned Noisette roses are perfect for screening a large area. Varieties such as the climbing 'Cecile Brunner' with its multitude of pink, thimble-sized blooms and 'Blush Noisette' with lilac-pink flowers are ideal. Both grow up to 15-20ft (4.5-6m) high and the same in width.

Wall shrubs

There are dozens of wall shrubs from which to choose. The blue-flowered Californian Lilac (Ceanothus) is ideal for a sunny spot. 'Burkwoodii', flowering in autumn and summer,

and 'Delight', blooming in May, are the hardiest varieties.

Carpenteria californica is another beauty for a warm wall. As it is slightly tender it is advisable to drape it with straw in the winter. In summer its display of large white flowers enclosing a mass of golden stamens is truly magnificent.

Colder spots of the patio can be effectively draped with orange, scarlet or yellow-berried Pyracantha, red-berried *Cotoneaster salicifolia* or any of the pink or white-flowered Quince or Cydonia varieties such as *Chaenomeles speciosa* 'Moerloosei'.

Conifers

A boundary of golden conifers, moderate in growth and non-intrusive, takes on a special appeal in winter. Ideal types that won't overpower you with their height are *Chamaecyparis lawsoniana* 'Lanei', 'Hillieri', 'Allumigold' and 'Stewartii'.

The blue-green forms such as 'Pembury Blue', 'Columnaris' and 'Ellwoodii' are also valuable for providing winter colour on the patio.

Fruitful screens

The white spring blooms of climbing cane fruits such as Blackberries, Loganberries and their hybrids can create a wonderful summer curtain, but you must make sure that you give them adequate support. A fruiting hedge of cordon or espalier-trained apple or pear trees is also pleasing.

Care

Whatever you plant, make sure you enrich the planting hole with plenty of humus-forming organic material, such as well-rotted garden compost, old manure or peat. A sprinkling of bonemeal also helps the plants to get established. Then firm the roots well into position and don't forget to use a stake to support trees or shrubs that might be exposed to buffeting winds.

Water regularly during dry spells and tie in any wandering shoots of vigorous climbers.

The variety of framework plants is large and it is always worth spending a little time browsing around garden centres, as these can be treasure troves for exciting species.

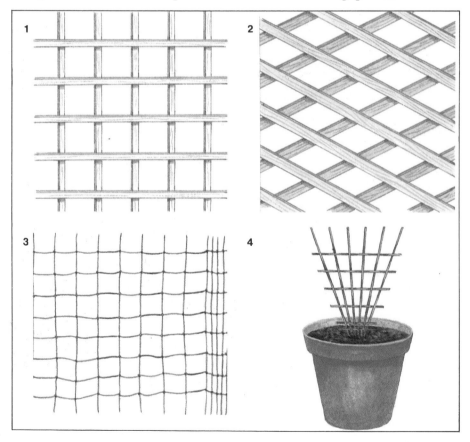

Trellis: a rigid framework is suitable for climbers and wall shrubs (1). Expandable wooden trellis is ideal for slender-stemmed Clematis (2). Use netting to give support to annual climbers (3), and plastic framework for small climbers in containers (4).

Top Performers

CLIMBERS	COLOUR/FLOWERING	HEIGHT	COMMENTS
Camspis radicans	Orange-scarlet, summer	12ft (3.6m)	Self-clinging, deciduous, needs a warm, sunny position, ferny leaves.
Clematis armandii	White, spring	9ft (2.7m)	Twining, evergreen, shelter from cold winds, trifoliate leaves.
Clematis montana 'Tetrarose'	Lilac-rose, spring	15ft (4.5m)	Twining, deciduous, tolerates cold walls, rampant.
Clematis 'Marie Boisselot'	White, summer	9ft (2.7m)	Twining, dediduous, best against a red brick wall, hardy.
Hedera helix 'Goldheart'	Gold splashed leaves	15ft (4.5m)	Self-clinging, neat habit, not intrusive, cold walls, evergreen.
Jasminum officinale 'Grandiflorum'	White, summer	8ft (2.4m)	Rampant twiner, deciduous, needs sunny position
Lonicera periclymenum 'Serotina'	Reddish purple, summer	12ft (3.6m)	Flowering late, its blooms have special appeal; hardy, rampant, deciduous.
Wisteria floribunda 'Alba'	White, spring	20ft (6m)	Magnificent against a dark background, keep away from eaves, robust, deciduous.
ROSES			
'Cecile Brunner' (climbing)	Pink, summer	20ft (6m)	Exquisite thimble-size blooms, repeat flowering, rampant, deciduous.
'Golden Showers'	Yellow, summer	10ft (3m)	Almost thornless, good for north walls or fences, deciduous.
'Parkdirektor Riggers'	Crimson, summer	12ft (3.6m)	Deciduous, repeat flowering, deep glossy leaves.
WALL SHRUBS			
Carpenteria californica	White, summer	6ft (1.8m)	Evergreen, richly scented, needs warm wall and winter protection.
Ceanothus 'Delight'	Blue, spring	9ft (2.7m)	Evergreen, foam of blossom, hardy, flowers freely.
Chaenomeles 'Crimson and Gold'	Crimson, spring	6ft (1.8m)	Deciduous, tolerates chilly positions, prune after flowering
Cotoneaster salicifolia	White, spring	9ft (2.7m)	Evergreen, willow-shaped leaves, scarlet autumn fruits, hardy.
Pyracantha 'Orange Glow'	White, spring	15ft (4.5m)	Evergreen, crimson berries, vigorous, hardy.
CONIFERS			
Chamaecyparis lawsoniana 'Pembury Blue'	Blue leaves	12ft (3.6m)	Neat, narrow pillar, handsome in winter, non-intrusive. Evergreen.
Chamaecyparis lawsoniana 'Lanei'	Golden leaves	15ft (4.5m)	Sunny appearance all year round. Evergreen. Can be trimmed.
FRUIT			
Blackberry Fantasia	White, spring	15ft (4.5m)	Largest and sweetest variety. Needs room. Makes good fruiting screen. Crops from mid August to late September.
Tummelberry	White, spring	8ft (2.4m)	Superior loganberry-like fruits from mid-July to August.
Apples/pears	White, spring	6ft (1.8m)	Grow as cordons to form fruiting screen. Any variety.

Clematis montana will tolerate a cold wall and always looks decorative.

The deciduous *Rosa* 'Golden Showers' is good for planting against north walls.

The Cotoneaster with its bright red berries is perfect for a colder spot.

A fan-trained apple tree can look most effective.

Bonsai trees are currently enjoying an increase in popularity.

Junipers such as *Juniperus chinensis,* 'Sargentii' are ideal bonsai subjects.

Bonsai such as *Larix kaempferi* are kept small by shoot pruning during the growing season.

Bonsai trees have been popular in China for hundreds of years and are currently enjoying a great increase in popularity over here too. If you have become enthralled by these enchanting little trees, shrubs and conifers, you will probably have bought one 'ready-made'. Alternatively, you may have decided to start one of your own.

Whatever you do, it is important to remember that bonsai are small, not just because they are grown in tiny containers, but because they are carefully pruned and trained. There is nothing difficult about this, and the same set of rules applies each year. The only variations likely to occur are as you progress to trying a wider range of plants, as these will grow at different rates.

A normal bonsai subject consists of a miniature tree in a container. Indeed, bonsai actually means 'plant in a container'. It can be a deciduous tree, such as Beech, Elm, Horse Chestnut or Maple, a conifer such as Scots Pine, Larch, Yew or Juniper, or a flowering tree.

Less simple examples of bonsai are those using a trailing or climbing plant. Favourite ones include the Wisteria, the Winter-flowering Jasmine (*Jasminum nudiflorum*), *Forsythia suspensa*, and the Weeping Willow (*Salix* x *chrysocoma*), which has lovely golden-barked shoots.

There are many different styles of bonsai, and mastering these can become a lifetime's obsession, but basically they fall into two categories. The first is concerned with the shape of the main stem or trunk, and the second involves those in which there are several trees in one container or, occasionally, one tree with apparently several main trunks. Trunks can be trained to twist and turn in all sorts of ways, to grow diagonally or cascading, and so on.

Where several trees are planted in the one container, the number should always be an odd one, because the Japanese regard these as being representative of immortality and age. The usual number is three or five, and any more would mean dealing with rather a large container.

Alternatively, it is possible to 'cheat' and to use only one tree by laying the main trunk flat on its side in the container and then retaining only those shoots on the upper side to give the appearance of several 'trees'.

Bonsai can be persuaded by the use of string, raffia and also wire to take on a variety of shapes and sizes.

Grow your own

If you want to start your own bonsai, you can collect seed from hedgerows in the autumn and sow it immediately in good compost. Leave the pots of seed outdoors throughout the winter, making sure they don't dry out, and then, when the seedlings start to appear, start training and pruning them. You can also obtain seed from nurserymen or from your own garden. Alternatively, you can use garden seedlings of Holly, Oak, Hawthorn and Sycamore.

Cutting remarks

Bonsai are kept small mainly by shoot pruning during the growing season, and then by root pruning at potting time. They are also sometimes shoot-pruned in winter, and leaf-pruned in midsummer, though this latter treatment is fairly drastic and is restricted to the strongest-growing types.

Shoot pruning basically consists of removing the young shoot tip when only 1in (2.5cm) long. You can do this with scissors, fingers or fingernails, and the cut should be made immediately above a leaf or a pair of leaves. This will encourage the growth of further side shoots which can, in turn, be pruned to the same length. Sideshoots grow at different rates, so pruning will continue over several months.

A sideshoot may also be removed entirely, and this is where some of the art of bonsai growing comes in. Vigorous varieties need this extra thinning, as they produce a lot of sideshoots, and the positioning of branches is important.

If you are dealing with a seedling, it should usually be allowed to grow to the required height before the tip of the main stem is removed, but sideshoots can be nipped back, as described earlier, from the first year onwards. If you are pruning a conifer, do not cut across the needles, but cut or nip the stem only.

Root pruning is the other main technique used to keep trees dwarf. This is done at repotting time, which may be every spring for the stronger-growing varieties, and every second or third spring for the rest. Give the plants a good watering the day before potting, then turn the plant out of the container. Remove some of the compost from the base and between the roots, so that they can be trimmed back by about a third. The exact amount of trimming depends on whether the tree is fast-, medium-, or slow-growing: the more root that is removed, the more its growth rate is slowed down.

Repot the plant in the same container, filling in with fresh compost, and water it in. By controlling the root growth like this, the top growth will also be kept in check, but remember to feed and water the trees normally to keep them healthy. Additional pruning includes winter shoot pruning, which is occasionally done to remove dead, weak or unwanted shoots; and leaf cutting, which is carried out on trees that are growing too fast. In the latter case, all the leaves are removed in late June, keeping only a short length of leaf stalk. The check on growth is considerable, though a new batch of leaves will appear before the end of summer; pruning should then continue normally.

Gentle persuasion

Apart from pruning, bonsai can also be persuaded, by the use of string, raffia and copper wire, to take on a variety of shapes and styles.

String and raffia can achieve a great deal, and this is probably the best way to start off. Use it to tie trunks to canes, to ensure vertical growth.

To encourage a cascading style, a piece of strong wire is pushed into the compost at the side of the container and bent over to the angle required. The stem of the tree is then bent over and tied to it, gradually tightening the ties and adding more as the stem lengthens. It is important to do this in stages, and to tie the tree down to its container to prevent the root-ball from being lifted out.

Copper wire needs to be heated to make it malleable and then cooled before it can be used. Wrap soft paper around it to avoid any damage to soft-barked trees. Plastic-coated wire can also be used, but looks rather ugly. In time, the wires are removed – usually after several years when the tree is set firmly in the required shape – but copper wires tend to harden when in position and can be difficult to remove without harming the tree.

Copper wire should be just thick enough to keep young shoots and trunks in place. Training should start as soon as the wire can be kept in position; it should be put on in spring and summer for deciduous varieties, and in autumn and winter for evergreens. Wind it round the trunk several times and then round the shoot you are aiming to train, placing the coils of wire about 1/4in (6mm) apart and extending the wire to just beyond the tip, so you will be able to continue training it as the shoot grows. You may need to rewind it after only a few months.

Make a focal feature out of bonsai such as an Acer.

Creating a water garden

A well stocked garden pond is more than a mere thing of beauty. A veritable hive of activity, it draws us to it again and again. Within its limpid depths goldfish, golden orfe, shubunkins or golden rudd glide and nose among an underwater greenery of oxygenating plants. A wealth of richly coloured marginals decks the sides to create interest throughout spring and summer. The surface is bejewelled with exquisitely cupped Water Lilies. And the splish-splash of a fountain has a hypnotic and therapeutic effect.

What's involved

If you've installed a polythene, PVC or butyl rubber liner, or one of the pre-formed fibreglass pools, you can fill it in with water, leave it for a few days for any chemicals in the liner or pool to disperse, and then plant.

If, however, you're planting a concrete pool, there's a serious danger of lime seeping from the concrete into the water. Your plants won't like this – they prefer a more acid environment – and it can have a disastrous effect on the fish you introduce, causing their fins to split, and may even kill them. The answer is to paint the dry concrete with a sealer, such as Silglaze, which neutralises the lime and converts the concrete into an insoluble compound.

Planting techniques

It is advisable to establish a thriving and well-balanced community of plants before adding the fish. And the best way of doing this is to plant them in small, special-purpose polythene mesh crates or baskets. Those with sloping sides fit snugly against the sloping sides of the pond.

Make sure your plants are thriving before adding fish to your pond.

Water Lilies are beautiful. First of all, line the crate with a special liner, sold specifically for this purpose, or use sacking. Cover the base with a few inches of heavyish loam or well-rotted turf which has completely disintegrated, set the roots in position, and pack more soil around the crown. To prevent the soil from escaping and muddying the water and fish from uprooting the plants, tie the sacking neatly round the roots to the base of the leaves, with plastic coated wire fixed to the basket as shown in the illustration *opposite*.

Never, never set a newly-planted lily on the bottom of the pool where it would be covered by 18in (45cm) or more of water – it would probably drown! Instead, position the crate on bricks or a large pot, so that it is only just beneath the surface. Then, when new leaves appear and leaf stalks lengthen, gradually lower the plant so that the leaves, or pads, are always floating on the surface of the water.

For a small patio pond, one or two lilies will effectively cover a large area and will both reduce light entering the water and keep it crystal clear.

Floaters are fun. They spread over the surface, creating beneficial shade which will keep fish happy during periods of hot weather.

The two most reliable ones are Frogbit *(Hydrocharis Morsus-ranae)*, with white, three-petalled blooms, small rounded leaves and roots that trail in the water; and a floating moss called *Azolla caroliniana*, which is actually a tiny fern with minute moss-like fronds that start off green and then assume a bright, reddish brown colour as the season advances.

Oxygenating plants are vital. These work by feeding on mineral salts and absorbing sunlight. In so doing, they deprive microscopic algae – responsible for the clouded, pea soup appearance of pond water – of the food and light they need to thrive, and result in bright, clear water. But this doesn't happen overnight: not surprisingly, it does take a little time for such a perfect balance to be achieved. Once the correct balance has been reached, it should not be necessary to change the water.

Apart from Hornwort, which has no roots and is simply placed in the water, they are best planted in small crates, like Water Lilies, and packed round with sacking. They are sold as bunches of cuttings, which are simply pressed into the soil.

Marginals, or water-edge plants, complete the picture. They are those plants that inhabit the zone of wet soil just in and just above the water line of a natural pond or river. Thriving in just a few inches of water, their glorious colour, attractive leaf shapes and interesting textures create an exciting fringe. They are all planted in small, medium or large crates, depending on size and vigour.

Introducing fish

If you remember that a 1sq ft (30sq cm) area of water is enough to support a 2in (5cm) long fish, it is then fairly easy to calculate the number of fish your pool will comfortably accommodate. For example, a 5ft (1.5m) x 4ft (1.2m) pool will take 20 fish about 2in (5cm) long, or eight fish about 5in (13cm) long.

One danger of over-stocking your pool is that fish will suffer from a shortage of oxygen, which often happens at night when oxygenating plants release carbon dioxide. Another danger arises when fish are introduced to a pool in which the mineral content differs widely from

Planting technique: line crate with liner, cover base with loam, set roots in position and add more soil around the crown.

To prevent soil from escaping, tie liner round roots to the base of leaves with plastic coated wire fixed to the basket.

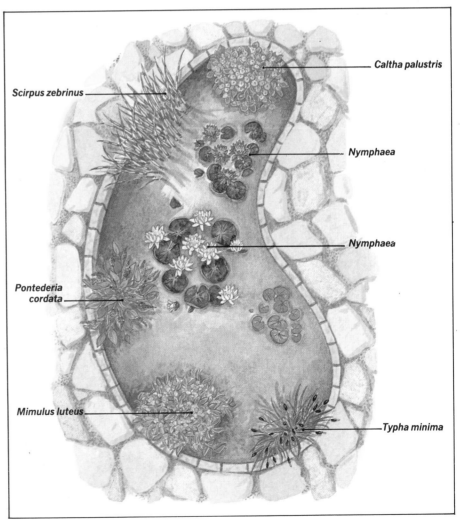

Scirpus zebrinus

Caltha palustris

Nymphaea

Nymphaea

Pontederia cordata

Mimulus luteus

Typha minima

that of the water in which they were before. The solution to this problem is to add a special water conditioner to the water before fish are released into it. This coats their gills and reduces their sensitivity to a new environment.

Pool care

Spring. Divide crowded plants and feed fish daily with high protein food to get them in peak condition in preparation for breeding. Plants should also be fed after the first year, using proprietary Water Lily pellets which are simply pushed into the soil around each plant. Repot every two years. Planting new plants is best done in late spring.

Summer. Top up the water level to keep it above the liner. This is especially important with a plastic liner, to prevent it from deteriorating when exposed to the air.

It's a good idea to install a fountain: this will help to aerate the water – which is particularly helpful on thundery days at this time of year when fish find breathing difficult.

Hose away blackfly from Lily leaves. Never use insecticide.

Some water plants grow with great vigour in their first season and will need thinning either during, or at the end of, the growing season.

Autumn. Net the pool against falling leaves, which rot and pollute the water with noxious gases. Cut off decaying leaves from all plants before they decompose in the water.

Winter. Install a pool heater to keep an area of water free from ice in order to avoid a build-up of poisonous gases. Alternatively, float a ball on the surface of the water and free it with boiling water as soon as ice locks it in. Then remove just enough water to leave a 2in (5cm) gap between ice and water so that fish can breathe.

Possible problems. If the water persists in staying a muddy green colour in spite of the presence of oxygenating plants, use an algicide, such as Acurel 'E' or Algimycin P.L.L., or fit a water filter. Long stringy Blankweed, another form of algae, is best removed by twirling it round a rake or stick and lifting it out of the water.

Your guide to pool plants

Name	Description	Depth of Water*
Water Lilies **White-flowered** *Nymphaea pygmaea* 'Alba'	Choice gem with tiny flowers just 2in (5cm) across	4-6in (10-15cm)
'Gonnêre'	Double blooms with distinctive green sepals	18-24in (45-60cm)
Pink-flowered *N. odorata* 'W. B. Shaw'	Attractively star-shaped, scented blooms	9-15in (23-38cm)
'Mme Wilfron Gonnêre'	Large, double rose-pink flowers	18-24in (45-60cm)
'Rose Arey'	Starry blooms with rich rose, slightly incurving petals	18-24in (45-60cm)
Red-flowered 'Attraction'	Glowing garnet-red blooms, petals tipped with white	18-24in (45-60cm)
'William Falconer'	The darkest red variety with contrasting golden stamens	18-24in (45-60cm)
N. x laydekeri 'Purpurata'	Bright wine red, ideal for tubs, sinks and very shallow pools	9-15in (23-38cm)
Yellow-flowered *N. marliacea* 'Chromatella'	Soft yellow blooms with bright yellow stamens, chocolate-blotched leaves	18-24in (45-60cm)
'Sunrise'	Deep sunshine yellow, large, slightly fragrant	18-24in (45-60cm)
'Helvola'	Sulphur blooms, ideal for shallow containers	4-6in (10-15cm)
MARGINAL PLANTS *Acorus calamus variegatus*	Green and yellow striped leaves. Height 2ft (60cm)	3-5in (8.13cm)
Butomus umbellatus	Flowering Rush with striking head of rose pink flowers. Height 2ft (60cm)	3-5in (8-13cm)
Caltha palustris 'Flore Pleno'	Double Marsh Marigold with thicky clustered petals. Height 1ft (30cm)	0-3in (0-8cm)
Cyperus longus	Ornamental Rush, much sought after by flower arrangers. Height 2ft (60cm)	3-5in (8-13cm)
Glyceria spectablis variegata	White and green striped grass. 2ft (60cm)	2-5in (5-13cm)
Iris kaempferi 'Higo'	Japanese or Clematis Iris, blue and white shades, double blooms up to 10in (25cm) across. Height 1 1/2ft (45cm)	0-3in (0-8cm)
Juncus effusus 'Spiralis'	Corkscrew Rush. Curious spiralling stems. Height 1 1/2ft (45cm)	3-5in (8-13cm)
Mimulus luteus	Monkey Musk. Small yellow flowers spotted red. Height 1ft (30cm)	0-2in (0-5cm)
Pontederia cordata	Pickerel Weed. Spikes of small Delphinium-like flowers. Height 1 1/2ft (45cm)	3-5in (8-13cm)
Sagittaria sagittifolia 'Flore Pleno'	Double Japanese Arrowhead. Flowers like double white Stocks. Height 1ft (30cm)	3-5in (8-13cm)
Scirpus zebrinus	Zebra Rush. Banded green and white, like porcupine quills. Height 2 1/2ft (75cm)	3-5in (8-13cm)
Typha minima	Japanese Reedmace. Brown, poker-like heads on stems 1 1/2ft (45cm) long	0-4in (0-10cm)
OXYGENATORS *Ceratopyllum demersum*	Hornwort. Curious whorled-leaved plant without roots that's simply placed in the water	
Elodea canadensis crispa (Lagarosiphon major)	Similar to Canadian Pondweed, with tightly curled leaves	
Myriophyllum spicatum	Milfoil. Most attractive with ferny leaves in neat whorls	
Hottonia palustris	Water Violet. Ferny leaves, stems topped with heads of white flowers	

* This is the depth of water between the top (rim) of the pot and the surface of the pool

Patio privacy

Create some secrecy on your patio with colourful climbers and shrubs.

BEING EXPOSED TO VIEW – whether to neighbours' prying eyes or those of passers-by – is the last thing you want when you're relaxing on your patio, chatting with friends, enjoying a drink or simply reading a book. Seeking seclusion isn't always easy. Neighbours' bedroom windows often overlook the garden and chain-link boundary fences aren't peep-proof. There are, however, ways round the problem – all you need is a little ingenuity.

Fences

Let's start, first of all, with boundary fences. Most are no more than 4-6ft (1.2-1.8m) high, which is adequate for most purposes. You can add extra height to the fence without adding extra weight by fixing trellis-work to the top. An additional 2-3ft (0.6-0.9m) can make all the difference, but do check with your local council's plan-

ning department that you're not extending to such a height that you need planning permission.

Trellis can then be draped with evergreen climbers, such as a sweetly-scented Honeysuckle (*Lonicera japonica* 'Halliana') or the spring-flowering Clematis (*C. armandii* 'Apple Blossom') which has handsome, tri-lobed, leathery leaves creating a dense screen. Ivies (Hedera) are another good idea. A most attractive Ivy for this purpose is the large-leaved, Persian Ivy, *Hedera colchica* 'Dentata Variegata', with leaves splashed with cream, gold and green.

If you have a very warm spot in your garden and would like to try something a little unusual, plant *Trachelospermum jasminoides.* This belongs to the Periwinkle family and rewards you with a profusion of fragrant, white, Jasmine-like flowers in mid- to late summer.

Hedges

A dense, noise-baffling evergreen hedge that even the most persistent dog cannot penetrate is the perfect solution to the privacy you're after, especially if it grows to 6-9ft (1.8-2.7m) or more and withstands a winter battering from gale-force winds. The hedge to go for is not the Leyland Cypress, the bane of many a garden where it has grown so tall that it's imprisoning its owners, but the common Holly (Ilex), which is prickly, yes, but troublesome, no.

There are many varieties of Holly. Try alternating the variegated 'Golden Queen', a male form, curiously enough, with 'Golden King', female, which will give you a profusion of scarlet berries against golden leaves.

Set plants in a double staggered row, about 18in (45cm) apart, in well-prepared soil. Tie plants to canes to prevent them moving in windy weather.

Another first-class contender is the evergreen *Cotoneaster lacteus*, which has deep green leaves with silvery undersides. The white summer flowers are followed by scarlet fruits in autumn.

Then there's Berberis. Most evergreen forms are low growing, but exceptions are *B. darwinii* and *B. stenophylla*, both robust arching plants decked with yellow, scented flowers in early spring.

If you're particularly keen on a hedge of conifers, opt for a closely-spaced planting of gold, blue and green varieties of *Chamaecyparis lawsoniana*, such as 'Dutch Gold', 'Green Pillar' and 'Pembury Blue' respectively.

Perennial climbers

Camouflage the patio itself by planting scented climbers to drape their sinuous forms from overhead beams or the screen block walling you've erected to keep the neighbours at bay. There are many glorious kinds, and they don't necessarily have to be evergreen.

It's great fun to plant a grape vine, such as the black-berried, full-bodied 'Black Hamburgh', which ripens at the end of August and is delicious eaten as a dessert; or 'Seyve-Villard', a white grape resistent to mildew and valued for its weighty crop, which ripens at the end of September. Both look attractive in the autumn, too, when their ornate leaves turn a bright yellow before falling.

Scented climbers are the most rewarding in the short term, so these are the ones you'll want to plant first. One of the finest of these is the Common White Jasminum, *Jasminum officinale* 'Grandiflorum', which has slender, fern-leaved stems that are heavy with white flowers in the summer. And then, of course, there are the Honeysuckles (Lonicera). Two wonderfully fragrant ones are the Early Dutch Honeysuckle *Lonicera periclymenum* 'Belgica', which is a concoction of rose-purple and yellow, during May and June, and the Late Dutch Honeysuckle *Lonicera periclymenum* 'Serotina', with reddish-white tinted flowers from July to September.

Roses are excellent for softening brickwork and timber and deserve a special mention. There are dozens to choose from, the best being those with the least prickly stems, such as 'Golden Showers', which has yellow blooms that turn creamy; and 'Handel', which has red and creamy-white petals. 'Climbing Iceberg' is another less vicious variety that blooms for most of the summer.

Cover bare walls with climbing roses.

'Madame Gregoire Stachelin' has deep pink flowers with a rich raspberry scent, endearing it to all who plant her, while the carmine buds of 'Pink Perpetue' open to give clear pink blooms.

Clematis – particularly the large-flowered hybrids such as the blush-white and pink 'Nelly Moser', mauve-pink and carmine 'Bee's Jubilee' and lavender-blue 'Lasurstern' – mingle well with Roses.

Climbing annuals

A quick and colourful screen to a height of 5-6ft (1.5-1.8m) can be achieved by sowing the climbing Nasturtium (*Tropaeolum majus*).

Its cousin, the Canary Flower (*Tropaeolum peregrinum*), is another hardy annual, which can be sown wherever you want it to climb. It has bright yellow flowers with a myriad of fringed, two-petalled blooms on twining stems, partnered by attractive leaves.

Taller and even more inspiring is the half-hardy Morning Glory (*Ipomoea tricolor*). Raise plants in gentle heat in early spring and plant them out when nights are no longer frosty. Give them a well-nourished site, laced with bonemeal, to help them ascend rapidly to 8ft (2.4m) and smother their stems all summer with pale blue trumpet-shaped flowers, each bloom lasting but a day.

Creating a little privacy with colourful and scented climbers and shrubs is a fascinating exercise. Take your time, choose wisely, and make that sun-soaked haven even more alluring.

Evening fragrance

IF YOU ARE OUT AT WORK ALL DAY you will probably make most use of your patio garden in the early evening. If this is the case, it is really worthwhile making a point of planting some of the plants that release their scents on to the evening air. The intoxicating perfume of Night-scented Stock, Honeysuckle or the white-flowered Tobacco Plant can give jaded spirits a real lift at the end of an exhausting day. And many of these evening-scented plants will also attract showy moths to your garden for your enjoyment.

There really is a magical quality about a garden at twilight. As the light fades, pale-coloured and white flowers become luminous, and stand out ethereally against their background of darkening leaves. Grey-leaved plants also assume a ghostly appearance and, as the spicy floral scents of the evening are wafted to our senses, the twilight garden becomes a place of enchantment.

One of the best plants for evening perfume is the Tobacco Plant *(Nicotiana affinis)*, which will flower continuously from June until the autumn. The white-flowered form has the strongest scent, and if you can grow a patch of this in your favourite corner of the patio where you sit during the evening you will get the full benefit of its fragrance. Interplant it with another annual, the Night-scented Stock *(Matthiola bicornis)* for a really heady cocktail of fragrance. The Night-scented Stock is grown mainly for the strong honey scent it gives off in the evening – its flowers are a drab, insignificant pale mauve, and it is best hidden among other, more showy blooms.

You can sow seeds of Night-scented Stock *in situ* in early spring, when the nights are getting warmer and longer, thinning the plants to 4-6in (10-15cm) apart. Seeds of *Nicotiana affinis* can be sown in gentle heat in February or March, and then planted outside in late May or early June.

The Sweet Rocket *(Hesperis matronalis)* has a strong violet fragrance, and is a true cottage garden plant, which William Robinson, the famous gardener, thought 'was amongst the most desirable of garden flowers'. As it is a short-lived perennial, it is best to raise fresh plants each year. Sow seeds in prepared soil outdoors in April.

An excellent choice to grow raised up in a container is the Evening Primrose *(Oenothera biennis)*, which opens its butter-yellow blooms only when night falls and emits an overpowering scent. It is also one of those desirable plants that flowers in the late summer after the mid-summer burst of bloom is over.

Raising scented plants in containers helps to bring their fragrance closer to us, and another good candidate for planting in a tub or trough is the Bee Balm – Bergamot *(Monarda didyma).* The clear pink form 'Croftway Pink',

Plant Bergamot, *above*, Tobacco Plants, *centre* and Night-scented Stock, *left*, to fill your patio with an intoxicating scent as twilight falls.

the rich violet 'Prairie Night' and the 'Cambridge Scarlet' forms are all valuable for their refreshing scent.

Abronia fragrans gives out a strong scent of vanilla. It is not a common plant, but is well worth searching for. It grows some 2ft (60cm) high and opens its flowers at sunset; in mild districts it can be treated as a perennial but in northern gardens it's best to grow it as an annual and sow seeds every year.

The attractive *Primula sikkimensis* bears striking primrose-yellow blooms on top of 2ft (60cm) stems that grow out of a rosette of long, narrow, dark green leaves. The honeyed fragrance of the flowers intensifies at dusk. In a patio garden this Primula would thrive at the edge of a pool where the soil is permanently wet.

Other Primulas that can be relied upon to reward us with scent late in the day are *Primula helodoxa* (Glory of the Marsh), which bears candelabra of bright yellow flowers; *Primula nutans*, whose lavender bells are borne on slender stems; and that old-fashioned double-flowered Primrose, 'Marie Crousse', that puts out a mass of rich purple-ruffled flowers edged with white. So strong and sweet is the scent it emits that you could be forgiven for thinking it came from a Cabbage Rose. Primulas are flowers of the spring and all prefer a cool, damp spot.

Many Honeysuckles fill the late spring and summer air with their honeyed scent. Finest among them are the Early Dutch (*Lonicera periclymenum* 'Belgica') and the Late Dutch (*L. periclymenum* 'Serotina') varieties. Early Dutch starts blooming in mid-May and finishes in summer, while Late Dutch begins its performance in mid-June and may not finish until autumn is almost here.

Both have rich, reddish-purple, yellow-flushed blooms, with a more intense red and creamier yellow in 'Serotina'.

Another Honeysuckle, an evergreen this time, that will scent the evening garden is *L. japonica Halliana*. This bears biscuit-yellow blooms in mid- to late summer, and their scent is intense on a warm night. Honeysuckles are marvellous for draping over overhead beams and pillars to soften and beautify them.

Try to find room for a tub, bowl or pot of Heliotrope, commonly called Cherry Pie. This bears deep violet-maroon-purple flowers, with an exceptionally sweet scent, on stocky stems 18in (45cm) high. You can sow seeds in early spring, and, once the plants are mature, you can take cuttings in late summer and overwinter them in a frost-free spot. These overwintered cuttings will flower earlier than plants grown from seed.

Clove-scented Pinks grown in clumps in spaces between paving slabs are generous dispensers of evening perfume. Some of the most strongly scented are the old garden varieties, such as shell-pink 'Inchmery', the 'overblown' double white 'Mrs Sinkins', and 'White Ladies', an amazingly free-flowering form laden with perfume. All these garden Pinks will do better if you give them a little lime (particularly if you have an acid soil) and some bonemeal to encourage vigorous growth.

Underfoot, you can plant Thymes so that they release their spicy aroma when you tread upon them. Peppermint is the smell that will come towards you when you brush your hands over *Thymus serpyllum* 'Annie Hall', which has bright pink flowers in summer. 'Pink Chintz' and reddish *T. serpyllum* 'Coccineus Major' are other var-

ieties you can use to carpet gaps in your patio paving.

The old shrub Roses are also gloriously fragrant. Particularly delicious are some of the Gallica Roses – the crimson and purple 'Charles de Mills', the dusky dark purple 'Cardinal de Richelieu' and the beautiful 'Belle de Crecy'. The first two grow into quite large bushes, but 'Belle de Crecy' seldom exceeds 3ft (0.9m) high and 3ft (0.9m) across. The Bourbon Roses and the old Hybrid Perpetuals also have several highly fragrant contenders: the shell pink 'La Reine Victoria', the warm pink with lilac 'Louise Odier' and the opulent, madder-crimson 'Mme Isaac Pereire'. Grow these vigorous (and quite thorny) bush Roses around the edge of your patio and they will fill it with their romantic, old-world perfume.

Roses, *above*, and Honeysuckle, *left*, are both gloriously fragrant and will add much to the balmy atmosphere of your evening patio.

Birds, bees and butterflies...

IF YOU ARE INTERESTED in helping to preserve the wildlife of our countryside, you could consider turning your patio garden into a miniature nature reserve. As modern farming methods destroy the meadows, hedgerows and woods that are the natural home of many birds, butterflies, moths and small creatures such as frogs, gardens of all sizes become ever more important in providing a safe home for these endangered species.

Many varieties of bird are easy to attract into a patio garden by offering food, and some kind of bird feeder can be provided even on a balcony garden or a window sill. In winter, particularly, the food provided by a thoughtful householder can be vital in ensuring the survival of the local bird population. A simple bird feeder can be made by filling half a coconut shell with a 'pudding' of table scraps and nuts bound together with dripping or lard. If you thread a string through the coconut holes before filling the shell with the pudding, you will then be able to hang it from a hook or a branch of a shrub or small tree. Tits, especially, will enjoy these coconut feeders. You can also hang a netting bag filled with scraps and nuts high up out of the reach of cats, and these will be enjoyed by a variety of small birds. If you can set up a bird table in your patio garden you will attract a greater variety of birds. All kinds of household table scraps can be given to your birds.

With luck this varied diet will attract to your bird table a surprising range of birds, even in a town garden. You can hope to see blackbirds, thrushes, chaffinches, several different varieties of tit, the house sparrow, robin, the greedy starling and perhaps even the shy little wren. Do not forget to put out a dish of fresh water – many birds die of thirst in winter when ponds are frozen over.

A bird feeder can do much to ensure the survival of your local birds, *top*. A Buddleia bush, *above*, will always attract bees as well as butterflies.

Remember, too, that birds eat many berries and seeds from the wild, and you can plant up your patio with plants and shrubs that will offer birds their natural food. Berberis and Cotoneaster are particularly suitable shrubs, and will provide attractive brightly coloured berries in autumn (until the birds devour them). Garden plants such as Honeysuckle, Sunflower, Scabious, Michaelmas Daisy and Antirrhinum will all provide birds with seeds to eat, as will wild plants, such as grasses, nettles, ragwort, teasels, blackberry and poppies.

As well as birds, you can attract bees and butterflies to your patio by planting the right kind of plants – those that are rich in nectar and often very sweetly scented. It may seem surprising that bees can be found in an urban setting, but many parks have their own beehives, and some keen bee-keepers will keep a hive on a roof garden or in a small town back garden. Bees will travel quite long distances in search of suitable food plants.

On the whole bees prefer blue flowers, and Common Sage is one of the best flowers of all for attracting bees. Lavender, Alyssum, Chives, Lemon Balm, Foxglove, Scabious, Thyme, Catmint, Teasels, French Marigolds and Nasturtium are all excellent bee plants and will give your patio a charming 'cottage-garden' effect.

Many of these bee plants will attract butterflies and moths to your garden as well. Butterflies find it difficult to feed from many of the double flowers found in gardens today, and they do not like red flowers. One of the best plants of all for attracting butterflies is the 'Butterfly Bush', or Buddleia, a hardy shrub that will grow almost anywhere. In late summer the mauve, honey-scented flower racemes of a Buddleia bush will attract Peacock butterflies, Painted Ladies, Red Admirals and Small Tortoiseshells. If left alone, a Buddleia will rapidly become too large for a small patio garden; it should be cut back hard almost to the ground each spring and, if it still grows too large, you can simply remove as many of the arching branches as you wish as they develop. On the whole, butterflies seem to prefer blue or mauve flowers. Plant a collection of Michaelmas Daisies, Catmint, Hyssop, Lavender, Scabious, Honesty, Marjoram, Heliotrope, Cornflower and Thyme to attract butterflies.

To provide the conditions butterflies need to breed, you must grow the plants the adult butterflies lay their eggs on, and on which the emerging caterpillars feed. Some of the commonest butterflies – and most colourful – lay their eggs on common stinging nettles. Plant a clump of these in a corner of your wildlife patio and you may attract a Red Admiral, a Peacock or a Small Tortoiseshell to lay its eggs there. Other, less common, butterflies that lay their eggs on nettles are the Comma and Painted Lady. A patch of Dock or Sorrel may be used by the Small Copper for egg laying.

While you will be fortunate if you can attract as many as half a dozen different butterflies to your wildlife patio, it is relatively easy to provide a home for many more moths. A very large number of moths seem to thrive in town gardens, given the right conditions, and many of them are very decorative. Most moths fly at night, and will feed on the night-scented flowers such as Honeysuckle, White Jasmine, Tobacco Plants and Night-scented Stock. Moths are not quite so specific as butterflies about the plants they will lay their eggs on, and a collection of wild plants such as Rosebay Willow-herb, Oxford Ragwort, Enchanter's Nightshade, Honeysuckle, Blackberry, Docks, Dandelions, Honesty, Plantains, Dead-nettles and grasses will support a wide range of moths.

You might also like to offer a home in your wildlife patio garden to that endearing little creature, the common frog. These have declined in number alarmingly in the last few years, and if you can provide a safe hatchery for even a few of them, this will help them to survive countrywide. It is a simple matter to set up a small pond – if you do not have one already an old sink or plastic baby bath sunk into the ground will serve very well. Put some earth at the bottom, and provide some washed stones or bricks in the water to give the little frogs somewhere to sit out of the water. Fill up the pond with rainwater. You can buy some

You can even rear frogs in your patio garden, *top*. The Red Admiral butterfly, *above*, loves to feed on plants such as *Sedum spectabile* 'Carmen'.

frog spawn or young tadpoles from your local pet shop in spring; at the same time buy some pond weed (to keep the water clear) and some live daphnia, which the tadpoles will feed on.

However small your patio, it can make a significant impact on the survival of wildlife in your area, at the same time allowing you to enjoy the sounds, sights and scents of the old country cottage garden.

Home and dry

GIVEN THE CHOICE, who would not prefer to use fresh herbs, rather than those that come freeze-dried in a packet? Herbs are at their very best used straight from the garden, but dried herbs can come a very close second. Not the dusty, faded relics sometimes available from grocers, though, but the real thing – home-grown herbs, dried at the peak of perfection and used within six to eight months, while they still retain their fresh green colour and pungent taste.

Stored in glass jars or hanging in bunches, they add a homely touch to any kitchen, while at the same time being on hand to liven up winter casseroles, soups and roasts. And you don't need a garden to cultivate herbs. Many varieties will grow happily in pots on the window-sill or a balcony.

Do-it-yourself drying is easy. Even on a first attempt it is possible to achieve perfect results every time, just by following a few basic guidelines. First, remember that not all herbs react well to drying. So which should you try?

Fortunately, most of the best culinary kinds do dry well. It might be worth working out which varieties you are likely to use, and roughly how much in a year, before getting started. And, while you're at it, why not dry small quantities of a few unusual herbs you may not have used

Above, Savory, fennel, sage, rosemary and lovage – even the tiniest garden can provide herbs for home drying.

before? You could also put your favourite herbal mixtures into small cheesecloth or muslin bags to make your own personalised bouquets garnis.

The choice is yours
The best results will be obtained from those culinary classics like parsley, chervil, marjoram, oregano, thyme, rosemary, sage, bay leaves and dill weed, which is just the foliage of ordinary dill.

More unusual varieties are lavender heads and leaves, for making infusions; scented geranium leaves, such as lemon or almond, to flavour cakes or salads; fennel and dill seeds for fish; or summer and winter savory. Savory has a piquant flavour rather like thyme, and is often used when cooking beans or other vegetables.

Other herbs useful for special teas and infusions are chamomile, which has a soothing and sedative effect; peppermint for stomach upsets; nettle as a tonic (but take care before using old plants!); and raspberry leaf, which makes a delicious, refreshing drink.

The time taken for herbs to dry varies slightly according to type, and is also affected by atmospheric humidity. But, on average, herbs dried naturally should take about seven to ten days or, in the oven, four to five hours. When 'done', herb leaves should feel brittle to the touch and crumble easily from their stems. Tough perennials, like bay and rosemary, may need a little extra help!

When you are freezing herbs, you can use small polythene bags, ice cube trays or plastic containers. Wash the herbs, and discard their stalks where necessary – there's no need to blanch them. Either chop them finely or use whole. If you are using ice cube trays, pack the trays first with chopped herbs, then cover with water. After freezing, take the cubes out of the trays and store in polythene bags in the freezer.

Preserve and protect

To de-stalk small-leaved herbs place the dried stems between two sheets of clean brown paper and go over them a couple of times with a rolling-pin. Stalks can then easily be picked out from the leaves. Make the paper into a funnel, and shoot the leaves into clean, dry, airtight jars. Plain glass jars must be kept out of sunlight, or your herbs will soon fade. Brown or green glass is kinder to their colour and will help preserve them.

Keep your stock cool and dry, and renew it every year – just as nature does.

Basil, chives, tarragon and mint are not quite so suitable for drying, as they lose most of their flavour in the process. However, these herbs can be put in bags in the freezer – frozen herbs give excellent results.

Pick of the crop

Herbs for drying should be harvested in early- or mid-summer, while the foliage is still young and a fresh green colour, and (except in the case of rosemary, where it doesn't seem to matter) before the plants start flowering. Avoid any shoots whose leaves are yellowing or diseased.

It is a good idea to wash herbs that may have been exposed to insect pests, traffic fumes, excessive dust or – even worse – cats and dogs. Better still, blanch the herbs by putting them in an enamel colander and dipping them in and out of rapidly boiling water. Rinse in cold water to refresh. This is not simply a hygienic measure: herbs treated in this way will also keep their colour better.

The traditional way to dry herbs is by tying them into small, loose bunches, and hanging them upside-down in a warm, dry, well-ventilated place away from direct sunlight. An airing cupboard, spare bedroom, shady conservatory or warm shed are the best places. Kitchens may be too humid, and greenhouses too sunny. However, even without an ideal spot in which to hang them, herbs can still be dried at home by laying them flat, and drying them in this way. Simply spread them out in thin layers on a sheet of plain brown paper, and turn them once daily during the drying process. Keep the temperature at 90°F (30°C) for the first 24 hours, then reduce this to 70°F (21°C) until drying is complete.

If space is limited, you can go one step further and 'force-dry' herbs in the oven. Just place the herbs on sheets of aluminium foil laid over the shelves, and set the oven to the lowest temperature. Or you can place the chopped herbs in a microwave on a double layer of kitchen paper and microwave on 'High' for 1½ minutes. Then remove from the oven and stir them with your fingers to check that they are completely dry.

Bunches of home-grown herbs hung up to dry in a north-facing room in late summer will add a decorative note, *above* and *top left* as well as providing freshly dried herbs to give piquancy to winter meals.

CHAPTER 7

Plant Postscripts

Start your own houseplant log book

Why bother to keep a houseplant log book, you may ask. Do it because it gives an instant handy growing guide as well as a precise record of your plants. By noting down their details you can anticipate their needs accurately and closely follow their progress over the years. These notes needn't take much time and they can really help you to improve your plants by reminding you exactly when and how to look after them – rather than in the haphazard way most of us treat them.

All you need to get going is a pen, a tape measure (you'll find out why later) and an empty address book, looseleaf file or some 5×3in (12×7cm) index cards and off you go. Like keeping a diary, it might at first seem difficult to find the time – but just like a diary, once it becomes a habit it's compulsive.

Putting a name to it
In alphabetical order, write down the name of the plant, plus its correct Latin botanical name – do you know it? Find out if you don't and write the names down alongside each other. Latin names are fascinating as they tell you some significant detail about each plant – perhaps its shape, or where it comes from originally.

Now jot down when you bought your new plant and the price, or who gave it to you. Remember to take your log book with you on shopping sprees and compare houseplant prices between shops and garden centres – this can be quite an eye-opener! Then, when you've had the plant for a while, you can look back to see where you got it and go back again if you had value for money.

Once you have a record of your plant's basic details, jot down what you should do to make it grow and flower to the absolute peak of perfection. First and foremost this means noting how much water it needs in summer and winter and how regularly – often there's a special little foible that a particular plant possesses. Add what type of fertiliser it needs, in what strength and, again, how often; when it flowers (if it does) and for how long; when it needs pruning, repotting and staking. All this will give you an at-a-glance guideline so you know how to look after your plant without guesswork or room for error. When you get your latest houseplant home – this is where that tape measure comes in – measure its height, and then, if you can, measure its diameter.

Then, in six months you can go through the process again and know exactly how much your plant has grown. If it should have grown and it hasn't, go to your records – check back over them and you should be able to spot where you went wrong. On the other hand, if your plant has grown

dramatically in all directions, you can feel justifiably proud and congratulate yourself on your wonderful green fingers.

By keeping a note of such points as when you water, you can be sure of giving precisely the right amount at the correct time and so avoid the commonest mistake of all, the dreadful crime of overwatering your plants.

Feeding and fertilisers
It can be even easier to forget when you last fed your plants, especially if you use those solid fertiliser sticks or tablets which last for about six weeks before needing to be replaced. Even a regular 14 day feeding routine can slip past unnoticed if you have been distracted by something like a holiday.

As it is impossible to remember the propagation details of all your plants, this is where a log book is really useful. You'll remind yourself of when a particular plant should be increased and how it is best done. By trying different methods for the same plant you'll get a good idea which is the most successful, both in the time it takes to root and for getting the healthiest plants in the quickest way. Also you can keep a check on the plants you have propagated over the years. Who knows, you might discover how Great Aunt Sally gets the Bizzy Lizzy cutting you gave her to grow into a huge year-round flowering plant, while you are lucky if yours flowers for two weeks!

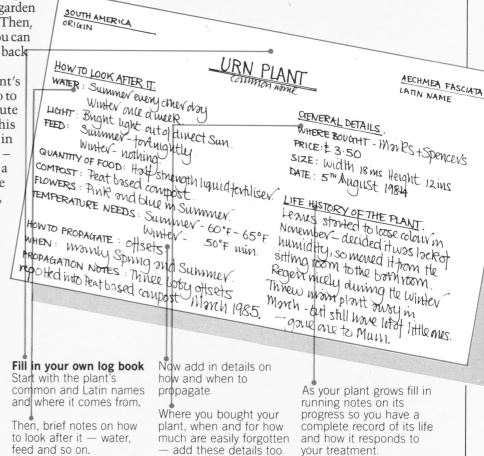

SOUTH AMERICA
ORIGIN

URN PLANT
common name

AECHMEA FASCIATA
LATIN NAME

HOW TO LOOK AFTER IT:
WATER : Summer every other day
Winter once a week
LIGHT : Bright light out of direct Sun.
FEED : Summer - fortnightly
Winter - nothing.
QUANTITY OF FOOD : Half strength liquid fertiliser.
COMPOST : Peat based compost.
FLOWERS : Pink and blue in Summer.
TEMPERATURE NEEDS : Summer - 60°F - 65°F
Winter - 50°F min.
HOW TO PROPAGATE : offsets
WHEN : mainly Spring and Summer
PROPAGATION NOTES : Three baby offsets
rooted into peat based compost
March 1985.

GENERAL DETAILS.
WHERE BOUGHT - Marks + Spencers
PRICE : £3.50
SIZE : Width 18ins Height 12ins
DATE : 5TH August 1984

LIFE HISTORY OF THE PLANT.
Leaves started to loose colour in
November - decided it was lack of
humidity, so moved it from the
sitting room to the bathroom.
Regrew nicely during the winter
Threw main plant away in
March - but still have lots of little ones.
- gave one to Mum.

Fill in your own log book
Start with the plant's common and Latin names and where it comes from.

Then, brief notes on how to look after it — water, feed and so on.

Now add in details on how and when to propagate.

Where you bought your plant, when and for how much are easily forgotten — add these details too.

As your plant grows fill in running notes on its progress so you have a complete record of its life and how it responds to your treatment.

KNOW YOUR HOUSEPLANT TERMS

Acid
Refers to soil/potting mixture/water, with a pH value below 7.0; indicates the absence of lime or other alkaline material (see *pH scale*).

Aerial roots
Roots growing on stems above the level of the soil. They serve a dual purpose: providing support by clinging to tree branches and for extracting moisture from the air. Often seen in Philodendrons.

Alkaline
Refers to soil/potting mixture/water, with a pH value above 7.0; generally indicates the presence of lime (see *pH scale*).

Annual
A plant which is grown from seed to flower within one year, after which it dies. Examples Capsicum and Celosia.

Areole
Peculiar to the Cactus family, a cushion-like sideshoot carrying hair and/or spines. Each areole flowers only once.

Axil
The angle between the leaf and its stem; any new growth from an axil is called an axillary.

Biennial
A plant that completes its cycle within two growing seasons.

Bloom
A harmless powdery or waxy coating on leaves or fruit of certain plants, usually of a whitish or bluish colour.

Bract
A modified leaf backing or surrounding a flower, often highly colourful and long-lasting. Example Poinsettia.

Bromeliads
Relatives of the pineapples, these are epiphytic plants (see *epiphyte*) which can grow supported on tree bark, without the need for soil.

Bud
An immature flower or leaf, often protected by overlapping scales.

Bulbil
A small immature bulb either at the base of mature bulbs or on the stems; a term also loosely applied to the leafy plantlets of certain ferns.

Calyx
The leaves surrounding a flower – usually green.

Capillary action
The natural physical force which causes water to move in narrow tubes, for example from the roots of a plant to its leaves.

Chlorosis
A condition in which leaves become pallid; an indication of insufficient nutrients in the soil.

Compost
Either decomposed plant remains or the mixture of soil and other ingredients used to grow plants in pots.

Compound
A leaf made up of two or more distinct parts called leaflets, or a flower composed of many florets.

Corm
The swollen base of a plant's stem which stores food and protects new growth; it fulfils the same function as a bulb.

Crown
Area at the base or centre of a plant from which top growth and roots emerge. Example Saintpaulia.

Cultivar
A variety of plant that has been artificially bred.

Cutting
A portion of stem or root used to propagate new roots which will develop into a mature plant (see also *leaf cutting*).

Deciduous
Plants which shed their leaves when inactive (usually during winter) producing new ones the following spring.

Division
Method of growing new plants by splitting the roots of a mature plant and potting the sections separately.

Dormancy
A temporary state of total inactivity, sometimes accompanied by a withering away of the top growth.

Drawn
A condition due to inadequate light or over-crowding; the stems become elongated and spindly.

Epiphyte
An 'air plant' generally living on tree branches or shallow moss, and deriving moisture and nutrients from the air and decaying matter, although not parasitic.

Evergreen
A plant that retains its leaves all year round.

Floret
A single flower that is one of many making up a larger compound flower head. Example the Daisy family.

Foliage plant
A plant that is grown indoors to display the beauty of its leaves.

Foliar feed
Liquid fertiliser that is sprayed onto leaves and is rapidly absorbed; it may also be taken up by the roots.

Forcing
The use of heat and/or light to induce growth or flowering ahead of the natural season; a term applied to spring bulbs.

Frond
An alternative term to describe the leaf of a fern or palm.

Fungicide
A chemical used to prevent disease and/or destroy fungus growth.

Genus
A botanical grouping of plants with similar characteristics; each is sub-divided into separate species.

Germination
The earliest stage of plant growth; when a seed begins to sprout.

Grafting
Joining a detached stem or shoot of one plant onto another that is still rooted.

Growing point
The point at which extension growth occurs; usually the tip of a stem or bud.

Hardy
Plants which are tolerant of cool conditions, many capable of surviving frost.

Heeled cutting
A cutting taken by pulling a sideshoot from the main stem with a strip of bark and wood attached.

Herbaceous
A plant that has a soft non-woody stem, and generally loses its top growth during winter.

Hybrid
A plant produced by cross-breeding two plants of different species or genera.

Hydroculture
A method of growing plants without soil; instead the pot is filled with pebbles and the plants are fed nutrients during watering.

Inflorescence
A head, cluster, spike or similar collection of small flowers grouped together on one main stem.

Insecticide   A chemical or organic substance used to combat insect pests.

Leaf cutting   A leaf (usually with stalk attached) used in propagation.

Leaflet   Any segment of a compound leaf.

Leaf mould   A component of some potting mixtures, consisting entirely of rotted leaves.

Leggy   A term describing spindly growth, when the stems are bare towards the base.

Midrib   The central vein (often raised) of a leaf, dividing it into two halves.

Moss pole   A plastic or wooden tube wrapped in moss, valued for its capacity to hold water and for training climbing plants.

Node   A joint or swelling on the stem of a plant from which leaves, buds or side-shoots appear.

Offset   A small plant that grows from its parent. It can be detached and grown separately.

Palmate   Three or more leaflets arising from a single point of attachment on the leaf-stalk, an arrangement resembling a hand. Example Fatsia japonica.

Peat   Partially decayed organic matter, valued in potting mixture for its capacity to retain air and moisture.

Perennial   A plant that lives for three seasons or more, usually indefinitely.

pH scale   A scale measuring acidity and alkalinity.

Photosynthesis   The process by which the leaves of a plant are nourished, requiring water, air and light.

Pinching out   The removal of a stem's growing point in order to encourage bushy growth from the dormant buds lower down.

Pinnate   Refers to a compound leaf with pairs of leaflets carried on opposite sides of the stem; if the leaflets are then further divided the whole leaf is called bipinnate.

Pot-bound   The crowding of roots within a pot which usually prevents healthy growth; some plants however do flourish if slightly pot-bound.

Potting on   The transferring of a plant to a larger container, allowing continued growth of the roots.

Propagation   The formation of a new plant from seed, or by using cuttings from a mature plant.

Pruning   The cutting back of a plant to encourage bushiness, better flowering and a more compact shape.

Repotting   Transferring a plant to a new container or renewing the soil, in order to revitalise growth.

Rest period   A season when a plant is relatively inactive, retaining its foliage but producing little or no new growth – compare *dormancy*.

Rhizome   A fleshy, usually horizontal stem (below ground); it is used as a storage organ and produces new buds and roots.

Rootball   A mass of potting mixture crowded with roots (as seen when a plant is taken from its pot).

Rosette   A cluster of leaves radiating from the centre, either on individual stalks or in an overlapping spiral. Example Echeveria, Saintpaulias.

Runner   An above-ground horizontal stem which roots at intervals to form new plants.

Scurf   Minute scales or particles on the foliage giving it a dusty, or mealy, appearance.

Sharp sand   A coarse sand, free of lime, sometimes used in potting mixture.

Spadix   A particular kind of flower spike (usually in the Arum family); a fleshy column with minute flowers spread over it.

Spathe   A large, often colourful, bract which surrounds and protects the spadix.

Species   A sub-division of a genus of plants, forming a distinct type; they are self-fertilising, and two plants of the same species can produce viable seed.

Sphagnum moss   A spongy bog moss used in the cultivation of houseplants because of its high capacity to hold water.

Spike   A flowerhead in which the flowers are virtually stalkless.

Spore   The tiny, single reproductive cell produced by such plants as ferns and mosses.

Stipule   A sheath which protects growth points, usually drying up and falling off when no longer needed. Example Begonia.

Stolon   A shoot that runs over the potting mixture carrying a new plant at its tip; differing from runners in that runners can root at their nodes and at their extremities.

Stomata   Microscopic breathing pores of plants, mostly found on the undersides of leaves.

Succulent   Plants with fleshy stems or leaves that function as water-storage organs. Example the Cactus family.

Sucker   A shoot that arises from below ground level and develops leaves and roots of its own.

Systemic   An insecticide sprayed onto leaves or watered onto the potting compost which enters the sap killing insects that feed on plant tissue.

Tendril   A thin but wiry organ which twines around a support and holds the plant firm. Leafstalks can act as tendrils.

Top-dressing   Replacing the top layer of soil or potting mixture in order to freshen the plant's growing medium.

Tuber   An underground swollen stem/root which stores food and enables the plant to survive over winter, and produce new growth next year.

Variegated   A term which refers to plants with patterned, spotted or blotchy leaves.

Vein   A strand of thicker tissue in a leaf which distributes moisture and nutrients.

Viviparous   Producing plantlets, without the need for seed, usually on the leaves or stems of the parent plant.

Whorl   A radiating arrangement of three or more leaves or flowers around a node on a plant's stem.

Xerophyte   Plants that are able to withstand very dry conditions. Example Tillandsia, Aechmea, Vriesea (air plants).

A case for transport

THE BEGINNING of the 19th century was the golden age of plant hunters, or as some people at the time preferred to call them, 'botanical travellers'. They were usually well educated, often very wealthy men, determined at virtually any cost to obtain plants that were unknown in cultivation. Huge conservatories were being constructed to house the treasures, and techniques had been mastered on the best ways of caring for the plants once they were brought into the country.

Prior to 1835, however, the business of transporting plants from one continent to another was a very hazardous one – they had to be transported by sailing ship, on the decks when space and the weather permitted and in the holds when it didn't. Packing was, by today's standards, pretty primitive (the plants usually travelled in slatted-sided wooden boxes, sometimes with crude glass tops), and on deck the plants were at risk from salt spray (not to mention the possibility of full-sized waves suddenly engulfing the decks). In the hold, lack of light could be just as deadly. Inexperienced officers aboard ship were detailed to look after plants that were often unknown quantities. Thousands of plants survived the journeys but hundreds of thousands perished.

An amateur naturalist inadvertently stumbled upon the solution to this problem. Nathaniel Bagshaw Ward, a doctor who practised in the dockland area of East London, had buried a butterfly chrysalis in some moist soil in a wide-mouthed bottle with a metal lid. He was surprised to find that within a week or two of setting up the bottle, some grass and a fernling had germinated in the soil. They lived inside the unopened bottle unattended for four years, until the metal lid rusted away.

Ward quickly appreciated what was happening: moisture was evaporating from the soil, condensing on the glass and trickling back to the soil. Theories about how plants lived were being shattered – it was clear that they could live without fresh air, for example. There was also an important practical consequence. Within closed cases, plants could be protected from all the problems of the outside world.

Two cases were constructed for transporting plants by sea to Australia; and the plants arrived in perfect condition. The cases were refilled with Australian ferns and shrubs, and in 1834 these journeyed through snow, ice and lashing waves on the deck of the ship as it rounded Cape Horn, through temperatures of 100°F (38°C) off Rio, to arrive safely eight months later in England in a temperature of around 40°F (5°C). Ward had hit upon the perfect way of bringing home tropical plants, and the Wardian case became a vital part of plant collecting. Later it became invaluable for sending plants from Kew Gardens to stock vast areas of the world with useful plants such as tea, coffee and rubber.

In the home, too, Wardian cases became a vital feature. Glass cases, modelled on the principle of the bottle but shaped like today's domestic aquaria, with sides and tops made from sheets of glass, were constructed to grow the more delicate thin-leaved ferns within the home in an environment protected from harmful domestic gas fumes.

A Victorian Wardian case, *above*, makes an elegant home for a collection of ferns. The modern case, *top*, is useful for displaying a number of tender plants.

Occasionally today you can still see a genuine Wardian case – in 1964 one was shown at the Chelsea Flower Show filled with colourful tropical plants including a miniature orange tree in full fruit. The original travelling cases were capable of being closed off completely, while the more decorative cases had access provided (and even clever watering devices built in). Today's equivalent are called terraria and come in glass or clear plastic, in all shapes and sizes. Although we no longer need to protect our houseplants from noxious gas fumes, growing in glazed containers remains very popular. When planting up a bottle garden, brandy balloon, sweet jar or old fish tank spare a thought for Dr Ward. No one seems to know or care, however, what happened to the butterfly chrysalis that started it all.

Plants of the rain forest

MANY OF OUR popular houseplants – such as Bromeliads, Begonias, Peperomias, Philodendrons and Pileas – grow in the wild as 'Epiphytes' in the steamy atmosphere of the tropical rain forests.

Epiphytes grow on other plants, but they are not parasites – they rely on their 'hosts' for anchorage only and take no nutrients from them. Most Epiphytes get their nourishment partly from the moist air and partly from the debris that collects around the leaf bases and roots. They can be found in any niche capable of supporting a plant and some make aerial roots to extract moisture from the air.

Rain forests are made up of several layers. The tops of the tallest trees soak up much of the sun, bear the brunt of tropical rain storms and winds, and provide shelter for the lower layers of trees and shrubs. Creepers and ground-hugging plants are at the bottom.

The rain forest is consistently warm. Dappled sun penetrates the upper layers, the air is heavily charged with moisture and there is virtually no difference between winter and summer. Some plants have developed a particular leaf shape to shed the virtually constant drip from the foliage of neighbouring plants. It rains regularly, but the water quickly drains away, and it is rare for plants to become waterlogged.

Some Epiphytes live high up in the top layers of the forest canopy. Here they are subject to hot direct sun, but the nights are much cooler and drying winds quickly rob them of the benefits of yesterday's rain. These plants develop tough, leathery leaves, often covered with scurf-like scales. Others live in the shelter of the canopy, and these usually have thinner, softer and smoother leaves.

Air plants such as Tillandsias, near the top of the trees, have virtually no roots and rely on the grey scales on their leaves to absorb all of their water and food needs. Bird's Nest Fern (*Asplenium nidus*) and Staghorn Fern (*Platycerium bifurcatum* and *P.grande*) are dramatic plants. The Bird's Nest Fern develops wide shiny fronds 3-4 ft (0.9-1.2 m) long (above a spongy mass of roots) spilling out from its host's branches. Staghorns make two kinds of fronds, the very

decorative antler-shaped kind (they are the fertile fronds that carry spores), and disc-shaped ones that grasp tree limbs and trap fallen leaves and other wastes on which they feed. Philodendrons climb up tree trunks and along the limbs by means of stout aerial roots, produced at every leaf joint, and their leaves are angled to collect maximum sunlight.

Because water and atmospheric moisture are plentiful, Epiphytes do not require an extensive root system. Instead, their roots cling tenaciously to the host plant, penetrating any fissure available and otherwise spreading out to soak up moisture. Soil is not needed, although the nutrients from forest debris are absorbed before they are leached away by the heavy rains.

Aeschynanthus and Columnea seed blown by the wind or deposited by birds into small pockets of moss or humus will sprout and quickly festoon large sections of tree branches. Here too can be found Peperomias, Begonias and Pileas and many other tropical plants, subsisting on very little soil but picking up their water and food needs in quite a different way to our garden plants and making a very flamboyant show of it.

To retain the rain forest's moisture, Bromeliads have evolved a central urn in the base of their leaves, in which water collects. These urns also act as drinking and bathing stations for many creatures. They can be filled with very murky 'soup' until flushed out by heavy rain.

It is a tribute to the adaptability of these plants that they are able to grow and thrive in a completely different environment — our living rooms.

The hot and humid tropical rain forest, *top picture*, is the natural home of the epiphytic Bromeliads, *above*, which have become popular houseplants.

How plants came in from the cold

THE POPULARITY of the pot plant as a decorative feature in the home has increased spectacularly since the end of the Second World War. Pot plants were of course an essential feature of Victorian living rooms, but the history of growing plants indoors goes back much further than that.

As early as the 16th century orangeries were being built in the great gardens of Europe. These were buildings designed to house exotic plants – mainly orange trees – that could not survive the winter outdoors, and they were often heated (indeed, they were sometimes called 'stoves'). As their popularity grew, in the late 17th and early 18th centuries, they became an essential adjunct to the grand country houses of the aristocracy, and a place where the ladies of the house could take a promenade in cold or wet weather.

Towards the end of the 18th century it was realised that plants needed plenty of natural light if they were to be grown indoors permanently. A new building technique then being developed enabled the first glasshouses to be built. These were metal (or sometimes timber) framed structures with sheet glass as infill. One of the earliest, and most elegant, was erected at Bicton in Devon about 1820. This was a semi-circular construction, backed on to a brick wall, and high enough to grow palm trees and other large plants inside. It was followed in 1840 by the great glass-house at Chatsworth, in Derbyshire, designed by the Duke of Devonshire's gardener Joseph Paxton (who later designed the vast Crystal Palace that housed the Great Exhibition of 1851). Many other, smaller, glasshouses were built during the 19th century, and a number of these – called conservatories – were attached to the main house, and formed a garden room.

As the idea of the conservatory spread (and as glass became cheaper) even the humblest home would have its mini conservatory – perhaps no more than a glass sided extension to the living room, or even a miniature glass-house fitting around a sash window. The impetus to grow exotic plants in the home received a tremendous boost from the spread of botanic gardens, where the general public could see growing outside and under glass the many exciting plants brought back from tropical and sub-tropical regions by the plant hunters of the 18th and 19th centuries.

The Botanic Garden at Kew was founded in 1759 and opened to the public in 1841. There visitors were able to marvel at the extraordinary range of tropical ferns, orchids and succulents on view; the Victorians took to palms, aspidistras, ferns, ivies and other foliage plants en masse, and a pot plant in the living room became the rage.

Snuffed out by gaslight

With the introduction of gas lighting, however, disaster threatened the indoor plant life. The incandescent gas mantels gave off toxic fumes and only the hardiest of plants, such as the aspidistra, could survive in this atmosphere. Fortunately help was at hand with the invention of the remarkable Wardian case – the sealed glass container that provided a micro climate in which precious plants such as rare ferns, caladiums, dracaeas, coleus and selaginellas could thrive protected from fumes and draughts.

After the First World War interest in houseplants dwindled, probably partly as a reaction against Victorianism. The current return to favour of the pot plant has almost certainly been helped by the widespread introduction of domestic central heating, which enables tropical and sub-tropical plants to be grown with relative ease. Modern architecture also favours large, picture windows that provide the natural light that plants need, and now that so many people live in flats in cities, the indoor plant offers a reassuring contact with nature.

The Palm House, Edinburgh Botanic Garden, and, *inset*, tree ferns in the glasshouse at Tatton Park, Cheshire.

The growth of mythology

THE EXTRAORDINARY INVISIBLE POWER that directs plant life, triggering seeds to sprout and grow, and mature plants to bear flowers and fruits, has been a potent source of myth and legend throughout Man's history. An archetypal 'earth mother' figure that cares for the earth and its crops is common to the mythologies of many cultures. To the ancient Greeks, this earth mother figure was Demeter (the Romans called her Ceres), and the annual cycle of seasons was explained by the myth of Persephone, Demeter's daughter. While Persephone was gathering flowers one day she was seized by Hades, god of the Underworld, and carried off to his gloomy kingdom beneath the earth. As Demeter searched frenziedly all over the earth for her daughter, the crops shrivelled and failed. Zeus, king of the gods, seeing that disaster threatened the world, sent Hermes to bring Persephone back from the Underworld. Unhappily, while she was in Hades' power, Persephone had eaten four seeds of a pomegranate – and was so condemned to return to the Underworld for four months every year. In the myth Persephone represented the corn seed, which disappeared into the bare earth during the winter, but emerged in the spring to grow and bear a crop.

In Norse mythology a mighty ash tree – called Yggdrasil – grows at the centre of the world, its branches spreading over the entire earth and its roots reaching down into the country of the dead. This world tree, connecting heaven, earth and hell, is found in other mythologies, such as that of the North American Indians, and it is possible that it forms the basis of the European maypole ceremonies, when young people dance around a ribbon-decked maypole on the first day of May. The fairytale of 'Jack and the Beanstalk', in which Jack climbs an enormous beanstalk to find himself in a land of giants, is also thought to derive from the myth of the world tree.

Many plants have a special significance in the mythologies of the ancient world. In Greece the fragrant Amaranth was sacred to the goddess Artemis, and its blossom was a symbol of immortality; it was used to adorn tombs and statues of the gods. Another plant from the Mediterranean region, the Olive, is to this day recognised as a symbol of peace. Ivy was a plant the Greeks held in particularly high esteem. It was dedicated to Bacchus, the god of wine, probably because it was thought that an infusion of the plant would counteract the effects of drunkenness. Greek poets were garlanded with a crown of Ivy, and in the Greek marriage ceremony the bride and groom were presented with a wreath of Ivy – it represented fidelity.

For centuries houses have been decorated with Holly and Ivy at Christmas, a practice frowned on by the Church, since it probably originated with the pagan Druids, who decorated their huts with evergreens in the winter to welcome the sylvan spirits.

Mistletoe also has pagan connections. For the Druids it was a sacred plant, capable of warding off evil. Young men would carry branches of mistletoe from hut to hut to welcome the new year – and the practice of bringing Mistletoe into the house at Christmas probably derives from this ancient custom.

Planted on the roof, Houseleek, *above*, was thought to protect the house from lightning. An arrow of Mistletoe, *right*, killed Balder, the Norse god of peace. After he was restored to life, Mistletoe was given to the goddess of love, who decreed that all who passed under it should receive a kiss.

The magic of plants

FROM EARLIEST TIMES Man has believed in magic and the supernatural and has enlisted the forces inherent in plant life to help him invoke the powers of good and evil. Witchcraft and magic were widely practised in medieval Britain, and many of the rituals used have been handed down to us in the *grimoires* – the ancient books of magic ceremonies. 'High magic' was used to invoke demons and spirits to carry out the magician's instructions – and in the elaborate ceremonies involved, plants and herbs had a crucial role. Magic potions – distilled from plants – would be drunk by the magician to help conjure the spirits to appear. Almost certainly, the plants used would contain hallucinatory drugs that could encourage the illusion of a visit from the supernatural world. In other rituals a mixture of herbs would be burnt producing a strange-smelling incense, that was thought essential for invoking the spirits. And while chanting his incantations to the demons, the magician would trace the occult signs necessary for his spell with a magic wand made of hazelwood.

There's no doubt that the hallucinatory drugs contained in plants such as Henbane and Deadly Nightshade were (and probably still are in some primitive societies) essential for the practice of witchcraft. The alkaloids they contain can produce the illusion of being changed into an animal – or a toad. A witch who chewed laurel or aconite leaves (both of them poisonous) would experience a series of convulsive fits and delirium – suggesting to observers that she was possessed by demons. The practice had its dangers, however. Too much of the poison would result in death.

Among ordinary country people the practice of 'low magic' was fairly widespread in the Middle Ages. This usually involved nothing more sinister than devising amulets to be worn as protection against evil spirits, and concocting love potions to secure the affections of a reluctant swain. To guard the wearer against spells and demons, a little amulet made out of red cloth would be filled with dried artemisia, betony and peony, and worn on a ribbon round the neck. The Periwinkle – known as the 'Sorcerer's Violet' – was believed to be very potent in exorcising evil spirits, and was also used in love potions. Its reputation for warding off demons went back to Roman times. In an ancient Latin Herbal by Apuleius, published in English in the 15th century, we read that 'This wort [herb] is of good advantage…against devil sickness and demonical possessions …if thou hast the wort with thee thou shalt be prosperous and ever acceptable.'

One of the most famous magical plants – and with one of the longest histories – is the Mandrake, or 'Satan's Apple'. The drug contained in Mandrake can produce the sensation of flying – probably giving rise to the belief that witches flew through the air at night on a broomstick. Its root can extend a staggering 5ft (1.5m) below ground and, because it is often forked, it was thought to resemble the human form. The ancient Greeks believed that if you fell down the hole left after the Mandrake was dug up, you would come out in Hades. In medieval times it was believed that anyone who dug up a Mandrake root would die, since the root emitted a scream on being tugged from the earth that was fatal to hear. Nevertheless pieces of Mandrake root, carved into fancy shapes as amulets, were thought to possess magical powers and were highly sought after. Since Mandrake root was hard to come by, pieces of Bryony root were often passed off as Mandrake, and in Henry VIII's reign, little images of Bryony root, shaped into the figure of a man, changed hands at high prices.

The sinister-looking and aptly named Deadly Nightshade, *main picture*, **contains a powerful hallucinatory drug that encouraged medieval witches to believe they could change into an animal. Little figures carved from the Mandrake root,** *inset* **(from a 15th-century book illustration), were prized for their supposedly magical properties.**

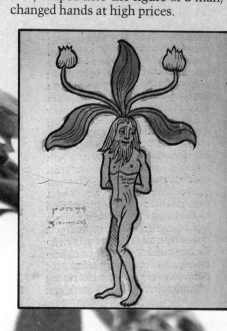

Old wives' tales

HANDED DOWN FROM GENERATION to generation by word of mouth, the ancient wisdom of gardeners is a mixture of common sense, based on practical experience, and superstition. Surprisingly, much of this gardening folk lore is now found to contain an element of scientific justification.

If you plant trailing Nasturtiums among your plants, the saying goes, you will not be troubled with whitefly. Although this sounds like a piece of superstitious nonsense, it seems to work – the deterrent may in fact be the volatile oil that is exhaled by the Nasturtium's leaves. Growing garlic among other plants is an ancient remedy for greenfly – even a single clove planted under a rosebush will protect it. It seems that the garlic roots may give out a substance that is absorbed by the rose's roots – and it is this that repels the greenfly. At any rate, this piece of gardening folk lore is (by some writers) guaranteed to work.

The old belief that seeds should be sown with a waxing moon (between new moon and full moon) was probably based on sound observation. Nowadays it also seems to be borne out by scientific research, which has established that the moon's phases affect the earth's magnetic field – which in turn affects plant growth. As plants are full of water, they are influenced by lunar rhythms in the same way that the tides of the oceans are.

Another curious piece of country lore is that old hair – either from animals or humans – placed in the bottom of a trench before planting beans would greatly improve the crop; science has now established that hair is rich in minerals and other elements essential for healthy growth. Banana skins (which are full of trace elements needed for growth) have long had a reputation for being good for roses if

Garlic, *above*, is said to have sprung up to mark Satan's first footprint outside the Garden of Eden. Planted under rosebushes, such as the Queen of Denmark, *inset*, it is reputed to deter greenfly.

they are buried beneath the bush; and a particularly tall story has been told about beer dregs (full of yeast) having a sensational effect when thrown on Hollyhocks – which then grew to over 18ft (5.4m).

Often regarded by modern gardeners as a useless weed, the wild Foxglove was highly prized in old cottage gardens in the belief that it stimulated the growth of surrounding plants and helped them to resist disease. Foxgloves were also thought to improve the keeping qualities of fruit and vegetables grown near them. It seems that Foxgloves do have some special qualities; modern flower arrangers know that including a few Foxgloves will ensure that the whole arrangement lasts much longer than usual. If Foxglove flowers are not wanted, the same effect can be achieved by infusing a handful of Foxglove leaves in boiling water, and adding the cooled liquid to the flower water.

The little Mexican Marigold, *Tagetes minuta*, was often to be seen in old cottage gardens growing as an edging along paths and flower beds. Old gardening lore has it that the Marigold controls weeds such as Ground Ivy and Couch Grass. But the more scientific gardener of today may be interested to know that the Marigold's scent, and the secretions of its roots, both have a beneficial effect on other plants growing in their vicinity. And, to give the old wives the last word, Marigolds growing among tomatoes will keep away whitefly.

The healing plant

THE HISTORY OF MEDICINE is inextricably linked with Man's discovery that infusions, lotions, potions and ointments made from plants had amazing healing and curative effects on injury and illness. The herbals of the ancient world that described plants and their qualities were not botanical or culinary manuals but medical reference books. The great physicians of ancient Greece and Rome – Hippocrates, Dioscorides and Galen – researched and recorded a great mass of information on the healing properties of plants, much of which is still valid today.

The pretty little wild flower Eyebright, for instance, has been valued for centuries for its properties as an eye medicine capable of preserving and improving eyesight. For many herbalists of the 16th century Eyebright was regarded as the specific cure for all eye diseases – and even today it is still recommended by modern herbalists for eye complaints. A simple preparation of 1oz (28g) of its leaves infused in 1 pint (0.5 litres) of boiling water makes a lotion that can be used (when cooled) to bathe the eyes three or four times a day – helpful in cases of tired or inflamed eyes.

The 17th-century physician and herbalist Nicholas Culpeper esteemed Eyebright so highly that he wrote in his famous *Herbal*:

> If the herb was but as much used as it is neglected, it would half spoil the spectacle maker's trade and a man would think that reason should teach people to prefer the preservation of their natural before their artificial spectacles . . .

Culpeper maintained that taking 'the juice or distilled water of the Eyebright . . . inwardly in white wine, or both, or dropped into the eyes for several days together helpeth all infirmities of the eye that causes dimness of sight.' He also believed that it 'strengthens the weak brain or memory'.

The traditional belief that Eyebright was good for the eyes was based on the ancient Doctrine of Signatures, which maintained that a plant carried on it signs of the affliction, or part of the body, that it would cure. 'The purple and yellow spots and stripes which are upon the flowers of the Eyebright,' the author of one ancient reference book tells us, 'doth very much resemble the diseases of the eye, as bloodshot, etc., by which signature it has been found out that this herb is effectual for the curing of the same.'

Lungwort good for lungs

According to the Doctrine of Signatures another common plant, Lungwort, was said to be an excellent remedy for lung disease – since the pale blotches on its leaves were thought to resemble diseased lungs. Even today a modern herbalist might prescribe an infusion of the leaves as a remedy for coughs and congested lungs.

A preparation from the Aloe plant is a very ancient purgative medicine that has been used since the time of ancient Greece. It was certainly in use in the UK in Anglo-Saxon times (it was recommended to Alfred the Great by the Patriarch of Jerusalem), and by the 19th century it formed the basis of many common domestic proprietary medicines. It is still used in several preparations that appear in the official pharmaceutical list in the UK and US, and is widely used in veterinary practice as a purgative for horses.

A preparation from *Aloe vera, below,* has long been used as a purgative. Lily-of-the-Valley, *right*, yields a drug that regulates the heart.

The flowers of the Lily-of-the-Valley yield a drug used in modern medicine to stimulate the heart. Safer than some other drugs used for the same purpose, the Lily-of-the-Valley drug regulates the action of a weak or disturbed heart, and at the same time strengthens it. Traditionally, Lily-of-the-Valley has been recommended as a remedy for many ailments, and water distilled from its flowers was known as 'Golden Water' and was thought to be imbued with very special properties. After describing how to steep the flowers in 'New Wine for the space of a month' one 17th-century writer claimed that the resulting wine was:

> more precious than gold, for if any one that is troubled with apoplexy drink thereof with six grains of Pepper and a little Lavender water they shall not need to fear it that month.

The 16th-century herbalist Gerard claimed that Lily-of-the-Valley water cured gout, and Culpeper recommended it for inflammations of the eye. He also believed that it 'strengthens the brain and renovates a weak memory' and that:

> The spirit of the flowers, distilled in wine, restoreth lost speech, helps the palsy, and is exceedingly good in the apoplexy, comforteth the heart and vital spirits.

The Violet is another attractive little wild flower that has a long medical history. A syrup made from its flowers was a popular laxative given to infants in the 19th century. Earlier herbalists maintained that Syrup of Violets was effective for a wide range of ailments, including jaundice, epilepsy, pleurisy, sleeplessness and ague. And, according to Gerard, Syrup of Violets 'has power to ease inflammation, roughness of the throat and comforteth the heart, assuageth the pains of the head and causeth sleep.'

Although many of these herbal remedies may seem quaint to us now, modern medicine is nevertheless based on the knowledge amassed by the old herbalists. A surprising number of medicines in the present-day official British Pharmaceutical list include extracts drawn from plants. And even where new drugs have been synthesised, in many cases they imitate, and were inspired by, the action of a traditional natural drug supplied by the plant world.

The purple and yellow blotches and stripes on the flower of Eyebright, *right*, were thought to be signs of the diseases of the eye that the plant would cure. A syrup made of Violets, *below*, used to be a popular laxative.

THE FOUNDATIONS OF MODERN MEDICINE are to be found in the old herbals. From earliest times, physicians had classified the wealth of accumulated knowledge about the curative properties of plants; in the 5th century BC Hippocrates, the 'father of medicine', compiled a record of over 400 plants and herbs valued for their ability to cure illness or alleviate pain. The Romans continued this tradition by cataloguing the herbal remedies of each land that they occupied.

By the 15th century, pharmacists (known as *aromatarii*, because the materials they sold were aromatic substances extracted from plants) were doing business all over Europe. The process for distilling pure alcohol had been discovered a century earlier, and this proved of great advantage to the pharmacists; many of the active principles in medicinal plants dissolve more readily in alcohol than in water. In addition, the discovery of new lands meant that a greater variety of new plants became available to the pharmacists. By the time that the New and Old Worlds had been thoroughly explored, the number of natural plants with known pharmaceutical action was enormous.

Up to the 18th century, physicians relied almost exclusively upon herbal and plant medicines; their bible was a huge work published in 1597 by the London herbalist John Gerard, which listed thousands of plants with curative properties. By the 19th century chemistry had advanced to the stage at which the molecular structures of individual plants could be identified; as a result major advances were made in understanding the healing qualities of some plant extracts and it was not long before chemists were able to put this knowledge to good use.

An excellent example of how medicine has profited from the plant world is aspirin. As far back as 2000 years ago a brew made from White Willow leaves was recommended for gout, or general aches and pains. During the 18th century chemists isolated in the plant one particular element (known as acetylsalicylic acid) that is capable of regulating the body's defence mechanisms – so reducing pain. This 'wonder drug' was eventually synthesised in 1899 as aspirin; and today this is the most common fever-reducing drug used both in the hospital pharmacy and in the home.

The British Pharmaceutical Society publishes a compre-

hensive list of all the approved medicines and drugs manufactured by the pharmaceutical industry, with details of their ingredients. Included in the *British Pharmacopoeia* are a variety of plant extracts – all still regarded as invaluable in the treatment of illness. Dandelion roots, for example, contain taraxcin which is especially therapeutic for liver and kidney complaints. Many of the patent medicines found in high street chemists contain dandelion root, which, depending on the dosage, acts as a strong stimulant to the digestive system. The roots of Belladonna contain atropine, which is a vital sedative indispensable for the

Henbane, *above*, is used in modern medicine as a sedative and as a liniment for the relief of rheumatism. *Below*, Dandelion roots are employed in many patent medicines as a tonic for digestive complaints.

Keep taking the medicine

treatment of eye diseases. Diluted with gelatine it helps to dilate the pupil of the eye, and the drug is invaluable in many eye operations.

Modern medicine would not be what it is today without the analgesic derivatives of the Opium Poppy – morphine and codeine. Morphine has long been the physician's main-stay for the relief of severe pain (particularly during the brutal surgery of the early 19th century), or in smaller doses as a nerve stimulant. Obviously morphine is not used in its natural state; it is combined with distilled water and alcohol to produce a tincture known as Laudanum, which, despite synthetic substitutes such as methadone, is still extensive-ly used. Syrup of Poppies was a popular remedy for coughs during the 19th century. Unfortunately parents and nurse-maids were apt to regard it as a miracle cure – because of the way it would pacify small children – without realising the dangers of unregulated use; many children died before the drug's potency was properly understood.

The common Foxglove (*Digitalis purpurea*) yields digita-lis, a drug which remains a vital part of medicine today. First mentioned in an early *Pharmacopoeia* in 1650, digitalis has since been shown to have three active elements – digitoxin, digitalin and digitalein – that are now used by doctors in the battle against heart disease. Depending upon the dose administered, digitalis acts as a cardiac stimulant or de-pressant, to regulate the heart's action.

For less serious illness, two plants are particularly valu-able: liquorice and eucalyptus. Each year hundreds of tonnes of dried liquorice root are imported into Britain; the pharmaceutical industry then extracts those oils which act as a demulcent, and blends them into some of the patent remedies we see in our medicine cabinets today. The distilled leaves of the eucalyptus are used to similar effect; eucalyptol is a strong stimulant and antiseptic which provides cleansing ointments for the skin, and forms the

Opium poppies, *main picture*, yield morphine, a valuable sedative still extensively used today. Digitalis from the Foxglove, *above*, is highly valued as a heart stimulant.

basis of many syrups and lozenges used to alleviate cold symptoms and inflammations of the mouth.

Even though the modern drug industry is now producing many synthetic remedies, the role of natural substances extracted from plants remains crucial in the manufacture of medicines. In the late 1950s, research into the composition of the shrub *Rauwolfia serpentina* (found in India and used locally as a sedative) led to the development of reserpine, a tranquilliser used to combat high blood pressure and treat mental illness. It is only quite recently that chemists have been able to produce a synthetic compound to replace quinine (from the cinchona tree), which has acted as an effective cure for malaria for over 300 years. Even antibiotics (substances capable of destroying living bacteria) can be found in plants; Burdock, for instance, is renowned for its ability to ward off infection. As medical research continues even more plants will undoubtedly be discovered to possess the power of healing.

What's in a name?

WHAT'S IN A NAME? Everything, it would seem – if it is a flower's common or country name. From primitive times, the flowers, roots and seeds of plants were central to the lives of countrymen and women, and it was inevitable that plants should acquire names that reflected the respect or affection in which they were held. Their medicinal uses, their appearance, the myths and magical properties they embodied were evident in the common names that have been handed down to us through generations.

The tiny-flowered Forget-me-not owes its name to tradition. Henry of Lancaster, later to become King Henry IV, was reputed to be responsible for this modest flower's haunting name. He adopted the flower as his emblem while he was in exile in France and, since his motto was '*Souviegne-vous de moy*' ('Remember me'), this became, by association, the flower's name. Another legend relates how, when Adam had named all the flowers in the Garden of Eden, he invited God to inspect his work. God's attention was caught by a tiny sweet-faced flower, and when He asked what it was called the flower was so terrified it could only stammer that it had quite forgotten its name. In the words of an anonymous Victorian poet:

No word the Almighty spake, 'till, having gone His round,
Again he passed the spot,
When, glancing towards the flower, smiling He kindly said:
'Good-night, forget-me-not.'

The origin of the name of the Cowslip, another favourite wild flower, has more earthy connotations. Ignored by grazing cows, the Cowslip's lovely nodding yellow umbels dot meadowland, along with that trap for unwary walkers, the cowpat or 'cu slyppe' (cow slime) from which, by association, this plant may well have got its name. The shape of its flower clusters – which resemble a bunch of keys – may have inspired two of its other country names, 'Key Flower' and 'Key of Heaven'. A bunch of keys was the emblem of St Peter – and in some old herbals the plant is called Herb Peter. One legend relates how, on one occasion, St Peter heard that some devious people were trying to gain admittance to Heaven via the back door; he rushed from his place as keeper of the pearly gates and, in his haste, dropped his bunch of keys. Where it fell to earth Cowslips sprang up.

Deadly Nightshade has a name and character altogether less cosy. Its other names – 'Devil's Cherries', 'Naughty Man's Cherries' and 'Devil's Herb' evoke Hell rather than Heaven, and indeed folklore insists that the Devil tends and trims it at his leisure. It is indeed deadly, every part of the plant being extremely poisonous. Its Latin name, Belladonna (Fair Lady), is said to arise from an old superstition that at certain times the plant assumed the form of an irresistible enchantress, upon whom it was fatal to rest one's gaze.

While Deadly Nightshade was feared, the Heartsease or Wild Pansy could not be more widely loved. Its many whimsical common names suggest the affection in which it is held – 'Love-lies-bleeding', 'Cuddle-me', 'Three-faces-under-a-hood', 'Jack-jump-up-and-kiss-me', 'Love-in-Idleness', 'Kiss-her-in-the-Buttery' – the list is almost endless. Legend suggests the flower was once snow-white, until it was struck by an arrow from Cupid's bow, mis-aimed at Diana; since that moment it has been 'purple with love's wound'. In Shakespeare's *Midsummer Night's Dream* Oberon used the juice of the Pansy to put a spell on the sleeping Titania, so that she would fall madly in love with the first living creature she saw when she awoke – it was the yokel Bottom the Weaver, with an ass's head. The popular name Heartsease probably arose from both its use as a love potion and its medicinal use in treating diseases of the heart. With a reputation for easing both emotional and physical heartache, it is not surprising that the much-loved Pansy is dedicated to St Valentine and lovers everywhere.

The charming – and increasingly rare – wild Cowslip, *above*, is said to resemble a bunch of keys, hence its country names 'Key Flower' and 'Key of Heaven'. Legend surrounds the naming of the pretty Forget-me-not, *top*, but its name may simply be due to the fact that its intense blue is unforgettable. Heartsease, or the Wild Pansy, *below*, has a multitude of common names.

On the right scent

THE POWER OF FRAGRANCE to affect our senses and to trigger an emotion or a nostalgic memory is considerable – the sudden waft of perfume from night-scented stock or tobacco plants in a summer garden at twilight is an experience like no other. Smells can influence not only our moods, but our actions – we recoil from a nasty smell, and are attracted by a nice one. And whereas the animal world supplies many of the really nasty odours, we are indebted to the plant world for most of the pleasant ones.

In the Middle Ages, far from being just a pretty smell, perfume derived from plants was thought to have the power of keeping the plague at bay; in 1560 it was recorded that a woman 'died of the plague, and they perfumed the house with grains of juniper' to cleanse it of the pestilence.

But the uses of perfume traditionally went far beyond that of fumigation. In ancient Egypt a young Casanova might employ as many as 15 different scents in an attempt to attract the opposite sex, while women concealed tiny globules of aromatic substances in their hair. A Roman might have used oil of mint for his armpits, palm oil for his jaws and oil of marjoram on his hair. And it is still common nowadays for us to use perfume for its supposed aphrodisiac qualities – and to use scented soaps, powders and bath oils to make ourselves attractive to others.

The word 'perfume' comes from the Latin *per fumum* ('through the smoke'), and is probably derived from the practice of burning incense – made from myrrh, cinnamon and other scented plants – in the temples to disguise the smell of burning sacrifices.

Then, as today, perfume was a rare and expensive product. It can take an acre of roses to produce one pound of aromatic

The use of aromatic plants has a long history. A young Roman might have perfumed his hair with oil of marjoram (*above*, marjoram growing wild in southern England); in the Middle Ages the scent of juniper (*below*) was thought to protect against the plague.

Two houseplants with a ravishing scent are the Honey Plant, *Hoya carnosa* (*below*), and the Sweet Orange, *Citrus sinensis* (*above*), which bears beautiful blossom and edible fruit. The handsome Cinnamon Tree (*above right*) yields the spice that is an essential ingredient of the aromatic pomander, or pot-pourri.

oil, which is why it is impracticable to produce home-made perfume. And even in this technological age, the old practice of making perfume is still an art – the same art that in the 1300s produced the first toilet water, called Hungary Water, from rosemary and alcohol. A formula for lavender water was recorded in 1615, and one for orange flower water (the main ingredient of eau-de-Cologne) in 1725.

A distillation of delight

Perfume is made from essential oils: from orange peel, for example, comes orange oil; from orange leaves comes petitgrain oil; and from orange flowers comes neroli. These oils are separated out by steam distillation and solvents, and one ton of vegetable matter may yield only a few pounds of oil. Some oils come from woods, such as sandalwood; some from roots, like vetiver; some from flowers and leaves, such as lavender or violet; others from rhizomes, stems, barks, fruits, seeds or resins. These essential oils are often mixed with animal secretions, like musk or civet, to provide the very special combination of odours we use as scent.

At home, it is easier to make a pot-pourri or pomander – a mixture of fragrant, dried flowers and spices kept in a container. In the Middle Ages these were thought to protect against infection and were also used to mask the odours of insanitary living; the pomander (a small china or metal pot, with a perforated lid, containing the pot-pourri) was carried by men – only later, in the 19th century, did it become a female ornament. Oranges covered with cloves and rolled in cinnamon, and small nosegays of fragrant flowers were also carried in the Middle Ages to ward off the plague.

Now that we have brought growing plants into our homes, we can make the most of the soothing and reviving properties of their marvellous fragrances. When you open your front door in the evening and the scent from your Jasmine or Hoya plant meets you and lifts your jaded spirits, you can reflect that this ability of a flower's fragrance to affect human moods and emotions is a very ancient and potent power of the plant world.

The potent plant

HOMOEOPATHY, A FORM OF ALTERNATIVE medicine that re-
lies mainly on remedies extracted from plants, was developed in the late 18th century by a gifted physician,
Samuel Hahnemann, who was born in 1755. He studied
medicine in Leipzig and Vienna and then practised as a
doctor in Germany. However, he soon became so disen-
chanted with orthodox medicine that he abandoned it in
favour of translating foreign medical books into German –
and in this way he came upon the theory that was to change
his life and result in the founding of homoeopathy, now one
of the most respected of the 'unorthodox' medical therapies.

While Hahnemann was translating William Cullen's
Materia Medica he found that he disagreed with that
learned Scottish physician's theory as to why quinine
(which is derived from the evergreen tree Cinchona, or
Peruvian Bark) could be successfully used to treat malaria.
Hahnemann knew that Peruvian Bark could actually cause
the symptoms of malaria in the people who were harvesting
it. He concluded that this must be a case of 'like cures like', a
very ancient medical theory going back to the time of
Paracelsus, and he determined to test this theory on other
substances.

For 20 years he experimented on himself, his family and
friends, and in 1810 published his own *Materia Medica*,
which recorded the action of some 67 remedies. He established that symptoms can be cured by giving to the sick
person (in minute doses) the very substance that would

The poisonous Monkshood, *above*,
yields the valuable homoeopathic
remedy Aconite that is used to treat
fear, anxiety, shock and fever. The
Wind Flower, *left*, is the source of the
remedy Pulsatilla, often prescribed
for timid, fearful women.

produce those same symptoms in a healthy person.

Moreover, his experiments showed that the more the remedy was diluted, the more powerful was its effect. In fact, homoeopathic remedies are so diluted that no trace of the original substance can be detected if the remedy is analysed, and this means that very poisonous substances such as Aconite and Belladonna can be used in homoeopathy quite safely.

Chamomile is one plant used in homoeopathy that has also been used for centuries in herbal medicine. The herbalists use it (in infusion) to alleviate nervous headaches and to calm the digestive system. In homoeopathy the remedy Chamomilla (derived from Chamomile) is prescribed particularly for restless or irritable babies and infants – a baby that cries without ceasing every night can be lulled to sleep by it. One doctor new to homoeopathy saw a dramatic example of its effectiveness. He was called out one evening to attend to a baby that was crying uncontrollably and jerking about in hysteria, so that it was quite impossible for the doctor to examine the child. He managed nevertheless to pop a powder of the remedy Chamomilla on to the baby's tongue – the child stopped crying immediately, and fell fast asleep!

One of the most valuable homoeopathic remedies is Arnica, derived from *Arnica montana*, or Leopard's Bane. It is used to treat any injury or bruising, and is invaluable in reducing the effects of post-operative shock, or the shock experienced after an accident. Arnica will stop bleeding, and is helpful after dental extraction; it has also proved

Homoeopathic remedies are also produced from two attractive plants often seen as houseplants. From *Cyclamen neapolitanum*, *below left*, comes the remedy Cyclamen, prescribed for lassitude; Pot Marigold, *above*, yields Calendula ointment, used for burns.

effective in treating the after-effects of old injuries that are still troublesome.

Several extremely poisonous plants have provided some of the most useful homoeopathic remedies. One of these is the deadly Aconite, or Monkshood, that has a reputation as a venomous poison stretching back into antiquity. In homoeopathy, however, it is used as a remedy for fear, shock and acute infection that is accompanied by a rapid rise in temperature.

Treating the patient as a whole

Homoeopathic prescribing is not limited solely to trying to find the remedy that will cure the symptoms the patient complains of. On a broader front, the homoeopathic doctor tries to treat the whole person, and will take into account all the mental and physical characteristics of the patient in arriving at the right 'constitutional' remedy for him. Once the patient's own constitutional remedy is found, it may be used over a long period to bring him back to full health. Homoeopathic remedies therefore tend to have their own 'profiles'. Pulsatilla, for instance, is extracted from the Wind Flower (*Anemone pulsatilla*) and is characteristically prescribed for passive people (usually women) of changeable moods, who are easily moved to tears.

The beautiful little hardy Cyclamen (*Cyclamen neapolitanum*) yields another constitutional remedy rather similar to Pulsatilla. It is prescribed for phlegmatic people who tire easily and generally feel disinclined to work.

Another well tried and tested homoeopathic remedy comes from a plant that can be enjoyed in the home as a pot plant – Calendula, which comes from the Pot Marigold (*Calendula officinalis*). This is used as an ointment, and is the standard homoeopathic remedy for burns.

A flowery language

TO THE VICTORIANS a flower was not simply a thing of beauty – it was an element in an elaborate language that became almost a cult. Following the publication in Paris in 1833 of *Le Language des Fleurs*, by Charlotte de Latour, the Victorians fell upon the English translation and made it their own. The 'language' described in the book was an intricate system of communication, in which each species of flower had a specific meaning, and by sending a carefully chosen bouquet to a loved one, a gentleman might, in effect, be sending an explicitly worded letter. The bluebell, for example, meant 'constancy', while the more sinister foxglove stood for 'insincerity' and the jonquil demanded petulantly, 'I desire a return of affection.'

In an age when young ladies were expected to be chaste, these flowery symbols provided an ideal way for sweethearts to express their feelings without loss of modesty or danger of hurt pride. So popular did this language become that it was described in rhyme:

There is a language, little known;
Lovers claim it as their own.
Its symbols smile upon the land
Wrought by Nature's wondrous hand;
And in their silent beauty speak
Of life and joy to those who seek
For love divine and sunny hours
In the language of the flowers.

The Victorians' enthusiasm for this new language had very little to do with botany and a lot to do with fashionable sentiment. With the other floral arts and crafts that were then becoming popular, it was a means for the *nouveaux riches* to idle away the hours indulging in rose-tinted nostalgia – another reminder of the 'simple rural life' that had been left behind by the industrial revolution.

The elaborate greetings cards of the Victorian age – that were often festooned with lace and ribbons – could carry two messages at the same time. Flowers decorating a Christmas card could transform it into a Valentine; peach blossom meant 'I am your captive', hawthorn pleaded for 'hope', and the peony confessed 'bashfulness'.

Distinctions of colour could also speak volumes. 'Slighted love' was the message of a yellow chrysanthemum, but a white one called for 'truth'; a red carnation whimpered 'alas for my poor heart', and a yellow one meant 'disdain'.

So complicated and widely used did this flowery language become that dictionaries were published to distinguish all the nuances of meanings, in order to prevent any unfortunate misunderstandings that might arise from a carelessly chosen bouquet.

In the language of flowers the beautiful pot plant Stephanotis, *left*, had a challenging meaning (see the glossary, *inset below*). The charming Bluebell (*below*, growing wild in woodland) stood for 'constancy'.

A glossary of flowers

Amaryllis: *pride*
Basil: *hatred*
Carnation (red): *'alas for my poor heart'*
Columbine (red): *anxious and trembling*
Daffodil: *chivalry*
Eglantine: *'I wound to heal'*
Forget-me-not: *true love*
Gladiolus: *strength of character*
Hellebore (Christmas rose): *'relieve my anxiety'*
Hemlock: *'you will be the death of me'*
Iris: *message*
Jasmine: *sensuality*
Kingcups: *desire of riches*
Lily-of-the-valley: *return of happiness*
Marigold: *grief, despair*
Nettle: *'you are cruel'*
Poppy (scarlet): *fantastic extravagance*
Quince: *temptation*
Stephanotis: *'you can boast too much'*
Tansy: *'I declare war against you'*
Verbena (white): *pure and guileless*
Wallflower: *fidelity in adversity*
Xanthium: *rudeness*
Yew: *sorrow*
Zinnia: *thoughts of absent friends*

ALMOST SINCE TIME BEGAN women have been exploiting the rejuvenating and restorative properties inherent in plants to improve their appearance. Infusions and lotions of flowers and herbs have been used to cleanse and soften the skin, and to condition and colour the hair; and, combined with other ingredients, plants have been used to make cosmetics to enhance (and subtly alter) the contours of the face. Even in today's sophisticated beauty products, plant extracts are still one of the main ingredients.

Until comparatively recent times cosmetics and beauty products were, of necessity, made at home. And now that technologically-produced cosmetics are proving to have many allergy-causing additives, the idea of once again making beauty preparations at home is becoming increasingly popular. Plants grown in a back yard, or even in the home as pot plants, are easy to harvest and use to make your own beauty preparations.

A plant that is immensely beneficial to the skin is Pot Marigold, which is easy to grow indoors in a hanging basket.

A simple remedy for badly chapped hands can be made by immersing a handful of marigold petals in half a cupful of cold-pressed almond oil. Leave this for a few days, then strain the oil, bottle it and use night and morning to smooth on the hands. An oily complexion can be improved with the use of marigold water. This can be made by pouring a pint of boiling water on to eight tablespoons of marigold petals and leaving to cool. This can be used as a tonic and astringent – pat it on to the complexion after cleansing.

Many plants have been used to dye or improve the colour of the hair. Henna (also known as Jamaica Mignonette and Egyptian Privet) is well known for the bright auburn tint it gives to the hair; the ancient Egyptians used the dried powdered leaves of the plant to make the dye, which they used not only on their hair but on their fingernails and the palms of the hands.

A rich brown colouring can be achieved in greying hair (it is claimed) by the use of a herbal dye made from sage leaves and black tea. Two tablespoons of black tea and two tablespoons of dried sage leaves are added to two pints of water and simmered for half an hour. The resulting dye is left to stand for several hours before being strained; it can then be massaged into the hair daily until the desired colour is achieved.

A simple beauty aid for a dry complexion is to rub it over with the inside of an avocado pear, *left*; the avocado oil softens the skin and has a long-lasting effect. Lavender, *below*, is used to make a fragrant toilet water that imparts a delicate freshness.

Gilding the lily?

Drab, lifeless blonde hair is said to respond well to a rinse with chamomile water. A cup of dried chamomile flowers can be added to one pint of boiling water and simmered for half an hour; when the liquid has cooled it can be strained and used as a final rinse after washing the hair. This chamomile rinse is said to restore the tone of blonde hair and bring out new lights in it.

Soothing and restorative baths are very easy to prepare using dried herbs and flowers. Lavender, majoram, bergamot, rose petals and the leaves of blackberry and raspberry are all very easily obtainable and can be used to make an excellent, refreshing bath. They should be first dried and then added (as a mixture) to a bowl of boiling water and left to stand for half an hour. The resulting liquid is added to the bathwater to give a cleansing and relaxing bath.

The herb rosemary was the main ingredient of the famous Hungary Water – the first toilet water known to have been prepared with alcohol spirits – which has been regarded by women since the 14th century as a valuable aid to preserving youth and beauty. The recipe for the toilet water was presented to Elizabeth, Queen of Hungary, and the lotion not only preserved her beauty well into her seventies, but was also believed to have cured her lameness. A simplified version of this beneficial toilet water can be made at home by mixing together half a cup of fresh rosemary leaves, a handful of fresh mint, and one teaspoon each of grated orange peel, ground cinnamon and grated nutmeg. Crush the leaves and spices together, and pour over them two pints of ethyl alcohol; transfer into a glass jar, cover with a lid and leave for two weeks. The liquid can then be filtered and transferred into a tightly stoppered bottle. It makes an invigorating body rub, and is also very refreshing when added to a warm bath.

Rosemary, *right*, was an essential ingredient of the legendary Hungary Water that was said to preserve a woman's youth and beauty into old age. Chamomile, *below*, makes a hair rinse that revives the highlights in blonde hair and acts as a tonic to both hair and scalp.

Soothing oils

AROMATHERAPY IS THE ANCIENT ART of treating the body with the essential oils of plants. This delightful practice is only now gaining popularity in Britain, but oils distilled from flowers, leaves, roots, bark and fruit rind have been used for thousands of years, not just as a basis for perfumes, but as stimulants, tranquillisers and cures for all kinds of mental and physical illness.

In India essential plant oils are still used cosmetically for their rejuvenating properties, and are also now put to therapeutic use to treat serious chronic conditions such as arthritis. The Ancient Greeks and Romans used essential oils as aphrodisiacs, while in China and Tibet they were employed to alter states of consciousness. In Ancient Egypt they were used for embalming the dead.

Aromatherapy was 'rediscovered' this century in Europe by a French chemist, Gatfossé, who discovered the wonderful healing properties of essential oils when he burned his arm in his laboratory. He plunged his arm into oil of lavender and, to his amazement, the pain disappeared almost immediately and the skin healed within hours.

The Austrian biochemist Marguerite Maury went on to develop beauty therapies using essential oils; treating the face and the area near the spinal cord, she found that she was able to slow down the effects of ageing and cure acne. Her patients reported beneficial side-effects, too: they slept better, found relief from migraine and arthritis and were generally more alert. Mme Maury also found that the reaction of her patients to any particular essential oil was highly personal; certain oils worked well on some patients, but had little effect on others.

Aromatherapy plant oils are generally used in combination, but each oil has its own individual profile. The essential oil of sage, *top*, is used to treat a range of conditions including aching joints, rheumatism, migraine and indigestion; oil of marjoram, *above*, is used for constipation and catarrh.

Mme Maury's work gained her a wide following and international acclaim, but scientists are still not able to say exactly why or how essential plant oils work. The theory is that their healing and rejuvenating powers are due to the vitamins and enzymes they contain; however, there may be other factors at work as yet undiscovered. But most of the increasing number of people who enjoy the benefits of aromatherapy are content to accept that it is yet another aspect of the magical power of plants.

Essential plant oils are what give flowers their smell, and herbs and spices their taste. In appearance they are more like water than oil. They are highly volatile and extremely potent, and need to be mixed with a bland carrier oil before they can be used.

When diluted in this way plant oils can be rubbed into the skin as a cosmetic or part of a massage treatment, inhaled or added to water. A few drops can scent a bath and soothe tense muscles. Mixed with water, the oil of your choice can be sprayed into the air to fill a room with its aroma.

The potency of the oil is released on contact with the skin. It combines the body's natural oil (the sebum) and passes through the pores into the bloodstream, and is carried to all parts of the body, giving a sense of well-being.

Elixirs of youth?

Plant oils can produce an astonishing range of effects. Oil of orange blossom and lavender stimulate the growth of new cells. Oil of fennel is also rejuvenating and can be used as an anti-wrinkle treatment; it contains a substance with similar properties to the hormone oestrogen. Oil of geranium soothes anxiety and lifts depression, while that of camphor has long been used as an antidote to shock and peppermint oil is known to relieve fatigue and sharpen the powers of concentration. Cinnamon oil is a stimulant, and oil of garlic possesses the extraordinary dual power of being able to raise the blood pressure if it is too low, and lower it if it is too high.

Plant oils can be bought from herbalists (and some chemists) that stock homoeopathic remedies. They should be kept in dark glass bottles, tightly stoppered, in a cool place, as they are highly sensitive to heat and light and quickly lose their potency if exposed to either. One drop of plant oil should be mixed with 50 drops of carrier oil for use – ideal carriers are almond and hazelnut oil, but sunflower, safflower or groundnut oil are cheaper alternatives. It is important not to apply any pure undiluted plant oil directly to the skin, as in its concentrated state it may be dangerous.

To discover the delights of aromatherapy for yourself, you can experiment with a small range of essential oils initially, noting how they suit your mood and your skin type. To improve the circulation, try oil of camphor or juniper; oil of cypress and orange blossom (which is also called neroli) can improve broken veins. An oily skin can be improved with oil of lavender, lemon or bergamot, while dry skin will benefit from rose, geranium or sandalwood oil.

Chamomile and geranium oils can be massaged into the body to relieve tension; oil of cinnamon, patchouli or jasmine will revitalise you if you are tired, while oil of rosemary will soothe muscles aching from overwork. Oil of ylang-ylang can be helpful when you are irritated, nervous or upset, and sandalwood is helpful for depression.

When used by professional aromatherapists, essential oils can have a very beneficial effect on many minor ailments. Oil of eucalyptus, for instance, can improve sinus conditions and muscular aches and pains. Oil of lemongrass has a tonic effect on the skin and improves open pores and acne. Oil of the black pepper plant is good for coughs and catarrh, while oil of cypress improves a sluggish circulation and calms an irritable disposition. Many other ailments – including high blood pressure, stomach ulcers, migraine, lumbago and acute depression – have been known to respond to the marvellous therapeutic qualities hidden in the essential oils of the plant kingdom.

The pink-flowered wild thyme, *top*, has antiseptic properties and its oil is used to treat colds, flu and skin conditions. Peppermint, *above*, yields an oil that is said to be beneficial in cases of diarrhoea and general debility; the oil of the cranesbill, or geranium, *below*, can be used as a massage oil for the treatment of dermatitis and eczema, or it can be added to the bathwater to make a relaxing, therapeutic bath to improve anxiety and depression.